THE COLONEL AND THE KING

"Elvis steps from the pages. You can feel him breathe. This book cancels out all others."   Bob Dylan

"Peter Guralnick's two-volume life of Elvis Aron Presley . . . is not simply the finest rock-and-roll biography ever written. It must be ranked among the most ambitious and crucial biographical undertakings yet devoted to a major American figure of the second half of the twentieth century."
                                                    New York Times Book Review

"Riveting . . . A masterwork."   *The Wall Street Journal*

"Nothing written about Elvis Presley comes close to the detail, authority, and uncondescending objectivity that Peter Guralnick has brought to his two-volume biography . . . Hypnotic."   *USA Today*

"Supple and altogether splendid . . . Guralnick writes evocatively, empathetically . . . He paints this world with perspective, respect, and great decency; it is one of the book's triumphs."   *Time*

THE COLONEL AND THE KING

Tom Parker, Elvis Presley and the Partnership that Rocked the World

PETER GURALNICK

WHITE
RABBIT

THE COLONEL AND THE KING

TOM PARKER, ELVIS PRESLEY

AND THE PARTNERSHIP

THAT ROCKED THE WORLD

PETER GURALNICK

WHITE
RABBIT

First published in the United States of America in 2025 by Little, Brown and Company
First published in Great Britain in 2025 by White Rabbit,
an imprint of The Orion Publishing Group Ltd
Carmelite House, 50 Victoria Embankment
London EC4Y 0DZ

An Hachette UK Company

The authorised representative in the EEA is Hachette Ireland, 8 Castlecourt Centre,
Dublin 15, D15 XTP3, Ireland (email: info@hbgi.ie)

1 3 5 7 9 10 8 6 4 2

A CIP catalogue record for this book is
available from the British Library.

ISBN (Hardback) 978 1 3996 3529 5
ISBN (Export Trade Paperback) 978 1 3996 3530 1
ISBN (Ebook) 978 1 3996 3532 5
ISBN (Audio) 978 1 3996 3533 2

All photographs are copyrighted by the photographer and/or owner cited,
all rights reserved.

Page i: At Elvis' twenty-sixth birthday celebration. *Courtesy of the Graceland Archives*
Page iv: In his Madison, Tennessee, office, ca. 1950. *Courtesy of the Graceland Archives*
Page viii: Colonel with the Bonjas, one of his many adoptive families, ca. *1955. Courtesy of Ron Bonja.*
Page xx: *Courtesy of the Graceland Archives*
Page 1: Andreas at seventeen or eighteen. *Courtesy of the Graceland Archives*
Page 330: *Courtesy of the Graceland Archives*
Page 331: Promoting Elvis, 1962. *Courtesy of the Graceland Archives*

Designed by Susan Marsh

Printed and bound in Great Britain by Clays Ltd, Elcograf S.p.A.

www.whiterabbitbooks.co.uk
www.orionbooks.co.uk

For Loanne Miller Parker and Jack Soden,

who opened doors for me that I could never otherwise have found

Contents

Finding the Colonel

I may not type good, but they sure do know what I mean up there.

— *Colonel Parker to photographer Al Wertheimer, summer 1956*

THIS BOOK goes back nearly thirty years. It goes back to the day that my wife, Alexandra, and I (and our friend and intrepid fellow traveler Ernst Jorgensen) were ushered into the repository of what amounted to a large part of the Elvis Archives, a nondescript, echoey warehouse not far from Graceland, in which all of Colonel Parker's vast collection of — well, of *everything* — resided. We were there at the invitation of Jack Soden, CEO of Elvis Presley Enterprises, who had extended his invitation with no preconditions after reading the first volume of my Elvis biography, *Last Train to Memphis*. And there we discovered an astonishing wealth of information, not just about Elvis, not just about Colonel's own remarkable life and career — it was, instead, a painstakingly preserved curation of nearly every aspect of what Colonel liked to call The Wonderful World of Show Business, all stored in the original dented file cabinets and battered black cube-shaped steamer trunks in which it had been accumulating for the past fifty or sixty years.

I can't begin to tell you how it felt — it was a little like entering Ali Baba's cave, as every sort of unlikely, and sometimes ungainly, treasure revealed itself: gas receipts tracking the Colonel's early travels with Elvis (and Eddy Arnold before him); contracts, itineraries, and court documents; box-office reports detailing the size and makeup of audiences in theaters, arenas, and makeshift venues across the country; oversized scrapbooks that chronicled every moment, it seemed, of Elvis' public life; and, of course, letters, tens of thousands of letters. With an open invitation from Jack (I was by now working on the second volume of my Elvis biography), Alexandra and I went back again and again over the next three or four years.

That was the genesis of *The Colonel and the King*—though I suppose it could be said to go back even earlier, to a letter I wrote to Colonel in the fall of 1994, as I thought about our own correspondence of the past few years and the book that he said he was still planning to write, though his efforts appeared to have stalled. (Yes, like every other writer, even the Colonel, it seemed, could be blocked).

"You know," I wrote to him, "I was thinking about one aspect of our last conversation: your letters. I really believe this would make a great book. You could tell your story through a selection of letters; they would convey not just the events themselves but the flavor of the events, the way you approached them; and you would not have to worry about putting together a whole new narrative.... Anyway, you may think I'm crazy, and if so just throw this suggestion out the window."

That was my mistake. "Your letter of November 8 read and carefully noted," Colonel replied with typical promptness six days later. "When you state: 'you may think I'm crazy' your suggestion is a little late." Oh, well. I guess after corresponding and sparring with him all this time, I should have known better.

Colonel's own book was always going to be called *How Much Does It Cost If It's Free?* In its quizzicality, its surface humor, and, unquestionably, its deeper meaning, it represented Colonel perfectly. (Just to set the record straight, he was always "Colonel"; he had claimed it as his first name since his initial elevation to the honorary title by the governor of Louisiana in 1948, unless you—or he—were referring more formally to the exalted status of his station, though, truly, there was no consistent rule.) The first reference to his book appeared in a *Look* magazine article in 1956 entitled "The Great Elvis Presley Industry," in the course of which he offered an alternative, almost instantly discarded title, "The Benevolent Con Man," and was described by reporter Chester Morrison as someone "with a reverence for money" and the willingness "to work hard for it." On the other hand, the writer, with uncommon writerly astuteness, got the impression that "if [he] didn't get any fun out of making money, the hell with it." And, as Morrison might have further suggested, you had to get up pretty early in the morning to fool the Colonel.

In fact, that was pretty much impossible, because Colonel got up earlier than anyone.

Soon after alighting upon that treasure trove of arcana and memorabilia (purchased by Graceland, along with the entire contents of Colonel's house and office in Madison, Tennessee, just a few years earlier), I told Jack Soden that we really had to do a book made up of Colonel's letters (it would have been a follow-up to our first shared project, *Elvis Day by Day*, which stemmed from the same source), and Jack without a moment's hesitation agreed. But then a number of strokes of fate intervened, including Lisa Marie Presley's sale of the Estate, and here we are thirty years later. And Jack is still at the helm at Graceland.

Originally it was just going to be the letters. I figured I could simply supply commentary, illuminating time, place, and circumstances, with a little bit of background on the various people involved. But then it occurred to me that the letters presented more than just an entry point into Colonel's external world. They in fact offered a reading-between-the-lines glimpse into Colonel's inner life as well, and if I wanted to take the opportunity to explore the story further (and I did), I needed to start thinking about a biographical portrait that could fill in some of the blanks.

It was around this time that I began talking to Colonel's widow, Loanne Miller Parker, about the book. I had known Loanne for nearly a dozen years at that point, but it was her unvarnished enthusiasm for the project, her willingness to help in any way she could, that set me off on paths I'm not sure I would ever have found on my own. Because Loanne had been not only a devoted (and I mean truly devoted) wife and companion for the last twenty-seven years of Colonel's life, she had also worked with him almost from the day they first met. She had been secretary and executive assistant as well as his companion on every one of Elvis' tours from 1971 on, where she soon took on an official role as RCA Record Tours secretary. She kept meticulous records and meticulous personal journals — and, while she admired Colonel as unreservedly as she loved him, she was determined to share them, if only to reclaim for him the place in history she knew he deserved. She remained resolutely cheerful right up till her death in 2020, but even when it was clear how difficult it must have been for her at times to call up some of the most painful personal details, she maintained an unswerving dedication to the truth, making no attempt to influence the way in which the story would ultimately be told.

Most of the earliest memories come from Loanne's recollections, not in her own voice, of course, but in Colonel's, as she recalled almost eidetically the tales her husband told her in his old age. They portrayed a bright, rebellious boy, a lost, lonely boy strangely desperate for affection, as he grew up in Breda, a bourgeois waterway city in the Netherlands, in a family that he never really felt part of. Many of the stories describe his search for a place in the world for himself. They invoke families who sought to adopt him, pranks that he devised to entertain and win the admiration of others; there was even a roving band of "gypsies" who took him in and taught him that you had to learn to survive by your wits in a world that was stacked against you.

He never explained to Loanne or anyone else just where this deep-seated sense of displacement came from, how he came to feel so alienated from both homeland and family — throughout his life he would always remain attached to the memory of his mother, whom he last saw when he left Holland for good at nineteen, but occasionally he would explode in altogether uncharacteristic bursts of emotion about his father, declaring angrily that he was a bad, bad man. He never told her anything more, Loanne said, though I wonder sometimes if this was a confidence she was simply unwilling to betray. It was only when he arrived in America, most likely as a stowaway on the Holland America line, that he found himself for the first time in a place that could accommodate his dreams, though tellingly, once again, even in America, many of his earliest memories describe seeking refuge, finding a family, a home, a safe haven, where he could at least temporarily feel secure.

I met Colonel in January of 1988, but, really, it was through our subsequent correspondence that I first got to know him. It was like a crash course in Colonel, in which from the start I was at a distinct, and unrecoverable, disadvantage. With all the goodwill in the world (though certainly with an agenda of my own), I told Colonel straightforwardly enough about the biography I was just beginning to write and my hopes that he might help me dispel some of the myths that had grown up around Elvis, and he just as straightforwardly — well, no, there was nothing straightforward about it. It was if I were playing chess with a grandmaster, and if at any point I might have thought I had gained some small advantage, he invariably blocked me. But not without first offering the same polite demurral: that if he were to help me, how could he refuse any of his other friends who might want his help—surely I could understand that. But then he always went on to offer *some* kind of help or point me in some useful direction, then adding, "But that's all I can tell you."

He invited me to his gala eightieth birthday celebration in Las Vegas in 1989. At the end of the evening, I approached him with all due deference just to thank him for his kindness. "I put you on the list," he declared with what appeared to be some asperity. I thought he might have misunderstood, or simply misheard, me, so I thanked him again—and again—until finally it dawned on me that what he was saying was: HE HAD PUT ME ON THE LIST.

And so he had. Which meant that, without his ever explicitly acknowledging it, he had given me not just the opportunity but his own personal imprimatur to meet perhaps two dozen of the most elusive and central figures in Elvis' life, and now it was up to me to make the most of it.

Loanne told me a number of times that Colonel *almost*—and I stress the word "almost"—decided to put his faith in me and submit to an actual, no-questions-barred series of interviews. But he didn't, and this may well have simply been kindness on Loanne's part. "He was so close," she told me, but at the last minute, she said, he would always pull back. But then, of course, as I learned from Loanne and everyone else, that was just Colonel's way. Actor George Hamilton, who went to Colonel for advice as a twenty-one-year-old newcomer to Hollywood and found a mentor for life, put it like this: "The Colonel always had a joke and a punch line which kind of framed him up." He tested you, and then, once you had proved yourself to him, he never doubted you—but he never stopped testing you either. It was the very act of helping you out, Hamilton said, that served as your admission into Colonel's large extended family, a family whose other members you might never meet but who, like him, were all a cherished part of Colonel's self-created world. With me it was something else, something far less, certainly, but I soon came to realize that the hoops he had me jump through (really just verbal hoops, but still . . .) were simply in service of my gaining admission, as he wrote to me, to his "file of literary friends that I know I can trust." And while I might have hoped to gain admission to another, more inner circle, if one existed, I was certainly grateful to take my place in that carefully designated file.

In the course of my research, through a series of small serendipities,

I was able to discover a number of other members of that "extended family" that George Hamilton spoke of, for whom Colonel became brother, uncle, substitute father, friend, and to whom he revealed himself in ways that he almost never revealed himself to the world. There were the Kufferaths, whom he met at twenty while serving in the army in Hawaii. The Bonjas in Alhambra, California, were the large family (there were ten children) of Colonel's longtime lieutenant Tom Diskin's older sister Helen and her husband, Ben. A teenage Brenda Williams and her mother, Clannie, initially met Colonel and his first wife, Marie, because they lived practically next door to them in Madison. From Colonel, Brenda said, she "got a standard of living. There were standards you were expected to [uphold] to represent yourself and your family. You just knew that the Colonel loved you, he was always respectful and tried to help, and you were the same with him." And you can see that same sense of closeness, that same unguarded yearning for connection, in his relationship with Abe Lastfogel, the powerful head of the William Morris Agency, a poor Jewish boy whose formal schooling, like Colonel's, had stopped at an early age. To outsiders the two must have seemed an unlikely pair, but each found something in the other that allowed them to connect with unfettered affection ("love" was a word frequently, and not lightly, invoked in their correspondence), and their loyalty to each other as both colleagues and friends never failed to stand up to outside challenges and frank expressions of professional disagreement (at least on Colonel's part) to the very end.

But most of all, there was Elvis. From the start, from the time that Colonel first saw him at the Louisiana Hayride in January 1955, Colonel placed his full faith and confidence not so much in the boy's talent as in the boy himself. Colonel Thomas A. Parker was at that moment one of the foremost figures in the country-and-western field, the top manager in the business, but at a time when no other country music promoter or major record label was prepared to make a serious investment in this nineteen-year-old regional phenomenon's career, Colonel was ready to set everything else aside in pursuit of a future that it seemed only he and the boy could see. The impact on them both was incalculable, but it was the unconditional trust that each placed in the other, the close intimate relationship that grew up from the start, that would remain forever a unique element in both their lives.

"Believe me when I say I will stick with you thru thick and thin and do everything I can to uphold your faith in me," Elvis telegrammed Colonel with rare and undisguised emotion when the sale of his Sun contract to RCA went through. "Again I say thanks and I love you like a father."

And when, less than eighteen months later, all their plans and dreams had succeeded beyond even their own wildest expectations (it's hard to believe either could have imagined how much more was still to come), Colonel wrote to Elvis: "I know that you have a certain quality in you the same as I have that can feel our way thru most any snowjob except if we lend a foolish ear. . . . I know that you understand me better than any-one for you have a very carefull Eye. I am a great deal like you, very sensitive, but only people I love can hurt me."

It was a bond that would never be broken, even long after it might have been better for them both if one or the other had chosen to break away. It was as if each had come to believe that without the other they would not be complete. "It's still Elvis and the Colonel," Colonel said after Elvis' death, with none of the cynicism that is so often attributed to him (and I must admit, until writing this book, that *I* would have attributed to him). "It will *always* be Elvis and the Colonel," he told Loanne. "I'll never stop trying to keep his name alive."

I didn't know Colonel in his heyday, when he could project a kind of imperious sangfroid, however self-amused and self-aware (and, yes, sometimes cruel), from a seat of unassailable power. I only knew him as an old man, of course—but there was never any question, he was still *Colonel*. I've tried to paint a picture not only of the Colonel that I knew but also of the Colonel that I knew him to be, with his mind running a million miles an hour, with his zest for life, in all of its multifarious possibilities, creative challenges, and clarion calls to battle, still undimmed. In the process, I encountered a good many challenges to my own preconceptions, and plenty of surprises along the way—but what would be the point of writing a book, of writing *anything,* just to end up where you'd planned on going all along?

My intention has always been the same: to present Colonel in the same freewheeling spirit that he presented himself, with all of his manifold contradictions boldly intact. Most of all, I hope you can see Colonel and Elvis in their fullest flowering, in the early years of their partnership, each in search of that ineffable goal in which they both so wholeheartedly believed, each in his own way uncompromisingly committed to its attainment. Surrender yourself, if you can, to their unremediated dream, set aside the myths that have grown up around them both, and give yourself over to an empathetic (and I don't mean credulous or uncritical, just human) reading of history. And when you read the letters, try to keep that same guideline in mind: read them as you would read any other unpunctuated teletype-scroll stream-of-consciousness outpouring of words and emotions, and remember Colonel's joyful adjuration to his old pal from Tampa, newspaperman Paul Wilder: "It is of course these funny letters and my feeling that One must enjoy his work or grow stale keeps me on the go, I can always bring myself right back into a happy medium by remembering how lucky we are, so let it snow let it snow I will always be somewhere to receive it."

A FEW WORDS ABOUT THE LETTERS

FIRST AND FOREMOST, I think it goes without saying, they speak for themselves.

Their bombast, their wit, the sheer energy that went into producing tens (and tens) of thousands of letters from a man whose education ended in Holland in the fourth or fifth grade unquestionably comes through, as he jousts, jokes, threatens, cajoles, introduces clever wordplay and parables to prove a point, sometimes all in the same letter, more often in a sequence of letters that show off his various epistolary styles in rapid succession.

I had originally thought I could present each letter complete and unedited—but that proved to be impossible. Colonel was simply too swift in his translation of thought to page, his manner of letter writing so often free of orthodox punctuation that I felt I couldn't allow *every* run-on sentence to simply run on without one or two signposts for the unwary reader. So I have added the occasional comma, even a period or two (for some reason Colonel seemed to have an unreasoning aversion to periods)—but always with a firm commitment to Colonel never to interrupt his free flow of expression. And I should note that long after personal secretaries took over the main task of typing Colonel's letters (this started sporadically as early as 1955 but did not become commonplace until the

1960s), not even their commitment to more orthodox forms of spelling and punctuation could still the wholly unorthodox impact of his words.

You will also notice from the ellipses that I have edited some of the letters for length. This is simply because, as much as the letters can be both instructive and entertaining in turn, Colonel was not a man of few words, or even a few million. He seemed to believe that once you've made your point, it never hurts to make it again. Not always, but often enough that here at least I think even Colonel might agree he could use some editing. Though, as he counseled his great and good friend Abe Lastfogel affectionately, in a multifaceted letter that did not need to be edited at all, "If this letter is too long, read it a little at a time."

What I have not done is tamper with Colonel's spelling or syntax in any way. That would be an insult to a man who invented his own unique form of expression as he went along; even his malapropisms (whether deliberate or inadvertent) make a point. This is a man of unadulterated originality, announcing himself in his adoptive language without hesitation or self-consciousness, and he needs to be permitted to speak both for, and as, himself, with all of his associative modes of articulation preserved intact.

And just remember the message that underlies so many of these letters: It's all about process. You can't lose a deal you never had. And if you can't find the fun in it, it really isn't worth doing.

BOOK ONE

....

HOW MUCH DOES IT COST

IF IT'S FREE

....

THE IMPROBABLE STORY OF

COLONEL TOM PARKER

PART I

....

BEFORE ELVIS

....

ONE

Boyhood

I was born with an adult mind in a child's body. I was frustrated a lot because I knew how to do things that my body couldn't carry out because of my small size. Because I didn't think like a child, no one understood me — in fact, I think they were afraid of me because I was different. I didn't want to be like other children my age, and wouldn't even try, so I was punished.

— Colonel Tom Parker, recalling his childhood in Breda, North Brabant, the Netherlands

H E WAS a strange child. Born in Breda, Holland, in 1909, Andreas Cornelis van Kuijk ("Dries") was the fifth of nine surviving children born of what appeared to be a marriage less of passion than of convenience. His father was a forty-three-year-old retired soldier named Adam van Kuijk, who worked as a liveryman at the Breda headquarters of a well-known Dutch cartage company. His mother, Maria Elisabeth Ponsie, was ten years younger than her husband, and her family made their living as "floating peddlers" along the waterways of Holland, selling goods of all sorts at the village fairs and town markets all along the rivers and canals. Adam van Kuijk, just out of the army after twelve years when they married in 1900, was by all accounts humorless and stern. Along with his job as a driver, he was in charge of the van Gend en Loos company's thirteen draft horses and provided with a large open living space above the stables. As part of the marriage settlement, his wife Maria's parents, Johannes and Maria Ponsie, moved in with the couple, an arrangement that seemed to weigh heavily on her husband, who had little time, evidently, for all the nonsense that went on with the Ponsie family and the flights of mood and fancy that it sometimes occasioned in his wife.

From the beginning, young Dries seems to have felt the weight of his father's disapproval, along with a sense of acute grievance that is difficult to explain in someone who in later years adopted the determination to always advance a positive view. "My father was no good, no good," he would say in later years in rare bursts of emotion, while always speaking of his mother with the greatest affection. Almost all of his early memories convey a sense of hurt and displacement. He was drawn to his elderly grandfather, Johannes, and looked forward to his regular visits with him at the old-age home to which he was confined after his wife's death. There the old man told him stories about his travels, about all the places he and his wife had gone, the people they had met—and he always encouraged the boy to express his individuality. But his grandfather died when Dries was eight, and he was just left with tales he would never forget that recalled the Ponsies' wandering ways.

Nothing he did merited his father's approval. "He had a heavy hand," he recalled, and his three older sisters, Adriana, Marie, and Nel, often came to comfort him and bring him food when he was banished to his corner of the boys' side of the loft in which they all slept. Each had warm memories of him as a child, seeing him as mischievous but never ill-intentioned. "He was very smart," said his sister Engelina, just sixteen months younger, "and I had a lot of fun with him at home. Some of us [appreciated him] more than others." To her, and her older sisters, he was "a very happy, very cheerful boy, always playing pranks." But all of them recognized the heavy cloud that seemed to hang over his head.

H E DIDN'T fit in at school—his mother had made sure to enroll him at the Catholic boys' school, St. Antoninus, despite the cost—but he had no interest in the subjects, and he rebelled against the discipline. The experience in fact seems to have instilled in him a lifelong mistrust of organized religion, as he openly challenged why priests should hold such a place of privilege.

Just as a measure of his discontent, he once estimated, "I ran away from home seventeen times in two years." Now, I don't think we need necessarily take this as a literal number (though, from my own observa-

Colonel's mother, Maria Elisabeth Ponsie van Kuijk. *Courtesy of the Graceland Archives.*

tion of the literalness and precision of his memory in later years, it may well be) to recognize the seriousness of his disaffection. His sisters all recalled the general consternation at his unpredictable disappearances, though none would ever hazard any real guess as to what led him to absent himself, other than the lure of adventure. To each of them, he was a cherished sibling, and possessed a power of imagination that no one else in the family seemed to have. When they were all getting ready to go to sleep at night, with the boys and girls in their separate quarters, the girls would open up the partition that divided them and beg him to relate one of his fanciful tales. "He never hurt anyone, but he was always up to something," said Nel, the third oldest of the girls. "He did everything that the others didn't dare."

To his second wife, and widow, Loanne, who knew him over the last thirty-five years of his life as a relentless, if very complicated, optimist who never passed a mirror without smiling, there was no question that he had at some point early on been deeply wounded. "He couldn't stand to be touched," she said, "even by those he loved most. From his memories it appeared that he was uncomfortable with caresses even in early childhood." He was never able, she said, to place his full faith in anyone, to the very end of his life. But in all the conversations I had with her, in which she frankly acknowledged the foibles of the husband she adored, she never once hazarded an explanation for his extreme sense of disaffection, whether because she felt it would be betraying a confidence that he was not about to offer anyone else, or because she simply did not know. I've sometimes thought that maybe she was speaking in a kind of code that she thought I would understand. And I wonder sometimes if maybe I do.

T HE FIRST few times that he ran away, as a very little boy, it may have been mostly to attract his mother's attention. But she soon learned to stop looking for him, and where he went when he explored first the streets, then the local countryside, no one knew. As he grew older he stayed away for longer periods of time and, perhaps inspired by his grandfather's accounts of the freedom of life along the waterways, spoke in later years of joining up with a roving band of "travelers" for several months, recounting to his wife, Loanne, how much he enjoyed their way of life and how much he learned from them.

Here, once again, I'm not altogether sure we can take him literally (I'm not sure Loanne did either), but there is no question of the allure that "gypsy" life had for him. In fact, he even wrote a brief screen treatment for movie producer Hal Wallis in 1958, in which Elvis would play a foundling, brought up by "gypsies traveling in wagons, sleeping outdoors," and, as Colonel suggested, living the kind of lifestyle that would show off Elvis' rugged versatility and allow him to stay free of the goody-good image that was killing Pat Boone.

Apart from the romance of the traveler's life, the one thing that intrigued him most was any form of entertainment that found its way into his otherwise circumscribed world. He had an aunt, one of his mother's sisters, who was an opera singer. She lived abroad, but every time she returned to the area, his mother took him to see her performance. He was so entranced by the spectacle, so drawn in by the music, that at the age of seven or eight he learned the arias to a number of the operas in which he saw her appear, and, as he recounted to Loanne, he would sometimes "walk through a pine forest near his home to a beautiful blue lake." There he would unburden himself of all of his cares and sing some of the arias he had learned, and the rich people who had houses along the shore would come out on their balconies and applaud. But, he told Loanne, he stopped singing when his voice changed, though he never lost his love of opera.

Of even greater impact was the fair that came to town the third Sunday of October every year. As Dutch journalist Dirk Vellenga wrote, "It took over the whole town, as its tents and stalls spread across the marketplace [and] all the way to the Kloosterplein, just around the corner from the Vlaszak, where the van Kuijks lived, [and] the normally dour town would temporarily become a place of music and laughter." The highlight for Dries was the van Bever family circus, a relatively small operation but a real circus nonetheless, with clowns and acrobats and, best of all, trained horses, all performing under a big top in a tent that had to be erected in every town they played. "He loved the circus," said his sister Engelina. He would hang around wide-eyed as they put up the tent, and soon he was volunteering for odd jobs, and then simply doing them if no one stopped him. He carried water for the animals without being asked, he helped the roustabouts, who fascinated him with their rough, freewheeling ways. No one questioned why he wasn't in school, and soon, in lieu of pay, he was rewarded with free admission to the circus, not just for himself but sometimes for his friends and brothers and sisters.

He loved the clowns, the way they entertained everyone with routines that, even if they were predictable, were so ingratiating that the audience responded with uproarious laughter every time. One of the clowns, it turned out, was some kind of distant relative, or perhaps just an acquaintance of the Ponsies, and he stayed with them whenever the circus was in town. Soon Dries was following him everywhere—he would pick up his discarded cigar butts and puff on them with the air of someone who knew himself to *be* somebody. Years later he could look back on the experience and say that this was the beginning of his lifelong love affair with what he would always call the wonderful world of show business.

With all of this as background, what could have been more natural than that young Dries should have sought to create a circus entertainment of his own?

At first it was a modest affair that he would present on Sunday afternoons when his father was at the local café. He charged his brothers and sisters and neighboring children a nominal fee for entrance to the "big top," a tent constructed of newspapers, which led to inevitable cancellations when it rained. The entertainment consisted of his own acrobatics, performed in scrupulous emulation of the acrobats that he had so closely observed at the van Bever circus, in addition to the various animals that he had collected and trained. He had a rabbit, some trained beetles, a number of sparrows that he had caught with small traps in the horse manure in the stables, and a goat that climbed stairs. The star of the show was a crow named Blackie, whom he had taught to do a few simple tricks, but when he tried to teach Blackie to deliver messages, the crow's strong stubborn streak kicked in, a trait that, he later ruefully acknowledged, was all too familiar to him.

Before long he decided to expand his circus and turn his father's heavy workhorses, whom he fed and watered every day, into performers. His model was the beautiful stallions in the van Bever circus, and he began by training the plodding dray horses to trot in circles, then to rear up, thrillingly, on their hind legs. Eventually, as Engelina's daughter, Mieke Dons-Maas, described it to biographer Alanna Nash, he "would walk on the backs of the horses, doing tricks and balancing acts as he jumped from one to the other." He was fearless, Engelina told her daughter, "even on the back of the meanest horse, the stallion who stood apart from all the others in another box."

This went on until one day his father, Adam, came home unexpectedly from the van den Enden Café and with a roar declared, not for the first time, that Dries was no son of his, that he would never amount to anything, and, after beating him to within an inch of his life, announced that he would be banned from having anything further to do with the stables.

HE QUIT SCHOOL AT TWELVE. He was in the fifth grade at the local elementary school after being expelled from St. Antoninus for his incorrigible clowning, and now he found himself expelled again for dramatically challenging his teacher's authority (she rapped him on the knuckles, he bit her on the leg and walked out of the school, never to return). He roamed the countryside, volunteered to work at a local farm doing what he enjoyed most, taking care of the animals, and with a friend from school, Cees Frijters, came up with a scheme to bring each of their families a real treat. The two of them, he told his sister Engelina, stopped by a local orchard and pretended to be foreigners. Dries, as the lead actor, was supposed to be English, and jabbered away in an indecipherable mix of made-up sounds, until at last the bewildered farmer gave them bags of apples just to get rid of them. They stopped off at the Teteringen orphanage on their way home, where he and Cees, he told Engelina, gave every one of the orphans an apple. What was left, they brought home for their families to enjoy. This was only one of his and Cees' many adventures. As Engelina's daughter told biographer Nash, "He would scheme, but always in a good way." Some might think him a bit of a rogue, she said, "but others had to laugh, because they had fun with him."

He got a job with a grocer for a few weeks, then went to work for a barber, but evidently his mind was not on his work, at least not the time he left a customer half shaved (his sisters liked to think the customer must have been drunk) and watched as the poor man stumbled out into the street to the amusement of passersby. Still, such was his charm, that, far from dismissing him from his job, the childless couple who owned the barbershop wanted to adopt him, though his mother, said Engelina, did not think much of the idea. Nor, unsurprisingly, did Dries, who, she said, "always wanted to be independent." To his sisters he seemed sometimes to be imagining a whole other life for himself, caught up in dreams of all the wonderful adventures that lay ahead.

In the spring of 1925 Adam van Kuijk became ill, and Dries prevailed upon his father to let him live with his mother's brother Jan Ponsie in Rotterdam, a bustling seaport of over five hundred thousand, which was just thirty miles away but a world apart. His father died shortly after, just ten days after Dries' sixteenth birthday, and he settled in comfortably with his uncle and his uncle's family. His uncle was an executive with Spido, a major shipping company, where he found Dries work in the shipping office for a time. But this was not the kind of life he craved, and in the face of Dries' constant importuning his uncle got him a job first on a Spido river taxi, then on a boat that delivered wheels of cheese all over the country.

His uncle formally adopted him, along with his five other minor siblings (the youngest was just seven), though the others all continued to live with their mother. Dries loved the city, he loved the water, and he appreciated the newfound comfort of his surroundings. He was fully grown now, nearly six feet tall, slim, with an expectant look, his hair neatly parted to the left—he was very particular about his appearance and spent much of his money on "fine clothes," which he sent home to his mother to be laundered. Whenever he returned home himself, he had expensive gifts for everyone, including, one time, cologne from a recent trip to Germany.

And yet he remained restless, moving from job to job, to his uncle's dismay. His sister Engelina put it down in part to his desire to make money (when he visited and their mother asked about his latest job, he would say, "I am no longer working there, because I can earn a [little] more"), but she also recognized that he simply "didn't like being told what to do," whether by his employers or by his uncle.

Soon he started absenting himself again, for a night or two at first, then for longer and longer periods of time. He couldn't explain it himself. In recollecting the experience, he said, "For some reason I had to keep moving," though if he had been pressed, he couldn't have explained exactly why.

And then one day he simply disappeared. In March of 1926 he set off for America, stowing away on the *Veendam* on the Holland America line.

To his consternation he found himself back home again in Rotterdam on March 30, less than one month later. He had been apprehended upon arrival in New York and sent back at the expense of the U.S. government. His uncle was understandably beside himself—but Dries explained it all away by saying that he simply hadn't had time to let his uncle know of his plans. And then, before summer had even arrived, he was gone again, his determination to escape to America undimmed.

This time, he succeeded.

TWO

America

D
RIES ARRIVED IN AMERICA for the second time in the spring of 1926, just two or three months after his first, failed attempt. He was a stowaway once again, once again on the Holland America line, but this time on a ship bound for Hoboken, New Jersey. From all that he told his family, it seems almost certain that he had been doing odd jobs for Holland America in Rotterdam, and very likely made friends at the shipping line who could help him refine his plan to evade the authorities both on board ship and at the port of arrival. What may have helped even more was making the acquaintance of a Dutch family who had recently immigrated to Hoboken. Whether he met them on board and they helped talk him through customs, as has been speculated, or somehow, in a city that boasted a large Dutch immigrant population, he simply found his way to their door, they were instantly taken with him and welcomed him into their home.

He was not quite seventeen years old.

Mostly he stayed indoors at first. The family thought he was shy, but he was not yet ready for the streets — he knew barely any English, and he did not want to be deported again. Instead, he read everything he could get his hands on — newspapers, handbills, advertising flyers — and listened insatiably to the radio. He peppered the family with questions about American ways, and they were utterly charmed, and concerned, about this young boy, seemingly without ties or family — they kept asking him, wasn't there anyone who would be worrying about him back home — and eventually they wormed out of him that he had an uncle in Rotterdam. When he wouldn't write to at least assure his family that he was safe, the mother of his new American family wrote to his uncle and aunt instead, astonishing the Ponsies, who had not heard from Dries in weeks and weeks, with the news that their ward was safe, and in America, and such a very nice, well-behaved young man. With that a correspondence began between the mothers of the two respective households and, upon learning that the Ponsies, too, had a daughter the Hoboken mother wrote to see if the girl might be able to come visit, even though she was several years older than her own ten-year-old daughter. Dries' cousin, Marie, surmised that the woman in America, who was clearly well-to-do, was probably homesick, "that must have been why she let Dries in and invited me to come, too."

The next the Ponsies heard, Dries was gone again. He had evidently vanished without a trace — not a word, not a letter, the New Jersey woman wrote to them. "Have you heard anything?" she plaintively inquired. "All we can suppose is that he's trying to join the American army. He talked about it sometimes."

But he had not. He had set off on his first full-scale course of adventures.

He spent the next eight or ten months hoboing around the country. This, he told his second wife, Loanne, in his old age, was where he really learned about life. He rode the rails from town to town, camped out in hobo jungles, and came to know how to seek out the men (and occasionally women) who might show a stranger kindness. He was, essentially, a loner but recognized that you needed not only friends but allies in this rough world. This was where he gained confidence in his English, questioning his fellow travelers not just about the meaning of words but also about American ways. He stopped over in a small Kansas town with one of his new friends and found work at a flour mill, living in a boarding-house where he curried favor with the landlady's daughter for extra portions at breakfast, but when he felt she might be taking his attentions too seriously he moved on. One time in a sweltering boxcar he saw an advertisement for a Chicago hotel that offered ice water out of the tap in every one of its rooms, and he vowed that someday he would make enough money to stay in a place like that.

When he reached Los Angeles, he worked briefly at Aimee Semple McPherson's recently opened Angelus Temple, after discovering that this was a place you could always get a free meal and bed if you showed up early enough and professed your faith in Jesus Christ. ("Be sure to get there by seven o'clock," he advised his Hollywood friends in later years.) He was, he said, even offered a full-time job there but turned it down

Andreas at seventeen or eighteen. *Courtesy of the Graceland Archives.*

because of his ingrained suspicion of organized religion and the way it preyed on ordinary people, desperate for belief. One of his few articles of faith throughout his long life was that you could never persuade anyone to do something for material gain that they didn't want to do, but you could fleece them out of all their worldly goods with the promise of heaven.

Once again he resumed hoboing, heading east on a trip that took a violent turn. Perhaps letting down his guard, he was beaten and robbed of all his possessions by a gang of ruffians, then driven out of the hobo camp and left in the freezing rain. He started off disconsolately down the road and, as it grew dark, was nearly at the point of surrendering to his feelings of abandonment and despair. It was, he said, the closest he ever came to thoughts of suicide. But then, he saw a light in the window of a solitary home and screwed up the courage to knock on the door. A Black man answered his knock, and he asked if he could sleep on the porch until the rain stopped. But the man wouldn't hear of it, he took him in and introduced him to his wife and children, and then the couple insisted that he stay with them until he was strong enough to resume his journey.

It was a traumatic experience that he never forgot, but in his telling of the story he never failed to mention that it was a Black family that had taken him in, which proved once and for all to him that human kindness was color-blind. And it led to a lifelong practice, once he had money of his own, of always having enough in his pocket to help those down on their luck at a time when they could actually use it.

But except for that single moment of despair, he never once lost faith that this was where he was meant to be, a land of promise and illimitable opportunity, a land where you could become whatever you chose to be and imagination alone could provide you with all the tools you needed for success. America was everything in his mind that Holland was not: proud, impetuous, braggadocious, daring, a society that was inherently generous in its appreciation of individuality and difference. He never again wanted to be anywhere else.

A T SOME POINT in his travels Dries found himself in Huntington, West Virginia, and here the story takes a turn. This is a place you will have heard of if you know anything about Colonel Tom Parker and the origin story that he would always provide some thirty years later when he first showed up in the public eye as the manager of the young recording star Elvis Presley. In this version of the story (it had many variants) Thomas Andrew Parker was born in Huntington on June 26, 1909, where his parents, who were otherwise childless, happened to be touring with a carnival. Sadly they died before he reached the fifth grade, and he was adopted by an uncle, scion of "The Great Parker Pony Circus," who gave him his own "pony-and-monkey act." Recognize any similarities? You can see how this all syncs up with the story as we know it (dropping out of school in the fifth grade, the pony-and-monkey act, being adopted by an uncle, the nomadic legacy of the Ponsies), just imaginatively transposed and transplanted more or less to another continent.

Well, in a way it was true. Huntington was indeed the birthplace of Thomas A. Parker in the more prosaic, though perhaps no less imaginative, origin story that he presented to Loanne, his constant companion for the last thirty-five years of his life. When he arrived in Huntington — how, he never explained — he came upon a small carnival, he told her, and the Parker family, who had the pony ride concession, seeing his unmistakable love of animals, and his adeptness at handling the horses, hired this shy but strangely self-possessed seventeen-year-old to help. Now, at this point I'm not clear on whether the Parkers were natives of Huntington or traveling with the carnival, but at any rate, much like the family in Hoboken, they were taken with this footloose young man who for whatever reason seemed at this point in his life to be merely drifting. When they asked where he was from, who his people were, he told them he was an orphan, and as they grew more and more fond of him (like the barber in Breda, not coincidentally, I would say, they had no children of their own), they offered to adopt him. For reasons of his own — let's just say he was ready, *at that moment,* to settle down — he embraced the offer and chose the American name of Thomas to go along with Andrew, an adaptation of his given name, Andreas, and even went so far as to allow himself to be baptized under his new name into his adoptive parents' faith. And then — well, then he disappeared again.

Here I hope you will permit me a digression of my own.

When, some ten or eleven years after his original arrival in Huntington in 1926, he registered for Social Security in Tampa, Florida, as a married, U.S.-born citizen, he listed his birthplace as Huntington, put down his actual birth date, but recorded his parents as "Edward Frank Parker" and "Mary Ida Ponsy [Parker]." And it occurred to me (and I'm sure others) that perhaps there was a clue in that. His real mother's maiden name was Maria Ponsie—but what about that "Ida"? And what about "Edward Frank"? I couldn't make any connection there, so could perhaps one or both of those names lead to a Parker from Huntington married to a woman named Ida?

No such luck. Or perhaps I was just taking Colonel Tom Parker too literally. Believe me, I struggled mightily to find some horse-raising Parkers in Huntington, some horse-trading Parkers, any Parkers at all who might have some connection, however peripheral, with a local or traveling circus. What I did find, with the help of some assiduous Huntington researchers, were a couple named Frank and Ida Parker, who lived in nearby Portsmouth, Ohio, a kind of sister city to Huntington, which was a railroad hub well into the '20s and '30s—but, no farm, no horses. And they were Black.

Okay, just indulge me one speculative twist more. When Loanne told me the story of how a seventeen-year-old Dries was set upon and robbed in a "hobo camp" and then rescued by a Black couple, the next stop on his journey, more or less (though I must admit this was not a neatly arranged chronological tale), was Huntington. And the Black couple were young, while the Parkers of Portsmouth were in their late fifties. So—who knows? We must always remember that Tom Parker, like his younger counterpart, Andreas, had a genuine gift for confabulation. Perhaps a young Black couple with small children made for a better story, even when he was relating it to his wife. Perhaps it simply taught a better lesson. (All of Colonel's stories taught lessons.) But I'm afraid I'm just going to have to leave it there. Feel free to make of it what you will.

My one certainty is that he was connected *in some way* to a family named Parker somewhere in the vicinity of Huntington, West Virginia. What he did, and for how long, after taking leave of the Parkers, is anyone's guess. By now he was fluent enough in English to make his own way in America—and with his gift for languages (he spoke some French, some German, some Romani, maybe even a little Yiddish), he could get along in almost any setting and find the kind of jobs he had been able to pick up in Holland with no real fear of apprehension. (Dries had always been proud of his practical and mechanical skills.)

I wish I could have talked to him about it — I wish *anyone* could have. But, even though he was clearly tempted toward the end, he remained unwilling to entrust his memories to scrutiny beyond a certain, limited point, and as Loanne pointed out, while he always loved to entertain friends and acquaintances with his stories, and never failed to relate them with the greatest of relish, he never provided any opportunity for interrogation, not even by his wife.

The one thing that we do know for sure is that on September 2, 1927, some sixteen months after he left home, he arrived back in Breda just in time for his mother's fifty-second birthday. He was, according to his brothers and sisters, the life of the party, dispensing gifts and conducting himself with a remarkable new sense of self-assurance and aplomb — but he made no excuses and he never said a word about where he had been. Two weeks later, at his sister Adriana's wedding, according to his Dutch biographer Dirk Vellenga, he behaved in such a madcap way as to seem almost unhinged. He stood on a table and recited a poem about "a boy who was bright and had a lot of talent [but because he was] lazy and lacking in motivation, ended up working as a bellhop." As the evening wore on, he danced a one-legged jig, following that up with a bawdy song. "A few people," Vellenga wrote, "glanced at his mother [to see] how she was responding to this behavior." But she was so glad to have her son home that she said nothing at all.

Some of the family thought that perhaps he had found his true métier at last, that, with his sly wit, he might be about to embark upon a career in the theater, as an entertainer of some sort, a clown or a comedian. But there is no evidence to suggest that he had any inclination to pursue anything of the sort, at least not at this time.

Instead, he settled into what could only have been a depressed kind of existence in his hometown. While America was booming, Dutch shipping was still suffering from the aftereffects of the First World War and the devastating impact it had had on the nation's principal trading partner, Germany. And it might be said that Dries himself had burned a lot of bridges — it seemed unlikely that he could look for much help from his uncle at this point. He finally found work at a shipping firm in Breda called Huyser, a regular customer of the delivery company his father had worked for. At first he simply loaded and unloaded barges, the kind of tedious work he had done all he could to escape. But Huyser ran a daily delivery service between Breda and Rotterdam, and before long he got a job as a deckhand, which suited his purpose by permitting him to resituate in Rotterdam, where he stayed at a kind of no-frills employee hostel that Huyser maintained above their offices.

That was his last known Dutch address.

In May of 1929, once again, he simply disappeared. The first his family knew of it was when a man from Huyser showed up at his mother's door with his trunk, saying the company couldn't store it any longer. "Nobody knew about it," his sister Engelina said. "He left all his possessions, his suitcase with clothing and his money, including his savings (because he didn't spend much), were still here. At that time I was so much younger, and I had my own life, but now I am old [she was eighty-six at the time] and think about it and [wonder] why did this happen the way it did?"

No one really knows for sure—either why or how—but let me fall back mostly on the Colonel's own account, primarily as related to his second wife, Loanne. He left Rotterdam on a freighter that appears to have had a number of ports of call. He was not a stowaway this time but worked in the ship's kitchen and anywhere else he could make himself useful. The ship docked in Curaçao in the Dutch West Indies, but this was not Dries' final destination. Instead, he appears to have signed on with a small fishing vessel of dubious lineage, which was impounded for rum-running in Mobile, Alabama. The captain was arrested, but the crew scattered in all directions. Dries found his way somehow to Atlanta, where, as he liked to tell the story, he saw a picture of beckoning Hawaiian sands (or maybe it was more like the illustration described in the July 15 issue of the *United States Army Recruiting News* of "soldiers on top of the mountains overlooking [beautiful] Pearl Harbor"), and with the assurance that this was where he would be stationed, he unhesitatingly joined the U.S. military, on June 20, 1929, six days before his twentieth birthday. He enlisted as Thomas Parker (serial number 6363948), acknowledging his Dutch birth and claiming that he had immigrated to this country in 1925. He was excited to be heading for the Island of Hawaii, where he would once again live on the water but be as far removed from his native land as he could imagine. He felt confident that in the army he would find both a safe harbor and an unassailable new identity, at least for the next three years.

THREE

Under Hawaiian Skies

The old man was walking a Russian Wolfhound in the park near the Royal Hawaiian Hotel. The Russian Wolfhound was an uncommon breed in Honolulu at the time, with its sleek, elegant looks, and the old man was taken with the gentleness with which the young man, his hair slicked down and carefully parted, knelt down and spoke to the dog. Without giving it much thought, he asked the young man what he was doing in Hawaii, and when the young man replied that he was in the army, stationed at Fort Shafter and far from home, the old man invited him to come to the house for Sunday dinner without a second thought. The old man introduced himself in a thick German accent as Carl Kufferath; he said he bred Russian Wolfhounds as a hobby. The young man introduced himself, with no discernible accent, as Tom Parker.

DRIES, now Private Tom Parker, had arrived in Hawaii in the fall of 1929 after a long voyage from San Francisco. He was stationed, first, at Fort DeRussy, near Waikiki, then transferred to Fort Shafter three miles outside of Honolulu, where he was assigned to the the antiaircraft section of the 64th Coast Artillery, whose principal job was to protect the island of Oahu against the possibility of air attack.

He wrote home not long after his arrival, assuring his family that he was well and alternately signing his letters André and Tom. He would send pictures from time to time, but he would never tell them where he was, or what he was doing. One snapshot showed him standing next to a big American car, maybe a Buick. "In another," said his sister Adriana, "he was sitting by a swimming pool." Since he never offered any details, the family wondered at first if maybe "he was a chauffeur for a rich man." In the pictures that have survived, he looks proud and self-assured, clearly pleased with the new place he has found for himself in the world. He continued to stay in touch with his family from time to time, and in

Private Thomas Parker,
64th Coast Artillery,
antiaircraft section,
ca. 1929. *Courtesy of the
Graceland Archives*

January arranged for five dollars a month out of his paycheck to go to his mother through the military finance office in Washington, which sent the money to Frans Laurijssen, Bankier, in Breda, where his sister Engelina picked it up.

He soon made friends in his regiment, cheerfully sharing duties, if not memories—but at the heart of his experience in Hawaii was the family of the old man he had met in the park. The Kufferaths would have stood out under any circumstances, but for young Private Parker not just the warmth of their welcome but the very diversity of their background provided him with some reassurance that there was a place in the world for him here. Papa Kufferath (Carl Theodor Jacob) was the son of a musical conductor in northwest Germany, his wife, Shin Hori, was Japanese, and they had met in Japan, where they lived for a time before moving to Hawaii twenty years earlier. All but two of the children (there were eleven in all, with the eldest born in 1896) had been born in Japan, Germany, or Tasmania, and all but those two would be interned for a time during the Second World War as suspected "enemy aliens." Although "Mama" Kufferath spoke scarcely any English, she was known to all for opening her house to anyone her husband or children might bring home, and she welcomed the newcomer with open arms. She urged him to eat up, this "Tommy" needed to put on some weight. "Get fat," she said, gesturing at his belly, and they all laughed.

Every Sunday he would come to the house, where he found a lively gathering of like-minded souls. He loved Papa Kufferath and was drawn to the dogs he raised, too, the beautiful borzois that were the mascots of the renowned "Wolfhound" Infantry Regiment stationed at Schofield Barracks. Tom spent time with the old man, walking and training the dogs, and he even accompanied Papa Kufferath to a dog show at Schofield, taking almost as much pride as Papa in the way the wolfhound Papa had donated to the unit performed.

But mostly he just cherished the time he spent with the family, who found Tom not only charmingly self-effacing but also, they all agreed, "one of the most intelligent young men" they had ever met. The two family members he was closest to were the youngest son, Arnold, sixteen years old and still a high school student, but just four years younger than Tom, and Bernhard "Sonny" Cordes, who was twenty-six and married to Arnold's sister Luise. Arnold was lean, athletic, an avid reader—he didn't smoke or drink and was often taken for a native Hawaiian because of the depth of his knowledge of the culture and the dark coloration of his skin. He had a quietly curious nature, not unlike Tom's, but it was Sonny, whose father was German, his mother Hawaiian, who was the real spark plug of the family. Sonny was a salesman at Aloha Motors in the heart of Honolulu, handsome, debonair, a real sport, with a natural, easygoing manner that made an impression on just about everyone he met. After dinner he and Tom would puff on cigars, drawing the moment out— Arnold had never seen anyone who enjoyed a cigar more than Tom—and then at the end of the evening the three of them would pile into Sonny's Model T and drive Tom back to the barracks.

After a while Tom started bringing some of his friends from the base. There was quite a bit of free time at Fort Shafter—it was generally known as "easy duty"—and the other enlistees, while they may not have been as

In driving cap, with Sonny Cordes, Hawaii, ca. 1929. *Courtesy of Gayle Kufferath Behnke*

Hawaii, ca. 1930.
Courtesy of the
Graceland Archives

far from home as Tom, were far from home nonetheless and seemed to very much enjoy their long afternoons at the Kufferaths'. And at the end of the day Mama Kufferath would always load them up with food, and Sonny would take them back to the base.

It was clear to everyone that Tom was feeling more and more at ease among his fellow recruits, exchanging small talk and complaints about everyday assignments and good-naturedly losing much of his pay to them in friendly games of craps. But he never let on to anyone, not even the Kufferaths, the secret of his origins. And of all his Breda acquaintances, he remained in touch only with his old schoolmate Cees Frijters, now serving with the Dutch army in Indonesia, with whom he communicated freely about his new experiences.

Sometime during the summer he told the Kufferaths that he was going to be transferred to the mainland in the fall. There was general consternation in the Kufferath family, but they had no doubt that Tom would do well wherever he went, and equally little doubt that he would return to Hawaii and they would all see each other again before long.

When they didn't hear from him at first, they didn't think much of it. As the years went by, despite all that happened (Papa Kufferath died, Arnold would get married, join the fire department, and have a daughter, and Sonny continued to prosper), they never ceased to talk about him. They always wondered what had happened to their friend Tom.

H E R E P O R T E D to his new assignment with the 13th Coast Artillery at Fort Barrancas in Pensacola in the fall of 1931. All went well at first. His three-year enlistment would be up in June, and as he wrote to his mother on February 9, he was not at all certain what he would do next. He had gotten her package, he wrote, and was pleased with the ties and socks she had sent him. As to the future, he concluded, "Everything is still the same. And I'll do the best I can do when my time is over. I can judge that much better when my time is over."

There was not much else to be said other than that he had no new photos to send her. Within a few months, he promised, he would send her a new one. And with that he signed off with greetings for the whole family. There is no hint that this would be the last known letter he would ever send to her. Except that at this very time the monthly allotments he had been sending home for the past two years (by now the sum had risen to seven dollars) abruptly stopped.

In March he took a monthlong furlough. He made good use of his time, traveling around Florida, he told his wife, Loanne, many years later, and connecting with the carnies and circus people who wintered in Pensacola. From all appearances he seemed to be settling comfortably into his new regimen, despite the fact that duty at Fort Barrancas was more demanding than anything he had experienced in Hawaii. He even reenlisted in June, seemingly in contradiction of what he had intimated to his mother, and shortly thereafter was promoted to private first class.

But then, two months later, after seven members of his unit had been granted leave and he had not, he granted himself a furlough on his own initiative. The army marked him down right away as absent without leave, and a week later, when he continued to be absent, he was demoted to private. He didn't return until February 17, 1933, with no explanation for his absence. Loanne got the impression from the way he talked about it fifty years later that he had simply caught up with some of his circus or carnival pals and gone off on tour with them, but she didn't really know. And if that was the case, one might ask, why bother to come back at all, why didn't he simply disappear, as he had in the past? Instead, he returned after nearly five months' absence, was sentenced to sixty days in solitary, and, upon release, according to biographer Alanna Nash, was so emotionally disturbed that he was placed first in the base hospital for observation, then sent to Washington for further evaluation at Walter Reed. On August 19, 1933, he received an honorable discharge with a certificate of disability that, according to Nash, cited reasons of "Psychic Psychogenic Depression" (he always said his medical discharge was for a bad leg that he had injured in the service), which may very well have been the outcome he had been looking for all along. But if it was, surely there were easier ways to get it.

So what does it all mean?

Loanne understandably discounted the whole story. She was convinced that he simply grew tired of the regimentation, as others have before and since, and, true to his nature, conceived of an ingenious, if inexplicably painful, way out.

If I had to guess, I would say that almost as soon as he reenlisted, he realized that he had made a terrible mistake. As anyone who knew Colonel Parker in later years would attest, he was not meant for a conventionally ordered life—at least not one in which anyone else was giving the orders. Nor in many ways was the abruptness of his departure radically different from the way Dries van Kuijk had always acted, just one more in a series of impromptu escapes he had been making since early childhood, though linked as it was—at least chronologically—with what would turn out to be a permanent estrangement from his mother, from his entire family in fact, it was certainly the cruelest in its consequences both for himself and those he loved.

It's hard to imagine that he was not discomfited for at least a moment or two by his inglorious exit from the army, but if he was, it didn't last long. For it was at this point that almost immediately, and seemingly without any hesitation whatsoever, he plunged into the glittering carnival world that had been beckoning to him for so long and from which, in one form or another, he would never depart.

FOUR

The Big Tent

THE CARNIVALS were at the height of their season by the time he got his discharge, but he had no trouble catching on with one of the smaller operations he had made contact with since arriving in Florida two years earlier.

By the spring of 1934 he had landed a job with the Johnny J. Jones Exposition, universally known as "The Mighty Monarch of the Tented World." It had fallen on hard times for a spell after the death of its charismatic owner three years earlier, but by the time Tom Parker joined, Johnny J. Jones had been thoroughly reconstituted under the direction of Louis "Peasy" Hoffman, a legendary figure in the carnival world. Hoffman, "a short, fat man with round glasses, an ever-present white hat, [and] an amiable but persistent attitude that rarely wavered," as Colonel's Dutch biographer Dirk Vellenga described him, was Tom Parker's conduit to Johnny J. Jones.

He had come to know Peasy Hoffman during the offseason in Tampa, a city of one hundred thousand that felt like a small town, where many of the shows wintered. One of the first lessons he learned was that the advance man (generally doubling as the overall promotion director) was the key to the success of the show. You needed, of course, to have the talent, Peasy advised his eager young student—but all of the shows had the talent and variety to open up the eyes of any audience that turned out to see them, especially in the more remote rural areas. It was the advance man, though, doubling as publicist and "community organizer," who got them stirred up to begin with, who greased the skids for a complex moving operation that set up shop in a new town every few days, who played an integral role in making sure that all licenses were properly obtained, that the local police force was sufficiently recompensed, that credit was established, and then extended if there were unexpected

New Year's Eve promotion, Tampa, December 31, 1934. Colonel is third from right. *Courtesy of the Graceland Archives*

forces (like three days of rain) to contend with, that handbills were printed and posted, newspapers notified—and all this *before* the show came to town.

For Tom Parker—"Tommy" to most of his elders—it was the opportunity of a lifetime. When the show left town, he left with it. He had no greater ambition than to learn everything he could at the feet of Peasy Hoffman and anyone else willing to instruct him. He had no hesitation about starting at the bottom—where else were you going to start if you were doing something you loved? If anyone had asked him what he liked most about the experience, he would have answered, *Everything—*

because, in reality, it was all he had ever dreamt of, everything that he had ever imagined.

As he would describe it with undisguised pride in later years, it was "like building a small village every week." Once the brightly colored trucks were unloaded off the flatbed railroad cars, the mechanics began bolting together all the pieces of equipment that made up the rides. The big tent had to be sited and erected first, then the smaller tents for the games and sideshows, all in such a way as to take maximum advantage of the allotted space. Miles of cable had to be laid, the generators tested, and at the end of a very long day you might finally get a chance for a few hours' sleep.

There was no predictable routine. He did anything and everything that was asked of him, working at the candy-apple stand, announcing and selling tickets for the rides, using his mechanical skills to help repair the games, pitching to the best of his still somewhat limited fluency in English for the sideshow or the penny arcade.

Whatever else he might do, he sought out every opportunity to work with, or simply take care of, the animals. He prided himself on his ability to communicate with them—he seemed almost to *identify* with them, whether it was a stray dog or cat, the performing horses, or the great pachyderms for whom he maintained an abiding fascination. He washed and watered the elephants whenever he could, and if he was lucky enough got to work with them and their trainers. Sixty years later he would write to country music star Garth Brooks in admiration of Brooks' spectacular high-wire act: "It reminded me of my circus days when I floated on top of an elephant." Which I'm sure he did, if only in imagination. And over the years he never missed a chance to visit the elephants he had worked with, should a traveling circus or carnival pass his way; he never failed to underscore his respect for their intelligence, discernment, and remarkable memory to anyone (and this could include his wife, a small child, a William Morris agent, or one of Elvis' retinue) he had brought along on the visit.

He soaked up everything he could from every experience. Unloading the trucks was a challenge at first. Well, not actually *un*loading—that was easy enough. But the first time he and his fellow workers tried to reload the equipment, he recalled, they were unable to fit it all back in again, as the boss just stood there, sadly shaking his head. "Everything came off

In later times with a later elephant, but who knows, perhaps the progeny of one of the elephants he worked with long ago. On the set of *Roustabout* with Elvis and Barbara Stanwyck, 1964. *Courtesy of the Graceland Archives*

that truck," he said, "and it will fit back. Now unload it, and do it right this time, because you're going to be here until you do." And by the next town, or the town after that, they were able to accomplish the task in just one or two tries.

Most of all he loved the warmth of a world that by its very definition provided a haven for outcasts, whether by choice or exclusion, a world that embraced its inhabitants without regard for pedigree or appearance. The clowns, the gypsies, the fortune tellers and mind readers, the dwarfs and acrobats, the "freaks," all constituted an astute, self-reliant community. ("We took care of each other," was one of Colonel Parker's most often repeated aphorisms.) He delighted in the special made-up language that they spoke to keep their business to themselves, he delighted in their ability to "read" the public, and each other. They had their own code of conduct, which relied on cleverness, resourcefulness, and mother wit, to survive in a world that, as he had come to view it, was never to be trusted.

And they possessed an unswerving loyalty to one another, and to the preservation of order in the set-apart world that they had built for themselves. In this world, a man's past didn't matter — it was all about the present, it was all about the future. The big bosses and specialty acts might travel and live on their private railroad cars, but he was happy to sleep on the merry-go-round, his worn clothing pressed in between two boards so it would look as neat and presentable as he could make it the next morning.

The cookhouse was the center of the carny world. Not only were you always guaranteed a good, nourishing meal, it provided a refuge and a gathering place after the midway had closed, a place not just for conversation but for all-night craps games in which carnival "scrip" was exchanged until payday arrived. Tommy Parker cherished every aspect of the experience; he had never enjoyed a greater opportunity for sharp-witted conversation, or a stronger sense of community, without ever being asked where he was from, or where he was going. The outside world was not so much the "enemy" as a necessary accessory to their own. And if the customers they called "rubes" occasionally felt they had been fleeced, the show folk rested easy in the same belief that underlay P. T. Barnum's philosophy and was soon to be immortalized by the vaudeville comedian and movie star W. C. Fields, "You can't cheat an honest man."

These were the people whom he would hold dear all his life. He would never cease to identify himself as a carny, and he ascribed nearly every one of the accomplishments of his fabled show-business career as something he had "learned from the carnies." And he never doubted for a moment that for all his awkwardness and unease, they appreciated him for who he was, a shy, oddly delicate, but enormously *eager* young man with new skills that revealed themselves every day and a desperate hunger for acceptance.

THE FOLLOWING year he went out with the Sells-Floto Circus, which had at one time featured Buffalo Bill's Wild West Show and would eventually be absorbed by the Ringling Bros. and Barnum & Bailey Circus. But while it was the realization of yet another childhood dream, perhaps because circus life was more regimented than the freewheeling life of the carnival, perhaps because once again he was starting at the bottom, he didn't find it as satisfying as the Johnny Jones Exposition, and in 1936 he was back with the carnival again. Only this time he was not alone.

He had met a young woman the previous year while she was working at the Hav-A-Tampa cigar stand set up by Royal American Shows on the grounds of the Florida State Fair. Marie Mott was twenty-six, just a year older than him, pretty, petite, outgoing in a way that almost immediately drew his attention. She lived with her mother and father and sixteen-year-old brother, Bitsy, along with her little boy by her first husband (she was just getting divorced from her second). She was bubbly, and she could be sharp-tongued at times, but for the first time in his life he was smitten. When her job at the Fairgrounds ended (she was, officially, dubbed "Miss [Cigar] Club" of Tampa), she started working at a coffee shop, and her new suitor fell into the habit of dropping by every afternoon for coffee.

When he came back from his season with Sells-Floto in the fall of 1935, they took up again as if they had never stopped, and he shared with her some of the secret dreams and ambitions that he had already begun to put into motion. On his own he had started to offer pony rides (he got the ponies from his showman friends) and set up a miniature animal show that included Dixie the pony, her colt Tiny, his dog Queenie, and a monkey called Peanuts. With this menagerie he did a special promotion at the Franklin Theatre for the opening of *Home on the Range,* starring Jackie Coogan and Randolph Scott, and there is a picture of him, erect and thin, with his hat tilted at a rakish angle, and Dixie, Tiny, and Queenie arrayed on the straw he had laid in a corner of the theater lobby. He also began a longtime practice of playing Santa Claus at the Maas Brothers department store, just down the street from the movie theater, where he not only embraced the role, he "shilled" for Santa, going out "on the streets around the store," as Dirk Vellenga wrote, "luring children and their probably less than willing parents into the department store's 'Toyland.'"

The two of them, Marie and Tom, went out together with Royal American Shows the following spring, leaving Marie's eleven-year-old son, Bobby, with her parents, and working both together and separately on the show. Royal American, which boasted the world's largest midway and the world's longest train (not to mention, according to Vellenga, "fifty-two rides, more than a thousand [employees] ... and enough electricity-generating equipment to light a city of forty thousand"), was

Man about town, Tampa, ca. mid-1930s. *Courtesy of the Graceland Archives*

at this point the undisputed king of the carnival world, and it would have been a thrill for Tommy Parker just to be there, let alone to be accompanied by his girl, who already knew many of the show folk from her own past associations. Marie sold tickets on the midway and worked the candy-apple stand, and everyone called her Mrs. Parker, even though they knew the two lovebirds were not yet married.

They returned to Tampa when the season was over and moved in with Marie's parents. Marie went back to work as a waitress, while Tom added steadily to his assortment of independent promotions. It was a challenge sometimes to find the money to pay for the placards and handbills he needed to generate business, but he struck up what would become a lifelong friendship with the printer he found to do the work. The first time he visited Rinaldi Printing on Howard Avenue, just north of Fig Street, he had just two dollars in his pocket, and the bill was going to come to ten, but the proprietor, Henry Rinaldi, looked the young man in the eye, assessed his character at a glance, and agreed to "carry" him for regular payments of one or two dollars a week.

Tom had never met anyone like Mr. Rinaldi before. In his late fifties, quiet, dignified, and a noted amateur historian, he had started the press in 1905 to publish his own books, one of which became the standard guide to South Florida until the Depression killed off the Florida land boom in the early 1930s. Rinaldi Printing was a well-established pillar of the city, but like every other business was affected by the hard times. Rather than let any of his workers go, Mr. Rinaldi started cooking lunch for them, and soon Tom, too, started showing up for lunch at his invitation. It was not a question of mooching, it was more a matter of learning, as Mr. Rinaldi dedicated himself to teaching the young man how to set up a business and offered thoughts and advice about how to deal with the public in a firm but kindly way. Before long Tom established a close friendship with Henry's twenty-two-year-old son, Clyde, who was just about to graduate from college. Father and son were equally taken with this lively young man so full of enthusiasm and ideas, so avid for knowledge about a world he had yet to fully experience or comprehend.

Tom and Marie went out again with Royal American the following year, but this time they took her son, who had the time of his life and acted as a kind of shill for a "Free Ham" giveaway (a free raffle ticket, that is, with the purchase of at least one Royal American ride), as he wandered the midway with a big ham on his shoulder, exclaiming, "Look what I won." Tom and Marie took charge of the pie car, too, that year, which was, in biographer Alanna Nash's description, "a kind of rolling casino with slot machines and games of chance for show people only." Tom not only presided over its official food-serving function, he almost invariably got caught up in the games of chance in which sometimes considerable amounts of "scrip" were wagered, and frequently lost, till the early hours of the morning.

But the high point of all his promotions was a gimmick he called "Wedding on the Wheel," which began with his going to the local courthouse to collect the names of every couple who had recently applied for a marriage license. Then, after a little bit of research, he would choose one of the lucky couples to be wed on the Ferris wheel. He had little trouble obtaining the wedding dress from "the best ladies' clothing store" in town by stressing to the owner how much business the free publicity would generate. Then he would promote the groom's suit in similar fashion, sometimes even managing a suit for the best man as well, plus "a wedding cake, bridal bouquet, groceries for the couple to start out married life, and [if he was lucky] even the bridal suite at the town's best hotel." That way, he loved to explain to latter-day listeners, all of the town's leading businesses had a stake in the carnival's success and would highlight Royal American in all their advertising, while the wedding party (always a big wedding party if his research was correct) would all attend and then pay to enjoy every ride and game on the midway. And there was never a single person in attendance who did not have a good time.

By now, with all this experience under his belt, he felt ready for bigger things, and so when the head advance man for Royal American quit, or was fired, in the middle of the 1937 season, Tom Parker confidently applied for the job.

He was turned down.

Various reasons were offered. Despite the success of Wedding on the Wheel, which everyone agreed had been slickly prepared and presented, he still was not ready. He might make a good junior advance man, he was told, but his ungrammatical speech and uncouth manner were simply not refined enough to deal with all the unexpected pitfalls that were bound to arise or, for that matter, all the local bigwigs that someone like Peasy Hoffman could so easily smooth over. He was told to wait, his time would come, he just needed a little more . . . *polish*.

But none of it made any sense to him, and he went ahead and got drunk, which he almost never did, starting with beer in the cookhouse, as he complained vociferously to his fellow workers, who just seemed to egg him on. As the evening progressed, he grew increasingly loud, and increasingly belligerent, until finally he marched right up to his boss and issued an ultimatum. Royal American at this point had a choice: either give him the job he deserved, or he quit. The result was a foregone conclusion.

Marie packed up, weeping and hurling recriminations at her "husband," who had shown such poor judgment in staking out a position from which he was too stubborn to retreat. And when he sobered up, he couldn't help but agree. He blamed no one but himself. It was the same mistake he had made in his hoboing days. He had become too self-confident, he had let down his guard. And he made a promise to himself there and then that he would never again drink alcohol to the point that it could impair his judgment in this manner. And, short of splitting a beer from time to time with one or another of Elvis' guys, he never did.

THEY RETURNED bedraggled to Tampa, where they once again took up residence at Marie's parents' house. As usual, Marie's mother and father moved out of their own bedroom to make room for the young couple, but they were delighted, as always, with the presents and souvenirs Tom and Marie had brought home from their travels. Marie went back to work as a waitress and Tom started up once again with all his various promotional gimmicks, renewing his ties with different movie theaters, expanding his animal shows and pony rides, and coming up with a "sleep endurance" contest at a local furniture store.

At some point, in a story he always loved to tell without, it seemed, too much regard for literal detail, he came across an elephant whose owner had suffered financial reverses and couldn't afford the substantial monthly feed bill. The way he told it, the poor animal was practically starving to death, so he took the elephant off its owner's hands, arranged with a local feed store to sponsor it in exchange for free sandwich-board advertising, and then found several other businesses in town that felt they, too, could benefit from similar publicity. And so, both he and the elephant thrived.

He was Santa Claus once again at Christmastime — it was a role he loved to play — but at the same time he could also be that spiffy young man in the double-breasted suit with a pocket square and white shoes taking part in the New Year's Eve celebration at the Park Theatre. In this role he convincingly played the freewheeling Rotarian, with the same bright faith in the nation's future as any other up-and-coming young businessman.

The following year he and Marie were both back out on the carnival circuit, only it was with L. J. Heth Shows this time, and this time he got the kind of job, as press agent and promoter, for which he had yearned for so long. It should have been a dream come true. It challenged all of his creative thinking, his tireless work ethic, and his staunch determination to maintain a positive approach at all times. He got a dog named Teddy and taught him to smile and do a few other tricks, and Teddy, who would be with him for a number of years, became part of the act. At one point in the season, they fell on hard times, and the carnival owner told him he thought they would need to lower the price of admission. No, Tom said without hesitation, he thought they should *double* the price of admission. And when the owner balked, or thought that he must have misheard him, Tom explained cheerfully that with the new price they could afford to offer a half-price refund to anyone who complained that they were not satisfied with the show. But hardly anyone ever did.

If this season of being-in-charge fulfilled many of his long-standing ambitions, for reasons that he was never able to fully articulate, or perhaps even understand, it turned out to be strangely unsatisfying. Marie's thoughts seemed more and more focused on settling down. They had both registered for Social Security the previous year, giving their residence as her parents' home, his employer as the Park Theatre. He was Thomas Andrew Parker, American-born in Huntington, West Virginia, on June 26, 1909, of equally native-born parents. And he signed the form in his customarily confident style.

Marie learned to cook all his favorite dishes, and while she could be confounded sometimes by his exacting standards, by what seemed like almost a fetish for cleanliness and personal hygiene, she was happy to settle into a domestic routine that might very well have led the rest of the world to think of them as just another happily married young couple. But whether she chose to acknowledge it or not (she did acknowledge her irritation that for whatever reason he refused to commit himself to the formal bonds of marriage), she couldn't altogether ignore that this was not the limit of her husband's dreams or aspirations. Those he confided to no one — he might even, she suspected, have had difficulty articulating them to himself.

They stayed busy. Marie had gotten a job playing piano at a music store, she was still with the Cigar Association, and she continued to waitress, too. As for Tom, he always found plenty to do. Everyone knew he was a hard worker, and one of the carnivals could always use his skills for several weeks at a time. He kept adding on to his portfolio of promotions and gratefully accepted advice from Henry Rinaldi not so much on how to conduct his business as how to make new connections by promoting himself. But mainly he appeared to be marking time. He seemed to feel, he *carried himself* in some indefinable way, as if he believed he was meant for better things.

FIVE

My Blue Heaven

G ENE AUSTIN was one of the first pop superstars. Bigger than Al Jolson for a time, bigger than Rudy Vallee; between 1925 and 1929, he had nine number-one hits, including such standards as "Yes Sir! That's My Baby," "Bye Bye Blackbird," and "Carolina Moon," and his 1927 recording of "My Blue Heaven," a rock 'n' roll staple for Fats Domino in the '50s, sold more copies (an estimated five million) than any single record until Bing Crosby's "White Christmas." He was, by all accounts, a great entertainer, with the ability to command any stage, but it was his relaxed, easygoing style that proved his most enduring legacy, influencing Bing Crosby profoundly and all those who would subsequently adopt Crosby's studiedly laid-back approach. All this was accomplished, he explained to his "nephew" (actually more like a third cousin) and protégé, Tommy Overstreet, a latter-day country star in his own right, by utilizing the microphone with an intimacy that previous recording techniques had not permitted. "What's the most important instrument when you're singing?" he demanded of his nephew. "Think about it. What's the most important instrument for you as a singer? You've got to learn how to hold that microphone and caress it and sing to it, so you can get the emotion through to the people. If you don't do that, everything else is whistling Dixie."

He was acknowledged by both Gene Autry and Jimmie Rodgers (the "Father of Country Music") as one of their greatest musical influences, and he provided each with personal and professional guidance. He formed a close connection with Fats Waller, too, the pioneering stride pianist and entertainer supreme, whose "Ain't Misbehavin'" he was among the first to record, with Waller accompanying him on piano over the objections of his otherwise all-white backing group. And while he sang for the most part in the kind of flutey falsetto favored by romantic crooners of the day, he insisted proudly that his was a falsetto with "balls." Which was a measure of both the delicacy and the forcefulness of his art.

By January of 1939, however, when he arrived in Tampa, Gene Austin had suffered a number of significant reverses. With the 1929 stock market crash, the bottom had fallen out of the recording business, and while he would continue to be a popular live attraction, accompanied by his own jaunty piano and the bass-and-guitar duo of Candy (Jonathan Joseph Candido) and Coco (Otto Heimel), who would soon become almost as well-known for their comedy bits as their virtuosic musical contributions, he never regained his popularity on the record charts. He did become something of a radio star, though, and he found work in the movies, too, in a succession of lively cameos, while enjoying intermittent success and failure in the cabaret business, rapidly acquiring, then just as quickly losing, ownership of various supper clubs and nightspots in a number of different cities. He remained, by his own description, a happy-go-lucky kind of guy, an unfailing optimist, who, far from saving his money, had, by his own admission, done everything he could to throw it away, placing his faith in a succession of people and opportunities that never quite came through.

His latest venture was a cowboy picture called *Songs and Saddles*, in which he starred as the singing cowboy in the white hat who chased bandits and saved the girl. Never really slim, at thirty-eight he made a determined effort to lose weight for the camera. He didn't have to brush up on his riding skills (he had grown up on a ranch and was a fine horseman), but perhaps as a concession to modern times, as often as not he chased the bad guys in his own motor home, called, appropriately, like the yacht that preceded it, "Blue Heaven."

As it turned out, making a movie outside of the Hollywood system presented difficulties he had not fully anticipated, problems of financing primarily (he almost immediately became a major investor in his own movie), but also distribution, and so he came up with a scheme to take the picture on the road and link it to personal appearances. From the outset this proved to be a challenge, as there were times when he was scheduled to appear in as many as three or four off-the-beaten-path towns in out-of-the-way markets in a single day.

That was how he found himself booked with his movie into the Park Theatre in Tampa, a more mainstream market than some, which had

Colonel, flanked by Gene Austin and Gene's fourth wife, LouCeil, with Louis Prima and Keely Smith at left, Las Vegas, 1957. *Courtesy of the Graceland Archives*

Songs and Saddles, 1938, with Gene singing, Candy on bass, Coco on guitar. *Courtesy of Barry Mazor*

Gene with popular Mexican film actress
Lupe Vélez. *Courtesy of Barry Mazor*

been a staple of his personal-appearance tours for the last five years. The
theater proudly announced his engagement for four shows a day immediately preceding each screening of his movie on January 28 and 29, 1939,
billing him with little exaggeration as "the outstanding recording artist
of all time" and promising that he would be accompanied by "Candy and
Otto [actually Coco]." In attendance both days was a young man named
Tom Parker, who introduced himself as someone who had done promotion work for the theater for years and would be only too happy to help
out in any way he could, should Mr. Austin require any assistance or
advice. And without being too brash about it, he wondered if with all the
complications that a tour like this entailed, Mr. Austin might not be able
to use the services of a good advance man and tour manager, which, the
young man explained, was the very job he had held with Royal American
Shows up until quite recently.

The young man carried himself with a degree of assurance that was
not unfamiliar to Austin. "He had a dynamic personality," Austin wrote,
"and told me of his lifelong background in carnivals and tent shows,
starting as a boy with his family," while stressing in particular his qualifications as "a crackerjack press agent and manager." Gene was sold, but
as he explained to Parker, unfortunately he didn't have a job for him at
the moment. He had to finish up this tour first, and he had a manager to
book all his personal appearances. Well, if anything ever came up, the

young man said. Of course, Gene replied, and filed it away for future reference.

The future was not far off. What happened next couldn't have been predicted. Or maybe it could, given the personalities involved. Toward the end of his movie tour Gene ran into a promoter named Billy Wehle, who had his own traveling tent show. Wehle immediately saw the potential of presenting a self-contained Gene Austin show and persuaded Gene that together they could get Gene back into the big time. They joined forces for the first time on February 25, 1939, in Valdosta, Georgia, in a show that would appear under a rapid succession of names but by April had more or less settled on Star-O-Rama of 1939. It advertised itself without undue modesty as "carrying a company of eighty people, including twenty lovely girls [in addition to] Gautchi and Sonnen, designers of dance divertissement, formerly at the Club Lido in Paris . . . and fifteen vaudeville acts selected from the leading nightclubs in the Americas and abroad [who would put on] a two-hour performance in its mammoth tented theater." All of this as a buildup to the show's presentation of its "bright star, Gene Austin, America's No. 1 song stylist, in person, together with his two colleagues of mirth and melody, Coco and Candy."

The show was an instant success. They drew as many as five thousand in Chattanooga, Knoxville, and Johnson City, Tennessee, playing on circus grounds and fairgrounds, or just in a big open field, but then, unfortunately, Gene and his new partner had a falling-out, as they discovered that each owed large sums of money to creditors, to the Internal Revenue Service, and in the end to each other. On July 8 *Billboard* reported that Gene would be taking over the show in three weeks in Raleigh under its new name, "The Ball of Fire Revue." By the time they arrived in Atlanta toward the end of August, it was called "Models and Melodies," though Star-O-Rama continued to be its prevailing name.

In Atlanta they encountered three days of heavy rain, and when the parking area became so mired in mud that they had to call off the show, Gene put on an impromptu performance for the patients at a local VA hospital. But the show by this time was so sunk in debt that Gene could no longer see a way forward. That was when he called the young man in Tampa who had been so eager to help out.

It was at least a fifteen-hour drive, but Tom and Marie Parker arrived the next day. Marie had strong misgivings — she grew emotional about leaving her son, Bobby, with her mother once again, about leaving friends and family behind. But Tom did not so much as blink. This was the call he had been waiting for; he felt as if fate had finally found him.

Under his direction, things turned around almost immediately. As Austin wrote, "It was obvious that Tom knew his business. In a short while he had the show going full blast, attendance was great, and it looked like we would never know anything but success and money."

Just as important, the two men, almost exactly nine years apart in age (Austin's birthday was two days before Tom's, a sign that neither one of them was incognizant of), were kindred spirits. Austin, too, had run away from home at the age of fifteen, in his case to join a traveling carnival, and he had led a life of adventure ever since. That spirit of adventure and invincible self-belief had not been daunted in the least by the unimaginable stardom he had attained in his mid-twenties. And now, at almost forty, he was just as determined to continue to discover new worlds. What they shared most of all, though, were two qualities not always combined in a single sensibility: on the one hand, both were thoroughgoing creatures of imagination; on the other, neither one of them knew the meaning of the word "quit." And so they careened around the South, setting up their tent wherever they could, a practice that to Austin's surprise Tom was particularly adept at, as Tom Parker single-handedly rescued the Star-O-Rama of 1939 from oblivion.

His promotional efforts were simple and effective, drawn directly from his carnival experience. For the most part he advanced the show by a week or ten days, doubling back to where he had left it once he had sufficiently seeded the ground. Placards were posted all over town saying only, in keeping with both his carnival training and his own gift for succinct messaging, "Gene's Coming!" Newspaper stories were planted, ads were placed announcing when and where the show would take place, always, unfailingly, "under the colossal canvas canopy." In each town Tom would find the most popular coffee shop, order as little as possible, stay as long as he was able, and pick up all that he could in the way of local news and gossip: who was influential, who might be open to the blandishments of the show-business world, who was a skinflint or a stiff-necked churchgoer that there would be little point in courting. Then he would make the rounds of promising local merchants and, just as with his "Wedding on the Wheel," give them a chance to provide heavily discounted goods to the show and thereby burnish their own reputations as sponsors of a performance that every man, woman, and child was going to want to see. In every town, Gene was advertised as frequenting this establishment or that, of employing the services of this single gas station or tire company. In one town, Gene drove only Chevys, in another Fords, and Tom supplied a sign for favored restaurant managers to display, announcing, "THE GENE AUSTIN SHOW EATS HERE." The show advertised twenty-five trucks, though they had only ten, and they didn't have enough serviceable tires for those, so he would send off four or five to the next town (as likely as not labeled GENE AUSTIN SHOW TRUCK No. 21 or No. 25), install them in place and remove the tires, which he would then bring back to the previous town, where they could serve the next batch of vehicles.

In Jackson, Tennessee, a young radio announcer and musician, Gabe Tucker, like nearly everyone else in town a fan of Gene Austin, went out to the Fairgrounds and was asked, as a representative of the press, if he'd like to meet the star of the show. "Well, I'd like to," he said, "but I'd really like to meet the man who was here before Mr. Austin hit town. The fella who made the arrangement for all those ads. As far as I can see, he didn't spend a single penny." It was, he said, the single best promotional campaign he had ever seen. And so he was ushered in to meet Tom Parker, marking the beginning of a lifelong association that would pick up again just five years later when Tucker started playing bass for Eddy Arnold, and continue, both professionally and personally, all through the career of Elvis Presley, and up until Tom Parker's death.

T HINGS CONTINUED to go well into the fall, but then, after a successful two-day stand in Mobile, Gene was hit with a lawsuit by his former partner, attaching all his profits, past, present, and future. Or, as he more delicately put it: "As the season ended most of the proud bulging bank account was [gone], and I had to find work to reopen the show the following season. I headed for Hollywood." Which is precisely what he did, playing various high-end supper clubs and niteries, including Sardi's, and signing on with Mae West, with whom he had previously worked, to contribute a song and a bit part to her costarring (and cowriting) venture with W. C. Fields, *My Little Chickadee*.

Tom and Marie Parker, meanwhile, "wintered" in Gene's hometown of Gainesville, Texas, with a skeleton crew from the show and virtually no money to sustain them. Gene worried about them a little when the thought crossed his mind. But he consoled himself that his hometown was a welcoming one — he just hoped it would be welcoming enough.

He needn't have worried. When he returned at the end of winter, he discovered that the Parkers had not only survived but thrived. Tom, it was true, had had to sell all the tires off all the trucks and put the trucks up on blocks, but he had a plan to get them back. A number of the show members mounted a brief rebellion against their unwanted confinement in the hinterlands, but Tom reminded them that knowing what a good guy Gene was, he was sure to pay them all bonuses once he had the money, and most of them stayed.

They took the show back out on the road in the spring of 1940 and once again enjoyed great success. Candy and Coco had remained in Hollywood, where each found many opportunities for employment (Candy Candido possessed a trick voice that soon got him a lot of voice-over work in cartoons and feature films like *The Wizard of Oz*), but Gene found a new backing group in Chattanooga, a youthful hillbilly-swing combo called the Fidgety Four, whom he promptly redubbed the Whippoorwills, after a line in "My Blue Heaven." They were all accomplished musicians, especially guitarist-leader Roy Lanham, but their experience in the entertainment world so far had been pretty limited, and they watched their new boss with a mixture of wonder and admiration.

"Parker kept asking Gene [where] he wanted to go next, and Gene would say, 'Well, wherever the loot's good,'" said bass player Red Wootten, who would go on to play with influential country artist Hank Thompson and on studio sessions with Frank Sinatra. The Whippoorwills were every bit as virtuosic as Candy and Coco, if not more so, and they delighted in the rackety jazz and improvisational feel of the show.

Gene immediately set the musical tone on his small traveling piano, attacking each song with a range of pianistic feeling that suggested a cross between the comic flair of Chico Marx and some of the latter-day fervor of a Jerry Lee Lewis. "We walked onstage with him without a sheet of music," said Wootten. "He'd just start singing and do a medley of twelve or fifteen different songs in one tempo, all kinds of tunes, and we'd have to follow whatever he played. . . . Everything we did in the tent show was

Gene (on piano) with the Whippoorwills: Red Wootten, bass; Roy Lanham, electric guitar; Gene's third wife, Doris Sherrell, on drums. At the Village Barn, New York City, 1941. *Courtesy of Barry Mazor*

pop music, [but then] Gene would turn around and do something like [Sister Rosetta Tharpe's signature gospel number] "This Train," [and] he could do that great." Or, as guitar virtuoso Merle Travis, one of the most influential across-the-board pop stylists of the twentieth century, recalled, Gene would survey his young trio with pride, then announce good-naturedly, "We gonna pee on the fire and turn the dogs loose, and we gonna turn [guitarist] Roy Lanham and his Diddlin' Duo loose on this old gut-bucket, hooked-joint blues that I wrote back when I needed money."

But then, once again, the show was beset with financial woes. As Gene put it: "It seemed like all the world had gone mad, [as] threats of war began to slow down attendance. We were saddled with the obligation of paying the back taxes, which . . . caused me to fall behind in meeting the deadline of the weekly payroll. [And then] other shattering misfortunes like storms, tornados, and hurricanes contributed to our hard times. . . . It was only Tom's knack of handling people," Austin wrote, that kept the show going, until the IRS swooped in when they were in Newport News at the end of July. That was when he was forced to tell Tom he couldn't go on any longer. "I called him into my office [and said], 'Tom, I can't go on paying eighty-five people, [plus] the taxman. I see no hope in sight. You'll have to tell the whole company we close the show Saturday night.'"

Gene then boarded a train for New York to see if he could find a way to make some "loot," and Tom and Marie headed back to Tampa in a thoroughly dejected state.

Tom tried to make the best of it. In retrospect, he told Marie, the abrupt conclusion could be seen as almost inevitable after all the mistakes that had been made before they ever joined the show. But it was an invaluable learning experience, wasn't it? Think of all the contacts they had made, all the knowledge he had gained at little or no expense, save for the long hours and hard work they had both put in. Think, too, of all the fun they'd had. And he had made a friend for life, which turned out to be truer than he could have imagined, as he ended up helping to support Gene in his last years, right up until his death in 1972.

Marie was not altogether won over and, undoubtedly out of deference to her, he agreed that perhaps it was time to settle down for a while. As if to mark his new seriousness he registered for the draft on October 16, 1940, though at thirty-one, with his previous military service and a bad back, it was almost certain he would never be called up. Two weeks later he mounted "a Welcome Home party for Tampa's traveling showfolk" at the Legion Casino, featuring numerous Royal American acts and a special return appearance by Gene Austin on Halloween night.

Then, on November 16, it was announced in the Tampa papers that "former circus man and animal trainer T.A. Parker" had taken a job as field agent and animal control officer with the Hillsborough County Humane Society on Armenia Avenue and that he and Mrs. Parker would be moving into the comfortable furnished apartment above the Society's headquarters that very day. As far as T. A. Parker was concerned, if he was going to stay home for a while, there could be no better job in the world.

SIX

The Hillsborough County Humane Society

T HE NEW JOB started right away. He had responded to an ad in the paper by the Humane Society, which, with a substantial endowment from two wealthy sisters, had been built a little more than ten years ago and had served under its original director ever since. The new applicant showed up in a professional-looking white coat he had borrowed from a gas-station-attendant friend, and the board was dazzled by both his qualifications and his demeanor. He himself was dazzled by the opportunities the new position would afford, which included not just a furnished apartment but the chance to work with animals and children, and to use his promotional skills to help an organization that, however amply funded, was still struggling to deliver the services for which it had been established.

The community was suitably impressed. As the *Tampa Tribune* wrote in its appreciation of the new field agent: "Ever since he was 15 years old, Parker has been in show business and handling animals. His uncle, Captain Bob Williams, gave him his first job helping train bears in an act for the Johnny J. Jones Exposition." Which, if not quite literally true, was certainly true to the spirit of the man. Moreover, the story went on, Parker had also worked for the Sells-Floto circus "as page boy in charge of horses," and, as if to further solidify his credentials, for the last two years had served as press agent for singer Gene Austin, traveling thirty thousand miles on the job. In addition, Mr. Parker's wife, Marie, would be working with her husband as the Humane Society's secretary.

He hit the ground running, setting out to improve the outreach, hygiene, cleanliness, and image of the Humane Society right away. He built new cages, rebuilt old ones, painted the Society headquarters in bold, solid colors, and began cleaning up the spacious grounds, which the *Tampa Tribune* described as looking more like an abandoned property than an up-to-date, modern animal-care facility. Over the next few weeks he made it clear in one imaginative promotion after another that he was there to provide his services for every dog, cat, horse, mule, goat, and every other type of pet and livestock in the county, while at the same time establishing an educational campaign for the detection and prevention of rabies and other animal-borne illnesses. On November 24, just a week after he himself had been introduced to its readers, the *Tribune* ran a feature on his wife, showing a picture of Marie Parker petting a pair of cats and looking radiant. She had never fully realized, she said, "the great love so many people have for their animals," but now, thanks to her husband's guiding example, she was fully committed to the job. And, just after Christmas, as if to put a cap on who the people of Tampa were getting for their new field officer, Tom Parker proudly hung a signed picture of Gene Autry (whom he had become acquainted with through Gene Austin) on his office wall.

On December 22 the *Tribune* announced the first Humane Society Christmas party, at which thirty-eight puppies would be given away by the new field agent dressed as Santa Claus, and every child in attendance would get a prize. There wouldn't be any refreshments because the Humane Society didn't at present have the funds, but there would be a four-piece string band led by the acting driver of the company truck. The following year saw the giveaway of one hundred dogs, as well as the participation of the "Bluegrass Buckaroos" and several well-advertised "midgets" from the Ringling Brothers circus, and each successive year showed marked growth in both attendance and enthusiasm. Over the next six months of Tom Parker's tenure there were any number of heartwarming and humorous stories, showing the new field agent's dedication to his duties and his flair for turning a commonplace incident into an event. In March there was a picture of the new "Emergency Ambulance," a presumably tongue-in-cheek repurposing of the Society's Ford coupe with a built-in cage in the back and the automobile's new designation painted in white letters on the trunk.

Soon "Dr. Parker" would open a maternity ward for expectant cats and, later, a "humane chamber" for euthanizing diseased animals. One story in the *Tribune* told of how he nursed a dog back to health by patiently feeding it from a baby bottle; another spoke of how long he cared for an abandoned dog that responded only to Swedish-language commands before finding it a proper home. Then there was the Mutt Parade, which extended over a full week in October 1942 and drew more than two thousand people on the first day alone under the big tent Field Agent Parker had set up on the Society's grounds. Though no admission was charged, the aim was to raise funds for further improvements, and it seemed as if every dog entered had a chance of winning a prize in some category of its own, including "Longest Tail," "Most Disobedient," "Longest-Haired," "Shortest-Haired," "Ugliest," and "Orneriest." Not a single incident or event, large or small, failed to receive coverage in the Tampa newspapers, and it was always Mr. Parker's energy, determination, and unfailing good humor that came through most clearly.

One of the stories he always liked to tell about his years with the Humane Society was the time that he got a friend of his from Ringling Brothers, Paul Horompo, to rescue a puppy trapped in a partially blocked twenty-four-inch drainpipe. (The newspaper headline read, "Midget Helps Recue Young Pup.") As the *Tampa Tribune* wrote, "Horompo crawled into the pipe with a rope tied around his ankle. He would dig awhile, then Parker would haul him back [and eventually] the puppy was drawn out sand-covered and quaking, but glad to be in the light again." The way Colonel Parker told it in later years, Horompo discovered early on that the puppy was barely wedged into the pipe, but, as a crowd gathered, his boss ordered him to stay where he was and continued to let out rope as if Horompo were descending further and further into the pipe. This man, Director Parker informed the growing number of onlookers, was bravely risking his life, and they should remain silent out of respect — which they did until at last Horompo emerged with the trembling puppy. Feel free to choose your version (I think I prefer the first), but either way it could only redound to the Society's good name and overall benefit.

But perhaps his most celebrated gimmick was his extravagant promotion of the Humane Society's pet cemetery, still going strong today, over eighty years later. He picked out a corner of the Society's rambling grounds, then hired a short, unprepossessing young man named Bevo Bevis, who lived just down the street from Marie's parents, to clear it. Bevo, who had been working in a local drugstore and at twenty-three was still living with his mother, was eager to help, but he was even more eager for the approval of Mr. Parker, whom he soon took to calling "Pop." Parker got a local dentist to furnish Bevo, whom he invariably addressed as "Mr. Bevis," with a long white smock to match his own, and charged him with building some small wooden caskets from scrap lumber. Then he got a local stonemason to make up a miniature gravestone for free. (It would serve as a sales tool for future customers, he said.) The wording on the gravestone simply read, "HERE LIES SPOT, A BELOVED AND FAITHFUL COMPANION," and Bevo, on whom he had conferred the title "General Manager of Perpetual Care for Deceased Pets," placed it in a prominent location in the cleared ground. With that, they were ready for business.

It turned out to be a profitable enterprise for the Society (and very likely for the field agent, too) and did nothing but burnish the reputation of both. As a final touch Tom offered to the bereaved pet owner, who had already paid something like fifty dollars for plot, casket, and headstone, the opportunity at a minimal fee to have fresh flowers placed weekly on the grave. The flowers were supplied by local florists happy to donate their day-olds to Mr. Parker for such a worthy cause. And if the bereaved ever happened to visit their pet's grave and find that the flowers appeared wilted, the Field Agent simply put on a long face and said, "I wish you could have been here yesterday when we placed them. They're a bit faded now, but they looked sensational then. Isn't that right, Mr. Bevis?" To which his newly married assistant and General Manager of Perpetual Care, who was just about to join the army, nodded his head in eager assent.

You could say it was a concatenation of genuine promotion and advanced legerdemain — and in later years some were inclined to assert (and they would certainly have been supported by Colonel Parker's own gift for mythmaking and fabulation) that it was all a product of Mr. Parker's dedication to self-advancement and self-aggrandizement — but nothing in the facts bears this out. And this was certainly not the opinion of most Tampans at the time.

When he was reappointed field agent in January of 1942, and then again in January 1943, he was showered with praise for his diligence and creativity, most of all for his dedication to making the Hillsborough County Humane Society a better place. As the *Tampa Tribune* put it some years later, when Parker arrived at the Humane Society, he found a "run-down, dirty, weed-covered [property]," but he left it a well-manicured, prosperous, forward-looking institution. And he accomplished this, the story noted approvingly, providing many humorous examples, by employing his well-honed "showman's pitch" to maximum effect. While clearly having a bang-up time himself.

For Marie it was like a dream come true. For the first time they had a place of their own, where she and Tom and her fifteen-year-old son could live as a family and no longer depend upon her mother and father's help. Also, as time went on, she became an enthusiastic partner in every aspect of the Society's operation, learning from her husband and admiring the ingenuity and skill with which he found solutions to what others might consider intractable problems.

Best of all, from her point of view, for the first time he became a full-fledged member of the greater Tampa community.

He joined the Exchange Club and gave speeches to just about every civic organization in town. At the suggestion of Clyde Rinaldi, who did all the advertising, postering, and ticket printing for the Humane Society, he joined the Optimist Club, an international organization dedicated to "Friendship, Sociability, Loyalty, Reciprocity," with over ten thousand members, and in 1943 he was elected sergeant at arms of the Tampa branch. The speeches he gave focused for the most part on his own forward-looking thinking, and he was even beginning to look the part of the prosperous Rotarian as he patted his expanding belly and puffed on an ever-present cigar.

And yet, gradually, inexorably, almost inevitably, he found himself drawn back into the world he had never fully left behind. He loved his new life, to be sure, but after his taste of success with Gene Austin, perhaps more to the point after his full-scale immersion in an experience he had sought all his life, how could he ever abandon a world that he felt certain was still beckoning to him, a world which, unlike the straight life of by-the-numbers civic success, offered no guarantees but presented you each day with new, hitherto unforeseen creative possibilities, new challenges to meet and overcome?

Throughout his three years at the Humane Society he never abandoned his old connections. He continued to do publicity stunts for the Park Theatre from time to time. He continued to offer free pony rides to kids. When Hollywood came to town, he supplied animals for their shoots and in the summer of 1942 had his picture taken with Gig Young, one of the stars of Howard Hawks' *Air Force*. He used his old carnival connections to help promote the Humane Society, and not just to rescue stray dogs from drainpipes either. Eleven members of Royal American Shows made a public display of joining the Humane Society just before going out on tour in February of 1941, and when Roy Acuff, one of the biggest stars of the Grand Ole Opry, was in Tampa for a show the following year, he was reported by the newspapers to have paid a visit to Tom Parker (whom he had undoubtedly met through Gene Austin) and put his name on the Society's membership rolls.

The promoter of the Acuff show was legendary showman J. L. (Joe) Frank, a gentlemanly forty-two-year-old veteran of nearly every aspect of the business, who had managed and masterminded Gene Autry's rise to Hollywood stardom and was presently guiding the careers of some of the Opry's biggest stars, including Acuff, his son-in-law Pee Wee King, and the Opry's newest star, Ernest Tubb. He was one of the first to put together the package shows, or revues (with an aggregation of well-known stars), that were changing the face of country music entertainment, and he was known throughout the business as a paragon of probity and dedication to his artists. As Pee Wee King observed, "He studied people [and] took a personal interest in the people that he managed and booked," while another performer made the point that "he always had a good word for the down-and-out musician." This was the man that Tom Parker apprenticed himself to, as Frank started bringing more and more shows to the Tampa area. In later life Colonel would often point to Frank, almost alone among his show-business acquaintances, as the source of many of the lessons he learned not just about the business but with respect to loyalty, character, and the necessity of having long-term goals.

His closest connection among the performers was Acuff, who had recently opened up the Florida territory for hillbilly artists. Acuff was unquestionably the artist whose music hit him the hardest and with whom, personally, he identified the most. In March of 1943, with the backing of the board of directors of the Humane Society, and under the auspices of J. L. Frank, he became the principal promoter of a two-night, four-show all-star run of nearly sold-out performances by Acuff at the 2,800-seat Municipal Auditorium. The *Tampa Times* called the show "a triumph for pure corn," while also noting that Acuff was introduced as "the greatest modern singer of American folk songs." And "he sent the crowd away," the paper further noted, "humming 'Precious Jewel' and other plaintive tunes he sings so well."

P ARKER SOON became invested in yet another aspect of Acuff's business. Western stars like Bob Wills and Pappy O'Daniel, among others, had long represented flour companies (for baking needs, for homemade pies, for every sort of country cooking), and Acuff signed on with Cherokee Mills in 1943 to manufacture Roy Acuff Flour, primarily for Florida sales. Tom Parker was almost immediately designated the company's local representative, and every Roy Acuff appearance was accompanied by an advertisement to: "BUY ROY ACUFF'S OWN FLOUR, Specially Blended for Roy Acuff by Cherokee Mills, Ask Your Grocer, TOM PARKER, Broker." With typical aplomb, he organized cooking demonstrations in theaters where his star was appearing. He would hire a cook to bake fresh biscuits in the lobby, then once the biscuits had been gobbled up, remind the well-fed crowd where they could buy tickets for the show and, if they were in need of flour, the grocery store where they could purchase it and — if they showed up at the right time — get Roy Acuff's autograph to boot.

Acuff was so impressed with the young man in fact that he invited him to move to Nashville and become his manager. Somehow, for whatever reason, perhaps because he felt the time wasn't right or, more realistically, he understood that at forty Acuff was as big a star as he was ever going to be and he didn't need Tom Parker to build his career (he was already making close to $100,000 a year), he demurred. But in later years Roy Acuff would always take credit for "discovering" Tom Parker. "I presume I was the first one ever to invite Tom to Nashville," he told Elvis biographer Jerry Hopkins. "I suggested he come to Nashville [and] meet the boys."

Which is more or less what he did, but on his own initiative and for his own purposes.

J. L. Frank had been telling him for some time about a young singer named Eddy Arnold, who up until May of 1943 had been the lead singer with Pee Wee King's very popular Golden West Cowboys. "Smilin'" Eddy Arnold (the nickname was almost instantly dropped, but it definitely suggested his winning personality) had joined the Cowboys in January

1940, and immediately instilled a new, crooning flavor in their music. When he left three years later, neither J. L. Frank nor Pee Wee King tried to discourage the man who had at this point become the band's most popular member; rather, they both urged him to strike out on his own and take the job he had been offered at WSM, the Grand Ole Opry radio station. Frank had told him from the start that if the opportunity to better himself ever came along, he should take it. And this was just such an opportunity.

Just two or three months later, in the summer of 1943, Tom read a story in the August issue of *Radio Mirror* entitled "Eddy Arnold . . . Marco Polo with a Guitar," profiling the twenty-five-year-old newcomer. With Frank's encouragement, and perhaps to test Roy Acuff's hospitality as well, he traveled to Nashville and met the young singer backstage at the Ryman Auditorium on the evening of an Opry performance. Through J. L. Frank he was well aware that Arnold was about to sign a personal management contract with Dean Upson, the Opry's powerful talent manager, but he knew from Joe Frank, too, the importance of long-range planning, so when he met the young man, he brought to bear all of his salesman's enthusiasm, speaking of all the work he had done for Mr. Frank in Florida and the various ways in which he was looking to expand his horizons. It was only when he mentioned his close connection with Gene Austin, though, that he felt he got the young singer's full attention. Eddy made it immediately clear that Gene Austin was one of his idols, and that as a boy he had ordered all of Austin's records "right out of the Sears Roebuck catalogue." From that point on, Parker stressed his connection to Austin so strongly that Eddy became convinced that it must have been Austin himself who had suggested that this strangely intense, brusque Floridian seek him out. As he later put it, "I was a young kid at that time, and Parker came up here and walked up and extended his hand."

And although both knew that no actual business was going to be transacted that day, that no actual business *could* be transacted, both came away from the meeting, undoubtedly for entirely different reasons, with a different feeling about the future. I'm not at all sure that either believed in fate, but it was clear that fate had something entirely different in store for them both.

In any case, without any discernible indication of just what that was, and over Marie's vehement objections and the dire warnings of friends that he would never find a more secure position than the one he held right now, on December 10, 1943, Tom Parker handed in his notice at the Humane Society. The board accepted his resignation with regret, and the Tampa papers loudly lamented his departure, touting all the improvements he had made not just in the physical plant but in the financial health and spirit of the place. But his mind was made up.

In December, almost certainly to assuage Marie, he bought an already furnished house on San Pedro Street in Tampa for $6,250, with a mortgage of $28.84 a month. It was the first home he had ever owned but then just after they moved into the new house, it was announced in the Tampa newspapers on January 21 that "Tom Parker, former county humane society field agent, has accepted a job as general agent for a Grand Ole Opry unit" which would be headlined by the wildly popular minstrel act Jamup and Honey and would include the newly emerging country comedian Minnie Pearl as well as new Opry favorite Eddy Arnold.

Whether it was fate or the beneficent intercession of J. L. Frank, or more likely some combination of the two, Tom Parker's course was set. For the next couple of months he was a man about town. "Ran into [movie star] Danny Kaye, [Brooklyn Dodgers manager] Leo Durocher, and Tom Parker, [on hand] to handle the exploitation on Roy Acuff's new pic," the *Tampa Times* reported on February 5. "It was a wholesome threesome, each the best in the business."

Then at the beginning of March he set out on tour with the conviction that he was at last embarking upon his life's work.

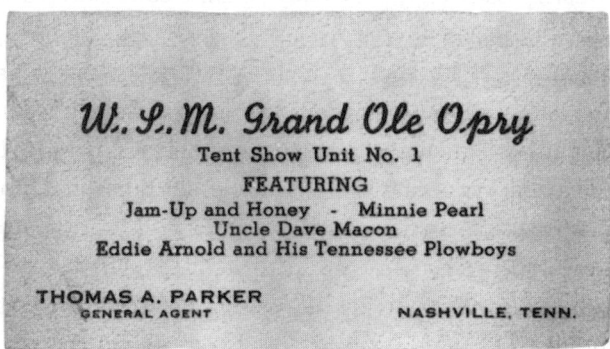

Thomas A. Parker's Grand Ole Opry Tent Show card, 1944.
Courtesy of Richard Weize and more bears archive

SEVEN

The Education of Thomas A. Parker

T HE JAMUP AND HONEY SHOW opened in March, continued through the summer, and played just about everywhere in the mid- and deep South that a traveling caravan could go. Jamup and Honey had put together the first of the Grand Ole Opry tent shows in 1940, aimed at bringing the hugely successful coast-to-coast radio program to the people with the tried-and-true methods of the circus and the carnival. It was the first time in many instances that audiences in Mississippi, Alabama, Florida, and Arkansas got to see the stars that they listened to religiously every Saturday night, and the response often approached mass delirium. Sometimes they played places that had never seen *any* kind of show before. In Jay, Florida, for example, a hamlet of fewer than five hundred people, in Honey's recollection, there wasn't a single person waiting when they arrived at four o'clock in the afternoon, but by the time the show was ready to start, "the traffic was so bad that two people got killed in it, [including] one poor old man who was coming down the road on a bicycle and got run over."

By 1944, when Tom Parker first joined the troupe, there were three Opry tent shows on the road. Roy Acuff was the first to break away from the original Jamup and Honey lineup to headline a show of his own; then his replacement, bluegrass pioneer Bill Monroe, did the same. All three crisscrossed a broad swath of territory, each laying claim to a particular route, but they operated in a mode of sodality and fellow feeling that seemed almost unique to show folk. Nashville newspaperman Jack Hurst quoted one member of the troupe fondly reminiscing about how the rival shows would check in on each other on the road. "There'd be talk like you

Tom Parker and Gabe Tucker, with the show, 1944. *Courtesy of Richard Weize and more bears archive*

Lining up for the show, Mobile, Alabama, 1944. *Courtesy of Richard Weize and more bears archive*

don't ever hear anymore. Like, 'How'd you do last week? Do you need any money? . . . I've got some I could loan you if you need it.'"

Jamup and Honey carried a full-sized tent, 80 feet wide by 220 feet long, with twenty-five roughnecks to move it, and nine or ten tractor trailers. The tent, which could accommodate up to 1,600 people, was set up each day in a different town, but never so far from Nashville that all the performers couldn't make it back for the Saturday night Opry show, a contractual condition that applied to everyone but the two headliners.

Nearly every aspect of it was familiar to Tom, from the siting and erection of the tent to the advance work that needed to be done in every town, and yet each day posed a new and welcome challenge, too. He slept no more than five hours a night, cared little about personal comfort and less about the appurtenances of success. He practically lived in the beat-up old Chevy International truck that he drove from town to town, accompanied only by a stray dog that he had picked up along the way and nursed back to health.

Under the big tent, Mobile, 1944. *Courtesy of Richard Weize and more bears archive*

His energy was focused on little but making sure that in its fifth sea-son this would be the best Jamup and Honey tour ever. But at the same time as they traversed the countryside, his admiration and certainty about Eddy Arnold only grew. Arnold's act was still unpolished, but his ability to connect with an audience, free from any of the usual hillbilly or minstrel-show embellishments, was uncanny. As expected, Arnold had signed with Opry talent manager Dean Upson and had even been put under contract by the RCA Victor Recording Company, though due to a protracted Musicians Union strike he had yet to make a record. But the fact that he still had another year and a half to go with Upson didn't faze Tom Parker in the least. He took every opportunity he could to get with the boy and offer friendly advice. And Arnold could see for himself how much the tour manager was doing for the show. The boy might be green, but Parker could see he was a keen student — and besides, his own situ-ation was improving all the time. Honey Wilds, the costar and organizer of the troupe, was certainly aware of the contributions that he made. "My father," Honey's son, David, told author Alanna Nash, "was a lot like Tom in that he was a very intelligent guy who worked really hard to either dominate a situation . . . or pretend that he wasn't as shrewd as he was. . . . Daddy had a tremendous appreciation for [Parker's] ability to get things done."

Tom went right back to work for Joe Frank when he returned to Tampa in the fall, which included promoting a few Opry-sponsored Eddy Arnold concerts in Florida at the end of the year. Then, in January, he went out with Ernest Tubb, whom Frank was managing, on a tour that Frank had constructed to take him off the Opry package shows and allow him to form a self-contained unit of his own. Tom was charged with most of the same responsibilities he had undertaken for Jamup and Honey, though this time the shows took place in theaters and auditoriums. Once again, he made sure to cement his relationships with everyone in the troupe — they all called him "Uncle Tom"— but he took on a new role, too. For the first time since leaving the circus, he became a performer, working up a comedy act modeled on the role of Frog Millhouse in the Gene Autry movies, as played by Autry's unassuming sidekick Smiley Burnette.

"As soon as Ernest walked out on the stage," recalled Nelle Poe, who with her sister, Ruth, formed the Poe Sisters, an integral part of the Tubb show, "Tom would start down the aisle, brushing people's shoulders off with a little broom [and] Ernest would just stop and stand there with his guitar and look through the crowd like he didn't know what was going on." Then the woebegone comic figure would shamble his way to the stage and talk a little bit with Ernest, who was acting even more confounded and "of course couldn't sing because people were just howling at this big commotion of Tom's. He was really hilarious." And Nelle Poe got the impression that Tom was aiming for "great things," she told writer Alanna Nash. "He always said, to me, 'I'm going to Hollywood someday.'"

But mostly during this strangely indeterminate period he was just waiting for Eddy Arnold. And as soon as Eddy's contract with Dean Upson was up in October of 1945, he and Tom Parker immediately struck a handshake deal, in which Parker would get 25 percent for taking control of all aspects of Eddy's career, from promotion to booking to road managing to dealing with the record company, the same percentage that J. L. Frank took for his services to each of the artists that he managed. But Tom Parker planned to concentrate only on Eddy.

I T WAS A MATCH made in heaven from the start.

In most ways everything was the same — he continued to do all the things he had done with the tent shows, and with Ernest Tubb, but now he was working for himself, for himself and a client in whose talent and potential, both artistic and financial, he wholeheartedly believed. There was something about the way Eddy delivered the sentimental old songs, the effortless way he crooned them with such heartfelt ease, that couldn't help but remind his new manager of Gene Austin. But it seemed like Eddy's smooth, modern delivery packed an even greater emotional punch, even if he never seemed to know quite what to do with himself onstage or how to use his hands. Once in a while some of the girls in the audience would respond with visible emotion to the opening notes of a song they recognized, a reaction that Gene, for all of his genial charm, could never elicit.

He was still out on the road on his own, doing all the advance work by himself, with Marie and her boy back in Tampa. Perhaps to make it up to her, they had finally gotten married that summer, on June 1, 1945, in Bay St. Louis, Mississippi, but Marie continued to waitress and pick up whatever odd jobs she could while they both waited for his gamble to pay off.

It was a slow process at first, even though he did everything possible to expand Eddy's territory. He set up bookings as far north as Pennsylvania and wherever else he could find them in the largely unexplored Northeast. He worked all the time. He had never slept much, but now he slept even less, as he dashed back and forth from town to town in an old Studebaker with a trailer that said "EDDY ARNOLD the TENNESSEE PLOWBOY and his Guitar."

He made sure that all the local businesses signed up to sponsor their shows, and the handbills he had printed up and the advertisements he placed in the local papers all employed the same familiar carnival tagline, "DON'T MISS IT."

He personally sold programs and songbooks at all of Eddy's shows, going up and down the aisles himself with a strong pitch and a sliding scale of prices. (He had long ago learned that you had to calculate what your audience could afford.) The merchandising concession had previously been given to the band on the theory that they could use the extra money, but Eddy's new manager made it clear that he was determined to maximize profits on every level—which included, with Eddy's approval, putting the band on salary in place of the profit-sharing arrangement they had had from the start. Many of the places they played had local tax exemptions for religious shows, so he always made sure that Eddy sang a hymn or two, which suited Eddy fine. Other locales provided exemptions for shows that exhibited livestock, so in those places he rented a small collection of farm animals, mainly pigs and chickens, whenever he could. This was the origin of the famous story of "Colonel Parker's Dancing Chickens"—of how he got the chickens to dance by putting them on a hot plate, and then charged money for the act. It was a story he loved to tell to wide-eyed listeners over the years, while some-times granting that this, of course, was something he would never actu-ally do, given his well-documented love of animals. But the vast majority of his listeners put their money on the myth.

"He was a ball of fire," recalled Eddy, who was by nature inclined to a more deliberate way of doing things. "He worked hard, he got up early, and he was a nondrinker. . . . He understood business, he was good with the record company, he was good with the personal appearances. . . . Actu-ally, he was good at everything! [And] he was absolutely dedicated to the personality that he represented." And as an unexpected bonus, he intro-duced Eddy to a world he had never hitherto suspected existed. "When we'd be in a town, and there'd be a circus, he'd take me and introduce me to these people. I met people that I never thought about meeting, because he was an old carny, and they help one another."

Over the years, Eddy would often chuckle about the unexpected lengths to which his manager's boldness and ingenuity could sometimes go. If a promoter claimed, as they sometimes did, that he alone held the exclusive right to sell merchandise in his theater, or simply asked for a bigger cut of the sales, Tom told him that was fine, they would just go ahead and play without an intermission. When the promoter panicked—what was he supposed to do without an intermission, that was when he sold refreshments and soft drinks, he had everything set up—Tom just shrugged his shoulders and pointed out that if he and Eddy couldn't sell songbooks and photographs, there was no need for an intermission. "About ten minutes went by," Eddy reminisced, "and the [promoter] came back to Parker. He said, 'You go ahead and sell your songbooks. It's all right. It's all right.'" Another time, in Chattanooga, the promoter

Eddy Arnold in Houston (note his manager, top right), ca. 1948–1949. *Courtesy of Shannon Pollard*

wouldn't come up with the second half of his payment before the show. "So Tom came back, pulled me aside, and said, 'Don't hit a note until I wave at you.'" And as the promoter, and the crowd, grew increasingly restive, Tom said to the man, "'You know, those entertainers are funny people. They won't hit a note unless I wave at 'em like that. Why don't you give me my money so I can wave.' He gave him the rest of the money." He was *stalwart*.

Eddy's new a&r man (or "producer") at RCA, Steve Sholes, who had just gotten his army discharge and returned to the company, picked up his recording contract at the end of the year, once again at a royalty of 1 percent. Because of the protracted musicians' strike, Eddy's first record, "Mother's Prayer" backed with "Mommy Please Stay Home with Me," hadn't come out until January 1945, when it sold well enough to warrant a second release in the spring, which had sold over 125,000 copies by the time Eddy and Tom Parker shook hands on their agreement.

That seemed like a fine start to Tom Parker, who at this point knew nothing whatsoever about the record business, though he was absolutely confident of his artist's potential. As far as he was concerned, the sky was the limit for Eddy Arnold—but he also recognized that at this stage he had little room for negotiation. Nor did he have any way of assessing the man he was dealing with at RCA, whom he scarcely knew at all. But Steve Sholes, a mild-mannered New Jerseyan of thirty-four who had started at RCA as a messenger boy in his teens, seemed agreeable enough, and Parker had learned in the carnivals and the tent shows that sometimes you just had to be patient and wait your turn.

Steve Sholes, as it turned out, not only had a feeling for country music, he had a true appreciation for the deep-seated emotion of Eddy Arnold's "heart music," and for his artistic instincts as well. At their very first session together, Sholes self-deprecatingly recalled, "I spent quite a little time trying to straighten out the meter in some of his songs, which was a lot of effort ill spent, because after we got the meter straightened out, the song didn't sound any good. So I said, 'Eddy, forget what I've said . . . Sing it the way you did in the first place!'"

More to the point, as Tom Parker would soon discover, Sholes, for all of his easygoing manner, was an ambitious man. As the person primarily in charge of hillbilly music at RCA, he was deeply concerned that his company had one of the poorest shares of the country market among all the major labels. In 1945, for example, RCA didn't have a single number-one hit on the country music charts, nor would they in 1946. What that meant, as Tom Parker saw it, was that the door was wide open for his artist, Eddy Arnold; RCA had only to recognize it.

It wasn't about the immediate payoff—it was *never* about the immediate payoff. But however much he believed in his artist and however bright he believed his future to be, at Christmas that year, as he and Eddy never tired of recounting, after months of hard work, they had a grand total of $100 to divide between them.

THE NEXT TWO YEARS were a time of extraordinary progress and growth. The bookings continued to increase to the point that Tom Parker had to turn down offers, and he was on the road almost constantly, whether his artist was or not. He was always looking for new opportunities, renewing old acquaintanceships and establishing fresh ones, taking out ads in the trades that called attention to the full scope of his artist's talents and the growing range of his activities. He was determined to expand Eddy's long-range prospects in ways the record company was not equipped to exploit or understand. (They were in the *record* business, after all. He was in the Eddy Arnold business.) He was not afraid to open up untried territories; he put out tentative feelers to venues that were not yet ready to book hillbilly acts; and he set up new, multiple-return engagements at the country music parks and "ranches" that were springing up all over the country, which, with their rides and carousels, offered down-to-earth destinations for country music fans to come back to year after year.

The peak of those early efforts came with Eddy Arnold's star billing at the first-ever country music show at Constitution Hall in Washington, D.C., which legendary East Coast promoter and disc jockey Connie B. Gay set up on Halloween night 1947. He had been doing more and more business lately with Gay, a highly sophisticated hillbilly with far-flung interests, whom he recognized immediately as a kindred spirit. Tom and Marie always stayed with the family, recalled Gay's daughter, Judy, affectionately. "[He] was a very kind man," she said, who loved going downtown for ice cream and scheming with her father, a proud native of Lizard Lick, North Carolina, on how the two of them could "make a buck with the hillbilly trade."

But however great the financial rewards from personal appearances were turning out to be, Tom Parker had become convinced that the future lay in radio, where there were no limits to geography or imagination. The Opry broadcasts, of course, had been the first way to get the name of Eddy Arnold out to all those prospective booking agents and promoters, but more and more his manager was coming to see that the Opry exacted too great a price from every artist appearing in its weekly presentation. Not only were you required to show up in person for nearly every one of its Saturday night shows, wherever, and however far from Nashville, you might be playing the night before, the Opry also took 15 percent of the gross proceeds from the personal appearances of any artist billed as a "Grand Ole Opry star."

Eddy's thirty-minute segment on the Opry was sponsored by Ralston Purina, the grain, cereal, and animal-feed conglomerate based in St. Louis, just as other segments were sponsored by such companies as Prince Albert tobacco, Royal Crown Cola, Cherokee Mills, and, soon, Nashville's own Martha White flour. It was with little more than this in mind that Tom Parker set out to break what he saw as the Opry's strangle-hold on his artist.

By dint of assiduous courtship of both the company and its founder, seventy-six-year-old William Danforth (author of *I Dare You!*, the self-help book that had been so influential on an entire generation, including future Sun Records founder Sam Phillips), he persuaded Purina to sponsor Eddy on a Saturday afternoon show on the Mutual network called *Checkerboard Matinee* (from Purina's well-known checkerboard motif), which would by early 1947 expand to noontime exposure every weekday as the *Checkerboard Jamboree*. Before long, both Eddy and Tom saw an opportunity to broaden their independent initiative even further, creating *The Eddy Arnold Show*, which they sold on their own across the country, furnishing each station that picked it up (three hundred by the end of 1947) with transcriptions that Eddy cut well in advance whenever he was in Nashville. This in turn emboldened them to drop "Grand Ole Opry Star" from Eddy's billing, thereby instantaneously increasing Eddy's personal-appearance income by 15 percent.

Eddy was nothing less than an equal partner in all this. A thoughtful, self-contained man, he was as ambitious in his own way as his manager, and what he valued most about Tom Parker was that Parker was willing to lead the way, and lead the way forcefully, without being burdened by the same regard for social niceties that he himself was temperamentally inclined to observe. They were a team. And if Eddy chose to express himself publicly with greater modesty of purpose, Tom was always there to take the heat.

He took such evident delight in every aspect of the business, to the point that it no longer felt like a business but a way of life. He treated the usual problems of the road — washed-out bridges, flash floods, flat tires, carburetor troubles — with a degree of alacrity that lifted them all up. One time in Birmingham, when the band was delayed by a punctured tire that Eddy and the comedian Rod Brasfield had to get out to fix, he got a fireman in the audience to give an extended talk on public safety. Then, as he recalled, "I was hunting up somebody else to do a stall act when the boys finally dashed in." He was never fazed or fussed. Tom never seemed to mind being seen as uneducated or uncouth. In some ways, Eddy realized, he even welcomed it. In dealing with the RCA brass, for example, or anyone else who took inordinate pride in their social or edu-

Colonel and his wife, Marie; Sally and Eddy Arnold; Jack Earns; and Hill and Range cohead Julian Aberbach, all top row. Center front unknown. *Courtesy of Richard Weize and more bears archive*

cational status, he was always happy to let himself be underestimated, but never at the expense of his artist's interests. "Earthy," Eddy mused, "I guess a lot of people might describe him; uneducated maybe. A lot of times people think they're dealing with a rube. 'Oh, I can take him,' they decide. They don't take him. He's ahead of 'em before they even sit down across a table . . . he fools 'em. They think, because his English might be faulty (he might say a word wrong here and there), 'Oh, I'll handle him.' They walk right into his web!"

B ETWEEN NOVEMBER 1, 1947, and November 6, 1948, Eddy Arnold topped the country charts for fifty-three weeks in a row, a figure never approached, let alone rivaled, in any popular music charts to this day. And that just set the stage for what by any measure would have to be considered an *annus mirabilis*, the kind of dominant achievement that has rarely been equaled, let alone surpassed, in the pop music field.

Standing orders for Eddy Arnold's new RCA releases outstripped those of any of his peers and, given the small number of accompanists that he used on his sessions, profit margins on the records far exceeded those of pop stars like Perry Como and Vaughn Monroe. The records were beginning to cross over, too, with "Bouquet of Roses" (at the top of the country charts for nineteen weeks) reaching number thirteen on the pop charts and selling well over a million copies.

So perhaps it should have come as no surprise when in September of 1948 Tom Parker informed the Grand Ole Opry that Eddy Arnold was planning on leaving the show altogether. It was a practical decision with which his artist fully agreed, he told Opry broadcasting station WSM's powerful sales director Irving Waugh, but he had two suggestions that he hoped might soften the blow. The first, which he was well aware Waugh was bound to turn down, was that Eddy, who at this point was by far the Opry's biggest star, be given a share of the show's profits. And when Waugh, one of the first members of the Nashville establishment to recognize the Opry's almost boundless earning potential, dismissed the idea out of hand, Parker presented the deal he had had in mind all along: that the Opry buy into Eddy's transcribed nationwide show for Purina and broadcast it whenever Eddy was unable to get back to the Opry on a Saturday night. At first Waugh thought he could get around what he took to be Parker's bluff. Others like Roy Acuff had left the Opry briefly, but they had always come back when they realized how much national exposure they were giving up. But Tom Parker had already sidestepped that issue. Eddy had two national radio shows of his own, and Purina was paying him quite well.

Irving Waugh realized that he had been outplayed as soon as he arrived at Purina's corporate headquarters in St. Louis to plead his case, only to discover that Parker had anticipated his move. He tried at first to stick to his guns, but Purina remained firm in their loyalty to Parker and his artist, and when, clearly at Parker's direction, they threatened to broadcast Eddy's transcribed show on Friday night on Nashville's other fifty-thousand-watt "clear-channel" station, WLAC, Waugh recognized that he had been beaten. "With the audacity of a young man," he said, "I told [them] that we couldn't permit a Country success on another station in Nashville." And he agreed to broadcast Eddy's show on WSM on Friday night, creating two half-hour live shows around it, which would soon become the basis for the highly successful Friday night Opry. It was his own fault, Waugh ruefully recalled. Colonel Parker had simply been smart enough to recognize the full breadth of Eddy Arnold's commercial potential, and the leverage it gave him, long before anyone else did. But then again, as Waugh, ever the good-natured realist, pointed out, Hank Williams would arrive at the Opry just eight months later.

As for the Colonel: "Mr. Danforth gave Eddy and me two shares of stock," he went out of his way to let me know some forty-five years later. They were worth two dollars apiece back then, he said, and $10,000 in 1994. He didn't know about Eddy, but as far as he was concerned, he wasn't ever going to sell them. They were a gift, he said, and a symbol of the enduring bond that continued to unite Eddy and him with Mr. Danforth.

Just two months after Eddy's departure from the Opry, when his contract with RCA came up for renewal in November, Tom Parker proposed a whole new way of doing business to Steve Sholes. Up till this point, Eddy had been working on the same 1 percent royalty that he had signed for in 1943 but now, after an unrelenting campaign by Parker, in which he hammered away at sales figures and never ceased to remind Steve that Eddy Arnold was RCA's number-one star, Sholes finally agreed to a new royalty arrangement of 5 percent, unheard-of for a country singer and top-of-the-line for a pop star on any label. Even more surprising, Sholes capitulated to Parker's demand that should any other recording artist's royalty rate rise above 5 percent, Eddy's would, too. And, in the kind of added-on side deal that is almost never memorialized on paper, Eddy also received contractual assurance that RCA would spend as much on promotion and publicity for their folk and hillbilly star as they did on any of their pop artists.

Steve did not put up much resistance to any of these conditions — Parker's arguments were totally supported by the facts, and there was no question in Sholes' mind that Eddy had earned this special treatment. He was only surprised that Parker, who had always shown a certain amount of circumspection in their dealings, was so adamant now in his demands. But he shrugged it off and merely tried to insert a standard noncompete clause stipulating that should Eddy receive an offer to advertise, or appear on any radio or television show advertising or promoting, a product that RCA itself manufactured, such as radio and television sets, phonographs, or any "cabinet" often containing all three, he only asked that Parker give RCA "the opportunity to meet any [such] offer [or] reimburse Eddy for his not appearing on such [a] program. . . . I am sure you agree that this is not unreasonable."

Parker simply crossed out the clause when he sent back the signed contract on December 4.

As if anything else were needed to cap this remarkable year, Thomas A. Parker was appointed an honorary Louisiana Colonel in October through an old carnival acquaintance named Bob Greer. This was something that tickled him all his life (he often joked about all the advantages that came from being a "phony Colonel"), though he never used the Colonel appellation in any of his official correspondence or duties in all his time with Eddy Arnold. What he did do, for undisclosed reasons of his own, was to insist that every member of Eddy's troupe (though certainly not Eddy), who up till now had almost universally called him "Popsy," address him henceforth as "Colonel." And so they did, though not in some cases uncomplainingly. And so everyone who went on to work or deal with him in future would forevermore. Joke or self-mockery (and some simply attributed it to the underlying neediness of a personality desperate to establish dominance), it would seem that at this point he should hardly have needed a title to shore up his self-esteem.

I N 1949, Eddy Arnold became the first hillbilly act to headline in Las Vegas, appearing at the El Rancho Hotel for two weeks in May. It was actually his first club booking anywhere. ("At that time," he said, "I hadn't ever really put an act together. I'd just sing my songs and let it go at that.") But Las Vegas was in fact merely a stop along the way. According to the press release that his manager gave out to the trades, he was on his way to Hollywood to make two cowboy movies — another first for Eddy — for Columbia Pictures. The contract called for a salary of $12,500 per picture against 15 percent of the profits, with a clause that Parker had fought to have inserted that gave Eddy control of the music. The movies, which were released the following January, weren't any good (Eddy's verdict: "I couldn't act"), but they made money and got Eddy's name in front of the public in a significant new way.

Even more significantly, the deal, like the Las Vegas booking, was negotiated through the William Morris Agency, the nation's premier talent agency, whom Tom Parker, knowing the limitations of his own experience in these areas, had worked long and hard to enlist on his artist's behalf. The immediate payoffs were obvious, but William Morris, Parker was convinced, could help carry his client (and, as it would turn out, future clients, too) to ever greater heights.

In August, undoubtedly emboldened by all these successes, he finally bought a house in Nashville, in Madison just outside the city and just around the corner from where Eddy Arnold lived. It was a comfortable three-bedroom, two-bath stone building, priced at $20,000, with a low-slung stone outbuilding behind the house that he almost immediately converted into an office. For Marie, it was what she had always been longing for, incontrovertible proof of her husband's success. She quickly made friends in the neighborhood and found a church she liked. She had started going out on Eddy's tours lately, selling tickets and doing whatever needed to be done, and when she and Tom visited New York she sometimes went shopping with Steve Sholes' wife, Katherine, or one of the other RCA executives' wives. But most of all, she treasured the time she got to spend at home with her husband.

For those who knew him only from his indefatigable life on the road or his hard-driving business negotiations, it might have been difficult to imagine what a homebody he was. Indeed, Marie and her husband had a relationship which many, including some in her own family, did not understand. In certain ways, he was intensely possessive of her and yet at the same time strangely remote—he had never been one for physical closeness, and he seemed uncomfortable in many respects around any woman that he had not known for a long time. But she had always believed in him, and with the success that his artist had now achieved, he had acquired some of the trappings of success himself. Perhaps above all, though, it was his unwavering loyalty to anyone who had earned his trust—to Eddy, to the banker in Madison who extended him credit when he really needed it, to the Rinaldis in Tampa who continued to do all of his printing—that reassured her of the stability of their own relationship, however different it might be.

Throughout the industry, on the other hand, Tom Parker was seen as an exemplar of the new brand of managers who were replacing the radio-station talent bureaus and serving the interests of their clients with a single-minded dedication that station bookers like the Opry's Artists Service Bureau, with a whole roster of talent to serve, simply could not match. Tom Parker was a legend among his fellow managers and promoters not just for his positive energy but for his extraordinary attention to detail. Even as his sole client's success grew and grew, he still did everything. He advanced the show, planned all the routes, wrote all the ad copy, sold programs and souvenirs at the shows, and settled all the box-office receipts. He was like a tornado, not infrequently disquieting those around him; his mind never seemed to stop working as he planned his next move. He kept up an endless stream of daily correspondence on the small portable typewriter that went with him everywhere, and when Eddy wasn't on the road, he remained a man in constant motion himself, looking for new and better deals for his client, with New York, Hollywood, Houston, New Orleans, and Chicago just a few of his revolving ports of call. And everywhere that Eddy was booked, he spelled out every detail of the engagement in advance, making sure not just that the terms of the contract were met to the letter, but that the promoter's commitment to both the show and the quality of its presentation was unqualified. "This is your show," he advised each promoter. "Get the most out of it."

And yet, for all that, an astute observer might have wondered if everything was as it should be. At times it appeared as if there was simply too wide a gulf, of outlook and temperament, between artist and manager to be altogether ignored. "The sky was the limit for him," Eddy observed with a mixture of admiration and chagrin. "A lot of things he'd do would kind of embarrass me." (And here Eddy might have been thinking of some of the stunts that his manager would pull, like having Bevo Bevis, Parker's devoted assistant at the Hillsborough Humane Society, now an all-purpose gofer for the troupe, strut around a crowded hotel lobby in what looked like a bellhop's uniform paging the star for no reason other than to call attention to his presence at the hotel.) More than once, Eddy would suggest half jokingly to his whirling dervish of a manager, "You should find a hobby," meaning golf or fishing. "You're my hobby," Parker would always say, either purposely misunderstanding or sometimes, Eddy suspected, not understanding him at all. And Eddy would simply resign himself to it. For how could things get any better?

I N THE SPRING of 1951, Purina, for whom Eddy Arnold had by now become the flag bearer for mill openings, conventions, fairs, and various other events that called for a public ambassador, agreed to pay him $100,000 a year for the exclusive radio rights to his services for the next two years. Three months later, in July, at the prompting of his manager, the deal was sweetened by another $17,500, and in December of 1952, it was extended in furtherance of a five-year arrangement with the NBC network, which, for an additional $100,000, secured exclusive television rights to Eddy Arnold's services. Part of the overall deal ensured separate payments to Tom Parker for his contributions to the promotion of various Purina events headlined by Eddy — which he didn't need to point out to his friends at the company were substantial in terms of both creative content and execution and thus appropriately recognized, independent of his managerial duties, in their own right.

There were additional benefits accruing to each of these agreements — one of the things Tom Parker had long since learned is that everything didn't have to be written down on paper so long as you could depend on the other fellow's handshake and, it went without saying, he could depend on yours — and all of them were designed to fit in with Eddy's new blueprint for his career.

For Eddy, a devoted family man with long-range plans of his own (he would make a fortune in real estate as one of the earliest developers of the exclusive Brentwood neighborhood in Nashville, to which he moved in 1951), wanted, as much as possible, to get off the road.

His manager didn't necessarily see eye to eye with his artist on this decision, but he did everything in his power to facilitate it. On June 8, 1951, he wrote Eddy a lengthy memo outlining the approach they would need to take, and emphasizing the steps they had already taken with respect to both long-term radio and television plans, to help effectuate this change. In accordance with Eddy's wishes, he would not be booking any additional dates for this year beyond those already under contract, which came to no more than fifteen or sixteen days in all, including the Purina dealers' shows and expositions.

"Should anything important come up that would be of tremendous interest to your career, we will of course take this up," he wrote, but otherwise he would respect Eddy's wishes entirely, and if the TV show developed as he hoped it would, he would not book any further personal appearances at all "except those directly involved with our sponsor on TV or Radio and only those that would be required from our sponsor. It is understood of course that should suitable workable TV or Guest appearance[s] become available from time to time we will take these as our schedule permit[s] as they are an important factor in our development.

"The personal appearance angle," he emphasized, would always be there if they needed it, "however we will from now on take this as a secondary spot in our work. I will at all times inform and take up with you when something important should come up and we will both make up our minds what-ever is best just like we have always done. However I do feel that we never want the information to get out that you do not want to play any dates, I understand to the letter why and agree, however for business reason[s] I will at all times advise any-one that we do not have time and have so much other work to do that we can only do so much of either.

"We are in a type of show business," he explained, "that a White Lie is in order from time to time to protect our interest and also the hard times and work we have put into this Field. . . . I am also right now going to even keep a closer watch on other people knowing our business. I know you will do the same."

As far as their agreement on just what that business was, he concluded, "I know that our families are right in trying to be home more, and you even more due to the children, and I will respect this you know that."

He did. And in keeping with this new resolution, when he set up Eddy's first full-scale tour of the West Coast in September of 1952, he made sure that it would be the best and biggest tour ever, bombarding every RCA regional manager and salesman in the area, all the Purina distributorships, all the RCA top brass in New York (many of whom promised to attend), and even the U.S. Department of Agriculture for Eddy's extensive work promoting their "Smokey the Bear" fire-prevention campaign on both record and film. No detail was overlooked in his determination to make sure everything went right and that his artist would not have to worry about anything but singing. He contacted every disc jockey and jukebox operator and provided every promoter with his usual, multi-page memorandum spelling out step-by-step exactly how each show was to be presented. Not a single element was left to chance, and, of course, the tour was an unmitigated triumph.

He was confident at this point that if anyone in the business was to bring up the subject of Eddy Arnold, the name of his manager, too, would immediately spring to mind. And just in case it didn't, if only to make certain that no one should miss just how much planning and hard work went into the making of a star, he made sure that every ad, every public service announcement, every thank-you message to DJs, distributors, the record label, the fans, gave a prominent place to the name of Tom Parker. As did the new business card that he had Rinaldi Printing make up for his artist, which proudly situated his own name at a jaunty angle in the top right-hand corner bordered by a checkerboard motif.

They were, he felt, an unassailable team.

F OR THE PERSONAL APPEARANCES that Eddy did continue to make, Tom and Eddy had long since put together a kind of self-contained revue, the type of variety show (with comedy skits, a strong supporting cast, and music that encompassed a wide range of musical eras and presentations) with which they had first started on the Jamup and Honey tent show. The difference, of course, was that the Eddy Arnold Show was entirely selected and paid for by the star and his manager.

In the summer of 1951, they added a new act, the Dickens Sisters from Chicago, three singing sisters, Nancy, Margie, and Patti Diskin, whose brother Tom had volunteered to serve as their manager and on-the-road protector. Since getting out of the navy, Tom had been working as office manager and general factotum for his best friend and high school classmate, Al Dvorin, who had a booking agency with an unending supply of specialty acts, including "Ventriloquists, Jugglers, Animal Trainers, Midgets, and All-Girl Orchestras." When Tom went to Dvorin for advice, Al told his friend that while he didn't want to lose him, this was a break that he and his sisters couldn't afford to turn down, and he all but pushed his more buttoned-up office manager out the door.

Tom and his new boss, Tom Parker, hit it off from the start. Tom Diskin was a bright, outgoing, mild-mannered young man, who, as Al Dvorin said, could organize even the paper clips on your desk. One might have thought there could be no two people with greater differences of

Colonel and Marie with the Bonja family. *Courtesy of Ron Bonja*

outlook and temperament than the "Two Toms," but Tom Parker instantly recognized the young man's qualities and capabilities. He learned he could trust him with the smallest details and count on him for the kind of loyalty you couldn't buy for any price. Soon he started relying on him not only to help set up the tours but to provide creative suggestions for their improvement. And he found in Tom Diskin someone who was able to provide the perfect foil for his own instinctively introverted nature, with the capacity to smooth over words that might sound rough coming out of his own mouth and represent policies that he knew would be best for all involved without ruffling any feathers. It seemed sometimes as if the two of them could almost finish each other's thoughts and sentences, though there was never any doubt about who was in charge.

Before long, he and Marie were drawn into the extended family life of the Diskins. (There were ten Diskin siblings and the second-oldest daughter, Helen, who lived in Alhambra with her husband, Ben Bonja, had ten children of her own.) Tom Parker became a second "Uncle Tom" to the Bonja family, and the two Toms and Marie visited them every time they were in California with a station wagon full of groceries. "It was always great to see them," recalled Ron Bonja, the second-oldest of the four boys. "When they arrived, it was like Christmas." Also, their second Uncle Tom was a very funny guy, prancing about in his suspenders, always indulging the kids with treats and jokes. They would all audition for Uncle Tom, singing popular songs like "Goodnight Irene," and he would solemnly — or not so solemnly — reward them with prizes and praise. After dinner he would sit back and light up a big cigar and tell them stories about show business and carnival days. Their home movies show a man comfortably disheveled and utterly relaxed, ensconced in the bosom of yet another family he was happy to embrace as his own. This second Uncle Tom, who would later be called Uncle Colonel, and not simply to avoid confusion, was always fun.

Within a year of their first meeting, Tom Parker had prevailed upon Tom Diskin to set up his own management company and booking agency, which, taking its name from Eddy's *Checkerboard Jamboree* radio show, would be called Jamboree Attractions and located in the basement of Tom Diskin's family home. Al Dvorin donated some office furniture and helped his friend get things going, and soon Al, a hulking bighearted man who looked like a gangster but always appreciated a good kidder ("The first thing I sent Colonel Parker," he recalled, "was a Top Banana hat, and he sent me back some Purina pens and a miniature covered wagon"), was fully enlisted in Tom Parker's business, too, providing "little people" and novelty acts for Purina mill openings, and entering into a lifelong association with Parker in which he played many different roles but is best known as the rough-hewn voice intoning "Elvis Has Left the Building" at the conclusion of all of Elvis' '70s concerts.

Jamboree Attractions, with Tom Diskin as a 25 percent partner, started somewhat haltingly at first as a convenient way to put the Eddy Arnold Show on the road without its star. Tom Parker was still in charge, Tom Diskin made that very clear to bookers, but he would be going out with the tour himself "to manage the show and attend to [the] details." In no time, though, it became an entity all its own, actively managing not just the Dickens Sisters but a whole host of country music performers, including Tommy Sands, a fifteen-year-old singer from Houston and Shreveport in whom Tom Parker had long taken an interest.

And while Jamboree Attractions (and its new publishing subsidiary, Jamboree Music) continued to use Tom Diskin's Chicago address as its

Colonel with a sixteen-year-old Tommy Sands (in cowboy hat) and friends, 1953. *Courtesy of Tommy Sands*

sole acknowledged place of business, and there was no overt mention of the other Tom's active participation in its management, Tom Parker was never less than a thinly veiled presence in all its activities — which, as time went on, made more and more sense to them both, given how little Eddy was now on the road and how much the overseeing of his long-term contracts and commitments came down to matters of "administration," which his manager attended to with all of his usual attention to detail but which failed to fully engage either his time or his interest.

NINETEEN FIFTY-THREE was shaping up to be their best year yet. Purina renewed its $100,000-a-year exclusive radio deal, and the five-year radio-and-television deal with NBC was finalized through the continuing efforts of William Morris. In exchange for NBC exclusivity, this would guarantee Eddy well over $50,000 a year with various fringe benefits, including extending his RCA contract, with its most-favored-nation clause, for the full length of the NBC term. In May Eddy would be playing at the recently opened Hotel Sahara in Las Vegas for the first time, a big step up from El Rancho, at $17,500 for a two-week booking. Prior to that, he would once again play the Houston Fat Stock Show (later renamed the Houston Livestock Show and Rodeo and billed as "the largest livestock and rodeo show in the world") at $21,500 for twelve days. And apart from the formalization of the NBC deal, he had been doing more and more TV, serving as the replacement host for Mrs. Parker's favorite singer, Perry Como, the previous summer and already booked to do the same for Dinah Shore in the summer of '53.

And then there was the Eddy Arnold string tie, a gimmick understandably dear to Tom Parker's heart. Eddy had always been partial to string ties, and as the slim Western version of the bow tie became more and more popular (Arthur Godfrey wore one; so, unsurprisingly, did the governors of Texas and Louisiana), his manager got the idea of creating a customized model. He discovered that the wife of Western-film-and-TV sidekick Andy Devine, an old pal from the Gene Austin days, had started a company that specialized in making the ties, and he commissioned scores of them with Eddy's name imprinted on the neckband. In the first year alone, he boasted to a reporter on a brief stopover in Tampa, he had given away one thousand to "radio and television stars, public officials, [and] disc jockeys," strictly as a promotional stunt. He himself would never be seen without one, he said, and in the picture accompanying the story Marie is shown making sure his tie is on straight. "If it would help Eddy Arnold," he declared with evident good humor, "I would wear earmuffs."

He was more than likely wearing a string tie when he received his second honorary Colonel appointment later that year, this time from newly elected Tennessee governor Frank Clement, whom he had helped in his 1952 campaign. He was genuinely tickled by the public recognition (like Elvis Presley's future discoverer Sam Phillips, he was a big fan of

Governor Clement's personality and progressive politics), but in fact he was more amused than impressed. As he told *Tampa Tribune* columnist Paul Wilder a few years later when one of the two Shetland ponies he had donated to the Florida Sheriffs Boys Ranch gave birth to a colt and the boys named it "Little Colonel" in his honor: "I must be the only phony Colonel who has a real Little Colonel named after him."

The only evident cloud on the horizon was a heart condition that had begun to manifest itself and culminated in a heart attack that spring, leading to a doctor's warning to lose weight and get off the road. Losing weight seemed out of the question, but, he rationalized, he had Tom Diskin now to take a lot of pressure off him. Still, even with Eddy's drastically reduced personal-appearance schedule, his manager, the newly crowned Tennessee Colonel, seemed to be traveling as much as ever, his mind too restless to settle down so long as there was a new deal to be made.

THE FIRST INKLING OF TROUBLE came in Las Vegas, just after Tommy Sands signed a full-representation contract with Jamboree Attractions, and his shadow manager was doing everything he could to get him signed to RCA. That is when it became clear to Eddy Arnold for the first time that he was no longer enjoying an exclusive arrangement with his manager. He confronted Parker, and Tom even offered to quit, but Eddy wasn't ready to take that drastic a step yet ("I just ignored him for several days"), and it seemed like they were back on a firm footing once again. For Mother's Day, *Billboard* reported admiringly, Tom Parker had set up a deal with every radio station in Las Vegas to play Eddy's new *To Mother* album and, just coincidentally, promote his Sahara appearance. And when the engagement was over, as usual they each went their separate ways.

But Eddy's feelings of resentment continued to fester ("I was displeased about the exclusivity; his take on me [of 25 percent] was for exclusivity"), and on August 21 he wrote a letter to his manager, which began, "Dear Tom, I really hate to write this letter," and went on to detail in the briefest and most civil of terms all the causes for his discontent, including the formation of Jamboree. "I am convinced," he wrote, "that our further association cannot work out and think upon sober reflection that you will agree with me. Of course, aside from this I do not agree with many of the methods you employ in doing business. Also, I had thought since your recent illness you would possibly slow down a bit so that it would make working with you a greater pleasure, however, it is my feeling that you have done just the opposite."

He wanted, he stipulated, "to make a cash settlement with you based upon a fair and equitable consideration." And he ended in the same straightforward but gracious manner that anyone who knew Eddy Arnold would have expected: "I wish to take this opportunity to thank you for the many things that you have done in my behalf, and assure you that in the termination of this arrangement I feel it best for the both of us and certainly I will be happier. We started as friends, let's end the same way."

Tom was devastated. Nothing like this had happened to him since his dismissal by Royal American, long before he knew the business, or even knew himself well enough to conduct business in the manner in which it needed to be conducted. He had let his guard down. He had been blind to any signs of trouble that under normal circumstances he would have picked up right away. And, once again, he had no one to blame but himself. He had let himself forget the fundamental inequities that the world was always prepared to set in your path.

It took him eight days, and several drafts, to formulate his four-page, single-spaced reply, and even then, while it can stand as a masterpiece of lawyerlike concision, running down close to a dozen carefully elucidated, closely argued points, it was, for all of his resolve to hew to the language of business, practically bristling with hurt.

"I have, from the first day we teamed up together planned for the future of you and the future of myself, not just to have it blown up," he wrote in an early draft, which pretty well expressed the theme throughout.

As you know I have invested a good deal of my earnings back into you as a personality which I always was happy to do. But not with the idea of letting some one person or representation department cash in without having any investment in you on what I have done towards building you into a First Class Attraction which you are today. [Furthermore], I will state that not being able to put the direct credit in words that you are responsible for fifty percent of your standing as an artist today and I am the other half with all the other elements tied-in to make this possible. Without these you or I could not have gone as far as we have.

There was more, much more. Where Eddy had brought up the matter of Jamboree Attractions ("My discontent has been increased since the organization of your agency known as the Jamboree Attractions"), his manager felt compelled to point out that not three months ago "this was straightened out in Las Vegas. Your desire there was voiced very strongly for me to remain with you and I did." And furthermore, it was hard to understand how it could have taken nine years "before you found out that my methods of business did not agree with you [even] when they somehow paid off. And I have never heard of anyone that I could not do business with again for you or anyone else in this field, except perhaps for some people that could not get the right deal that would have been good FOR THEM ONLY AND NOT FOR YOU AND I. . . .

"In making our settlement," he stresses more than once, "there is no place for either one of us to bring up our faults, dislikes, mistakes or shortcomings of which I like any other human have my share." And then he accepts without objection Eddy's suggestion that they use Eddy's lawyer, Bill Carpenter, as an intermediary in the negotiations — so long as it is understood that Mr. Carpenter's role will be that of "a friend and not an attorney for I know that he is a fair person and will be just as fair with his advice if I need it as he will be with you." At which point he reminds Eddy that "I am not able to get worked up in my condition and will do my utmost to control myself. Should we somehow misunderstand and let our emotions run away with ourselves," he adds in what is perhaps his most telling admission, "I will depart from the meeting as a very unhappy person but not a defeated one." And he would "remain Mr. Carpenter's friend [and] understand that this can have no relation between us at anytime. And I will respect his trust in me for this will never cause me to waiver in my belief that he will do whatever he feels is right for you."

In the end it was worked out in a manner that seemed fair to all. Tom Parker would receive $60,000 (roughly $710,000 in 2024 money), representing perhaps a 20 percent commission on a full year's work, and in exchange forfeit all interest in any and all ongoing or future deals, including the ones with RCA, NBC, and Purina that he had so painstakingly initiated. But then, in steadfast service to the amicable spirit he was determined to maintain, Eddy wrote in a side letter that "you are authorized to book me for ten (10) personal appearances during 1954." Which would serve as a template for Tom Parker's continuing involvement in Eddy's career over the next twenty-five years, including prestigious Las Vegas bookings in the '70s, after Elvis Presley had returned to live performing and established himself as Las Vegas' reigning star. And it permitted them to continue as they had started, in Eddy's words, as friends, which they remained until Thomas A. Parker's death forty-four years later, when Eddy spoke with characteristic affection and restraint at the invitation-only memorial service at the Las Vegas Hilton.

What followed was perhaps even more surprising than what preceded it. Others might have sat around salving their wounds and living off a cash settlement that could easily have carried them for three years without ever having to think about money. But Colonel Tom Parker — for it was from this point on that he assumed the sobriquet almost without exception with all newcomers to his world and, increasingly, with old acquaintances as well — instantly went back to work.

On September 14, just ten days after the settlement, he proposed to Steve Sholes that he assemble an RCA package tour to showcase some of the label's finest country artists, an idea that Sholes immediately embraced, though it took another three months to agree on terms and finalize all the details. It took even longer to do all the meticulous work of coordinating dates and finding venues that could accommodate all of the artists' different schedules, but in the end the RCA Victor Country & Western Caravan kicked off in Asheville, North Carolina, on April 25, 1954, concluding in Little Rock on May 9. The Colonel had added four dates to RCA's original ten, making the argument to Steve Sholes that they could reach far more people with this expanded schedule, and, with careful control of costs, he could bring it in for the same price. "The outcome must be victory [on every level]—time, effort, and money," he wrote to Tom Diskin in an internal memorandum not intended for RCA consumption. "We must sell records. We must have a good show. We must do it right [or else] learn how to clean auditoriums and get jobs as janitors."

The outcome was indeed victory. The tour was, from everyone's point of view, an unqualified success, carried out with all of Tom Parker's customary aplomb. Nor was Parker's ability to handle every situation that came up and tamp down every potential crisis lost on its headliner, Hank Snow, a feisty thirty-nine-year-old Canadian transplant who in the last three years (under the aegis of Steve Sholes) had become one of the top stars in the new country music firmament. (His "I Don't Hurt Anymore" would soon become the number-one hit of 1954.) At the end of the tour Snow wrote to his new friend, Tom Parker, about "one of the greatest record promotions I have ever been connected with." And it wasn't just the promotion, it was the care and concern that Parker showed to every artist. He particularly appreciated the way that when he went out onstage, Parker was always "down front giving me a hand." And he signed off, "Your friend always, HANK SNOW."

O N NOVEMBER 6, 1953, *Billboard* informed its readers that "Col. Tom Parker, of Jamboree Attractions, Madison, Tennessee, in a phone call from New Orleans reports that he has inked a pact with Hank Snow." The pact included personal management, personal appearances, and recording, radio, and TV on an exclusive basis, and would go into full effect at the start of the new year.

Even before then, Colonel Parker embarked upon an ambitious campaign of letter writing and promotion in which he contacted everyone he had come to know on even the most cursory basis in his nine years with Eddy Arnold. (Steve Sholes wrote back to Hank that he was certain the association would be "beneficial to all concerned," and he was looking for even bigger and better things in the future for Hank Snow.) He inundated William Morris, too, with energetic ideas and suggestions, while launching what amounted to an all-out assault on every major booking agent in the country. At the same time, he began negotiations with RCA for a new five-year contract, while establishing a 50-50 partnership with Hank in a joint booking agency, song publishing, and promotion company to be called Hank Snow Enterprises–Jamboree Attractions (or vice versa, it was never clear). All of which was undertaken with the implicit-bordering-on-the-verge-of-explicit aim of proving that what he had accomplished with Eddy Arnold, he could accomplish again — or possibly even surpass.

The new year began with a flurry of announcements and personal, promotional, and television appearances, culminating in an all-star,

Colonel and Hank Snow, for Purina, 1955. *Courtesy of the Graceland Archives*

"record-breaking tour of the Southwest and the West," booked prior to the Snow-Parker association but expertly promoted by the Colonel. (Veteran promoter A. V. "Bam" Bamford, a longtime associate, declared in *Cash Box* that in all his years of putting on shows "we have never had as successful a tour.") That tour was immediately followed by the first to go out under the banner of Hank Snow Enterprises–Jamboree Attractions.

That inaugural tour began in Roswell, New Mexico, on February 14 and was once again headlined by Hank, but this time, rather than feature a group of Grand Ole Opry stars, it took as its model the self-contained Eddy Arnold Show. The supporting cast included the Duke of Paducah, who went back to Jamup and Honey days; a young singer from Henrietta, Texas, named Charline Arthur, who had been featured on the RCA Caravan after Colonel Parker helped get her signed to RCA; Hank Snow's son, Jimmie Rodgers Snow (also an RCA recording artist); and a promising new singer from Memphis, Tennessee, named Elvis Presley.

PART II

....

A PARTNERSHIP OF EQUALS

....

EIGHT

The Beginning of It All

H E FIRST BECAME aware of the boy in early 1955 through an old pal in Texarkana, Arkansas, a DJ, radio personality, and promoter named Ernest Hackworth who went by the name of Uncle Dudley. Hackworth, who, like so many other promoters, worked on his own shows as a country comedian, reported that this kid from Memphis had drawn more than eight hundred people to a little schoolhouse in New Boston, Texas, on January 11, which was a heckuva draw for an unknown artist whose name he usually got all jumbled up.

Oddly enough, Colonel was later reminded, he had actually been told about the boy two months earlier by another old colleague, Oscar Davis, who was wont to say he had made several fortunes (true — he had managed Hank Williams at the height of his career) and lost even more (equally true). Davis, a smooth-tongued, silver-haired operator who went back even further than Colonel in the world of carnivals and show business, was a peerless pitchman, always immaculately dressed, always sharp as a tack—in the view of a mutual acquaintance who did business with them both, he differed from Colonel in only two ways. Unlike Colonel, Oscar Davis looked the part, "he looked like the man with the money"—but also unlike Colonel (with whom you could operate with complete confidence on a handshake basis) you couldn't trust a word that he said.

Oscar had hit a rough patch lately and was advancing an Eddy Arnold tour for Colonel when he met this Presley boy in Memphis and had even gone to see him perform at some little club where the kid had really gotten the audience worked up. But for one reason or another, it seemed like Oscar wasn't emphasizing the point too strongly, or maybe Colonel just wasn't listening that closely (with Oscar Davis, you didn't want to

Tampa, July 31, 1955. *Courtesy of the Graceland Archives*

over-listen), so it wasn't until Uncle Dudley spoke to him the day after the New Boston show that he paid attention.

This time there was no hesitation.

He and Tom Diskin went to see Presley perform at the Louisiana Hayride three days later, and he was so knocked out, not so much by the music — he really wasn't sure at first what to make of the music — as by the reaction of the crowd, that he got in touch with Presley's manager, a Memphis DJ named Bob Neal, right away. Within a week he had him booked on the Hank Snow tour that was about to begin in New Mexico on February 14. Even before the start of the tour, apparently on the strength of the Hayride performance alone, Colonel approached Steve Sholes about signing him to RCA, but as it turned out, the head of Presley's little record label in Memphis, Sam Phillips, wouldn't hear of it, in fact he seemed almost insulted by the idea, so Colonel was forced to let Steve know that it looked like Presley was "pretty securely tied up" for the time being.

From the very first dates on the New Mexico tour, the boy's talent — not just his talent but his drive, and especially his capacity for growth — were unmistakable. When asked some eighteen months later if he took credit for Elvis Presley's unparalleled success, the Colonel uncharacteristically demurred. "I think Presley was a star from the first day he ever started going into show business," he said. "I knew I could help him, [but] I think anyone could have helped him that knows something about show business."

It was astounding, the speed with which it happened.

Everywhere the Hank Snow–headlined revue played, the clamor over Presley's performance only grew, and many nights he took the show. Hank Snow tried to hide his reaction, but Colonel could not help but be aware of it and all the ways his client's wounded vanity played out. The boy never seemed to notice, though; he clearly thought the world of Snow, and Colonel did all he could to smooth things over, pointing out that everywhere they went, they were breaking attendance records, which surely had to be considered a tribute to the star of the show.

Things could not have been going better, in fact, for the new partnership between Colonel Tom Parker and Hank Snow. Record sales were up, and due to his assiduous efforts, Colonel never tired of reminding Snow, all sorts of new, high-paying opportunities in radio and television were starting to open up. The trades attributed these rapidly expanding horizons to a unique artist-manager relationship which *Cash Box* would describe as "based on loyalty, mutual respect and a common objective," not to mention the uncommon efforts of Tom Parker, "a colorful personality [with] a natural flair for showmanship [who is] known from coast to coast . . . and respected for his sound business principles [and his] policy of doing more than he has promised."

But, tellingly, Colonel didn't book Elvis with Hank again until May, while Hank continued to do record-breaking business on his own.

O NE OF the stumbling blocks — the *principal* stumbling block — to his doing more with Presley was the boy's manager, Bob Neal, who seemed infuriatingly unsusceptible to persuasion, promotion, or even recognition of his own (let alone his artist's) ever-increasing opportunities. During a brief break from touring at the beginning of March, Colonel wrote to Tom Diskin, clearly disheartened by his inability to make any headway with Neal. "I don't see much use in wasting any [more] money or time on Presley till we know that they need us, and only when they contact us direct for help in some way." Things were slow in the business in general, he noted, but he had not given up on improving Hank's royalty situation with RCA, or maybe even moving him to his old friend Randy Wood's Dot label (though in all likelihood, here he was merely musing out loud, for his own and Tom Diskin's benefit, about something that would almost certainly have been little more than a negotiating ploy). Meanwhile, he thought he would set up another strong ten- or fifteen-day tour for Hank, "keep getting special deals lined up," and focus on getting him another guest shot on TV with Perry Como.

But as frustrated as he was by the Presley situation, he was not about to give up. Finally, on March 29, he was able to come to some sort of agreement with Bob Neal for a two-week series of one-nighters in Florida with Hank Snow, but he couldn't resist needling Neal while at the same time trying to steer him toward a more realistic appraisal of the situation. Neal had to pay more attention to business, he wrote with unfeigned indignation. He had to get the Colonel a complete supply of photos and records right away. And most important of all, the boy was never going to get anywhere so long as he was on Sun Records. "I am finding out that in some places they have never heard of Elvis. . . . This I am not saying to knock, as you well know but to drive home the fact how sad it is that this boy does not get the spread he needs on his records." And when Neal failed at this task, as at every other, he wrote again — and again.

THE FLORIDA TOUR was a triumph beyond anything that could have been imagined.

On the first date, in Daytona Beach on May 7, Mae Boren Axton, a forty-year-old high school English teacher and sometime songwriter from Jacksonville, who had been doing advance press work in the area for the Colonel for the last year or two, witnessed a kind of crowd reaction she had never seen before. A well-educated woman from a prominent political family in Oklahoma (her nephew David later became governor of the state and a three-term U.S. senator), she had grown up, she said, with "no idea" of what hillbilly music was, but she had come to like it from all the promotion work she had done for numerous hillbilly jamborees over the last few years. Now, in her capacity as Colonel's designated press officer, she undertook to conduct an interview with Elvis before the show, one of the first real interviews he had ever done, she imagined, judging from his polite, tongue-tied responses — but then she was almost struck dumb herself by the altogether unexpected explosiveness of his act. At one point she ran across one of her former students while Elvis was still onstage, "and she was just right into it, didn't know who he was, none of them did. But she was just ahhhh — all of them were, even some of the old ones were doing like that. I looked at the faces — they were loving it. And I said, 'Hey, honey, what is it about this kid?' And she said, 'Awww, Miz Axton, he's just a great big beautiful hunk of forbidden fruit.'"

In Orlando, four nights later, the crowd called for Elvis to come back when Hank Snow took the stage, and could not be quieted during Snow's performance. The reporter for the local paper, a complete neophyte to this kind of music (it provided "a poignant contrast to Metropolitan Opera in Atlanta, I must say," she acknowledged to her readers), gave a reasonably enthusiastic account of the entire evening, "but what really stole the show was this 20-year-old sensation, Elvis Presley, a real sex box as far as the teenage girls are concerned. They squealed themselves silly over this fellow in orange coat and sideburns who 'sent' them. . . .

Following the program, Elvis was surrounded by girlies asking for autographs. He would give each a long, slow look with drooped eyelids and comply. They ate it up." Which evolved in the blink of an eye into a full-scale riot in Jacksonville, when, at the conclusion of his act, Elvis announced, "Girls, I'll see you all backstage."

"I heard feet like a thundering herd," Mae Axton recalled, "and the next thing I knew I heard this voice from the shower area, and Elvis was on top of one of the showers looking sheepish and scared, and his shirt was shredded and his coat was torn to pieces . . . he was up there with nothing but his pants on and they were trying to pull at them up on the shower." The Colonel, said Mae, "and I don't mean it derogatorily, got dollar marks in his eyes."

But I think even Mae would be willing to admit that this was a reductive picture of a man she had come to admire for both his intellect and determination. Because she could tell even then that from Colonel's perspective Elvis Presley was not just another passing fancy to be cashed in on and forgotten, he was, potentially, a once-in-a-lifetime phenomenon.

WITHIN DAYS Colonel was hard at work trying to set up another Florida tour. Once again, Bob Neal's refusal, or simply inability, to take a businesslike approach was an obstacle, but one which Colonel was confident he could overcome. On May 25 he wrote to Neal in what could be taken as a lesson in coercive persuasion: "I was most happy to do what I could to help Elvis and you in getting him across in these new markets. . . . I am always glad to work with both of you, I am not one of the type of personalities that tries to cut out a manager, as you well know a good many would do. . . . If ever you wish to tie in with me closely and let me carry the ball I will be happy to sit down with both of you and try to work it out." Evidently that must have struck a chord with Neal, who instantly initiated a phone call, which in turn prompted a second letter from Colonel, spelling out terms and conditions and laying out "the protection I must have to enable [me] to tie these things up and not be fanning the air and spent my money foolish."

He felt no need to mention it at the time, but the second Florida tour, scheduled to begin in just two months, would take place without the presence of Hank Snow. Snow instead would be heading up a West Coast tour of his own, his first all-out assault on that market, which would be operating under the direction of Tom Diskin and conclude with a triumphal appearance at the Hollywood Bowl. Colonel made sure that Hank understood that he was not abdicating managerial responsibility, that every aspect of the tour would be plotted out by himself and Mr. Diskin, and that it would, of course, be fully supported by RCA. But in fact Hank couldn't have been more pleased, and if he were to be perfectly honest about it, he would not miss the presence of Presley in the least. And it wasn't as if he were losing anything on the deal. As a partner in Hank Snow Enterprises-Jamboree Attractions, he stood only to gain by the addition of another big moneymaking tour in whose profits he would be a full participant.

In the meantime, while fully engaged in the setup of both tours, Colonel continued to go back and forth with Bob Neal about the smallest, and largest, of matters. He dangled the promise of two weeks in Las Vegas ("The [club] owner is a good friend of mine"), which surely he would have had difficulty delivering on, but Neal didn't bite. He continued to hector Neal about his inattention to business ("I have been waiting to hear from you," again, and again, and again), without any tangible results. Finally, he arranged to meet with Neal in person about a whole panoply of issues, including, once again, trying to shop Presley's record contract to a major label, about which he believed they had finally reached agreement, only to hear back from Neal three days later: "Hold off any further announcements regarding Elvis until I have more time with him."

On June 25, Colonel wrote to Tom Diskin in what appears to be barely concealed, barely punctuated frustration. "Get it in your mind that there is no future in anything but big deals, no small time stuff it takes as much time and no money can be made of it. You have to believe this so strongly that you will let no one get your time and ear on junk deals. Everytime we have become involved in something small [and here it is hard to believe that he is not for the first time wondering if this is how the whole Elvis experience will turn out] we have lost time money and get nowhere."

Just how discouraged he must have been feeling is evident in the entirely unaccustomed rush of emotion that he pours into what he writes next to Diskin, with whom he has been working in perfect harmony for three years now without ever once communicating just how much the younger man's contributions have meant to him. "The future looks very good for you if you want to make it that way," he writes, in a passage posing as well-meant advice for a junior partner who needs bucking up, but which could just as easily be taken as a confidence-building message to Colonel himself. "I will always protect you all I can/and I know you do the same. You are good for me and I know that I do understand you better than any-one could. Your closer to me than any-one ever has been and will be, and I know you understand me."

THE RETURN to Florida, beginning on July 25 and ending seven days later with a benefit show in Tampa sponsored by the Sertoma Club and Clyde Rinaldi, proved to be even more spectacular than the first tour. The all-star cast was headlined by comedian-actor Andy Griffith, but it was Elvis who took the show every night, astonishing not only the audience but his fellow performers. Once again there was a riot in Jacksonville in the course of which Elvis once again had his clothes torn off, something the Colonel made sure to mention two weeks later in an exhortatory letter to Sam Weisbord, one of William Morris' most senior West Coast agents.

He was enclosing a set of action pictures he had had taken in Tampa, he wrote to Weisbord. (One of them would become the arresting cover of Elvis' first RCA album some eight months later.) He was also enclosing a selection of his records. "He is presently on a small record label and they have sold this year over 100,000 of this boy's records already, and they have no distribution whatsoever. . . . This artist seems to me to be right in line for motion picture material, television, and a stage career. . . . With the right training and advice and good material the possibilities are unlimited. His exposure on the stage does 75% towards the public accepting this artist. The talents that are hidden in this personality are unlimited."

He didn't hesitate to invoke Hank Snow, another well-regarded William Morris client, who "has done much to expose the talents of ELVIS PRESLEY, as he has taken him more or less under his wing and has been plugging away on all his personals and blowing the bugle about ELVIS PRESLEY."

And he summed it all up on a not altogether unexpected note. "I can only go so far without the help of friends like you towards making the

Andy Griffith, the star of the show, and Colonel, July 31, 1955. *Courtesy of the Graceland Archives*

world aware of such great talent. You have forgotten more than I'll ever know about how to bring this out in an artist and I'm asking you for advice to carry on and get the best results out of and for ELVIS PRESLEY and all of us."

He copied the letter to Harry Kalcheim, the head of William Morris' New York office, who had been instrumental in helping to broaden Eddy Arnold's appeal with key supper-club and television bookings. And he continued to bombard Steve Sholes at RCA with letters and telegrams, ostensibly under the guise of tipping him off to something that Colonel was good enough not to want him to miss.

This might all be taken as Colonel's usual method of operation, of course—and in many respects it was. But the lack of caution, the abandonment of all of his usual, carefully calibrated reserve, was something new. Certainly he had felt the same kind of full-blown belief in Eddy

Arnold and the vast potential of his talent — but he had always proceeded with an element of circumspection, taking each incremental step only after he was confident of the success of the last. With Presley he was making no such allowance for failure. If the boy failed, he was leaving himself nothing to fall back on. Because here it was not just Elvis Presley's musical talent that foretold an almost limitless future (though that may well have been enough in itself), it was his spongelike ability to absorb and reshape everything that he took in and experienced, his seemingly inexhaustible appetite for self-improvement. As Colonel would one day remark in comparing Presley's talent with that of Gene Austin, his first superstar, both were "individual artists [who] have a feeling inside them for what they are doing which you can't teach anyone." And as he was quick to point out with more than just a smidgen of irony, "I, as a salesman and drummer, know this [better] than the average guy."

WHAT TURNED OUT to be the start of the real negotiations began in August, in the immediate aftermath of an incident in Batesville, Arkansas, on August 6. Elvis had evidently engaged in some "off-color" jokes and general misbehavior with his bass player, Bill Black, the comedian in the band, and, the promoter wrote, a number of customers had asked for their money back. After ascertaining from the Duke of Paducah, who was featured on the show, that the complaint was legitimate, Colonel immediately sent back a refund of $50.

But he also wrote to Neal on August 22 with a stern warning: "You must definitely set up a new deal with ELVIS where he gets on the stage as a singer, stays on the stage as a singer, and comes off like a singer.

> There is always enough comedy on any of my shows that they don't have to do comedy. To be exact, I just can't have any more comedy on ELVIS PRESLEY'S part of the program. . . . ELVIS has great talents and he does not have to resort to smutty comedy to sell his attractions. When we ask for more money for ELVIS we definitely must give better production or we should sell him as a comic, and you know how much we can get for him doing that.
>
> I think the most important thing is that he needs guidance. He is young, inexperienced and it takes a lot more than a couple of hot

records in a certain territory to become a big named artist, level-headed, courteous, and carry the responsibility that goes with being a star as ELVIS wants to be. There is no way we can play this down — even if we tried — as we would only be fooling ourselves and would be out of business in no time. My reputation is more important than my friendship and belief in the talents that ELVIS has. He can cash in on this to the fullest, but he must contribute all the qualities that I know he has or can have if he makes up his mind to do so.

It's hard to know just how literally this should be taken. On the one hand there is no question that Colonel was serious. He had always maintained prim, almost Victorian standards in the presentation of his shows — they were intended, he insisted to artists and promoters alike, to be good clean fun for the whole family. On the other hand, would he have actually cut Elvis loose, would he have simply walked away from his vision of the future?

I think it is perhaps safest to say that he calculated both the risk and the people involved. He was positive that the boy didn't mean any harm — he was a good boy from a good family and he knew the difference between right and wrong, as Colonel always insisted in pitching Presley's talents, and as he firmly believed. Nor did he have any doubt that Bob Neal, too, would be upset to learn of the complaints. Perhaps more to the point, though, Bob Neal was not the kind of man who could stand up to the pressure of being perceived to be in the wrong.

It turned out that it was his threat to walk away that finally turned the tide, that and a letter he had managed to extract from Neal and Mr. and Mrs. Presley in the midst of the Batesville crisis (his parents were still their twenty-year-old son's legal guardians), granting him sole and exclusive representation of Elvis in nearly every way, most of all in "the build-up of Elvis Presley as an artist . . . in any way possible."

And yet there continued to be an almost endless exchange of communications between him and Neal, most of it on Colonel's side, as he sometimes patiently, more often less than patiently, tried to school Neal in the realities of the business, while Neal for his part almost invariably failed to grasp the point. In September there was a break of almost three weeks after Neal wrote to Colonel that he and Elvis were "quite disturbed" by Colonel's upcoming bookings and prices, and Colonel wrote back indignantly, and in considerable detail, that Neal and Elvis could have it any way they wanted. He would be "most happy," he wrote, to make a settlement at the end of the current tour and "dissolve our relationship . . . because I see no point in carrying this situation on under the present working conditions if I am to be questioned everytime I make a deal."

This went on for longer than would have seemed possible — it's hard to say who was keeping whom on a string — until on September 17 Colonel sent Elvis a letter, enclosing a copy of his letter to Neal acquiescing to Neal's demand for a dissolution of their association. "I hope that we will be able to work again together in future," he wrote to the boy, with suggestions of "a good many irons in the fire that may come thru as we go along," and he signed his letter, not without calculation, "Your Pal The Col."

There was never any question of the outcome. Despite Neal's plaintive talk of a "pleasant parting," there was no real parting, and they remained in a kind of undeclared limbo for the next month. (There were, among other things, many already booked dates for Colonel to fulfill and collect his commission on.) And so Colonel continued to go about what he imperturbably declared to be his business, which was primarily to find a new label for his artist (and, really, he only had RCA in mind), with or without the help of anyone other than his loyal lieutenant, Tom Diskin.

He had never wanted anything more.

H E ENLISTED EVERYONE in the operation to win over Elvis' parents, who, despite having signed that official letter of authorization, continued to be put off by what they took to be Colonel's blunt "big city" ways. He called on both Hank Snow and Hank's son, Jimmie, who had become close to Elvis from their tours together, along with his old friend the Duke of Paducah, whose folksy homespun humor Vernon and Gladys Presley both appreciated and enjoyed. "They were country people," observed Jimmie Rodgers Snow, who would later leave show business to become a well-known evangelical preacher. "They were poor, hardworking people. Colonel was too slick. And I think they were more concerned about sticking with Bob Neal and things that were working, just like anybody else that's hardworking. The idea was to explain to them that they had to progress and go forward." As to his father, Snow said, "They liked my dad. They were impressed by stardom, like anybody. And Colonel was smart enough to realize that he could not directly [influence] them, so he utilized anybody that could."

Not surprisingly, he also continued to call upon every important associate, past and present, he could think of, masterfully cultivating all his contacts at William Morris as well as every one of his RCA connections going back to the start. He enlisted the Aberbach brothers, too, whose powerful Hill and Range song publishing company had originally sought out Eddy Arnold and presently had a partnership publishing deal with Hank Snow. And while he never showed any flagging of energy or enthusiasm in his everyday business (including plans for a spectacular Hank Snow–Bill Haley–Bob Wills tour scheduled to follow up on the great success of the current Snow-Haley tour), it seems obvious in retrospect that his mind was on only one thing.

But he still had the problem of his partnership with Hank Snow. He had been growing increasingly disenchanted with Snow, who, for all of their success together, simply had too inflated a view of himself to permit any meaningful collaboration. Perhaps more significantly, unlike Eddy Arnold (whom Colonel, even in the aftermath of their bitter breakup, still considered to have been a true partner), Snow had a vision of the future that was built entirely on the past. For all of his drive and determination, his emergence from a difficult childhood combined with a sense of exclusion that Andreas van Kuijk should have been uniquely able to identify with, Hank Snow simply could not imagine the world that Colonel believed Elvis Presley was about to step into, the revolutionary changes that Colonel believed even more firmly he was destined to create. And so, although it went against all of his instincts, all of the hard-earned lessons he had taken from his earliest days in show business and all of the principles that he would continue to espouse for the next forty years — that loyalty overrode everything, that you never went back on a contract or a personal commitment — Colonel finally determined that if and when he was ever able to get the boy signed to RCA, he would have to walk away from Hank Snow.

It was his name alone that was on the agreement with the Presleys and would continue to be on all future documents, he rationalized, it was he alone who would continue to conduct the on-again, off-again negotiations with the record company — and throughout it all, Snow never exhibited the slightest curiosity about the proceedings, except to speculate that at some point there was likely to be a great deal of money coming their way.

WHEN IT HAPPENED, it happened quickly.
On October 20, Colonel had Mr. and Mrs. Presley telegram him with a carefully worded text that he had provided for them to sign, empowering him "to act as our sole and exclusive representative in all negotiations pertaining to the recording contract of Elvis Presley [with] no other person or persons . . . authorized to represent Elvis Presley." They would be bound by his decisions, the telegram said, "as we feel that you will be for the best interest of Elvis Presley."

A week later he heard from Neal that he was "very much upset" by what he had just learned from the Presleys, but by then Colonel had already returned from New York, where, armed with his new authority, he had initiated formal talks with RCA.

At the start of those talks, on October 24, he had telegrammed Sam Phillips from the Warwick Hotel that "Elvis Presley and his parents Mr. and Mrs. Presley have requested and authorized me to handle all negotiations towards affecting a settlement of the Elvis Presley recording contract with you. . . . If interested will you please advise me your best flat price for a complete dissolution and release free and clear."

An agitated Sam Phillips called him back almost immediately. *What the hell are you doing?* Sam railed at this man he barely knew but knew well enough to dislike intensely. *What gives you the right to sell something you don't even own?* Was Tom Parker (he'd be damned if he'd call the man by his phony title) trying to ruin him? Once his distributors heard that Elvis' contract was up for sale — even though it wasn't — "this could cost me my company. You're not just messing with an artist contract here, you messing with my life."

Colonel waited him out, and when he was done simply asked, if he *were* to sell Elvis' contract, what would he want for it?

"He didn't say how much he was thinking," Phillips recalled, "just how much would I take. So I said, 'I hadn't really thought about it, Tom. But

I'll let you know.' So he said, 'Well, look, think about it, and let me know.' And I thought about it about thirty seconds and called him back."

The price that he named — $35,000, plus several thousand dollars he owed Elvis in back royalties — was more than anyone had ever paid for a popular recording artist (by comparison, Columbia had paid $25,000 for the contract of Frankie Laine, an established star, in 1951). But after making a few little clucking sounds, Colonel didn't even bother to argue — there would be no point. He had learned by now how passionate Sam was about his little record company, so he simply told Sam he would do the best he could.

What he didn't tell him, because it would have just inflamed him even more, was that RCA had already made an offer of $25,000, which they presented in two different forms of payout for him to choose from. It was, he recognized, an extraordinary offer in and of itself, but not enough to satisfy Sam Phillips, and RCA chief legal counsel Coleman Tily made it perfectly clear that it was their final offer, there would be no further discussion of the matter.

Over the next few days he heard from Steve Sholes and Sholes' boss, Bill Bullock, that RCA was not going to budge; however much Sholes and Bullock would like to sign the boy, the money simply wasn't going to change. Nonetheless, Colonel set up a meeting on Saturday, October 29, at Sam's brand-new radio station in Memphis, WHER, "the first all-girl station in the nation," as Sam proudly branded it. The meeting was held on the very day the station went on the air after a number of technical glitches and delays, and for all the stress that Phillips was under, Sam seemed persuaded by Colonel's point that there was no reason for theatrics on either side, this was a *business* meeting in the end, however difficult the decision to sell Elvis' contract might have been for Sam to come to.

Only the three principal parties representing Elvis' interests were there: Colonel and Tom Diskin, Sam, and Bob Neal, who by now seemed not just to have accepted the situation but to have enthusiastically embraced it. After making a token attempt to get Sam to come down on his price ("Well, you know $35,000 is a lot of money, Sam, there's not a lot of people who believe in this thing"), Colonel simply set to work hashing out an agreement that would essentially memorialize Sam's terms: $35,000 for Elvis' contract and recordings, along with the recognition that Sam would not be held responsible for any unpaid royalties and his commitment to stop distributing Elvis' Sun records at the end of the year. The agreement would take effect on November 1 and be secured by a nonrefundable down payment of $5,000, to be transmitted by midnight on November 15.

And only the Colonel knew the money wasn't there.

There was no room left to maneuver. The only bluff he had to fall back on was his unshakable calm in the face of RCA's desperate plea that he listen to reason, he was going to lose the deal if he didn't come to his senses. But he remained impervious. Despite the stakes — and his recognition that things could never go back to the way they had been if he failed — he continued to articulate the philosophy that had carried him through his entire career so far: you can't lose a deal that you never had. And he continued to act as if he were in possession of a secret that no one else — certainly not his RCA counterparts — knew.

On the morning of the last day of the option he received a telegram from RCA Manager of the Single Records Department Bill Bullock, meeting all his terms and guaranteeing "Thirty Five Thousand [Dollars] to Sun Records, Five [as a nonrecoupable bonus] to Presley, three television guest appearances and complete promotion coverage." Because time was so tight ("The banks close here at Two PM," he couldn't help but remind Bullock), Colonel volunteered that he would be "very happy to handle everything" on his end and advance the $5,000 that was necessary to secure the deal. And he couldn't resist the opportunity to stick the needle in a little bit further by suggesting (and one can only imagine how firmly his tongue was lodged in his cheek), "Personally, I believe the price too high [but] tomorrow he may go up again."

In a follow-up letter to Coleman Tily later in the day, he wrote with new authority (well, not new to him, but new perhaps to Tily, a proud Princeton graduate, who would soon get used to it), "There are many details to be worked out to protect this setup and it would be best for you to come here [to Madison] and we can go on to Memphis [together] . . . I am very proud to [have] advanced the money for RCA as I am a stock holder anyway."

And so it was that on November 15, 1955, ten months to the day from the time he had first seen Elvis perform at the Louisiana Hayride, the deal was done.

At the RCA contract signing, Sun studio, November 21, 1955, with (left to right) Colonel; Gladys, Elvis, and Vernon Presley; RCA attorney Coleman Tily; and Bob Neal. *Courtesy of the Graceland Archives*

THE SIGNING CEREMONIES at the Sun studio six days later were an intimate affair, including Elvis and his parents, Sam Phillips, Bob Neal, the Colonel and Tom Diskin, a couple of regional RCA representatives, and Coleman Tily. In the end Colonel had gotten almost everything he wanted, including a $1,000 bonus from Hill and Range to secure their upcoming publishing deal with Elvis. The only thing he might have been disappointed about was RCA's insistence that the purchase price of $35,000 would be accounted against one half of Elvis' forthcoming royalties until it was fully paid off. But he didn't put up much of a fight on that point, because, for one thing, he was confident the boy would have nothing to worry about financially, and for another he was absolutely certain that his success would register on such a stratospheric scale that there would be no trouble securing him a new, much better contract before too long. For some reason the only signature lines provided on the contract were for H. Coleman Tily for Radio Corporation of America and Elvis and Vernon Presley, but Colonel appended his signature at the bottom as Elvis' sole and exclusive representative.

Hank Snow flew in from Nashville for the ceremony, and though he missed the actual signing, he looks pleased as a peacock in the pictures taken at the Hotel Peabody in Memphis afterward. He and Colonel drove back to Nashville together, and he never asked a single question. ("I don't think my dad realized at the time what had happened," said his son, Jimmie Rodgers Snow, who seemed to understand better than his father ever would just *why* it had happened.)

As for Colonel, I would imagine he spoke about anything and everything but Elvis Presley's new contract on the drive home — he and Hank Snow had extensive plans going well into the next year, and oddly enough they would continue to do business, if on an understandably reduced scale (and Snow would continue to seek favors, and Colonel would continue to dispense them), long after Hank realized, to his lifelong consternation, that he had been cut out of the Presley picture.

But what Colonel was thinking — well, one can only speculate. He may have lingered for a moment to savor his triumph, a triumph that had come against all the odds, and in the face of dire predictions from all the naysayers who never fail to crowd the sidelines. But you can be certain, he wouldn't have lingered long. Throughout his long life, Andreas van Kuijk's mind never focused on anything but the future, and he was well aware that now the real work would begin.

By the time he got back to Nashville there was a telegram awaiting him that said more than any mere business deal ever could. "Dear Colonel," it read:

Words can never tell you how my folks and I appreciate what you did for me. I have always known and now my folks are assured that you are the best and most wonderful person I could ever hope to work with. Believe me when I say I will stick with you thru thick and thin and do everything I can to uphold your faith in me. Again I say thanks and I love you like a father — ELVIS PRESLEY

NINE

Defending Elvis

The writers are having a Field Day with this new personality.
I am sure one of them will come up with a good writeup before long,
as they also will get tired of writing the same thing all the time.
I have always remembered, and practiced the old saying: "One never
wins anything when one gives up," and I'm not a quitter. As long
as the LIGHT BEAMS, I will turn it on!

— Colonel Tom Parker in response to repeated criticism of Elvis,
June 1956

MUCH OF COLONEL'S JOB for the first two years of their association consisted of defending Elvis against the fears, insecurities, importunities, and demands coming at him from all sides, and in particular from every element of the business that was threatened by a talent so startling, so revolutionary, so original and new. Starting with the record company, RCA, but including the booking agency, William Morris, that was so vital to all of their plans, the television industry, and, of course, the Hollywood hierarchy.

His first challenge was to secure the national television exposure that RCA had promised but that it quickly became obvious they were not going to deliver on anytime soon. Initially he turned to his longtime friend and ally, Harry Kalcheim, at William Morris, but when it became clear that Kalcheim wasn't taking the urgency of the matter any more seriously than RCA, he called on a freelance agent named Steve Yates, and Yates did the job, getting Elvis four appearances (with an option for two more) on CBS' Saturday night *Stage Show* hosted by swing-era legends Jimmy and Tommy Dorsey.

Signing with the William Morris Agency, New York City, January 31, 1956, with William Morris agents Nat Lefkowitz and Harry Kalcheim (seated). *Courtesy of the Graceland Archives*

Kalcheim was livid. But as Colonel made clear to him, his allegiance was first and foremost to his client. "Harry you know as well as I do offering a new artist is one thing but selling One is another," he wrote to his old friend. "I can't go for a pitch that my artist has been submitted and then wait till you hear from some-one that wants him, that way you can write One hundred letters and just sit and wait till some-one comes up with a deal. . . . If I waited for some-one to call me with deals all the time, I would have to start selling candy apples again. Nuff said." Kalcheim made a show of protesting, but he had come to know Tom Parker well enough not to be put off by his bluster. He made sure, too, that William Morris' longtime head, Abe Lastfogel, heard all about Tom Parker's new find, who Harry was now convinced (as much as anything by Parker's inexorable commitment) might very well possess some of the vast artistic and commercial potential that his manager was claiming for him.

The issues with RCA went deeper. Even before the first session, in Nashville at the beginning of January 1956, it was clear that Steve Sholes had no idea how to even address Elvis, let alone suggest suitable songs for him to record. He adopted an avuncular, almost patronizing approach, which Elvis responded to with the kind of smoldering resentment you might expect from a just-twenty-one-year-old artist with deep-seated insecurities, to be sure. But if that was what Sholes was thinking, he was missing the whole point, for Elvis Presley was a young artist with an almost untrammeled belief in himself as well.

Colonel had always liked Sholes, at forty-five his near contemporary. He was just the kind of jovial, easygoing-on-the-outside a&r man that Eddy Arnold and Hank Snow needed — he never got in the way, and both Hank and Eddy appreciated the record-company support that his seniority ensured. Now, with Elvis looking askance at every song suggestion he made ("Shiver and Shake" and "Wham! Bam! Hot Ziggety Zam" were among the more egregious), Colonel assessed the situation and since he had no plans to be at the session himself (he had long ago determined that this did not lie within his sphere of operations), he told Sholes there wasn't much he could do to help. Steve was just going to have to figure it out for himself.

As it turned out, the session was no more successful from an a&r man's point of view (an a&r man, like a Hollywood producer, is supposed to control the situation) than the lead-up to it. The one song to which Elvis was fully committed, Colonel knew, was the song that Mae Axton had given him at the Country Music DeeJay Convention in Nashville in November — she told him it would be his first million-seller, and if he recorded it, she would even give him a third of the songwriter copyright. And then when she played it for him, he liked it so much he said, "Hot dog, Mae, play it again." And promised her right then and there it would be his very first RCA single.

"Heartbreak Hotel" was an odd, unapologetically morbid number, a slow, heavily accented blues that had been inspired by a newspaper story about a man who committed suicide and left a note saying, "I walk a lonely street." Mae had come up with the idea of putting a hotel at the end of that street, a hotel where the bellhop's tears kept flowing and the desk clerk dressed in black. To Sholes it made absolutely no sense. Leaving aside his own musical inclinations, "Heartbreak Hotel" was completely different from the jaunty, buoyant mood of Elvis' five Sun singles, and the gloominess of the lyrics was only amplified by the RCA engineer's clumsy attempt to replicate the richness of the Sun sound by placing a mike and an amp at opposite ends of the long hallway at the front of the building, resulting in a cumbersome echo effect. Still, Elvis put everything he had into it, and whatever Sholes' personal reservations may have been (and they were many), the heavy overlay of echo combined with drummer D. J. Fontana's rim shots created a powerful, emotion-laden atmosphere of upbeat despair.

The only other songs they got that first day were two of Elvis' current r&b favorites, Ray Charles' "I Got a Woman" and the Drifters' "Money Honey," which from Steve Sholes' point of view, however popular they might be in live performance, and however exuberantly the boy performed them in the studio (for he seemed to treat the session itself as if it were a live show, wearing pink pants with a blue stripe up the side and playing to an audience that wasn't there), were hardly the stuff of pop stardom. The next day, to Sholes' relief, Elvis finally got around to two of the mainstream pop ballads that he had suggested, but even these were marred by Sholes' almost inexplicable failure to get the backing quartet, the Jordanaires, who toured with Eddy Arnold, that Elvis had requested. Instead, he assembled a mismatched trio consisting of Jordanaires leader Gordon Stoker and Ben and Brock Speer of the Speer Family gospel quartet, who had recently signed with RCA. And while Elvis never challenged Sholes directly, in conversation with Stoker he made his displeasure plain.

It was, all in all, an unpromising start, made all the more so by the reception that Sholes got when he returned to New York with the tapes. In fact, Sholes said, his superiors were so put off by what they heard that they wanted him to turn right around and go back to Nashville. "They all told me it didn't sound like anything, it didn't sound like his other record[s], and I'd better not release it, better go back and record it again."

Sholes countered that it had taken him two days to get this much, if he went back it would just be throwing good money after bad. Besides, they would have an opportunity for another pair of sessions in New York at the end of the month, in between Elvis' first two television appearances on *Stage Show*. And in any case, they needed to put something out right away.

So, with little conviction, RCA released "Heartbreak Hotel" on January 27 — and, as if to bear out everyone's worst fears, it failed at first to make any real impression. Worse still, Sun Records had put out a single, "Blue Suede Shoes," by a new artist named Carl Perkins, some four weeks earlier, which represented everything that Sholes had been hoping to get out of Elvis Presley (bright, bouncy, *dynamic* rock 'n' roll), and it was taking off like wildfire.

The New York sessions didn't do anything to remedy the situation. Once again Elvis ignored Sholes' song suggestions, rebuffed his advice, and treated the vast, high-ceilinged RCA studio on East 24th Street as little more than a rehearsal space for him to work up a half dozen of his blues and r&b favorites. Sholes did get him to start out with a hopped-up cover of "Blue Suede Shoes," but after thirteen takes, they still hadn't come up with a version to rival the authority of the original, and Sholes could scarcely have been reassured when the boy declared that it was no use doing any more, they couldn't do better than Carl's.

But then, at Presley's urging, they launched into a song with which Sholes was surely familiar because it came from an artist whom he had worked with extensively in RCA Victor's "race" series, blues singer Arthur "Big Boy" Crudup. Crudup had written and recorded the original version of "That's All Right," Presley's Sun debut, and now, out of the blue, Elvis delivered a masterful version of another Crudup song, "My Baby Left Me," in which for the first time the band really coalesced and began to sound like a unit.

This was progress, certainly—but it was little consolation to Steve Sholes. Once again, he complained bitterly to his old friend Tom Parker, he had gotten nothing from the session that sounded like a hit single to him. And once again he got no help from Parker, who was adamant in his refusal to become involved in discussions about the manner or content of Elvis' music in any way. That was his artist's business, Colonel reiterated, and he had full confidence that his artist knew his business.

Meanwhile Sholes' boss, Bill Bullock, alarmed at the turn things were taking, wrote to Colonel on March 7, pointing out all the shortcomings of what he viewed as Colonel's small-market approach to business and, with charts of sales potential and actual sales performance (poor) in more than a dozen major cities, suggested that it was time for a change. Even though it had at this point sold three hundred thousand copies, "Heartbreak Hotel" still had not registered on the national charts, and the way Parker was going about things, Bullock wrote, bore little resemblance to the strategy he thought they had both agreed upon: to create as many sales in the pop market as in the country-and-western. "You must remember," he reminded the young man's manager, "that we too have a big stake in this artist"— and they couldn't simply sit around and wait till summer to try to break him in the "big selling popular record markets."

Colonel's reply was the soul of deflection, as he thanked Bullock for all his good advice ("I agree with you 100%") and ticked off everything he was doing at this very moment, all the dates he had set up (none of which, as it happened, were in the markets that Bullock was talking about), all the obligations he was under, and all the work he was continuing to do for Hank Snow and Eddy Arnold, also, it need hardly be said, RCA recording artists. At the same time, he couldn't emphasize too much, "We have to be very careful the kind of package we build around Elvis," who was, the barely less-than-explicit argument underscored, a unique artist who had to be treated as such — and he couldn't do anything further about personal appearances anyway until Elvis had his screen test at the end of the month. In a P.S. he inquired innocently whether Bullock had ever received the Tennessee country sausage that Colonel had sent him, after Bullock let him know how much he had enjoyed it at another RCA executive's housewarming.

Harry Kalcheim, too, weighed in from time to time with the same sort of well-meant advice, to which Colonel responded with the same sort of shoulder-shrugging indifference. Kalcheim wholeheartedly agreed with Bill Bullock that Parker should be booking Elvis in more "northern spots." He wondered if Tom might be interested in a two-week engagement at the 3,600-seat Paramount Theatre in New York if William Morris could land it. But Colonel stuck to his own single-minded course, barely sniffing at the offer and indicating that he would only be interested if it paid a minimum of $50,000 against a percentage of the gross, and then only if he and Elvis had approval of all the other talent on the bill. Obstinacy or genius? Kalcheim might have wondered, but he might also have wondered if Tom Parker wasn't leaving himself wide open to second-guessing.

RCA put out the first album on March 13, simply entitled *Elvis Presley,* with one of the action shots that Colonel had commissioned in Tampa the previous year, crudely highlighted in shivery block letters of pink ("Elvis" down the side) and green ("Presley" across the bottom). From Steve Sholes' perspective, it was a slapdash affair in which neither he nor anyone else at RCA had any more confidence than they did in the single.

In the end, because of the lack of acceptable new material, he had cobbled together twelve tracks, including five unreleased Sun outtakes to go with the seven masters he had been able to cull from the RCA sessions. ("Heartbreak Hotel" was not included because of the prevailing belief in the record business at that time, to which the Colonel fully subscribed, that you did not cut into the sales of a still-active single by making it available as an album track.)

Just how little commitment there was to the album can be seen in the cursory liner notes, which describe how "Elvis Presley, RCA's new recording artist, has zoomed into big-time entertainment practically overnight" and conclude weakly, "His belting style stands out vividly on records and in personal appearances and accounts for his universal popularity, especially with the teen-age audience."

And yet, and yet — and I feel obliged to append this as a personal note, even though I can't imagine this was in any way part of Colonel's master plan — the album is a genuine masterpiece. (So is the cover photo, which isn't even accompanied by a credit.) If we were to award Steve Sholes a single accolade for all his early work with Elvis Presley — but it is a very high accolade — it would be to have assembled and sequenced an album that, however haphazard its origins, remains an enduring work of art. Even the cover, with its iconic image and its iconic pink-and-green design, became both a prototype and a symbol, with the 1979 Clash album, *London Calling,* clearly emulating it in both color and design, while the photographic image itself has come to stand for the wild, almost (but not quite) anarchic spirit of rock 'n' roll.

Moreover, for all of the pessimism at the record company, the album took off from the start. By mid-April it had sold 150,000 copies and stood at number three on the LP charts. And by this time, too, "Heartbreak Hotel" sales had finally accelerated to the point that on April 21 it was number one on the pop and country charts (and on its way to number three on the r&b charts), where it would remain for most of the next two months.

None of which solved Steve Sholes' immediate problems. If anything, it only added to them. Sholes was still faced with the challenge of recording a second album, which, he told Colonel, was irrevocably locked into a November release date. He begged, he implored his friend Tom to help him out of his dilemma, to propose some way to set things up on a different, and more workable, basis. "I know you have Elvis on a heavy personal appearance program and I certainly can't blame you," he wrote, but he *needed* more material. Then, when the deadline for recordings for the new album had already passed, he begged Colonel once again to intervene. "As you know," he wrote, "after this current release, we will be left with one unreleased side here at the Company." He would do anything, he said, to avoid the problems they had encountered in the past — he was prepared to record Elvis wherever and whenever he liked.

But Colonel was unbudgeable. He was not about to cave to external pressure of any sort, let alone put pressure on his artist to supply the market with more product that it did not need. He told Steve Sholes what he had already told both Bullock and Sholes several times already: If RCA didn't like what he and his artist were doing, if they weren't satisfied with the results they were getting, then clearly Elvis Presley was on the wrong label, and he would be happy to release them from their contract "so you [will] not have to take all this buffing around."

In any case, he and his artist had bigger fish to fry.

E LVIS HAD his screen test for veteran movie producer Hal Wallis (*The Maltese Falcon, Casablanca,* most recently Tennessee Williams' *The Rose Tattoo*) on March 27, 1956, and it was every bit as much of a triumph as Colonel had hoped it would be. Not only were Wallis and his longtime business partner, Joe Hazen, who had an exclusive distribution deal with Paramount Pictures, impressed by Elvis' undeniable box-office appeal, they were impressed with his acting potential as well, while RCA, for all of their nervous nay-saying, were so excited they made special arrangements to show the screen test at their annual convention in June.

What happened next was the kind of thing Tom Parker had spent all his life trying to avoid. He found himself in a position where he had no idea what to do. "I pretended to know a lot about pictures," he reminisced toward the end of his life, "but I didn't have a chance with these guys."

He had been guided through every stage of the process so far by William Morris head Abe Lastfogel, who, thanks to the prodding of Harry Kalcheim, had involved himself to a far greater degree than he ever would have with any other promising new talent. He had come to appreciate Tom Parker, too, who like himself had clearly learned everything he knew

Colonel and Abe Lastfogel. *Courtesy of the Graceland Archives*

by the seat of his pants. (Lastfogel, the child of Yiddish-speaking Russian immigrants, joined William Morris as an office boy at the age of fourteen, in 1912, when he recognized "it was time to quit school and get a job.") Lastfogel went to bat for Parker in getting Hal Wallis to agree to an option clause which would permit Elvis to do one outside picture a year. Throughout the negotiations Wallis was adamant that he wanted an "exclusive," but the agency was able to win him over in the end by employing Colonel's argument that this was a purely theoretical issue in any case. With all of his recording obligations and the lucrative personal-appearance schedule that Colonel Parker had him on, how could Elvis possibly have time for an outside picture?

Otherwise, for all its thirty-nine-page length, the agreement was pretty much cut-and-dried. It was as good as you could get, Lastfogel, a soft-spoken man who knew the business backwards and forwards (he had represented Al Jolson when Jolson signed for *The Jazz Singer,* the first "talkie," in 1927), assured him. They could negotiate for another six months, and they weren't going to do any better than this for an untried, unproven talent like his boy: a straightforward one-picture deal that started out low, at $15,000, but included options for six more pictures, with the price gradually escalating to $100,000 for the last.

The Wallis-Hazen offer was finalized by William Morris lawyer Ann Rosenthal within a week, and, Wallis and Hazen made clear to her (and she made clear to Colonel), they expected it to be signed right away. But, no matter how much Abe Lastfogel reassured him, he still did not feel right about the contract. He said he would have to study it some more.

He went over the agreement again and again with Ann Rosenthal, knocking out a few points, applying the same combination of common sense, intuition, and improvisatory skills that had guided him all his life — but he did not know the language. And he was aware that Ann Rosenthal did not take him altogether seriously *because* he didn't. Abe Lastfogel advised Hazen and Wallis that they needed to channel every-thing through the Colonel, he was "most sensitive" on this point, and he dragged out the signing process as long as he could. But in the end he signed.

I used to think — I have even written at length — that Colonel accepted the terms without blinking, because he was so sure of his own ability to alter those terms by dint of willpower and perseverance once Elvis had proved himself. The results would certainly seem to bear out that thesis. By the end, by the time they made their last picture with Wallis, in 1967, Colonel had managed to get Elvis' salary up to $500,000 plus 20 percent of the profits (a bargain price he would offer no other studio, Colonel hastened to assure Wallis), with no end of fringe benefits for both himself and his artist. But in fact, however logical my explanation might be, I was wrong. In one of the few recorded instances of Colonel looking backward (it was against his philosophy), he never stopped beating himself up for giving in to Abe Lastfogel's argument that *this was how it was done*. In fact he made clear just how dissatisfied with himself he was when he wrote to Lastfogel the following year, after they had become the best and—to the outside world at least, most improbable—of friends, and declared with unexpected animus just how much the decision still rankled.

He appreciated everything Abe had done for him, he wrote. "I can understand that you have a great deal of mileage behind you with the Movie Studios, and I respect your thoughts and suggestions whenever you advise me." But, he said, he couldn't help but "think back to the time, a little over a year ago," when nearly every William Morris agent had told him all the things that he *couldn't* do. He and Ann Rosenthal had managed to correct some of the most egregious terms of the contract, but Abe knew—this was the underlying theme of the whole letter—it was still far from right. And if Abe didn't know that, he did. And just in case there was any doubt, he spelled it out.

> I am not interested in any way, to sign any contract with anyone, when I feel that the clauses are not in line with our [require-ments]. . . . I have learned a great deal from you and I am grateful. I think I have done a good many turns to show my loyalty to your office. . . . However, I must also feel that I am doing the right thing for ELVIS. I would much rather blow a deal than to feel that I have taken the easy way out, just to get a contract. Let nature take its course. . . .
>
> My loyalty is with you, and you know it [but] I will always keep my own freedom in making up my mind when I feel that things are not right for us. I have been brought up the hard way in Show Business. . . . I have been in and out of so many towns, cities and hamlets— playing shows in barns, stockyards, auditoriums, school houses, auction sales, ball parks, home shows, theaters and what have you, that I know what we must do for the customers—and what they will buy.

"PRESLEY is a special set-up and must always be handled as such, or it will not last," he continued with conviction. And until it was proved otherwise, he didn't know anyone better than himself to manage that setup, which required not just legal language but dedication and belief, intimate connection and empathetic understanding. Ultimately, success in any business came down to trusting your own judgment and remaining true to your principles, no matter what all the people around you who were so free with their advice told you. And it seemed abundantly clear, both from his very frankness and his overall tone of loyalty and respect, that he was not including Lastfogel in that company. "I hope this clears up some of the details that I always have in mind," he concluded. "If this letter is too long, read it a little at a time."

IN THE WHIRLWIND

I DON'T THINK I need remind you that this is not a biography of Elvis Presley. It is, rather, intended as an introduction to the life and career of Colonel Thomas A. Parker (né Andreas van Kuijk), and there was no time more busy, or more consequential, in that life and career than the summer and fall of 1956. It was as if the world had been turned upside down by the meteoric success of a single twenty-one-year-old popular recording artist, as triumph built upon triumph and the breadth of Elvis Presley's achievement seems to have exceeded the capacity of anyone but the artist, his manager, and Elvis' original discoverer, Sam Phillips, to imagine.

Everyone knows at least some of the elements of the story. Elvis sold over twelve million records in that one year alone, practically monopolized the 1956 singles charts (with one or another of his songs holding the number-one spot on the pop, country, or r&b charts for something like eighty weeks), reached 82.6 percent of the national audience with his first appearance on *The Ed Sullivan Show* in September, and became an international movie star.

But for Colonel it was simply an invitation to ever greater and more expansive challenges and actions. He continued to meet every sign of doubt with his familiar (and by now almost numbing) litany of cheerleading advice, which boiled down to three words: Stay the course. When restraint was urged, when RCA or William Morris or Hal Wallis or anyone else grew fainthearted in the face of withering denunciations from the press or clergy with respect to his television appearances that spring and summer (the *New York Daily News* deplored "the sight of young (21) Mr. Presley caterwauling his unintelligible lyrics in an inadequate voice, during a display of primitive physical movement difficult to describe in terms suitable to a family newspaper"; the *New York Journal-American* described "an exhibition that was suggestive and vulgar, tinged with the kind of animalism that should be confined to dives and bordellos"; and the Catholic weekly *America* simply advised: "Beware Elvis Presley"), Colonel merely shrugged his shoulders and predicted confidently that this, too, would pass.

And in the end he was always right, because Elvis' very success in the face of all the threats of banning and boycotts made the case for him. Ed Sullivan, by far the biggest force in general-entertainment television both at the time and for the decade to come, was said to have vowed never to have Presley on his Sunday night show because of his threat to public morals. Then on July 1 Steve Allen showcased Elvis (wearing white tie and tails, both for comedic purposes, and to silence the critics) on his new Sunday night show and thrashed Sullivan in the ratings. Just eleven days later Sullivan announced that he had changed his mind and would be booking Elvis at an unprecedented $50,000 for three appearances in the fall and winter. Which was fine with Colonel as far as it went, he was happy to let William Morris handle the negotiations, but, after the experience with Steve Allen, he wasn't going to sign any contract, he told Harry Kalcheim, unless it guaranteed his artist "complete control of presentation as to songs," including "sole selection of musical accompaniment and instrumental and vocal group if any."

So far as recordings went, he stuck to the same intractable mantra: his artist, and his artist alone, would call the shots as to what, when, and where he recorded, he would be the sole arbiter of song selection and its manner of delivery. Despite all of Steve Sholes' pleas, there had been just one session in the aftermath of the sensational success of the first album in March, and that one session had produced just one song. It must, then, have come as something of a relief to his a&r man when Elvis called for a session to take place at RCA's New York studio on July 2, the day after his Steve Allen appearance.

The primary purpose of the session, as Sholes understood it, was to record "Hound Dog," the Latin-flavored Big Mama Thornton blues that Elvis had been performing to an increasingly frenetic reaction in his live

Colonel, Elvis, Ed Sullivan. *Courtesy of the Graceland Archives*

shows for the last three months. It was his performance of the song on *The Milton Berle Show* just three weeks earlier which had ignited the firestorm of moral indignation that had broken out around him. But for all the excitement that the song generated in live performance, Elvis had remained skeptical that he could create the same effect in a recording studio. He saw the song, in his guitarist Scotty Moore's words, as a kind of "novelty" number, always effective for capping off a show, but needing a very different kind of treatment if it were to produce the same impact in the studio.

This is where Colonel entered the picture. He had no more interest in influencing his boy's artistic choices in this matter than any other, but it would appear that he now suggested to Elvis, without insisting on the point, that there was a commercial angle to this, too. He had seen the response that the song got on the show every night — and there was no doubt in his mind that Elvis was drawn to the song simply by the energy and enthusiasm with which he performed it. That was where he left it — it was Elvis' decision entirely, but he was not unhappy when Elvis made up his mind to record the number.

The session itself, as observed by a twenty-six-year-old freelance photographer named Al Wertheimer, who had been hired by RCA on a short-term basis to take some shots of their new artist in March, then rehired to document his appearance on *The Steve Allen Show*, started slowly. Steve Sholes took a largely passive role as the engineer got his mix and the musicians started to get a feel for the song, but seventeen takes went by without coming close to a satisfactory master. The drums, always the driving force in the live show, weren't working right; Scotty, Wertheimer noted, was groping toward his guitar solo; and the Jordanaires, present with Elvis in the studio for the first time after their television appearance with him the previous night, were having difficulty finding their place. Steve Sholes was becoming visibly concerned, and it was getting more and more obvious that he was anxious to move on, but Elvis, who exhibited few points of stillness in any other aspect of his life, maintained absolute concentration. "In his own reserved manner," wrote Wertheimer, "he kept control, he made himself responsible. When somebody else made a mistake, he sang off-key. The offender picked up the cue. He never criticized anyone, never got mad at anybody but himself. He'd just say, 'Okay, fellas, I goofed.'"

With the twenty-sixth take Sholes was satisfied that they had it, but Elvis wanted to keep going. And so they did, until, after the thirty-first take, Sholes announced over the PA, "Okay, Elvis, I think we got it," and Elvis reluctantly agreed to listen to playbacks. "He sat cross-legged on the floor listening intently . . . absorbed and motionless," Wertheimer wrote, until finally "he slowly rose from his crouch and turned to us with a wide grin, and said, 'This is the one.'"

Then, almost as an afterthought, after a late lunch of sandwiches and soda pop, he recorded a new number called "Don't Be Cruel," which would become as much of a benchmark in Elvis' recorded pantheon as "Hound Dog," picking it out from a stack of acetates that Freddy Bienstock, the new song rep from Hill and Range and a Viennese cousin of the Aberbachs, had picked out for the session. Once again he brought to bear the same single-minded focus that he had given to "Hound Dog," though this time he seemed more relaxed, and the song took on a lilting, almost offhand kind of feel, as Jordanaires leader Gordon Stoker duetted with Elvis on the chorus, and drummer D. J. Fontana laid Elvis' leather-covered guitar across his lap and played the back of it with a mallet for an additional snare effect. It was hardly a formulaic approach, and it was clearly one that left the nominal a&r director baffled. When, after twenty-eight takes, they finally got the sound that he was looking for, Elvis pronounced, "That felt good," and, though it was late, called for another playback of an acetate that he had listened to at the beginning of the session. This was a pleading ballad called "Any Way You Want Me" that Steve Sholes had brought in, and he polished it off in just five takes before finally bringing the session to a close at nine o'clock.

Sometime during the afternoon, Colonel dashed off a brief letter to RCA Vice President and General Manager of the Record Division Larry Kanaga, which made little reference to a session he had not attended but offered a tongue-in-cheek prediction of his own. "I think," he wrote, "our recording of 'Hound Dog,' which I manipulated from the start, will be a big seller; it may even be big enough for you to make a special emblem to use a 'Hound Dog' [as the official RCA insignia] instead of the 'Victor Dog.'"

When he met up with Elvis in the restaurant car the next day at the beginning of their twenty-eight-hour train ride to Memphis, Colonel asked how things had gone at the session. Pretty well, Elvis responded. Reaction to *The Steve Allen Show* had been good, by and large, Colonel said, purposefully ignoring the reaction of Elvis fans who were outraged that he had been forced to sing "Hound Dog" to a sad-eyed basset dressed, as if to mimic the singer in his own formal getup, in collar, bow tie, and top hat. "Glad to hear it," Elvis replied.

This appeared to be their routine, reported the photographer, Al Wertheimer, who had decided to hitch a ride to Memphis on his own initiative on an assignment that had turned out to be more momentous than he could ever have anticipated. "The Colonel would start the conversation," Wertheimer later wrote, "and Elvis would end it. 'It's gonna be good to get back home. I'm sure your folks'll be mighty glad to see you,' said the Colonel. 'Yeah, it'll be good to see 'em.'"

"HE'S A VERY amusing guy," Elvis said about his manager to Colonel's old pal, newspaperman Paul Wilder, in Lakeland, Florida, the following month, in an interview for *TV Guide*. "He plans stuff that nobody else would even think of. Oh, I could tell you lots of things, but I don't have the time right now." In another interview, when asked what kind of specific advice Colonel had given him, Elvis responded: "Everything. In other words, he's the one guy that really gave me the big breaks. . . . I don't think I would have ever been very big without him. Because he's a very smart man."

As for Colonel, he felt no need at this point to call further attention to himself—he was content for the most part to let Elvis' success speak for itself. To Wilder, in a brief exchange interrupted by screams from the audience as the show began, he conceded that his experience might have helped advance Elvis' career on a faster track than it would otherwise have taken. But patience, too, was a big contributor. "Making contracts where perhaps someone would offer a certain amount of money and I thought this artist was worth more, and I held out for my price. I've lost some deals, but I've gained some others by waiting." How about promotion? Wilder asked. Well, yes, Colonel conceded, promotion was all very well, but it was the press, radio, the public, the fans, the RCA Victor people—"there is no way to pinpoint how much they [all] contributed." And after he had gone through the whole litany of credits, he added, "And I think we should all be grateful [to] Sun Records in Memphis, Tennessee, that brought his first record out. . . . [But] the credits for this artist go mostly to his parents. They've encouraged him—his father and mother have been very patient. They have a great deal of anxiety when he's on the road. They worry about him." And whether because it was all he had to say on the subject, or the sound of Elvis' stage show was growing louder, that was the end of the interview.

With Harry Kalcheim, he was somewhat less circumspect. "As to your question how Elvis is getting along," he wrote, unable to hide the pride he took in his boy but still obscuring the meaning of his words to anyone who did not know him well, "I think he is putting all he has into what he is doing. . . . Time will tell, if he will gain the strength personally with the experience to buff himself for greater things to come. I will do whatever is in my power to protect him as long as he is willing to listen, for even a poor teacher is a good teacher if the pupil will listen."

For all of his professed modesty, there seems little doubt that he had every reason to believe that Elvis would continue to listen. Colonel remained as determined as ever to maintain a perceptible distance from his artist's personal life, which he was as convinced as ever was the correct managerial course. He had no interest in interfering with the boy's private life, except when he needed to be protected against himself. There was that damned girl from Biloxi who traveled with him, *publicly,* on the same Florida tour where he did the interview for *TV Guide.* Colonel had nothing against her, for propriety's sake she even brought a girlfriend along with her, but she was the kind of girl who couldn't help drawing attention to herself, as "she reportedly stroked [Elvis'] brow between stage shows," the *Miami News* informed its readers. "Furthermore, June Juanico, 18, the Biloxi beauty whom Presley evidently prefers to aspirin, admitted that Elvis is as unsteady in love as he is on the stage." Before the story came out June had met Elvis' manager briefly, and he was polite enough in a distant sort of way, but now, in her recollection, he came storming into the dressing room before the first show. His gaze went first to June, then back to Elvis, and he had the newspaper story in his hand. "Son, we can't have this kind of publicity," he declared, face red, eyes flaring, rapping the newspaper loudly against his palm. "You've got to do something about this."

Elvis did. In the presence of his manager, he told another reporter, "I got about twenty-five girls I date regular. She's just one of the girls."

"They show up sometimes eight at a time," chimed in the Colonel, seemingly restored to good humor, "all claiming they're his 'steadies.' One girl even claimed she was my daughter, and I don't have a daughter."

If he had been a person more inclined to self-scrutiny, it might have occurred to him that on this occasion he had perhaps gone too far, but the boy didn't seem to hold it against him. In any case, it was at just this moment that the offer for an "outside" picture that he and Abe Lastfogel had been angling for all summer finally came through. Within days he and Elvis would be heading for California, and the girl, Colonel was sure, would be forgotten. It wasn't really her fault, he supposed. She just didn't seem to understand how much was at stake. And it was out of character for Elvis to lose his head this way. He wasn't concerned if the boy got up to the usual hijinks that any young fellow might get up to — they were not going to jeopardize his future. The boys around him, generally one or two of his cousins and a big fat boy named Arthur Hooten, didn't seem to have any idea of how to act, but they were good, harmless company for his boy, and he had Marie's brother, Bitsy Mott, who officially worked security, to watch over them anyway. They never thought to intrude on the private conversations that took place behind closed doors between him and his artist, and if they had they wouldn't even have begun to understand.

Nor, Colonel suspected, would anyone else. In a strange way he felt like he had found in Elvis a true confidant. It was as if the two of them understood each other perfectly, they could communicate a mutual sense of exclusion that neither was comfortable revealing to anyone else. And now, with their first movie about to start (the deal had come through just days before shooting was scheduled to begin), they were getting ready to embark upon yet another uncharted adventure in which everyone no doubt would underestimate them both and yet they would emerge triumphant. And he was positive the boy knew it, too.

W ORKING OUT the deal with 20th Century Fox had proved just as daunting in its own way as the initial Wallis negotiations, except in this case the outcome was altogether different, and when they reached a resolution, it came together very fast. New studio head Buddy Adler, taking note of the fact that Elvis had an option clause in his contract with Hal Wallis, and well aware that Wallis had nothing prepared for the foreseeable future, approached Abe Lastfogel with his offer at the beginning of August. They had nothing specially written for Elvis, Adler told Lastfogel, but they could slot him into a Civil War Western called *The Reno Brothers* that was scheduled to start shooting on August 22. They had already signed Richard Egan and Debra Paget, two solid box-office draws, but he could offer Elvis a strong secondary role as Clint Reno, the youngest of the Reno brothers (and, not coincidentally, the love interest of Paget, a renowned screen beauty). This would give the boy a wonderful opportunity to work with real professionals, he said, and they were prepared to pay him $25,000, $10,000 more than Wallis was going to pay for his first Paramount picture.

Lastfogel dutifully conveyed the offer to Tom Parker, but he was not surprised by the manager's response. (And while the language may well be apocryphal, the message definitely is not.) "That's fine for me," the Colonel calmly replied. "What about Elvis?"

Lastfogel got the offer up to $75,000 in fairly short order, but if he expected to be greeted with thanks and praise, he was sorely disappointed. Colonel said he thought he had made his terms clear: $100,000, and not a penny less. Abe Lastfogel would have spluttered if it been in his nature—but he had to admit that he was a little disconcerted. And disbelieving. "You're just going to lose the deal," he told his friend, certain not only that this was true but that it was the argument that would change Parker's mind. But it didn't, not in the least. Parker flung back at him the adamantine bedrock of his philosophy: There was no way anyone could lose a deal they never had. And so Abe Lastfogel was forced to go back to Fox and state the Colonel's nonnegotiable terms, and perhaps to his surprise (though I wonder if Abe Lastfogel was ever surprised) Fox came up with Tom's price on August 13, one week before Elvis would be required to report to the studio. Not only that, the contract included options for two additional pictures, at $150,000 and $200,000, and before they were done talking, Colonel got all his other demands, too: song publishing for any songs used in the picture; his own office on the lot, a very *small* office to be sure, "right next to the donicker," Colonel was sure to point out to visitors, explaining that "donicker" meant "toilet" in carny talk; salary payment for the secretary he was about to hire anyway; a screen credit as "Technical Adviser," and, ultimately, a verbal promise from the Greek shipping magnate Spyros Skouras, who owned the studio, that his artist would receive a $75,000 bonus if the show exceeded $5 million in profits. Which it did. And though the promise was never delivered on, Colonel needled Abe and Skouras mercilessly to drive home the point that while he knew the money itself was not important to either one of the parties ("I'm sure neither of us will go out of business"), he had no doubt that Skouras as an honorable man would want to fulfill his promise.

He quickly found a home on the lot, even if it was only the anteroom to Elvis' modest dressing room—though the dressing room, too, became part of his "office" whenever Elvis was on set. In Buddy Adler he immediately recognized a kindred spirit, however different their backgrounds. Adler, a bright, universally well-liked man from a comfortable, middle-class Jewish background, had great plans for the studio. (Among other things he was in the process of setting up a million-dollar program

On the set of *Love Me Tender,* with Elvis' cousin Gene Smith. *Courtesy of the Graceland Archives*

for training young actors with fabled "Method"-trained acting coach Sandy Meisner, an approach to acting of which every other major studio disapproved.) But what Colonel liked most about him was that here was a man who knew the nuts and bolts of his business and yet could still imagine a world beyond the realm over which he presided.

He was a kidder, too, who invariably responded to Colonel's gags with gags of his own. Every time Adler or one of the studio bigwigs visited his office, he had his new secretary, Trude Forsher, another Viennese-born relative of the Aberbachs, and Elvis' boys stage some kind of tableau for their benefit. "Everyone look busy," was the watchword, as they all grabbed a pen and paper or blew up promotional balloons — or they might pick up an empty Coke bottle and jabber into it as if engaged in a high-level long-distance call, while Trude or Tom Diskin busied themselves with more credible everyday tasks. On the other hand, if Abe Lastfogel stopped in for a visit, everything was on the up-and-up, and Trude acted as hostess, serving everyone what they wanted, as if it were a kind of formal tea party (though generally without any tea). One time, according to writer

Alanna Nash, Colonel had Trude direct Buddy Adler and a Fox associate to Colonel's "West Coast office," which turned out to be the men's room with a sign over the door, where Colonel was sitting on a closed toilet while a fully clothed Arthur Hooten sat on a stool in the shower pretending to take dictation with a steno pad.

All of which, clearly, was taken in the spirit in which it was offered. As Colonel wrote to Adler one time not long after they finished the picture (there is an extensive record of correspondence — this is just a taste): "You are a refreshing personality, but also a very smart and intelligent operator. . . . It is with great satisfaction and pleasure that I can call you my friend, because you are always sincere, even when you are snowing." And he presented Adler with a business proposition on the third page of his not exceptionally prolix letter. "If you ever need a producer to produce a picture that will make people see it five times before they understand it, I am the man," signing off (if merely to indicate that "snowing"—or the fine art of the put-on — could only be regarded as a positive collegial value) as "Head Snower, Colonel Parker," as opposed to his sign-off two weeks earlier, "Colonel Thomas A Parker, Executive Associate Producer."

He was probably even closer to Fox's fabled head of publicity, Harry Brand, who had been instrumental in promoting the careers of everyone from Shirley Temple to Marilyn Monroe and was known throughout the industry as the "Herald of Hyperbole." Colonel and the sixty-one-year-old Brand exchanged extensive gag letters back and forth, but he was by no means above offering this Hollywood legend promotional advice. "I like[d] the old window cards I used to put up when I was with a small circus," he wrote to his new colleague one time, "we had nothing on it except wait for the big show even when there was no other show coming in before us, but some of them waited and we did business." 20th Century Fox could do well to learn from this example, he suggested. "We know that no One ever reaches all the people all of the time, but some of the late comers can be best served all the time by working at it. People that like pictures and shows are all alike, some like One or the other but none will ever come back if they are snowed into something and find out later they could have waited and seen it for free [i.e., on television]. So my slogan is, SELL SOMETHING FOR MONEY ONLY IF NO ONE ELSE CAN GET IT FOR FREE AND YOU NEVER GET ANY COMPLAINTS." To which, like Buddy Adler, Harry Brand would never respond in anything but equally enthusiastic kidding fashion, because they all took each other seriously in that midcentury manner that esteemed wit, and the snappy comeback, as the surest sign of intellectual engagement.

Speaking of needling, he didn't fail to pass along the good news of his Fox contract to Hal Wallis, whom he had taken to refer to with intimates like Harry Kalcheim as a man who "gets hot and cold. Hot, when the press notices are good and cold when they are adverse. You know the old saying about missing the boat, I don't think Mr. Wallis knew when it was sailing." Wallis' partner, Joe Hazen, was practically apoplectic when Colonel informed him, in great detail, of how well the people at Fox were treating him. In one typical memo Hazen told Wallis about a meeting he had had with Colonel and Harry Kalcheim in New York, where Colonel boasted "about all the wonderful deals that had been proposed to Presley," most of which he had turned down. "He recounted that Fox gave him (the Col.) an office with a secretarial staff and a car and chauffeur at his disposal," and suggested that Wallis and Hazen might like to do the same and that perhaps he should be hired as an adviser in connection with their picture, too, "since he knew how to handle Presley." You can sense that Hazen, not in the least a kidder, is barely able to contain his loathing when he concludes, "I let this comment pass."

Even before the Fox contract came through, Colonel concluded a sweeping marketing deal with a thirty-eight-year-old merchandiser named Hank Saperstein. Saperstein was a veteran of highly successful campaigns for television shows like *Super Circus, Ding Dong School, Lassie, The Lone Ranger,* and *The Life and Legend of Wyatt Earp,* but, as *Variety* noted, this would be the first all-out merchandising campaign in memory aimed at teens, not "moppets." He had been introduced to Saperstein through William Morris and rapidly put together a deal for the exclusive right to exploit and commercially promote the Elvis Presley image, which was secured by a $35,000 deposit by Saperstein against 50 percent of whatever profits their enterprise generated. By the time that *The Reno Brothers* started shooting, Saperstein's campaign was in full swing, with something like eighteen licenses and twenty-nine products, many of which (belts, scarves, skirts, jeans, lipstick, lockets, charm bracelets, publications, and Western ties) were laid out on the hood of Saperstein's car in a publicity shot taken on the movie set. By the end of October the program was really getting into gear, with thirty licenses and fifty products to be marketed through Sears, Montgomery Ward, W. T. Grant, and Woolworth, among others, and *Variety* was endorsing Saperstein's prediction of $40 million in retail sales over the next fifteen months. This would come to $18 million wholesale, which at the customary 5 percent licenser's royalty would mean $900,000 for Saperstein and the recently christened Elvis Presley Enterprises to split.

This was the kind of deal that Colonel dearly loved, and he was fully engaged in every aspect of it, sometimes to Saperstein's annoyance but more often with a sense of mutual dedication to their shared task. As *Look* magazine noted in as extensive a feature on Elvis Presley as had yet appeared in a mainstream publication (though it was in reality about the Elvis Presley *phenomenon*), "Hank Saperstein and Tom Parker are a great pair. They are sardonically gay, as [topical comedian and satirical commentator] Fred Allen used to be. The Colonel sometimes drops absentminded ashes from his good cigar onto the folds of his plumpness. Hank is younger, handsomer, taller and he doesn't sag anywhere. Both of them have a reverence for money and work hard for it. But both of them give the impression that if they didn't get any fun out of making money, the hell with it."

Colonel's two recurrent points of difference with his new partner—and they were not, as he saw it, issues of character, but, rather, Saperstein's "sloppy" manner of doing business—had to do, first, with a simple commitment to always keep your word and, in a related matter, paying everyone you did business with the moment they fulfilled their obligation to you—because, after all, they were in business, too. "You should never ask me," Colonel wrote early on, "if this is still my idea. When I promise something I mean to keep it for better or for worse." Dissatisfied with Saperstein's lack of obvious response, Colonel took it upon himself two months later to provide the younger man with a six-page manual of instruction, laying out all the various organizational failures of his way of doing business. "[You] cannot retain all the money that you take in, some must be spent for competent help," he wrote. "I have thought a long time before writing this letter Hank, but I have checked and watched the operation, and there is a definite lack of co-ordination on the whole project [and] even for a boy that failed in math like I did in school [it] does not sound like somebody is looking after your interest very well. . . .

"The most important fact pertaining to this letter is that we trust each other," he concluded with the kind of practiced deflection that he brought to bear in even his most confrontational moments. "You can rest assured that all the mistakes, and remarks I made in this letter can probably be pointed also towards me. Except one. I pay my bills right on the [day they are submitted]. It is a religion with me and gives me a great deal of satisfaction and peace of mind. I am quite disturbed when people that have served well must be aware of the lack in receiving compensation that is rightly due them. Take care of yourself and read this letter like you know I want you to read it. It can only make for a better relationship. Your Pal (Have I got salt?)"

Saperstein seems to have taken the criticism well enough, and they went on to make a lot more money together. Summing up his experience some thirty-five years later, he told Elvis biographer Peter Whitmer that the Colonel certainly talked like a carny, acted like a carny, he even *said* he was a carny—"but he was one hundred percent honest." And he had one unforgettable piece of advice when it came to selling, the same advice he had offered Eddy Arnold when Eddy wanted to change the course of his career. "Don't turn any[one] down. You never know when you might need him." Instead of an outright rejection, he told Saperstein, what you needed to do was to "just price yourself out of the market"—until the market changed, that is, and it was time to do business again.

It is very amusing when you say you hope that finally I am getting some much needed rest when I have to be here everyday from morning till night and then at night stick around to keep the rats away. . . . I should take my [own] advice, close my shop up and take off for two or three months. Then again I wonder rightly so, what a mess you people would be in, trying to tie the ends together when I am not around.

— Colonel to Harry Kalcheim, end of summer, 1956

COLONEL WASN'T BLUFFING, he didn't feel like he could take a minute off, there was just too much to do. That was what he said not just to Harry Kalcheim but to Abe Lastfogel, to whom he was growing more and more close, and who was offering him the same counsel. "Dear

Tom," Abe wrote affectionately at the start of filming on *The Reno Brothers*, "it's very gratifying for me to be associated with you in the representation of Elvis Presley. . . . I always enjoy working with you because you are so wise and constructive. Warmest regards . . ." And while it might well be argued that Lastfogel would most likely have kind words for almost any colleague at the start of a new venture, there is no question that, after the bargaining session they had gone through with Hal Wallis, he saw Tom Parker in a very different light, far removed from the usual run of Hollywood hustlers, with whom, to be fair, he had his own form of knowledgeable rapport. Parker, he confided to Hill and Range cohead Julian Aberbach, possessed an originality of thinking that he had never run into before — Parker was teaching him how to scrutinize and "refine contracts that [William Morris] had with motion picture companies in ways that [Lastfogel] had never imagined."

From Aberbach's own sophisticated point of view, "Tom Parker was one of the most creative men I ever met," even though in other ways Julian viewed Colonel as provincial in the extreme, ignorant of the ways of the cosmopolitan European world that Julian and his brother Jean had grown up in. Most of all, as Julian saw it, the limitations of Tom Parker's vision became most evident when it came to matters of finance, where for the Aberbach brothers tax shelters and tax avoidance practically amounted to a religion. "He told me he had no more than four years of school. And in some ways [that showed in almost every way] he had an inferiority complex. He was very, very careful to pick out people to do business with. He expected total collaboration. But in return he also gave his total commitment. And he stood by his word 100%. Once he promised something, he always kept his promise."

On October 13, just eleven months after Elvis had signed with the label, Colonel presented Elvis with a new RCA deal which completely upended the terms of the previous agreement. The new contract set aside all the onerous obligations to which Colonel had previously agreed, substituting in their place a commitment by RCA to what amounted to close-to-a-million-dollar deal. The way the new contract would work (and this is a vast oversimplification) was that RCA would guarantee non-returnable payments coming to a minimum of $910,000 over the next ten years as best I can figure, including "advances" against royalties (of which $430,000, $80,000 more than the first five years' guarantee, had already been earned), plus nonrecoupable bonuses, with any royalties beyond those already earned to be added on, as due.

It was not much of a gamble on RCA's part (though Colonel still had to convince them that his intricately worked-out formula was to their advantage as well as his artist's), as sales continued unabated. According to *Variety,* in what was generally conceded to be the best year ever for the record industry Elvis' sales were so overwhelming that they were putting a crimp in all other singles sales. They were so great in fact that RCA was forced to utilize outside pressing plants for the first time to press his records, which accounted for two-thirds of the company's entire singles output.

Everyone wanted to know the secret of Elvis' success, and Colonel as usual played along. The secret, he wrote runically to Harry Kalcheim six months after the new contract was signed, "is a very simple one, that very few people can figure out. . . . I think I have somehow stumbled on to a new medium along with a great artist, of course to make it work. . . . The [limited] exposure on TV is of course one answer but, the main answer I will reserve to put into my book some day and I sincerely believe it will surprise many Desk Experts."

Needless to say, the world is still waiting.

H E WAS GRATEFUL to Harry Kalcheim for many things, but perhaps most of all for bringing him and his artist to Abe Lastfogel's attention from the start, when everyone else was ready to simply write them off as a novelty act. Harry was his oldest friend at the company, dating back to Eddy Arnold's first TV and Las Vegas bookings, and he never shrank from unburdening himself to Kalcheim, even if as often as not the manner of his unburdening might come in the form of scathing diatribes, which Kalcheim always seemed willing to take in the spirit in which he knew them to have been offered. Along with Tom Diskin, who remained uniquely able to follow Colonel's every thought while at the same time speaking (well, writing) in a voice that was indistinguishable from his mentor's, Colonel revealed himself to Kalcheim in a way that he would not often risk with others.

He boasted to Kalcheim in an almost touchingly transparent manner of his growing closeness to Harry's boss. In fact, he informed him immediately the first time he was invited to have dinner with Abe and his wife at the Hillcrest Country Club, the Jewish golf and country club that had been started in 1920 as a response to the almost universal policy of "restricted membership" at every other club in town. (This was widely understood to be the basis for Groucho Marx's famous remark, "I wouldn't want to belong to any club that would accept me as a member"— but, perhaps needless to say, he did.) "As usual," Colonel hastened to assure his friend of the dinner conversation, "I promoted Harry Kalcheim." It wasn't long before he would be describing Abe Lastfogel and himself to Harry as thick as thieves: "Whenever I am on the Coast," he wrote, "we now seem like the Two Golddust Twins as we do work so very closely together, and what a pleasure it is working with him even if we do not always agree, that of course makes it good learning for me."

It was the kind of relationship that he had not experienced since his early days with showman-promoter Joe Frank, and before that with Tampa printer Henry Rinaldi, where he gladly surrendered the lead and accepted the older man's mentorship, while at the same time basking in their approval of his quickness and humor.

Whenever Marie was in town, which he sought to ensure more and more often lately ("At least," he wrote to Kalcheim, "I [will] have someone to confide in who won't run out and repeat my stories"), they would get together with their wives at Hillcrest, just a mile or so from the Beverly Wilshire, where for the time being Colonel was in residence. (Lastfogel, a confirmed hotel resident, had a permanent suite there, and made sure that Colonel and Elvis had good accommodations when they arrived for the start of filming at Fox.) Abe's wife, Frances, was a bold, brassy woman, a former vaudeville star as Frances Arms (née Armhaus), who had rivaled her good friend Sophie Tucker and believed she still would if she hadn't given up her career for marriage. She constantly reminded her husband of this, mostly in a genial way, and was generally known, in pretty much the same sort of way, as the "boss" of Abe. "She had a mouth on her," was one common way of putting it, but almost everyone agreed that she was both 100 percent loyal and astute.

It's hard to imagine the two couples as a dinner foursome, and even harder to imagine Frances Lastfogel's interaction with Marie, but perhaps it all came down to their husbands' unfeigned uxoriousness. Tom frequently wrote to Abe of all the ribbons his wife had won at the local flower shows in Madison. ("Hers are the best as far as I am concerned. I told her to put some of Frances perfume on [them] . . . to get a ribbon for outstanding perfumed flowers from her own yard.") He even boasted of all the help he was to her in keeping up her garden when he was at home and she was off visiting family in Tampa. ("I have been watering the flowers all Day for Marie. . . . I told her I could prove it by the water bill next Month that each flower got at least 5 gallons of water every Night.")

As the relationship deepened, the tone of the letters grew fonder and fonder, not infrequently signed with love on all sides, though it must be admitted more often by Abe, for Colonel, as must be clear by now, remained uncomfortable with a simple sign-off. With Abe, though, there were probably more undisguised expressions of emotion than with any other acquaintance — except perhaps one. What each valued most in the other was their unwavering commitment to loyalty, proven in practice again and again, and their deep-seated belief in the values (or perhaps it was just the value) of show business, in which they had both found their true identity. It was as if, for all their differences in background and outlook, they complemented each other in ways the public at large could never have understood. As writer Frank Rose, by no means an uncritical fan of the Colonel, described it in his history of William Morris, *The Agency,* Parker might have the appearance of "a sharpie who told everyone who'd listen he was only in it for the money, but hidden in the pall of cigar smoke was a man who was loyal and square and true." Lastfogel, on the other hand, whom Rose described as a "little square man whom people called 'the Pope'" in recognition of his unimpeachable integrity, also possessed the cunning of "a big-time wheeler-dealer who knew every trick." And each recognized the complexity that lay behind the mask of the other.

The bond between the two would be forever sealed — if indeed it needed sealing — by a tour the Colonel undertook to take over in March of 1957 as a favor to his friend, the one time he ever really strayed from his single-minded devotion to his artist, Elvis Presley, in their twenty-one-year association. The tour was intended to promote the career of Hugh O'Brian, star of *The Life and Legend of Wyatt Earp,* a top-rated television series, by breaking him into the increasingly profitable pop music market. When the William Morris agent who was supposed to

promote the tour had to bow out at the last minute, Colonel unhesitatingly leapt into the breach, even investing $25,000 of his own money, as
he wrote to Harry Kalcheim, solely because of the agency's "kindness
toward our office [and] the many favors and gestures extended to me."
Though he couldn't help adding, as if Harry or the agency might forget,
"There are many things that we do far and beyond the call of loyalty, duty
and service and I sincerely hope that these little extras are not taken for
granted by some people as it's much easier to go fishing than to take [on]
a chore like this."

He was more than proven right.

The tour was a disaster, and while there were many possible explanations or excuses (including O'Brian's lack of observable singing talent)
that could have been advanced, Colonel dismissed them all with a wave
of his hand. There was no scapegoat to blame, Tom Diskin wrote in his
boss's name to all the principals of the tour. What it all came down to
was that while no effort had been spared to let the public know that "the
attraction was to appear in town, they just didn't bother to come to see
it. . . . With Hugh O'Brian's interest in mind it is best for the artist's sake,
that as little comment as possible be made about this tour." This report,
Diskin concluded, "is prompted by the Colonel's wish that all connected
with the tour should have an accurate picture of the time, promotion,
talent and money that went into this tour."

Abe Lastfogel was mortified. He sent Colonel a check for $10,000 to
cover roughly half of his losses. Colonel sent it back with a note. "My
Dear Brother Abe," it read. "It was indeed good of you to mail me the
enclosed check, I know you only did this to show me you and Frances
have money. The only real thing I know by your letter is, that I will never
go Hungry as long as both of you are alive. . . . So put it back where it
came from, I am in show business and we do not take money from any-one
[unless we have earned it]. I am over 21, and should know what I am
doing. . . . This was One hunch [that did not pay off but] I did it, so I also
learned by my losses. I at all time believed in the project and that was
One reason I did not give up, but did everything possible to make it go.
[Signed] Love Your Pal Tom." To which he received a reply the next day,
"To tell you my feelings in words would be superfluous." Or as Colonel
wrote to Harry Kalcheim, "I know where my support lies . . . and that is
more important than money."

And when William Morris gave an intimate, closed-even-to-the-stars-they-represented celebratory gathering for the eighty-fifth anniversary of the agency's founding, and not coincidentally eighty-fifth birthday party for their beloved chairman emeritus, Abe Lastfogel, in June of 1983, of the two hundred or so guests, the only outsider present was seventy-three-year-old Colonel Thomas A. Parker.

B UT THAT WAS in the future. In the meantime, amid a swirl of pre-tended misunderstandings and hurt feelings ("The Colonel is upset about being ignored," Joe Hazen wrote to his partner in October of 1956), Hal Wallis finally reentered the picture. This came about as a direct result of the frenzy of anticipation that had built up around the upcoming release of Elvis' motion-picture debut, *Love Me Tender*, which had been very quickly renamed after Elvis recorded the song four days after his arrival at the Fox studio. When "Love Me Tender," the song, went gold on September 28, the day of its release and eight weeks prior to the movie's opening, Wallis and Hazen were forced to recognize that a rival studio was about to have a smash Elvis hit, despite their own view (which Hazen didn't hesitate to share with Colonel Parker) that it was "a crap picture."

Colonel didn't bother to argue. The commercial success o ʹthe movie spoke for itself. (When it opened nationwide on November 21, it was showcased at 575 theaters and proved a formidable rival to two of Holly-wood's biggest productions, *Giant* and *The Ten Commandments,* for box-office supremacy.) But he was still renegotiating Elvis' contract in a tortuous back-and-forth with Wallis and Hazen, steadfastly supported by Abe Lastfogel in his polite but insistent way, until the day the Wallis movie, *Loving You,* started shooting. In the end Colonel once again got everything he wanted: an office on the studio lot (an improvement on the office he had on the Fox lot — and, just to be clear, according to *Loving You* screenwriter-director Hal Kanter, no other personal manager got similar treatment from any of the studios); explicit recognition by the producers of his own importance to the success of their venture (his credit as "Technical Adviser," the same title he had gotten for *Love Me Tender,* was the least of it); and a bonus of $50,000 in the form of two separately negotiated payments, bringing Elvis' salary up from the contractual figure of $15,000 that Wallis had been so adamant about, to a barely acceptable $65,000. (Both Colonel and Abe Lastfogel insisted to the end that it should have been $100,00 to match Elvis' Fox salary.)

At Colonel's suggestion, Hal Kanter flew to Memphis to meet Elvis and drive to Shreveport with him for his final appearance on the Louisiana Hayride. The drive, Colonel wrote to Hal Wallis, should "help them to get to know each other better." To Kanter, a highly regarded screenwriter who had started out writing comedy skits and gone on to become a well-known television director, it appeared as if this might be his opportunity, at thirty-seven, to break into major-motion-picture directing. A native of Savannah (though he was Jewish, he said, "my feelings are still Southern — I think"), he had been impressed when Wallis showed him Elvis' screen test, and had been tailoring a script to suit Elvis since the summer. In Memphis, though, it seemed as if the two of them were circling each other warily until Elvis expressed admiration for the Sy Devore velvet sport shirt the director was wearing and he took it off and gave it to his star. That was the first time Kanter got a sense of "the sweetness of the man," and he determined to try to work that quality into the script. The next night they set off on the eight- or nine-hour drive to Shreveport, passing through empty towns connected by long, deserted stretches of highway. Elvis was driving, his cousins Gene and Junior Smith (who made up most of his very small cohort at that time) were asleep in the back seat, Kanter recalled, "and we passed a dog, an old dog howling in the night, and Elvis said how much he envied that dog. 'That dog has a life of his own,' he said. 'He goes out at night, and he's doing this, and he's doing that, and nobody knows what he's up to, but he's having more fun — and when the sun comes up he's back under the porch sleeping, and nobody knows what a wonderful life he's living during the night.'"

TEN

Elvis and the Admiral

I have always respected every-one [here at RCA] in their own jobs,
but you know that I dont [just] sit here and smoke cigars hoping
for something to happen.

— *Colonel to RCA Vice President Bill Bullock, 1958*

COLONEL CONTINUED to keep all the wheels spinning — at RCA, with Hal Wallis, with his entrepreneurial partner Hank Saperstein, with everyone and everything in fact in every department and every way that could possibly benefit his artist, with the sole exception of personal appearances, whose number at this point had been drastically reduced, and television, from which he felt they had gotten all the benefit there was to be gained.

For the most part he was confident that everyone at RCA knew their proper role, though he had to remind them from time to time, in the most exuberant of spirits, just who was in charge. With Bill Bullock, who for all intents and purposes had replaced Steve Sholes as their primary contact at RCA, he had taken to referring to the record company as "our firm" and identifying everything he did, and everything he advocated, as being as much for the company as for his client. ("You seem to be unpretentious of my remark of being associated with RCA on a dollar a year basis, for me as an advisor," he wrote to "Lt. Colonel" Bill Bullock with customary deference, "and it intrigues me tremendously. Receiving such a small annuity should give me a tremendous voice in the operation.") He had advice for everyone, including Frank Folsom, the august president

On the set of *Loving You,* January–February 1957. *Courtesy of the Graceland Archives* of the label's parent company the Radio Corporation of America and widely hailed as "one of the nation's leading Roman Catholic laymen"— and for the most part everyone seemed to appreciate it and respond in the same convivial spirit with which it was offered. "Seriously, Tom," RCA Vice President and General Manager Larry Kanaga wrote on the eve of his departure to take over the talent agency GAC, "it is very difficult for me to tell you how much your friendship and help has meant to me." It had, he said, "brightened up many a dull day," and taught him many valuable lessons over the years.

At the same time it would have been virtually impossible for him to refrain from reminding every RCA executive with whom he had business of any sort that their deal for Elvis was worth more than the paper it was written on. As he wrote to Bill Bullock, "I guess I am one of the few Managers that have so many verbal agreements not in writing." And, on another occasion, he reminded Bullock (again) that he really needed to explain "the setup we have on our business" to other RCA executives who might not be as "up to date on . . . the many verbal agreements other than those listed in the contract we now have with the Company," as there were so many details "that we did agree on but could not be injected into the contract at that time."

And why was that? Well, quite simply, the most-favored-nation clause that was embedded in the contracts of so many other RCA artists stipulated that should anyone else signed to the label get more favorable terms — a higher royalty rate, for example — they would, too. Which would obviously cost the company a great deal of money if the real terms of RCA's agreement with Elvis were spelled out in the contract. But Colonel had long since figured out how to get around such unnecessary formalities and secure for his artist terms far in excess of what could be written down on paper. And he was not going to let those commitments, just as strong as anything more conventionally documented, lapse, simply because of a change in personnel. As he wrote to Howard Letts, even higher up in the RCA chain than Bullock, the lack of a written record was "not too important to me as long as I am doing business with you." But he *was* concerned about "what would happen in event you would leave the Company for any reason whatsoever." And he expected some form of irrefutable reassurance.

When it came to marketing, though, there was no room for debate. Here Colonel had certain fixed principles, which revolved around a single immutable rule: if you had a product the public wanted, there was no substitute for market scarcity as an inducement to sales. This was a lesson he had first learned from Joe Frank, and he saw no reason to add any refinements to it now. The same principle applied to movies, television, records, even personal appearances, but most of all to the scheduling of Elvis' record releases. His mantra, repeated early and often, was, "We must be careful not to smother the market," and he took great pride in the way he chose to exploit that market as well. He directed every detail of the marketing campaign, right down to the smallest elements of design, which, far from exploring any fancy new advertising techniques or methodology, relied on the tried-and-true methods he had learned in the carnivals and tent shows: directness, simplicity, repetition. If it had been up to him, he might simply have fallen back on Oscar Davis' old line: "DON'T YOU DARE MISS IT!" All copy and content had to be approved by him, and if it wasn't, then the product might have to be recalled, as Bill Bullock learned to his dismay when he was forced to recall eighty thousand covers of what would turn out to be one of Elvis' all-time bestselling albums, *Elvis' Golden Records,* because, as Colonel reminded him, "We had a complete understanding for us to have approval." And, just for the record, Colonel's complaints were not without merit in this instance.

On the other hand, while there was no question that he believed completely in his own ideas, he was always ready, he told Bullock, to be proved wrong. And if someone else came up with a better idea — which, so far as he could ascertain, had not happened yet — he was more than willing to concede the point. "I have always been happy to bring my ideas to you," he wrote cheerfully in the midst of a discussion about merchandising, "and I also know that some of them stink . . . but One only needs a few good setups from time to time to make it pay and all the bad ideas are soon forgotten. . . ."

"I am now preparing myself for the lambasting I will get from all sides when I goof up, and the time must be near for me to goof as I have been too lucky for too long." But, he concluded philosophically, "I will be in good company as you of course will be with me when we are called upon the red carpet."

Elvis with Bill Bullock (left) and Steve Sholes. *Courtesy of the Graceland Archives*

There was one point, however, on which he was unwilling to budge. This was, quite simply, that it was his artist, and his artist alone — not the Colonel, not the company, not the a&r department, not the critics or the naysayers — who was in charge of the music. And it was his artist's judgment in every respect that was going to prevail, whether it had to do with the sound of the records, the feel of the records, where and when he chose to record, even the order in which the songs that he chose for release should be put out. When in the middle of the summer of 1957 Sholes and Bullock were trying to pressure Colonel to get Elvis to select the songs that he would record at his next session for the Christmas album that Colonel himself had instigated and for which he had devised the most elaborate packaging and promotion campaign, he simply told them, "I spoke to Elvis and it is impossible to pick those tunes till we start recording. . . . He may at the last minute find another tune that he would like better, if this is too late there is nothing else we can do but forget about it. I cant create something that is impossible to work out. I do not blame Elvis for not putting himself on record that he is going to record a certain number and later feels it does not work out."

As he wrote to Steve Sholes on another occasion, "Elvis is completely aware of what is going on and this situation has been brought to his attention." But then, maybe to emphasize his point, more likely just to get Sholes' goat, he couldn't resist adding dryly, "I have never interfered with the selection of songs or records, but only handle the business end which keeps me pretty busy."

Busier and busier, in fact. Record sales continued at the same unprecedented pace—new gimmicks and new sources of income were constantly opening up, and Colonel dismissed any suggestion that Elvis was "slipping" (there had even been talk at RCA that their newest star, Harry Belafonte, one of Mrs. Parker's favorites, might soon rival Elvis in sales) with a casual flick of his cigar. There was plenty of room in the business for everyone, he said. "We all know that every artist must level off at some phase of the business. Fortunately, I have enough foresight to prepare myself for such an event and still be happy. . . .

"Remember my slogan—'One must come down to be able to get on top again'. There is no place as far as I am concerned about being on the top, except a snow man on top of the Himalaya Mountains, and I don't think they are making records up there. If they did, they would melt anyway in the heated conversations that are held at the buck passing meetings."

ELVIS'S SECOND MOTION PICTURE, and the first in which he played the lead role, *Loving You*, turned out to be a big box-office success, and Hal Wallis felt vindicated—at least up to a point. Of course, it would have been a bigger hit, Wallis and his partner, Joe Hazen, couldn't help but remind Colonel, if he and Elvis hadn't gone ahead and made that dreadful Fox picture first. To which Colonel countered relatively mildly that he and Elvis were well aware that *Love Me Tender* wasn't going to win any Academy Awards, and that everyone agreed that *Loving You* was a much better picture, but more to the point, he wanted to be sure Wallis was aware that he and Mrs. Parker had spent the week of the movie's New York opening working the lobby of the Brooklyn Paramount with folios and photos to help raise money for hurricane relief.

For all the goodwill and bonhomie that he was willing to put in evidence, however, it would be impossible to overestimate how angry Colonel still felt about the deal he had signed almost at gunpoint (though, to be fair, he blamed no one but himself). "I now know more than ever that I should have held out for my First deal with Wallis," he wrote to Abe Lastfogel in July, as if Lastfogel needed reminding. "There is of course no way possible for us to come out under this setup other than blow a lot of money."

Two months later, he underscored his point by suggesting that he could hardly be expected to come out to the West Coast and set up his office there on a semipermanent basis with the money that Wallis was offering. This time, he emphasized to Lastfogel, he was expecting much better representation from Morris than he had gotten on the original deal. "I am not complaining," he said, "but only want to go on record in plenty of time."

He did at least concede to his friend that the agency had done a good job on the picture they had just concluded for MGM, the one "outside" picture for 1957 that they were promised in their contract with Wallis. He had bypassed Fox, with whom he continued to have the most cordial of relationships, but their very respectable offer of $150,000 was far eclipsed by MGM's guarantee of $250,000 plus an almost unheard-of 50 percent of the net profits over $500,000. *Jailhouse Rock* (for which Colonel proposed as alternate titles either *Don't Push Me Too Far* or *Trouble Is My Name*) also provided Elvis with the kind of rugged rebel role that both he and Colonel had been seeking, and of course provided him with endless opportunities to remind Hal Wallis that not everybody was a piker. Which paid off to some degree at least, Colonel might have admitted, though only under duress, because Wallis eventually raised Elvis' pay for the next Paramount picture, now scheduled to start just after the new year, to $100,000, four times what he was contractually guaranteed, but still, Colonel felt, hardly sufficient for a star of his magnitude.

What was beginning to concern him more and more, though, was his growing suspicion that, however well his artist was being compensated financially, the motion picture industry as a whole was not taking Elvis' artistic aspirations seriously. From the beginning their aim — *his* aim and

Elvis, Tennessee Williams, Colonel, Laurence Harvey, and Hal Wallis, on the set of *G. I. Blues,* 1960. "He was the most gallant of men," Tennessee said of Elvis. Williams did everything he could to get Elvis to play the part of Val Xavier, the character inspired by Elvis in his play *Orpheus Descending* (later the film *The Fugitive Kind*), but even he recognized that it was an unrealistic expectation. *Courtesy of the Graceland Archives*

Elvis'—had been to see him take his place with James Dean and Marlon Brando in the forefront of genuinely revolutionary contemporary actors. ("This boy Elvis Presley has the same type of personality and talents along the line of James Dean," he had written to Harry Kalcheim in November 1955, before Harry even knew who Elvis Presley was.) As he wrote to Abe Lastfogel in the summer of 1957, in the first of several letters on the subject, "Regarding the story Wallis has in mind [this was the upcoming Paramount picture, for which they were still negotiating a contract, which would turn out to be *King Creole*] I believe we must have some idea what it is and if Elvis will feel at all like doing the type of picture Wallis is planning, I know he is not at all interested in doing a repeat of the type of pictures we have just made all 3 of them are somehow of the same order with the Second picture somewhat better and the Third a pretty good acting part in this type story. [But] I cant understand the thinking of any studio to want to keep on this same idea."

Or, as he wrote to Elvis in August, presenting him with an astronomical new offer that MGM had just put on the table: "The money is not as important right now to make a picture if the story is not right for you. . . . I agree with you that I would like to keep the next picture down to a real story and perhaps no singing other than the title song where they do not see you sing at all but acting only." If Elvis didn't like the role, as Colonel suspected he would not, "I would much rather break off trying to get a deal on this story with Metro now — and have them look for something better to your liking."

Which would appear to have been the last word on the subject, although it turned out to be a moot point anyway, when Hal Wallis blocked them from making a second outside picture that year, and the following year Elvis was drafted.

THERE WAS no question in Tom Parker's mind that they were going in the right direction — and that they were doing it together. He spent a great deal of time and effort on his communications with Elvis, trying to find the right tone to convey what needed to be said, sometimes serious, other times jocular, alternately caring and breezy, but always with the purpose of underscoring that the two of them were in this together, by themselves, and that whatever he did was intended to serve one goal, and one goal only, Elvis' best interests. Perhaps the most revealing of any of the letters he wrote to Elvis is one he wrote in April of 1957, which touched on many subjects but whose naked essence can be summed up as follows. (See the Letters section for more of this very long letter.)

> You can let me have your ideas on this anyway you see it, but remember that the strength you have lies in how we handle the proper business setup along with your talents. Your talent is your own, you are tops in this and there has never been a time except when I knew

you were in trouble that I stuck my nose in this, and only then when you asked me what I thought. I know you can barrel any of this better yourself; at the same time I also think I am as good as you are with your talents in smoking out the best for us. This I appreciate you knowing and having the confidence in me on this, as I can also see your strength in buffing people off towards me when they try to get you involved in making a business deal. I also buff them off when they try to sell me on a song as I tell them Elvis picks his own songs; if he likes them or a certain song then he tells me and I'll get him the best deal I can. . . . I know that you have a certain quality in you the same as I have that can feel our way thru most any snow job except if we lend a foolish ear. . . .

I know that you understand me better than any-one for you have a very carefull Eye. I am a great deal like you — very sensitive — but only people I love can hurt me.

And perhaps in a canny attempt to underscore all that they had in common, perhaps simply out of the affectionate regard he had come to feel for both of Elvis' parents (more likely from a combination of the two), he brought Gladys Presley, the person who occupied a singular place in Elvis' heart, directly into the picture. "When we all think back," he wrote, explicitly including the entire family, "we can count on One hand the real friends we all have and those that are still with us even if things look gloomy and rough. Advise is free even when its bad or good, but to get advise from people that have nothing to show for themselves for knowing so much is always something to be carefull about tak[ing]. Remember my slogan how much does it cost if its Free. . . . Your mother was very wise when she told me that she judged people by what they did and were doing, not what they had done that was wrong."

And, after three pages more of very specific practical advice, it was signed, as always, "Your Pal, Admiral Snow to you," just another twist on a joke that for Colonel alone had endless permutations but for communications between himself and his artist — who, like his mother, was well aware of all the phonies that surrounded them — had its own special meaning in the secret language that they shared.

PERHAPS BECAUSE the boy was so much younger, perhaps because he himself was so much more experienced now, he felt comfortable bringing up subjects for discussion with Elvis that he never would have raised with Eddy Arnold. He would never have tried to talk politics with Eddy, for example — Eddy had very decided ideas of his own. But with Elvis he was not above steering the boy in directions he believed Elvis would have wanted to go, if he simply had more information on the matter. He actively encouraged Elvis to endorse Adlai Stevenson in his own way in the 1956 presidential campaign ("I don't dig the intellectual bit, but I'm telling you, man, he knows the most") because Stevenson's nomination would give his friend, Tennessee's progressive governor Frank Clement, a chance at the vice presidential slot.

Similarly, when the world reacted with outrage to the Soviet Union's invasion of Hungary that fall, Colonel, in an unprecedented gesture of untempered idealism, urged Elvis to take part in a benefit concert for Hungarian relief ("I sincerely believe this to be a very good effort for us . . . to do all we can to help"), and when that appeared to have at least temporarily stalled, made sure that the subject was brought up in Elvis' third and final appearance on *The Ed Sullivan Show* in January. Sullivan, who had himself been a major advocate for the movement, introduced Elvis as "feeling so keenly about Hungarian relief" that he urged everyone watching to contribute whatever they could and wanted his fans to know that he had chosen the song he was about to sing, Black gospel pioneer Thomas A. Dorsey's classic composition "Peace in the Valley," in support of the Hungarian cause.

But perhaps his most outspoken political action was one in which his hand was not even seen. An unfounded rumor had sprung up in the Black community in the spring and summer of 1957 that Elvis Presley was a racist, that he had said — in Boston, where he had never performed, on a national TV program on which he had not appeared — "The only thing Negroes can do for me is buy my records and shine my shoes." Nothing could have been further from the truth, but as Colonel well knew, countering a rumor like that was a practically impossible task. So when *Jet* magazine, a pocket-sized publication that billed itself as "The Weekly Negro News Magazine," requested an interview with Elvis — at a time when Colonel was blocking all interviews with *anyone* — he gave his okay for *Jet*'s star reporter, Louie Robinson, to come on the set of *Jailhouse Rock* and give Elvis a chance to speak for himself.

Elvis seized the opportunity, as Colonel knew he would, speaking freely with Robinson and declaring, "I never said anything like that, and people who know me know I wouldn't have." He cited his attendance at Black churches like East Trigg in Memphis, presided over by the trailblazing Memphis preacher, gospel composer, and civil rights leader, William Herbert Brewster, and called attention to all the influences he had absorbed from Black music, both sacred and secular. He could never hope to surpass the achievements of great artists like Fats Domino or the Ink Spots' Bill Kenny, he told Robinson, who interviewed a number of Elvis' Black friends and acquaintances, going all the way back to Tupelo, and concluded his story with a quote from an unnamed "business associate" of Elvis, which the writer clearly endorsed. "It's a stupid rumor. To Elvis people are people, regardless of race, color, or creed. . . . He doesn't even think along those lines. It's not in his nature."

Which, whether it put the rumor to rest or not (and, as Colonel would have been the first to point out, you were as likely to put a stop to a rumor as you would be able "to chase a gopher into a mousetrap"), certainly satisfied Colonel's sense of fairness and racial equality, something he had felt strongly about ever since being rescued by a Black family, probably the first African Americans with whom he had ever personally interacted, on his first visit to America in 1926, when he knew so little of the world and yet hoped for so much.

At times he worried about the boy. He would scarcely be human if he didn't. Mostly he worried not so much about his being led astray as being taken advantage of by the boys around him. They should be more grateful, he felt, in keeping with his oft-repeated motto, "How much does it cost if it's free," though how could they be more grateful if more was not expected of them? "May I suggest," he wrote to Elvis in the same lengthy letter that contained his own surprising outpouring of emotion, "that you assign or I will for you each One of them some part of service to help you and to look after things to make things easy for you, and put them at least for the time being on the payrole for some small fee so you can deduct all those expenses rather than perhaps being called on it later [by the IRS] as being none deductible." And then, as if to show Elvis that this was more than a simple matter of self-interest, he laid out a lesson that he hoped the boy might take to heart, one of the hard-earned truths that he had himself learned from personal experience. "All those boys . . . must know by now that it is your kindness and friendship that make these things possible for them to be with you. They would have to work if they had a job and would not have half the fun or eat as well and sleep as nicely at the same time. The responsibility is not yours for them to be looked after but theirs to make things more pleasant for you so they can at least feel they mean something other than going along for a free ride."

But if he had some limited success in this area, he had no success whatsoever when it came to Elvis' personal finances. At first Colonel made a point of explaining all the details of all the deals he made, but it quickly became apparent that Elvis wasn't interested, and soon Colonel involved Elvis' father, Vernon, who was plainly concerned about what he considered to be his son's reckless spending. Colonel wrote Elvis and Vernon any number of letters about making provision for the future, about setting money aside for the enormous tax bill that would soon come due, even about taking out liability insurance for the pool that had just been installed at their new home, Graceland. With the exception of the pool insurance, it all appeared to fall on deaf ears.

Colonel opened a bank account for Elvis at his own bank in Madison with a personal deposit of $1,200 and a letter from the assistant bank manager congratulating the young man on the "fine success you are making in your own field, also as having Mr. Parker as your manager and agent." He had known Mr. Parker a good many years, Mr. A. H. Vaughan assured his new client, and he couldn't be in better hands. Elvis soon emptied the account.

Sometime later, Colonel encouraged Elvis to buy government bonds, and at one point even enlisted RCA in setting aside royalties for that purpose, but once again the effort was doomed to failure, because the moment Elvis felt a financial urge, he raided the account.

In November of 1956, he had Tom Diskin write Vernon a letter detailing all the money Elvis had made in that first year, complete with meticulous charts and a record of all sources of income and disbursements. Of the first $300,000, Diskin wrote, Elvis would retain only $64,000 (a tax rate of approximately 80 percent), and on all subsequent income the tax rate rose to 91 percent, as it did for all unincorporated high-income earners (like baseball player Ted Williams, for example) in 1956 America. He further advised Vernon, "For Elvis's sake and for your own do not get out on the limb by over-spending. We can't impress too strongly upon you that Elvis, you and Mrs. Presley read this paragraph over a few times so as to be fully aware of the large amount of money that must be set aside for your income taxes. And remember, it is almost impossible to become a millionaire. The Colonel has advised you about this all along and wants you to understand this fully so that you won't have any problems when Uncle Sam asks for his share."

He did everything he could to explain things to Vernon and Gladys and draw them into a confidential inner circle that included no one but himself and their son. He even inducted them into his self-proclaimed and self-administered high-end celebrity-packed Snowmen's League of America (for further enlightenment see the next chapter), assuring them that as "one of the few female members of this club wich include Snow-ess Marie Parker and Martha Raye, she [would have] nothing to worry about. . . . Snow-ess Gladys will be able to outsnow either one of these members." The Presleys should just "be sure and display this letter to Potentate Snower Elvis so he can approve your membership at once. [Signed] High Potentate Snower." And then, on the next line, he added jauntily, "Admiral Colonel Private Parker," no differently than if he were writing to close personal friends.

He set Elvis up with an accountant who had already extricated him from the tax situation that Bob Neal had left him with and made sure that he had a Memphis lawyer he could trust. More than that, though, he couldn't do, because, however much he tried to break down social barriers and proffer sound financial advice, Elvis and his father thanked him politely but made it very clear that, so far as their personal finances were concerned, they were determined to go their own way, and after the first year, he made few serious attempts to intervene.

There were those in the business who, either knowing their own proclivities or the temptations to which other colleagues of theirs had fallen prey, could be excused for thinking that Colonel was dipping his hand uninvited into some of his artist's hard-earned cash. But the Elvis business, as Colonel explained to his old friend Sammy Weisbord at William Morris (and as the Aberbachs and all the prim-and-proper account executives at RCA well understood), was really very simple, with a double-entry bookkeeping system set up at his Madison, Tennessee, office to make sure that every source of income was precisely registered and recorded.

"My Artist," he wrote to Weisbord, "does not ever get involved in the business end, somehow Elvis seems to want it this way and so far it has worked out pretty good. . . .

> I smoke things out screen out the phoney deals and free setups and only present details to him that are cut and dry as to understanding how much and what do I have to do. . . . I don't handle his money investments or his personal expenses, these are handled by his Father Lawyer and Accountant in Memphis, it is much better this way. When he gets his checks [which, as Colonel explained, were made out directly to Elvis by RCA, Hill and Range, the movie studios, any of the entities with which they did business, with Colonel's own 25 percent commission already removed], he can do whatever he feels he wants to do with it on the advise of the people that he has to handle this, not me.

> I handle my own, I pay all my own expenses run my own office, handle all our own transportation office expenses out of my earnings and this way we have no transaction as to how much I paid out for advertising and other expenses as my artist is not involved in this and does not share in it in any way. Its the cleanest setup I know of any artist Manager re-lationship.

A T THE end of October Elvis embarked upon what would be only his fourth personal-appearance tour of the year. Like the others, it would be brief (in this case a whirlwind four days), and like the others it was to be promoted by Lee Gordon, a recent protégé of Colonel's from Detroit who had brought rock 'n' roll to Australia with such luminaries as Bill Haley, Big Joe Turner, Little Richard, and Gene Vincent, and was determined against all odds to get Elvis there, too. Gordon, who sometimes claimed to have been stationed in Australia during World War II, and had made a second professional home there for the last four years, was a man after Colonel's own heart, an entrepreneur of imagination and daring, who was always prepared to take a chance and put everything he had on the line. (Just a few months earlier, Colonel had refunded $10,000 of his own money to Gordon for the disastrous Hugh O'Brian tour,

Promoting the show: Al Dvorin, Colonel, Lee Gordon, and Tom Diskin, in Hawaii, first week of November, 1957. *Courtesy of the Graceland Archives*

because, as he wrote to Abe Lastfogel, "I felt he only went in on my say-so [and] I was wrong.")

Tom Diskin's old friend from Chicago, Al Dvorin, had produced each of Elvis' 1957 tours, including merchandise sales and, in his full-time job of talent broker, supplying all the acts. Dvorin, who had appreciated Colonel from the first for his integrity as much as his sense of humor, was almost as tickled by Gordon's audacity, though, as he put it, "I didn't have the highest regard for his ethics." Colonel had his own doubts about Lee, though they had more to do with the man's judgment than his honesty. As he wrote to Gordon's business partner in Detroit, Art Schurgin, who had remarked with some amusement that Colonel might have Lee just where he wanted after his "extremely generous" financial gesture: "Perhaps [now] he will listen more to my advise and not get snowed so easy by phoneys, or well wishers that have nothing to show for knowing so much." Which, as it turned out, was a little overoptimistic, but long after he realized he would never succeed as Lee's teacher, he remained the staunchest of friends, providing moral and financial support when Gordon's life fell apart and he was hospitalized for increasingly severe episodes of depression and schizophrenia. In the end, when Lee died in London under mysterious circumstances at the age of forty, it was Colonel who provided the funds for his wife to return to Australia.

Gordon in any case was at this point still talking about an Australian tour for Elvis when they began their four-day, three-city tour in Oakland on October 27, 1957. Colonel, who had already investigated how long it would take to sail to Australia (Elvis was still honoring his promise to his mother not to fly) and concluded that it was an impossibility given their present schedule, indulged Gordon by suggesting, why didn't they just roll the dice for a quick add-on date in Hawaii, as a kind of geographical compromise? Gordon won — or so the two of them said — and to the chagrin of Al Dvorin, who had promised his wife he would be home by November 1 ("It almost cost me my marriage," he later reflected ruefully), Colonel announced that they would indeed be extending the tour. He and Tom Diskin and Al Dvorin and Lee Gordon would be leaving for Hawaii immediately following Elvis' final show at the Pan Pacific Auditorium in Los Angeles on October 29 to do the advance work necessary for a concert now scheduled to take place in less than two weeks.

Five days later the *Honolulu Sunday Advertiser* ran a concert poster ad announcing "!!! IN PERSON !!! ELVIS PRESLEY NEXT SUNDAY 2 SHOWS 3:00 P.M. and 8:15 P.M.," with tickets scheduled to go on sale the following morning at Honolulu Stadium. Two days after that, Elvis, along with half a dozen of his friends and relatives, boarded a ship scheduled to arrive in Honolulu the day before the concert.

Colonel meanwhile was hard at work pitching the show. What had given him the idea, he told featured *Honolulu Star-Bulletin* columnist Cobey Black, were the twenty-one thousand Christmas cards (out of a four hundred thousand national total) Elvis had received from the Islands the previous year. This was enough to convince him, he said, with I'm sure an observable twinkle in his eye, that Hawaii had more than enough fans to support not just one, but two, shows on short notice. Cobey Black in any case was utterly charmed, as she does not seem to have been by

Elizabeth Taylor's new husband, hard-charging Hollywood producer Mike Todd, the previous week. Heading her story "He's a Promoter and a Gentleman," she clearly caught Colonel in a carefree mood, "a soft-spoken, molasses-moving Southern gentleman," as she described him, perhaps with tongue a little bit in cheek, who regaled her with "home-spun candor after a week [of] Todd's pressure cooker." He appears to have been just as taken with her, not even bothering to allude to his story about rolling the dice with Lee Gordon, though, in recounting the tale to another *Star-Bulletin* reporter, he suggested that at this point, for all he knew, they might even decide to go on to Australia. In response to a question as to whether he would continue as Elvis' manager for the entirety of his artist's career, he assured Black that even though he was nearing fifty, he planned to be in the business a long time. "For my next promotion," he offered, "I'm going to try to get that little dog in Sputnik II [the second Russian spacecraft, which had launched just a few days earlier, with a dog named Laika as its sole passenger]. Seriously, honey, he'd be great on a personal appearance tour. And I could get a good deal on dog food."

But for all his "homespun candor," he didn't tell her, or anyone else, his real reason for taking that bet.

THE FIRST CALL Colonel made upon his arrival in Hawaii was to the old number he had for the Kufferath family, who had been so good to him when he was stationed at Fort Shafter over twenty-five years earlier. It came as something of a shock to learn that Papa Kufferath, whom he had originally met walking a Russian Wolfhound in the park not far from the hotel where he was now staying, had died many years ago, and he made plans to place a lei on his grave at Diamond Head Cemetery the next day. But first he accepted the family's immediate invitation to dinner. He then asked if Grandma Kufferath could be put on the phone, and although she was native Japanese and spoke very little English, she was thrilled to be speaking with "Tom," who had left so many years ago, and promised to make him his favorite Japanese noodle dish for dinner.

He spent much of the next few days before Elvis' arrival on the tenth with the Kufferaths, who peppered him with questions about all the

Placing a lei on Papa Kufferath's grave, first week of November, 1957. *Courtesy of Gayle Kufferath Behnke*

things that had happened to their dear friend Tom since his departure from the Islands twenty-six years ago. One can only imagine he answered their questions lovingly, but sparingly, as they confessed that when they listened to all the news reports on the radio about Elvis' imminent appearance, they had never dreamt it could have anything to do with the return of their old friend.

For his part, he was delighted to see that Arnold, the Kufferath he was closest to, just sixteen when they last met, was married and moving up in the Honolulu Fire Department, while his wife, Anna, worked full time as a dental assistant and their thirteen-year-old daughter, Gayle, was a passionate Elvis fan. Sonny Cordes, six years older than Colonel, was still selling cars and just as dashing as ever, while his wife, Luise, Arnold's older sister, welcomed him, too, with open arms. Grandma just fussed over him like he had never been away, she let him know, by word and gesture, how delighted she was to see him again — he hadn't changed a bit except, she indicated, by pointing to his stomach approvingly, she was happy to see he was no longer the undernourished young man she had tried so hard to fatten up.

They had wonderful get-togethers at Arnold and Anna's house, and at Arnold's wealthy brother Carl's, too, where Colonel lay out by the pool with a reflector and baked in the sun all day. At one time or another the

With old friends Sonny Cordes (left) and Arnold Kufferath, and Arnold's daughter, Gayle, in front; first week of November, 1957. *Courtesy of Gayle Kufferath Behnke*

whole extended family was present, more than a dozen of them, uncles and aunts and cousins and children and wives, and Gayle's mother, Anna, prepared fresh-caught mahi-mahi specially for their visitor. They were just as he remembered them, good, kind, down-to-earth people, and he and the Kufferath family all made vows never to allow themselves to be separated again. And in fact they weren't. Every time Colonel returned to Hawaii with Elvis for films and concerts over the next sixteen years, Arnold took time off from the fire department to serve as his chief local lieutenant and make sure that everything was arranged just as he wanted, and even after Elvis died they remained in touch until Colonel's own death.

The whole family went to the show at Honolulu Stadium at Tom's invitation and had the best seats in the house. Grandma alone, whose love for Elvis' music was exceeded only by her granddaughter Gayle's, failed to attend, but at eighty-five her absence from the screaming crowd, where her granddaughter's screams would be among the loudest, was understandable.

The shows were a great success, confirming the Colonel's frequent and loudly stated faith in the Islands. The afternoon and evening shows at the Stadium drew nearly fifteen thousand people and took in $32,000. Colonel even added a third performance the next day at Schofield Barracks where he and Papa Kufferath had attended the dog show featuring the wolfhound that Papa Kufferath had donated to the "Wolfhound" Infantry Regiment as a mascot. The concert was intended primarily for military personnel and their families and was advertised only by notices on the local posts. But it still drew ten thousand people and its success was heralded in the barracks newspaper, the *Hawaii Lightning News,* which proclaimed: "You gotta give it to him—he's a great showman! . . . The hottest thing to hit this post since the Honest John [a mobile rocket system first deployed in 1954], Elvis led his audience, majority teen-age girls, into a state of mass hysteria."

It is doubtful that Tom Parker could have been happier. The Kufferath family photographs show a man utterly at peace with himself, a man seemingly living the life he had been meant to live all along, as he puffs happily on his cigar while wearing a white shirt, a Western tie, and a contented smile. There is not a hint of a shadow hanging over him.

ELEVEN

Colonel at Play

It is of course these funny letters and my feeling that One must enjoy his work or grow stale keeps me on the go, I can always bring myself right back into a happy medium by remembering how lucky we are, so let it snow let it snow I will always be somewhere to receive it . . . I Can always go back to catching Dogs for a living in event I am kicked out of the Club.

— *Tom Parker to Paul Wilder, September 1957*

COLONEL WAS NEVER kicked out of the club, of course — he started it. But more about that later.

And in a certain sense he was always at play. He was always at work, too — there was no real distinction between the two, as you will undoubtedly have gathered by now. It would in fact be impossible to imagine a more unrelenting work schedule than the Colonel maintained, not simply in terms of the number of hours he devoted to his client, whether in action or in contemplation (generally speaking, both simultaneously) but also in terms of the number of hats he wore and the agility with which he changed them.

But, and I hesitate to even broach the subject, it seemed almost as if, with his artist so firmly established, record sales soaring to ever-greater heights, and the three movies released by the end of 1957 among the most profitable box-office hits of 1956–1957 (while earning his artist a total of $415,000 before profit participation) — it seemed almost as if Colonel was bored.

Okay, I'm not going to try to defend that statement. I can hear Colonel's voice ringing in my ears: he was *never* bored. How could anyone *ever* be bored when there were so many exciting new challenges to be dealt with every day? But, nonetheless. . . .

Colonel had another avenue of creative expression in mind.

The first mention appears to have showed up in a *Look* magazine feature on November 13, 1956, entitled "The Great Elvis Presley Industry." This was the story that focused for the first time on the Elvis Presley phenomenon rather than the controversy surrounding him. But it focused equally astutely on the man behind the phenomenon. As its author, Chester Morrison, noted with reference to Colonel's carnival background, "Colonel Parker is happy, but he is certainly not unsophisticated, and he has seen the Tattooed Lady. He genuinely loves those people who come to the carnival, because every last one of them buys a ticket." And when Morrison was enterprising enough to pursue the subject further, he learned from Colonel, in what would qualify as a genuine exclusive, that Elvis' manager was "writing an autobiography that should find a place in every home. He calls it *The Benevolent Con Man,* but his alternate and better title is *How Much Does It Cost If It's Free?*"

I don't know if the idea had occurred to Colonel before (maybe his literary aspirations dated back to his early, dreaming days in Holland), but it was definitely reinforced when he got a letter almost before the story hit the newsstands from *True: The Man's Magazine,* addressed to him care of *Look,* inquiring if he had any plans for his work in progress. If he was as good a con man as he said he was, Associate Editor Don McKinney wrote by way of introducing himself, perhaps he could "con us into writing a story on you and your multifarious exploits." More to the point, the autobiography itself might be a perfect piece for the magazine. They would have to condense it, of course, and they couldn't afford the kind of money that the manager of Elvis Presley might be used to, but *True* could offer him a platform to "spread the gospel" to its more than two and a half million readers. And who knew where that might lead?

Colonel wasted no time in getting back to Associate Editor McKinney, assigning the task to Tom Diskin, who responded in what amounted to Colonel's own words and spirit, though not spelling or punctuation. "Colonel Parker," Diskin wrote, "asks me to advise you that he lays no claim to being a 'con' man in the Look magazine article. His autobiography complete with a whole array of options and hidden clauses is already committed and he thinks it should be off the press for a sneak preview sometime around 1959 or thereabouts. You can, however, count on his buying the monthly issue of TRUE which he has been doing for some time."

Sneak preview or no sneak preview, it appears to have given him the impetus to plunge headlong into a project based on what was very likely little more than a throwaway line. (Remember: if there was any con to it at all, it was a *benevolent* con.) Though it's hard to believe he was ever serious about actually *writing* a book (but who knows?), he started scribbling notes for both its subject and its purpose right away. It was going to be, he wrote in his neatly serviceable hand, "a study of people . . . what can be learned about people," and not just famous people either. ("Not too much about Hollywood," he specified, "that's the sequel.") Rather, it would include "the waitresses, the bellboys, the cabdrivers," anyone in fact who incorporated the qualities of energy, conscientiousness, and invention that Colonel prized. And though it would be "not strictly autobiographical," it would tell the story of a man who had only completed the fourth grade and how he had learned to make up for it by "keeping the mind sharpened up." It would share his experiences in the circus and on the carnival midway, "with traveling shows, with Gene Austin [and] the Humane Society," and his encounters over the years "with people looking for something for nothing and when they got something what the cost was." It would reveal some of his secrets but make clear that there was "no secret to con jobs — when it happens it's done so smoothly always, after that the dawn hits." But most of all it would strike an overwhelmingly positive tone, telling wholesome tales and offering "free advice to young talent" while portraying the magical qualities of the world that he had discovered and in which he so happily resided. And it would come with special ad space reserved for "character photos" and show cards in the layout.

As if to motivate himself even further, he wrote down some of the "outstanding personalities" he had met over the years, which broke off at forty-five but clearly was going to run on to a great many more if he stuck to his task. The list included Joe Frank and Gene Austin and Royal American owner Carl Sedlmayr, along with any number of other, less well-known carny friends, "local people in Tampa," Eddy Arnold, "Earl the Doorman," and "Pete the Greek." Abe Lastfogel, Harry Kalcheim, and Mr. Danforth (the founder and owner of Ralston Purina) were, of course, included, too, not to mention Bevo Bevis, RCA corporate president Frank

Folsom, and Tennessee governor Frank Clement. All the people, in other words, who had captivated and not infrequently influenced him, all the people he loved. He wanted his book to be "the most up to date and funniest book ever written about show business," as he described it to one colleague, "the only book," as he described it to another, "with a good story of show business."

But that appears to have been the end of it, at least the writing part of it, though he continued to speak of his book, with its never-less-than-enticing title, *How Much Does It Cost If It's Free?* (and even got a $1 million offer for it from a major commercial publisher as late as 1988), right up until the day he died. What he got caught up in instead was the *marketing* of it, into which he put fully as much energy as he ever could have had he actually sat down to compose it.

He did broach the subject to writer Hal Kanter in January of 1957, at the start of filming of *Loving You*. The Colonel, Kanter told me years later, with a certain amount of mordancy, was "a very amusing man. He came on like a truckload of turkeys, cause[d] a great deal of flurry, and then, suddenly, he's gone. He came to me once while we were working and said, 'How would you like to write my biography? Maybe you'd like to write it with me.' I said, 'Well, maybe, what have you got there?' He said, 'All I have is a title, [but] I know the title will sell.'" He told Kanter the name of the book, and Kanter agreed, it was a great title. "'Number two,' he said, 'it's going to be an instant best seller.' I said, 'How do you figure that?' 'Because RCA is going to buy 10,000 copies of it and take a full-page ad on the back cover.' He had it all figured."

As he expounded further upon the subject over the years, sales prospects and profit margins only continued to grow. To *Tampa Tribune* columnist Paul Wilder, who knew a good gag when he heard one, he presented a variation of the same thing he had told *Time* magazine in 1960. In Wilder's version a guy from New York called Colonel, sounding like "he was going to crawl through the phone," and asking how much for a half interest in the book. When Colonel told him $100,000, there was silence on the other end, and Colonel asked him if he was still on the line. "He said yes—but I must be nuts. I told him he might be right, but for one hundred thousand dollars it did not matter. He said he would have to talk to me about it, so I told him I would have to charge him for my time, at least $2500 per hour. . . . He asked me something else, but I could not

With Steve Sholes (left) and RCA corporation president Frank Folsom. *Courtesy of the Graceland Archives*

answer him as I did not know if he was good for the money, so I hung up. I hope you agree with me that I did the right thing—after all, I did not want to cheat anyone."

But perhaps its truest realization came in his teasing description to Bill Bullock, who was by now his strongest advocate (and principal prankster-in-training) at the record company. He repeated his promise to reserve the back cover of the book for RCA "at a special rate of $2500 Twenty Five Hundred Dollars" but suggested that "it would be a good idea to have a letter on this in my files as we do not know at present when the book will be finished and we would have to be sure that the Company is buying this ad as we have no trouble unloading this important space to some-one else this would be of course the only advertising in this important book regarding Records and other material RCA Victor has for sale."

With that out of the way, he emphasized all the advantages his book would bring to the company.

> I feel that I am giving the company a very good rate having been with you folks such a long time and the value of the advertising will more than pay for the cost, we will of course let you furnish the plate and the layout for this ad at no cost to us. We will at least give you a Six Months notice in advance before the book will be re-leased so you can order at least enough copies for the Company as I know you will want to present a copy to each Fieldman and Distributor, as much information regarding record sales and promotion gimmicks will be included in this great publication. . . . Price of the book will be $10.00 Ten Dollars . . . wich is plenty cheap when you can learn so much from it and also will be able to realize so much information on what went on in the past that many of my friends were in on from the start.

There is no record that any money ever changed hands. Which is a shame — I think RCA would have gotten its money's worth. But on the other hand, maybe just listing the names of all those who had helped influence and inspire him along the way, while referencing the lessons he had learned from them and in some cases what they had learned from him, was enough to constitute a kind of autobiography.

Except, of course, none of those names or experiences went back to a time prior to the arrival of a wide-eyed sixteen-year-old boy in Hoboken, New Jersey, some thirty years earlier, or, for that matter, to any of the people or experiences that helped shape him over the next seven years, before he found a place in the world he had for so long yearned to join. The book, in other words, would unquestionably paint a picture of the American Dream, but there would be nothing in it to suggest just what it was that might first have kindled that dream.

B UT BY THIS TIME Colonel's mind was already off and running as he explored other, ever-more-fertile outlets for his antic energy.

At the very same time that he first began to excite interest, whether real or ironic, in his notional autobiography, he announced the formation

Colonel with Abe Lastfogel (left) at a Hollywood photo session for the gospel album *His Hand in Mine,* August 15, 1960, more than two months before the actual recording session in Nashville at the end of October. *Courtesy of the Graceland Archives*

of what would almost instantly become his crowning creative achievement. This was a wholly fictitious, but highly complex, organization called, variously, "The Snow Club," "The Snowmen's Association of the World," "The Royal Order of the Snowmen's League," and "The Snowmen's League of America, Ltd," which, with "Ltd" distinctly optional, pretty much became its official name. As for himself, he was variously self-appointed "Chief Snower," "Snow Chief," "High Potentate," "Imperial Potentate," "Benevolent Snow Coner," and at his most grandiose, "Chief Potentate and Founder and High Mogul." But whatever the designation, he presided over an organization that he alone had created, an imaginary club of no fixed address, bylaws, or visible means of support, whose membership was limited to men and women of goodwill. (Yes, women, too — they were called "Snowess-es" and included Mrs. Colonel; Mrs. Presley; the redoubtable Mrs. Lastfogel; the manager of the Gotham Hotel in New York; and Minnie Pearl, one of Colonel's personal favorites.) In fact, the only bar to membership — and it must be admitted, it wasn't always strictly enforced if the inductee was of sufficient standing in Colonel's world — was the absence of a sense of humor or, to put a finer point on it, an inability to engage in the same deflective terms of emotional intimacy that the High Potentate himself practiced. This was the highly evolved technique, disguised as off-the-cuff badinage, that permitted Colonel to tell his story in a way that both revealed and concealed at the same time — which, as it turned out, was an integral part of every Snowman's training.

The name of the organization, whichever of its variants you might choose to employ, derived from the Showmen's League of America, an organization founded in 1913 by "a small group of dedicated 'out-of-doors showmen' [to] cater to the needs and wishes of carnival people everywhere, through good times and bad," with legendary globe-trotting show-business pioneer Buffalo Bill Cody ("Buffalo Bill's Wild West Show") serving as its first president.

Colonel revered the organization, and one of the proudest achievements of his life was the League's recognition of him on his eighty-fifth birthday with a special commemorative book. And yet, as fanciful as his own organization may have been, in many ways it served as broad a social purpose as the Showmen's League. For, just as Abe Lastfogel and his fellow *landsmen* formed the Hillcrest Country Club to offer a place of refuge in a land of exclusion, Colonel, too, feeling an equally acute sense of rejection, invented a club of his own to which all of his pals, whether highborn or lowborn, whatever status they may or may not have achieved in the everyday world of outward appearance or financial success, could gain admittance under the same sweeping democratic rules. It was a club in which doormen and waiters, a Bombay shipping agent (who sent him elephant figurines for his collection) and hotel clerks, could take their place with studio heads, plutocrats, and presidents (Lyndon Johnson was eventually so honored, though he may only have been vice president at the time), and to which no one was ever recorded as having turned down admittance, perhaps because it was widely advertised by its founder as costing nothing to get in but $10,000 to get out. ("We've never lost a member yet," was the Chief Snower's proud boast.)

It was dedicated, of course, first and foremost, to the fine art of bamboozlement (a fancy word for "snowing," which itself fell somewhere between "selling" and "persuading"—or, let's be honest, not all that far

Santa visits the set of *Wild in the Country,* along with Hal Wallis, Christmastime 1960.
Courtesy of the Graceland Archives

removed from good-natured "conning"), but its purpose, like every one of Colonel's enterprises, even the most commercially consequential ones, was clear from the start: to make work fun and "to have fun while working." But then, as if to confound the expectations of some of his more aggressive snowers (in many cases, not surprisingly, some of the purest examples of material success on the Snowmen's League rolls), he insisted from the start that "all snow jobs have to be honest." Even more to the point, he adjured his captive audience: "Never snow anyone other than to do good" (this might require a little bit of a logical leap, but there is no question from the number of times he repeated it that Colonel was serious). One other rule "you must always abide by," he wrote to his old pal Paul Wilder in Tampa, was to "allow other snowers to snow you from time to time even if you know you are being snowed." And, above all, "Never take advantage of anyone you have been able to snow under." For, after all, weren't they all members of the same club?

It started out big and kept getting bigger. Among its first inductees were Milton Berle, Bob Hope, legendary PR men and professional kidders Harry Brand and Howard Strickling (who could have started a society of their own), Nick Adams, Andy Griffith, charter member Lee Gordon, RCA president Frank Folsom, Abe Lastfogel, and, quite naturally, Hal Wallis and Joe Hazen, each of whom Colonel felt compelled to warn that the other had "tried in every way possible to keep you out of this exclusive club." By the end of the year Frank Sinatra and Sammy Davis Jr., too, had been inducted, along with Spencer Tracy, Bing Crosby, prominent Hollywood restaurateur and congenial impostor (to both the Russian throne and American citizenship) "Prince" Mike Romanoff, and a host of comedians, columnists, small-time DJs and promoters, and designated "Mosquito Manure harvesters." All responded with warm, often witty letters of appreciation for the signal honor they had been accorded, with only Bing Crosby striking a different, characteristica ly sincere, tone, as he wrote, "I am happy that you were pleased with wl at I had to say about your young man, Elvis Presley. I honestly think he's a great performer and under your astute guidance, he's going to be a big star for a long time."

It was a running gag that took on a life of its own. In the first few months, Colonel had Snowmen's membership cards made up, modified, revised—and then revised again. From the start the League established its own singular language, a language stemming entirely from Colonel's own gift for rapid-fire and original self-expression, which was further stimulated by the competitive efforts of some of the brightest lights in the entertainment business. Sometimes when he felt things were getting out of hand, Colonel might reprimand a new recruit for "trying too hard." As he wrote to one: "We of course can understand that you tried to impress us at once with a big snowjob—the reaction of new part-time members has always been that way—and most everytime they snow themselves under by doing this, I hope this does not happen to you." Which, understandably, more often than not, only spurred the new-born Snower on to new heights.

Before long Colonel put together a booklet for members, its subtitle proudly proclaiming it to be a "Confidential Report Dealing with Advanced Techniques of Member Snowers," underneath a cartoon drawing of a genial snowman, in top hat, scarf, and corncob pipe, with a shovel over his shoulder. Its table of contents alone, wrote Elvis biographer Jerry Hopkins, "qualified it for a position in classically nonsensical literature."

But why just its table of contents, you might ask. Because in fact the small book that Colonel produced — though it contained a page or two of Acknowledgments to "the following" (who, of course, were not named in the space provided but saluted as a "team notably skilled in evasiveness and ineptitude"), and there was a dedication to "Those Pioneer Snowmen who were called but didn't answer and thus set the stage for even greater strides in the direction of the unknown"— consisted for the most part of thirty-two pages deliberately left blank for the Snower to do with as he or she pleased. There was a special page toward the end reserved for a "Complete Listing of Paid-Up Members in Alphabetical Order" (also blank) and a space reserved for each member to paste in their own picture for a fee of ten dollars as well as another bordered blank space, also for sale.

The table of contents, on the other hand, perhaps to make up for this lack of evident content, set out to summarize the various forms of snowing, or at least *some* of them, with nods to the "melt and disappear" technique and the concept of "directional" snowing (which required the ability to make one's approach simultaneous with one's departure) as well as some of the indirect (and possibly autobiographical?) consequences of the snowing life with respect to forward motion ("with sufficient training one can develop the ability to go nowhere with devastating results") and sociability ("it sets the member apart and sometimes can lead to exile").

He saved his most intricate piece of logical inversion for last, however, in which, as if to restore confidence in a thoroughly confounded membership, the High Potentate explained in three paragraphs how he had managed to lower the per-unit cost of each book to zero. Just how had he achieved this almost unimaginable financial feat? Well, it was simple, he modestly explained. First, he increased the quantity of the order to the point where the cost per book was virtually erased. But then, when he realized how much of a burden storing such a vast quantity of books would place on the printer (presumably his good friends at Rinaldi Printing), he thoughtfully cut back on the order, thereby "permitting the printer to run these off at a reduced loss to himself for which he was very grateful." It was, the Colonel concluded, yet another "sterling example of a good snowman's willingness to see the other man's problems and show the greatest understanding without financial involvement."

And then, as if for a pièce de résistance ("I hope that this is not a vulgar expression," he wrote to a secretary in Paramount's legal department, whom he was considering for Snow membership and who had used the phrase in a letter to him), he embellished the final page of the book with a popular inspirational quotation from Fra Giovanni, a Franciscan monk of the fifteenth and sixteenth centuries, whose architectural works (the Loggia del Consiglio in Verona, among others) were as celebrated as his artistry, scholarship, and archaeological studies. He was in other words a real person, and this particular quotation was said to have come from his "Letter to the Most Illustrious the Contessina Allagia degli Aldobrandeschi, Written Christmas Eve Anno Domini 1513."

"There is nothing I can give you," the High Potentate quoted, a little incorrectly but certainly in the spirit, "which you have not / But there is much while I cannot / give you you can take."

I think I can safely state that there is no one who would have been more gratified than Colonel to discover that this inspirational quote was a fake, created by British polymath Greville MacDonald as a Christmas greeting in 1930, as was firmly established by the British Library in 1970.

"MANY HAVE BEEN CALLED, BUT FEW HAVE ANSWERED"

PAUL WILDER, the *Tampa Tribune* columnist, asked him once just what this enigmatic statement, so often invoked by Colonel, might mean. "Well, to tell you the truth," Colonel responded (though Wilder may well have wondered, *What truth?*), "I don't know myself."

It went back to a gag told by an old comic on the Gene Austin tent show, he said. "I never could figure out what it meant, but he got a good

Bevo Bevis (center) in earlier days, ca. 1948, with his employers Eddy Arnold and Tom Parker.
Courtesy of Richard Weize and more bears archive

many laughs and I always acted like it was a good joke so as not to show
him I did not know what he meant. And since he did not know what it
meant either—he never knew that I did not know. And the fans in the
tent always laughed and since they had already bought a ticket—this
made it a very good joke."

Colonel was having a good time. He had built a protective network
that included all his old pals and many new ones, too. He continued to
keep up a steady stream of palaver with all of his fellow kidders of long
standing—with Oscar Davis and Gabe Tucker and Al Dvorin and newcomer Lee Gordon, too, along with Bevo Bevis, who had been around
since Dogcatcher days when he had been hired as a lost young man by
Field Agent Parker, and he still called Colonel "Pop" in gratitude. With
the Humane Society Colonel had bestowed upon him the grandiloquent
title of "General Manager of Perpetual Care for Deceased Pets," and after
working as factotum without portfolio during Colonel's time with Eddy
Arnold, he now found himself showered with all kinds of extravagant
Snowmen's League honorifics, from "Corporal at Guard" to "Vice President

in Charge of Looking Out the Windows," to "Head Mosquito Hunter" and sometimes even "Chairman of the Buckpassing Committee."

With or without the honorifics, he was always listed prominently in Snowmen's League literature, taking his place just below Vice President Tom Diskin on the League's three-man Board of Directors. As the Colonel wrote to one old friend, "If you do not know who Bevo is, he has been with me for about 20 Years off and on and he always feels that he is One of the Family." And to another, as if to emphasize how integral, and integrated, Bevo was into the whole program, "Bevo seems to be pretty well fogged up by your greeting, I hope someday you will have the privilege meeting him as you will never forget Bevo. He sticks and how."

Some might have thought Colonel's tone inappropriate. Many — and not just those outside the tent — might very well question why Bevo should be the unwitting butt of so many of Colonel's gags ("Parker orders Bevo around mercilessly and bawls him out in public," reporter Ed Linn wrote in the January 1958 issue of *Saga* magazine). But Bevo would almost certainly have argued that no one should feel sorry for him — and not just because, as Linn went on, his employer "protects him, supports him [and] seems to have a genuine affection for him." Much more to the point, he considered himself in on the joke, which, as any observer could plainly see, was the same for everyone, even the Colonel, who mocked his own titles and pretensions as much as anyone else's.

The joke, in other words, was not on anyone — it was, rather, something they all embraced. And no one was more appreciative of it than Elvis, who, while he never participated actively in the Snowmen's League (I'm sure his manager felt it would have been beneath his dignity), was in every respect the First Snowman. He never tired of the tales that Colonel told of how when they first arrived in Hollywood, everyone had taken them for rubes — but look at them now! It was an implicit understanding that the two of them shared, and shared with no one else. It was their common bond.

THIS WAS the Colonel, then, a man in full, standing six feet tall and weighing close to three hundred pounds, something his doctor was not happy about in the least (he had by this time suffered several small heart attacks) but that he was not inclined to do much about. By now, at

Colonel receives an award as "the most outstanding talent manager in the business" from former Opry manager and Artists Service Bureau head Jim Denny at his Madison, Tennessee, office, late March 1957. *Courtesy of the Graceland Archives*

age forty-eight, he was recognized throughout the industry as "the most outstanding talent manager" in the business, in the words of an award that he received from former Opry manager and Artists Service Bureau head Jim Denny in the spring of 1957. Or, as fellow impresario and industry stalwart Hap Peebles put it more sweepingly, "I think a great deal of the prestige in country music during the past few years is due in no small way to your untiring efforts and the experience you have had in show business that has enabled you to bring the country music out of the doldrums."

Nearly everyone in the pop and country music community at this point would have agreed, including Abe Lastfogel, just about anyone in the know at RCA, and maybe even Hal Wallis, however reluctantly. What they saw in Colonel Tom Parker—well, what didn't they see? For all of his personal eccentricities (and it must be admitted, even in this highly eccentric company his eccentricities definitely stood out), it was his intellect that compelled attention most of all, what Abe Lastfogel called his gift for looking at familiar objects and practices in a way that seemingly no one else had ever looked at them before. He was, it was generally agreed, a man of a different order.

None of his fellow managers or promoters would even think of trying to outmaneuver or outwit the Colonel (well, maybe Oscar Davis), and if they did they were quickly disabused of the notion (Oscar Davis again). For all of his hustle and bustle, for all of his bluster and outsize personality, this windmill of a man had reinvented their world, and in the process created one of his own, in which for the first time he felt truly at ease. There was not a single moment in his well-filled day that he did not enjoy, there was not a challenge he was not eager to meet, and he had an artist of whom he couldn't be more proud. The army was hovering, it was true, but as worried as Elvis was, Colonel had no doubt they could overcome that, too, perhaps even turn it to their advantage.

He wrote poems—doggerel in the Dutch manner—that commemorated births, deaths, engagements, and other social occasions, both private and public, in rhyming, loosely scanned couplets. Some of his lengthiest efforts celebrated the fellowship that all Snow members shared. At Christmastime he sent out a picture of himself in a Santa Claus outfit, just as he had dressed up for the children at the Maas Brothers department store in Tampa twenty years before. He never tried to hide his background, in fact he celebrated it, unfailingly citing his dogcatching days, his circus and carnival experiences, his lack of formal education, as the very qualities that made him different (and by implication perhaps lifted him above the common herd), sprinkling clues that might have led the curious observer to look further into his history, but they never did.

He was, to all appearances, comfortable at last in his own skin. As he wrote with unguarded sentimentality in his "Welcome to New Snowers":

> *Now you are like one of us*
> *In fair and snowy weather. . . .*

You know how CLOSE we are,
Like snowflakes on the window,
But never let your snow befall
On some unworthy fellow

And yet, and yet (and please don't ask me to interpret this), at the conclusion of what one might certainly have expected to be an equally sentimental — more like joy-filled, really — twelve-month countdown to Christmas, he wrote:

The tree was small and empty
The packages were fakes
But we gave each other presents
Boxes of phoney snow flakes

TWELVE

Preparing for the Future

*WE PLAN TO GO RIGHT ON LOOKING AFTER ELVIS PRESLEY
PRIVATE ELVIS PRESLEY THAT IS. . . . AS FAR AS I am
concerned Elvis is in the service but we are not, so we now must
even work harder to keep his name alive till he gets out. This I feel
we can do if every-ONE PITCHES IN ALONG THE RIGHT
TRACK AND MY MAIN PLAN IS NOT TO OVEREXPOSE
ELVIS IN ANY WAY. THE WAY BUSINESS IS TODAY, ONE
MUST BE VERY CAREFULL AND PLAN EVERYTHING
THE BEST WAY POSSIBLE.*

— Colonel Tom Parker to Bill Bullock, RCA, April 1958

PUBLIC SPECULATION about Elvis' draft status, which had been widespread for over a year, had reached a fever pitch by the time he finally got his induction notice in December of 1957. Neither Elvis nor Colonel had given any thought to trying to get out of it. This was a time, remember, when every young man, whether prominent sports figure or movie star, was subject to peacetime military call-up (barring certain broad but well-defined exemptions), and every regional area, including Memphis, had to meet its quota. Most professional athletes and entertainers received assignments which allowed them to pursue their professional vocations (entertainers for the most part served in a designated branch called Special Services), but Elvis and Colonel were firmly opposed to this course — and each had reasons of his own, as well as a single shared reason.

The shared reason, as naive as it might sound, was, quite simply, a matter of patriotism, which entailed gratitude to a country that, in dif-

Hal Wallis visits Elvis in Germany, ca. August 18, 1959. *Courtesy of the Graceland Archives*

ferent ways, had rewarded them each with so much. They also shared an awareness of the public perception that had labeled certain well-known performers as "draft dodgers," but for Elvis it was as much a matter of self-image as public perception. Elvis, who had grown up a shy and reclusive only child, was determined to serve "like any other soldier" for the same reason that if, in his first year or two of national success, he was publicly challenged (which happened on more than a few occasions in the early years), he could not back away from a physical fight. For Colonel, on the other hand, the decision to bypass Special Services rested on his single unbending principle of doing business: you never gave anything away for free, and you never cheapened your product by permitting it to become too readily available.

And so, looking ahead to the future, Colonel had begun his own tactical preparations long before Elvis finally got his call-up notice. One of the first elements of that preparation was to educate Elvis as much as possible (though in this instance, Elvis was not a particularly eager student) on the importance of the many forms of remuneration that could be generated without the necessity of his being in the public eye. Song publishing, for example. Colonel had done his best from the start to emphasize how much publishing income from the songs that Elvis recorded (which hopefully others, too, would record, seeking to emulate his success) could add up, but now he redoubled his efforts. "It will be long after sales are slowing down and things are running at an easy pace," he reminded Elvis in April of 1957, "that you will be getting revenue off these tunes." But then, in addition to publishing, there were also, of course, the many lucrative promotional and exploitation campaigns that he had initiated (such as, but not limited to, the merchandising deal with Hank Saperstein for trinkets, lipstick, scarves, skirts, lockets, and Western ties)—these, Colonel stressed, would be of great value to him during the two years he was likely to be in the army, and all "without having to [do] anything personally as far as services are concerned."

But most of all, his job with Elvis, as he saw it, was to help restore his sense of equilibrium, to help him regain faith in his destiny. Because Colonel knew that whatever he might say for public consumption, there was an element in Elvis—and not a small element either—that felt the acute unfairness of it all: the unfairness of being drafted at the height of his success, the unfairness of having so much taken away from him, the very unfairness of fate, which, Colonel would agree, had always been kind to them. But then, just as he was finishing up basic training at Fort Hood in Killeen, Texas, and waiting with the rest of his company to ship out to Germany, something almost unimaginable happened.

Elvis had been living off base with his parents and grandmother ever since Colonel discovered (and his sergeant confirmed) a loophole in army regulations that allowed a soldier to live off post if he had any legal dependents living nearby. By the end of June 1958, Elvis had moved his family to Killeen and established residence there—but then his mother, who had always been his staunchest supporter, believer, and friend, suddenly grew ill and, within days of returning to Memphis for treatment, died of what her doctor could only diagnose as a "clotting phenomenon" that had attacked her liver and other internal organs.

In the immediate aftermath of her death, Colonel had done everything he could think of for Elvis and Vernon. At Vernon's request he had

Family portrait, July 1955. *Courtesy of the Graceland Archives*

seen to all the practical details of the funeral, and he took care of the more than one hundred thousand condolence cards and letters that came in from all over the world—but he simply didn't know how to address Elvis' almost unspeakable grief. He had witnessed the way it had expressed itself. Along with everyone else at the service, he had seen and heard Elvis cry out at the gravesite, "Good-bye, darling, good-bye, I lived my whole life just for you," then, after four of his friends half dragged him into the waiting limousine, piteously blurt out, "Oh God everything

I have is gone." And he had no idea how to comfort the boy. And so, while Elvis remained frozen in his grief, Colonel was just as clearly frozen in his inability to help the one person in the world he would have most wanted to protect.

All that he knew how to do — and he could not have failed to recognize that this must be little consolation indeed — was to present Elvis with evidence that all of their previous good fortune had not simply been a fluke, that the future still lay within their grasp.

To that end he had, first, to nail down the movie deals, which appeared to have gone sideways for the moment, as much as anything, Colonel felt, due to the studios' lack of belief in the incandescent talent of an artist who had proved himself again and again. It was Colonel's job to rekindle that belief, without compromising his client's interests in any way or selling them short. As he wrote to William Morris head Abe Lastfogel, his principal ally and friend, "I feel very strongly that we [need to] work out . . . the same set up we had when Elvis was drafted." And that is what he set out to do.

With respect to Hal Wallis, who appeared to be balking at the idea that their deal even remained in place as written, since Elvis was unable at this point to fulfill his contractual obligations, Colonel directed Last-fogel to let Wallis know that he was thinking of booking "a pretty long set up of personal appearances [for 1960], at least 25 or 30 of them." These, clearly, would take precedence over making movies with Wallis, and they would pay better, too. I'm not sure that Colonel was altogether serious (it seems even more doubtful that Hal Wallis would take the threat seriously), but it was absolutely essential to Colonel to stake out a position of strength in the negotiation. And in the end he prevailed, overcoming threats of lawsuits and not infrequent declarations on both sides that they had reached a point of no return, until in October he finally emerged victorious with an agreement by Wallis and his partner, Joe Hazen, to pay $175,000 against 7.5 percent of the gross receipts for Elvis' first post-army picture, with options for three more pictures on comparable terms. (Just for the sake of comparison, that picture, Elvis' third for Wallis, would have paid $25,000 under what once were taken to be the ironclad terms of the original contract.)

He went at 20th Century Fox in the same uncompromising spirit, accusing them at first of welching on an agreed-upon deal, then redrawing the terms of the contract so that Elvis would get $200,000 for the first film in a two-picture deal and $250,000 for the second, with 50 percent profit participation in each. At the same time, he simply walked away from MGM in disgust when they acted as if they didn't remember any of their promises. (That deal was renegotiated in January of 1961, a year after Elvis' return from Germany, by which time it had evolved into a four-picture deal worth $2 million, plus, once again, 50 percent of the profits.)

The almost evangelical language with which he delivered the news to Elvis in November speaks of how much he knew was riding on this. He was well aware from the letters and phone calls that he had been getting from Vernon that Elvis was in a bad way. For even though both Vernon and Elvis' grandmother were living with him in Germany (taking advantage of the same rule that had allowed him to live with his family in Killeen), he had yet to emerge from the dark mood that had set in with his mother's death.

It wasn't hard to see why he should equate her devastating loss with the situation in which he now found himself, a "lonely little boy 5000 miles away," as he described himself to a girlfriend. But Colonel was well aware of the dangerous allure of self-pity, something he had trained himself with great effort to avoid from childhood on. His pressing mission, as he now saw it, was to convince Elvis to once again take control of his life.

They would all be better off now, he announced in his November 18 letter, spelling out the details of all the deals he had just concluded. Elvis could now consider his worries over, and he hoped that this would prove to the boy once and for all that there would be no backsliding. "This now brings our picture setup in line with a very healthy setup for the future," he wrote. In fact, he informed both Elvis and Vernon, "Elvis will do even better this Year than he did last Year even while he is in the service."

Colonel knew that this kind of news could not erase the inconsolable loss of his mother, or even Elvis' underlying resentment at the unfairness of his fate, but as long as Elvis was stationed in Germany he kept up the barrage of good news (sometimes just news, more often than not advice), day after day, week after week, as he and Tom Diskin dispatched dozens and dozens of letters, telegrams, and phone calls that put him in what amounted to almost daily contact with his boy.

Colonel hosts Hal Wallis (left) and RCA's Bill Bullock on the set of *Blue Hawaii*, 1961. *Courtesy of the Graceland Archives*

W ITH RCA the work went on as before. Colonel was by now so accomplished at the task that sometimes it seemed almost a matter of rote. He hectored, he joked, he cajoled, he invoked unwritten understandings, while all the while cheerfully lambasting longtime colleagues and new ones alike. But above all he made clear that his commitment to Elvis was unequivocal. As he wrote to RCA Records General Manager George Marek, before Elvis had even entered the army, "There is no need for anyone to panic just because he has been called to military service. . . . We should all [just] put on a new working jacket to show him we are still in front with him [and] if we stay on the ball, we can have a ball game every day with a winning team. We cannot be anything but happy that the end of the rainbow is a long way off."

Most of all, of course, he never stopped looking for new ways to improve the RCA deal. There's no need to go into any great detail here. But at a time when the future of Elvis record sales could have been considered to be most in doubt, Colonel was seeding the ground for substantial increases in both artist and publishing royalties, saw to it that recoupment of studio costs by the company would be eliminated (thus effectively putting Elvis in complete charge of his sessions, as few other artists were at the time), and got a new clause added to the basic agreement that turned over control of all photographs, printing, and promotion to Colonel and Colonel alone. In other words, Elvis and Colonel would derive the financial benefit not just from all the normal publicity campaigns and promotions that he dreamt up but, after taking possession of RCA's voluminous catalogue of Elvis publicity shots, Colonel's company, All Star Shows, would draw an annual fee of $15,000 to supply something like half a dozen photographs.

"Just remember, Anne, that we do everything," Colonel wrote to an infuriated Anne Fulchino, RCA's Press and Information Administrator and one of Elvis' earliest boosters at the company, who had watched all her carefully assembled files carried off. "So there will be no misunderstanding, we plan to handle our situation as we always have in the past, strictly from our own setup without any coordination whatsoever pertaining to tie-in's regarding the press or other publicity media. . . . The simplest thing for your office to do is give them the same answer as they do in New York—[you] have no information."

"HONORABLE TENN COLONEL THOMAS A. PARKER"

D EALING WITH THE ARMY, as it turned out, had proved to be the least of Colonel's problems.

From the start, from the time he first accompanied Elvis to his induction in March 1958, where he handed out balloons advertising the new Hal Wallis picture, *King Creole,* to the crowd that had gathered outside, he had little difficulty taking command of the situation. From Memphis he set out for Fort Chaffee in Fort Smith, Arkansas, where Elvis was to be processed for the next three days. A caravan of cars containing newsmen and fans had followed the army bus out of Memphis, and there were more than a hundred civilian fans, forty or fifty newsmen, and another two hundred dependents of military personnel on hand to meet the bus when it finally pulled in at eleven fifteen that night, with Colonel—who upon his arrival sometime ahead of the bus had volunteered to help the beleaguered information officer—heading up the greeting committee.

The newsmen were determined to cover every aspect of the new recruit's experience, including his first standard-issue military haircut the next day and a phone call home to his mother from a public phone booth. When reporters sprinted after him, Colonel stepped in. "I think he's entitled to talk to his mother alone," he said, blocking their way.

After three days Elvis was shipped to Fort Hood in Killeen, Texas, on March 28, for basic training and advanced tank instruction. Once again Colonel showed up in the office of the camp's information officer to offer "his services, advice, and moral support," as writer Alan Levy observed, before the bus carrying the new recruits even arrived. Lieutenant Colonel Marjorie Schulten was less receptive initially than her Fort Chaffee counterpart ("Well, Colonel," the ersatz Colonel shrugged, "you're the boss"), but everything was smoothed over the next day, when Colonel met with the fort's commanding officer, Major General W. Paul Johnson, and acquainted him with some of the unanticipated complications that might arise from having a celebrity like Elvis so publicly on display. His letter to General Johnson the following week expressed his gratitude for the general's consideration and singled out for praise all the officers who had carried out their tasks so efficiently (including Lieutenant Colonel Schulten) and done so much "to make our stay a pleasant One at Fort Hood." He then signed off "Respectfully, Thomas A. Parker," with a postscript that explained, "I am leaving the Tenn Colonel tittle [sic, as per usual] off as my signature, as Private Elvis Presley has been calling me Admiral lately."

Elvis shipped out to Germany three months later, on September 22, after an elaborate farewell ceremony and a press conference orchestrated by the Colonel (with the help of E. J. Cottrell, assistant chief of information for the Department of the Army in Washington) at the disembarkation point at the Brooklyn Army Terminal. That in turn was followed by the release of a five-and-one-half-minute interview-and-sound-effects EP (extended-play) recording called *Elvis Sails,* which reached number two on the EP charts, just one of the many promotional "gimmicks" that Colonel proudly brought to Elvis' attention.

Once Elvis arrived in Germany, Colonel established an almost exclusive relationship with Cottrell, with whom he was soon on a first-name

Induction day, March 24, 1958. *Courtesy of the Graceland Archives*

After the first army haircut, with Tom Diskin (left), March 25. *Courtesy of the Graceland Archives*

basis (they were "Ed" and "Colonel Tom"). It was Cottrell who oversaw to Colonel's exacting specifications every detail of Elvis' contact with the outside world. With respect to the army's various efforts to enlist Private Presley in one public performance or another, Colonel had little trouble persuading Cottrell that this would put the army in a very precarious position for all the extensively developed reasons he had enunciated to so many who had sought Elvis' services for free over the years. It could, for example, he wrote to Cottrell early on, "be of great expense [and] if not presented properly . . . leave all of us open for bad publicity." It could be the worst kind of security disaster. It could engender resentment of both Elvis and the army for the special treatment he would be perceived to be receiving. Whereas the way things had been handled to date, with Elvis treated "just as a soldier, so far has been very good for Elvis and also for the Army."

Cottrell would appear to have been in full agreement, as he wrote back effusively to "Colonel Tom" about what a pleasant experience it had been to be associated with him—and "educational," too. He would do all he could to accommodate Colonel's concerns to the fullest extent, so long as it was consonant with his duties. And so he did, even so far as to visit Elvis at his post on a trip of his own to Germany the following year, reassuring Colonel that Elvis, while maybe a little homesick, continued to be "a darn fine soldier," who had the admiration of his commanding officers and all those who served with him. Colonel Tom should be very proud.

Colonel never seems to have given any serious thought to visiting Elvis himself. As he wrote to Cottrell with what one can only assume to have been a certain amount of disingenuousness, "We had thought [of] perhaps going over there ourselves to double check everything, however after thinking about it very carefully I do not believe that this would help any, as it would look like we are sticking our nose into the Army wich you know I have no right or intention of ever doing." And perhaps, irrespective of concerns about a passport or his unrenounced Dutch citizenship (and you may think me naive, but, given all his talk of a world tour at this time, I'm really not sure how much of a problem he perceived this to be), he may well have judged wisely.

He was content in any case to rely on volunteer proxies like Ed Cottrell, Jean Aberbach and Freddy Bienstock of Hill and Range (who made sure that Elvis' two-week Paris furlough in June of 1959 came with a full complement of diversions), and Hal Wallis, who offered Colonel a berth in his stateroom for the Atlantic crossing he was about to make in order to film location scenes for Elvis' first post-army movie, *G. I. Blues*. Colonel merely passed this off as, and with, a good joke, while steadfastly refusing to allow Elvis even to visit the location shoot, let alone recite a single line of dialogue, lest he jeopardize his hard-earned "just like any soldier" status.

He could, of course, always have sent Tom Diskin, whose loyalty he trusted implicitly, but for reasons of his own — and I'm not going to even speculate — he didn't. (He did in fact volunteer Diskin's services to Fox for some business that the studio deemed essential, but when they learned that they would have to pay all expenses, as well as the salary of Diskin's replacement for the two weeks he would be gone, they swiftly lost interest.) And so the two Toms continued to operate out of the confines of Colonel's compact, five-person Madison, Tennessee, office, dubbed variously (and not inaccurately) as the Madison branch of Wallis-Hazen Productions, RCA Records, and the William Morris Agency.

It occurs to me that by presenting Colonel's actions so cavalierly, and in so compressed a form, I am perhaps doing a disservice to all the planning, the long-range thinking, and the sometimes necessarily seat-of-the-pants

Elvis' army discharge, March 3, 1960. *Courtesy of the Graceland Archives*

improvisations that went into Colonel's complicated campaign — but there was never a moment when he lost control, and never a moment when he lost sight of his primary objective, which was, quite simply, to keep Elvis' spirits up while maintaining his finances in the same healthy state.

And when it came time to start thinking of Elvis' upcoming March homecoming, Colonel got Ed Cottrell to introduce him to his boss, Major

With army brass, March 3, 1960. *Courtesy of the Graceland Archives*

General William W. Quinn. He visited General Quinn in Washington in September of 1959 with the explicit aim of making sure that Elvis' return to civilian life was handled in the same low-key manner that the rest of his army service had been — well, kind of. There were, Colonel explained to the general, over twenty competing civilian organizations (including several in his hometown of Memphis), all clamoring to stage a big event to celebrate Private Presley's discharge, but, as he had Tom Diskin write to Ed Cottrell in the aftermath of his Washington visit, it would hardly be fair to give a single organization primacy, let alone create so much fuss about one soldier's return. "Since no one gives a big homecoming for the other boys who have served right alongside Elvis," Diskin wrote, even as Colonel was writing the very same thing to Elvis, "there's no reason for a lot of fanfare just because a guy happens to be a widely known personality — sort of a continuation of the equality system."

Or, as he wrote to Abe Lastfogel about his visit with the general, "[While] the meeting was a pleasant one, I gave them nothing but good will, wich they can collect on after Elvis gets out of the Army. . . . I was able to cool off several projects wich some of them pitched at me wich would be good for Elvis, they say — however, when I agreed on everything as long as we got paid they somehow felt it was not too important a deal, so I went along with them and agreed that we should do nothing. But they did thank me for helping out."

To be fair, though, Colonel did do everything he could to cooperate with the army's needs, so long as it did not involve a free performance. This included lending Elvis' name to a nationally syndicated article, "What the Army Taught Me," which ran in *This Week* magazine not long after his visit to General Quinn. "Don't try to be different, you won't win," Elvis wrote in a pastiche of surprisingly honest, but warm, reminiscences. "The Army's bigger and older than you are."

The army, then, was left in nominal charge of all ceremonies attendant on newly promoted Sergeant Presley's return to civilian life — which meant in effect that Tenn. Colonel Thomas A. Parker was in full command of the event that took place in the wake of Elvis' arrival via military transport at McGuire Air Force Base, near Fort Dix, New Jersey, at 7:42 A.M. on the morning of March 3, 1960. Hundreds of fans had gathered in a driving snowstorm, and by midmorning a full-scale press conference for over one hundred newspaper, television, radio, and newsreel reporters and photographers had been convened at the Colonel's behest. Frank Sinatra's nineteen-year-old daughter, Nancy (who had just announced her engagement to Colonel's longtime protégé Tommy Sands the day before), was on hand to present Elvis with a gift of two formal lace-front shirts from her father and also, not coincidentally, to serve as unofficial publicist for her father's "Welcome Home Party for Elvis Presley" television special, which was scheduled to be shot in three weeks. (It aired on May 12.)

"The Colonel went through that day like a force of nature — just this fierce constructive energy," observed RCA publicist Robert Kotlowitz, later to become one of the creators of *PBS NewsHour*. Before the day was over, Kotlowitz told writer Alanna Nash with something close to genuine admiration, he would see everyone in Colonel's path — generals, RCA executives, and seasoned reporters alike — bend to his will. "None of the relationships I saw [that day] were in any way conventional or even normal. You did what he told you to do, or if you didn't, he was finished with you."

"THE 91% TAX CATEGORY"

THE ONE PROBLEM still hanging over them — for which even Colonel was beginning to despair of a solution — was something he had never anticipated: taxes. And it was the single problem that he never seems to have fully addressed in his communications with Elvis and his father, because, after all, what would be the point? This was a problem that it was up to him to fix, and if he couldn't, well, there would be plenty of time for recriminations later.

He had set up Elvis' RCA contract on an elaborate schedule of deferred payments that had been recommended to him by the top tax lawyers at William Morris and Hill and Range. RCA's legal department, too, had offered their thoughts and assured him that this was the kind of deal that they and every other major label had with their biggest stars. (In 1951, for example, Nat "King" Cole had entered into a deferred-compensation agreement with Capitol Records, which ten years later had grown to retained earnings of approximately $1 million.) And yet for no apparent reason, starting in mid-1957, the IRS seemed to have come after Elvis alone. It wasn't long before they appeared to have reached the conclusion that he would need to pay full income tax on the more than $1 million that he had earned in 1956 and 1957 alone, rather than take roughly $100,000 year in payouts over the next ten years, as specified in his RCA contract. Which, with an income-tax rate of 80–90 percent, would clearly be ruinous.

At first, the lawyers assured Colonel that it was all just a mistake that could be easily rectified. By early 1958, however, as the IRS demands grew louder, it became evident that RCA was starting to take the matter seriously. In February Steve Sholes wrote to Colonel, with a certain amount of bureaucratic circumspection, that the company had held a meeting of all "the top record personnel," and while it was generally thought that some progress had been made, Sholes conceded that everyone appreciated the "powder keg" that Colonel and Elvis were sitting on. By April it had become clear to everyone that this powder keg could very well go off, and Colonel wrote to Sholes, in a separate self-typed addendum to a normal course-of-business letter, that he was sending his accountant and attorney to New York to confer with Warren Ling and Coleman Tily, two of RCA's top legal and financial experts, informing him further that the

IRS had written to him that the "RCA Victor Contract will not hold up and they are going to attack the contract as not being legal."

He need hardly remind Sholes, he continued to type in one very loosely punctuated single-sentence opening paragraph, "one of the main reasons we made such a contract for such a long time [was] we were told that there were many such contracts with RCA Victor artist and that had not been stopped." To which he added with barely suppressed indignation (or maybe not suppressed at all), "We of course do not know wich way to move at this time as we have not had any information regarding this from RCA Victor, since all parties will be involved it can only be handled by all concerned." As for where it could all lead, Colonel did not leave much room for doubt. "After they have filed the papers there will be plenty of publicity on this matter as it seems rather unfair to have this brought up just on Elvis while he is in the service and not on some others that have had these type of contracts for Years, somehow if a contract like this is no good there is no need to make long terms contracts anymore with any-One for it does not mean anything."

In June of 1959, with the situation looking, if anything, even more dire, Colonel dispatched his lawyer, Elvis' lawyer, and their respective accountants to Washington to put the case before what appeared to be an ever more unsympathetic Internal Revenue Service. "If the ruling should be against this contract," he wrote once again to Sholes, "we will all be back where we started 4 Years ago, with some new plans to be made to see how we can work this out so Elvis and myself wont be holding the bag all by ourselves. . . . After all the company had [Howard] Letts fly out to California to work out this new contract and on their advise we of course went along with the deal. I know they cant help it should the ruling be against the contract, but we cant either. . . .

"I don't have much hopes that it will be in our favor," Colonel concluded with as naked an admission of pessimism as he had ever publicly permitted himself (though, on second thought, perhaps it was for a more veiled political purpose), "as they claim it was done to beat the taxes."

It went on like that month after month, with little to suggest the prospect of a successful resolution. Even as late as mid-January 1960, after a series of conferences and calls and memorandums and meetings with all the top RCA executives, Colonel had come to the conclusion that if things went against them, he could see no other solution than for RCA to pay out the vast sum of Elvis' money that they were holding so that he and Elvis could simply pay their taxes. If it came to that, Colonel proposed, the company could subsequently put Elvis on the books as an employee with a regular weekly salary. And with an elaborate series of calculations that perhaps only he fully understood, he worked out a formula by which Elvis would be paid $160,000 a year with five one-year options (yes, adding up to roughly $1 million), with RCA bearing all costs of production and promotion and no royalty calculations whatsoever.

There is no record that anyone at RCA came up with a more practical solution, and it would appear that Colonel's plan was still being held in abeyance when, for unexplained reasons (or at least for reasons that I do not understand), the IRS finally dropped its case, and Colonel and Elvis were able to sign a modest three-page letter of amendment to the basic RCA agreement on March 1, 1960. It has certainly occurred to me that the reason this letter was so modest (it offered only the most minimal improvements on the extant contract) was that neither Colonel nor RCA were prepared to thumb their nose at the IRS just yet. But just one year later, in a further letter of amendment, there was a great deal more for both Elvis and the Colonel. For one thing, in addition to the ongoing weekly payments from his original 1956 contract, Elvis' annual guaranteed payments were bumped up to $400,000 and extended to 1967, with four additional one-year options. I wouldn't go into all this in such detail (I mean, doesn't everyone have tax problems?) except that, as I'm sure many readers have already noted, it serves in many ways to counter the picture that has emerged in recent years of Colonel's lack of financial acumen. Which has served to reinforce the even more widely accepted view that Colonel was strictly a practitioner of the short con.

In some ways this is understandable, I suppose, because of Colonel's widely circulated declarations (wisecracks? aphorisms?) about taxation. (Just bear in mind: one of Colonel's first rules of doing business was that it never hurts to be underestimated.) In June of 1960, for example, he proclaimed to a reporter from the *New York Journal-American* that he and Elvis were proud to be in the 90 percent tax category, without, of course, alluding in any way to the bruising battle they had just been through. "Elvis and I look at it this way. We're luckier than a whole lot of people. . . . We never had it so good, and we know it." Somebody, he declared, "has got to pay the government for the country we've got." Or, as he put it to

Lloyd Shearer of *Parade* magazine at about the same time, "Elvis and me got one job: to keep [him] in the 91 percent bracket. It would be unpatriotic . . . to go below that figure."

CLANNIE AND BRENDA

E VEN AS all these challenges and calls to arms were weighing on him, and even as he continued to travel back and forth between Hollywood and New York and Washington, D.C., with no hint of slowing down, Colonel found himself spending more time at home in Madison than he had in years. And, not surprisingly, as he had throughout his life, going back to a time before he met the Kufferath family in Hawaii in 1929, he found himself another family.

Clannie Williams met Marie Parker at the beauty shop in downtown Madison in the summer of 1958, and the two of them hit it off right away. Mrs. Williams, a divorced mother with two teenage children at home, lived just down the street from the Parkers. When Mrs. Parker told her husband about this nice woman who could really use a job, it was only natural that Clannie, a bright, easygoing person who always saw the positive side of things, should be hired to help out Tom Diskin's sisters Patti and Mary. And so she went to work right away in the low-slung stone building directly behind the matching three-bedroom stone house, in which Colonel had long ago set up his office.

Patti and Mary Diskin, who with their brother lived in a little house in the Inglewood area of East Nashville, just five minutes away, each had their separate tasks. Mary, the elder by fifteen years (she was the oldest of ten children, Patti was the youngest) did the books, and Patti did a little bit of everything. Clannie Williams was given the job of assembling the voluminous scrapbooks which Colonel had kept as a record of his life from the Humane Society on.

Work started early each day, as soon as Colonel came down the back stairs from his house and the three Diskins arrived from their Inglewood home. Everyone went promptly to work at their appointed tasks, but in a spirit of comity everybody's doors (except Colonel's when he was conducting confidential discussions about business with Tom Diskin or on the phone) were always open. At five the Diskins would all leave, and

Clannie Williams in front of
Colonel's Madison office. *Courtesy
of Brenda Williams Cohen*

Colonel would return to the house, where Marie had cheese and crackers prepared for him, and he would put his feet up and smoke a cigar as the two of them watched TV.

Clannie Williams fit right in from the start. She was efficient, she was outgoing — and she had a good sense of humor. As her daughter, Brenda, observed, the Parkers were homebodies, but before long Brenda and her mother were not just accepted but adopted almost as part of the family. Brenda, who was still affected by her father's leaving, started going to church with Patti at St. Joseph just two doors down from the Parkers' home, and Patti became her godmother when she converted to Catholicism for a time. The three Diskins were all ardent churchgoers; Mary and Patti attended Mass every morning before coming to work, and all three of them attended services every Sunday.

Even though he continued to address her formally as Mrs. Williams for the longest time, Colonel and Mrs. Parker started inviting Clannie and her daughter to dinner, and Clannie returned the favor. Marie was a good cook, Brenda said, "typical Southern style" like her mother, and the Colonel clearly relished his meals, whether it was his wife or Clannie

Brenda Williams with Colonel and Marie and Marie's granddaughter, Sharon Ross (front), in Florida. *Courtesy of Brenda Williams Cohen*

Williams who prepared them. The Diskins were frequent dinner guests, too — it seemed to Brenda sometimes like the Colonel and Marie's entire circle of friends in Madison "was just the Diskins and us."

One time, Colonel asked her to stay with Marie when he had to be away on business, and after that she did it as a matter of course. (Marie didn't like to be alone, but Colonel didn't like for her to be alone either.) On weekends that she stayed over, Brenda went to the Baptist church with Marie, but, she noticed, Colonel never joined them when he was home. The first summer after her mother started working for the Colonel, he and Mrs. Parker asked if they might take her to Tampa on a two-week vacation, so she could meet Marie's grandchildren, and her mother, naturally, said yes. They stayed at a little mom-and-pop motor court with a pool right by the ocean, and that was where she first learned to swim.

It was all new and exciting, and when they returned she felt even closer to both Colonel and Marie. But it was Colonel to whom she was most drawn. In the office, amid the great swirl of activity that was always going on around him, Colonel could seem gruff at times, but he was never unkind. "I guess sometimes he used to storm around the office, but he had a warmth about him. I used to call him Uncle Colonel, out of respect. He had a big personality, but he [could be] quiet, too. You just knew that the Colonel loved you." Everyone in the office responded not so much to Colonel's commands as to his wishes — it was a beehive of activity, never swamped but constantly working, a close-knit team of five handling a global enterprise.

FOR MARIE it was an idyllic time in their marriage. If she could have chosen, it would have gone on like this forever. "Marie and I are closer than ever," Colonel wrote to one old friend around this time, and he spoke proudly of both her and the grandchildren in letters to colleagues like Steve Sholes and Abe Lastfogel.

He was proudest of all of her gardening activities — she was an active member of the Garden Club of Madison, and they employed a full-time gardener to keep up the lush plantings. They had a housekeeper, too, who came in several times a week, which was a big help to Mrs. Parker, whose health seemed to be a matter of growing concern, as she suffered from a number of difficult-to-diagnose complaints, including just "feeling low," that put her in the hospital several times for observation without the doctors ever being able to come to any kind of conclusion.

They each had their hobbies; Marie was always adding to her collection of china roosters and chickens, just as Colonel cultivated his extensive assortment of ivory elephants in the basement. Marie was thrilled when Colonel got involved in various forms of civic activity, like leading the effort to pay off the mortgage on the Madison city park or raising funds for the local hospital. To lift her spirits, Colonel kept trying to get her to go to Hawaii with him, and in August of 1959 he finally succeeded, and she seemed delighted with the way she was treated, like a real celebrity.

The two of them were so devoted to each other, Brenda observed, if in a slightly old-fashioned kind of way — and yet at the same time they were so different. Marie didn't possess Colonel's warmth or generosity of spirit, particularly when dealing with those she considered "beneath her"—and she was always quick to place her own preferences first, even if it meant quarreling with those around her. Colonel, on the other hand, for all of his shrewdness and exacting standards, "was always respectful and he always tried to help. And you were the same with him. I got a standard of living from him," Brenda said. "I don't remember him ever sitting me down [and lecturing me], I just remember regular conversations. You just knew there were standards you were expected to [uphold] to represent yourself and your family. You were expected to have good values and good morals. You just knew it."

Being with Colonel was always fun. He was even-tempered, rarely got mad, and if he did, he was quick to get over it and crack a joke, just to make you feel better. He was always interested in her opinions, too. During the run-up to the Democratic convention in the summer of 1960, Marie told her she had better keep her strong John F. Kennedy views to herself, because Colonel was good friends with Lyndon Johnson, but he never tried to change her opinion, and she and her mother remained staunch Kennedy supporters.

After Elvis got out of the army, Colonel was away from home more often, and Brenda stayed with Marie more frequently. She was fifteen years old now and developing interests of her own, and for the first time she started to feel the confining nature of the relationship. Marie liked to have her do her hair, but the conversation was always "Colonel this and Colonel that, everything was about the Colonel," and sometimes when she was staying at the house, she felt a little bit like a prisoner. Marie liked to play a game with marbles, something like Chinese checkers but with rules that Marie seemed to make up as she went along, and Brenda came to dread it, because "if you beat her, she would storm off, she'd go storming through the kitchen and the dining room and every other part of the house, wiping her nose and crying. You know, as an adult, I didn't like games for the longest time, [because of the way] she would get so mad."

In the summer of 1961, they all went back to Florida, but this time for the whole summer because Elvis was making a movie there. Her mother spent the first part of the summer with them, but then Marie's grandchildren came and stayed, and she saw a side of Colonel she had never seen before. Sometimes in the evening, he would gather all the children around him—he included Brenda, even though she was four

Mexican president Adolfo López Mateos picks Eddy Arnold's guitar, with Eddy Arnold, Colonel, Senator Lyndon Johnson, and his daughter Lynda Bird (far right) observing, at LBJ Ranch, October 18, 1959. *Courtesy of the Graceland Archives*

years older than Sharon, who was eleven now, Tommy was only nine — and he would tell them stories. Well, they were all part of the same story, Brenda decided, they were all about himself when he was a little boy "and how he ran away from home. I don't know how old he was, but he hoboed and caught freight trains and would eat snow sandwiches in between two stale pieces of bread. Colonel had these big blue eyes, you know, and he would open them up so wide [till] you could see the whites all around them, and then the tears would start coming." She didn't know if the tears

On the set of *Follow That Dream,* Crystal River, Florida, summer 1961: Colonel; Brenda and Clannie Williams; Marie's granddaughter, Sharon Ross; Marie; Elvis. Elvis' costar, Anne Helm, is to his left, and the two boys in front are twins who play twins in the movie. *Courtesy of Brenda Williams Cohen*

were real or not, but she was positive that the stories, in some way or another, were. "I got the impression he was from somewhere else from the stories — I don't know how. But I just knew he had a hard life as a boy, and when he told us about it, he would get tears in his eyes. And we would get tears in our eyes, too."

THE FOLLOWING two summers Brenda went out to California with the Parkers and stayed with them at their homes in Beverly Hills and Palm Springs. She met some of Colonel's friends, Abe Lastfogel and Fox publicity chief Harry Brand in particular, and Colonel and Marie took her out one time to an exclusive Hollywood restaurant, Chasen's, where she was thrilled to be introduced to Frank Sinatra and his date,

Natalie Wood. Colonel took her to the Hillcrest Country Club, too, for one of his regular lunches with Abe Lastfogel — he explained to her that it was an all-Jewish club, and she understood immediately, because, growing up in Madison, she had felt a sense of exclusion first for being a Catholic convert, then for being a Kennedy supporter when all of her friends at Church of Christ believed that all Catholics were going to hell. Colonel made a joke of it by introducing her around as Brenda Williamstein, just as he would sometimes refer to himself within the confines of the almost exclusively Jewish William Morris Agency, in what can only be taken as a shoulder-shrugging gesture of solidarity, as Zeke Parkenstein. For the most part, though, during those two summers in California, she was confined to the apartment in Beverly Hills or on weekends at Colonel's new home in Palm Springs. Marie never went out, not even to the grocery store, and so she was stuck either inside the house or out by the pool. And she couldn't help but think that whatever feelings of affection the Parkers still had for her, the real purpose for her being there was to look after Marie.

Clannie Williams went on working for Colonel till well after Elvis died, and Brenda always stayed in touch with both Marie and him, but she went to work right after graduating high school and didn't spend as much time with them after that. She and her mother and her first husband all went out to Las Vegas to see Elvis' show not long after he opened there in 1969. (It was the first time she had seen him perform since she and her girlfriend, Patsy, had watched him on *The Ed Sullivan Show,* and then gone out in the yard and screamed their heads off.) But her memories of Colonel never dimmed — to Brenda Williams "he was charismatic. And, you know, he was such a decent guy, he was a family man, and maybe he just kind of made people his family because he didn't feel part of his [own].

"It just breaks my heart," she says, "when I hear people say what a bad man he was. I remember the Colonel as determined and strong, a very kind, decent, shrewd, smart, tender-hearted, intelligent man. As you know, he was my father figure, and I really loved him. I am sorry to say he probably had no idea how much I loved him or what an influence he had on me. I hope I have learned the lesson of letting people in my life know how much they mean to me."

"ARE YOU LONESOME?"

T HE WORK NEVER STOPPED.
Wherever he was, whether it was Florida, California, or what he liked to call his "lonely outpost" in the "Madison, Tennessee William Morris office," even if he was supposed to be on vacation, he was always working. Or, as he liked to say, his mind was always working. Probably most of all during the time that Elvis was gone.

He estimated at one point that during Elvis' two years in the army he sent out some four thousand congratulatory telegrams and letters. They went to movie stars, longtime colleagues, columnists, reporters, magazine editors, other musicians, recording executives, and politicians, and celebrated births, birthdays, holidays (Mother's Day, Father's Day), stage and movie openings, anniversaries, and everything in between, all in the name of "Elvis and the Colonel." He was always finding new ways to generate income, whether it came from licensing some of the publicity photographs that he had recently acquired from RCA back to RCA on special promotional deals or giving the Loew's theater chain the exclusive right to display a photograph of Elvis in the gold suit that Colonel had had made for him at a bargain-basement price of $2,353. He got $23,907 from RCA for a reissue of *Elvis' Christmas Album* and another $9,395 for the booklet that went with it, while special deals for various other photo albums brought in another $12,500.

He traveled to Georgia, Alabama, and Florida to promote the rerelease of *Jailhouse Rock,* while he and Al Dvorin came up with the idea of an Elvis Presley Midget Fan Club at the Music Operators of America Convention in Chicago in April of 1959. (Al Dvorin represented a lot of "little people," including Eddie Gaedel, the only midget ever to appear in a Major League Baseball game.) He made a big splash as usual at the Country Music DeeJay Convention in Nashville. And he and Tom Diskin made sure that all the fan clubs were kept fully informed and fully engaged. He did everything, in short, to keep Elvis' name in front of the public, while lacking the ability to present Elvis himself, and at a time when other big-name artists' sales were dropping and the industry itself was in a well-documented slump, Elvis had seven Top 10 hits, including two number ones, plus an album, *Elvis' Golden Records,* that spent fifty weeks on the LP charts.

But Colonel had even higher hopes for all the new projects he had in the works that were just awaiting Elvis' return.

E LVIS' METICULOUSLY STAGED homecoming drew crowds of up to two or three thousand on a modified whistle-stop train run between Washington, D.C., and Memphis. Frank Sinatra's "Welcome Home Party for Elvis Presley," which had been in the works for close to a year now, looked like it was going to create as much of a stir as his last television appearances, on *The Ed Sullivan Show*, three years ago. But it was the initial recording session, on which so much was riding, that proved to be the greatest triumph of all.

Much to everyone's surprise, Colonel, who almost never attended any of Elvis' recording dates, showed up at the first of two staggered sessions in Nashville. (Each of these sessions consisted of three consecutive three- or four-hour segments interrupted only by half-hour breaks.) Steve Sholes and Bill Bullock joined Tom Diskin and Colonel in the control booth, along with Nashville a&r head Chet Atkins, publisher's rep Freddy Bienstock, and engineer Bill Porter, and with more than a dozen musicians and backup singers, and five or six of Elvis' guys on the floor, it would have been impossible to miss the weight of expectation. According to Jordanaire Ray Walker, it was almost eerie when Elvis himself finally walked in the back door. "He hadn't made a sound—you couldn't have heard it if he had—but everybody, just like we were on pivots, turned, and there he was."

There was a lot of nervous joking around at first, plenty of talk about Germany and Elvis' newfound enthusiasm for karate, but for all the conversation and laughter, you could sense the jitteriness in the room. When Elvis finally kicked off the first tune, Bill Porter said, he could feel the Colonel, Sholes, and Bullock almost breathing down his neck. "They didn't say anything, but they wouldn't sit down until he got it down." But then when he did, said Porter, you could hear an almost audible sigh of relief, and everything just fell into place as if he had never been away.

It wasn't until the second of the two sets of sessions, though, which took place two weeks later, in April, that Elvis got around to fulfilling Colonel's request. Colonel had never asked him to record a song before (and never would again), but he had been after Elvis for over a year now

Elvis and Marie, Las Vegas, July 1960. *Courtesy of the Graceland Archives*

to record "Are You Lonesome Tonight?," a heartfelt ballad from the '20s, which he said was his wife Marie's favorite song. He knew Elvis might find it a little old-fashioned, it was certainly different from Elvis' usual approach, but even with its dramatic Shakespearean recitation, he thought it would be right for his "new style," and he had a hunch that it could be a big hit with his new adult audience, too.

Elvis hadn't gotten around to it during the first four-and-one-half-hour session, or at the second one either, which ran until 3:45 A.M. on April 5. The final session began after a fifteen-minute break at four in the morning, and he didn't start with Colonel's song this time either. But then, after a spirited version of Clyde McPhatter's "Such a Night," "he chased everybody out of the studio," Chet Atkins recalled, and asked for the lights to be turned down. "Well, I turned around and looked in the studio," said the engineer, Bill Porter, "and the lights were all out, and I couldn't see what the hell was going on, and then I hear the guitar and the bass and the Jordanaires humming a little bit, and Elvis started to sing. And then all of a sudden he starts talking right in the middle of it! If you listen closely, you'll hear them bumping the microphone stands because there were no lights." The level, said Porter, was completely wrong, but the feel was completely right.

"That was the only song I ever recommended to him," Colonel mused to me in 1993. "He cut that for me as a favor—he thought he was doing me a favor."

But there was something Colonel didn't know.

What Elvis never let on was that he had been working on the song for almost as long as Colonel had been pestering him to do it—in fact, a beautiful, home-recorded version from that time emerged in 2018 on the collector label, Follow That Dream. So that while Elvis may have given Colonel the strong impression that he was merely indulging his manager by acceding to his request, "Are You Lonesome Tonight?" was in fact a song he cared so deeply about that when he didn't get it right in the studio at first, he begged Bill Porter and Steve Sholes to "throw that tune out, I can't do it justice." But in the end, of course, he did.

This may have been one of the few times that Elvis ever put one over on the Admiral. And he never let him in on the joke.

THIRTEEN

The Past Arrives

E LVIS' RETURN HOME, in March of 1960, was among the most extensively covered news events of the year. In Eindhoven, in the Netherlands, Dries van Kuijk's older sister Nel saw the famous photo of Elvis getting off the train in Memphis in his dress uniform, with a bulky older man in scarf, overcoat, and narrow-brimmed fedora standing in the doorway behind him.

She was struck instantly by how much the man looked like her youngest sibling, Jan, now a policeman in Amsterdam. She pored over the picture. Dries had been on her mind lately. Their widowed mother had lived with her in Eindhoven until her death in 1958. Though she rarely spoke of her "lost son," she burnt a candle for him every week at church and never gave up hope that someday he would return.

Nel didn't tell anyone else in the family at first (it was a family that had never been close and was even less so now), but she did try to get in touch with this man who was evidently Elvis Presley's manager, at first through the Dutch fan club, then with letters to America, none of which received an answer. Finally, at the end of the year she brought the matter to the attention of her brother Ad, just twelve when his sixteen-year-old brother first set out for America. Ad was something of a figure of mystery among his more sober-minded brothers and sisters, none of whom trusted him much. He had had a checkered career in business and was the only member of the family (apart from Andreas) who had ever been abroad, having spent two unaccounted-for years in Switzerland just prior to Germany's invasion of the Netherlands, leading some in the family to think he must have been some kind of "spy." He was currently running

The famous photo of Elvis' arrival in Memphis following his army discharge, March 7, 1960. *Courtesy of the Graceland Archives*

Ad van Kuijk Jr., summer 2023, Oostburg, the Netherlands. *Courtesy of Jorrit Van Der Kooi*

a combination tea shop and catering service in Breda but was as dissatisfied with this as with all of his previous business ventures.

Ad had never really known his brother, but that didn't much matter—as the rest of the family correctly perceived, he was the only one of them with the motivation or drive to go looking for him. "Let me tell you a story about my family," his son, Ad Jr., a kindly man who has taken on the role of trying to explain his family over the years, said to me in answer to what he may have considered a naive question. "The eldest brother of the Colonel, Sjef, was born in 1900. Once I was with my father in Breda. We took a walk, and we met a gentleman, and my father started a conversation with this gentleman, and [since] I was educated not to interfere in this conversation, I stepped out and let the two men talk. After a while the conversation ended, they left each other and I waited and then asked my father who was this gentleman? And my father said, 'That was Sjef, my eldest brother.'"

As to why his father took up the challenge of connecting with this long-lost brother, well, in one way, Ad Jr., an only child, intimated, the answer may have been obvious. But on the other hand, he suggested, his father was as much of a mystery to him as he was to everyone else. "My father was always in the distance. He only [wanted] what he wanted, he told only what he wanted to tell, and if he didn't want to [reveal it], then you could forget it, it came never."

It soon became evident that Ad had no more idea how to proceed than his sister did. He tried some of the same things she had tried, but with no greater luck. And it didn't take him long to come to the conclusion that writing a letter in Dutch was never going to work. But it was simply too good an opportunity to miss, and it turned out there was a solution. Ad Jr. was an eighteen-year-old language student at university in Utrecht studying to be a high school German teacher, and as part of his studies, he had learned to write letters in French, English, and German. So he said to his father he could write a letter to his uncle in English, at least he could try. He worked on the letter for several days, trying to get just the right tone, say the right thing, not scare his uncle off. In the end, with his father's help, he composed a brief, respectful note, which posed the very simple question, "Are you really my uncle?" And then they waited for a reply.

C OLONEL WAS extraordinarily busy in the first month of 1961. He was in the midst of preparations for not one, but two benefit performances which (despite an exceedingly lucrative movie schedule extending over the next four years) represented a momentous return to live performing after an absence of nearly four years.

The first was planned for Memphis, to benefit more than two dozen Memphis charities plus Elvis' own personal project, the long-dormant Elvis Presley Youth Center in East Tupelo, which to Elvis and Colonel's consternation had not advanced one bit since Elvis' donation of all the proceeds from his performance at the Mississippi-Alabama Fair and Dairy Show on the Tupelo Fairgrounds in 1957. Colonel threw himself into the promotion of the show, even getting into a friendly competition with the mayor over who could sell the most tickets (it was no contest) and securing early commitments from all the RCA bigwigs to attend. "There will be no passes," Colonel announced ebulliently to the Memphis press, for what would surely turn out to be "the greatest one-day charity show box office in the country's history," and indeed when the show was staged on February 25 (with a matinee performance added), it raised $51,612, which Colonel scrupulously apportioned to each of the designated charities.

The second concert was, if anything, even more ambitious, though it had come about largely by happenstance. It was prompted by a story Colonel read in the *Los Angeles Examiner* on December 4, 1960, anticipating the nineteenth anniversary of the Japanese bombing of Pearl Harbor. The piece spotlighted the stalled plans to erect a memorial to the victims of that bombing on the site of the USS *Arizona,* whose more than 1,100 officers and enlisted men remained entombed beneath the water. Three hundred thousand dollars had been raised over the course of the past fifteen years, but the Pacific War Memorial Commission was still $200,000 short of the funds needed to construct a monument in time for the twentieth anniversary of the attack the following year.

The story was the result of a letter sent out to over 1,600 mainland newspapers by George Chaplin, editor of *The Honolulu Advertiser,* asking that they consider running an editorial on or about December 7 with an appeal for funds. The appeal brought in about $20,000 from all over the country, but it also brought a telephone call to Chaplin from the Colonel. "Parker said Elvis was coming to Hawaii to make the film *Blue Hawaii* — and that if we could get an appropriate arena, and the tickets, ushers, lights, et cetera were for free, then Elvis would donate his services." Chaplin seized on the Colonel's offer and cleared it with the navy, explaining that if they were able to raise $50,000 they would have enough to complete the "bare essentials" necessary for a Memorial Day dedication. He then issued an official invitation to the Colonel to come to Hawaii.

Colonel arrived on January 7 to solidify arrangements with the chairman of the Memorial Commission, and held a press conference at the Hawaiian Village Hotel on January 11. Every penny that was raised would go to the fund, Parker announced, while stipulating that he and Elvis would pay for the talent on the show out of their own pockets. "This is the real McCoy, fellas. This is no gimmick. . . . You know, Elvis is twenty-six (last Sunday was his birthday), and that's about the average age of those boys entombed in the *Arizona.* I think it's appropriate that he should be doing this." And then, once again, he reminded every dignitary present, along with all potential attendees, that "everyone's gotta buy a ticket — the governor, Admiral Solomons, Admiral Sides, commissioners —

everyone, even me. Everyone in that hall will be a contributor to the *Arizona* fund."

But Colonel being Colonel, he couldn't — or wasn't about to — just leave it at that. Somewhere in between conception and execution he came up with another idea. This could be a television special. And not just any television special but, as he pitched it, "the greatest TV package ever presented either by one sponsor or sponsors for a one shot deal in the history of TV."

He expanded upon the idea at a special meeting of RCA, NBC, and William Morris executives on January 16, just days after his return from his initial trip to Hawaii. He recounted in rapid-fire fashion the almost instantaneous conception and acceptance of the benefit concert, describing, whether apocryphally or not, all the commercial opportunities that he and Elvis were passing up, including an Australian tour — he ticked off all the support they had in Hawaii from the local business community and media, and then he pitched the plan for the special, which would cost NBC a contractually guaranteed $150,000 up front, with $100,000 going to the *Arizona* Fund, $50,000 for musical expenses, and perhaps another $150,000 for all additional expenses, with (and I'd like to think this was a bargaining chip, since it seems like a little bit of overreach, even for Colonel) the negative and all rights reverting to Colonel Parker and the Presley organization after a single showing. It would be, he declared, practically a giveaway, for what was certain to be "the highest rated program of 1961."

As he boldly conceived it, the show would have "no production . . . all the filming would be in the raw, merely as it happens," and it would end the following day on a barge decorated with flowers, which, accompanied by a boat carrying Admiral Solomons plus a second navy boat, "would go out to the *Arizona* where the memorial is being built [and] Elvis would place a wreath . . . and sing 'Peace in the Valley,'" with the Jordanaires, dressed in military uniforms, providing vocal backup.

As if to reinforce the viability of the plan, RCA vice president Bill Bullock advised the committee that since coming out of the army Elvis Presley had been responsible for 18–19 percent of RCA's gross business, and Abe Lastfogel pitched in with William Morris' unqualified endorsement, pointing out that Elvis' most recent appearance on television, on the 1960 Frank Sinatra "Welcome Home Party for Elvis Presley," had drawn 65 percent of the viewing audience, though he sang only two songs. At one time, Lastfogel said, people might have considered Elvis Presley an oddity, but "that phase is all finished"; at this point there was no mistaking who he truly was.

The proposal was considered very seriously, a budget was drawn up, and all the logistics explored, and if, ultimately, it was turned down for good reason (among other things, it seemed doubtful that Hawaii had the capacity to transmit the show in color), Colonel wasn't fazed in the least. In the end, he and Elvis gladly paid for all expenses (each wrote a check for $27,000)—as far as Colonel was concerned, all of this would only serve as a prelude to something even greater. He was still fixated on the idea of taking Elvis on a world tour. As he had written to Abe Lastfogel a few months earlier, "I am still operating under the same banner to pick up some of our neglected personal appearances throughout the world, which are definitely much more lucrative within the same time period as it takes to make a picture, if we were to utilize that many play dates." And if not a world tour, then that long-promised tour of Australia for Lee Gordon at the very least. But all of that was going to have to wait.

T HIS WAS THE CLIMATE, then, in which he received his nephew's polite, deferentially phrased letter.

It's hard to imagine what he must have felt. In a world that still relied upon ocean travel, he had constructed what he believed to be a foolproof, if highly idiosyncratic, identity for himself, which had now unraveled on the basis of a single photograph, one of thousands of universally disseminated images, none of which had ever prompted an inquiry.

About a month before Ad Jr.'s letter arrived, he had in fact felt compelled to post a notice directing everyone in the office in capital letters: "DO NOT OPEN ANY MAIL FROM HOLLAND ADDRESSED TO COLONEL OR TOM." Perhaps he hoped that that this would staunch the flow of correspondence that had begun with his sister's recognition of his face in a Dutch magazine. But then, in light of this new, much more explicit challenge, he did something very uncharacteristic.

He did nothing.

Colonel, that most indefatigable of correspondents, who prided himself on his instantaneous response to any and every letter that reached

him, whether business or personal (the sheer volume of his correspondence, tens of thousands of letters, each personally composed, attests to
both the compulsiveness and the energy of his letter writing), waited a
week, then another two or three.

Now, it's true, there was a lot of business calling for his attention —
and not just the matter of arranging two full-scale benefit concerts. There
was also the ever-present issue of renegotiating the Hal Wallis contract
yet again, which he concluded for the time being on January 6, stabilizing
the remuneration for the next three Paramount pictures at $175,000 for
the first and $200,000 for the next two, with profit participation. Then,
on January 20, he cemented a four-picture deal with MGM at $500,000
per picture plus 50 percent of the profits. Which meant, as he announced
jubilantly to Bill Bullock, that they were "completely sold out for motion
pictures through 1965, which of course enhances the value of this great
artist for your company also." He accomplished each of these tasks with
typical alacrity and dispatch. But when it came to the letter to his nephew,
which he finally composed on January 31 and typed in his own distinctive
style (with "Master" added to his nephew's name on the envelope seemingly as an afterthought)— well, judge for yourself.

It began in the third person, as if written by someone only vaguely
acquainted with the Colonel, requesting that the young man not write
again and instruct all those who had been sending letters that had been
"getting into the fanclub and other hands" not to communicate anymore
until "we have been able to contact Mr. Parker regarding this seemingly
personal matter. . . . I am sure you will agree that this matter if it involves
Mr. Parker must be handled very carefully and privately."

The letter writer would not be seeing Mr. Parker again until April or
May, in either California or Hawaii, when he would take up such letters
as he was able to read (presumably only those in English) with him in
person. "You know as well as we do," he admonished his young correspondent tellingly, "that at times it is better to let the past be as it is and not
re-open old wounds, if this should be the case I am sure Mr. Parker has
felt the same longing and hopes as all of you but must have had a very
good reason and many problems so not to bring them to any of his people
at any-time, I know he is not that sort of person if he could help it."

There was more along these lines ("Believe me Mr. Parker feels for
you and all the other members of your Family the same as you must

feel")—until suddenly, in the two syntactically challenging sentences that conclude this one-page letter, the real Dries astonishingly emerged.

"Bear with us," he wrote, "and we will try to help in some way to at least make-up for any mistakes some-one may have made without meaning to do so.

"Remember me to all of them and if you can understand the meaning in this letter completely you will know and the others will also know this is the only way we can try to solve this for you.

"Sincerely and with Thanks

"[Signed with a neat, cursive signature] Andre"

In Breda there was an understandable mix of elation and confusion. "It was a little strange," Ad Jr. reflects with a dry chuckle today. And yet at the same time he and his father were very excited. "We saw possibilities. Perhaps if we could continue this contact, there would be a possibility for my father to go to America and meet his brother. So together we made a strategy not to frighten him [because] we had the impression that the Colonel was frightened perhaps of blackmail."

What the strategy came down to was setting up communication through a business colleague of Ad Sr.'s in Breda, also named van Kuyk though he was not a relative (the spelling of this fairly common Dutch family name appears to be interchangeable), who had immigrated with his wife to Hackensack, New Jersey, two years earlier. Noud van Kuyk gladly took on the role of intermediary, and from that point on all correspondence was strictly domestic and in English, all exchange of information and plans came from an innocent address in New Jersey, and Colonel stuck to his word that once all his present, very important business was done, he and his brother would indeed have their reunion in Los Angeles, probably at the end of April, after location shooting for Elvis' new movie was completed in Hawaii.

COLONEL SPENT much of February and March attending to preparations for the two benefit performances. Even before the success of the February 25 Memphis shows was assured, the majority of his attention was focused on the USS *Arizona* benefit a month later. The challenge was to raise the $50,000 he had virtually guaranteed in the cramped four-thousand-seat Bloch Arena, a venue which Colonel had initially opposed (he would have preferred a larger theater in downtown Hono-lulu) but accepted on the recommendation of the Pacific War Memorial Commission because of its location on the Pearl Harbor base itself. All efforts needed to be bent on selling the exclusive run of $100 tickets, he emphasized again and again, if they wanted to meet their stated goal. Don't worry about the cheaper seats, he told the local businessmen, who had signed on for this as they had signed on for every other aspect of the promotion, he would make sure that every one of those tickets was sold once he arrived in Hawaii by ship on March 8, seventeen days ahead of the show. "Be assured," Tom Diskin, the only other principal in what otherwise amounted to a one-man show, promised the Commission's executive secretary, "Colonel Parker will come off that gang plank loaded with ideas."

He made sure once again that many of the RCA top brass would attend (he was well aware, he acknowledged, that this was a considerably greater commitment than flying to Memphis from New York, as nearly every one of them had just done), and he even extended an invitation to Hon-orary Snowman Lyndon Johnson through the vice president's longtime aide Walter Jenkins. "Believe me, this is no gimmick," he wrote to Jenkins. "It would be a great honor to have the Vice President or Secretary of the Navy there with us on that date." And if that proved to be impossible, a congratulatory telegram would be much appreciated.

A telegram from the Secretary of the Navy duly arrived, and in the end, after a last-minute contribution of $5,000 from Elvis and the Colo-nel, which was matched by Commission Chairman H. Tucker Gratz, the show realized over $62,000, more than enough to get the commission's long-stalled plans off the ground and allow the memorial to progress to completion and dedication a little more than a year later.

Colonel was enormously proud that his and Elvis' efforts had paid off, and he was equally gratified by the uninterrupted flow of favorable pub-licity off the back-to-back charity concerts. On March 8 Elvis addressed a combined session of the Tennessee state legislature on what the state had declared Elvis Presley Day, and a month later the Hawaiian legisla-ture passed a resolution expressing that state's gratitude and appreciation for the remarkable efforts of Elvis Presley and his manager.

But for all the pride he felt in the success of the two events, and the tangible reward for all his efforts, Colonel's greatest pride was reserved

The Kufferath family at Bloch Arena, March 25, 1961. Front row: Arnold Kufferath's sister Mathilda; Arnold and his wife, Anna; Sonny Cordes' wife, Luise; Arnold's sister Vera, his daughter, Gayle, and Gayle's cousin Lydia Spencer. Second row includes Arnold's brother Carl and his family. *Courtesy of Gayle Kufferath Behnke*

for the performance that his artist had put on at both shows. He had never seen Elvis more fully engaged, more full of vitality and unselfconscious exuberance. "[He] grabbed the mike as if he were trying to eat it," the *Memphis Press-Scimitar* reported of the Memphis show, while the newest Jordanaire, Ray Walker, who had never sung onstage with Elvis before, was startled by the transformation that took place. "He just had kind of an effervescence about him. He would do some unexpected things and do them so well we'd forget to come in. Then he'd turn around and grin and call us a name."

In Hawaii, he egged on the band with an enthusiasm not just for what they were able to do, it seemed, but for what they permitted *him* to do, indicating his approval of their performance with grunts and exclamations that had little to do with the audience but more to do with his self-delight. Watching, as he had once watched Eddy Arnold and Hank

Snow with equal attentiveness perhaps but not quite the same captivation, Colonel found himself caught up in the moment almost as much as his artist. He was of greater resolve than ever now to get Elvis back onstage. You couldn't miss the electric spark that ran through him when he was performing, the rapturous sense of freedom that seemed unable to find its way into his motion pictures.

But at the same time Colonel was not about to give up any of his side games either. "Dear Mr. Johnson," he wrote cheerfully to the vice president, "we have just completed raising more than $62,000 for the USS Arizona Memorial Fund at Pearl Harbor. Now more than ever we feel it proper to let you know that we are willing able and available to serve in any way we can our country and our president in any capacity, whether it is to use our talents or help load the trucks. Sincerely, your friends, Elvis and the Colonel."

THE COLONEL REMAINED in imperturbable good humor throughout the filming of the new picture. He spent a great deal of time with the extended Kufferath family, more than a dozen of whom attended the concert in the $100 section at Colonel's expense. Both Arnold Kufferath and his brother-in-law Sonny Cordes helped Colonel out with many of the personal arrangements for his extended stay at the Hawaiian Village, making sure, among other things, that his telephone lines were set up correctly and that his suite was stocked with four cases of the mountain spring water that he favored in advance of his and Mrs. Parker's arrival.

Arnold was able to take time off from his job with the fire department to serve as Colonel's driver, adjutant, and personal aide, pitching in anywhere he could throughout the filming. "My dad," observed his seventeen-year-old daughter, Gayle, "just helped Colonel out with whatever needed to be done. He was a very giving person, real kind, not trying to impress anyone. I think he worried [at first] when Colonel called to pick him up that Colonel would expect a fancy car, but it was just our old station wagon." And as it turned out, Colonel, whom her Dad called "Tom," because that's how he had always known him, couldn't have cared less. The previous year Gayle had stayed with Uncle Tom and Aunt Marie for two weeks in Hollywood, meeting Shirley MacLaine at Colonel's birthday party on the set of *G. I. Blues*. The *Honolulu Star-Bulletin* had covered her

With Hal Wallis, on the set of *Blue Hawaii*, 1961. *Courtesy of the Graceland Archives*

visit with a story headlined "Island Girl Meets Elvis at Hollywood Party," noting that "the Kufferath family has known Parker for 30 years [since] he was stationed at Schofield Barracks."

On-set, it seemed as if his return to the Islands brought out all of his latent impishness, as he interviewed tourists, using the aluminum tube from his cigar as a microphone and identifying himself as a representative of Radio Pineapple, and hypnotized Elvis' boys for Hal Wallis' amusement. One day he halted shooting by walking in front of the cameras and demanding a conference with Wallis. Wallis, who thought at first that something might be seriously wrong, inquired as to just what the problem was. "Read the contract, read the contract," Colonel replied testily, although by now even Wallis was beginning to catch on. "You know, if Elvis provides his own clothes, he gets ten thousand dollars more." Wallis surveyed the scene, in which Elvis was wearing nothing but a bathing suit and riding a surfboard, and arched his eyebrows. "He's wearing his

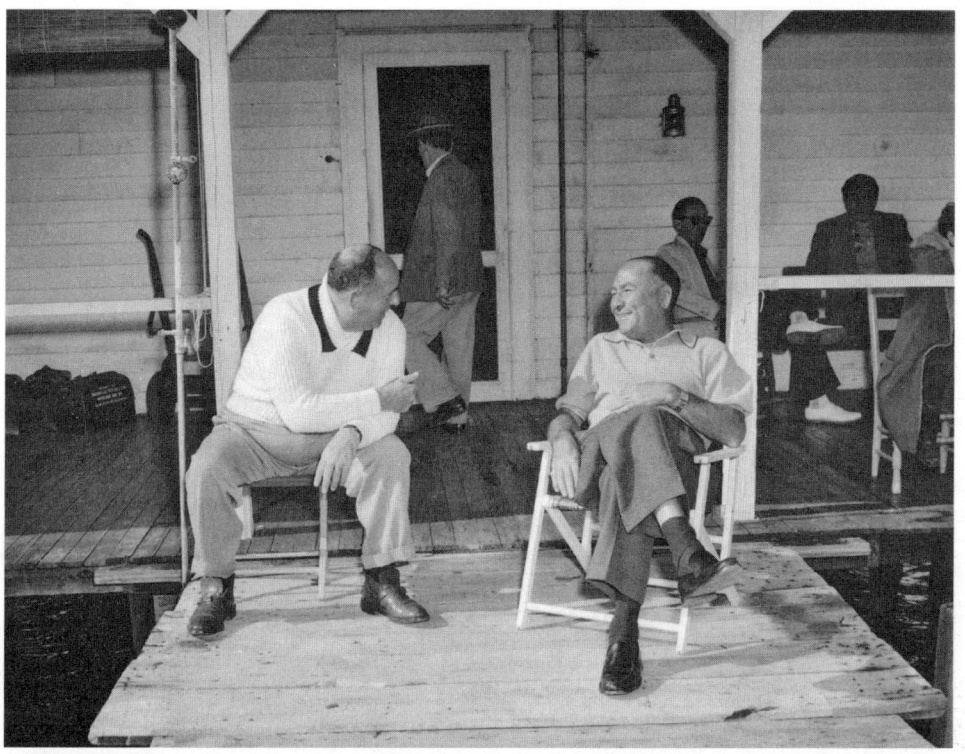

And on the set of *King Creole* three years earlier. *Courtesy of the Graceland Archives*

own watch," declared the Colonel without batting an eye. And the scene did not proceed until he took off the watch.

Nonetheless, Wallis remained unfazed. By this time he felt his official Snowman's status had conferred upon him immunity to Colonel's antics, and in any case he couldn't have been more pleased with the way the film was going. After what he considered to be the disaster of Elvis' last two pictures, *Flaming Star* and *Wild in the Country* (both for 20th Century Fox), in which he took on serious acting roles, with scarcely any music and little impact at the box office, he finally had Elvis in the kind of movie he had wanted to make with him all along. *Blue Hawaii* was a predictable, fast-paced musical comedy, with a meticulously recorded soundtrack that could have fit right into a Bing Crosby travelogue (the title track was in fact a song Crosby had recorded for another Paramount film in 1937), all amid spectacular Hawaiian sights and sounds and the kind of "production values" that were the hallmark of every Hal Wallis picture. (This was, it might be noted, the setting, if not the theme, Colonel had been pitching to Hal Wallis since 1958.)

Location shooting in Hawaii concluded on April 17, and by April 20 Elvis was back on the Paramount film set. The following day Ad van Kuijk flew from New York to Los Angeles, along with his friend Noud van Kuyk and his wife, Bep. He had arrived at New York's Idlewild Airport twelve days earlier and had been staying with the van Kuyks in Hackensack ever since. He had visited Times Square, the United Nations building, and a Western theme park in New York State where he had had his picture taken with a wrinkled Indian chief in headdress, and he and the van Kuyks had even gone bowling.

Ad seemed to be thoroughly enjoying this little interlude—the kind of American vacation his brothers and sisters could never have dreamt of—but at the same time he couldn't help but wonder what his brother had in store for him next. Finally he got word—he would have four days in Los Angeles with Dries before flying back to New York on the twenty-fifth for the flight home the next day. He had come equipped with a number of grandiose plans which he hoped might catch his brother's fancy, even bringing with him a blank check from the Dutch promoter and impresario Ben Essing for any amount Elvis Presley's manager might like to fill in. (In 1964 Essing would book the Beatles for two shows.) He had also contacted *Rosita,* the same magazine in which his sister had first seen Dries' picture, and while they do not appear to have agreed to sponsor his trip (it was Ad Jr.'s belief that his uncle provided the financing), they at least promised to pay him for his story. But if he was under the illusion that he was going to be able to dictate—or in any way influence—the terms of his visit, he found out right away that he was mistaken.

"FROM THE [moment they met]," said his son, Ad Jr., "the Colonel made clear: I decide what the program is during your visit. I decide. I am the boss." There were to be no photographs, either of Dries, or of his home. There were to be no "uncomfortable" questions. And Colonel had planned virtually every minute of his brother's stay, with a young William Morris agent named Irving Schechter driving him and Mrs. Parker around, sometimes accompanied by the van Kuyks, on what amounted to a sightseeing tour. They visited the MGM studios and

Knott's Berry Farm, Ad took pictures of the Miramar Hotel in Santa Monica, the fashionable shops on Rodeo Drive, and Los Angeles' imposing Union Station, along with various other locations in and around the city. And each night Ad and Dries' wife would return to his brother's snug modern apartment at the Beverly-Comstock, a mixed residential and hotel building complex provided at the expense of William Morris and at the instigation of Abe Lastfogel, who cherished his regular lunches with his friend at the nearby Beverly Wilshire Hotel where he lived, and their frequent get-togethers at the Agency, just blocks away.

But as per his agreement Ad took no pictures, although his brother appears to have thoughtfully provided him with a random assortment of publicity shots, mostly taken at Colonel's home and office in Madison, Tennessee, that he could show to anyone he pleased and pass off as intimate glimpses of his famous brother Colonel Parker relaxing at home in Hollywood. For Ad, after all his dreams of movie-star glamour and entrepreneurial opportunity, it must have been a crushing disappointment. In the evening (and they were all early evenings, because Colonel was up at five each morning and out of the house), Dries might relax in his bathrobe as they sat in front of the big RCA console TV that he boasted was a grateful gift from the record company. There was an array of gold records on the wall, and Elvis pictures and memorabilia everywhere, as well as artificial flower arrangements and a small sampling from Marie's extensive teacup collection.

There was a piano, too, which Marie loved to play, lighthearted, bouncy tunes for the most part in addition to what Ad recognized as hymns, presented in much the same manner. She was clearly, it must have struck her brother-in-law from the days that they spent together, a bright, energetic person. But at the same time she had obviously been thoroughly instructed by her husband not to give anything away. And when Dries cleared his throat and addressed him directly in that old-fashioned guttural Rotterdam accent, Ad never failed to respond politely with news of the family, prompts that he hoped might lead them to more productive topics of conversation. But they never did.

The one thing that the two of them always seemed to get stuck on was their mother's death. When he first arrived, Ad had presented his brother with Maria Elisabeth Ponsie van Kuijk's "mourning card," almost as if it were a proof of identity, but Dries kept returning to what he claimed to be his original reason for cutting off contact with home. At the end of the war, he said, he had met a man from Tilburg who had served in Holland's Princess Irene Brigade. "He told me that Mother had died. She was in fact my only true tie with Holland, and when she was dead Holland was dead for me." And while Dries now realized that the information he had received was incorrect, there appeared to be nothing Ad could say or do to restore that sense of connection.

On his brother's last day in Los Angeles, or perhaps it was the day before, Dries unexpectedly asked if he would like to meet Elvis, and, after summoning Irv Schechter, he took Ad to see his artist.

There are a number of different versions of the story, each of which had its own variations. In some, the meeting took place in Elvis' bungalow on the studio lot. In others, which Colonel's second wife, Loanne, believed to be true, the young William Morris agent drove Colonel and Ad to Elvis' home in Bel Air, though whether Schechter simply waited in the car or went in is not universally agreed upon. What *is* agreed upon, wherever the meeting took place, and whether or not any outside observers were present, was that Colonel made no attempt to disguise the relationship, he simply introduced this skinny, dark-haired, almost vulpine-looking middle-aged man who spoke virtually no English as "my brother"—which Elvis appeared to accept with equanimity, never breathing a word of the relationship to a single soul.

Long after the fact, after Elvis was dead, some of Elvis' cohorts, none of whom had ever had the slightest suspicion that Colonel was not from *somewhere* in the South, if not literally from Huntington, West Virginia, doubted that this meeting could possibly have taken place, suggesting that Colonel would never have entrusted such vital confidential information to their boss, when everyone knew that Elvis couldn't keep a secret. But, evidently, at least this one time he did.

Ad kept his side of the bargain, too. He never said a word to any of his brothers and sisters about the substance of his visit, about anything their brother had said or promised, other than, "He sends you all his greetings." But he made it clear that Dries had no interest in hearing anything further from any of them or staying in touch at all.

He delivered his story to *Rosita,* but his account was so fanciful, his son observed, that some members of his family were not convinced that he had gone to America at all. The story appeared in three successive issues in July and was made up for the most part of well-worn tales that Ad, or more likely the magazine, had gleaned from a 1960 article in *Time* magazine and fan-club publications, along with a few family stories. The "exclusive" photographs that accompanied it amounted almost entirely to snapshots Colonel had sent to his old school friend Cees Frijters when he was in the army and stock photos of Elvis and the Colonel, along with two snapshots of Ad's arrival in New York. And when Colonel spoke in what was purported to be his own voice, it was to spin stories that were so outlandish as to be just plain laughable, introducing one extended anecdote, for example, by suggesting that for a time he and his wife had been so destitute they couldn't even afford a postage stamp. "Sometimes we had to live on a dollar a week. We slept in horse stables behind the horses. I did all kinds of things then. I went to the Indian territory, where I pretended to be a big wise white man. It so happened that sometimes I really predicted the future." With the war, he said, "I organized parties for the army, and that's how I got into the world of show business. . . . I've been a dogcatcher, and I sold hot dogs. But I didn't want you to know all the things that I did."

It was Dutch journalist Dirk Vellenga's theory that Ad concocted this weird mélange in order to purposefully confuse the reader. "From the beginning," said Ad Jr., "it was clear that my father wanted to protect the Colonel and not give any trouble. He had a fear perhaps that there could be problems for the Colonel if he were too bold with [his] answers and articles, and so he was very careful about [his] position." The very ridiculousness of the story was the reason "no magazine or newspaper picked it up," wrote Vellenga, who came to Breda in 1973, at age twenty-six, to work for the newspaper *De Stem,* and would go on to do much of the pioneering research into Andre van Kuijk's early life and origins. If anyone even thought about digging any further, Vellenga said, they gave up "after a meaningless conversation with Ad van Kuijk, who stated that he wanted to forget the whole thing." And so, as hard as it may be to believe in this hyperconnected age, while everyone in the Netherlands was well aware of the true identity of Colonel Tom Parker, the rest of the world remained blissfully unaware.

It was Ad Jr.'s abiding suspicion, and Colonel's widow Loanne's firm belief, that Colonel continued for many years to send money to his brother through the van Kuyks. But Ad Sr. seemed to take any sums he received not as money intended for the family but as funds specifically meant to help him out in his various business ventures. The rest of the family, who never learned of the money, was split in their feelings, though not in their belief that they were being lied to by their brother. But in a family that had never had any cohesion to begin with and was now scattered across the country, there was no real impetus for dealing with either Ad or Dries, and, despite his sisters' fond recollections of their mischievous little brother, the family as a whole seemed stuck in a permanent state of disgruntled disinterest.

Ad Sr. intimated to his son that Dries had made three promises to him, but his father never shared with him what they were. One of them, Ad Jr. believed, was a commitment to help his father move to America, but that never came to pass because his mother, who had always been her son's principal defender and, besides that, had no interest in emigrating herself, put her foot down. She was not about to see their only child leave his university studies in Utrecht, she said, when he was so close to achieving his baccalaureate degree. Which in fact he did and went on to teach high-school German very happily for the next thirty-nine years. Ad Jr. never found out what the other two promises were (though one might surmise they had something to do with money), because, as he observed, his father was not in the habit of sharing confidences with anyone.

As for Colonel, he was more committed than ever to working out a plan for Elvis to return to live performance. But first he had to fulfill all their film commitments. After completing *Blue Hawaii,* which would turn out to be the biggest box-office hit of his career, Elvis went on to make two movies in rapid succession for United Artists at a salary of $600,000 apiece plus 50 percent of the profits. He next completed another film for Hal Wallis, once again set in Hawaii, in early May of 1962, and started on the first of the four films in the new MGM contract four months later. By then, though, Colonel had worked out a plan for entirely revamping Elvis' career.

The idea was for RCA to finance a tour in which Elvis would appear in forty-three cities under the sponsorship of RCA's forty-three distributors, with a press conference in each city and a guaranteed overall payment of over $1 million. The tour would be under the aegis and sole direction of Colonel's umbrella company, All Star Shows, and to prove his good faith Colonel even put off a second MGM picture till the following year in order to have two months free and clear for touring.

The talks went on for some time, but then, it seemed, RCA got cold feet — perhaps it was simply that they were not in the touring business — and Colonel wasn't interested in their proposal to scale the number of dates down to eleven for a flat $500,000. It wasn't worth doing if it wasn't going to be done right, Colonel said, and if RCA lacked the nerve to back what would undoubtedly have been one of the Biggest Tours in Show Business History, it was better to wait. He was sure other opportunities would come along.

They never did — at least not for another seven years, when Colonel made another million-dollar deal, this time with the International Hotel in Las Vegas, which agreed to pay Elvis $125,000 a week for eight weeks' work in 1969 and 1970. And subsequently Elvis did return to touring for the last seven years of his life. But after Ad van Kuijk's visit in 1961, there was, for whatever reason, whether judiciously considered or out of a newly reawakened sense of caution, no more talk of a world tour.

PART III

....

SUSPICIOUS MINDS

....

FOURTEEN

Lateral Thinking

T HERE'S A LOT MORE to the rest of the story, obviously. There were a lot of deals, there were triumphs and failures, and an unimaginable amount of money was made, but this is intended as an introduction to Colonel, primarily in his own words. For more details on the business of Elvis, the intricacies of the negotiations, the staggering sums that were at stake, and the ways in which the money was spent, you can check out any number of sources, including the second volume of my Elvis Presley biography, *Careless Love*, where this all gets plenty of attention.

Suffice it to say that with the spectacular success of *Blue Hawaii* (it was the fourteenth-highest-grossing film of 1961, though it was released in November, and by the end of 1962 it had earned a profit of $2.7 million), the die was cast. As Colonel summed it up for *Variety* in January 1964, Elvis had made fifteen pictures (amounting to eleven films since his army discharge in March of 1960), and they had earned $75 million in box-office receipts to date. His film salaries for the last year alone added up to $1.5 million, with "50% of [the] films' profits due on top of that figure."

As to the quality of the films, the Colonel was always happy to volunteer that once the deal was made, the studio took over. After all, "What do I know about production? Nothing." As far as winning an Oscar went, Colonel had a similarly disingenuous response. If anyone came to him looking for Elvis to take a salary reduction because of the Oscar-worthiness of their picture, all they had to do was to pay him his regular salary up front, and if Elvis won an Oscar, Colonel would be more than happy to refund the money. There had been, Colonel added, no takers to date — and unlikely to be any. "We don't have approval on scripts," Colonel con-

Colonel and Hal Wallis in paper hats that Colonel had specially manufactured for promotion purposes, with a display celebrating the release of G. I. Blues, fall 1960. *Courtesy of the Graceland Archives*

tinued on this theme, "only money. Anyway, what's Elvis need? A couple of songs, a little story and some nice people with him."

It was, as usual, a bravura performance, but you will notice, there's no talk of lofty cinematic goals, there's no mention of Marlon Brando or James Dean, or any of the other actors Elvis admired, as there always had been at the start (and long past the start, in Colonel's correspondence about future projects). Nor is there any acknowledgment of the commercial failure of the two serious, nonsinging pictures that Elvis did for 20th Century Fox (*Flaming Star* and *Wild in the Country*) in between Hal Wallis' *G. I. Blues* and *Blue Hawaii*—which undoubtedly had something to do with the choices made. Instead, *Variety* simply took Colonel's carefully calculated portrait of self-regard at face value, quoting his mantra,

"Look, you got a product, you sell it," as if there were not even a smidgen of irony in it. And to his evident delight, nearly everyone else bought the pitch: this was Colonel Parker, the self-proclaimed carnival barker with a host of good stories, who told more than one reporter with relish (and with even greater relish for the way in which they in turn capitalized on the carefully constructed image), "The [Hollywood] big shots are afraid to be seen with me. Saves a whole lot of time."

Now and then a reporter chose to look past his rube-in-Hollywood act — his old pal in Tampa, Paul Wilder, for one, and, later, Elvis biographer Jerry Hopkins — and that seemed to delight him even more. "The Colonel," Hopkins wrote in the '70s, "projected an image of cornpone simplicity," but that was simply "camouflage." The Colonel, according to Hopkins, had developed a process of illogical "lateral" thinking which could be compared to that of Maltese philosopher Edward de Bono, even if Colonel's philosophy, perhaps best expressed in the literature of the Snowmen's League of America, came first. "Lateral thinking," as Hopkins explained it, involved "pattern-switching," or approaching a problem indirectly and then doing something so entirely unexpected, or even outrageous, that it generated both laughter and reassessment, in either order. And what could be more Colonel than that?

In 1961, Colonel made his one and only stab at developing a movie of his own. He had always said, from the time he first went out with Ernest Tubb in pre-Eddy Arnold days (this was the tour on which, in addition to serving as road manager, he had forged an onstage role for himself as a country comedian), that he wanted to make his mark in Hollywood — and indeed he could certainly be said to have done that. But now, beyond merely guiding his artist's career, he sought to acquire the film rights to naturalist Joy Adamson's current number-one bestseller, *Born Free,* which told the story of how she and her husband had raised a lion cub named Elsa after Elsa's mother was killed. Though Colonel's reading habits were generally limited to informational nonfiction and the trades, his deep love of animals had never waned, and through William Morris he made a modest offer for the book. Adamson's publisher responded that a number of leading film companies had been in touch with higher offers, but they would still like to know just what Colonel Parker had in mind. But that was the end of it. Colonel simply withdrew, suggesting meekly that he did not have the wherewithal to compete with the major studios

Celebrating his fifty-first birthday two or three days early on the set of *G. I. Blues,* June 23 or 24, 1960, with Marie by his side, Elvis in uniform, Nick Adams in his Johnny Yuma–*Rebel* hat (left), and Hal Wallis peering over Colonel's shoulder. *Courtesy of the Graceland Archive*

in rendering the "authenticity" that such a picture surely deserved. And so we will never know what Colonel might have made of this opportunity, just as we will never know what might have happened if Hal Wallis had taken him up on his offer of a screenwriting collaboration that would create for Elvis more "rugged" roles. But then both were well outside his area of expertise, and as one of his close friends (like all of his close friends a keen admirer of Colonel's acumen) observed, "He wouldn't play a game he didn't know how to win."

He did, however, continue to freely dispense advice, both business and personal, and do everything he could to advance the careers of young protégés like Tommy Sands, actor Nick Adams (in addition to helping get Adams his starring role in the television series *The Rebel,* he was godfather to Adams' daughter, Allyson), and, most recently, screen newcomer George Hamilton. For the twenty-one-year-old Hamilton, who came to him looking for guidance after costarring in *Home from the Hill* with Robert Mitchum (a publicist at MGM told Hamilton that the Colonel

With George Hamilton,
fall 1963. *Courtesy of the
Graceland Archives*

was the one man who could steer him through the Hollywood labyrinth),
it was a personal connection that would come to mean as m ich to him
as any other friendship in his life. (Some years later, Colonel would serve
as best man at his wedding.)

It was clear from the start that Colonel liked Hamilton, but he couldn't
really give him any advice, he said, because that would mean taking away
from his managerial obligations to Elvis. (Hamilton was never sure
whether he meant time or money, or neither.) But he could offer the
young man an opportunity. He had a thousand little papier-mâché elephants, and all Hamilton had to do was to pay him $1,000 for the ele-
phants and they would have a deal. Hamilton scratched his head — it was
going to be hard for him to come up with $1,000, and he couldn't under-
stand how this was going to work to his advantage — but he made the deal,
and when he came back to Colonel after selling all the elephants, it was
perfectly evident that he had passed the test.

It was Colonel who got him the lead in MGM's *Your Cheatin' Heart*,
the life story of country music legend Hank Williams, a couple of years

later, and, although he turned elsewhere in Hollywood trying to understand this business he had entered without plan or preparation (George Hamilton, as anyone who knows his work will surely be aware, is nothing if not a man-about-town), it was Colonel alone who gave him useful information, knowledgeable insights, and irrefutably wise counsel. As Hamilton saw it, "The Colonel always had a joke and a punch line which kind of framed him up," but once you proved yourself to him, Colonel never doubted your intentions, though he might very well question your judgment.

"I don't think he ever trusted anybody fully," said Hamilton, who possessed a rare gift for reading between the lines of Colonel's aphorisms. Even his most fantastical stories, Hamilton was certain, pointed to some deep-seated absence in his life. The very act of helping you out, he came to realize, was tantamount to his adopting you into a family whose other members you might never meet but who, like him, were all a cherished part of Colonel's self-created world.

Allegiance to, and from, the Colonel was uncompromising. "Whatever he wanted, you better commit to do—yes, like the elephants! He would give you things to do and see if you would vary from them. And I never did. I knew that if I ever needed [anything], he would give it to me. But I would never ask." In the end, Hamilton said, the greatest lesson he took from Colonel might seem surprising to those who knew him only for his easygoing debonair manner. "I learn[ed] to be a loner. People always thought I had a lot of friends, but the truth of the matter was, I had a lot of acquaintances but I never depended on any of them, not one of them. That taught me strength. And I to this day don't depend on anybody. The Colonel taught me that. Now, is that good? I don't know. It was a survival technique. But the Colonel taught me to depend on myself and to figure it out. And to make sure that the person you're with is someone you want to saddle up with; otherwise don't be near them."

E LVIS, who had absorbed many of the same lessons from his mentor over the years, had reached what could only be called a point of stasis in his movie career. As Colonel proclaimed, his artist's movies had only continued to grow in commercial success, which one might imagine should have given him the power to call whatever shots he liked. Instead, he just seemed to walk through his roles — whether as a race-car driver, the skipper of a fishing boat, a bush pilot, or a glorified beach boy — with an indifferent professionalism, delivering his lines almost as if he were in a hurry to get rid of them. As he said in later years, with what appeared to be a curious lack of interest in either taking or assigning blame, "I don't think anyone was consciously trying to harm me. It was just Hollywood's image of me was wrong, and I knew it, and I couldn't say anything about it, couldn't do anything about it. . . . I had thought that they would give me a chance to show some kind of acting ability or do a very interesting story, but it did not change, it did not change, and so I became very discouraged. They couldn't have paid me no amount of money in the world to make me feel self-satisfaction inside."

On the other hand, the studio recordings that he made independent of the movie soundtracks not only continued to provide that satisfaction but set some of the most ambitious goals of his recording career. In the immediate aftermath of recording *Elvis Is Back!*, as fully realized and thought-out an album as he ever made, he recorded an exquisite gospel album in the fall of 1961 and for the next two and one half years continued to produce music of rare beauty and aspiration. He looked for songs to expand both his range and repertoire and found them in the ballads of songwriter Don Robertson and the songwriting team of Doc Pomus and Mort Shuman as well as the Italianate arias to which he had always been drawn. He seemed to be seeking to forge a new artistic identity composed of equal parts bravado (the arias) and vulnerability (the utterly naked, painfully wounded fragility of many of the ballads). His very willingness to put his name on two songs, including "That's Someone You Never Forget," which could be interpreted from its delivery as a brokenhearted tribute to his mother, might have seemed to an outside observer evidence of a barely cloaked desire to reveal himself.

It should also be noted that what could very well be taken as the pinnacle of his movie career (though I understand there will be a lot of disagreement with me on this point) came in a dream sequence inserted into the splashy big-budget (Colonel argued vociferously that it was way *over* budget), big-production extravaganza with explosive screen newcomer Ann-Margret, *Viva Las Vegas*. The musical theme for the sequence was the deeply romantic Pomus-Shuman ballad "I Need Somebody to Lean On," and it provides the most telling moment in the picture, if one of its most atypical ones, as the Elvis character, troubled over the failure of his relationship with his cinematic and real-life love interest, Ann-Margret, wanders in a kind of meditative fugue and the song becomes his inner voice. It is his purest acting in the entire film, as we see him in an overhead spotlight shot, singing with a quiet sincerity that belies the surface charm of the rest of the show. One can only imagine the satisfaction that Elvis must have felt as words, music, and image all come together for once.

But that was a rare, if not unique, movie moment. And I think even Colonel realized that his artist could use more of a challenge — they both could — but somehow his inner voice, the extraordinary intuition that had always served him so well, failed him now. Maybe it was the pressure of keeping up the almost unstoppable march of success, maybe it was nothing more than the enveloping comfort of that success, but he was simply unable to come up with a sufficiently engaging solution for them both.

Colonel tried to break the all-too-predictable cycle when he canceled the second MGM movie of 1962 in anticipation of the forty-three-city tour that he believed RCA had signed on to — but then when that fell through, they went on to make *Fun in Acapulco* (shot entirely in Hollywood at Colonel's insistence) for Hal Wallis.

And so they continued to pursue the path of least resistance, each in his own way, these two men who had believed so fervently for so many years not just in themselves but in each other. And, seemingly, both did everything they could to blind themselves to the change.

FIFTEEN

The Jewels in the Desert

IT WAS AT THIS POINT that Colonel retreated to the desert.

He had started going out to Palm Springs at Abe Lastfogel's invitation in the late '50s. They stayed at the Spa Hotel, where Abe and his wife Frances, lifelong hotel residents, kept a permanent suite, and he and Abe would enjoy the steam room, the hotter the better, every Saturday morning.

Then Abe suggested, Why not have a place of his own? It would probably be good for Marie, too, who was suffering more and more from a multitude of maladies. William Morris owned some properties in Palm Springs, Abe said, and Colonel could just be installed in one of them, a modest house on Regal Drive, as a kind of permanent resident. Not long afterward, Abe "loaned" him another, more suitable William Morris–owned property, a comfortable, streamlined home on Vista Vespero, with three bedrooms and three baths, and there Colonel remained, while continuing to maintain his principal residence at the Beverly-Comstock in Los Angeles, also a William Morris property.

Colonel took great pleasure, and great pride, in his new home, just as he did in the meticulously maintained property in Madison. He loved the informality of his new life. He loved the hot, dry desert air and watching the sun come up every morning with Marie's cat, Midnight, by his side. Sometimes he would just sit out on the patio by the pool in his bathing suit for much of the day, reading the newspapers and the trades and puffing contentedly on his cigar. He swam at least once a day—he was a surprisingly graceful swimmer, and it eased the constant back pain which he always said dated back to carnival days but which his doctor suggested might abate (along with his ongoing heart problems) if he would just try to lose some weight.

Celebrating Abe Lastfogel's birthday, Colonel-style. *Courtesy of the Graceland Archives*

Marie seemed to be doing a little better. She had her cats and a new collection of cat figurines, she enjoyed playing the piano, and sometimes she would even play for visitors. But she remained easy to rile, and everyone who visited was expected to play Yahtzee with her and pretend not to notice her constant cheating. Colonel never played himself, he just watched the goings-on with what could only be described as a patient, inscrutable expression.

He didn't spend much time indoors—that was Marie's plastic-wrapped domain. He put all of his energy, and much of his imagination, into the ever-expanding area around the pool, which would soon come to include a fifteen-foot-wide by six-foot-high barbecue setup built of desert rock, with built-in ovens, grills, a sink, and assorted other appurtenances. Before long, he added a walk-in freezer, a wet sauna, an enclosed whirlpool, and a small steam room. There was a little rock waterfall garden

Colonel's office at 20th Century Fox. The office could be dismantled and moved to another studio for Elvis' next picture at the drop of a hat. *Courtesy of the Graceland Archives*

with a miniature Dutch windmill, another windmill on top of a white trellis, and an assortment of elephant figures composed of every material and of every dimension. There were times he could content himself with puttering around in his own private realm for days on end, and if he didn't have anything better to do, he would busy himself organizing and rearranging the contents of Marie's refrigerator, taking out every item of food and carefully inventorying it before putting everything back in a new, more carefully considered order. She would survey the process wordlessly, but sometimes when he was out of earshot, she would say to a friend, "I wish he'd stay out of my refrigerator. I can't find a damn thing."

It might have seemed like a kind of well-earned retirement to some, a welcome respite from the whirlwind of activity that had engulfed him for the last fifteen years, but Colonel would surely have bridled at the thought. It could not be said that he wasn't working as hard as ever — that he wasn't putting together as many deals, some of them negotiated in the steam room of the Spa Hotel, where, he chuckled to Abe Lastfogel, if you turned the heat up high enough, they would always give in. But no matter how many needling letters he wrote to RCA just to make sure they were on the ball, no matter how much time he spent making improvements to his new home or busily revamping his offices at the various movie studios, extravagant installations memorializing a life spent in show business (just try to imagine all the Elvis trinkets, stuffed animals, balloons, pennants, and assorted memorabilia surrounded by dozens of blown-up photographs in no discernible order or mood), they could scarcely substitute for the life itself. It was almost as if all his imaginative powers were being employed to create a collage of pictures and objects that only he could fully decipher, an ever-shifting display meant to suggest some of the crazy life force that had always animated him, and that was still very much alive in him. There's no doubt in my mind that Colonel was as capable as ever of amusing himself with these and other similar distractions. But it leads me to wonder (and I have no pat answers, honest): what exactly was he distracting himself from?

H E BEGAN to set up meetings with Elvis in Palm Springs. Elvis at first took the attitude that this desert retreat was strictly for old people and he would only stay briefly, at most overnight, at the Spa, simply to satisfy his manager's whims. But he soon came to realize that Palm Springs could be a retreat for him as well, where no one concerned themselves with his comings and goings and he could fly girls in and out without anyone taking notice. Before long he leased a house for himself, not too far from Colonel's but far enough to ensure a suitable amount of privacy.

They both began to visit Las Vegas with increasing frequency at around this time. Not together, at least not as traveling companions, but not coincidentally either. Each enjoyed Las Vegas in his own way. For Elvis it was a kind of twenty-four-hour playground in which time had no

Elvis celebrates his twenty-seventh birthday at the Hotel Sahara in Las Vegas, with Sahara owner Milton Prell, January 8, 1962. *Courtesy of the Graceland Archives*

meaning and he had no obligations. And while Colonel was confident that Elvis could take care of himself, especially with his newly appointed coterie-of-friends-and-relations team foreman, Marty Lacker, happy to report directly to Colonel on anything that was going on (unlike longtime head Joe Esposito, who had been temporarily deposed), he could feel doubly assured that everything was under control. He knew, too, that he could always rely on his old friend, Milton Prell, owner of the Sahara casino and hotel (known for many years as the "Jewel of the Desert") where both Elvis and Colonel stayed, to let him know if anything were to be amiss. He had first met Prell when Eddy Arnold played the Sahara in 1953, not long after it opened, and Milton always looked out for them both, even throwing Elvis a lavish twenty-seventh birthday party when he and his guys were all holed up there in January of 1962.

But Colonel's Las Vegas was very different from Elvis' Las Vegas. Because little as he might have looked like one (to take on any of the flamboyance of the city's outer trappings would have been a clear violation of his mordant sense of wit), Colonel was a *player*. And he was drawn to the city's action in the same way that he had always been drawn to the high-stakes financial games he played with high-priced attorneys and corporate executives alike. For all of his show of unassailable confidence, maybe *because of* it, Colonel had never been afraid to lose. Take it or leave it, he had never been afraid to walk away from the game.

Elvis and Colonel with Lynda Bird Johnson and George Hamilton, on the set of *Spinout,* spring 1966. *Courtesy of the Graceland Archives*

"He had this need to get to Las Vegas," said George Hamilton, though he never fully understood why. It was never "with the object, I'm going to gamble. It was always he was going to do something else. But then he would get me to play roulette or craps with him — and he was an amazing player. I knew about Monte Carlo and places like that, because I'd gone there a few times, but I'd never seen this kind of gambling. The Colonel knew all the hard ways and odds and everything — but it didn't matter. [Because] he played every number. I mean, how could you win if you played every number? I just — it was just bigger than life. I'd never seen anything like it. I'd seen a lot of movie stars, but I never saw anybody play the way he did."

He never risked too much, and he never lost too much. He was confident that he knew exactly how much he could afford to lose and still maintain the cash reserve that he would need to have on hand if Marie's health were to worsen badly. But if anyone should ever remonstrate with him on the subject, he would just flare up. It was his money, he had earned it, he would assert angrily, and he had the right to do with it whatever he chose.

SIXTEEN

The Magician

ELVIS MET LARRY GELLER at four o'clock in the afternoon on April 30, 1964.

Geller, a twenty-four-year-old hairdresser at Jay Sebring's fashionable salon, arrived on Elvis' doorstep as a substitute for his regular hairdresser, who had just quit. For the first hour or so the talk was little more than polite conversation. Then, as Larry finished spraying and shaping his hair, Elvis suddenly turned to him and said, "Larry, let me ask you something. . . . What are you into?"

Geller, who had devoted himself seriously to spiritual studies for the last four years, had no doubt that there was something out of the ordinary in the question and didn't hesitate in his response. "I said to him, 'Obviously, I do hair, but what I'm really more interested in than anything else is trying to discover things like where we come from, why we are here, and where we are going.' As I'm saying this, I'm thinking he might think I'm some kind of a kook, but while I was talking, I noticed that Elvis' eyes were lighting up. He said, 'Man, just keep talking, just keep talking.'"

After that, it could be said, everything changed.

It's a complicated story, and I don't mean to diminish it in any way by shortchanging its importance in Elvis' life. But for the purposes of this narrative, it should be sufficient to say that Elvis' spiritual education filled a deep emotional need for him, a void left by the devastating death of his mother six years earlier. The meeting with Larry Geller brought about an almost immediate shift in Elvis' life and interests. Right away he started reading books like *Autobiography of a Yogi* and *The Impersonal Life*, studying the works of Gurdjieff and Madame Blavatsky — he was, as Larry Geller observed, like a man dying of thirst in the desert, "requesting

With Elvis and Larry Geller, 1966. *Courtesy of the Graceland Archives* a new book almost every other day. . . . It was never enough for him to simply read a book; he had to absorb it, think about it, question it, link its thoughts and ideas with all he had read before and things he had heard people say. Elvis dog-eared pages, highlighted passages, and jotted notes and questions on the endpapers and throughout the margins." It commanded his attention day and night, it became the centerpiece in all his conversations with the guys, who were by now almost universally referred to as his "Memphis Mafia."

And he didn't go into the recording studio for anything but soundtrack recordings (and sometimes not even for those) for the next two years.

N OW, MANY REASONS have been advanced for this. All, I believe, with the utmost sincerity.

The most popular (both the most emphatic and the most empathetic) is that this was Elvis' rebellion against what had become the stultifying sameness of all his movie roles, the complete absence of any sort of creative challenge. In this scenario the Colonel is cast as the villain, and Elvis as the Promethean figure seeking to throw off his chains. And, again, I don't mean in any way to downplay Elvis' frustrations or intentions. But, it must be remembered, it wasn't the movies that Elvis gave up (which, not coincidentally, delivered over $3 million in his two-year absence from the recording studio); it was the music. And I would suggest that it was not so much the movies' lack of creative sustenance as his own almost total absorption in his spiritual studies that kept Elvis away from what had been the one driving force of his life ever since he was a small child.

For Elvis this was a time of great excitement, exhilaration, and discovery. He reported for work at the studio each day, knew all his lines, and delivered them in his customary manner. But it was obvious to everyone he couldn't wait to get off the set as soon as possible, just so he could go back to his texts. As Larry Geller said with customary acuity, "For Elvis, reading wasn't a passive activity; each book promised a new adventure, a new way of viewing things." And he did everything he could to get everyone around him equally involved in his new passion.

For the guys it was alternatingly frustrating and bewildering to various degrees. For one or two of them it was a source of genuine excitement.

But most took to mocking Larry openly, referring to him as the Swami or Rasputin or the Brain Scrambler and making cracks to his face as well as behind his back. Looking back on it, Elvis' then nineteen-year-old fiancée Priscilla Beaulieu summed up best how great a change this represented in all of their lives.

"Larry was a total threat to us all. He would spend hours and hours and hours with Elvis, just talking to him, and he wasn't anything that Elvis represented; he didn't represent anything that Elvis had believed in prior to that time. Everyone wondered who he was, what he was doing there, what they talked about. When I first met him, I thought, Well, he's not so bad, he's really harmless. But then Elvis went the other way and became harmless, unthreatening, energyless — he became passive. Which was the total opposite of what he had been before. He read books studiously for hours and hours. He had conversations with Larry for hours and hours — he was going on a search for why we were here and who we were, the purpose of life; he was on a search with Larry to try to find it. You know, Larry would bring him books, books, books, piles of books. And Elvis would lay in bed at night and read them to me. That was the thing when you dealt with Elvis: if he had a passion for something, you had to go into it with him and show the same love he had for it. Or at least you had to pretend to."

Colonel would certainly have agreed. Whether rightly or wrongly, he saw Larry as a charlatan. More to the point, like Priscilla, he saw him as a threat, one who had driven a wedge between artist and manager in a way that no challenge or crisis in their nearly ten years together had been able to. And he had created a situation in which, with record sales sharply falling and the record company constantly on Colonel's back, he was not even able to get his artist to fulfill his contractual obligations.

And yet, almost unimaginably, he could not broach the matter directly for fear of risking an irreparable break. And so, for the time being, he kept his own counsel. But not so much that Larry was under any illusions about what Colonel thought of him. One time, he wrote in a memoir, he went to the Spa Hotel in Palm Springs for a steam bath, and the woman who collected the steam-room fees registered instant recognition. "'Oh, you're Larry Geller!' she exclaimed, as if she had been looking for me. 'Yeah,' I answered, confused. 'I heard about you,' she said. 'I understand that you're a magician. Colonel Parker told me so.'"

IT SHOULD PERHAPS come as no surprise that Colonel's initial solution to this problem took the form of a business deal.

The most immediate crisis that needed to be dealt with was that Elvis was seriously in arrears on the recordings that he owed to RCA, and RCA, by virtue of Colonel's strict policy of never giving them anything more than what they absolutely needed at the moment, had virtually nothing left in their vaults. With Bill Bullock retired and Steve Sholes sidelined by corporate politics, Colonel's dealings with RCA over the last couple of years had been minimal, coming down to little more than gags and complaints. But in the summer of 1965, with record sales at an all-time low and movie contracts only certain (though very profitably certain) for another two years, he entered into negotiations with Bullock's successor, Harry Jenkins, to improve and extend the 1962 agreement.

As usual, the new agreement, which was concluded on September 21, came in the form of a brief, barely four-page letter to Elvis, which, though permeated with the usual combination of idiosyncratic angles and hard-to-decipher consequences, fundamentally stood as just one more modification of the original 1956 contract. But while on the surface the letter merely provided a one-year extension of the present agreement, through 1972, with an additional two-year option on his services, the financial benefits for both artist and manager were extraordinary.

To begin with, RCA would raise its guaranteed annual payments from $200,000 to $300,000 (since there was currently about $1 million owed in back royalties, the total would come to $2.1 million in guaranteed payments over the next seven years, with only $1.1 million left to be recouped), with all of these contractual payments split 75–25 between artist and manager. RCA would in addition pay out a $300,000 nonrecoupable bonus, to be split 50–50 between Elvis and All Star Shows (the Colonel), along with an additional $25,000 bonus to each party on January 1, 1966. The basic 5 percent artist royalty arrangement that had been established with the original 1956 contract remained in place; these royalties went against the $1.1 million that had to be recouped. The "bonus" royalties, on the other hand (2 percent domestic, 1 percent foreign, which Colonel had first negotiated at a slightly lower rate in 1960 and which were split 50–50 because of their definition as special payments outside the scope of the regular contract), were free of encumbrance and were to be paid out, no matter how much in arrears Elvis' recoupments might be. Finally, the $27,000 annual payment that RCA had made to the Colonel since March 1, 1960, for consultation, promotion, licensing of photographs, and general counsel and advice, was upgraded to $30,000, with all arrangements explicitly acknowledged and signed off on by Elvis.

It was all in all a remarkable contractual upgrading for an artist whose record sales had declined by about 40 percent since 1960 — and for his manager.

But what was most important about the agreement, as was so often the case with Colonel's intricately woven negotiations, was something that was not written down or otherwise memorialized in the agreement itself. In concert with Harry Jenkins, Colonel had enthusiastically embraced the idea (and I have little doubt whose idea it was) that Elvis would, in Jenkins' words, deliver "two good new singles, possibly more important one new Christmas single, [and] a complete brand-new religious album" the following year — and Jenkins hoped very much it would be *early* in the following year. The key to it all from Colonel's point of view was the religious album. As always, he had advocated strongly for the Christmas single because of his belief in the perennial appeal of seasonal recordings — but it was the gospel album that Colonel felt, both from experience and in light of Elvis' current dedication to spiritual matters, that would be indispensable to getting Elvis motivated again.

By early 1966 his instinct proved right, as Elvis threw himself into preparations for the new recordings. Red West, his friend since high school, who in addition to serving as Elvis' double in fight and action scenes, had found acting work in Hollywood and started writing songs himself, had recently bought a second tape recorder to better demo his songs, and he and Elvis' army buddy Charlie Hodge started taping songs that they thought Elvis might be drawn to — and not just gospel songs either. Soon the three of them started recording some of those songs in three-part harmony, with Elvis as often as not taking the bass part on gospel songs, Hawaiian numbers, and Western classics like the Sons of the Pioneers' "Tumbling Tumbleweeds" or "Cool Water." It was akin, really, to a renewal of the soul; just rediscovering the joy of singing led Elvis to further expand his listening tastes, which in turn motivated him to undertake greater vocal challenges. He listened to Caruso, Mario Lanza, and Hank Williams; Judy Garland, Aretha Franklin, and Odetta singing an album of Bob Dylan songs; Peter, Paul & Mary and the Rolling

Stones. He grew so consumed with admiration for Jimmy Jones, the great bass lead for the Black gospel quartet the Harmonizing Four, that he announced to Colonel that he needed to have Jones, who appeared to have left the gospel scene for parts unknown, on his session, and Colonel had Tom Diskin and Freddy Bienstock institute a search. (They were unable to locate Jones, despite diligent efforts.)

In the meantime, Harry Jenkins was getting more and more nervous and started prodding Colonel as February turned into March, March into April, and they still did not have a recording date. These were the kinds of letters that in the past Colonel might have written to the company. They reminded him of his obligations, and under any other circumstances he would certainly have blown up at the unwonted presumptuousness of their tone. But he put up with Jenkins' nagging reminders with remarkable equanimity, because he was convinced that until Elvis delivered, this was the only way the game could be played.

And then, when Elvis finally entered the studio on May 25, there was no longer any cause for concern.

The four-day session turned out to be one of the high points of Elvis' career. Not only did he deliver the seminal gospel album *How Great Thou Art,* one of the cornerstones of his latter-day reputation, he recorded four strong r&b tunes, a beautiful version of Bob Dylan's "Tomorrow Is a Long Time" that he had picked up from the Odetta album, and he even got to do an up-tempo duet with one of his childhood idols, Jake Hess, lead tenor for his all-time favorite gospel quartet, the Statesmen.

On the one hand, Colonel felt vindicated.

But not vindicated enough that he could feel any more at ease. Because his troubles with Elvis were hardly over. It was perfectly evident that Larry remained as immovable an obstacle as ever. And, in seeming contradiction to all of his newfound spiritual impulses, Elvis' spending was getting even more out of control.

There was a flood of letters from Vernon. They had bills due, they were overdrawn at the bank, he didn't know how they were going to make their quarterly tax payments. Somehow Colonel always came through, as often as not wheedling the money out of RCA for some new contractual demand or buried understanding—but at the same time neither he nor Vernon was able to make a dent in the overall problem. Because, no matter how much money Elvis made (and in 1964 his total income exceeded

$2 million, the equivalent of $20 million in 2024 dollars; by 1966 it was well over $3 million, with his tax rate stabilized at approximately 33 percent), he always managed to spend more. Nor did it have anything to do with the acquisition of wealth or property. In this respect he was like his manager, though, of course, their lifestyles were entirely different. Elvis seemed to simply enjoy *spending money,* whether it was on his friends, on the many worthy causes to which he, like his manager, sub-scribed, or on his own creature comforts. So, somewhere around this time, Colonel took to keeping $1 million in a regular savings account at the City National Bank that he would never touch, just in case things ever caught up with Elvis in the way that he and Vernon most feared.

It seems noteworthy, too, that for the first time he began to speak of retirement, though never in anything less than his usual kidding terms.

The world should not be surprised if he quit the fray before too long, Colonel declared to British music reporter Chris Hutchins, who detected a somewhat more chastened mood lurking beneath the rodomontade. "Sooner or later," he said, "someone else is going to have to take the reins." And he gave an interview to his friend James Kingsley at the *Memphis Commercial Appeal* in early 1966 which was apparently intended to reas-sure Kingsley, and the world at large, that reports that he was leaning toward withdrawing from the hurly-burly (even Sam Phillips had written to ask if Elvis' contract was for sale) were not to be believed. "Heck yes, I would retire, and so would my boy, Elvis — if we received enough money," he declared. "But if we retired, who in the heck would want us?" There were hundreds of people who depended on Elvis for their liveli-hood, he pointed out, as if speaking to a secret listener, for whom he appended a message that seemed even more explicit. "The bigger an attraction you become, the more responsibilities you face.... Elvis is big enough to bear up under [those] responsibilities ... and he also loves to work. I honestly believe that he will become one of the industry's great actors in the future."

It all seemed so by the book. But as it happened, Colonel was more serious than anyone knew.

For one thing his own health (heart, back, neck, his ever-increasing reliance on one or another from his assortment of decoratively embossed canes) seemed uncertain. Marie's was even worse. And, too, more and more of his longtime associates and contemporaries, like Bill Bullock, were retiring, whether by choice or not. But of greater concern, he confided to his second wife, Loanne, in later years, was that for the first time he was starting to become worried about "the instability of his artist." He had been on the verge, he told her, of letting Elvis know at this point that "he no longer wanted to manage him."

But he didn't.

Instead he made another deal.

In the fall of 1966, just eight or nine months after the last RCA contract went into effect, he began working on a new arrangement with both Elvis and RCA.

If they were going to go on like this, he told Loanne long after Elvis' death (if, in essence, he was going to be required to deliver an income for his artist that Elvis was always going to exceed, while in addition complaining to all and sundry that Colonel was forcing him to do things he no longer wanted to do), then he needed to change the terms of their engagement, and the nature of their business relationship would have to be recognized for what it was: a "joint venture" in which each of them had their separate tasks but to which they both contributed equally. In other words, a true partnership.

By the beginning of the new year, he had worked it out, and, after scrupulously explaining every aspect of the new arrangement to Elvis and Vernon, he sent it off to William Morris, RCA, and Elvis himself for signature.

This was the crux of the new deal:

To all intents and purposes, it extended the RCA contract that they already had by six more years, meaning, as Elvis cheerfully telegrammed RCA Operations Manager Norm Racusin, "it will be at least 1980 before there is a divorce." Elvis would continue to receive $300,000 a year against royalties for the next four years, with $225,000 to Elvis and $75,000 to Colonel, and there would very likely be bonus payments negotiated by Colonel from time to time on one pretext or another, which would (as always, since they were outside the contractual obligations) be split 50-50. But—and this was the catch—for the first time all royalties earned over the guaranteed amounts, or "flat payments," as they were termed in Colonel's explanatory letter to Elvis of January 2, were to be

On the *Roustabout* set, 1964. *Courtesy of the Graceland Archives*

treated as bonus payments as well and thus subject to the same 50-50 division between artist and manager.

Now, in some ways this might not seem like such a substantive change (after all, Elvis was still guaranteed a great deal of money, and there were elements of this understanding in previous deals), but it is not difficult to recognize the inherent dangers of this approach. There would always be the temptation to reduce the sum total of guaranteed payments and broaden the definition of just what were to be considered "bonus payments." And in fact the seeds of this approach were already contained in the new agreement, as the guaranteed annual advance against royalties was reduced from $300,00 to $200,000 after four years, and for the last five years of the contract (from 1976 through 1980) there were no guaranteed payments at all. But that was far in the future, and Elvis signed off on the new understanding with a flourish, telegramming Colonel from Memphis:

DEAR COLONEL. THE GREATEST SNOWMAN ON EARTH HAS CAUSED ANOTHER STORM. LOOKING FORWARD TO ANOTHER GREAT FORECAST FROM YOU RESPECTFULLY ELVIS

And, to be fair, Elvis' income never fell but only continued to grow and grow. And neither man ever chose to look back and label this moment as any kind of a benchmark in their relationship. But more and more I've come to wonder if things between them were ever really the same.

Everyone signed off on the deal. All the *i*'s were dotted, all the *t*'s crossed, and Colonel clearly felt that this represented a much fairer adjudication of each party's interests and the roles that each of them played. Elvis may well have, too. As Priscilla said, "Colonel basically [said], 'I work only for you. I have no other plans, and if you want me, you get all of me.' What could Elvis say to that? It was true, and he certainly wasn't going to sever the relationship after all those years and [all] that they'd accomplished together."

Colonel articulated his views without apology or equivocation over the years. Their relationship represented a unique confluence of forces. He was not just a one-artist manager, he was a one-man operation, who, rather than going out and hiring expensive outside firms, provided all services himself. He took care of all publicity, marketing, and record and concert promotion, in exchange for his managerial fee, 50 percent of which, he told *Variety* in 1964, perhaps just to make a point, went right back into Elvis' business. And that may well have been true.

And yet, for all his protestations it was clear that some part of him felt, if not guilty (and I don't think it was that), at least misunderstood. Throughout the years he continued to explain himself in uncharacteristically defensive fashion. As he said to me one time without prompting, just after the publication of my book *Last Train to Memphis* in 1994, which he assured me he had carefully reviewed, there was just one thing that bothered him (and it wasn't necessarily in the book): how many people still faulted him for what they mistakenly believed to be an across-the-board managerial fee of 50 percent. "I never took more than 25 percent from the movies, from the [publishing]," he said, "but I took 50 percent when Elvis and I did a joint venture." And then he went on to explain at considerable length, and in a manner which, while it was not inaccurate, seemed strangely prolix for this particular conversation, that this was the kind of manager he had always been: that unlike so many other managers (and he named some), who blithely collected their commissions on four or five different artists, none of whom they had any personal involvement with, he always went out with his artist personally, "I went into each town with my staff, set them all up, and then played them. And Elvis [always] got his guarantee, he got his expenses—he got his plane paid for, his hotel, his band, and anything we made over that, we split 50-50. And," he concluded, with what I would like to think was a twinkle in his eye, "he didn't [even] have to pay me a salary!"

HOWEVER PLEASED Elvis may or may not have been with the outcome of the RCA negotiations, it did not improve communications in the least. And there was no abatement in his spending.

In fact, if anything things got worse in that respect, as he discovered a new passion: horses to begin with, and then the dream of a ranch to go with them. And not just a ranch, but a kind of commune on which he and the guys could live together, ride together, work together, and study together.

It started with his going out to find a bay horse as a Christmas gift for Priscilla, but it was only days before he decided everybody, including

Colonel and Vernon go riding. *Courtesy of the Graceland Archives*

wives and girlfriends, should have a horse, too, and in one irrepressible burst after another the little house behind Graceland where Elvis' cousin Billy Smith and his family had once lived was bulldozed to make way for a riding ring, and the old barn, which hadn't been used in years, was completely renovated to accommodate its new population. "Elvis would go out in the barn every day and every night," said Marty Lacker, now co-foreman, with the return of longtime head Joe Esposito. "He fixed up a little office for himself and wrote the names of the horses on the stalls with a big red marking pen. He'd write notes to himself like 'What I'm Going to Buy Tomorrow' and 'What I'm Going to Do Tomorrow.' And he would clean up the barn and buy new tack. He just loved it."

Then one day, as he was returning from a horse-buying trip in Mississippi, Elvis spotted an immaculately maintained 160-acre cattle ranch called Twinkletown Farm, with a lighted sixty-five-foot-high white cross, just across the state line, and he purchased the property pretty much on the spot.

In no time he had bought more than two dozen vehicles, half a dozen house trailers, and six horse vans, along with tractors, miscellaneous ranch equipment, septic tanks and water lines, and a quarter mile of temporary plywood fencing which would have to serve until the $12,000 eight-foot-high wooden fence that he had contracted for could be built. In all he managed to pay out well over $100,000 in approximately two weeks, an orgy of spending that seemed to momentarily pacify Elvis but horrified Vernon, who complained to Colonel that he had been forced to put Graceland up as collateral for his son's purchases and he didn't know where it was going to end. According to Priscilla, who was no more sanguine than Vernon about Elvis' spendthrift ways but found it easier to act like a good sport: "Vernon literally begged him to stop, but Elvis said, 'I'm having fun, Daddy, for the first time in ages. I've got a hobby, something I look forward to getting up in the morning for.'"

Meanwhile, despite numerous attempts, Colonel had been unable to get in touch with him at all, even as the deadline for his arrival in California for the start of a new movie had passed — and then, after Colonel got the studio to agree to a week's postponement, he had to ask for another week when Elvis claimed to have saddle sores. "We have spent hundreds of dollars," Colonel wrote angrily to Marty Lacker, "on telephone calls [in] the last three weeks and have received practically no information whatsoever. This must stop." But it didn't. He heard little from Marty but, much more tellingly (and one would have to think insultingly), nothing at all from his artist.

Elvis finally showed up at the United Artists studio for costume fittings on March 6. Two nights later, in the early morning hours, he fell. He told Joe he had hit his head on the bathtub, and Joe called Colonel right away. Everyone assumed it was the pills and "medications" that Elvis had been taking in ever-increasing numbers (it had started with amphetamines issued in the army, but soon it was downers, too, and now other drugs that had been deemed a doorway to spiritual enlightenment), and after consulting with Elvis and getting a doctor to come out with portable X-ray equipment, without any preamble Colonel lit into them all. *What were they thinking?* he demanded. *What did they think their job was? Why did they let him get this way?* Someone was going to have to be with Elvis twenty-four hours a day—even if they had to go to the bathroom with him. From now on, he declared, things were going to be different.

Then, with Elvis just sitting there and not saying a word, he announced that there were going to be some more big changes. From now on they would not be going to Mr. Presley with their personal problems and concerns. If they had any concerns that needed to be addressed, they would take them to Mr. Esposito, who would once again be the sole person in charge. "Some of you," Colonel said, looking at Larry Geller, "think maybe he's Jesus Christ, who should wear robes and walk down the street helping people. But that's not who he is."

Shooting on the new film started up two weeks later under familiar enough auspices, but true to the Colonel's instructions Larry was no longer allowed to spend any time in private with Elvis. Haircutting sessions, once the occasion for grand philosophical discussions, were now limited to half-hour time periods that were strictly chaperoned. Hostility toward Larry reached new, undisguised heights, and Elvis didn't even bother to show his secret sympathy. "You know," he said to Larry one day out of the blue, "those masters of yours have hidden motives. They're trying to control people's minds and use them for their own damn purposes."

Less than two months later, Elvis and Priscilla were married.

This was something that Colonel had been advocating for strongly for nearly three years, ever since it became obvious that Priscilla, after arriving from Germany as a seventeen-year-old and moving permanently into Graceland, was here to stay. Elvis had promised her father, a career air force captain, that she would be chaperoned at all times and that someday she and Elvis would marry. That day had better come soon, Colonel had started to grumble, warning Elvis with increasing directness that this whole thing could blow up into a scandal they couldn't control, even if her father didn't force the issue by going to the newspapers, or the courts, with claims of bad faith and broken promises.

The ceremony took place in the private living quarters of Colonel's friend Milton Prell at the Aladdin Hotel, which Prell had recently purchased.

Colonel was in charge of all the arrangements. He told Elvis that it would be impossible for all of Elvis' guys to attend, given the confined space of Mr. Prell's suite, so invitations to the ceremony itself would have to be limited to Joe and Marty, who were, in a last-minute series of diplomatic maneuvers, his two best men, and his cousin Billy Smith. The others would just have to content themselves with the reception afterward in the spacious Aladdin Room. None of the guys had been informed beforehand, and none of them were happy, but with the exception of Red West, they all swallowed their pride and waited in their rooms to be called. Red hit the roof. He cursed Elvis up and down — he hadn't brought his wife out here to be humiliated like this, he shouted, and as for Colonel, he said, he would beat the shit out of that old sonofabitch if he so much as saw him.

But he didn't. He and his wife, Pat, stayed in their hotel room, until he was able to catch a flight back to Los Angeles.

"We were both so nervous," Priscilla said of the wedding. "I don't think either of us was aware of who was there and who was not. We hadn't slept all night long and were escorted into the room with the judge [Nevada Supreme Court justice David Zenoff, a friend of Prell's, who married them] and everyone already there. We should have had Red there. Elvis [later] agreed: that was not right. And he understood how Red felt. But never did he think it would not be forgiven. It was an oversight. Now, it could have been manipulative; I wouldn't put it past Colonel. And I think, too, from Red's point of view, this was a time when Elvis should have taken a stand. There were all those times he didn't as far as business was concerned. But this was personal. I think basically that's where Red was coming from. Elvis didn't take a stand."

SEVENTEEN

Reawakenings

ND THEN, for no readily discernible reason, it was as if the fog lifted. Elvis returned to the recording studio in late 1967, and then again in early 1968, and while the three r&b-oriented singles that came out of these sessions did not do particularly well on the charts, they clearly heralded a renewed sense of purpose.

Six months later, in June of 1968, he began work on the one-man NBC television special that has been widely branded as the "'68 Comeback Special" (a title to which Colonel strongly objected for its implication that Elvis had ever been away), though its actual title was, simply and sufficiently, *ELVIS*.

The way it came about was, once again, a matter of commercial serendipity. By the end of 1967 the movie deals had run out (Hal Wallis couldn't even get the Paramount studio to pay Colonel's promotion costs for their last picture together, instead paying $3,500 out of his own pocket), but he had been in touch with NBC's West Coast vice president Tom Sarnoff about doing something together for some time. Originally, in 1965, he had proposed a picture that NBC would finance and premiere domestically on the NBC network, then roll out in theatrical release throughout the rest of the world. By late 1967 he had come up with a scheme whereby NBC would get Elvis for his first television appearance in eight years, and in exchange the network would finance a motion picture which it could either produce itself or farm out to a mutually agreed-upon studio. The entire package would come in at the bargain price of $1,250,000 ($850,000 for the movie, plus an additional $25,000 for the music; a mere $250,000 for the special, with $125,000 reserved for a

"If you're looking for trouble": Elvis performing the opening number of the "'68 Comeback Special." *Courtesy of the Graceland Archives*

second showing). What this all meant, Colonel explained to Sarnoff, was that his client would be getting the $1 million that he long since demanded for him as a simple mark of respect, but NBC would be getting Elvis Presley at a steal.

Not surprisingly the original idea was for a Christmas special, a seasonal tie-in which, of course, always appealed to Colonel. In addition to all the other favorable financial benefits, in the formalization of the contract on January 16, 1968, Colonel ensured that ownership of all rights to the show would revert to Elvis after three years, with a maximum of three rebroadcasts at a rate of $125,000 per showing; then, several months later, almost as an afterthought, he got the network to agree to turn over all audiotapes free of charge to RCA for whatever use the record label chose to make of them.

Elvis was still busy finishing up *Live a Little, Love a Little,* his twenty-eighth picture, when Colonel met with Alfred di Scipio, vice president and artistic director for the show's sponsor, the Singer Company (no longer a sewing-machine-only concern), on May 8. At that meeting, according to a widely circulated memorandum, di Scipio with the full support of Bob Finkel, the NBC producer assigned to the show, "was able to convince Parker that the program ought not to be a purely Christmas oriented show but rather a program which would . . . tell the story of Presley as the initiator of a style of music which has become an integral part of our contemporary musical culture."

I imagine it took Colonel a moment or two to get used to the idea, but once he was assured that the show would continue to be a one-man special, and that at least one Christmas song would be retained, he never sounded a note of protest, and in the immediate aftermath of the meeting encouraged Finkel to speak directly about the new format to Elvis himself. A week later Finkel reported back, according to another intercompany memo, that he saw what he took to be a very encouraging endorsement of the show's new focus on Elvis' part, when Elvis made the "rather revealing statement . . . that he wants this show to depart completely from the pattern of his motion pictures and from everything else he has done." Which led Finkel to ask himself the question, "Who was I going to get to do it?" And within a week he had hired a talented young director named Steve Binder, who had recently formed a partnership with audio engineer Bones Howe. (Finkel had previously worked with

Colonel celebrates his fifty-ninth birthday on the '68 Special set with Steve Binder, Bob Finkel, and Elvis. *Courtesy of the Graceland Archives*

Binder on one or two projects, and Bones, he learned, had assistant-engineered some of Elvis' early West Coast recordings.)

They would be perfect, Finkel thought, and indeed they were.

I wouldn't bother going into such detail, except that I am well aware this is not the way the story is generally told. In most versions Colonel is portrayed as a villain, the bad guy who, for whatever reason (the reason generally cited is almost always control), fights ferociously throughout the production to keep Elvis from expressing himself in the manner that Elvis desperately desires. But if you keep reading (or if you simply take into account the dating of the memos), you will see that this is not the way it happened. Colonel was not just a willing but an enthusiastic collaborator — well, collaborator might be going too far, because he did not play any creative role in the show. But, according to the accounts of nearly every other participant, from Al di Scipio and Bob Finkel to Bones Howe, he was an enthusiastic *booster*.

Elvis, in any case, threw himself unreservedly into the show even before they got into the rehearsal studio in mid-June. When Steve Binder and Bones Howe brought the script to him for suggestions, they told him,

"We don't want you to like it one hundred percent"—but he did. And he spoke with depth and insight not just about the music but about the political situation in this country, too, about the devastation that he felt over Bobby Kennedy's and Martin Luther King's assassinations. And then, once rehearsals started, none of the guys could remember seeing him work so hard, none had seen him show a more uninhibited commitment to simply making music.

Colonel on the other hand simply amused himself. Bob Finkel, anticipating trouble, had given himself the assignment of keeping Colonel happy on the set (or at least distracted enough so that he didn't throw up any of the roadblocks for which he was famous). But there were no roadblocks, and Finkel was shocked at how much he was captivated by the other man's imperturbable charm and good humor. Colonel had commandeered the two William Morris agents assigned to him to dress up as Buckingham Palace guards, so Finkel in turn reinvented himself as Admiral Finkel, requisitioning a Lord Nelson outfit from the costume department and appearing in three-quarter-length breeches and tricornered hat.

At Colonel's insistence the two of them played a game called Honesty, in which Colonel thought of a number, Finkel put up $20, then tried to guess the number—and was, predictably enough, almost invariably wrong. Once or twice, just when Finkel figured he would never win, Colonel announced that he had finally guessed right and forked over $20 with a long face, but over the course of two weeks of rehearsals, the executive producer in charge of Colonel Parker calculated that he must have dropped close to $600. Finkel considered himself under ordinary circumstances a man of conventional sobriety, and he sometimes wondered at himself, and at the strange hold the Colonel seemed to have on him. "I did funny things—he would do things to me, and I would do them back to him. I went to him one day, and I said, 'Colonel, I'm going to beat you at these things. If I beat you and you admit it, I want your cane. I want to hang it up on my wall.' And he agreed." In the end, Finkel got to collect on the bet, but only when, after taping had been completed, he had the giant letters spelling out E-L-V-I-S on the show assembled on the lawn of Colonel's Palm Springs home. "I had the letters sent down with a generator, and when he got there, they were flashing. I have his cane on my wall today."

The gags were one thing. Elvis' engagement was another. "My boy likes you a lot," Colonel told Billy Goldenberg, the music director, who was being given a very hard time by the guys for what they judged to be his highfalutin ways. (You can interpret that any way you like.) "Is there anything you want me to do, to make it easier for you?" Colonel asked him. And he showed a genuine interest in Goldenberg ("He wanted to hear everything about my background, he'd say, 'Tell me about yourself. What's your life like? What do you want to do?'") that served effectively to accomplish that end. But most of all, without ever overtly admitting it, he was caught up in the carefree, unrestrained *enthusiasm* that his boy showed for every aspect of the show. It was a little like what he had witnessed at the USS *Arizona* benefit, that sense of sheer exultation that had overtaken Elvis onstage, which had in turn led Colonel to do everything in his power to set up a world tour at that time.

I have no record of whether or not he was present when Elvis performed the number that closed the show (he first recorded it in the studio, then performed a live vocal to the backing track), but no one could have missed the raw emotion that Elvis put into the song. It was called "If I Can Dream" and had been written at Steve Binder's request to suggest what he believed to be some of Elvis' deepest and most idealistic feelings. Under any other circumstances, it might have seemed like little more than a well-intentioned liberal statement about peace and brotherhood and universal understanding, but it is not the lyrics that command attention. It is, rather, the pain and conviction, the out-of-control abandon in Elvis' voice, as he sings of a world "where all my brothers walk hand in hand," then, in each of the recorded versions, almost screams out the last line: "Please / let my dream / come true / Right now."

There is no way of neatly summing up the meaning of the moment. But for Colonel, whether present or not, it provided a rare opportunity to simply bask in his boy's triumph. And to envision all the subsequent triumphs it might lead to.

Two days after the show's December 8 broadcast, he entered into talks with Kirk Kerkorian, owner of the still-under-construction International Hotel in Las Vegas, about an extended booking at what would become the city's largest showroom when it opened in July. Nine days later, despite a deluge of lucrative television offers, he accepted Kerkorian's proposal of $400,000 for four weeks, with an option for a second engagement in December and a most-favored-nation clause. It would be a challenge, he conceded to Elvis, who had just completed his next-to-last contracted film, but it was the kind of challenge from which neither one of them had ever shrunk. In fact, it was a clear-cut imperative, if only because *no one had ever done it before.*

Elvis in the meantime was just about to begin a historic series of recordings at Chips Moman's American Studios in Memphis. This had come about for a variety of reasons (among other things two of his guys were employed by the studio), but most of all, I would like to think, because Elvis was now committed to looking for musical challenges of his own. Everyone knew that Chips Moman, the thirty-one-year-old cofounder of Memphis' seminal r&b label, Stax, was a discerning-bordering-on-demanding music producer, with a string of over sixty recent pop and r&b hits over the last eighteen months and a stable of songwriters and musicians who came close to embodying the freewheel-ing, time-denying spirit of Sam Phillips' Sun Records. No one at Ameri-can, or at Sun for that matter, just went through the motions; working with Chips required passionate musical commitment. And that is exactly what Elvis gave, in what amounted to twelve days of lengthy sessions (up to ten or twelve hours a day) stretched out over more than a one-month period.

The result was music of uncommon feeling, forcefulness, nd beauty. Much like the 1960 *Elvis Is Back!* sessions, every song was sung with conviction and purpose (I feel a little guilty shortchanging you of any description of the hard-won process, but check out *Careless Love* for details), and it seemed incontrovertible that Elvis was once again caught up in nothing but the pure joy of making music.

And Colonel? Well, of course, Colonel wasn't there. He made no more of a musical contribution than he had to any of Elvis' earlier epochal musical achievements. That was not his job, he would have said (he *did* say over and over again, from the start). And he left it to Tom Diskin and Freddy Bienstock to haggle over the publishing arrangements on the one song that really mattered, "Suspicious Minds," a beautifully articulated piece of meditative pop that Chips had brought to the session. This pretty much sent Chips Moman, who gloried in his own abrasiveness ("I'm kind

On the set of *Change of Habit,* spring 1969. *Courtesy of the Graceland Archives*

of a stubborn fellow. I guess I believe in what I do enough, so I think if a guy's hiring me [to do a job], I believe that's what he's hiring me for"), around the bend. If they wanted the publishing so bad, Chips said, they could have their money back and stick it up their ass. Eventually, with RCA representative Harry Jenkins' support, Chips actually won the day, but Colonel stayed out of it, perfectly content, as he had been watching the NBC television special come into focus, to see Elvis once again so engaged. Because, as he once told Steve Sholes and Bill Bullock long ago, the music was his artist's business and he had full confidence that his artist knew his business.

THE GOPHERS IN THE DESERT

B Y THE TIME that Elvis opened in Las Vegas on July 31, the first single to come out of the American sessions, "In the Ghetto," had reached the top of the pop charts. It was the first number-one hit in seven years for Elvis (number one in *Cash Box* — in *Billboard* it only reached number three). Perhaps even more significant was its social message, which was a good deal more explicit than "If I Can Dream," which had itself reached *Cash Box*'s Top 10. "Suspicious Minds," the second release from the American sessions, was his second number-one hit, later that year.

For the Las Vegas opening Colonel papered not just the town but the entire state. (As he told Elvis jokingly, "The gophers in the desert [will] know you're here! Believe me, everyone in town will know Elvis Presley is coming, but you're the only one that can bring them in.") To promote the booking, he had preempted over two hundred forty-eight-foot billboards, took out double-page ads in all the newspapers, secured taxicab tops and bus-stop benches for on-the-go advertising, kept five hundred radio spots going throughout the month, and curried favor with every radio personality in town.

On the night of Barbra Streisand's closing show (Streisand had opened the International, after Colonel turned down an extra $100,000 for Elvis to fulfill that role because he was not going to subject his artist to an untried and untested room), Colonel and his crew, armed with hammers, ladders, and staple guns, were putting up posters, glossies, banners, pennants, and oversized cardboard records, so that by morning you would

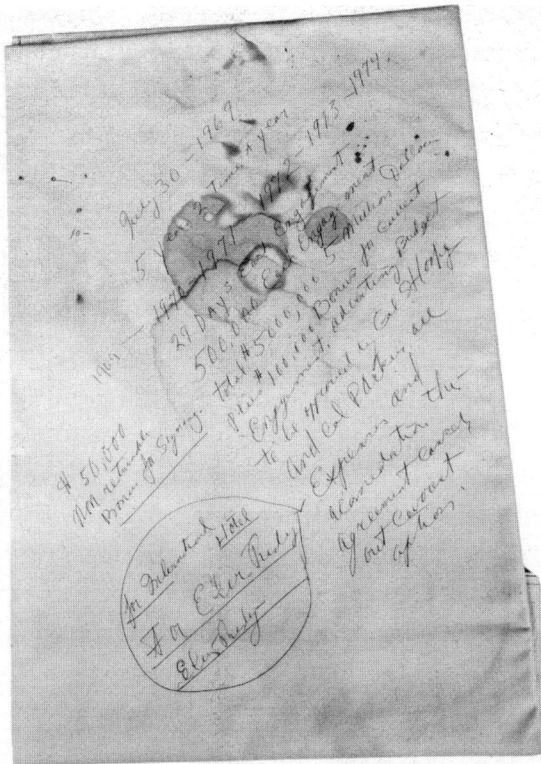

The Tablecloth Contract.
Courtesy of the Graceland Archives

never have guessed that this was anything but a theme park dedicated to Elvis Presley. And when Elvis opened two nights later, there was Colonel himself, dressed in a long white butcher's smock that announced "ELVIS INTERNATIONAL IN PERSON," as he welcomed fans and celebrities alike with W. C. Fields aplomb.

Elvis' opening night performance bore out all the planning and preparation on both their parts. Elvis had put together a band from scratch and ran through over 150 songs in almost two weeks of rehearsals. Now he took control of the stage as if he had never been away, as he displayed a giddiness and freedom that seemed as joyous as it was spontaneous. Before long he had everyone in the star-studded audience on their feet roaring their approval. Even waitresses who had "recently struggled through the ennuied debut of The Divine Barbra," as the *Los Angeles Herald Examiner* put it, "were visibly swooning."

No one backstage after the show could forget the unabashed emotion shown by both Elvis and Colonel. None of them had ever seen anything like it before. Colonel's body was visibly shaking as the two men approached each other, then wordlessly embraced. And then, all at once, it was over, and Colonel steered Elvis toward the press conference he had set up on the spur of the moment midway through the show.

For Priscilla it was as if Elvis' performance were showing her a man she had never seen before. "On the stage he [had] this look, you know, prowling back and forth, pacing like a tiger, and you look and you say, 'My God, is this the person that I —?' It was difficult to attach who he was to this person onstage. It was incredible."

Later that night Colonel met in the hotel coffee shop with International president Alex Shoofey, who suggested that they should just tear up the contract they had recently signed. As far as he was concerned, the International was prepared to exercise its option on the spot and agree to the financial terms Colonel had originally demanded. And so, on a stained pink tablecloth, Colonel outlined the terms of the new deal, which raised Elvis' salary to $125,000 a week retroactively, with an extension to two engagements a year for five more years, thus guaranteeing Colonel's yardstick demand of $1 million a year for eight weeks' work through 1974.

COLONEL IN LOVE

L OANNE MILLER was not at the opening, though she had gone to work for the International earlier that year. A thirty-four-year-old divorcée from Covington, Ohio (the divorce had only recently gone through), she was working as a secretary for the hotel's executive director. In that capacity she had been instructed to attend a meeting between Colonel's staff and key International executives, but she had been told by her boss to say and do nothing — she was just there to fill out the International's numbers.

To her consternation — well, maybe more than that — she found herself sitting between Colonel and International President Alex Shoofey in the dining room of owner Kirk Kerkorian's private villa on the grounds of the Flamingo Hotel. Her biggest challenge, she recognized, was not just to keep out of their line of communication, but to keep out of their line of sight. "I was continually leaning forward or backward, so as not to block their line of vision of one another." She was so paralyzed by the situation that she remembered nothing about the luncheon except for one exchange between Shoofey, who would soon become her new boss, and this strange, brusque man, who seemed so utterly sure of himself even in the company of such powerful men. "Mr. Shoofey mentioned to Colonel that with their deal there would be 'other goodies'—and he made an 'under the table' gesture with his hand. Colonel's immediate reply was, 'Everything is on top of the table or forget it. We don't do business that way.'"

She didn't see Colonel again until the following January, just before Elvis was to open in Las Vegas for the second time, when, after taking notes at another meeting between Colonel Parker and her new boss, she was asked to do some typing for the Colonel in the evening. She was reluctant at first—"I didn't know if Colonel's motives were strictly work, and work was all I was interested in"—but she was told by Shoofey's executive assistant that work was all the Colonel ever had in mind. Nonetheless she dressed down for the occasion—she didn't want there to be any misunderstanding—and she reported to Colonel's office-residence complex of six rooms on the hotel's fourth floor in jeans and a flannel shirt. Everything went fine until, at the end of the evening, he started asking a number of personal questions and then, when he walked her to the elevator, he kissed her on the cheek. "Uh-oh," Loanne thought to herself. Now it really *was* beginning to seem personal.

But even though he invited her to sit with him and Tom Diskin and his friend from RCA, George Parkhill, at several shows over the course of the engagement, she never detected anything overt in his manner toward her. One thing that was unmistakable, though, was his deep sense of isolation, though it never interfered with his attention to business. Or the steady stream of kidding that was always accompanied by a twinkle in his eye but almost never by outright laughter.

Soon they started spending time together, and Colonel reserved a suite at the Sahara, so they could have dinner together once in a while, or simply spend an hour or two with each other between shows. When Elvis started touring in the fall, Colonel called her every day from the road. One time, in order to help her sleep, he put together a cassette that he had recorded by the ocean, with Tom Diskin providing sound effects. He called her from Palm Springs whenever he was at home with his wife, who Loanne knew had to have someone with her at all times due to her failing health.

Then, toward the end of the year, Colonel called her from Hollywood to explain that he had "a major problem" and needed her help for a big meeting that was scheduled to be held at the MGM studio. "Several times," she recalled, "he emphasized how important the meeting was going to be and the great importance of all the people who would be attending." She flew in on her day off and met him at the studio, then followed Colonel and his staff with some trepidation to the huge doors of the MGM conference room. "Colonel asked, 'Jim [this is Jim O'Brien, next to Tom Diskin one of Colonel's most trusted lieutenants], is everyone present for the meeting? And where is Miss Miller's book to take notes? You know how important this is.'" O'Brien quickly produced a notebook and pen, and Colonel motioned for Loanne to precede him into the room.

> I walked through the doors trying to look confident, and immediately stopped in my tracks. The conference room had been set up in a very professional manner with water pitchers, glasses, pads and pencils placed in front of every leather chair at the long rectangular mahogany table. And seated in each chair was — a huge stuffed teddy bear!

"I told you they were big and important," Colonel said to her, but at least, he reassured her, she didn't have to take dictation. "They don't really talk too much."

Soon after, she moved in with him, very quietly, very privately, in a suite at the Royal Inn on Convention Center Drive, close to the International. Sometimes, during the week, she would cook an early dinner before Elvis' first show, but on weekends he always flew to Palm Springs to look after Marie.

LOANNE LOVED to listen to his stories, especially when he had an audience of young William Morris agents or PR men who had never heard them before or friends, for that matter, who never tired of hearing them again. But she soon came to realize that the stories, with their loose, expandable story lines and, always, the snappy punch line at the end, were more in the nature of "fables" than linear accounts. He loved to talk about hoboing across the country, tell stories of desperate times, and good times, too, but for all the intimacy that she and Colonel shared, however much it seemed he wanted to confide his feelings to her, she couldn't help but sense all that he was leaving out. He told her a little about the army ("He detested it — he said he hated losing his freedom to go when and where he wanted"), more about traveling with the circus and the carnivals, but he never said anything about his family, his child-hood, in anything but the most emotionally and geographically disguised terms. I don't think it really surprised her when he finally told her years later of his real origins, of how his father had treated him — but I wonder sometimes if she ever felt betrayed. And I hope she didn't.

Living with Colonel, she said, was learning to live with constant criti-cism. "He was a wonderful man, but not an easy one," she told me. And, with a clarity of vision that in no way undercut her single-minded devo-tion to him, she came to see him as "an introvert who had to learn to act like an extrovert in order to survive. When Colonel was not confident, he bluffed his way — and for him that worked." Loanne was by nature a very optimistic person, and she came to see "all the adjustments he had to make throughout his life" as obstacles he had overcome. "I'm [still] dazzled at his ability to assume new roles."

One time she was out on the road with him advancing Elvis' first, extended '70s tour, and Colonel saw a story in the Salt Lake City paper about a traveling circus that had just arrived in town. He took her to the show that afternoon, and afterward they went backstage, where he traded stories with all the show folk, performers and roustabouts alike. She had never seen him so relaxed, all his worries and cares just seeming to melt away. "He was like a child again," she said, "all wide-eyed and happy to be back in the world he had known." She only wished she were able to spark such moments herself, she would have given anything to see him so jaunty and at ease more of the time — but, whatever the challenges of the relationship, she knew for a certainty that this was one of the happi-est times in her life.

EIGHTEEN

On the Road Again

THE TOURING STARTED almost without warning or even proper
preparation.

It had begun with a kind of trial run prompted by the persistence of a brash young manager and promoter named Jerry Weintraub.
Weintraub had recently acquired a partner, Tom Hulett, cofounder of
Concerts West, the biggest concert promotion company in the country
(Jimi Hendrix, Creedence Clearwater Revival, and Led Zeppelin, among
others), and they first approached Colonel in Las Vegas in the summer
of 1970. Colonel was intrigued by Weintraub, who did all the talking and
was not above underscoring the monumental significance of the enterprise he was promoting, so, in his customary fashion, Colonel gave the
two of them a task to accomplish.

All they had to do was come up with $240,000 for four dates on a
six-city tour that was scheduled to begin in less than a month. That, and
follow the Colonel's instructions to a T.

They did — and evidently they did their job well enough that Colonel
gave them another chance to prove themselves on a more carefully considered (but not *too* carefully considered) eight-day-long tour in November. But this time he raised the stakes. This time, he told Weintraub, he
was going to give Weintraub and Hulett's company, Management III, the
entire tour, but in exchange they were going to have to present him with
a $1 million deposit as an earnest of their good faith.

Once again they rose to the challenge, but not before Colonel conveyed to Weintraub something he was not sure the promoter fully understood (or to be more accurate, what he was certain that Weintraub did
not understand): that the fans came first, that no one was to be given
precedence over them, that they were to be considered at all times the
"privileged customers." And as long as he worked with Weintraub, for the

Tom Hulett, in a buoyant mood. *Courtesy of the Graceland Archives*

next seven years, he felt obligated to repeat that message — and he was never sure that it was getting through.

Weintraub's partner, Tom Hulett, on the other hand, was clearly a young man who knew his business. He knew the buildings and the building managers, and he proved his mettle on the first date on the first tour when he set up a big-box sound system for Elvis with both broadcast and monitoring capabilities. On Colonel's instructions, Tom Diskin had provided Hulett with a stage diagram that mimicked the Las Vegas setup as much as possible, so that when Elvis walked out onstage he would feel comfortable. Hulett had nearly finished the installation when Diskin spotted the giant speakers being moved in. What the hell are those? he demanded, and when Hulett said it was their sound system, the normally mild-mannered Diskin said, "We don't use sound systems. There's one in the building." That was when Tom Hulett realized, Oh, of course, they hadn't toured since 1957 — there were no sound systems then.

Landing in Phoenix for the first date on the first tour, September 9, 1970. *Courtesy of the Graceland Archives*

In the end, it was agreed that the decision would be left to Elvis. At the start of the show, Hulett said, "I was a nervous wreck. "I'm standing right by the side of the stage ready to pop the button to turn the system off, and Elvis starts the show, and in the middle of the first three notes, probably for the first time in his life, he heard himself. And he stopped and looked to his left and smiled and said, 'Ladies and gentlemen, we're going to have one heckuva show tonight.'"

The eight-day second tour, in November, was an unqualified success. Elvis' Las Vegas show had started to get a little goofy around this time, but there was nothing perfunctory about his performance on the tour. And at its conclusion Elvis and Colonel had $500,000 to divide on the newly established two-thirds–one-third basis they had adopted for live engagements (these would soon include Las Vegas), whose success was largely dependent upon the energy and inventiveness of Colonel's promotion. The monetary return told them both that they could make a lot more money on the road than they could in Las Vegas. Or at this point, for that matter, from making movies.

Just one year later, in November of 1971, they launched a full-scale, twelve-city tour on which Elvis performed with a consistent display of both discipline and enthusiasm. (I can testify to this, at least with respect to the Boston concert I attended.) And at the end of that tour, there was more than $800,000 to divide after expenses, more than twice as much as they could have realized in four weeks in Las Vegas.

At first they both loved it—it was an adventure for them both. For Elvis it offered the thrill of making music, if not exactly off-the-cuff, at least outside the constraints of a showroom setting. And it gave him the pure, undiluted pleasure of playing directly to his fans, the ones who had been there from the beginning and from whom, to the end of his life, he always seemed to draw both strength and affirmation. For Colonel, it was just good to be back in the game, doing what he had always done, selling tickets, advancing the show, renewing old acquaintances (it seemed like he knew every building manager, ticket seller, sheriff, local politician, and concessionaire in the business), and never failing to deliver a sold-out crowd to his artist. Every night he watched the show from his perch beside the stage speakers, every night he watched Elvis blow the crowd away, and then he waited until Elvis was safely back in his hotel suite, before taking off again for the next city.

His scripts for the radio advertising in each city never varied—they were identical to his carnival pitch in the '30s, the same singsongy rhythm, something along the lines of "Hurry, hurry, hurry," repeated three times, then the name, place, and date, concluding with "Don't you miss it." He never allowed the spots to be prerecorded but gave them to the local DJs to deliver, so that they would feel a built-in connection to the show. But woe betide the DJ who departed from the script. It had to be delivered exactly as written, because, Colonel said, it was composed as a call to action—the same rhythm, the same urgency of message, he said, that the radio and TV evangelists employed "to make people do what they wanted them to do."

"We were like a family," said Al Dvorin, who went almost as far back with Colonel as his onetime employee, Tom Diskin. Everyone, it seemed, just picked up where they had left off. For Colonel and him, it was just like it had always been—the jokes, the routines, the constant attempts to top each other never changed. Al, a big man, was always complaining that the bed in his hotel room was too small. When they got to Oklahoma

City Colonel told him he'd better take a look at his room and make sure it was all right. When he did, he said, he was confronted with the biggest bed he had ever seen. Colonel had pictures taken of him propped up in it, and then he had postcards made, so that Al could write to his friends and show them how well he was being treated.

"All the years I was on the road with him, he always looked after my dietary [needs]. I explained to him that I didn't eat pork, I was brought up kosher. So he always had vegetables, fruit plates, broiled fish, whatever. If there was a party for Elvis, there was a special meal for Al Dvorin." Which, Al chuckled, really pissed Jerry Weintraub off. "I think it was because Jerry had a very Orthodox upbringing, and he got away from it, so it used to bother him that I wouldn't eat the 'shit food.' But in those days Parker used to eat Jerry's ass out. And he would always make Jerry get something special for me if he was the host! Colonel always liked to play with you."

THEY STEPPED UP the touring in 1972, and Elvis netted personal income of close to $4 million from concert appearances alone (excluding Vegas) out of total taxable income of almost $6 million. At the end of the year, having grown more and more exasperated by what he considered to be Jerry Weintraub's half-hearted commitment to his artist and his business (Weintraub seemed more committed to his management of John Denver, who had his first two big hits in 1971 and 1972 with "Take Me Home, Country Roads" and "Rocky Mountain High," than to the Elvis tours), Colonel ditched Weintraub and got RCA to form what amounted to a shell corporation called RCA Record Tours. With RCA Record Tours, there was never going to be any doubt about who was in charge, and they committed $4 million to support a projected fifty dates over the next year, with Tom Hulett remaining, in effect, Colonel's second-in-command.

At this point the troupe consisted of seventy or seventy-five members, including tech people, equipment handlers, orchestra members, and concessionaires. They traveled in three leased planes, with two complete stage setups transported from city to city on eighteen-wheelers. It was in a sense a far cry not just from the tent shows of the 1940s but from what looked now like their free-and-easy jaunts across the country in the

'50s, but in one essential way nothing had changed. For all the technological innovation and logistical sophistication, there remained one person, and one person alone, on whose judgments the success of the tour depended. Colonel was still leading the charge.

He took great pride in the way that both he and his artist had once again proved themselves to the world — and yet he couldn't sweep aside the nagging worries. By the end of the third tour of the year, he was unable to ignore just how much things had changed for Elvis as the newness wore off. Reviewing his second International engagement of 1972, *Los Angeles Times* pop music critic Robert Hilburn wrote that Elvis was operating at "only about 60% of his musical potential"— though that was an improvement on his previous appearance, where, Hilburn had written, he was "merely going through the motions." Sometimes in his live appearances around the country throwing out souvenir scarves to the fans seemed to take on greater importance than the songs. And the effect of the pills that he was taking in ever greater numbers was more and more in evidence both onstage and off. He couldn't seem to help himself, as he exhibited mood swings veering from giddiness to grandiosity, which were in turn punctuated by frequent bursts of anger more often than not precipitated by his ongoing separation from Priscilla.

Anyone looking at the situation from a loftier height might well have worried about where all this was going (many did), but they might also have concluded (though Colonel would have vehemently disagreed) that his manager was contributing as much to the problem as the artist. Or perhaps blame could more fairly be assigned to an ever-increasing inability on both their parts to lay their cards on the table — just to be straight with each other.

For Colonel at this point, even Loanne was aware, was proving to be more and more a victim of his own emotions — was increasingly subject to his own irrational impulses, his own suspicions and fears. Perhaps as much as anything due to the physical demands that touring made on a sixty-three-year-old man not in the best of health, his fitfulness was often on display, and he would lash out sometimes with no other purpose than to relieve some of the pressure that he felt coming at him from all sides in a manner that a younger Colonel Parker would never have permitted himself.

"He would get very disappointed when he would give someone a task and they did not perform it [up] to his standards," said Loanne, who was by now traveling with the tour as the official RCA Record Tours secretary and ensuring that all of Colonel's personal needs were met. "He would complain about this person or that person, 'They're not trying! They're not doing their job!' I would tell him, 'They *are* trying. They just don't have your abilities.'" But no matter how hard she tried to calm him down, she rarely succeeded, and as often as not he turned against her, too. One time (this was a little later) he began shouting at her over one inconsequential matter or another, and she asked why he always had to get so upset with her when he knew she was only trying to help. He gave her "a hard look," she said, but then he seemed to let down his defenses and open himself up to her in a way that he almost never did.

She knew how much crap he had to put up with, he said, but he had to keep his mouth shut for the sake of the show. (She might have contradicted him there, but what would have been the point?) There were times, he said, when he was afraid he might explode. "Who can I shout at except you? You love me, you understand. So help me when I need to shout, or else I'll just blow up and then there'll be no more Colonel."

She knew that was as close to an apology as she was ever going to get, and she was satisfied with that. She didn't doubt his love, but she knew, for all the happiness they had found together, what a solitary creature he would always be. She wished she knew what it was in his childhood that had hurt him so badly — but she knew there was nothing she could do to help him, because he was never going to talk about it. But what worried her even more was something that was happening now, something that she herself was witnessing and yet could do nothing about. Because Colonel, that most rigorously disciplined and iron-willed of men, was clearly in the grip of something he could not control.

NINETEEN

Secrets and Lies

A s SOMEONE who had always seen life as an uncertain bet, Colonel had been drawn to gambling from an early age. In the army it was not unusual for him to lose a week's paycheck in a friendly game of craps, or later, in the carnivals, he used carnival scrip as surety until payday came. But it had never been a problem. He and Marie had saved their money till they could buy a modest home in Tampa, and then in Nashville they had bought a more extensive property when they could afford it. Even after he started visiting Las Vegas regularly in the '60s, his losses never really added up — sometimes they were not even losses, although more often than not they were. But since Elvis had started in Vegas three years before, things had changed in a way that no one could ever have anticipated, and Colonel's gambling, which was now on full public display in the casino lounge, had become almost part of the show.

In 1970, a reporter for *The New York Times,* on assignment for what turned out to be a very positive (if not very accurate) feature on Elvis in *The New York Times Magazine,* casually described Colonel's presence at the roulette table, where, he noted with wry amusement, this "combination of con man and Santa Claus . . . had a system: he covered *all* the numbers." Which, while it may not always have been a winning system, the reporter remarked, fit right in with the whole Santa-Claus-in-summer image.

But in fact Colonel did not have any system at all — unless (and this is the inexplicable part) it was a system for losing. Colonel, everyone who knew him agreed, was a brilliant tactician, a man who could calculate complicated mathematical problems in his head and figure the odds in any game of skill. But he didn't play games of skill. Instead he played blackjack, craps, roulette, the wheel of fortune, games in which there was no chance of winning in the long run, and everyone watched, as he stood

A grizzled Colonel. *Courtesy of the Graceland Archives*

with a fixed, unreadable expression on his face and lost vast sums of money, up to $800,000 at a single sitting.

To his old friends it was almost inconceivable. To song publisher Julian Aberbach who went back to the very beginning with Eddy Arnold: "This was a man who never spent any money, who at one time had in excess of five million dollars [I'm not too sure about this, but Julian could well be right]—until he arranged for Elvis to go to Vegas. After that, things were never right."

Colonel had even warned Elvis' guys when they first started going to Vegas to be sure not to get caught up in the trap. "Don't get crazy," he told Joe Esposito, "and get hooked on gambling, 'cause the hotel and casinos will own you." Now they all talked about whether the casino owned the Colonel, but nobody ever knew for sure, because whatever might actually be going on, as longtime member of Elvis' retinue Lamar Fike said, "you never could pierce that veil."

With Jerry Schilling (left) and Joe Esposito, ca. 1980. *Courtesy of the Graceland Archives*

He could forget about all his pains and problems when he was gambling, Colonel told Loanne, who against all her instincts actually broached the subject to him early on. It was, she came to realize (or rationalize?), his "defense mechanism to cope with the stress." But at the same time, she came to see that it was rapidly taking over their lives. One night she finally addressed the issue head-on. It was May 21, 1972, she noted in her journal, and he had stayed up all night in the casino gambling. "When he came upstairs to the suite," she told me, "I was extremely upset and told him that apparently gambling meant more to him than I did, [and] I felt my relationship with him should continue on a business basis only. Peter, I was seriously worried about the effects on his health. I tried talking to him about the toll [it was taking on him]. But this was Colonel's addiction," she concluded sorrowfully, "and a person guards their addiction under any and all circumstances." And, she added at another point, in a not-quite-parenthetical afterthought, "He never lost more in the casinos than he could afford. And he always made sure Marie was well cared for financially."

That may have been true as far as it went, and many of Colonel's friends even speculated that he might in some way be "fronting" for the casino — in other words, the casino might be discounting his losses, like many other high rollers', because of all the business he drew in. But one can't help but wonder to what extent all the contractual twists and turns, which were undoubtedly to Elvis' benefit but sometimes benefited Colonel even more, may have been prompted by Colonel's ever-increasing need for money to offset his losses.

Nothing in his dealings with either the International or the Hilton, which took over ownership of the hotel in June of 1971, would suggest that Elvis was ever shortchanged by that need. In fact, Elvis remained the highest-paid performer in Las Vegas, and his deal only improved as his performance faltered. But Elvis' performance, his erratic onstage behavior, his seemingly uncontrollable spending were all subjects that Colonel could never talk about with Elvis. As Joe Esposito noted, "Colonel had always told him, 'I'm not going to tell you what to do with your money — you do what you want to do. Your money is yours.' It's like Elvis would go out and spend a million dollars on the ranch or something like that, which was crazy, while Colonel was out there gambling. So what could he say?" They were locked in a relationship of mutual denial, just as they had always been linked by proximities of character and temperament not visible to the outsider. "As different as they might appear, they had the same kind of egos," said Jerry Schilling, among the youngest and most objective of all the guys. And neither of them, Jerry said, ever wanted to display vulnerability — to each other or anyone else.

Tom Diskin became so concerned that he confronted Colonel directly, but Colonel just blew up at him and banished Diskin from his sight. "I came into this world with nothing," he railed at his longtime partner with a fury that barely masked his defensiveness and fear, "and it doesn't bother me one bit to go out with nothing. I don't have any children. Who am I hurting?" And when Al Dvorin attempted to intervene — "I told him, 'Tommy just talked to you because he loves you'" — Colonel would have none of it and simply repeated what he had said to Diskin.

"It made me sick," said Al. He had never seen Colonel so out of control before—he had never seen Colonel out of control. And though the breach with Diskin was soon mended, it was not something that either one of them could forget.

THINGS SEEMED at pretty much of a standstill with Elvis.

"He was still good," said Jerry Schilling. "You wouldn't have known it [as an outside observer], but he—he slowed down. And he started getting into other things."

Ten months after his last recording session, Colonel and RCA were finally able to get Elvis back into the recording studio at the end of March of 1972. The intent of the session was to come up with a hit, something that Elvis had not had in some time (sales had declined precipitously over the past two years, from a reasonable expectation of three-quarters of a million to a current level of 250,000), but in the Los Angeles studio Elvis adamantly refused to record the one song that everyone (the musicians, the guys, his producer, Felton Jarvis) was certain would be a hit, the up-tempo, rock 'n' rollish "Burning Love." Instead he focused on songs that expressed deep feelings of depression and loss, and the mood in the studio was one of almost unremitting gloom. In the end, he did record "Burning Love," and it did turn out to be a big hit, even though it was clear that he could not entirely put his heart into it, and the lachrymose titles of the songs he focused his attention on—"For the Good Times," "Separate Ways," "Where Do I Go from Here?," and "Always on My Mind"—told the real tale of the session.

He had several different doctors on call, any one of whom would deliver exactly what he ordered from the *Physicians' Desk Reference* guide, from the usual uppers and downers to liquid Demerol and an assortment of other heavy-duty painkillers.

His girlfriend Joyce Bova, a twenty-five-year-old staff member of the House Armed Services Committee in Washington, who had been as much the reason for his unexpected visit to Washington in December 1970 as the Bureau of Narcotics and Dangerous Drugs badge he received from President Nixon (the BNDD would soon be absorbed into the DEA), knew that their relationship was over when she came to visit him in Las Vegas in February of 1972. Before she left, she tried to talk to him about the drugs, but she was unable to penetrate his shell of messianic conviction. People listened to him, he told her, "because I know what they want and need. Like you. You should listen to me more. . . . I know what's good for you, baby. One day they'll all listen." His message, he said, was under-standing. "We all have divinity inside us, Joyce," he said. "Some of us just understand it more."

> I took the plunge. "Elvis, if we're gods, or at least have this 'divinity' in us, why do we need drugs?"
>
> "Silence is the resting place of the soul. It's sacred. And necessary for new thoughts to be born. That's what my pills are for . . . to get as close as possible to that silence."

T HERE WERE TRIUMPHS, to be sure. Elvis' first, and what turned to be his last, appearance in New York City, at Madison Square Garden, turned out to be a triumph as much of image and public relations (playing New York City was very different from playing Fort Wayne, Indiana) as of musical firsts. In a feat of extraor-dinary legerdemain, Colonel was able to build a series of three concerts, with a fourth added and a press conference thrown in for good measure (the four shows sold out instantly and grossed $730,000), into a monu-mental historic event. "Once in a great while," *The New York Times* declared, "a special champion comes along, a Joe Louis, a José Capablanca, a Joe DiMaggio," and Elvis, the reviewer wrote, was that "champion, the only one in his class." Colonel laid down a logistical marker as well when he insisted that an album commemorating the event had to be made instantly available in the face of RCA's protestations that it simply could not be done. But, of course, *Elvis as Recorded at Madison Square Garden* was manufactured and released just one week after the last of the con-certs, rising to number eleven on the charts and going gold (more than five hundred thousand units sold) just two months later. Meanwhile "Burning Love" reached number two on the singles charts by the end of October, effectively restoring Elvis to the top of the commercial market-place and once again positioning Colonel exactly where he wanted to be in his always ongoing negotiations with RCA.

Las Vegas, August 1972. *Courtesy of the Graceland Archives*

There was a second, hastily arranged MGM documentary, too (it began the day after the Los Angeles recording session ended), which would chronicle the April tour. It had its musical moments, particularly some of the off-the-cuff gospel rehearsal footage, but its real highlight was an audio-only interview conducted by the film's two directors (but prompted by the advocacy of Jerry Schilling), in which Elvis offered notably candid, at times even introspective thoughts on his life and career, casting much of what might have been carried off with an athlete's or entertainer's ready-made collection of clichés in a fresh and thoughtful light. It served as well to highlight the well-founded thinking behind Colonel's long-standing dedication to synergy, as the film generated increased interest in Elvis' concerts, while at the same time adding $250,000 to the $1 million they were already guaranteed for the tour by Management III and RCA Record Tours.

And yet, as much money as they made, and as much as Colonel could point to statistical benchmarks, Elvis only seemed to need more money, and the calls and letters from Vernon accelerated in both their number and their desperate tone. The thank-you notes were less frequent, too, and in fact the more support that Colonel provided, the more income he generated, the more he felt that he and Elvis were at cross-purposes, the more it seemed his involvement was treated as, at best, a kind of unwelcome intrusion.

A ND, OF COURSE, Colonel was beset with other worries. Marie was never far from his mind.

He would call her two or three times a day from Las Vegas, even put old friends on the line to try to cheer her up. She made it clear, both to him and to others, that she couldn't understand why he had to be gallivanting off to Las Vegas all the time. And once the touring started, it was worse. He had people with her twenty-four hours a day—cooks, nurses, housekeepers, companions. But when he was able to enlist the help of old friends like Brenda Williams' mother, Clannie, or George Hamilton's new wife, Alana, they never lasted long—Marie's testy, even hostile behavior always drove them away. He was home every weekend except when they were on the road, and he tried to entertain her sometimes with a little hand puppet (sometimes it was just a sock), which he would animate with a squeaky little voice, doing his best to coax a smile out of her.

She barely left the house anymore, spending all of her time indoors, while he baked in the sun. When friends visited, he liked to put on his chef's hat and apron and barbecue on his elaborate cooking setup. He had a phone with an extra-long extension cord so he could conduct business by the pool. And he could spend hours at a time just hosing off the patio area or cleaning his ovens and grills. "Oh, he's just an old coot," Marie would say sometimes, shaking her head, as if, one of the visitors remarked, she wasn't really buying his story. Or had simply heard it too many times.

The holiday season remained special for him. At Christmas, Colonel continued to don his Santa suit. In 1971, just before the holiday, he flew to Las Vegas and took a carload of toys to the children at St. Jude's Ranch for Children. The following year, in addition to his usual home calls as Santa to the mothers of his Palm Springs neighbors Frank Sinatra and Liberace, he dressed up in his Santa suit for the Sinatra Medical Center and received a letter of thanks from both Frank and his mother, signed by Frank as "The Little Snowman."

Loanne tried to tell him that he should take pride in the fact that he was still the manager of the world's number-one entertainer, that there wasn't a single person in the business who didn't seek his approval or advice — but that didn't seem to help.

"Elvis," a reporter had asked at the New York City press conference, "are you satisfied with the image you've established?" "Well, the image is one thing," Elvis replied, "and the human being another. It's very hard to live up to an image."

Colonel might very well have said the same thing.

Everyone saw him in a certain way — many people kept their distance, no doubt out of a combination of fear and respect. But the human being that hid inside that grizzled image was, in his own way, as vulnerable as the young boy who had first come to this country at the age of sixteen, terrified of all the trials that lay ahead but determined not to shrink from them.

What Elvis needed now, he was certain, was a challenge. And so did he.

He announced just what it would be at a press conference set up between shows on September 4, 1972, the final night of Elvis' current Las

Vegas engagement. He had gotten the idea for a worldwide satellite broadcast performance from watching the live broadcasts of President Nixon's historic trip to China in February. The first thing he had to do was to sell Elvis on the idea, then convince RCA and Tom Sarnoff at NBC to go along. The fact that it had never been done by an entertainer before was, of course, the very thing that intrigued him. This unprecedented television event would be called *Aloha from Hawaii.* It would reach the largest audience ever to see a television show at one time, Colonel's press handout trumpeted with an alacrity not always confined to the facts, "in excess of one billion people" (take all of this as a little bit of poetic license: among other things, after premiering live in the Far East, the show would not be broadcast until later in the day in Europe, and not till April in America), and would also represent "the first time in the history of the record industry" that an album (the follow-up soundtrack) would be released simultaneously on a global basis.

Flanked by a poster board drawn up according to the Colonel's speci-fications with six rows of Elvis Summer Festival hats, each festooned with the name of a country in which the spectacular would be broadcast, RCA Records head Rocco Laginestra congratulated both the entertainer and his manager on their bold leap into the future while the Colonel beamed. As he had stated to reporters in an earlier press release, "It is the intention of Elvis to please all of his fans throughout the world." And if it was "impossible for us to play in every city" throughout the world, perhaps, it was implied, this would serve as evidence of their good faith.

PART IV

....

CODA

....

TWENTY

Loss

T HE *Aloha* concert was filmed on the night of January 13–14 and was an unparalleled triumph, just as Colonel had known it would be. He believed it could be the start of a whole new day. As he wrote to Elvis at the show's conclusion, "I always know that when I do my part you always do yours in your own way and in your own feeling in how to do it best. That is why you and I are never at each other when we are doing our work in our own best way possible at all times.... You above all make all of it work by being the leader and the talent. Without your dedication to your following it couldn't have been done."

But then, very quickly, things returned to the way they had been, only worse. Elvis, who had lost a great deal of weight for the show, immediately regained it all, and then for the first time was forced to cancel several of his February shows at the Hilton while delivering erratic performances at many of the rest.

It was as if he had exhausted his limited fund of focus and commitment. His mania, too, seemed to be growing more and more out of control, as he entertained fantasies of killing Priscilla's new live-in boyfriend, karate instructor Mike Stone, and pushed Red West to the point that he actually made contact with a reputed contract killer, who said he would do the job for $10,000. Red had no idea what he would do if Elvis told him to go ahead and give the guy the money; he didn't think he could actually do it, but, with the hold Elvis exerted on them all, he wasn't sure he could stop himself either. He stared into Elvis' eyes when he delivered the news, and Elvis was silent for a moment before answering. "Aw, hell," he said at last. "Just let's leave it for now. Maybe it's a bit heavy. Just let's leave it off for now."

Everyone had their theories about what was wrong, with Elvis' increasing consumption of (mostly) prescribed medications being the

Aloha from Hawaii, January 13-14, 1973. *Courtesy of the Graceland Archives*

first, last, and most logical explanation, but Joe Esposito offered a more probing description of the world in which they all lived. "Everything we did, we drove into the ground. What it would take somebody else ten years [to get tired of], we did in six months. Sometimes he'd get you so frustrated—I think he enjoyed doing it. You'd get pissed, and I don't know if it was a test to see if people'd still be with him, but then he'd sit and talk to you, and there was just something about him—he'd smile at you, and he could convince you of anything. Sometimes I thought about leaving, but I liked him too much, and I figured things were going to change. Everyone was just waiting for that day to happen."

In the meantime, Elvis and Colonel's joint business venture had reached its tipping point with the sale of Elvis' masters to RCA in 1973.

The record company had approached Colonel in late 1972 with a proposal to buy out Elvis' back catalogue. RCA, of course, like any record company, already owned the master recordings and the right to market them in perpetuity. That was never at issue, not even with Colonel. What was constantly at issue, in endless nagging skirmishes that never seemed to be fully resolved, were matters of royalty payments, the actual use to which the catalogue could be put (over which Colonel, whether by custom or contract, maintained absolute control), and other contractual elements that had never been put down on paper but that Colonel was always hinting might prove to be embarrassing to the record company if they were ever revealed to the world.

RCA's vice president in charge of financial affairs, Mel Ilberman, was now proposing to do away with this source of conflict once and for all by buying out Elvis and the Colonel. In exchange for a single lump payment the artist would give up all claim on future royalties, his manager would give up any potential grounds for troublesome dispute, and RCA would establish in perpetuity their right to do whatever they wanted with all the music that had been recorded to date, using it to build up the RCA Record Club (one of Ilberman's pet projects), exploiting the back catalogue in a manner the Colonel would never allow, and wiping out all the disputes over foreign royalties, container deductions, and European album content with which Colonel had continued to bedevil them for years.

It was a gamble virtually unprecedented in the record business, which, like both Colonel and Elvis, dealt almost entirely in "now money" and put very little faith in the future. ("Catalogue" was a much-derogated concept; publishing was where you built up a backlist, because a song could always have a new life, as opposed to an artist.) But, surprisingly, Colonel was against it for any number of reasons — though ultimately what it really came down to were matters of control. (Certainly no one could ever accuse Colonel of having blind faith in the future.)

Elvis and Vernon, on the other hand, were all for it, for reasons of their own. Well, just one, really: Elvis' desperate need for money. Vernon outlined to Colonel the mountain of debt they were facing; he was afraid at some point they might actually lose Graceland, and in addition to his son's profligate spending (which both of them knew they could not control), Elvis would soon be facing a substantial divorce settlement with

Priscilla for which the money was simply not at hand. If Colonel wouldn't handle the deal, Vernon said, he and Elvis might just go to Elvis' personal attorney, Ed Hookstratten—he was sure Hookstratten would be happy to step in. (Although from my conversations with Hookstratten I doubt that he would have.)

It's hard to say whether this was the convincing argument, but it didn't really matter because Colonel was sure at this point that there was no way of persuading Elvis and Vernon that what they wanted so badly was not to their long-term benefit. And so he entered into talks with Mel Ilberman at RCA, professing great reluctance—but also sensing an exceptional opportunity.

Ilberman was facing his own challenges as well. When he first proposed a buyout offer of $3 million to the record company, "the financial people," he said, "were very upset." But then to his surprise, RCA president Rocco Laginestra, whose flair for the dramatic had led him to embrace the *Aloha* satellite-broadcast concept from the start, lent his wholehearted support—and with Laginestra's imprimatur he was able to carry the day.

He and Laginestra flew to Palm Springs, confident that there would be no problem finalizing the deal.

Colonel heard them out, then just shook his head.

Three million dollars wasn't close to enough, Colonel said, it wasn't even in the ballpark. After the success of *Aloha*, Elvis would need to have at least $5 million. Ilberman was ready to shrug his shoulders and walk away, but then to his consternation Laginestra went for the deal on the same basis that he had gone for *Aloha* (and Colonel had pitched it): it was a bold action that had never been undertaken before.

"I was pissed," Ilberman said, "because I thought we could have gotten it for four or four and a half." But given Laginestra's enthusiasm (and his position at the company), he didn't say anything and contented himself with the knowledge that at least they had a deal. Or so he thought—until they went out to dinner at the Spa Hotel, and Colonel kept introducing all these perplexing qualifications. "The Colonel continued to talk in terms of there still would be restrictions on the catalogue—and Laginestra really didn't know what the Colonel was driving at, but I did, and I was very upset. I kept raising the issue: we've got to have the catalogue free and clear, without any restrictions. And he asked me for some involvement in packaging in the future for [his promotion company] All Star Shows, and I said yes. And I did promise that on future packages I would use the new stuff as well as the old, so that he and Elvis would be getting [some] income. And that's how he got the rest of [what he wanted]." But even Mel, a longtime admirer of the Colonel, was surprised at how much he took for himself.

Because as it turned out, the buyout deal became the signifier of a new understanding between Elvis and Colonel. Up till now their limited partnership had been conducted with relative restraint, as Colonel continued to take his usual 25 percent managerial commission on everything guaranteed by the contract, with the 50 percent partnership applying only to what could be termed "profits" from the original deal or "bonus payments" beyond the contractual guarantee. But now, with the catalogue buyout, they became for the first time full 50-50 partners in every aspect of their business dealings except for touring, which would continue to be divided on a two-thirds-for-Elvis, one-third-for-Colonel basis.

But even more than that (and you'll have to bear with me on all these computations), in the end the buyout deal itself became something like the tail that wagged the dog. Because in addition to the $5.4 million that the buyout itself came to, there was a new contract extension that guaranteed $500,000 a year against royalties and, unlike the present one, was divided under the terms of the new agreement 50-50 between Elvis and Colonel. Moreover, at the conclusion of its seven-year term, Elvis and Colonel would each receive a $100,000 bonus, not to be counted against royalties.

In line with Ilberman's determination to keep the catalogue unencumbered, Colonel got a number of contractual guarantees of his own. He was to receive a $50,000-a-year consulting fee for the duration of Elvis' recording contract for assisting RCA in the "development of merchandising and promotional concepts" and for supplying RCA with "merchandising and promo materials," plus $10,000 a year for exploiting merchandising rights for the duration of the expired contract. Finally, for his assistance in helping RCA Record Tours in "planning, promotion and merchandising in connection with the operation of the Tour Agreement" as well as the records made under the Record Agreement, in essence for the seven-year duration of the new contract, he was to receive a grand total of $1.35 million ($150,000 the first year, $200,000 every year thereafter) plus 10 percent of RCA Record Tours' profits off the top.

In all, the Colonel was guaranteed $1.75 million on top of his $2.6 million share of the buyout itself (he only took $100,000 of the first $400,000 of the purchase price, as if it alone were the contractual guarantee, the $5 million the "bonus payment") and the $1.75 million that he would get as his share of the new recording contract. Which meant that Colonel would receive roughly $6 million to Elvis' $4.5 million from all of the deals combined. (This might be likened to a professional athlete's seven-year contract for approximately $75 million in 2024 dollars, with his agent getting 57 percent of the money.) Taking touring money into account (at least $15 million, with Elvis getting $10 million, but only after Colonel collected his 10 percent of tour profits beyond the promoter's guarantee), the overall package could be seen as close to a true 50-50 joint venture — which was undoubtedly how Colonel did see it, in one of the numerous alternative accounting approaches that he took to every commissionable transaction. And that is how he always explained it both to contemporary colleagues like William Morris lawyer Roger Davis (who, like many of Colonel's professional associates, was largely in agreement with the arrangement) and, later, to reporters and would-be biographers like me. The explanation never varied. He was having increasing difficulties with his artist, who, however unique his talent and potential continued to be (perhaps even because of that very uniqueness), required far more managerial attention than the normal, everyday client. As did a career which, through Colonel's own unique contributions, had risen to previously unimaginable heights. Moreover, by restricting his practice to a single client, Colonel was making substantial financial sacrifices, and to compensate for those sacrifices it was necessary to structure a different kind of deal. Which is what he and Elvis had done. Theirs, he always concluded, was nothing less than a true partnership.

Once the deal was completed, Colonel brought the papers to Elvis at his home on Monovale Drive in Los Angeles to go over each and every one of the six linked agreements, all of which required Elvis' affirmatory signature. He and Tom Diskin were driven there by his longtime aide George Parkhill, who lingered indoors with Diskin and Vernon while Colonel went out to the pool to confer with Elvis. Then they all gathered around Elvis' desk in the living room, as Colonel and Diskin went over the permutations of every deal with both Elvis and Vernon, after which all the agreements were signed and witnessed (that was Parkhill's primary function), with a copy of each left for Elvis on the desk.

Elvis and Vernon were elated. Elvis was so excited that he boasted about the deal to his guys and even outlined some of the specifics, something he had never done before. Once again, he said, Colonel had pulled the wool over everyone's eyes. It was almost karmic with Colonel, he told his karate instructor Ed Parker one time, the way that money came in one door just as it was going out the other — so long as the two of them kept their wits about them, he said, there would always be plenty of money to go around.

But the cosmopolitan Viennese-born song publisher Julian Aberbach, who had always recognized Colonel's unique talents and qualities, took a different, and decidedly more acerbic, view. It was Las Vegas that had seduced the Colonel, he said, and his gambling losses that had caused him "to do something that there was no excuse for, and that was selling all of the royalties of Elvis Presley back to RCA for $5 million, which were worth in my opinion $100 or $200 million." Although Julian was a very savvy financial analyst, I'm not so sure about the figure — this would mean taking a very long view — but one thing he was certain of was the cause. "I think it was because he recognized that [the way things were going with Elvis] there wasn't long to go." And after that, Julian said, "things with Elvis were never right."

E LVIS AND COLONEL fired each other in the early morning hours of September 3, 1973, just after Elvis' closing show in Las Vegas.

This was triggered by Elvis' reaction to what he felt was the Hilton's mistreatment of his favorite waiter, which led to an extended onstage denunciation of Barron Hilton, the Hilton chain, and the whole Hilton family. "Adios, you motherfucker, bye bye, Papa, too / To hell with the whole Hilton Hotel, and screw the showroom, too," he improvised at one point in what could be described as an "X-rated version" of "Love Me Tender."

Colonel and Loanne were sitting in their usual booth. "He turned to me," Loanne recalled, "and he said, 'I've never been so embarrassed in my life. I wish I could just crawl under this table right now.'" Adding, not at all as an afterthought, "Who does he think he is? How am I ever going to face the Hilton people? He can't get away with this." And as soon as the show was over, he stormed backstage to confront Elvis.

The full story can be gleaned, at least insofar as psychological details can be fully discerned from a one-sided correspondence (and I think they can here), from Colonel's four emotion-racked letters to both Elvis and Vernon in the Letters section in the back of this book. All the pent-up anger, all the bottled-up resentment and hurt on both sides, can be deduced, I think, even in the absence of any written response from Elvis, as all of these long-suppressed feelings come bubbling to the surface.

The next few months provided a sad denouement, with virtually no contact between the two of them and Elvis' extended hospitalization at the end of October for what was diagnosed as "iatrogenic and volitional polypharmacy" supplying a melancholy end note to the year.

Colonel heard from a number of sources that Elvis was putting out feelers for a new manager. The only advance notice that he got that he might actually be hearing from Elvis were brief telephone calls from Vernon and longtime Memphis Mafia member Sonny West just before Christmas. When Elvis called, Colonel recalled in a brief written account that he composed for Loanne in the mid-1990s, "I asked [him] what he wanted. He said, 'When are we going on tour?' I told him I could not answer that since he had never replied after he told me [in September] that he wanted to make a fair settlement [for the dissolution of their contract]. 'Well,' he said, 'I want to start working.'" And once Colonel gathered that "he wanted to carry on with me as we did before, I asked him if he was in shape to do this, [and] he said, 'Right now I am ready.' So I started to put him back to work. [And] it was great for a while. But at least we did not work him until he was ready."

It's hard to know what to make of this, except that clearly there had been no resolution, nor would there be one for the last four years of Elvis' life. As Loanne wrote with painful honesty, "I don't think either of them trusted the other one totally after that." And while there were public rumors toward the end that Colonel was thinking of selling Elvis' contract, neither one seems to have seriously considered leaving, because, despite all the resources that each had at his command, neither one of them felt (and I'm sure both would have vociferously disagreed) that they had anywhere else to go.

Nothing changed. There were few shared moments, no real intimacy.

Elvis, as has been amply documented, sank deeper and deeper into a crushing cloud of drugs and depression that never lifted; his health continued to suffer, and so, understandably, did his performances, with only the occasional show to lift his spirits.

As for Colonel, even as Elvis' problems became more apparent, his did, too, if not to the public at large, certainly to those who knew him. It was not unusual now for him to spend twenty-four hours at a time in the hotel's casino, and as his worries about Elvis' health and state of mind grew, so did Loanne's about Colonel's health (both physical and emotional) and state of mind. One time, right after Elvis' December 2, 1976, opening at the Hilton, he spent over two days straight in the casino before returning to their suite at 2:00 P.M. on Sunday, where he would remain in bed for the next two days. Always, at moments of stress, he retreated to the casino, and there was nothing Loanne or anyone else could do about it. "Colonel dreaded starting a tour," Loanne said, "and would spend as much time as possible in the casino before we started out. At the end of a tour he would celebrate by gambling." And she no longer even attempted to talk to him about it, because, as she had long since come to recognize, an addict "will use any excuse to justify their addiction."

Colonel continued to advance the tours by a day or two, waiting for Elvis' plane to arrive before taking off for the next city — and not infrequently, in the small-bore game of retribution and retaliation that each now played, Elvis would keep Colonel waiting on the tarmac, sometimes (perhaps especially) in the pouring rain.

There was no talking to Elvis about any of it. On the rare occasions that Colonel attempted to bring up the drugs or the lackadaisical performances, Elvis offered the same rationalization that Colonel himself would fall back on if anyone dared criticize his own behavior: *I know what I'm doing.* One time Elvis fixed him with an appraising look and said, "I don't tell you what to do with your life, I don't interfere with it [and] I don't want you to get involved in [mine]." But for the most part his boy just did his best to avoid him. "He's so cunning," Colonel told Loanne, with little sense of self-awareness or irony, "he doesn't want me to see him when he's in bad shape, and when he does see me, he knows that I know."

On July 28, 1976, after a desultory performance, in Hartford, Connecticut, Colonel went backstage to talk to Elvis about the show but, upon returning to the hotel, he told Loanne Elvis had been too groggy to respond. "What can I do?" he said to her despairingly, as if she might actually have an answer. "The real Elvis," he said (his words were practically embedded in her memory), "is sharp and clever, but the person I saw tonight didn't even recognize me. No one knows how much I miss the real Elvis. If only I knew how to bring him back. I miss my friend so much." And then he started crying—he seemed unable to control himself, as the tears came pouring down.

Loanne had never seen him give way to his emotions like this before, and she would never see him quite like this again. She wished she had the words to comfort him—but surely some part of her must have wished that Colonel had someone who could confront *him,* too, who could somehow bring back the real, unencumbered Colonel to her.

You have only to look at the letters over the last two or three years of Elvis' life—to Vernon, to Elvis, to Tom Diskin and Tom Hulett—to grasp the whole inexorable story. They paint a picture of frustration, bafflement, and despondency; they underscore the desperation on all sides.

For the fans, and for the guys around Elvis, there remained the dream of an overseas tour. Going to places he had never been, playing to fans who had never seen him perform, might provide him with just the lift he needed, could present him with the kind of challenge he had always risen to in the past. But there never was any overseas tour, and history has come to believe that the underlying reason was that Colonel could not go with him because he was not a citizen and didn't have a passport. (Although this was not known at the time, Colonel's reluctance at any point in the last ten years of Elvis' life to entertain talk of foreign tours or, for that matter, set foot outside of the country himself, was the subject of much uninformed speculation.)

It's possible that this was the true explanation, or that it was at least in part true—but I don't think it's the whole story by any means. When Tom Hulett came back from taking the Moody Blues to Japan in January 1974, he and Colonel spoke at length about the logistics of Elvis embarking on just such a tour. Hulett and Jerry Weintraub even introduced Colonel to Nagashima Tatsuji, the Japanese promoter of the Moody Blues tour, who had brought the Beatles to Japan in 1966 and who was fully

Colonel and Tom Hulett.
*Courtesy of the Graceland
Archives*

prepared now to offer Elvis a $1 million guarantee. Tom Hulett was the
one person Colonel would have trusted to take Elvis out on such a tour
on his own—there was no question of Tom's loyalty (it had been well
tested during the period of Elvis and Colonel's estrangement), and Colonel had always admired Tom for not just his deep knowledge but his love
of show business. But as the two spoke, their conversation quickly shifted
into a mutually understood code, in which the key word was "security."
How could Elvis go to Japan, with its strict drug laws, how could he pass
through all the customs stations he would have to clear in Europe if it
were not to be a single small-country tour, without his prescribed medications? And who was going to carry those medications for him? Certainly his doctors would not be willing to take that risk, and his guys—well,
that wasn't even worth discussing.

But there was something else. In the end neither one of them was
convinced that Elvis actually wanted to go. Elvis had asked to see Hulett

in his suite at the Hilton just after his return from Japan. Before he went up there, Tom said, "All the guys were saying, 'He wants to go to Japan. He's going to bug you about going to Japan.' But when I got up there, never once did he ask me about going to Japan. Just asked me how it was." And Hulett got the further impression that whatever was not being said (and Hulett suspected there might be quite a lot, because Elvis was not at all naive when it came to how much exactly he was willing to risk, or even reveal), however excited the guys might be about foreign travel, "Elvis just was not interested in all the hassles."

I N 1977, in what amounted to one last attempt to "challenge" Elvis—or, as many of Colonel's most persistent critics believed, particularly in the aftermath of the broadcast itself, for no other reason than to derive one last payday—Colonel negotiated a deal with CBS to shoot yet another performance special in June, in the midst of the fifth tour of the year. Colonel had demanded $750,000 and full ownership of the show, and in later years he would always say, I believe with some degree of remorse (though perhaps it was just purposeful disingenuousness), that he never thought CBS would meet his price, and when they did, what alternative did he have but to bring it to Elvis? And when, on April 12, he did, Elvis gave the project his wholehearted approval.

It was just twelve days since the moment that Colonel and Tom Hulett had been dreading for so long finally arrived: on March 31, in Baton Rouge, they had for the first time been forced to cancel a performance, along with the rest of the tour. But after only four days in the hospital, Elvis assured Colonel that he was fully recovered, and he was back on the road again by April 21.

Tom Hulett, ordinarily the most hardheaded of realists, allowed himself to believe that the CBS special might be just what Elvis needed. So, apparently, did most of Elvis' entourage. Perhaps the best (and kindest) way to suggest what they were all feeling (and this would have to include Elvis himself) is that they all continued to believe, some *part* of them continued to believe, that Elvis would rise to the challenge, as he always had in the past. Colonel himself, Loanne said, spoke to her about how "the Satellite show had motivated Elvis to get in shape, and he hoped the TV special would [do] the same." They all seemed to think that Elvis could "recapture his form if he really wanted to," she said, shaking her head (though one wonders if Colonel could really have been so credulous). "In retrospect, it all seems [so] strange." For the 1977 special was a sad spectacle, the kind of failure that, just a few years before, neither Elvis nor Colonel could even have contemplated, let alone allowed to happen, and after its initial broadcast it was never shown on television again.

Tom Hulett knew right away. And while there's no record of what Colonel thought, it's not hard to guess. Loanne was devastated. But for many in the company, at the time it felt like just another show, and it was not until it was broadcast on October 3, seven weeks after Elvis' death, that they would recognize the reality of what they had participated in. Myrna Smith, the de facto leader of Elvis' female backing group, the Sweet Inspirations, called her boyfriend, Jerry Schilling (who by now was working for the Beach Boys at the start of a managerial career of his own), the night of the show. Jerry asked her how it had gone, "and I said, 'It really went great.' But afterwards, when I watched [the broadcast] I just burst out crying. We were all wearing blinders."

E LVIS was pronounced dead at Baptist Memorial Hospital in Memphis on the afternoon of August 16, 1977, the day before his sixth tour of the year was scheduled to begin in Portland, Maine.

Colonel got the news in Portland. He and Loanne and the regular advance crew had arrived late the previous afternoon, and he had taken them all out to dinner, regaling them with familiar stories and jokes. They all had breakfast and lunch together the next day at the hotel and mapped out everything that needed to be done both for the opening-night show and for the upcoming tour. Around 4:00 P.M. Colonel got a call from Joe Esposito that Elvis had been taken to the hospital. Then there was a rapid succession of calls from Joe and from a sobbing Vernon Presley, who was barely able to speak.

Colonel told Loanne right away.

"He was calm, too calm," she later recalled. She was sure he was in shock, as, without further discussion and a blank, unreadable look on his face, he assembled everyone and told them they had work to do. He called Barron Hilton first, then he and Tom Hulett started making calls to cancel the tour, while a wide variety of tasks and responsibilities were delegated to others. The show plane had to be turned around. So did the Nashville plane carrying Tom Diskin, Felton Jarvis, and some of the Nashville-based musicians. Ticket refunding had to be set up in every city, and people who had bought tickets for the two Portland concerts had to be notified by newspaper and radio ads right away. Throughout it all Colonel remained resolute and calm, but, Loanne said, "he was talking and moving automatically, as though he had thrown up a wall between his inner self and the outer world." She was deeply concerned about him — she was deeply concerned for them all. She understood what the others were going through, but Colonel was no more willing to let any of them show their feelings than he was to reveal his own. Part of her wanted to reach out to them, but, given Colonel's state of mind, she was unable to.

That night, amid what Loanne called an "ominous calm," they all had dinner together as usual. "None of us wanted to [be] there, but Colonel insisted we had to maintain a normal atmosphere for the public. He told us, 'We have to be strong. We owe Elvis that. We must make him proud.'" He told them they would be leaving for Memphis the next morning.

Later, in their room, he told her he was worried about Vernon. His health was already severely compromised, and Colonel was concerned that he might not be able to survive this. They needed to get to Memphis right away, Colonel said, because he was going to have to help Vernon with all the funeral arrangements. Vernon had asked him to do that with Gladys' funeral, but this was going to be much harder. Everything had to be dealt with very sensitively, Colonel said. Otherwise, it could just be turned into a circus.

Loanne told him she would need clothes for the funeral. All she had with her were the everyday clothes she had packed for the tour, and she needed something more suitable. To her dismay Colonel blew up at her. "If the clothes you packed were good enough for Elvis when he was alive," he said in what appeared to be a mix of anger and disbelief, "they should be good enough to say goodbye." The only reason for a fancy outfit, he said, would be "to make an impression on others. Elvis will be satisfied to see us wearing our work clothes because he will know we are still on the job." And nothing she said, none of her pleas, would change his mind.

They left Portland at eight fifteen the next morning. On the plane Colonel once again addressed the grief-stricken crew. "I don't want to see anyone crying or making a scene when we get there," he announced. "I expect each of you to remain calm and on the job for Elvis. We have to keep our minds clear and show a united front in spite of our sorrow. There will be no emotional outbursts of any kind. We will honor Elvis by controlling our emotions and remaining dignified. We are still working for Elvis, and we want him to be proud of us. That means being strong and taking care of business even under these difficult circumstances. I mean it — NO TEARS. If you need to cry, then go off and do it in private."

"I think," said Loanne, who was surely as taken aback as anyone else, "Colonel spoke these words as much for himself as for the rest of us. I believe he felt that if he allowed himself even a little emotion, he would lose control of his emotions entirely." For the duration of the flight he remained grim-faced and expressionless while everyone else, including her, stifled their tears, though every so often one of them would wipe their eyes and catch the glance of another.

Colonel went to Graceland as soon as they arrived. When he returned, Loanne said, he was utterly crestfallen. Vernon had told him he didn't need any help, he would handle the funeral arrangements himself. Colonel was hurt, but more than that he seemed for the first time to be at totally loose ends. "He wanted Elvis to know he was [still] doing everything possible for him," Loanne said. And now he couldn't.

The morning of the funeral, he sent Tom Hulett back to his room to change, reprimanding him for dressing up in a way that Elvis wouldn't recognize. He himself was attired in his customary baseball cap, seersucker pants, and a blue short-sleeved shirt. ("Elvis wouldn't recognize me without the cap," he whispered to Loanne, as they sat in the back of the room.) He never approached the coffin, because, he told her, "I want to remember him like he was when he was alive." At some point he was able to get Vernon alone in the kitchen. No one could miss the intensity of their colloquy, as Colonel tried to impress upon the grieving father the urgency of the situation, the need to act right now even in the midst of mourning. The vultures were circling, he said, already there were probably half a dozen unscrupulous hucksters and fly-by-night manufacturers making plans to move in and create thousands of unlicensed Elvis products whose profits should rightfully belong to Elvis' nine-year-old daughter alone. Vernon's gaunt handsome face reflected a sorrow almost beyond expression; it was hard to tell how much he was able to take in, but he seemed to assent almost mutely to every one of Colonel's impassioned pleas.

Colonel and Loanne flew to St. Petersburg the next day, registering at the local Hilton under assumed names. He couldn't do the work that needed to be done, he told her, if he were under constant public scrutiny — but she thought more likely it was simply because he needed room to breathe. The Rinaldi family offered him office space at their printing plant in Tampa, and he set up shop there with his small team. He was determined to do everything in his power to protect Vernon and Lisa Marie. Even if everyone else around him went to pieces, he told Loanne, he needed to be strong. And he needed to figure out a way to deal with those vultures — he simply did not have the resources to deal with them on his own.

At William Morris' suggestion he got in touch with Harry "Bear" Geissler (Geissler's business and home were situated in Bear, Delaware), an independent entrepreneur of modest accomplishments up until now, whose company, Factors Etc., had only recently made a fortune on a merchandising campaign for William Morris client Farrah Fawcett-Majors. Not only that, Factors had gone after every bootlegger and small-time grifter hawking unauthorized Farrah Fawcett-Majors products and shut them down with lawsuits that he promised he would bring against all the low-level scammers and con men now seeking to profit off Elvis.

In the meantime Vernon sent Colonel a letter on August 23, reaffirming his faith in Colonel's judgment and his desire to maintain the full partnership that Elvis and his manager had formally established at the beginning of the previous year. "I am deeply grateful," Vernon wrote, "that you have offered to carry on in the same old way, assisting me in any way possible with the many problems facing us." And once he had finalized the agreement with Factors, which, in addition to a minimum payment of $150,000, guaranteed that Factors would pursue all legal means to uphold the Elvis trademark at their own expense (the contract was backdated to August 18, two days after Elvis' death, to safeguard the Estate's claim), Colonel traveled to Memphis to go over all the details of the deal with Vernon, along with any other business immediately at hand.

He made deals that were good for Elvis and that were good for him. (By now, with the 50-50 understanding reaffirmed, the two were virtually synonymous.) He negotiated with NBC to rebroadcast both the 1968 special and *Aloha from Hawaii* in an arrangement that initially brought $461,625 to both himself and the Estate, and another $400,000 for subsequent showings. His own contract with RCA for ongoing "advice, promotion, and counsel" was extended for another two years with personal compensation amounting to $675,000, while both he and the Estate received approximately $2 million apiece for record deals he made in the three years following Elvis' death. In addition, he secured a personal payout to Vernon of $50,000 from RCA "as Payment in full for counseling, advisory and exploitation services [for] the 'Our Memories of Elvis' album" as well as exclusive representation by William Morris for other business opportunities that might come Vernon's way. There would, of course, continue to be publishing royalties, adding up to nearly $1.5 million over the next two years, as well as ongoing profit participation in Elvis' many motion pictures, which came to something like $275,000 in income for the Estate.

The Factors deal, meanwhile, exceeded its initial $150,000 guarantee by at least $50,000 in its first three months of operation, and Factors immediately launched the first of what Factors would claim amounted to some four hundred lawsuits to defend both the Estate's proprietary interests and their own.

Throughout it all Colonel conducted himself with his usual imperturbable confidence and calm, falling back on the same public face he had always chosen to adopt (one in which wry amusement was undercut by what appeared to be an air of carefully calculated indifference), which was in turn embraced by both press and public with the same credulous amusement they had always extended to Colonel's antics. "It's just like when he was in Germany," he said to one reporter (or was said to have said, because I think many, if not most, of these statements may well have been apocryphal). "Nothing has changed." To another he declared, "Elvis didn't die, the body did." Adding (did he really say this?), "We're keeping up the good spirits. I talked with him this morning, and he told me to carry on." But always the underlying message remained. "It's still Elvis and the Colonel." Or as he told Loanne, "It will *always* be Elvis and the Colonel. I'll never stop trying to keep his name alive."

Loanne alone saw the inner turmoil. But she was well aware that she only saw what he permitted her to see. He kept telling her that he needed to be strong to protect Elvis. But he rarely spoke to her about the past, about his and Elvis' early days together. And he never spoke to her about the time he had first seen the boy in early 1955, when he had been so electrified by both his talent and his promise that he was prepared to abandon all of his previous, carefully laid-out plans for success and stake everything on a gamble that no one else would ever have dreamt could pay off in the way that it did. It was without question the most remarkable moment, a moment of greater heat and intensity than anything else he had ever experienced in his long career in show business, and it had led to a relationship unlike any other in his life. As he had written to William Morris agent Harry Kalcheim long ago, "I will do whatever is in my power to protect him as long as he is willing to listen, for even a poor teacher is a good teacher if the pupil will listen." But now the teacher was left to carry on alone.

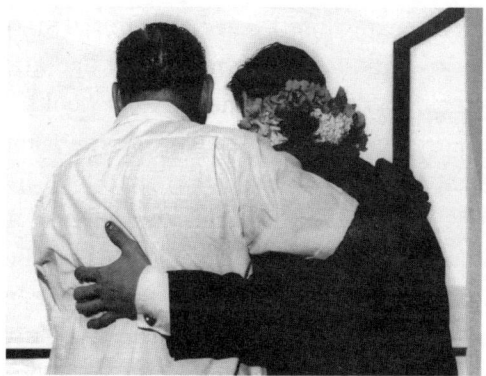

Aloha: After the Show. *Courtesy of the Graceland Archives*

THE PUBLIC MASK never slipped. It was the character he had chosen to inhabit most of his adult life. Once, though, speaking to *Los Angeles Times* reporter and critic Robert Hilburn at an "Always Elvis" fan festival that he had put together a year after Elvis' death, the mask cracked.

It was the end of a long day, Hilburn wrote, and Colonel was tired. He had signed many pictures as well as copies of the poem he had written for Elvis (like all of his poems, it was written in the Dutch-doggerel style of his youth, ending, "We will play your songs from day to day / For you really never went away"), for which he charged just one dollar, with all proceeds going to Las Vegas' Sunrise Hospital Medical Center. He was clearly pleased with the success of the event, not just the turnout but the warmth shown to him by the fans, the way they kept wanting to extend their conversations about Elvis, their *connection* with Elvis, through him.

"We made a hell of a team," he said to Hilburn, after waiting for the crowd to disperse so he could be sure that his conversation with the reporter would not be overheard. "I thought we'd go on forever, but—"

"He stared out into the distance," Hilburn wrote, "leaning on the cane he carried in later years and pausing as if trying to figure out what more to say.

"'Sure,' he said, softly, answering a question that hadn't been asked. 'Sure, I loved him.'"

TWENTY-ONE

After Elvis

LL OF HIS CLOSE FRIENDS AGREED: Colonel was never the
same. He was still without question the Colonel — witty, com-
bative, never anything less than a formidable force — but he had
been reduced somehow, he had lost some of the relentlessness of his
never-less-than-inscrutable personality.

He never took on another client, although he was certainly approached
and was free with his advice to young artists and his informal promotion
of the careers of performers as disparate as George Strait and a very
young Celine Dion.

He never wrote his book.

In 1988 two of his still-loyal Management III promotion team members, Paul Gongaware and Mike Crowley, obtained a million-dollar book
contract for him from a major publisher. I can attest from my own
experience in publishing that it was a very good contract for what the
publishers described as "an unusual book peppered with all [your] wonderful anecdotes . . . the life and times of a truly picaresque hero." But,
even though it conformed to every one of his major demands, he turned
it down. Nor, to my knowledge, did he ever allude to this very real offer,
but instead, if anyone ever asked about the progress of his book, simply
railed against publishers in general, the whole culture of publishing,
which "only wanted dirt — and I'm not a dirt farmer." Sometimes he
might add, "I've got the book right here," pointing to his temple. But what
it came down to in the end, I think, apart from the natural fear that every
prospective writer has in approaching a blank sheet of paper, was his
ingrained belief that the artist always wore the white hat and no amount
of money could ever get him to change hats with his artist.

He managed the Estate's affairs until 1980 when the Shelby County
Probate Court appointed a thirty-eight-year-old Memphis attorney

Colonel and Loanne. *Courtesy of the Graceland Archives*

named Blanchard Tual as guardian ad litem to look into the interests of Elvis' daughter, a minor, now her father's sole surviving heir in the aftermath of Vernon Presley's death the previous year. In 1981, after the guardian ad litem submitted two lengthy reports, a lawsuit was filed by order of the court on behalf of Lisa Marie, essentially to separate the Colonel from any further connection with the Estate, as well as recover some of the funds which the ad litem guardian clearly felt had been misappropriated. The lawsuit, which the Estate, whose executor trustees included Priscilla, Elvis and Vernon's accountant, and the National Bank of Commerce, entered into with great reluctance because they did not agree with the findings of the court (they were enjoined by the judge to act as litigants on behalf of Lisa Marie), alleged "collusion, conspiracy [and] fraud" on Colonel Parker's part, and focused largely on the sale of the RCA masters and the various joint-venture and partnership agreements that had been in place since 1967.

Needless to say, Colonel fought back, and in 1982 he filed a countersuit demanding that he be paid the $1.6 million he said he was owed as a result of forgoing his full commission the last year of Elvis' life. In his sharply worded written responses to the original report, he offered point-by-point rebuttals to each of the charges, suggesting with thinly veiled contempt (in fact, not veiled at all) that Blanchard Tual, the court-appointed lawyer, should find someone to acquaint him with the niceties of contract law, not to mention some of the realities of show business. Tual's report, Colonel declared, not entirely without reason, failed to grasp not just the purpose but the myriad financial benefits of many of the deals he had negotiated, whether they had to do with merchandising ("Had Colonel been a Polo Lounge manager," he wrote, "he would never [have] initiated merchandising. But Colonel is a showbusiness manager and set about to enhance Elvis' performances with the color and excitement that fans came to expect") or the royalty rate that Elvis received on post-1973 record sales, which, Colonel pointed out acerbically, far from being fixed at the rate spelled out in the contract, "because of RCA's fine relationship with the Colonel . . . were [frequently] updated by amending letters."

In sum, he concluded, "Mr. Tual should refrain from guessing what took place and then make it appear as if that's the way it was."

In all of the permutations of the various lawsuits and counter lawsuits Colonel never gave ground, save in one respect, and it was so unexpected that it could only be described as shocking. After nearly fifty years of disguising, fictionalizing, and denying his true identity, he revealed at long last just who he was, and where he was from — and not for anything that appears from a layman's point of view to have been a very compelling reason.

It's certainly true that there had been increasing rumors in the wake of Elvis' death that Colonel was Dutch. (Remember: this was seventeen years after the revelation in the Dutch magazine *Rosita* that he in fact was — which, despite the ever-increasing pace of global communications, was universally ignored.) And, with the publication of Albert Goldman's best-selling biography, *Elvis,* in late 1981, these rumors had been to all intents and purposes confirmed. But it was only when he launched his own countersuit against the Estate and its executors in March of 1982 that Colonel himself did not simply concede the point but loudly announced that the rumors were true.

To what end, one might ask. And why now? Let me quote from Colonel's affidavit, without, I'll admit, being able to make any claim to fully understanding its purpose. "I am advised by my attorneys," Colonel declared—and here I'll substitute my own imperfect language for the various case-law citations—he had been advised, he said, that the removal of his lawsuit from state to federal court was improper, because the federal court lacked jurisdiction "since I am not a citizen of the US or any foreign country." Upon which he went on to reveal the details of his birth and his enlistment "in or about 1929" in the U.S. Army, where he "did willingly swear allegiance to the government of the United States of America. I did not seek or obtain the permission of the Dutch government to serve in the U.S. Army [and] as I am now informed, my failure to seek and receive such permission . . . effected an automatic forfeiture of my Dutch citizenship." Nor was he a U.S. citizen, "having never become a naturalized citizen of this country or of any other." He was, in other words, as he would state dramatically to a number of publications in the aftermath of this revelation, "a man without a country."

Well, maybe so—although in the end this argument, so far as I can see, proved to be something of a red herring. Because, really, it never seems to have been fully tested—it appears in fact merely to have served to delay the proceedings. But maybe that was the point. And if that was the case, it worked. Because, in June of 1983, all the parties settled.

The proceedings at this point had dragged on for almost two years, to the advantage of absolutely no one, least of all the Estate, which, with RCA payments held up by the lawsuits and none of the fresh sources of income that Colonel's dealmaking might have brought in, could ill afford to bleed any more money on costly lawyers' and accountants' fees. The end result—one of the end results, anyway, in a fairly complicated dispersion of everyone's interests—was that in an out-of-court settlement Colonel received more than $2 million (considerably more than the $1.6 million he had originally sought, almost all of it paid by RCA), with his financial interests permanently severed from the Estate's.

But even as the lawsuits were still going on, in fact just two months after filing his own countersuit, Colonel communicated through his lawyer (who stipulated that this should in no way be taken as affecting his position as a litigant) that he was prepared to do everything in his power, without recompense or precondition, to help the Estate with their plans to open Graceland to the public in June of 1982. Which was in fact something Colonel had urged on Vernon within days of Elvis' death for a number of very good reasons (primarily having to do with merchandising) and something he felt even more strongly about now.

One day he simply called Jack Soden on the phone. Soden, a thirty-five-year-old investment banker from Kansas City who had recently been appointed head of what would soon be called Elvis Presley Enterprises, had met Priscilla through the money-management firm he worked for in his hometown, and the two of them hit it off. It didn't bother her that he had no experience in show business. "I just liked his positivity," she said, and it was that very positivity, along with a vast reservoir of common sense, practical curiosity, and unassuming charm, that propelled them forward in their determination to learn all that they could about how to open up a private home to the public (which included brief visits to Monticello, Mount Vernon, and the Hearst Castle in San Simeon) in a very short period of time.

"We were in a race to open," Jack said, "and then one day my secretary comes rushing into my office (my office at the time was my two-bedroom apartment at the Meadow Oaks Apartments, practically next door to Graceland) and said, 'There's a man on the phone who says he's Colonel Parker.' So I got on the phone, and he told me he had been reading things about our plans and asked me a number of questions. And then he said, 'I'll be happy to be a resource for you.'" And Jack shouldn't concern himself in the least with the lawsuits. There was no quarrel, he said, between Jack and himself, or even between himself and the Estate — they were simply enmeshed in a larger battle that had been precipitated by the Court and, he was sure Jack would agree, the opening of Graceland was in the best interests of all concerned.

Jack wasn't really able to take advantage of Colonel's offer (even if there had been more time, it seems unlikely the Court would have looked very kindly on any renewed association with Colonel), because by now Jack and Priscilla were totally caught up in just getting everything ready in time. It was a little like putting on a full-scale production without so much as a dress rehearsal. But they opened on schedule on June 7 with their hearts in their mouths (and fourteen Dodge vans to shuttle visitors back and forth from the parking lot across the street)— and they were a success! And the success just continued to grow. And Jack, whose generosity

With Jack Soden at Graceland, ca. 1988. *Courtesy of the Graceland Archives*

of outlook and practical vision continued to serve Elvis Presley Enterprises well over the next forty-plus years, would always think of Colonel Parker as part of that success, if only in spirit.

Through Jack's and Priscilla's combined efforts, and with the active assistance of Barron Hilton (for whom Colonel continued to serve as a paid consultant), Colonel was welcomed back into the Elvis world in 1987, when he orchestrated an Elvis festival at the Las Vegas Hilton. Colonel booked Elvis' friend Wayne Newton as the headliner, and put together an exhibit of Elvis memorabilia and artifacts, which would be shown in what had once been Elvis' thirtieth-floor, four-bedroom suite. Nothing would be for sale, he told *Nashville Banner* reporter Pat Embry on a brief trip to Madison to gather up some posters and memorabilia for the exhibit. It would be strictly "a tribute to a great artist, because to me [it's] not a real tribute when you sell a lot of merchandise." He had just gotten back from Graceland, he told the reporter. He had stayed there for two days as a guest of Jack Soden's, and "you can tell 'em the Colonel said, they're doing a beautiful job."

He himself had been giving some thought to opening up a museum at his home in Madison, he went on, almost as if the idea had just occurred to him. He was doing some work on the property now. If he decided to go ahead with his plan, it would be called "Colonel Parker's Wonderful World of Show Business"—but he thought it might just be too much trouble. It might be easier simply to sell the property and the collection. Which would be a shame, he said, because if he went ahead with his plans to convert the house into a showplace, it would be "the only real authentic memorabilia place open that [would] look like it's always been."

In the wake of his visit to Graceland and the Vegas tribute, he was officially embraced by Graceland when he was invited to celebrate what would have been Elvis' fifty-third birthday, on January 8, 1988. Colonel was very chipper ("It's been too long," he said at one point, "but things are working out") and delivered an engaging address that acknowledged his warm reception by both the fans and the Estate. His only complaint was that he and his fellow featured guest Steve Binder (the director of Elvis' celebrated 1968 television special) had each received the same award. "Don't you think," he said, but not before first praising Binder generously ("I don't think there was any producer [who] could ever . . . get the talent out of Elvis like Steve"), that given his length of service, "mine should be a little bigger?"

THAT WAS WHERE I first met the Colonel.

I had just started work on my Elvis biography, and I was there solely because Colonel Parker was advertised as one of the featured guests. To my mind this presented me with a rare, and what might turn out to be a unique, opportunity. I was well aware that Colonel hardly ever did interviews, and, knowing the rarity of his public appearances, it seemed doubtful that I would ever get a chance to actually meet him, so I thought (and you can take this with a grain of biographical salt), maybe if I was in the same room with him, I could absorb a little bit of his aura.

But then, as it happened, at the invitation of my good friend Knox Phillips (Sam's older son), I found myself sitting with the Phillips family, and when Sam, whom I would soon start interviewing extensively for the Elvis book, said he thought he would go over and say hello to his old friend Tom (never "Colonel"—and the "old friend" part may have been

Colonel, Sam Phillips, and a thrilled bystander at Colonel's eightieth birthday party, June 24, 1989. *Photograph by Sally Wilbourn*

more than a little ironic), I chose to embrace the opportunistic gene that all writers are said to be born with (if only) and tagged along. Not long after that very brief introduction, I wrote to Colonel, saying how much I had enjoyed our meeting and telling him a little about my book, about my serious intentions, most of all (and most embarrassingly of all) how I hoped he might rethink his policy of not doing interviews but instead see this "as an opportunity to set the record straight."

Needless to say, he did not take me up on my offer, but he did write back right away, greeting me not with his customary salutation of "Friend Peter" (that would have to wait until the second letter) but a gracious acknowledgment of "the honesty of your request" and an offer to put my name "in a file of literary friends that I know I can trust."

Thus began a correspondence that more closely resembled a chess game in which, with all the goodwill in the world, I attempted to gain an advantage on the Colonel, and he, with all the goodwill in the world, blocked me every time.

The upshot — well, the upshot of our first year of correspondence — was that he invited me to his eightieth birthday party at the Las Vegas Hilton in June of 1989, a wonderful occasion in and of itself, at which I met many luminaries in the Elvis world as well as the moving men who had recently moved Colonel and Loanne into their modest Spanish-style home in a development not too far from the Strip.

At the end of the evening I went up to thank him. He was sitting on a throne-like chair surrounded by various images of elephants, including a giant ice sculpture behind him, tusked and trumpeting, with Sam Phillips standing just to his left. The two of them were engaged in a spirited discussion that had to do with the events that had occurred between October 29 and midnight on the night of November 15, 1955, essentially the sale of Elvis' contract by Sam's Sun record label to RCA.

They were going at it hammer and tongs, each armed with what appeared to be an unbreachable memory accompanied by a steel-trap intellect unprepared to concede the possibility of error. The discussion was proceeding not week by week, not day by day, but hour by hour, with neither giving any quarter and each telling the same story—but from an entirely different point of view.

This might have gone on all night, but I had to catch a plane, so I inserted myself into a rare pause in the conversation, stated my name, and congratulated and thanked the Colonel. He looked at me a little balefully, I thought, and then said in a surprisingly thick, guttural accent: "I put you on the list." Well, I know, I acknowledged with some puzzlement—of course he had put me on the list, how else could I have been invited? This went on in an Alphonse-and-Gaston sort of way for quite a while until the obvious finally dawned on me. What he was saying was: HE HAD PUT ME ON THE LIST.

And so he had. Which meant, quite simply, he had given me the chance to meet maybe two dozen of the most elusive and central figures in Elvis' life, and while I was certainly not so ill-bred as to bring up the subject of my book at Colonel's birthday party, I recognized the opportunity I had been provided—and, finally, the manner in which it had been offered. And so I followed up with letters to Tom Hulett, Freddy Bienstock, Julian Aberbach, and many others, whom I might never otherwise have gotten the chance to talk to if, quite simply, for whatever reason (and I hesitate to even speculate on the reason) Colonel had not— PUT ME ON THE LIST.

MARIE PARKER died in 1986. At the end she could neither feed herself nor speak, and her death was attributed to "chronic brain syndrome," stemming from a "massive benign brain tumor" that had been discovered just four years earlier after remaining undetected for years.

In 1990 Colonel sold the contents of his Madison home to the Estate. He had been seeding the ground for several years now by continuing to allude both publicly and privately to his not fully formed thoughts about possibly turning the Madison house into a museum — or maybe just selling the collection to an unnamed collector, more often than not Japanese, for an unnamed sum, more often than not $5 million.

He and Jack Soden had become friends by this time (he even extended a framed lifetime management contract to Jack's one-year-old daughter), and once he discovered that Graceland had a toll-free WATS line he started calling once or twice a week. "They were long rambling calls," Jack recalled, "often covering the same subjects as the previous call." But they were always interesting, and Jack never lost sight of the fact "that I was talking to one of the truly legendary characters in the evolution of American entertainment. Colonel kept saying, 'You should have all this stuff [in Madison],' and I'd go, 'Yes, we should. And when are you going to give it to us?' And he'd just laugh."

Then one day, Jack said, the lightbulb went on. Colonel was not just talking about the Elvis memorabilia. He was talking about everything in the four-building compound. "I thought, Oh, I'm doing this all wrong. He needs, he wants somebody to care about it all — the beds with the headboards that looked like wagon wheels. Marie's porcelain chickens, all these little [relics] just locked away in time. And I remember the day I called him and said, 'We've thought it over. We want everything. We want the furniture. We want the linen in the closet. We want the pots and pans. We want Marie's chickens. We want everything.' And all of a sudden it was a whole new negotiation."

It didn't take long — but first there was a slight hitch.

Against his better judgment, Jack, a conscientious steward of the Estate, had allowed himself to be persuaded by sound legal advice to include all the standard legal language and extended contemplation of every conceivable contingency that might, or might not, arise, in the twelve- or fourteen-page contract that he sent to the Colonel. "Colonel was furious — he practically hung up on me when we spoke." What he wanted, what he now *demanded,* as Jack had known he would from the start, was a simple, two-page agreement, in plain English, like all of his RCA contracts — and thanks to Jack's persistence that is what he got. The final agreement was little more than a page. It was signed by Colonel on October 23 and called for a single payment of $1.25 million to be made by bank check and handed over to Tom Diskin on-site. Jack directed pickup of the entire collection three days later, as stipulated in the contract — he had done his homework beforehand and had all the contents inventoried and the layout of the four buildings mapped out for precise reassembly in a Memphis warehouse. Someone with a less than generous cast of mind might have pointed out to Colonel that the buying price didn't come close to the $2 or $3 million he had always insisted was his floor, but who would have had the temerity to say that (except maybe Tom Diskin, who believed he had taken a low payout on the $2 million-plus out-of-court settlement he had agreed to in 1983 and was furious that, in his opinion, once again his longtime employer had done the same)— but then Colonel would surely have countered that this way Elvis and the Colonel would be together forever and "Colonel Parker's Wonderful World of Show Business" would have a home. The only real drawback was that this would of necessity mark the end of negotiations. "I knew he was having fun," Jack said. "He was trying to, you know — he probably wanted to negotiate something till the day he died."

But there would, of course, be other matters to negotiate, as Jack would soon discover to his consternation. Because Colonel was always going to be a dealmaker, even if to all appearances there were no deals left to be made.

Colonel and Loanne married on October 26, the day that Elvis Presley Enterprises picked up the collection in two eighteen-wheelers, two moving vans, and an assortment of private vehicles owned by Graceland employees. They had bought their new home together the previous year as "a single man and a single woman," but now when Colonel wrote to Jack about some additional items he wanted to ship to Memphis for the collection, Loanne affixed her signature proudly at the bottom as "Mrs. Colonel."

THE MAN I came to know over the next few years was as keen as ever and (almost) as self-amused. Not infrequently he offered me friendly warnings and advice, sometimes one and the same thing. (See if you can pick out a theme.) "I don't want to see you made a patsy," he said one time, then at a later point in the conversation, "Peter, don't get conned." These were intermixed with his own guarded, but I think sincere, professions of friendship, which more often than not incorporated a similar message. ("I want to be your friend," he declared early on, "but I ain't gonna be your patsy.")

Thanks to the good offices of both Jack Soden and Priscilla Presley, he remained in good standing in the Elvis world, though understandably, after the accusations in the ad litem report, he never regained his former status. And, equally understandably, it never ceased to bother him, though (I'm not going to add a third "understandably" here) he would never admit it. He was called upon on various public occasions, including the unveiling of the Elvis stamp in 1991, to greet fans and serve as an unofficial ambassador of goodwill. He did a handful of interviews, in which he parried the familiar questions with all of his customary skill, if not the full range of his old inventiveness. And he made a rare trip to Palm Springs for his induction into the Palm Springs Walk of Stars in 1994.

He claimed to have no regrets. *What would be the point of regrets?* he always said. "I sleep very good at night," he would never hesitate to proclaim, as if that proved his point. And yet, in every interview, in almost every casual conversation, he brought up the same lingering questions, whether or not they were actually asked. His much-misunderstood 50-50 partnership with Elvis. Why no manager looking out for his client's interests would ever have accepted the deal that Barbra Streisand offered Elvis for *A Star Is Born*. His reluctance (and Elvis and Vernon's insistence) to enter into the RCA masters deal. I won't rehash his answers here (and I'm not discounting them out of hand either)—it's just that to me they betray what I can only call, and Colonel would vehemently deny, an ineradicable sense of self-doubt.

At some point he wrote a poem so unabashedly personal it seems almost impossible to ignore. It was called "To My Friends" and was markedly different from any of his usual poems, which were composed for the most part for a range of ceremonial occasions. "Sometimes we do not let one know," it began, "How much we care and tell them so. . . .

> *They say I'm tough and sometimes cold,*
> *But I'm really just as good as gold.*
> *We all get hurt from time to time*
> *And to forget the pain, it takes a while.*
> *So if you're right and I am wrong*
> *Please remember the good I've done.*

His fall from grace weighed heavily on him, too, in a manner that he could no more directly address. One time he worked himself into such a state that he summoned Jack and Priscilla to a meeting in Las Vegas to demand that he be taken care of in the way that all his years of service demanded. He wanted $1,000 a week as a Special Consultant — and even that, he said, was hardly enough.

Loanne was beside herself with embarrassment. "I pleaded with him, but there was nothing I could do. I [refused to] be any part of it. Colonel was just terrible to them. He was rude. He just wasn't himself. But to their credit they heard him out."

Jack sent him a letter two weeks later from Graceland. It was a very nice letter — a very kind letter, putting things as gently as he could. "We have decided," he wrote, "that such a relationship, while good in terms of acknowledging our respect for your wisdom and experience would [not be] the highest and best use of your unique body of knowledge." But then, after thinking about it, he wrote another letter the following day, upbraiding Colonel not just for his rudeness but for his subsequent threats to take legal action if his demands were not met. None of this was worthy of him, Jack said, least of all the way he had treated Priscilla, who had always been his greatest champion. "Colonel," Jack concluded, "I have appreciated our talks over the years and I have great respect for [you]. Nevertheless, I have felt compelled to get the above off my chest. I would like to remind you that you have periodically heaped harsh criticism on me and others in our organization and fully expected us to take that criticism in stride. I heartily recommend that you do the same. Don't be overly upset. Write [your] book."

Colonel never said a word to Loanne about the letter, though he knew she had read it. "I was just so embarrassed for him," she said. "He would never have done anything like that before"— especially, as she well knew, when he was holding none of the cards.

COLONEL was clearly diminished by the time of his gala eighty-fifth birthday celebration, once again thrown by Barron Hilton, but he was no less engaged. There were still deals to be imagined, advice to be given. Through Mike Crowley, formerly a junior member of Colonel's Management III promotion team and a loyal Colonel acolyte, he met alt-country singer and "Zen cowboy" Jimmie Dale Gilmore, who was enjoying considerable success under Crowley's management. Gilmore was so enthralled he spent an entire off day with him on a busy tour, just listening to his advice and recollections. Colonel engaged another of Crowley's clients, the very talented but not very well-known Monte Warden, to play his eighty-fifth, and in the aftermath of the performance, which at Colonel's request, consisted primarily of Monte's original compositions, talked him up every chance he got, even going so far as to call William Morris to see if they couldn't do something more for this very talented young man.

He was also a great fan of rising country music superstar George Strait, who in 1987 had been the first to sell out the Hilton showroom in his debut performance since Elvis had sold it out (as the International) eighteen years earlier. Colonel never missed an opening and had lots of words of encouragement and advice for Strait, who in his self-effacing way always seemed flattered by the attention. But Colonel felt that Strait was missing an opportunity for real growth; he was convinced that Strait could be a movie star, too, and to that end he brought him to the attention of Jerry Weintraub, now a film producer (*Diner* and *The Karate Kid*, among others). The resulting picture, *Pure Country*, released in 1992, was moderately successful, but it turned out to be Strait's first, and last, true feature, because he simply was not that interested in movie stardom, preferring instead a quiet private life that included ranching and roping. But Strait always made clear his gratitude to Colonel, and Colonel always remained a firm fan.

H E BECAME increasingly housebound over the last few years, but thanks to Loanne, who cared for him vigilantly, he was still able to enjoy his life.

They went out to lunch every day at one or another of the restaurants that he favored, the Hilton coffee shop more often than not, but also the Hungry Hunter, a favorite Italian restaurant, or a local meat and three. They always sat at the same table, and the staff knew them and knew all of Colonel's favorite dishes. After lunch they invariably ended up at the Hilton casino, where Colonel played the $25 slots with the same grim attentiveness that he had once shown the roulette wheel. Then they would go home, where Colonel spent much of the day reading or watching the news or studying the televangelists on TV. He was always fascinated by their pitch, and, as a dispassionate student of human nature, he never failed to be amused by the transparent nature of their hypocrisy or the seemingly unregulated flow of the vast amounts of money that they collected. He might speculate about how they got away with it to one visitor; to another he suggested that this would be a great subject for a book. But as professionally curious as he was about the rhythm of their patter and their variety of promotional techniques, he was never tempted to reconsider the view that he had first formed when he worked at Aimee Semple McPherson's Angelus Temple as a young man just arrived in this country: that the evangelical mission was altogether different from the entertainment world in which he had cast his lot. The world of entertainment, for all its tinsel and glitter, never failed to give the public what it wanted in exchange for their hard-earned dollars. The televangelists, on the other hand, as he saw it, preyed upon ordinary people desperate for belief with promises they could never fulfill.

Old friends stopped by to visit. He remained close to a few of Elvis' chief lieutenants, especially Jerry Schilling, who was now fully embarked on a managerial career of his own, and even Lamar Fike, the clown of the outfit, stayed in touch. Old pals from the carnival world still visited occasionally, though their numbers were noticeably diminishing with age, and Colonel always made sure that Loanne knew exactly who they were and how much they meant to him. He called Eddy Arnold regularly and sent unprompted notes to old acquaintances, assuring them that he still loved them while transparently seeking assurances of love in return.

"My brain is like twenty," he told me one time, and if he forgot things once in a while, he was inclined to say, it was because "sometimes there's so much up there there's no more room." "Every morning," Loanne said, "he woke up convinced it was going to be a wonderful day."

He spoke more extensively than he ever had about growing up in Holland, self-contained anecdotes mostly combined with loving memories of his mother—but there was never any clue as to how, or why, he had been so badly hurt. He spoke affectionately of his sisters Nel and Engelina, and grumbled about another sister, Marie, who had wasted so much of her life as a nun before finally seeing the light and leaving the convent. His interest in news of his surviving family waxed and waned, but on one subject he remained adamant: he had no interest in either seeing or being in direct contact with any of them again. Engelina's daughter, Mieke, at one point got his carefully guarded home phone number and explained to Loanne in broken English how much it would mean to her mother, who was suffering from cancer, to speak to her brother Dries once again. Loanne carried the message to Colonel but then was forced to carry his almost pitiless message back. "The Colonel," she said, repeating as best she could his exact words, "said he doesn't wish to speak with anyone from Holland."

Loanne couldn't understand it. It seemed so needlessly cruel. She could only theorize that maybe he was trying to protect her—she wasn't quite sure from what. She knew that he had long since come to believe that all the gifts and money he had sent home in the wake of his brother Ad's long-ago visit, had been appropriated by his brother, and as a result the gifts had long since stopped. That hardly explained his need to erect so impenetrable a wall against all the others, though—surely they were not at fault. But she could see no way to bring the subject up.

One time a young Dutch filmmaker named Jorrit Van Der Kooi approached him in the Hilton casino with his camera running and, after some idle chitchat in Dutch, asked Colonel directly why he seemed to have no interest in being in touch with his family. "He grunted at me in English," Jorrit said. "'They live their life and I live mine. I know how they're doing. My brother Ad came to visit me. He is dead, you know.'" Jorrit, whose English was only rudimentary at the time, didn't understand him at first. "He switched to Dutch and in a kind of Rotterdam accent said: 'Dood, Ad is dood.'"

A year or two later, as his health declined, a young nephew — or perhaps it was a great-nephew, Loanne was never sure which — wrote a thoughtful letter in very good English, and for the first time it seemed Colonel might be tempted to reply. Loanne urged him to think about it — after all, the young man wasn't asking for anything — and when Colonel hesitated, she persuaded him to put the letter under his placemat at the kitchen table. He kept it there for weeks, but in the end he told her to tear it up. When she remonstrated, he fixed her with a look and said, "You're my family now."

In the last year of Colonel's life, Loanne said — not long before he died, on January 21, 1997 — all the hurt he was hiding, the sense of abandonment she had so long suspected was lurking behind the public mask, surfaced in a way she could never have fully anticipated.

Would she go with him, he asked one day, seemingly out of the blue, *if he were forced to go to another country to live?*

Of course, of course, she said. Didn't he know by now that she would do anything for him? And I'm sure in her own irreproachably positive way she was confident that he did. But one can only imagine how heartbreaking it must have been to realize that, after all their years together and all the confidences they had shared, he could still harbor such unassuageable fears.

BOOK TWO

·····································

THE LETTERS

·····································

1955

"Colonel" Tom Parker, who had only recently begun to insist on the universal use of that honorific to address him (in fact, only since December of 1954, when he had begun managing Hank Snow, the number-one country-and-western recording star of that year), first became aware of an obscure twenty-year-old Memphis artist named Elvis Presley on January 12, 1955.

He and his lieutenant, Tom Diskin, went to see Presley perform on the Louisiana Hayride in Shreveport just three days later, and he was as knocked out by the crowd's reaction as he was by the music. Within a week he had him booked on the Hank Snow tour scheduled to begin in New Mexico on February 14.

But before that tour even began, Colonel had Tom Diskin, a native Chicagoan who frequently served as a second voice for his employer, write a letter to George Ferguson, head of the WLS Artists Bureau in Chicago. (WLS was the home of the National Barn Dance, which predated the Grand Ole Opry, the hallmark of country music radio, by more than a year.) The letter minced no words in expressing Colonel's extravagant regard for the young man's talent and potential, while at the same time advancing the interests of two of his longtime clients, June Carter and country comedian Minnie Pearl.

It is the tone of Diskin's letter, the unrestrained, let's just say it, *over-the-top* enthusiasm of his and Colonel's words, that stands out most here. This is a point made all the more evident in retrospect by the fact that even as he was just beginning his management of Snow (whom he was determined to elevate to the same heights as his previous client, Eddy Arnold, by far the biggest star in country music up till that time), Colonel seemed ready almost to set everything aside in pursuit of this new, unproven phenomenon.

And just to amplify how big a gamble this was likely to be, neither Ferguson nor any of the other booking agents and promoters whom Colonel contacted with similar expressions of belief was able to find a spot for Elvis on any of their shows. ∎

"We have a new boy that is absolutely going to be one of the biggest things in the business in a very short time"

Mr. George Ferguson   January 27, 1955
WLS ARTIST BUREAU
1230 W. Washington
Chicago, Illinois

Dear George:

Just to say hello and let you in on a few things.

We have a new boy that is absolutely going to be one of the biggest things in the business in a very short time. His name is ELVIS PRESLEY. Currently he is on the Louisiana Hayride and on a small label Sun records. He gets the girls excited the way Frank Sinatra used to do it. And he's as good looking as all heck. I really know that you'd get terrific reaction on the TV show with this boy. He's a hot box office attraction and everybody is trying to get him for repeat dates where he has appeared . . .

Sincerely,
Tom Diskin
HANK SNOW-JAMBOREE
ATTRACTIONS

Did I tell you about June Carter? Doing great as a comedian. If you have an open date let me know and I'll see what we can do on price. She gets as good reaction as Minnie [Pearl] on the shows.

———————

Over the next four months, Colonel did everything in his power to advance the young man's career. Even before the Hank Snow tour started, he wrote to Steve Sholes, Eddy Arnold and Hank Snow's a&r man (producer) at RCA, and Harry Kalcheim, the William Morris booking agent with whom he had worked to expand Eddy Arnold's career, with little tangible result. He contacted every major promoter he knew (that constituted virtually every major promoter), telling them of this great new artist who might need "lots of buildup before he is a good investment" but they could rest assured he *would* be a good investment —

The iconic photo: Tampa, July 31, 1955. *Courtesy of the Graceland Archives*

but once again the results were disappointing. The main stumbling block, though, was the boy's manager, a Memphis DJ named Bob Neal, to whom he tried to convey the prospect of a limitless future, a vision that Neal simply seemed unable to grasp.

Finally, on June 21, Colonel appeared to have persuaded Neal to let him take the reins, writing to Steve Sholes, "Elvis Presley will be working thru our company as of July 24. If you have a strong interest in trying to secure EP for RCA let me have your thoughts."

That very day, despite a sensational weeklong tour of Florida the previous month on which Hank Snow had headlined but Elvis stole the show, Neal reneged on their understanding, saying only: "Hold off any further announcements regarding Elvis until I have more time with him."

On June 25, the day before his forty-sixth birthday, Colonel wrote to Tom Diskin, with whom he had worked hand in glove since 1951 but who now appeared to be entertaining thoughts of quitting the road. The letter is a rare, if not unique, example of Colonel expressing doubt or discouragement about any course of action he has ever taken. Under the guise of providing Diskin with a pep talk, he involuntarily reveals that he may be the one needing the pep talk, offering up a transparent confession of vulnerability all the more surprising from a man with a lifelong aversion to intimacy. ∎

"Get it in your mind that there is no future in anything other than big deals. . . . You have to believe this so strongly that you will let no one get your time and ear on junk deals"

Dear Tom;   June 25th, 1955

Thanks for the speaker, you could not have gotten me anything better [as a birthday present].

Handle the HANK SNOW TOUR, your in complete charge, take this off of me, so I will not have to worry about it. You know the deals. . . . you know that I wanted you to be home this long for reasons of your Mother yourself and the family, I know they appreciate it, it has been rather hard for me to handle as much work as I have the last 4 weeks, but I know you will balance it out in many ways, your setup also will work out much better for you, as the signs show it. Get it in your mind that there is no future in anything other than big deals, no small time stuff, it takes as much time and no money can be made of it. You have to believe this so strongly that you will let no one get your time and ear on junk deals. Everytime we have become involved in something small we have lost time money and got nowhere. You can do much better than you have been doing when you believe this, I know you can do it when you make up your mind, and you can make up your mind when you want to make it up. . . .

I am not an office man, but can sell anything that anyone else can sell. Go at it, take charge of the tour, handle your end of it with confidence and look after HANK. Take things off of him as much as possible [and] dont get bogged down. . . . the future looks very good for you if you want to make it that way, I will always protect you all I can and I know you do the same. You are good for me and I know that I do understand you better than any-one could. Your closer to me than any-one ever has been and will be, and I know you understand me. . . .

> Marie said hello.
> Tom

And yet, not surprisingly, he persisted. After a second sensational Florida tour, this time without Hank Snow, who had his own simultaneous West Coast tour with Tom Diskin at the helm, Colonel made his first all-out approach to the William Morris Agency, the premier talent agency in the country, with whom he had worked so successfully to get Eddy Arnold television shows and supper club bookings. He was still at this point frustratingly far from taking over Elvis' management from Bob Neal, but his exhortatory letter to Sam Weisbord, one of William Morris' most senior West Coast agents, while cannily referencing his primary client Hank Snow's successes (he and Snow were on-paper partners in the success of Presley's bookings under the shared rubric of Hank Snow Enterprises–Jamboree Attractions), stands as irrefutable evidence of the totality of his conviction and commitment. ■

"The possibilities are unlimited"

Mr. Sam Weisbord   August 17, 1955
William Morris Agency
202 North Cannon Drive
Beverly Hills, California

Dear Sam:

  It was nice talking to you on the phone while in Hollywood. Sorry we couldn't get together at the office as time was pressing.

  The Hollywood Bowl for HANK SNOW was a great success. Not only was the attendance very good — over 12,000 — but percentage-wise also. San Diego was a sell-out on Sunday night and also Town Hall Saturday night after the Bowl appearance. Will appreciate any guest shots or situations that you can move HANK SNOW in on as he is a great artist and has a tremendous following in California.

  I am mailing you a complete set of pictures on ELVIS PRESLEY, the new boy I told you about on the telephone . . . also some of his records. He is presently on a small record label and they have sold this year over 100,000 of this boy's records already, and they have no distribution whatsoever. The photos are action shots that I had made in Tampa, Florida, during ELVIS PRESLEY'S engagement at the Armory, Sunday, July 31 [one of these would be used seven months later as the iconic cover shot for Elvis' first RCA album], with a couple of studio shots included that were made in Memphis. This artist seems to me to be right in line for motion picture material, television, and a stage career. He has ability, although inexperience since he has only been working about a year, but with the right training and advice and good material the possibilities are unlimited. His exposure on the stage does 75% towards the public accepting this artist. The talents that are hidden in this personality are unlimited with the proper exploitation.

  I can only go so far without the help of friends like you towards making the world aware of such great talent. You have forgotten more than I'll ever know about how to bring this out in an artist and I'm asking you for advice to carry on and get the best results out of and for ELVIS PRESLEY and all of us.

  I am sending this same package to Harry Kalcheim with a copy of your letter and I have a feeling that there will be a close association in time to come pertaining to this artist.

Promoting Hank Snow, at the Country Music DeeJay Convention in Nashville, November 1955. *Courtesy of the Country Music Hall of Fame and Museum*

HANK SNOW has done much to expose the talents of ELVIS PRES-LEY as he has taken him more or less under his wing, and has been plugging away on all his personals and blowing the bugle about ELVIS PRESLEY. In Jacksonville, Florida, I had to get four officers to take the boy off the stage as the young fans tore his clothes and shirt off him.

I sincerely believe a screen test is in order. I'll wait to hear from you.

Your Pal,
The Colonel

The back-and-forth with Bob Neal continued, until, just around the time of his letter to Sam Weisbord, Colonel saw an opening, when he got complaints about a show that Elvis had headlined in Batesville, Arkansas. Presley, the show's promoter wrote, had indulged in some highly objectionable "smutty comedy" with bass player Bill Black. (You'll have to supply what "smutty comedy" 1955-style would be like.) You can read Colonel's letter as an honest statement of principle (it is), a principled proffer of advice (it is), or as an almost in-your-face way of telling Bob Neal that he wasn't up to the job (he wasn't). There is nothing hypocritical here — Colonel was committed to putting on a good clean show, and as he made clear, from his beginnings with Eddy Arnold in 1945 to Elvis' Las Vegas performances thirty years later, he was not prepared to stand behind a performer who insulted his audience. But at the same time the letter appears to have done its stealth job, too, as over the next three months a bewildered (and overmatched) Bob Neal found himself tending toward the same conclusion that Colonel had been steering him toward all along: it might perhaps be time to turn the job over to the Colonel. Though, of course, there would be any number of unpredictable twists and turns in between. ■

"I think the most important thing is that he needs guidance. He is young, inexperienced, and it takes a lot more than a couple of hot records in a certain territory to become a big name artist, level-headed, courteous, and carry the responsibility that goes with being a star as ELVIS wants to be"

Mr. Bob Neal   August 22, 1955
Radio Station WMPS
Memphis, Tennessee

Dear Bob:

It was nice talking to you on the phone yesterday. It is regrettable that the Batesville situation was goofed up. I know there are always two sides to every story, but after talking to Mr. Lyon [the promoter of the White River Water Carnival festival in Batesville] on the telephone and getting the story from the DUKE OF PADUCAH [a featured performer and an old friend of Colonel's who was a staple of the festival], somehow ELVIS must either have been sick or upset, as he surely was not himself. May I suggest that if you can see your way clear [to] a refund of at least $50 to the Batesville people — which you can handle direct or I will handle for you, as it is very important for ELVIS PRESLEY to maintain the best relationship with sponsors. One bad sponsor can undo full years of work just from bad publicity alone.

You must definitely set up a new deal with ELVIS where he gets on the stage as a singer, stays on the stage as a singer, and comes off like a singer. There is always enough comedy on any of my shows that they don't have to do comedy. To be exact, I just can't have any more comedy on ELVIS PRESLEY'S part of the program. If I had received one gripe, or two or three, I would understand that you can't please all of the people all of the time, but from all sources — my connections, friends, people I work with, customers — the complaints have been dominant in all situations and I think we are very fortunate to be able to nip this before it is too late. ELVIS has great talents and he does not have to resort to smutty comedy to sell his attractions. When we ask for more money for ELVIS we definitely must give better production or we should sell him as a comic, and you know how much we can get for him doing that.

I think the most important thing is that he needs guidance. He is young, inexperienced, and it takes a lot more than a couple of hot records in a certain territory to become a big name artist, level-headed, courteous, and carry the responsibility that goes with being a star as ELVIS wants to be. There is no way we can play this down — even if we tried — as we would only be fooling ourselves and would be out of business in no time. My reputation is more important than my friendship and belief in the talents that ELVIS has. He can cash in on this to the fullest, but he must contribute all the qualities that I know he has or can have if he makes up his mind to do so. You, as his manager, carry the biggest part of this responsibility. I don't know whether you have ever thought about it that way. They don't say this ELVIS PRESLEY, the first thing they say is who is his manager to let it go on — then they say who books him here, and it all falls back on our shoulders. You know that I am only quoting the things I've heard — I was not there — but the complaints are overwhelmingly the same, so there must be something that happened. . . .

I am sure you know how to handle this situation, and impress upon ELVIS the importance if he plans to stay in show business. It is important for him to be on time as per contracts, just as much as he is looking for the money when he finishes playing — even more so the buyer is looking for the talent to be on time and do the job he is paying for. I know that if I had not collected the money in Batesville in advance they would not have paid us for part of the show without a gripe. You must be firm, Bob — this is not something to play with. I have some clients that would cancel him out even while he was on the stage if they thought it would hurt their business, and definitely would not pay for something that they didn't bargain for. There is a time to play for ELVIS but he must not do it too close to his working agreement.

I don't know of any stronger words than to say it is a lot easier to undo all the good things you and I have done, and ELVIS will be just a floating memory no matter who handles him, because he has to please the masses and also the people that invest in him.

Get back to me with your thoughts and also let me know in plenty of time whenever you want me to move in on the record situation and the [Horace] Logan set-up [the extension, or curtailment, of Elvis' one-year contract with the Louisiana Hayride, which Horace Logan managed]. The New Orleans deal for ELVIS could be tremendously important for his career, as with two performances there he has not created the following that I thought would be his. I know it is there — this is his opportunity to wake them up.

Regards,
The Colonel
By Georgine Keeney
Sec'y to Col. Tom Parker

It worked, up to a point — and then it didn't. Bob Neal continued to go back and forth, agreeing to certain conditions and then retracting his agreement. So, in effect, a month later Colonel quit (although, as usual, he allowed Neal to make the first move), but not without informing Elvis (with whom he had had virtually no direct communication up till this time, and certainly no personal correspondence) of his regrets. There are so many little touches — Hollywood, "stop by here on your way home," all the "irons in the fire"— it is clear Colonel was not really planning on going away anytime soon. And as it turned out, true to his expectations, there was no need. (And you will note that this letter, unlike the last, was not typed by a secretary.) ∎

"I hope that we will be able to work again together in the future"

Mr ELVIS PRESLEY   Sept 17, 1955
Richmond, VA

Dear ELVIS;

Enclosed is a copy of my letter to Bob Neal, in answer to his letter received here a few Days ago, advising me that to desolve the agreement we have upon proper settlement would be much better all the way around, this of course I agree on, as it seems that I am never able to keep working along a regular line of order from time to time.

I hope that we will be able to work again together in the future, after everything has been worked out such as proper settlement with me as agreed upon, and I will of course plan to work the markets that I have opened up for you, as I have Bob Neal's promise that I will be protected in these markets.

I also have a good many irons in the fire that may come thru as we go along and I will expect these to be carried out after coming to some understanding. I have just mailed a deposit check for $1000. for the October 19-20-21-22-23rd engagements with the ROY ACUFF SHOW wich I sold direct with Bob Neals understanding and approval.

If you have time stop by here on your way home and see my place, also pickup your speaker wich of course I promised you some time ago. I will also give you the special blowup for your home that I had made in Hollywood while I was there last Month.

Give my best to Bob Neal and your Parents and Mr Diskin.

Sincerely
Your Pal The Col.

By the end of October, with Colonel finally, firmly, in charge, he began the process of selling Elvis' Sun Records contract to RCA. First he got Elvis' parents (and guardians — Elvis was still twenty years old), Vernon and Gladys Presley, to send him a carefully composed telegram (the format of the telegram was sent out under the signature of Tom Diskin, whom the Presleys found to be a more congenial connection, but there is no question that Colonel dictated every word) authorizing him to be their son's exclusive representative. Then, in an even trickier diplomatic maneuver, he got Sun Records owner Sam Phillips to name his price, which turned out to be the unheard-of sum of $35,000, plus $5,000 to cover back royalties. RCA for three weeks was stuck at a figure well below that sum, but finally on November 15, 1955, agreed to Sam Phillips' and Colonel's demands. ■

"WE FEEL THAT YOU WILL BE FOR THE BEST INTEREST OF ELVIS PRESLEY"

MR & MRS VERNON PRESLEY   OCT 20 1955
2124 LAMAR ST PHONE 484921 MEMPHIS TENN

DEAR MR & MRS PRESLEY FOLLOWING IS THE COPY FOR THE WIRE AUTHORIZING COL PARKER TO NEGOTIATE A RECORD CONTRACT ON BEHALF OF ELVIS. "DEAR COL PARKER, WE HEREBY AUTHORIZE YOU TO ACT AS OUR SOLE AND EXCLUSIVE REPRESENTATIVE IN ALL NEGOTIATIONS PERTAINING TO THE RECORDING CONTRACT OF ELVIS PRESLEY THIS AUTHORIZATION TO INCLUDE THE SETTLEMENT FOR THE PRESENT CONTRACT WITH SUN RECORDS AND FULL AUTHORITY TO NEGOTIATE A NEW RECORDING CONTRACT WITH A MAJOR RECORDING FIRM NO OTHER PERSON OR PERSONS ARE AUTHORIZED TO REPRESENT ELVIS PRESLEY IN ANY RECORDING CONTRACT NEGOTIATIONS OTHER THAN COL PARKER AND WE WILL BE BOUND BY YOUR DECISION AS WE FEEL THAT YOU WILL BE FOR THE BEST INTEREST OF ELVIS PRESLEY SIGNED MR & MRS VERNON PRESLEY AS GUARDIANS FOR ELVIS PRESLEY". SEND THIS WIRE TO COL PARKER CARE THE HOLIDAY MOTEL ROUTE 3 MECHANICSBURG PA, COLONEL IS NOT ONLY INTERESTED IN GETTING ELVIS ON MAJOR LABEL BUT WANTS TO GET THE BEST, POSSIBLE DEAL FOR HIM NOW AND FOR THE FUTURE YOU CAN BE ASSURED THAT YOU ARE PUTTING THIS IN MOST CONFIDENT HANDS KINDEST REGARDS TO YOU AND ELVIS

TOM DISKIN

"Please advise me your best flat price for a complete dissolution and release"

WESTERN UNION STRAIGHT WIRE

Mr. Sam Phillips   Oct 24, 1955

SUN RECORDS

706 Union Ave.

Memphis, Tennessee

IMPORTANT: TO BE DELIVERED = NOT PHONED.

Dear Sam:

Elvis Presley and his parents Mr. & Mrs. Presley have requested and authorized me to handle all negotiations on an exclusive basis towards affecting a settlement of the Elvis Presley recording contract with you and the Sun Record Company. If interested will you please advise me your best flat price for a complete dissolution and release free and clear of the talents and recording services of ELVIS PRESLEY and also to include the masters of all Elvis Presley recordings now held by your firm and your associates if any. It is of course understood that you will [be] allowed to service your distributors and dealers with the releases that are currently on sale and for a reasonable period of time. Advise me here at the Warwick Hotel in New York City, by wire today as I will have to leave here in the morning.

Kindest regards,
Colonel Tom Parker

On November 14, with the RCA agreement still hanging in the balance, Colonel responded to a well-intended suggestion by William Morris agent Harry Kalcheim that he might be able to get Colonel's new client a "short," that is to say a fifteen-minute film which would run ahead of the feature in movie theaters (like a cartoon) and could serve to expose Elvis to a wider audience. Colonel's first reaction was outright indignation — Elvis Presley was a major talent whose most obvious point of comparison was the recently deceased James Dean, who was not only an actor of deep emotional depth and a symbol of youthful rebellion but, along with Marlon Brando and Montgomery Clift, one of Elvis' biggest movie idols. The brief correspondence that ensues indicates that Colonel may have had a somewhat imperfect understanding of the movie business at this time, but once again it shows his faith in his artist's unlimited potential.

The first letter, uncharacteristically cautious in its expression, is in response to Kalcheim's initial suggestion, but it heats up from there. ■

"On the order of James Dean"

Mr. Harry Kalcheim   November 14, 1955
William Morris Agency
1740 Broadway
New York 19 NY

Dear Harry:

Regarding Elvis Presley you have the complete publicity kit and information wich I sent you at the same time that I sent it to Sammy Weisbord. I would be interested in making a picture with this boy, however we must be very careful to expose him in a manner befitting his personality wich is something like the James Dean situation. . . .

> Your pal
> [Signed "Tom"]
> The Colonel.

....

To which Kalcheim, who at this point clearly holds the upper hand and is not yet a true believer, responds with some bewilderment the following day.

....

Dear Tom:

. . . RE: ELVIS PRESLEY

I wrote you to find out whether he would do a short. Your note has me rather perplexed as you speak about handling him on the order of James Dean. My purpose in getting him into a short and on Universal lot is to expose him to the studio people. Agree with you that he has tremendous potential. Let me know immediately if I can proceed with the short. . . .

Kindest regards.

Sincerely,
WILLIAM MORRIS AGENCY
[Signed "HK"]
Harry Kalcheim

....

Whereupon Colonel, doing all he can to make up for lost ground (and doing a pretty good job of it) now that the RCA deal has been agreed upon, reasserts forcefully, but in carefully calculated terms, his view of the matter.

....

"Believe me, if you ever follow one of my hunches, follow up on this one and you won't go wrong"

Mr. Harry Kalcheim   November 17, 1955
William Morris Agency
1740 Broadway
New York 19 NY

Dear Harry:

Thanks for your letter dated November 15th. When I mentioned on the order of James Dean, I only meant that this boy, ELVIS PRESLEY, has the same type of personality, and talents along the line of James Dean. Since the unfortunate accident of this artist a few months ago, I thought perhaps that Warner Bros. may have had some plans prepared to use this artist which will now have to be shelved due to this unfortunate accident of the late James Dean.

Believe me, if you ever follow one of my hunches, follow up on this one and you won't go wrong. I now have exclusive representation on this artist for motion pictures, television, radio, personal appearances in theatres, as I told you before. If you do come up with a situation that we should take ELVIS PRESLEY to the Coast give me some advance notice and I will work it out. . . . This rabbit you can rest assured has already been pulled out of the hat. . . .

My best to the family.

Sincerely,
The Colonel

On the day he signed with RCA, in a signing ceremony at the Sun Records studio, with his parents, Bob Neal, Colonel Parker, Sam Phillips, and various RCA executives in attendance, Elvis telegrammed the Colonel: ■

"I love you like a father"

November 21, 1955

Dear Colonel, Words can never tell you how my folks and I appreciate what you did for me. I have always known and now my folks are assured that you are the best and most wonderful person I could ever hope to work with. Believe me when I say I will stick with you thru thick and thin and do everything I can to uphold your faith in me. Again I say thanks and I love you like a father. Elvis Presley

One of the key elements of the RCA contract was that RCA would secure for their new artist a minimum of three national television appearances. They didn't. Colonel then entrusted the William Morris Agency with the task. They didn't do anything either — at least not quickly enough to suit Colonel. Therefore, he took matters into his own hands, using an independent agent to book four appearances on CBS' Jimmy and Tommy Dorsey–hosted *Stage Show*, with an option for two more. He didn't waste a minute in letting his old friend and colleague Harry Kalcheim know what he thought of Kalcheim's inattention to business. ■

"If I waited for some-one to call me with deals all the time, I would have to start selling candy apples again"

Mr Harry Kalcheim   Dec 16, 1955
William Morris Agency
1740 Broadway
New York City New York

Dear Harry;

   . . . Regarding your note on ELVIS PRESLEY. Knowing you as I do I will be very frank; Some-one is giving you a bum steer regarding Bob Neal advising the producer [of the Dorsey brothers' *Stage Show*] to get in touch with Steve Yates [the independent agent, who ended up booking the show]. . . . Bob Neal does not advise any-one to contact any agency but myself First so we do not run into any snags. Steve Yates called me with an offer for the Gleason show One shot, and the price he gave me was way out of line so I told him what I wanted for PRESLEY and he got it. I called you up right after this and asked you why your man had not worked on this setup. . . . Only after we had already been talking and confirmed the 4 dates did the producer called Yates and asked him what William Morris had to do with it. . . .

   Harry you know as well as I do offering a new artist is one thing but selling One is another, I cant go for a pitch that my artist has been sub-mitted and then wait till you hear from some-one that wants him, that way you can write One hundred letters and just sit and wait till some-one comes up with a deal. So till I get up there lets just leave everything as is, and I am not exclusive with any-one for the time being, for we surely will have to clearup a few details or we will always be in hot water and have misunderstandings. I dont think that this artist was pitched full force for the reaction that I got on my own deals have been very good and so far we got nothing from William Morris. Steve Yates did a good job with this deal and some-one just did not get on the ball in time to nail this down. If I waited for some-one to call me with deals all the time, I would have to start selling candy apples again. Nuff said, I just spoke to you and you know my feelings towards you and William Morris but I cant let my friendship keep my artist from working, so lets all dig-in and keep things rolling. I think this will work out for the best of all of us. But I do hope that your man will at least dig in a little more often and tell every-one so they will know who they should call. My best to you and the Family.

                        Your Pal
                        [Signed "Tom"]
                        The Colonel.

1956

In the early months of 1956, after what nearly every one of the RCA top brass considered a disastrous initial recording session in Nashville (though it produced "Heartbreak Hotel," and three sides which would be featured on Elvis' epochal first album, the RCA executives wanted to discard the entire session and send Steve Sholes back to Nashville to try again), the company was nearly as frustrated with what they took to be Colonel's provincial approach to national promotion. Bill Bullock, manager of the Single Records Department and effectively Steve Sholes' boss, wrote to him on March 7, 1956, and made it abundantly clear that everyone's patience was wearing thin. "You must remember that we too have a big stake in this artist," Bullock dyspeptically reminded the Colonel. Had Colonel forgotten what they had all agreed upon: that the idea was to break Elvis as a pop singer in major markets such as New York, Chicago, and Detroit? Colonel had done nothing so far to indicate that he had any intention of keeping his part of the bargain. Nor had his artist, he implied, as evidenced by the manner in which he conducted himself in the studio, where he appeared insistent on going his own way.

Colonel's reply was short and, if not directly to the point, made its point by agreeing 100 percent, but really not at all. He was prepared to defend his artist and his artist's choices at all costs. And he never changed his approach, never played the cities that Bullock cited, and never suffered the consequences that Bullock and all the other RCA marketeers predicted. And, of course, both in the manner and substance of his address, he claimed at least equal status with every one of them, while providing each with a shipment of country sausage. ■

"We have to be very careful the type of package we build around ELVIS"

Mr. W.W. Bullock, Manager   March 9, 1956
Single Records Department
RCA Victor Record Division
155 East 24th Street
New York (10), New York

Dear Bill:

Thanks for your letter regarding ELVIS PRESLEY, and all of the information.

I am well aware of the problems, and agree with you 100%. You also know that I am doing everything possible to co-ordinate, but I have a lot of pressure from this side, also from distributors, record managers, and commitments that I must fulfill on obligations that were made before I took ELVIS over, and there are a good many. . . . However, there is nothing I can do on personal appearances definitely until ELVIS has completed his screen test in Hollywood at the end of this month.

We have to be very careful the type of package we build around ELVIS. At the same time, I am keeping [two other prominent RCA artists] HANK SNOW busy, and also setting up dates for EDDY ARNOLD.

Everyone has been very helpful, and I will call on you if there is any way you folks can help me, and I appreciate your offer to do so.

Your Pal,
The Colonel

cc: Messrs. Steve Sholes, Larry Kanaga, Howard Letz [Letts], Chick Crumpacker

P.S. . . . Did you ever receive the sausage that I ordered for you, which I promised you and the Mrs. at Joe Carlton's house warming? If not, advise, as several packages seem to have gotten lost.

E ven after things had "settled down" to the point that Elvis, after more than two months at the top of the pop, rhythm and blues, and country charts with "Heartbreak Hotel," was beginning to be recognized as not just another rising star but an uncategorizable phenomenon, the company was still in turmoil over some of the choices that he was making and the continued lack of concern for their concern from his manager. After Elvis' controversial second appearance on *The Milton Berle Show* on June 5 (the one that was described by one New York television critic as "an exhibition that was suggestive and vulgar, tinged with the kind of animalism that should be confined to dives and bordellos"), Harry Kalcheim wrote to Colonel to express both his and the agency's (and unquestionably RCA's) uneasiness. It is interesting that, from the tone of his letter, Kalcheim appears to still think that he occupies the superior position and that his friend Tom may actually listen to what he has to say. (See Colonel's reply below.) ■

"The comments on Elvis around here, on his show Tuesday, were not very complimentary"

Col. Tom Parker   June 7, 1956
P.O. Box 417
Madison, Tenn.

Dear Tom:

The comments on Elvis around here, on his show Tuesday, were not very complimentary. The comments have come in from the junior members and friends of our various associates. They also felt he didn't look too good and that he had a very tense look on his face all through the first number.

In connection with the Steve Allen Show, want to make sure that he comes in looking like he did on his first Berle Show, with plenty of rest for a couple of days prior to his appearance. Also would like to suggest that he watch his numbers and if possible get some numbers where he doesn't shake as much as he did on the show Tuesday night.

Know you understand these suggestions are constructive and are for his good.

Kindest regards.

Sincerely,
WILIAM MORRIS AGENCY, INC.
[Signed "HK"]
Harry Kalcheim

Whatever Harry Kalcheim might have hoped he would hear back, he can't have been altogether pleased with the reply that he got, as Colonel wasted no time, and minced no words (though I'm sure he expended a good deal of thought), on his immediate response. ∎

"I have always remembered, and practiced the old saying: 'One never wins anything when one gives up,' and I'm not a quitter. As long as the LIGHT BEAMS, I will turn it on!"

Mr. Harry Kalcheim   June 8, 1956
William Morris Agency, Inc.
1740 Broadway
New York 19 NY

Dear Harry:

. . . REGARDING ELVIS APPEARANCE on the BERLE SHOW: Just like in the BOB MITCHUM days, the writers are having a Field Day with this new personality. I am sure one of them will come up with a good writeup before long, as they also will get tired of writing the same thing all the time. . . .

As for the STEVE ALLEN SHOW — we will just have to see what happens. I can understand every situation, and will do whatever possible to work things out right. You must realize that I have been buffing [possibly "bluffing"?] this situation for some time, and will continue to do so, but not at the expense of covering up an impossible situation when it arises. I have always remembered, and practiced the old saying: "One never wins anything when one gives up," and I'm not a quitter. As long as the LIGHT BEAMS, I will turn it on!

> Your friend
> The Colonel

In the aftermath of Elvis' appearance on *The Steve Allen Show,* on July 1, where he was forced to don a tuxedo and sing "Hound Dog" to a basset hound, Colonel was determined to regain control for his artist. Ed Sullivan, by far the biggest force in general-entertainment television both at the time and for the decade to come, had vowed never to have Presley on his show, but when the ratings for Steve Allen's debut show came out and showed that for the first time he had been soundly beaten in his Sunday slot, he got in touch with William Morris and offered an unprecedented $50,000 for three appearances. (By comparison, Elvis got $7,500 for *The Steve Allen Show*.) Harry Kalcheim relayed Sullivan's offer, but Colonel was more concerned about the terms of the contract. And, not to jump the gun too much, but in the end, after some hard bargaining, he got exactly what he wanted, which guaranteed his artist "complete control of presentation as to songs," including "sole selection of musical accompaniment and instrumental and vocal group if any." ■

"I will do whatever is fair but must insist on complete control"

HARRY KALCHEIM   July 12, 1956
WM. MORRIS AGENCY
1740 BROADWAY
NEW YORK CITY, NEW YORK

... SUGGEST YOU HAVE SOMEONE MOVE IN ON THE SULLIVAN SETUP TODAY AND TRY TO CLOSE SAME OR GET OFF ON SOMETHING ELSE BEFORE WE GET TANGLED UP TOO MUCH. ... SPOKE TO SULLIVAN TODAY AND THERE SEEMS TO BE SOME MISUNDERSTANDING REGARDING PRESENTATION OF PRESLEY. I WILL DO WHATEVER IS FAIR BUT MUST INSIST ON COMPLETE CONTROL OF PRESENTATION AS TO SONGS. WE HAD TOO MUCH ADVERSE PUBLICITY ON LAST SHOW REGARDING ELVIS BEING TIED DOWN TOO MUCH, AT LEAST TEN TO ONE. ...

By the end of the summer Colonel was feeling overworked and, it would seem, underappreciated. (Despite his show of supreme self-confidence, Colonel was never without the need for approbation.) He had been going on all cylinders (his usual mode, but still...) ever since the previous fall; Elvis was in the midst of shooting his first motion picture, *Love Me Tender*; and Colonel had just initiated a mammoth merchandising deal, something far beyond anything ever attempted with a pop singing star before, with a thirty-eight-year-old specialist-market merchandiser named Hank Saperstein. All of his friends were advising Colonel that he needed to take some time off. He seems to have appreciated their concern, but he scoffed at their advice. As he wrote to Harry Kalcheim at the end of August, "It is very amusing when you say you hope that finally I am getting some much needed rest when I have to be here everyday from morning till night and then at night stick around to keep the rats away. Hollywood's rats that is." At the same time he was clearly exhausted after working sixteen to eighteen hours a day, seven days a week, for his single client. Let's just say he felt beleaguered as well as understandably proud. But don't feel sorry for Colonel Tom Parker. As you will see from his caustic sign-off (I don't know if this is the actual sign-off, because nothing further of the letter survives), he has not lost any of his edge, as he brutally dismisses Hal Wallis, the producer who signed Elvis to his first movie contract but who has not yet come up with a vehicle to star him in. Hence *Love Me Tender* is being made for 20th Century Fox on a clause that Colonel had insisted be inserted into the Wallis contract: his artist's freedom to make at least one picture a year with an outside studio, despite Wallis' protestations that he needed an "exclusive" deal. ■

"One cannot bluff his way through a pile of work when one has to do it oneself"

Mr. Harry Kalcheim   September 6 1956
William Morris Agency
1740 Broadway
New York 19 NY

Dear Harry:

Thanks for your letter, between you, Abe Lastfogel, Marie [Colonel's wife] and a lot of people I should take my advice, close my shop up and take off for two or three months. Then again I wonder rightly so, what a mess you people would be in, trying to tie the ends together when I am not around, which of course would go on regardless one way or the other.

I guess its a weakness in me, that the only decisions I can make are the ones that envolve a lot of people and somehow I am always unable to make a decision that envolves just Marie and I. May be I run out of tape one of these days and then I can't go on. But its gratifying to know your kind thoughts which gives me strength to go on just a little longer.

One cannot bluff his way through a pile of work when one has to do it oneself, however if this is possible I would be very happy to pay for it. I think you would do the same because I know you are always under pressure and not practicing what you are preaching to them. . . .

Regarding the Hal Wallis situation I understand he will make his picture in December. Somehow Mr. Wallis gets hot and cold. Hot, when the press notices are good and cold when they are adverse. You know the old saying about missing the boat, I don't think Mr. Wallis knew when it was sailing.

At some point during this time period, in this fragment from an undated letter, once again to Harry Kalcheim, Colonel gave his unvarnished view of both his client's potential and his ability to nurture it. ∎

"Even a poor teacher is a good teacher if the pupil will listen"

. . . Regarding Elvis, as to your question how Elvis is getting along, I think he is putting all he has into what he is doing when he is working. Time will tell, if he will gain the strength personally with the experience to buff himself for greater things to come. I will do whatever is in my power to protect him as long as he is willing to listen, for even a poor teacher is a good teacher if the pupil will listen. . . .

Your Pal,
THE COLONEL

The merchandising deal worked out better than anyone (except Colonel) could have expected. By the time *Love Me Tender* started shooting on August 22, 1956, Hank Saperstein's campaign was in full swing, with something like eighteen licensees and twenty-nine products, including belts, scarves, skirts, jeans, lipstick, lockets, charm bracelets, publications, and Western ties. By the end of October the program was getting into even higher gear, with thirty licensees and fifty products to be marketed through Sears, Montgomery Ward,

W. T. Grant, and Woolworth, among others, and *Variety* was endorsing Hank Saperstein's prediction of $40 million in retail sales over the next fifteen months.

Colonel had his reservations, though, not about Saperstein's honesty but about his methods of doing business — and so he set about trying to educate Saperstein. He wrote several letters to his partner in this joint enterprise, one of the very few instances in which Colonel relied on another's expertise to steer the ship. You may be surprised at the kind of advice that was offered, which centered around principles of hard work, ethical considerations, frugality, a scrupulous regard for the other guy's problems, and painstaking bookkeeping. It should probably be noted that he only offered advice like this to those he believed could benefit from it.

I'm placing this letter out of chronological sequence because it refers to a situation that began in the fall of 1956, when he let Saperstein know that he expected to be taken seriously. "You should never ask me if this is still my idea," he wrote in November, "for when I promise something I mean to keep it for better or for worse. Its just like getting married, and so far — me being married has been very good for me." ∎

"Even for a boy that failed in math like I did in school [it] does not sound like somebody is looking after your interest very well"

Mr. Hank Saperstein   January 23 1957
410 South Beverly Drive
Beverly Hills, Cal.
PERSONAL DELIVERY.

Dear Hank:

Having been out here about a week, trying to get things in order, I like to go on record, so you can decide immediately on the best way to handle the following, as I am now under tremendous pressure for no reason at all. . . .

As I told you several times before Hank, I always lay my cards on the table. I have no skeletons in the closet as far as you are concerned. I pointed out several times that I did not think that you had the organization to follow up properly the tremendous responsibilities that you are now involved with. Such as, following up on your merchandise, on our licenses, checking royalty statements completely for corrections and fol-low up letters when statements are lagging behind.

There does not seem to be any follow-up to keep these people on the ball and happy, as they keep writing us. We send the letters on to your office and that is the last we hear of it. . . .

Even for a boy that failed in math like I did in school that does not sound like somebody is looking after your interest very well. . . .

One cannot retain all the money that you take in, some must be spent for competent help. I spend at least 50% of my income in making a proper relationship with all factors in my business. I am a pretty good worker, but I would not be where I am today, if I had not relied on other people to support me and help me carry out my ideas in my type of work, for which I have to pay. And the better supporters I hired, the better my returns. . . .

I have no secrets from you pertaining to our business and I can only be helpful with my suggestions when I can find out what I like to know. There are several things that do not jibe with our understanding that we have whether they are verbal or in writing.

The only satisfaction I have received so far is, knowing that you are honest and sincere in whatever you are doing. This gives me at least the strength to try and figure out a way of helping you secure a better and sounder foundation in whatever you are doing.

I sincerely believe that you are doing everything you can, but that you are trying to do it alone, either because you don't have confidence in some of the people that are available or to get the most out of every Dollar you take in.

This is very smart but only if you can retain all the Dollars, but not when you save one and lose three some other way. Because when you miss a deal that could make us money, you also hurt our income besides your own.

I have thought a long time before writing this letter Hank, but I have checked and watched the operation, and there is a definite lack in co-ordination on the whole project.

May I suggest that you go over your entire situation and you may even make more money by doing less, but doing it on a stricter policy.

I definitely know that bills must be paid promptly when the service has been rendered. I do not delay any of my payments when they are due to anyone. When I spoke to you on the phone regarding splitting up the six page advertising we run for the holidays four ways, 25% for me, 25% for Elvis, 25% for Special Projects and 25% Elvis Presley Music, you said that it was a great and fair idea. Just have Tom [Diskin] mail you the bill and you will send the check immediately.

You must have put the check in your shaving kit when you went to Paris, so far Tom has not received it, although we paid the bills when the ads came through.

What you need is not a good man Friday, but a good man every day of the week, and if you cannot find one, call one in. We will try to hire one away from somewhere, because if you find someone who is not working, beware, there is something wrong, or he would not be available.

The most important fact pertaining to this letter is that we trust each other, we have at least that satisfaction.

You can rest assured that all the mistakes, and remarks I made in this letter can probably be pointed also towards me. Except one. I pay my bills right on the [day they are submitted].

It is a religion with me and gives me a great deal of satisfaction and peace of mind. I am quite disturbed when people that have served well must be aware of the lack in receiving compensation that is rightly due them.

Take care of yourself and read this letter like you know I want you to read it. It can only make for a better relationship.

Remember me to your family.

> Your Pal,
> (Have I got salt?)
> Colonel Parker

When it came to matters of personal finance, Colonel was always scrupulous about giving Elvis (and from the start Vernon, too) very specific advice without treading too heavily on their toes. He wrote to Julian Aberbach, cohead of Elvis' song publisher, Hill and Range, that he needed to boil down how payments worked for Elvis' father in clearly understandable terms, and with Vernon he had Tom Diskin reiterate (once again, in clear, understandable language, which probably would have gone on for twice the length without adding anything of substance, if Colonel had written it himself) the perils of assuming that if you earned $1 million (in an age of 80–91 percent taxation) you could retain $1 million.

Not all of this is altogether clear to me. As best I can figure, the 1956 edition of Elvis Presley Enterprises was a kind of shell corporation for Elvis to pay the band, his own and their hotel and travel expenses, and any other business expenses that could be treated as deductions, while Special Projects was the joint merchandising arrangement with Hank Saperstein referenced above. There's a good deal of other (good, I think) financial advice in the early days, including numerous suggestions to buy government bonds. Colonel even opened up a savings account in Elvis' name at his own bank in Madison with a personal deposit of $1,200 and a letter from the assistant bank manager congratulating the young man on the "fine success you are making in your own field, also as having Mr. Parker as your manager and agent." Unfortunately, none of this advice ever really took, and the bank account was soon depleted, the government bonds cashed in the moment Elvis felt a financial urge. ■

"Remember, it is almost impossible to become a millionaire"

Mr. Vernon Presley   November 2, 1956
1034 Audubon Drive
Memphis, Tennessee

Dear Vernon:

Enclosed you will find the following:

1) Elvis Presley Statement of Earnings as of October 31, 1956 and attached you will find two checks:

> RCA Victor Royalty Check $75,000.00
> Elvis Presley Music, Inc $13,416.00
> Note that Special Projects, Inc. earnings check has been deposited in the Elvis Presley Savings Account at the First American National Bank Madison, Tenn. The savings account including the above check for $8,661.47 now has a balance of $21,436.26

2) Record Royalty Statements with a breakdown of record sales and royalties.

New RCA Victor Record Contract which provides for royalty payments over a period of years.

Agreement for Elvis's endorsement of the RCA phonograph.

Special Projects, Inc. earning report breakdown

3) Elvis Presley Enterprises blank checks #1044 through #1062 which require Elvis's signature on the end stub. These checks will be needed for the forthcoming tour and I have enclosed a return envelope so that you can send them right back to us after Elvis signs them. These checks are not valid unless they also have the Colonel's signature on them.

4) A chart showing income tax due on earnings at various levels. In brief you can see that with net earnings of $300,000.00 the tax due is $235,480.00. In other words on the first three hundred thousand dollars Elvis gets to keep about $64,000.00. Many items such as the extra cars, furniture, etc. are not deductible so you can see how very important it is that you do not lose sight of the fact that you actually get to keep about twenty percent of the money that is earned. Anything over $300,000 you get to keep only 9% or nine cents on every dollar that is earned. So for Elvis's sake and for your own do not get out on the limb by over-spending. We can't impress too strongly upon you that Elvis, you and Mrs. Presley read this paragraph over a few times so as to be fully aware of the large amount of money that must be set aside for your income taxes. And remember, it is almost impossible to become a millionaire. The Colonel has advised you about this all along and wants you to understand this fully so that you won't have any problems when Uncle Sam asks for his share.

Best to you all from all of us.

Sincerely,
[Signed "Tom Diskin"]

PS: The Colonel is talking to the real estate man so play it cool for he can get a better deal when they know that you are not over anxious.

1957

Colonel almost immediately found a home in Hollywood. With the exception of his dealings with Hal Wallis (whom he came to like, though he never stopped blaming himself for the first contract he signed), Colonel loved his new Hollywood surroundings, taking them as a natural extension of his beloved carnival world, in which he lost no time establishing himself on an equal footing (primus inter pares) with moguls and publicity men alike.

Buddy Adler was the recently installed head of 20th Century Fox when Elvis made his first picture there — but more significantly he was a creative thinker and most important of all a great kidder. Never underestimate the importance of the kidding culture in all of Colonel's dealings, wherever he found himself in his life's journey. He keenly relished the rarely less than affectionate matching of wits, the constant challenge of coming up with new gags, though never, he would always insist both explicitly and implicitly, at the expense of a fellow kidder. Still, it should always be noted and renoted: Every joke has a serious meaning (or perhaps that should be serial) for serial kidders like himself operating on the highest professional level.

As he wrote to Adler in an earlier letter, he hoped Adler would keep him in mind "if our stock goes down [and] there is an opening in your life-stock division at the studio, for I have the distinction of being the only manager that used to be a dog catcher. Please do not release this information to [Fox publicity director, and fellow kidder par excellence] Harry Brand as I feel sure that he has an inside line to the American Humane Association and he may check up on my qualifications."

At the time of this note, Elvis was shooting his second picture (his first for Hal Wallis), *Loving You,* at Paramount, hence the many inside jokes and references. ■

"It is with great satisfaction and pleasure that I can call you my friend, because you are always sincere, even when you are snowing"

General Buddy Adler   January 29 1957
Executive Snower
Twentieth Century Fox
Beverly Hills, Calif.

My dear General:

Your letter dated January 29th 1957 has been received at our snow head quarters at so and so so studio. Knowing that you would be unhappy if I mentioned the name of Paramount Studios, I didn't mention it.

First, I wish to thank you on behalf of myself and Elvis Presley for the 16 mm print of "Love Me Tender". For the sake of good relationship with my artist and the deep respect he has for your friendship, kindness and generosity and anything else that would sound good, if I knew how to spell it—I delivered the print with a real production to Elvis on the set a few minutes ago, advising Elvis that this print was for him from you.

I sincerely believe this was the right thing to do. Since Elvis lives 227½ miles and 400 feet from Madison Tenn. It would require a tremendous amount of travelling expenses, to tot it back and forth from my basement to his basement.

Would it be possible, or could you be persuaded, befuddled befogged or bewildered into making up another print and allow me to either pay for this, or trade it out in Elvis Presley merchandise of which I have several lockers full, such as hats, pins and "Love Me Tender" buttons.

If this is possible, please advise me and I will leave shipping instructions with your office, as I would like this print shipped to my home, Box 417 Madison, Tenn.

For the following reasons getting an extra print for my own use at home for free from you will put me in an embarrassing situation, when I make another deal with you, as I will have to knock at least something off, and this my conscience would not allow me to do.

It was a great pleasure to see you. You are a refreshing personality, but also a very smart and intelligent operator. It takes a good snower not to be defrosted by your ability to snow. I gave credit to Harry Brand for being the head snower at Fox, but you are far superior with your spray of snow.

It is with great satisfaction and pleasure that I can call you my friend, because you are always sincere, even when you are snowing.

I would appreciate very much, if you would not show this letter to Harry Brand, as I have reason to believe that he has a grapevine into other studios. I was amazed at Paramount they did not know him in the press department, and I believe Mr. Brand was deeply hurt when I told him so. He should not have felt so bad, because they did not know me either.

I am sorry we could not get together on a deal, but I am also happy that I am welcome at the studio for lunch, even if I do pick up my own check most of the time, unless I bring a live-one in from the outside.

If you don't know what a live-one is, I suggest you check with Harry Brand who is well acquainted with the vocabulary of the carnei [sic] language. If Harry Brand does not know, you have a personality that is connected with your studio in some sort of capacity, what it is I don't know, but he goes under the name of Bill Smith, who has qualified himself in my estimation as a King Potentate Snower, of all snowers on the Fox Lot.

I will be leaving for Tennessee in a few days to stay home for a week and bring Mrs. Parker back with me. If there is anything you need from Tennessee that I can get into my bag on top of my clothes and still not carry any overweight baggage, let me know and I will pick it up, such as a stick of smoked sausage or midget ham, as any overweight baggage must be paid by you, if I am requested to fulfill your order. . . .

If you ever need a producer to produce a picture that will make people see it five times before they understand it, I am the man.

My price will be determined by the money that will come in, if people see it over and over.

Knowing that you are very busy, I am making this letter as short as possible. If I do not receive an answer from you, don't worry about my feelings, as I will understand. Should I receive an answer you will then qualify to reach the first plateau in the Harry Brand Snow Man's Association, which means that you will be qualified to freeze the fox tail of the 20th Century Fox enabling him to wiggle sideways instead of up and down, without breaking the ice.

Snowingly yours,
Your Pal,
Head Snower, Colonel Parker

P.S. I spoke to Harry Brand regarding the story in Hedda Hoppers column. Looking forward to see this story next year, as I love to be back with you folks. I will always have a warm spot for the fine treatment we received at 20th Century Fox. If you bog down in production call on the Colonel.

O ne of the ways Colonel kept himself amused, or at least always in practice, was to ignore no letter received, whether from a fan wanting to know whether Elvis had secretly gotten married (he hoped that Elvis would tell him, Colonel courteously replied, though as an adult he certainly wasn't obligated to), a hotel clerk, an old carnival friend, or a shipping agent in India who was a big Elvis fan and whom he inducted into the Snowmen's League, a recent "club" born entirely of his own fecund imagination, which occupied more and more of his time throughout 1957. (See subsequent correspondence, especially his letter to Paul Wilder, for further meditations on, and definitions of, snowing.) In this particular instance, he received a letter from a woman in the Paramount Legal Department (extension 331), billing herself as "Secretary Paramount Studio Club, Sports Car Club." She related how members of her club were "constantly searching for something to adorn their cars" and at their latest sports car "ralley" one of the participants had shown up with the " 'piece de resistance'— an Elvis Presley badge." Everyone had been so excited that she wondered if it might be possible for the club to acquire a few more badges for the badge bars on their cars, while also issuing "an invitation to you and your 'gang' to accompany us on any of our rallies." Colonel replied the following day — and if the Sir Fin Kipper sign-off throws you, just consult your tarot cards. ∎

"Please do not criticize this letter for spelling, as you have several words that are out of kilter"

Miss Blanche Baker   January 31 1957
Legal Department.

Dear Miss Baker:

Your letter dated January 30th received. Noticing on the letter-head that you must be in the legal department we cannot take your letter into consideration until you fully and legally sign your letter.

Before we can go to the extensive preparation of presenting your request to our "Snow Man's Board" we must have a complete explanation, explaining your proposition.

Not having finished school past the 5th grade, I don't know whether you mean 331 badges or 331 extensions.

If you desire to pursue this matter any further, I suggest that you take it up immediately with one of our 9 secretaries in our dressing room office 102, Paramount Studio, but do not disturb us during lunch, as we carry our own lunch and eat in the dressing room.

To entice you to immediately take action on this request we are sending you one badge which must be returned if you do not receive the other badges after you request them from us.

The word "piece de resistance"—I hope that this is not a vulgar expression, as I have never seen this before, would you please explain it for me. The reason I am in doubt is that you had the letter delivered without a stamp. This gives me the opinion that you could not send it through the mail.

Do we receive a free sports car if we secure the badges?

You must be specific in stating exactly how many badges you desire. This does not mean that you will get them. We do have available special packages of souvenirs, at a reduced rate, if you pick them up yourself.

Please give this letter your immediate attention, as our badges go fast.

We do not allow anyone to use imitation badges, since you are working in the legal department, I am sure that you can get legal advice without charge, as I gather from your letter that you are an experienced request-orette which means exactly what you are asking for.

Please do not criticize this letter for spelling, as you have several words that are out of kilter. It was a pleasure hearing from you and I am replying respectfully with your request "hoping to hear from you soon". If I had written any sooner, I would have written before I received your letter.

Respectfully yours,

SIR FIN KIPPER
Super—Intendant
Elvis Presley Badges, Free Loading
Department.

———————————

E ven in the midst of Elvis' period of greatest success, Colonel still had time to promote the career of singer Tommy Sands, with whom he had worked for nearly eight years, ever since Tommy was twelve. Colonel had believed in him from the start, got him signed to RCA, recommended him for a film biography of Hank Williams that would not get made for another seven years, even pushed him to Steve Sholes as a suitable substitute for Elvis in early 1955, when it looked like neither Bob Neal nor Sam Phillips was ever going to come around.

Sands finally got his break with the live broadcast of "The Singin' Idol" on the *Kraft Television Theatre* on January 30, 1957, in which Sands starred as an Elvis type, with a conniving manager strongly resembling Colonel Parker. His song from the show, "Teen-Age Crush," rose to number one on the pop charts shortly thereafter, and with the release of *Sing Boy Sing,* a motion picture adapted from the teleplay (for which Colonel, in a masterly strategy of indirection I can't even begin to describe, made sure he got the role), twenty-year-old Tommy Sands was at last a full-fledged star. Colonel couldn't have been prouder. Tom Diskin, who had been just as involved with his career almost from the start, was just as proud. And Tommy never failed to express his gratitude to Colonel, who had never given up on him, even when he was at his lowest ebb.

The correspondence presented here starts with Sands' emotional telegram to Colonel on the very day of the television show's live broadcast — in fact, it would appear, just before. The second letter, from Tom Diskin, a little more than a month later, speaks for itself, while the third is as notable for Colonel's playful, but unmistakably affectionate, tone as for its generosity of spirit.

Take this triptych of letters, then (just a brief sampling from a lengthy, and always loving, correspondence), as a small measure of Colonel's deep-seated belief in all of his artists — not just Elvis. Though, if we're going to be absolutely honest, most of all Elvis. ■

"I'll always consider it an honor knowing you"

COL TOM PARKER   1957 JAN 30
KNICKERBOCKER HOTEL HOLLWOOD CALIF

DEAR COL: THIS SHOW I'M DOING FOR YOU I'LL ALWAYS BE GREATFUL ILL ALWAYS CONSIDER IT AN HONOR KNOWING YOU TONIGHT I'LL TRY TO LIVE UP TO YOUR EXPECTATIONS

TOMMY SANDS

Tom Diskin. *Courtesy of the Graceland Archives*

"Any time you face a difficult problem or decision you can call on us"

Mr. Tommy Sands   February 11 1957
6536 Franklin Ave, Apt. 4
Hollywood, Calif.

Dear Tommy:

The Colonel and I want you to know how very happy we are at the reaction you have received as a result of your performance on "The Singing Idol".

As you and your mother both know, the Colonel and I have absolute confidence in your ability to rise to the top in the show business world and we feel proud of the fact that we played some small part in this.

While it was mentioned by you, we are waiving our commissions for booking you on the Kraft Show.

Elvis, too, was very happy for your success and he well remembered the fine support you gave him when you were a disk jockey in Shreveport.

I am sure you and your mother both know, that any time you face a difficult problem or decision you can call on us.

Best wishes for your continued success from Elvis, the Colonel and myself.

Sincerely,

TOM DISKIN

"I dont think I am a real Colonel at that but a snow Colonel"

Col Tommy Sands   August 22nd 1957
Hollywood, California

My Dear Colonel;

Thanks for your letter Mr. Diskin mailed same on to me while I was down in Tampa with Bobby and Marian [Colonel's wife Marie's son and his wife] and Bitsy [Mott, Marie's brother and Elvis' sometime security man] for a visit.

Boy you must have really done a master snowjob to be promoted to Colonel so soon, it has taken me Years of Snowing to get mine, and every Once in awhile I dont think I am a real Colonel at that but a snow Colonel.

The [royalty] check from the tremendous Music firm [Colonel and Tom Diskin's mostly defunct publishing company, Jamboree Music] you received is enclosed, since I am no longer associated with this large firm I am unable to take any money from that source even if it came from you. His royal Highness Tom Diskin received this firm as a present from myself and the board of directors some Years ago after we had a meeting to either burn the company or give it away, since burning the company would have required the expense of using good matches we thought it cheaper to give the firm to its Vice President Tom Diskin, I was so amased when your check arived the other Day as I never dreamed that that much money could come from this broken down music firm, however One always learns. Tommy I know how you feel and I appreciate your thoughts and also know that you want me to have a present, please keep the check give it to your Mother or buy something for yourself, you tried hard when you did the songs for wich this royalty payment is received by you.

If you want to do something for the Col, why dont you fix up some sort of award for services in the line of duty or whatever you call it, and this I can hang in my office or a statue of some sort with your picture or some highclass real sincere snowjob. I am leaving here tomorrow for Seattle as we play 4 dates up that way next week, I will be on the Coast for a few days in about Two Weeks and will try to get together for dinner or at least brush up on our snow course. Give my best to your Mother, Mrs Parker went down to Fla ahead of me, and I brought back her Mother and also my old pal Frankie Conners the Tenor you remember him from the Shamrock he always works on our shows as I try to use old friends in the business that need the work. [It should be noted that Frankie Connors opened most of Elvis' 1956 and 1957 shows, and Colonel did his best to help Connors' daughter, Sharon, with a movie tryout.]

Take care of yourself, tell Molly B, Tenn Ernie, Cliffie Stone [all performers on the star-studded Los Angeles–based country music television show *Hometown Jamboree*] and all the rest of our friends hello for me. And keep up the good work.

Regards from Mr. Diskin. Your Pal. The Colonel

———————

By 1957 Colonel had found in Bill Bullock the staunchest of allies. Bullock, who had been at RCA in one capacity or another since 1926, when he was nineteen (this was the same year that sixteen-year-old Andreas van Kuijk AKA Colonel Tom Parker first arrived in America), had locked horns with Colonel over just about everything following Elvis' initial arrival at RCA, but by now had either been persuaded by Colonel's logic (it happens) or by the unprecedented success of his artist. Or perhaps it was simply that Bullock, along with nearly every other top RCA executive (with the singular exception of Colonel's old friend Steve Sholes, who had so deftly guided Eddy Arnold's recording career but did not take to Elvis — or more to the point, vice versa), had been won over by Colonel's (and I hate to say it, but it's true) unassailable charm. Another man might have been satisfied with this result, but Colonel was not about to rest, or, for that matter, let anyone else rest, on his laurels. He continued to needle Bullock, who took the needling in the affable spirit in which he believed — correctly, I think — it was being offered. And Colonel, of course, never missed a chance to remind Bullock of all of RCA's obligations, written or unwritten, to his client — and of his insistence that the company live up to every one. Colonel also enlisted Bullock in his ongoing fight against the "buck-passing" ways of the corporate world — something to which Bullock, who unlike Steve Sholes was blessed with a keen sense of humor, not to mention an appreciation for the varieties of human behavior, happily acceded. As he did to his provisional promotion to "Colonel" status (well, "Lt. Colonel") in the letter that follows. ■

"MANY HAVE BEEN CALLED, BUT VERY FEW HAVE ANSWERED"

Mr. Bill Bullock   March 13, 1957
RADIO CORPORATION OF AMERICA
155 East 24th Street
New York City, N.Y.

Dear Bill:

The "Sleeve" on "ALLSHOOK UP" received. Thank you for same — it looks very good.

Seems a little odd that the way ELVIS is selling records and albums that with the release of the SACRED EP this week that there wasn't even an ad in the trade papers — Billboard, Cash Box — announcing this tremendous new medium for ELVIS when everyone else has a big ad in the trades this week. There has been no advertising on ELVIS to speak of on "TOO MUCH". I would appreciate some comment from the "Buck-Passing" Department on this. The services we have rendered from this end towards expediting material for covers on records and albums to me has been far and beyond the call of duty. You can interpret this in your own way, or put it in the suggestion box at VICTOR. I will be delighted if you will suggest that I will have nothing to do with anything pertaining to promotion of records on the MGM picture as it will release me from a tremendous responsibility, that is, unless we can come to some form of a reciprocated understanding. RCA VICTOR seems to be laying off people and I have a feeling that some of the extra work is being piled on the Managers of the Artists — me being one of them. If this is not so, you will at least get a good laugh out of it.

I have no objections to your reading this letter at the next "Executive Buck-Passing" meeting. Remember my slogan "MANY HAVE BEEN CALLED, BUT VERY FEW HAVE ANSWERED" and the title of my book is, "HOW MUCH DOES IT COST IF IT'S FREE?". I got the inspiration for this title from my association with RCA VICTOR, and you of course will receive due credit when the book comes out. Your reaction to my comments when my book is out will be immaterial to me as I will be out of the business by then, so don't lose any sleep over it. My only regret is that when I was a dog-catcher that I didn't pick up all of the "Nipper" dogs [the RCA symbol] in sight at that time.

If ever there should be an opening for a superb "SNOWER", I feel that I am well qualified to be considered as I have had great training since I have been associated with your organization on a "One-Dollar-A-Year" basis.

Regards,

THE COLONEL

Cc: MR. STEVE SHOLES, MR. LARRY KANAGA [General Manager of the RCA Record Division]

"Remember my slogan —'One must come down to be able to get on top again'"

Lt. Colonel Bill Bullock   March 20, 1957
RCA VICTOR
155 E, 24th Street
New York 10, New York

Dear Colonel:
Your letter dated March 15, received. Was forwarded from the Hollywood office. I am now back in Madison, as you know.

Thank you for the records of Harry Belafonte. Mrs. Parker appreciates them very much.

Regarding the Executive Buck Passing meeting, which you state will be held this week, I am not too enthused about this meeting, as nothing seems to happen at these meetings but "passing the buck" and none of these bucks seem to be coming my way.

You seem to be unpretentious of my remark of being associated with RCA on a dollar a year basis, for me as an advisor, and it intrigues me tremendously. Receiving such a small annuity should give me a tremendous voice in the operation. Let me go on record at this time and see if you can secure more money for my advisory capacity and let me have nothing to say in the operation of the company. It would be much more profitable for me. . . .

Received the phone call from a Memphis newspaper advising me that an RCA Victor executive had quoted "Belafonte outselling Presley, two to one". This does not matter to me, however it should have been much better if it had been in the paper in Timbuctu instead of Memphis. We all know that every artist must level off at some phase of the business. Fortunately, I have enough foresight to prepare myself for such an event and still be happy.

As I said before, Elvis Presley will most likely be the first artist at RCA that they will say, "he is slipping" when he sells only a million records for release. I believe that I can rightly take a bow when I state that a great percentage of the sales of his records and popularity are based upon my policy of not over-exposing this artist, which I would have done if I had listened and bowed to the tremendous pressure I received for the first six months of his popularity, from all sources.

Sometimes we overlook the basic responsibility we all have toward prolonging the life of an artist. I can only refer you to my track record with Eddy Arnold, which I also limited to a certain type of exposure for many, many years and his sales remained very solid up until the time that he changed his methods of operation in all fields. This great artist could still be brought back into the big seller class, but only with proper handling and advice.

Eddy has great quality in his artistry and will always have a loyal following. There is no one more aware of all the responsibility of being tied into a record company than I am, having been now associated for more than ten years, from the bottom, half way up the ladder. Remember my slogan—"One must come down to be able to get on top again". There is no place as far as I am concerned about being on the top, except a snow man on top of the Himalaya Mountains, and I don't think they are making records up there. If they did, they would melt anyway in the heated conversations that are held at the buck passing meetings.

You are fortunate in having such executive snowers as [top RCA executives] Larry Kanaga, Howard Letts, Sagebrush York[e] and Potentate

Snowers, Sholes, Merrick [Marek] and others available to you with their advice. You spray one of the finest snow sprays ever seen by me, and I have seen the best.

Yours for better snowing and understanding.

Frigidly Yours,
THE COLONEL

Colonel's relationship with Abe Lastfogel, longtime head of the William Morris Agency, was perhaps the most important professional relationship of his life as well as one of his closest personal friendships. It started out strong — but only because Colonel proved not just his audacity but his creative genius to Lastfogel. (Parker, Lastfogel remarked very early on, had shown him how to scrutinize and "refine contracts that William Morris had with motion picture companies in ways that [I] had never imagined.") Their closeness only continued to grow in intimacy, mutual respect, and (astonishingly for two such solitary individuals) love, until Lastfogel's 1984 death. The nature of their relationship is perhaps best exemplified in a 1957 exchange of letters following Colonel's single surprising side trip away from his exclusive representation of Elvis Presley, when at Lastfogel's request he undertook to promote a tour to launch the singing career of television star (*The Life and Legend of Wyatt Earp*) Hugh O'Brian. Despite the most meticulous planning and preparation, it was, to put it mildly, a complete disaster, and Lastfogel tried to make amends by sending a check for $10,000, half of Colonel's losses on the tour — well, read Colonel's response for yourself. The next day Lastfogel simply wrote, "To tell you my feelings in words would be superfluous" and signed off with love for both Tom and Marie Parker. ∎

"I am in show business and we do not take money from any-one except if you had been a partner"

Mr. Abe Lastfogel   April 17, 1957
William Morris Agency
1740 Broadway
New York City New York.

Abe Lastfogel. *Courtesy of the Graceland Archives*

My Dear Brother Abe:

It was indeed good of you to mail me the enclosed check, I know you only did this to show me you and [Lastfogel's wife] Frances have money. The only real thing I know by your letter is, that I will never go Hungry as long as both of you are alive, this is more important than the check now. So put it back where it came from, I am in show business and we do not take money from any-one except if you had been a partner, You know I would not have mailed you Ten Thousand Dollars if I had made Twenty thousand, so why should you share in the losses if you would not have shared in the profit.

I am over 21, and should know what I am doing, if my little venture somehow helped Jules [William Morris agent Julie Sharr] off the hook with his client and showed him that One must be on the ball to keep an artist rolling I have done the job I set out to do. This was One hunch I had [to] do, and I did it, so I also learned by my losses. I at all time believed in the project and that was One reason I did not give up, but did every-thing possible to make it go.

Peter Shaw [another William Morris agent] has been in touch with me on MGM, [William Morris legal counsel] Ann Rosenthal is holding off on the contract with MGM till I return, I also have been reading the Fox contract she gave me, and believe me you and I will have some fun knocking out some of the very nice clauses for Fox. I am sure you will agree with me on most of them, and those that you do not agree on with me, we can have lots of fun finding out who will win, you or I.

Marie should be back Tonight from Florida after taking care of the kids down there, I sure did miss her, as I am not a very good house-keeper and cant cook, she surely has been busy looking after the Family down there. . . .

Give our best to Frances and take care of yourself, I do appreciate the offer of the check but I cant take, and I wont take it even if you should return it, so save the postage and your time trying to do so.

Love Your Pal Tom.

Colonel continued to offer frequent advice to Elvis based on a mutuality not just of interests but of temperament (at least as Colonel emotionally describes it here), something that few outsiders, including, especially, Elvis' band of brothers and hangers-on (who would come to be known as the Memphis Mafia), would never have suspected or acknowledged. This is certainly the longest single letter Colonel ever wrote to Elvis, not even rivaled by the voluminous correspondence he maintained while Elvis was stationed in Germany during his army service. It is a densely packed, single-spaced 3,000-word letter, including what amounts to a 1,000-word postscript, and at the risk of challenging your attention span I'm going to include almost all of it, up till its lengthy sign-off, which begins without even a hint of writer's cramp, "Now for some other information that I know you will want to have."

Think of it as existing in three parts: the practical, with, as usual, lots of suggestions about how to contend with everyday problems; the educational, like his ongoing reminder (I don't think any of Colonel's reminders were singular) that having the songs he recorded in his publishing company was not just some arbitrary rule but would ensure him income long after his performing days were done; and then there was the personal. What we see here is an explosion of emotion rarely to be seen coming from Colonel in any form. What prompted it — worry perhaps over the limit-testing behavior that some of Elvis' boys were indulging in, the extraordinary measures needed to maintain extraordinary success, or just a gush of his deepest, truest, seldom-expressed, and long-suppressed feelings — I just don't know.

This is one of many self-typed letters, but even more than most it lacks any kind of logical punctuation or paragraphing, so I'm going to add some to provide as clear a path as possible for the reader while doing my best not to interrupt Colonel's spontaneous emotional flow. ■

"I know that you understand me better than any-one for you have a very carefull Eye. I am a great deal like you, very sensitive, but only people I love can hurt me"

Dear Elvis;   April 18, 1957

After sending you the wire last Night, I thought I [would] also follow this up with a letter. I am working on the loan setup for the $50,000 Your Father spoke to me about. It is not a good idea to try and handle this thru RCA Victor, as the special contract I made to prolong the payments is such a savings on income tax over a period of Ten Years that it would be foolish to do anything that may impare this setup, so after talking to [RCA General Manager] Larry Kanaga and getting his views that the only way they could do it is to have them okay a loan with a bank, it is better to handle this on our own plan some other way, wich way I do not know at the present but I hope to come up with something sensible and good for you and your parents.

Regarding the recording session for RCA Victor, here is the best plan I can think of for your setup. First we have a very important obligation to MGM Pictures to do a first class job on recording the tunes for the picture [*Jailhouse Rock*] with nothing else on your mind but the picture recording before anything else. Second after we get the picture on its way we can work out a schedule together suitable to you to record some for RCA Victor either while we are on the Coast after the picture is well on its way (you could do this over the week-end perhaps sometime in early June while out there) or record after the picture is finished. At least we can talk about the victor recording after all the recording for the MGM picture has been finished.

If you remember we had a bad deal the last time at Paramount. We were recording for RCA Victor about the same time we had to get the recording session in for Hal Wallis, this was not good either for you and not fair to the Hal Wallis contract as your voice was not up to par. This was due to the fact that you had too much recording to do all at One time there. I also take part of the blame to let myself get snowed into this type of schedule, but we all try to be fair to all concerned. This time we do not have to get involved that way so lets not do it. Here is my plan, think it over and I know you will feel that this is the only fair way to do it. Also for you and for the Metro-Goldwyn-Mayer Picture, as they are also paying a top price for your services; along with the fact that we will be in on the profit of the picture, this can mean a tremendous income in later Years from this picture.

Second, We have gotten you a Third interest in all the songs in the Picture you are to do, not counting that they will be in Either Gladys or [Elvis] Presley Music [Elvis' two publishing firms, both set up by Hill and Range], insuring a steady income for the firm from this all along. So the picture recording session is First on the list, than the starting of the picture production, after that we will do our best to work out something with Sholes to record for RCA Victor while there, but nothing before that time period.

Third, it is also important that any tunes you have and like are passed on to Jean and Julian [Aberbach] so they can see if they can get a deal for you either in the Presley or Gladys Music or participating — Remember, if it was not for your having a piece of all the songs they have been able to tie up so far, you would not be getting these weekly salary checks and bonuses and royalty payments we all have been getting right along. Just check your income and see what has been coming in from these tunes that we would have had nothing to show for if we had not gotten a deal of some sort on them thru Jean and Julian. There are many writers and publishers that are watching to see you do some tunes where you are not in on, so they can turn Jean and Julian down, saying, Look, Presley did this tune for Sam Jones without being in on it, he likes our tune so we handle this ourselves — and you would be up the creek. I am sure you know what I am talking about, there are always good snowers when they can snow any-one in to doing something for nothing. It will be long after sales are slowing down and things are running at an easy pace that you will be getting revenue off these tunes that Jean and Julian were able to get you a piece out of. Just remember what we did with the Fox tunes [for Elvis' first film, *Love Me Tender*] where you shared in every-one of them all along. I am suggesting to Jean that he has Freddie [Freddy Bienstock, the Aberbachs' cousin, and Hill and Range's personal representative to Elvis since July 1956] or Grelun [Landon, a longtime RCA and occasional Hill and Range employee, who had worked with Colonel since Eddy Arnold days] travel along on the train with all the dubs from the MGM picture so you will have plenty of time to listen to them on the train.

You should do nothing but work on those tunes First and get them out of the way, Sholes has nothing to do with the recording for MGM, we can handle this directly and in your own style and way of doing them without worry-ing about doing a record session at the same time. I am sure that you will come up with enough good material out of this MGM session that we will have plenty of good material on hand to work into an album and some singles from the picture. Remember, our strengt lies in not having too much in the can so they cant use any material that we may not want to use later. You have been following a very good patern of handling the recording setup, Let's keep it that way, untill we decide its better to do something else.

You can let me have your ideas on this anyway you see it, but remember that The strengt you have lies in how we handle the proper business setup along with your talents. Your talent is your own, you are tops in this and there has never been a time except when I knew you were in trouble that I stuck my nose in this, and only than when you asked me what I thought. I know you can barrel any of this better yourself; at the same time I also think I am as good as you are with your talents in smoking out the best for us. This I appreciate you knowing and having the confidence in me on this, as I can also see your strengt in buffing people off towards me when they try to get you involved in making a business deal. I also buff them off when they try to sell me on a song as I tell them, Elvis picks his own songs; if he likes them or a certain song than he tells me and I'll get him the best deal I can with Jean and Julian. What would be the use to make a good deal on any song before you even know what it is, and perhaps you dont like or do the song, we would be getting one hundred percent out of nothing, except it would have taken up your time and mine.

I know that you have a certain quality in you the same as I have that can feel our way thru most any snowjob except if we lend a foolish ear. Always remember, the well wishers did not try too hard to find you when you was living on Getwell [where Elvis and his parents rented a modest home in Memphis in 1955] and trying to figure out where you could get some money to buy things for your Mother and Dad with. I can always remember the tears in your eyes and your Mothers when I was able to give you your First $5000 Check when I made the Victor deal; it has always been amusing to me how many people have been trying to [take] credit for this deal, even some people that did not even come to Memphis when the deal was made. I will always treasure the wire I received from you and Vernon asking me to handle the record deal even before I was even involved with you any-more than trying to help.

When we all think back we can count on One hand the real friends we all have and those that are still with us even if things look gloomy and rough. Advise is free even when its bad or good, but to get advise from people that have nothing to show for themselves for knowing so much is always something to be carefull about taking. Remember my slogan how much does it cost if its Free. . . .

Your mother was very wise when she told me that she judged people by what they did and were doing not what they had done that was wrong. . . . You would find out very quick how many friends would come to your house if all at once they found out you were broke and had to move into a tent and borrow money to eat on. Perhaps some of them would be kind enough to tell you that those Two Donkeys I gave you would taste pretty good if cooked right, and the only advise they could give you then would be it would save you from having to feed the donkeys. Now dont think that all your friends are like that, not the real ones, only the phonyes wich are at present in pretty good numbers all over the place here and there. They say, We are worried about our boy elvis slipping, but they do not say, In case he does we will be here to see that he will want for nothing, for we love him so very much and always have ever since he got on the top.

I know that you understand me better than any-one for you have a very carefull Eye. I am a great deal like you, very sensitive, but only people I love can hurt me, no one else.

Now for some other information that I know you will want to have. . . .

....

And here he fills Elvis in, indefatigably, with two more pages on practical matters along with further advice on his retinue of friends, stressing utility (each should do a certain job), tax issues (in order for their services to be tax-deductible, they all need to be on the payroll), and self-worth ("so they can at least feel they mean something other than going along for a free ride"), before signing off. . . .

....

Happy Easter to you, Mother and Dad, Mrs Parker arrived back from Florida last Night, so now I will at least get back to normal at home. Bevo [Bevis, Colonel's oddball but 1,000 percent loyal aide-de-camp, who had been with him since dogcatcher days] is still snowing the girls whenever he can. Mr Diskin, his Sister and Mother left for Chicago for Easter. We will stay here at home. Take care of yourself and I hope to have the other deal on the loan for the repairs worked out by Tomorrow or at least by Monday, wish me luck.

Your Pal
Admiral Snow to you.

Mr Diskin also wishes all of you a Happy Easter.

Colonel continued to maintain his close relationship with Harry Kalcheim, responding to Kalcheim's solicitude about him with warm professions of fellow feeling. But even here he is not above a bit of fun. Harry, he is sure, like everyone else, would like to know the secret of Elvis' success. Well, Colonel (still Tom in this instance) will be glad to reveal it — but not until the publication of his book! (For more on the subject of his book, which became an increasingly important part of his ever-evolving story, see below.) ∎

"The secret on Elvis' record sales is a very simple one, that very few people can figure out"

Mr. Harry Kalcheim   April 19, 1957
Wm. Morris Agency
1740 Broadway
New York 19, N.Y.

Dear Harry:

Thanks for your letter. I am back again with a sore neck, however, Marie is back from Florida and looking after me. I hope to be feeling better by next weekend as I have to go back to the coast for the M-G-M picture.

The secret on Elvis' record sales is a very simple one, that very few people can figure out. I have learned that since Hooper [television] ratings went out and some of the other ratings they use on TV and Radio, that they are very good to sell clients but very seldom bring in real money deals. I think I have somehow stumbled on to a new medium along with a great artist, of course to make it work. I always remember the early days of Eddy Arnold that this gimmick worked very well for him and it surely is working for Elvis in many ways.

The exposure on TV is of course one answer but, the main answer I will reserve to put into my book some day and I sincerely believe it will surprise many Desk Experts.

There is not much news. I received a check from my brother, Abe Lastfogel for half of the losses on the Hugh O'Brian show Tour. This I returned for I had no plans in the past to give him half of the profits if I had made money, and, I also think he was trying to impress me that he had money. I know where my support lies however, and that is more important than money. I also believed very strongly in the attraction so I made a mistake. Also, did it 75% to help Julie [William Morris agent Jules Sharr] out of a spot.

Marie said hello. Remember us to your family.

Sincerely,
The Colonel

This is one of the few instances of bringing an old pal, far removed from the hurly-burly (Barton Wilson, formerly a Texas-based DJ and promoter, was now living in Peru), up to date on his doings. I think Colonel's pithy summary of events provides a glimpse of the pride he took in his achievements, with due allowance for false modesty (humblebrag?), which is an interesting perspective in itself. Note the Australian tour he says he is planning for his artist with his latest protégé, Lee Gordon, an American manqué who has made his fortune promoting rock 'n' roll in Australia. Gordon had gone in with Colonel for the first time as promoter of Elvis' spring tour of the Midwest and Canada and was truly a man after Colonel's own heart. An entrepreneur of rare imagination and daring, he was always prepared to put everything he had on the line, possessing much of Colonel's zest for life (and for the deal), while unfortunately lacking his mentor's impermeable core of common sense. ∎

"Elvis is a very strong personality with worlds of talent, and of course, we both were lucky to run into each other"

Mr. Barton Wilson   April 21, 1957
Lima, Peru

Dear Barton:

Your letter dated July 9, 1956 was delivered to me here in person at 4:30 pm today, Easter, by your friend, Mr. Socol. At least that sounded like his name. I thanked him and he talked to Marie in the yard before leaving. He said he had been trying for some time to deliver the letter here to our home but had had some time finding the place and as our phone number is not listed, you know how it is, However, I now at least have some word from you. . . .

Regarding ELVIS PRESLEY I have been handling him now about a year and a half. However, before that time I used him on a good many of my road shows as an act. As you may know, I managed Hank Snow for about a year before taking over Elvis completely. Now we have completed two Pictures, one for 20th Century Fox, "LOVE ME TENDER", and one not re-leased to date, "LOVING YOU", for Hal Wallis, a Paramount Picture. We start in production early May on a picture for MGM at Culver City, California. . . .

I am enclosing a few photos for your station. Thought you will want them as always. I also have been handling all personal appearances for EDDY ARNOLD for some time. Eddy does not do much anymore except his records and he has his TV films on the market. We are good friends and he calls on me often. Sorry to hear about you and Dorothy [Wilson and his wife, Dorothy, had recently divorced], however, such is life. I am happy to say Marie and I are closer than ever if we could be any closer.

Elvis is a very strong personality with worlds of talent, and of course, we both were lucky to run into each other. He has the talent and I do have a great deal of management experience and know so many people in the business that can help us.

We have been very lucky in the way we planned his career as I am handling him on a special setup of not to overexpose him in any medium. We do very few personals and very little TV so he has been able to remain fresh for all mediums, as folks do not see him often in person or on TV this makes for good Box Office results and also tremendous record sales. His records are doing great all over the world. . . .

I have a friend of mine in Australia, Lee Gordon, who had a tour with us last Month. I had planned to take the show to Australia with him, but due to the new picture set-up at MGM, we played the dates over here.

You don't seem to remember that the name Eddy Arnold was Spelled Eddy instead of EDDIE. You of all people having promoted the best show we ever had in San Angelo, lets get on the ball, boy. . . .

Well this is about all the news. We have been down here now since 1949 and guess we will be here for awhile as it is hard to sell a place after one has it all fixed up. Someday we hope to move back to Florida with the grandchildren down there. . . .

My best to you,
Your Pal, Tom Parker
Manager, ELVIS PRESLEY

I n the first year of their association, when by virtue of Elvis' constant touring they were rarely apart, Colonel's letters to Elvis consisted of large dollops of advice, frequently flavored with a shared sense of humor, starting with Colonel's self-reassignment to "Admiral." In 1957, with touring severely reduced and Elvis' moviemaking schedule proving more predictable, Colonel dedicated himself more and more to the teaching role to which he always assigned himself. With this letter, we can see both his closeness to his artist and, I think, a little of Colonel's concern that his pupil, who is increasingly showing an independent streak, not escape the classroom altogether. The main point of the letter, as always tucked inside a joke, is that Elvis needs to feel comfortable about his ongoing *Jailhouse Rock* soundtrack recording sessions; if he doesn't, without needing to be overly explicit about it, Colonel wants his artist to know that he is, as always, prepared to do battle for him. ∎

"I NEVER GIVE THESE BRAINWAVES THAT COME MY WAY MUCH THOUGHT UNTILL YOU INDICATE TO ME PERSONALLY THAT YOU WISH TO DO SOMETHING FOR THE BETTER"

ELVIS PRESLEY * MOVIE STAR*　　　　　　May 2nd 1957
VERY IMPORTANT*

DEAR ELVIS.

　　MRS PARKER SHIPPED ME A PIECE OF THE COUNTRY BACON YOU LIKE SO WELL AND SO DO I. IF YOU WANT ME TO HAVE THIS COOKED WELL DONE FOR LUNCH LET MR DISKIN KNOW BY RETURN PIGEON AND I WILL HAVE IT COOKED SO I CAN ALSO EAT SOME FOR LUNCH.

　　THERE IS A POSSIBILITY THAT EDDY ARNOLD MAY STOP BY TODAY BEFORE RETURNING TO NASHVILLE, HE MAY HAVE LUNCH WITH ME HERE, IF SO WE OF COURSE WOULD LIKE TO HAVE YOU AND YOUR TROUPE JOIN US AT THE TABLE, SINCE OUR DEPARTMENT IS GROWWING DAILY IN PERSONAL I WOULD OF COURSE LIKE TO KNOW HOW MANY OF THE TROUPE YOU WANT AT THE TABLE WITH YOURSELF EDDY AND THE COLONEL SO I CAN DO THE PROPER SNOWJOB IN ADVANCE FOR A EXTRA LARGE TABLE AND FOG-UP EVERYTHING IN THE PROPER PRESLEY PARKER MANNER IN ADVANCE.

　　IF YOU RATHER HAVE THE BACON COOKED AT THE HOTEL I CAN ALSO HANDLE IT THAT WAY, AS YOU KNOW MY SNOW-PLOW WORKS IN ALL DIRECTION SINCE I HAVE RECEIVED MY TRAINING FROM THE NEAL LOGAN [MOST LIKELY BOB NEAL-HORACE LOGAN] COLLEGE OF POTENTATE SNOWERS.

　　WHILE I AM ON THIS SNOWKICK THIS MORNING WILL YOU BE GOOD ANOUGH TO ALSO INDICATE IF THERE IS ANY NEED FOR YOU AND I TO TALK ABOUT THE SESSION TOMORROW IN EVENT YOU ARE DOING ANOTHER TUNE THAN WHAT IS PLANNED. I SEEM TO BE GETTING A WAVELENGT INDICATION FROM THE BRAINTRUSTS THAT THIS MAY BE IN THE OFFING, AS I NEVER GIVE THESE BRAINWAVES THAT COME MY WAY MUCH THOUGHT UNTILL YOU INDICATE TO ME PERSONALLY THAT YOU WISH TO DO SOMETHING FOR THE BETTER, I AM WAITING WORD

"COVER THE NATION"

Thomas A Parker
Exclusive Management

"ELVIS PRESLEY"

P.O.
417
MADISON,
TENN.

May 2nd 1957

ELVIS PRESLEY * MOVIE STAR*

VERY IMPORTANT*

          DEAR ELVIS .

               MRS PARKER SHIPPED ME A PIECE OF THE COUNTRY
BACON YOU LIKE SO WELL AND SO DO I. IF YOU WANT ME TO HAVE THIS COOKED
WELL DONE FOR LUNCH LET MR DISKIN KNOW BY RETURN PIGEON AND I WILL HAVE
IT COOKED SO I CAN ALSO EAT SOME FOR LUNCH.

THERE IS A POSSIBILITY THAT EDDY ARNOLD MAY STOP BY TODAY BEFORE RETURNING
TO NASHVILLE,HE MAY HAVE LUNCH WITH ME HERE,IF SO WE OF COURSE WOULD LIKE
TO HAVE YOU AND YOUR TROUPE JOIN US AT THE TABLE,SINCE OUR DEPARTMENT IS
GROWWING DAILY IN PERSONAL I WOULD OF COURSE LIKE TO KNOW HOW MANY OF THE
TROUPE YOU WANT AT THE TABLE WITH YOURSELF EDDY AND THE COLONEL SO I CAN
DO THE PROPER SNOWJOB IN ADVANCE FOR A EXTRA LARGE TABLE AND FOG-UP EVERYTHI
IN THE PROPER PRESLEY PARKER MANNER IN ADVANCE.

IF YOU RATHER HAVE THE BACON COOKED AT THE HOTEL I CAN ALSO HANDLE IT THAT
WAY,AS YOU KNOW MY SNOWPLOW WORKS IN ALL DIRECTION SINCE I HAVE RECEIVED
MY TRAINING FROM THE NEAL LOGAN COLLEGE OF POTENTATE SNOWERS.

WHILE I AM ON THIS SNOWKICK THIS MORNING WILL YOU BE GOOD ANOUGH TO ALSO
INDICATE IF THERE IS ANY NEED FOR YOU AND I TO TALK ABOUT THE SESSION
TOMORROW IN EVENT YOU ARE DOING ANOTHER TUNE THAN WHAT IS PLANNED,I SEEM
TO BE GETTING A WAVELENGT INDICATION FROM THE BRAINTRUSTS THAT THIS MAY
BE IN THE OFFING, AS I NEVER GIVE THESE BRAINWAVES THAT COME MY WAY MUCH
THOUGHT UNTILL YOU INDICATE TO ME PERSONALLY THAT YOU WISH TO DO SOMETHING
FOR THE BETTER,I AM WAITING WORD ON THIS, IF I DO NOT HEAR FROM YOU ON THIS
I TAKE IT, THAT YOU ARE ONLY DOING A GOOD NEEDLING JOB FOR SOME-ONES
ATTENTION AND SNOWJOB ALONG WITH IT TO SMOKE SOME-ONE OUT .

KNOWING HOW BUSY YOU ARE WITH YOUR SNOWSETUP WILL YOU LET MR DISKIN
KNOW YOUR DESIRES AT ONCE SO I CAN GO ON WITH READING THE MGM CONTRACT
WICH I NOW HAVE IN MY OFFICE AND NEEDS A GREAT DEAL OF TRIMMING DOWN.

               SNOWINGLY YOURS THE ADMIRAL.
PS I CAME BY TO SEE YOU LAST NIGHT BUT I UNDERSTAND YOU WERE DICTATING .

Courtesy of the Graceland Archives

ON THIS, IF I DO NOT HEAR FROM YOU ON THIS I TAKE IT, THAT YOU ARE ONLY DOING A GOOD NEEDLING JOB FOR SOME-ONES ATTENTION AND SNOWJOB ALONG WITH IT TO SMOKE SOME-ONE OUT.

KNOWING HOW BUSY YOU ARE WITH YOUR SNOWSETUP WILL YOU LET MR DISKIN KNOW YOUR DESIRES AT ONCE SO I CAN GO ON WITH READING THE MGM CONTRACT WICH I NOW HAVE IN MY OFFICE AND NEEDS A GREAT DEAL OF TRIM-MING DOWN.

> SNOWINGLY YOURS
> THE ADMIRAL.
> [A handwritten X]

PS I CAME BY TO SEE YOU LAST NIGHT BUT I UNDERSTAND YOU WERE DICTATING.

A few weeks later, Colonel once again consulted with Elvis on which path Elvis wanted to pursue (though here it seems evident he had his hand on the scale), in a letter whose form of address was derived from the wallaby Elvis had recently received as a gift from his Australian fans, which he would soon bestow upon the Memphis Zoo. ∎

"I have been bombarded befuddled befogged bewillderred and snowed under"

Dear Walaby; The First.   May 14, 1957

I have been bombarded befuddled befogged bewilderred and snowed under the past Few Months to have you do a Television show on a spec-tacular for RCA.NBC in Color. they have told me everything under the sun how good this would be for you for exposure, they came up with a pretty good offer several times but I turned them all down, with respect to our motion picture work and for reason I know are best for us. So I told them that our next TV show for any sponsor we do would be $50.000 Fifty thousand dollars as I want to do only One or Two TV shows this Year and with a setup like that we would blast the whole country with

May 14,1957

Dear Walaby;The First .

I have been bombarded befuddled befogged bewilderred and snowed under the past
Few Months to have you do a Television show on a spectacular for RCA.NBC in
Color. they have told me everything under the sun how good this would be
for you for exposure,they came up with a pretty good offer several times
but I turned them all down,with respect to our motion picture work and
for reason I know are best for us. So I told them that our next TV show
for any sponsor we do would be $ 50.000 Fifty thousand dollars as I want
to do only One or Two TV shows this Year and with a setup like that we
would blast the whole country with the advance publicity as they say we
will never get it from no One.well maybe we wont,but at least you will
not be overexposed like some of the top stars that are now working for
nothing as they are worn out on TV. I am only writing you this note so
you know what is going on,please indicate by marking either Yess if you
think you should work cheaper or NUTS if you think I should keep snowing for
the $ 50.000 . I will guide myself either way you want to go.

YESS IF YOU WANT TO CUT THE PRICE _-_/---_-_--------

NUTS IF WE BATTLE TOGETHER ON GETTING TOP MONEY ----------_-_--------
TO INDICATE MY DESIRE MY VOTE IS NUTS AND OF COURSE OUR TO--

the advance publicity as they say we will never get it from no One. well maybe we wont, but at least you will not be overexposed like some of the top stars that are now working for nothing as they are worn out on TV. I am only writing you this note so you know what is going on, please indicate by marking either Yess if you think you should work cheaper or NUTS if you think I should keep snowing for the $50.000. I will guide myself either way you want to go.

YESS IF YOU WANT TO CUT THE PRICE
[Handwritten "NUTS"]
NUTS IF WE BATTLE TOGETHER ON GETTING TOP MONEY
[Handwritten "OK"]
TO INDICATE MY DESIRE MY VOTE IS NUTS. . . .

H ere Colonel spells out as plainly and frankly as possible his philosophy of contracts and contract negotiation to Abe Lastfogel, his principal ally and best friend. He does not spare himself, citing his own naivete and willingness to settle for less when they first entered into negotiations with Hal Wallis a little more than a year ago — but he spares Lastfogel even less. His regret over the Wallis contract that he signed on April 25, 1956, has only increased over the past thirteen months, but his anger over the poor professional advice he feels he was given and that against all of his better instincts he accepted has grown even more. Perhaps most saliently, he insists, in a four-page, single-spaced letter, that Lastfogel hear him out, and then hear him out again, not just in spite of but *because of* their friendship. ■

"It seems to me that sometimes we all get too hasty to make a deal and are sorry for it later"

Mr. Abe Lastfogel   May 22, 1957
William Morris Agency, Inc.
151 El Camino
Beverly Hills, California

Dear Abe:

I just received your letter dated May 20 with reference to my being "needlessly excited" when Tom Diskin advised me of Phil's statement regarding the MGM checks. I was not excited—I only thought it proper to call you.

Tom Diskin works for me and it is his duty to inform me whenever things are not going as they should. My instructions were for him to be on the look-out for a check from MGM on Friday—as per agreement. When he did not receive it, he checked with Phil [presumably a William Morris agent or lawyer]. Phil told Diskin that someone at MGM had advised him the contract was not signed and there would be no check until it was signed. I could have called MGM myself and handled this matter but, since the Morris office represents us on these matters, I do not think I was out of line in any way, in bringing you up to date. Tom Diskin has told me again—"It happened just that way".

Regarding the MGM contract:—I am not interested in any way, to sign any contract with anyone, when I feel that the clauses are not in line with our agreements. I agreed to have Elvis Presley make the picture for certain amount and to have him there, ready for work. The other terms must be worked out. What I will agree to, after I read the contract, is entirely up to PRESLEY and me. There are many terms in these movie contracts that are completely against our setup, in our type of work. If movies were the only thing we could do, I could understand these terms. But we have been able to do a great deal more than motion pictures. What I should agree to regarding the MGM contract, I can only decide after I have double checked it after all corrections I gave Ann [William Morris legal counsel Ann Rosenthal] have been made.

I can think back to the time, a little over a year ago, when I was advised by one of your representatives that the Wallis contract had been checked by the Morris Office and everything was okay and ready for us to sign. I went over the contract with Ann at Las Vegas and we knocked out more than forty details that would have been signed by us if I had listened to Lenny [Hirshan, a young William Morris agent]. I feel that we have a complete right to double-check and either agree or, disagree on terms other than the fee we agreed upon and the time to report for work.

I also have a letter advising me that it would be impossible for us to share in any receipts of a loan-out from Wallis. Marty Jurow had advised

Harry Kalcheim that this could not be done. But after Ann and I went over the contract and did get a deal, I feel sure that it is very important to double-check all contracts more than once. I can understand that you have a great deal of mileage behind you with the Movie Studios, and I respect your thoughts and suggestions whenever you advise me. However, I must also feel that I am doing the right thing for ELVIS. I would much rather blow a deal than to feel that I have taken the easy way out, just to get a contract. Let nature take its course.

We are giving MGM and the other studios a great deal more than what the contracts call for in the way of exploitation, promotion, and time and money making phone calls. Getting Radio and TV Stations to plug the pictures, doing our own promotion. Gimmicks which we do not have to do — for these deals are not in the contract, but we do them all the time. Mr. Buddy Adler will be very glad to confirm this. Also, Joe Hazen and Hal Wallis. I am not going to sign any contracts that will leave us wide open, to be used in a commercial field by Theater Managers and local promoters in connection with us making a motion picture.

I am watching with a great deal of interest, the way Tommy Sands is currently being over-exposed. He only started two months ago and is just about milked out by his handlers in just about every field possible.

The Pat Boone Tour is, from all reports, bogging down all along the line and this should have been a big tour. I do not claim to know everything but, I think you must agree that, I try to plant my seeds first, before mowing the hay. There is nothing I do, that in some way does not help the Morris Office at the same time. I see no reason for a book-full of terms to make a picture, when we okay a picture. No one has told us that we must agree to all these clauses.

Should we make another deal with any studio, I will have to read the contract terms first, before I decide whether or not we can get together. This will do away with us having to go over all these deals and we can make up our minds as to what we can and cannot do. We can get together with the Studio and they can advise us — "yes or no".

It seems to me that sometimes we all get too hasty to make a deal and are sorry for it later. This, I try to stay away from. You know me well enough, that I could have had many deals, other than through the Morris Office and on our own terms. My loyalty is with you, and you know it. I will always keep my own freedom in making up my mind when I feel that things are not right for us. I have been brought up the hard way in Show Business. I think that I know which way we can go and stay in business. The things that work for the movie stars, do not always work for us. I have been in and out of so many towns, cities and hamlets — playing shows in barns, stockyards, auditoriums, school houses, auction sales, ball parks, home shows, theaters and what have you, that I know what we must do for the customers — and what they will buy. Television has proven to me, a great many of these points.

I could go on for hours, telling you of the deals, wherein I was advised I should have taken, when I turned them down. After I made the deal my way, the same people advised me — "It was certainly smart that you held out. We did not understand exactly what you meant, but now we can see it". I always remember the saying, "Don't put too many eggs in one basket — they may break". The same applies to our business. Even now, from time to time, I get a pitch to play a hotel or some club with PRES-LEY, when you know as well as I do that this would be a great step downwards in his career.

PRESLEY is a special set-up and must always be handled as such, or it will not last. The service required for this artist is not available, other than through personal contact and understanding. One can't break in an agent to do this, as they would bog down. I have no gripe with anyone, except to ask for complete understanding in the way I must handle this personality. Anytime, anyone can show me they can do a better job, and that it would be better for PRESLEY, I would be the first to work along with them or step aside and let them take over. I have not met anyone willing to take the personal gamble on this. I seem to be able to get a great deal of advice all along, but no one to pay the bills if things don't work out the way they planned.

This also applies to the WYATT EARP-HUGH O'BRIEN TOUR. Any of the promoters who worked with me, were all paid by me. I was the only person involved with the money. I paid all the bills. I had no partners in any of the towns. I was the only one who lost. No-one else. Everyone was paid in FULL. I even gave Lee Gordon back his ten thousand he had put up, as I felt he only went in on my say-so. I was wrong, so I let him out completely. I returned his money on the first date in Denver.

I have learned a great deal from you and I am grateful. I think I have done a good many turns to show my loyalty to your office. We can't always have everyone like us. I am always aware that all of us have shortcomings in our work and we can't cover these up by trying to be especially nice to people so that they don't see them. I have no dislikes for any man, and I never try to fool anyone with a phoney friendship.

I respect Ann Rosenthal's help and suggestions. She understands me very well and I have always been very understanding in accepting her suggestions, where originally I thought she was wrong, but after she explained them I knew she was right. Perhaps I am a little old-fashioned in my beliefs — that people take my word, when I tell them not to worry. I always say — "The fact that we report for work is a good sign of our respect and understanding".

It's like my banker — A long time ago, I needed $500. I had no security. I asked one of my friends to loan me the $500. He said — "What can you put up"? I told him — "Nothing but my promise to pay you back". He said — "Try the bank". I did, and got the money. I have not seen my friend since, but I am still banking with the same bank. This worked out good for me. Now I could loan him the $500, but I don't know where he is and I know he won't ask me. I know where the bank is, but they don't need it, so I feel that my friend did me a big favor by turning me down. If he should ask me for $500 now, I could tell him — "Try the bank". They gave me the money upon his advice to — "See the bank". It just goes to show that we never know when we are right or when we are wrong.

Remember me to Frances. I hope this clears up some of the details that I always have in mind. If this letter is too long, read it a little at a time.

Marie joins me with her best.

> Your pal
> THE COLONEL

Two months later he cannot help but return to the Hal Wallis matter and remind himself as much as Lastfogel that, with MGM and Fox negotiations pending and, once again, a battle with Wallis looming, they need to keep all their newly established precepts in mind. All of which adds up, once again, to his repeated declaration that neither he nor his artist is about to be fooled again.

Just as a postscript, with every picture that Elvis made for Wallis over the entirety of their eleven-year association, Colonel always managed to improve the deal. ∎

"I also know the old saying One should not change Horses in the middle of a stream, however there are many farmers that have always an extra bag of Oats on the other side trying to get them accross faster rather than see One of the Horses turn around and eat better by going back"

Mr. Abe Lastfogel   July 24th 1957
William Morris Agency
Beverly Hills California

Dear Abe;

Thanks for your letter dated July 22nd, to date I have not received the Metro Contracts for checking. . . .

Regarding the Fox contract I am not aware that we have any other than the Picture LOVE ME TENDER wich we have already completed and have been paid for except the bonus as promised, the terms and clauses in the Fox contract were not explained to me over the phone other than the amount of money for the One picture and the amount for the Second and Third Picture, but I never agreed on a certain time to make these pictures as it was never mentioned over the phone as far as I know it could have been a picture every 6 Months or every Two or Three Years, just because it is in the contract Fox made up did not mean that we would agree to some of the clauses in it. We have a complete right to disagree on those details as we never knew them till I read the contract anyway and the fact that we did not sign them at that time is enough for any-one to know that some things would have to come out.

I will depend on you to advise me what will have to be done on the Wallis setup, There is of course no way possible for us to come out under this setup other than blow a lot of money to make a picture for Wallis, if we could have ELVIS go out to the Coast on his own and stay there to make the Wallis Picture without us setting up our staff and other gimmicks wich ELVIS needs and wants done, he could just come out even, this of course is impossible as I know he has no desire to go to Hollywood without his regular following with him. I also know that this is no fault of Mr. Wallis, but with his drawing power and LOVING YOU doing okay all over the Country I do think they should re-write the contract for this Artist as it is only the fair thing to do, RCA Victor did it for the same reasons. And we did not have to prod them very much. You of course will be much wiser than I to come up with AN ANSWER ON THIS.

We also have done a great deal of promotion on the Wallis picture from our end to help kick it off and advance promotion, wich is much more than Mr. Wallis gets from many of his stars, also knowing that we do not have a percentage deal either, I now know more than ever that I should have held out for my First deal with Wallis when I was talking to Harry Kalcheim [and] Marty Jurow and should never have let any-one talk me into taking a deal like that, I have enough proof that I never was very happy with this First contract and there are enough reasons wich Ann [Rosenthal] will remember why I knocked out so many clauses out of the Wallis contract this was all I could do at that time.

I can very well understand your thinking on the First picture for us to report for work First and work out something better only after we start the picture, I do not believe this same idea will work this time, DO YOU?

I also know the old saying One should not change Horses in the middle of a stream, however there are many farmers that have always an extra bag of Oats on the other side trying to get them accross faster rather than see One of the Horses turn around and eat better by going back. . . .

Your Pal
And Old Friend The Colonel.

Colonel initiated the idea of Elvis recording a Christmas album in the late spring of 1957. He proposed deluxe packaging with a gatefold cover and a lavishly illustrated interior booklet which would advertise Elvis' entire catalogue. This was music that Elvis loved, Colonel declared, and he was sure his fans would love it, too. And, not at all coincidentally, it would provide a perfect vehicle for perennial promotion. Which certainly proved to be the case, as *Elvis' Christmas Album* turned out to be the biggest-selling album of his career, selling an estimated twenty million units in various permutations over the years.

But, as compelling as Colonel's arguments were, when RCA insisted that the recording had to be completed by a certain date and Elvis said he wasn't yet ready to make the song choices, Colonel's response to both Steve Sholes and Bill Bullock was the same one that he had given them from the start: his artist called the shots. And if that meant no Christmas album, despite all the planning and expense that had already gone into it, so be it.

As Colonel frequently said, You can't lose a deal that you never had. Bluff? Annoyance? Disbelief that a bureaucratic deadline was going to stand in the way of a project in which everyone so firmly believed? I don't know. But the album got made on Elvis' schedule (along with a remake of "Treat Me Nice" from the *Jailhouse Rock* soundtrack), as always to Elvis' exact specifications. And Colonel once again reaffirmed the principle, in a series of letters to Bullock and Sholes, that his artist was in charge of all artistic decisions — and that he was prepared to defend those decisions in each and every way. ∎

"I do not blame ELVIS for not putting himself on record that he is going to record a certain number and later feels it does not work out"

Mr. Bill Bullock   July 24th, 1957
RCA Victor Division
155 East 24th Street
New York City New York

Dear Bill;

There's not much news, I advised Stephen [Sholes] that we will mostly record late in August or early Sept as ELVIS wants to recut some of the Jailhouse Rock tunes for commercial release. He's not sold on the sound track. Regarding the Xmas album I'm awaiting word from ELVIS also on this as he is working on tunes and trying to decide if we should do this album at this time. Take care of yourself and I hope to be able to get away for a Week or so before long. We are still working on the books here.

Sincerely,
Tom.

Mr. Stephen H. Sholes, Manager   July 24th, 1957
Artist & Repertoire, Single Records
RCA Victor Record Division

155 East 24th Street
New York 10. NY

Dear Steve;

I have just received word from ELVIS that he does not wish to record in Nashville, he also informs me that he has been listening to some of the records from Jailhouse Rock and he feels that he wants to cut some of them over for commercial use rather than use the sound track. I plan to work out my schedule so that we can either record sometime late in August or early Sept most likely on the Coast, we of course by that time will know about the Xmas LP also.

I think ELVIS is talking about "Jailhouse Rock" and "Treat me Nice" and some other tunes, he was going to wire me the titles, as soon as I know for sure we will wire you or write you the titles. Now you can plan your vacation as you wanted, I have not been able to get away from here as we are still working on our books and also the contract is being checked pretty closely. What will come out of it I have no idea, time will tell. There is not much news. Diskin returned from his trip with Eddy Arnold and told me Eddy did very well. . . .

Kindest regards,
The Colonel

Mr. Bill Bullock   August 6th 1957
RCA Victor Division
155 East 24th Street
New York City New York

Dear Bill;

I hope to be able to take off for a Week or so by Tomorrow, I will try to go somewhere where no One can find me so I can at least get a little rest.

Regarding the names of the tunes for the Xmas LP, I spoke to ELVIS and it is impossible to pick these tunes till we start recording Sept 5th on the Coast with Sholes as, if he should cut this special album, he may at the last minute find another tune that he would like better, if this is too late there is nothing else we can do but forget about it, I cant create something that is impossible to work out, I do not blame ELVIS for not putting himself on record that he is going to record a certain number and later feels it does not work out. If nothing else we may have to work out an EP for Xmas instead. . . .

Sincerely
Tom.

It's not clear just what MGM ("Metro") script is being referred to here, but, as you might deduce, Elvis didn't do the picture. (With the army years intervening, he would not in fact make another MGM film for five years.) But the degree of consultation and collaboration, and the seriousness with which both Elvis and Colonel were seeking dramatic roles, is, if not surprising, at least revealing. If only we had Elvis' response. (But we never do.) ■

"The money is not as important right now to make a picture if the story is not right for you"

Dear Elvis;   August 3rd 1957

Enclosed is the Metro Story [script] received from Mr. Lastfogel—

Read it, and let me have your thoughts as soon as possible—I do not know if you would like this type of role—I do believe that any question regarding a song is out, other than perhaps the tittle song where you would sing the tittle song but not be seen singing this thru-out the picture—I have a feeling that you would not like to play this type of role right now, perhaps at a later time, however it is up to you to let me know. In this case we surely do not have to take this type of role as we have no deal at Metro and they cant hold us to you playing this picture—but we do owe them an answer—even so far we dont have an offer I guess they want some idea that you would like to play this role before going into trying to make a deal with me. So advise me as soon as you have read enough of the story so you know if you would like to do a picture like this or not.

The money is not as important right now to make a picture if the story is not right for you, With Wallis we would have trouble turning down stories too often as we have no story approval on contract bases, also the same with 20th Century Fox, however we can always work on this when the time comes. I agree with you that I would like to keep the next picture down to a real story and perhaps no singing other than the tittle song where they do not see you sing at all but acting only. Except of course if it was a tremendous musical and even a musical we would have to [be] sure it is the right story at this time.

I would much rather break off trying to get a deal on this story with Metro now — and have them look for something better to your liking so I would not waste a lot of time working on a deal, as you know I am trying to get even a little better deal than the other deal at Metro. . . .

> My best to all of you.
> The Admiral.

PS Mr Diskin will also give you his thoughts.

I t would be easy to dismiss Colonel's persistent complaints about the Hal Wallis contract as haggling over money — and over the years this argument has tended to devolve into the idea that Colonel Parker was just haggling for more money for Colonel Parker. Which is certainly true up to a point. Whatever the increase in his client's income, it certainly redounded to his own financial benefit. But Colonel never lived lavishly and never acquired any savings or property to speak of. What I would suggest he was looking for — *always* — was respect: respect for himself but, even more, for his client. Nor was he in any way above rehashing the past, as should be evident by now. The game, as he saw it, was always about improving your situation. Here he is in the midst of making the case that Hal Wallis has almost a moral obligation to increase Elvis' salary for the next picture to $100,000 (four times the contractually specified amount) after all the success that Elvis' first two pictures (including the one for Wallis) have enjoyed. In the end, after much huffing and puffing, that is what he got. But far more important to him, as I think this letter makes clear, was that his artist be taken seriously, both as a star and as an actor. And for that he was prepared to use every tool at his command, including (implied) blackmail.

Well, judge for yourself. ■

"I know he is not at all interested in doing a repeat of the type of pictures we have just made"

Mr. Abe Lastfogel   September 13, 1957
William Morris Agency
151 El Camino
Beverly Hills California.

Dear Abe;

As I have not heard from you as of this Morning I feel that something must have gone wrong with the Color TV set that I had orderred for you and Francess from Marie and I. Let me know what happens.

I also received the notice from Hazen [Hal Wallis' partner, Joe Hazen] and have forwarded same on to ELVIS, I also wrote Ann Rosenthal my thoughts on this setup, I am now waiting to hear from you regarding Hazen on the money we asked for last Week. AS you already know it will be impossible for me to come out there and maintain my office under the setup we now have with Wallis, I will of course be there a Day or so to get ELVIS started off but I will have to return home and keep my office running from here, the returns that we receive under the present setup would not pay for our expenses not even counting the tremendous expense that ELVIS has with his Buddies. One of course can say he does not have to bring them out with him, however they are part of his make-up and he works much better with his Buddies around him to keep him company at Night and pal around with.

Regarding the story Wallis has in mind I believe we must have some idea what it is and if ELVIS will feel at all like doing the type of picture Wallis is planning, I know he is not at all interested in doing a repeat of the type of pictures we have just made all 3 of them are somehow of the same order with the Second picture [the Hal Wallis production, *Loving You*] somewhat better and the Third [*Jailhouse Rock*] a pretty good acting part in this type story. I cant understand the thinking of any studio to want to keep on this same idea.

Regarding the songs if any in any future picture we will be very care-full in doing any tune on records other than the tune that we feel will be better than anything we may already have in the can, we always have the final say-so when and what to re-lease on records, this has nothing to do with making a picture, the recording company cant give permission to any studio that they will re-lease a certain record at a certain time except if we agree, this also applies to any other recording we do even if it is not in a motion picture.

AS soon as you hear from Hazen and Wallis regarding the extra money we ask for let me know, also about the story, I will also expect a much better re-lation setup with the Morris office than we had on the last Paramount picture.

WE had a great deal of buck passing between your representative and the Studio and your office wich did nothing for the good of our working setup — I sincerely hope that we will be able to have the same pleasant re-lation as we did at Metro with the least trouble. I handled a good deal of clearing up on things that should have been handled by your office at Paramount, this I do not mind at all except I dont want to be put in the middle on trying to cover up for any-one.

I believe that ELVIS is an important client for any office and he deserves whatever service he may need thru us from the Morris office, I am not complaining but only want to go on record in plenty of time so we can start off with a clean slate and not a lot of buckpassing after we get out there, this is a very important setup it does not work like some other personalities and we need no undue pressure from any agent at anytime, I am almost like One of your own people looking out for the interest of the Morris office and you know this very well.

I hope things are well with you and take care of each other, Marie joins me with best wishes along with our hopes that you have A NICE VACATION.

Your Pal
The Old Colonel.

Colonel was always going to have his fun with Bill Bullock, but the serious point here — and it's one that recurs frequently in their correspondence — is that he does not want Bullock (or anyone else at RCA) to forget that ALL points in the contract must be strictly adhered to, whether written or unwritten. Elvis' contract had been built up by now to a point far beyond that of any other pop star — but not on paper. The reasons for this were numerous, but the fundamental reason was the most-favored-nation clause that every big star with a sentient manager has in their contract. What this meant was that if Elvis got paid more than anyone else on the label, the biggest stars needed to be paid that much as well. As a result, many of the deals that Colonel made were worked out according to a complex algorithmic table that Colonel devised and few were going to understand without his patient guidance — or they were simply not written down at all. As he writes here, with disingenuous tongue in disingenuous cheek, "I guess I am One of the few Managers that have so many verbal agreements not in writing and my mentality is of such proportion that I forget sometime." Meaning that no one at RCA had better forget, and that they had better make sure that their unnamed successors-to-come would remember, too. But the greater underlying message amid all the buck-passing contests to which he alludes? Well, you might think it was, Don't underestimate me, I'm not going away. But actually I think the message was aimed just as much at his friend Bill Bullock and conveyed the same uplifting advice: Don't underestimate yourself. (And to the reader in the face of all the challenges that Colonel's self-typed run-on stream-of-consciousness style provides in this letter: Don't underestimate yourself.) ∎

"I am now preparing myself for the lambasting I will get from all sides"

Mr. Bill Bullock   September 19, 1957
RCA Victor Division
New York City New York

Dear Bill;

Your letters received everything seems to be shaping up okay. Mr. Tiley [RCA chief legal counsel Coleman Tily] called me also Today and I explained some of the details to him.

Bill Bullock. *Courtesy of the Graceland Archives*

Regarding the Xmas Album I feel that this should be a real booster all along the line, I know I will be watching with real interest on the outcome.

I am thinking up some special ideas for next Year regarding merchandising if I can come up with anything I will advise you, it seems we have been able to role some of these ideas in pretty good. As I told you on the phone Today the Day's are back where One must come up with special gimmicks as the pressure now is off from buyers except on a special interesting setup believe me the pictures are helping a great deal along this line with the advance orders and we surely do not want to under-estimate the Field Reps who are doing a tremendous job by tying in all along the line. . . .

I also know that this will wear off if we do not from time to time move in another way, now by putting this Xmas LP out as a special and during Xmas at that you will be able to move a good many other sales at the same time.

As I told you Today on the phone I have always been happy to bring my ideas to you and try to work them out with the company and I also know that some of them stink at times but One only needs a few good setups from time to time to make it pay and all the bad ideas are soon forgotten.

IF you remember many times things look bad and we may think its no use — but somehow they all fit together, many of our problems are unknown to people who are right in the middle of things but they cant see them as they are busy with their own problems however our problems also are the Company's.

I am now preparing myself for the lambasting I will get from all sides when I goof up, and the time must be near for me to goof as I have been too lucky for too long with my ideas. However I will be in good company as you of course will be with me when we are called upon the red carpet — There is One thing for sure it will be One of the best Buckpassing contest's that will ever be held when that happens as you and I do have plenty of background along that line.

I guess I am One of the few Managers that have so many verbal agreements not in writing and my mentality is of such proportion that I forget sometime, after you figure this out I know you will advise me the answer. . . .

When Mr. Marek [RCA's new General Manager George Marek] the other Day told me that RCA Victor had done a great job on ELVIS I of course agreed with him on that point except to state that ELVIS also had done the same for the Company and that many of the problems we handled ourselves also protected the other people that we did and are doing business with, I remember several times when I ask[ed] you and others if the company was not in accord with what we did regarding ALL THE BAD PUBLICITY WE AT THAT TIME WERE GETTING we would re-lease them so they would not have to take all that buffing around, So all in all I think things have turned out pretty good, I dont think any One person any-where could ever claim credit for PRESLEY except perhaps the fans all over the world. IF any-one does have the ability to waive that magic spell I sure hope they use it on others also for I know a couple of great artists that could use a little magic spell right now. The whole deal boils down to hard work by every-one in the entire field.

Save this letter for your snowfiles someday you will get a good laugh reading it when you are chairman of the Board, you can always say I could have known the Colonel better, if I had only been able to read his snow-letters better. Give my best to [RCA officers] WARREN LING, STEPHEN SHOLES*SNOWER TILY*DAVIS, BURGESS, WELKER, FINN, MCCUEN. AND SOME OF THE INTER-MEDIATE SNOWERS. SOME DAY I HOPE TO GET BACK INTO THE GOOD STANDING OF COL TILY AND GET HIS PERMISSION TO USE THE NIPPER DOG AGAIN ON MY SNOW-LETTERS, OF COURSE WHEN THIS HAPPENS I WILL CHARGE FOR IT.

MY BEST THE COLONEL.

By late 1957 Colonel's antic invention, the Snowmen's League, was taking up more and more of his creative energy and time. (Does this tell us something about his artistic inclinations — or even how little the intricacies of the business, while they always engaged him, actually fulfilled him?) Here he writes an indulgent letter to Paul Wilder, the columnist at the *Tampa Tribune* who had always boosted him during his time at the Humane Society, attempting to instruct him on the philosophical precepts of the League. Wilder was the reporter assigned at Colonel's insistence to interview Elvis for the highly influential weekly *TV Guide* at the beginning of the 1956 frenzy. The interview outraged fans (it outraged even his future biographer — me) for its flat, unvarnished, almost sneering tone, though Elvis acquitted himself beautifully. And until recently I had no idea who Wilder was — and I'm still not sure how this changes the tone of the interview in any positive way (is it possible Colonel's old friend was just a poor student?)— but it turns out Wilder was a great kidder, too. ■

"It is of course these funny letters and my feeling that One must enjoy his work or grow stale keeps me on the go"

Mild Snower Paul Wilder   Sept 25, 1957
Tampa, Florida

Dear Part-time Member;

Your Snow letter received here at our censor office for snowletters — I am somewhat atakin [sic] back with your letter — I never would have thought that you would answer so soon and with such a mild snowletter. We of course can understand that you tried to impress us at once with a big snowjob — the reaction of new part-time members has always been that way — and most everytime they snow themselves under by doing this, I hope this does not happen to you. . . .

Regarding any information on this outstanding Snowclub for your fine paper the Tribune — Any of our members have to be good enough snowers so they can make up their own snow stories for newspapers without calling on any of the top snowers, there is One rule you must always abide by — and that is, One never Snow's any-one other than to do good. Never take advantage of any-one that you have been able to snow under, allow other snowers to snow you from time to time even if you know you are being snowed. Bevo Bevis our associate snower First Class advises me that there are no dues, there are no aims, there are no by-laws only in-laws and they cant belong to the snowclub. You tried so hard to snow in your last letter that we knew at once you had just been admitted into the Club, dont try so hard as you may snow yourself right out again.

We plan to go on our Fall Florida Safari to get a new supply of Mosquito Manure for our Christmas orders this Fall. In event you should need any you of course as a member can get it wholesale. Bevo is now making all the plans for this Safari you can write him direct for information on where and when they will leave from the place they never arived at.

Now back to normal business for a few lines, I am more or less violating the rules of the club by INJECTING PERSONAL BUSINESS HOWEVER I Can always go back to catching Dogs for a living in event I am kicked out of the Club.

The new MGM Picture Jailhouse Rock will be released late October, we are leaving tomorrow for Tupelo where ELVIS is doing a benefit Friday to raise money for a recreation Center they plan to build in his name at Tupelo. . . .

Say hello to the Family for me and I am glad you are enjoying the records — It is of course these funny letters and my feeling that One must enjoy his work or grow stale keeps me on the go, I can always bring myself right back into a happy medium by remembering how lucky we are, so let it snow let it snow I will always be somewhere to receive it. . . .

> Your Pal
> Tom.

All the usual Hollywood disputes and contretemps continued, I'm sure to Colonel's considerable divertissement, with William Morris stuck in the middle. Here they are articulated in a letter to a young agent named Lenny Hirshan, who for some reason Colonel took a dislike to (he may be the agent-in-waiting Colonel is referring to obliquely in his September 13 letter to Abe Lastfogel when he declares, "I believe that ELVIS is an important client and he deserves whatever service he may need thru us from the Morris office"). This musing and remonstrance about the future is prompted by a yet-unnamed and evidently still to be fully scripted *King Creole,* which would turn out to be Elvis' fourth picture (his second for Hal Wallis), and the last he would make before going into the army in March of 1958. As you can see, the rise in price to $100,000 has yet to be resolved and will only be concluded to Colonel's complete satisfaction days before the picture starts shooting. ∎

"We now have done 3 musicals and to do another picture of the same type would be foolish"

Mr. Lenny Hirshan   October 7th 1957
William Morris Agency
Beverly Hills California.

Dear Lenny;

Your letter dated Oct 4th received thanks for same, On this Hal Wallis setup I am not ahead with any-one, so far we have no idea what the story is like or if there are any songs in the story that we will have to check on and know about, it seems to me that time is running out and we will again be under pressure on this setup, there is also a good possibility that I may not come out to the Coast on this picture as due to tremendous work at home and the expenses involved out there I will see if I cant handle most of the details from here, I will have Tom Diskin there at least to get the ball rolling. We are also waiting for confirmation regarding the $100,000 we asked for at Lunch when you were there with Mr. Lastfogel and so far we have not heard a word. . . .

Bring me up to date on all details now so we will know what is ahead and what should be done, you know as well as I do that the story will have to fit Elvis way of thinking before we start something that we cant finish, we now have done 3 musicals and to do another picture of the same type would be foolish, even if I thought the other way I know Elvis is very much concerned about the next story and we will have to watch this very closely. The same apply's to any songs that are worked out with our publisher that are to be in the picture for if they are not the right tunes we of course do not record them on [RCA] records as this is our own business and has nothing to do with making motion pictures.

There is no other news at this time I am still waiting to hear from Mr. Hazen and Wallis regarding our luncheon we had before we left the Coast, Elvis also is asking Daily for some idea on the story setup, as you know he does not work overnight on a story and it will only delay everything if we get this at the last minute. AS you state in your letter in case we want to make revisions we must read the story First before we can get together on that.

Sincerely The Colonel.

The Colonel's true identity was always something of a mystery, even to those who knew him well, but it was more a matter of slightly bemused speculation than anything that anyone might be seriously concerned about. There were many individuals with floating origin stories in those days, particularly in the world of show business and entertainment. "Prince" Mike Romanoff, for example, a prominent Hollywood restaurateur and Snowman par excellence, was warmly embraced, and openly described, as a "professional impostor"— to both the Russian throne and American citizenship, among other equally spurious claims. The catch for Colonel is that while he certainly craved publicity — perhaps credit most of all — at the same time he seems by now to have recognized the dangers that too much publicity might pose to his carefully contrived origin story. Here he instructs Harry Kalcheim on just how to deal with any inquiries that might come his way. His excuse for not giving anyone information is the same one he relayed to me some forty years later: if he helped me, he said, he would have to help everyone. ■

"I stopped doing any interviews as none of them came out with the facts the way we gave them"

Dear Harry;   Dec 2nd, 1957

. . . Note in your letter regarding people asking you about myself, I know you must have this happen every once in while, we get a good deal of it here. However due to the fact that there have been about 5 stories out on me in the past 2 Years in newspapers and some books, I stopped doing any interviews as none of them came out with the facts the way we gave them, also it did not look proper for me to be in the limelight all the time, as you know I stayed in the background a good deal when I had EDDY ARNOLD, some of the writers that did write stories got whatever information they could gather from some people and as they of course sell these stories they seem to fit them into a patern where they can get the most money, some have been fair in reporting whatever they could find out as they found it out, some wrote with a bad feeling that could very well stem from having been turned down for personal interviews, some received information from perhaps people that are jealous or perhaps had some complaint or other who knows, we do know that some of the stories have such a phoney touch to them in the way it is written only we that know can enjoy the reading of them as we know wich is wich for sure. If its too bad, the folks that know me know better, and the people that do not know me will most always think a long time before believing everything they read, someday when I will have the time and write my own story in its entire form with the facts as I know them, and also know they can be checked, almost all the other stories will become comic strips to any-one with a sense of humor. One of the main reasons that I am unable to give any-one an exclusive story at this time is very simple, I have many Friends that have asked me to allow them to write the story, if I gave it to One the others would feel bad or would figure I was shopping for a better deal, so when I do write the story I will pay for the writers and sell the whole package all at One time including motion picture rights and what have you to the Highest bidder. Marie joins me with the best to all of you. Your Friend The Colonel

Colonel's relationship with Vernon and Gladys, shaky at first, had improved considerably after two years of uninterrupted success, and while it cannot be said that he was ever able to fully overcome Gladys' mistrust, to Colonel's credit he never stopped trying. He had a more easygoing relationship with Vernon, and their shared worry over Elvis' improvident spending served to bring them together more and more over the years. This appears to be an awkward attempt to bring both parents into the inner circle, as he inducts them into his exalted and exclusive (not so much maybe — and yet... and yet it was) Snowmen's League. You'll note who gets the most extravagant compliments, and I'll leave it to you to speculate as to what Snow-ess Gladys' real thoughts might have been. ■

Vernon, Gladys, Elvis at home on Audubon Drive, summer 1956. *Courtesy of the Graceland Archives*

"TO THE CHIEF SNOWER AND SNOW-ESS"

DEC 19TH 1957

TO THE CHIEF SNOWER AND SNOW-ESS VERNON PRESLEY AND GLADYS PRESLEY, DEAR SNOWER MEMBERS, AT A SPECIAL MEETING Today at SNOW HEADQUARTERS WITH SNOWER BEVO BEING IN CHARGE I WAS ABLE TO SNOW HIM INTO ALLOWING BOTH OF YOU INTO THIS GREAT SNOWCLUB, SNOWER ELVIS PRESLEY BEING ABSENT FROM THIS GREAT SNOW MEETING WILL HAVE TO APROVE THE CARDS WHEN YOU RE-CIEVE THEM AS HE

SEEMS TO BE THE HIGH POTENTATE SNOWER AT PRESENT,
SNOWER CLIFF AND LAMAR NOT HAVING PAID THEIR SNOW-
DUES THIS YEAR MAY VERY WELL BE DEFROSTED OUT OF THE
CLUB.

IT IS UNDERSTOOD THAT SNOW-ESS GLADYS IS NOW ONE
OF THE FEW FEMALE MEMBERS OF THIS CLUB WICH INCLUDE
SNOW-ESS MARIE PARKER AND MARTHA RAYE, KNOWING THAT
SNOW-ESS GLADYS WILL BE ABLE TO OUTSNOW EITHER ONE
OF THESE MEMBERS SHE HAS NOTHING TO WORRY ABOUT.

I HOPE THAT YOU WILL TREAT THIS MEMBERSHIP WITH
THE OUTMOST RESPECT AND CONFIDENCE AND KEEP UP IMPOR-
TANT SNOWJOBS AT ALL TIMES, WE WILL JUDGE BY NEXT YEAR
AT OUR ANUAL SNOW MEETING IN IGLO ALASKA DURING
THE STRAWBERRY SEASON IN DECEMBER IF PERHAPS ONE OF
YOU WILL BE PROMOTED TO HIGH POTENTATE SNOWER OR
SNOWESS.

BE SURE AND DISPLAY THIS LETTER TO POTENTATE SNOWER
ELVIS SO HE CAN APPROVE YOUR MEMBERSHIP AT ONCE.

SNOWINGLY YOURS
HIGH POTENTATE SNOWER
ADMIRAL COLONEL PRIVATE
PARKER.

Exclusive manager Uncle Travis and associates.
ALSO ENCLOSED IS A CARD FOR UNCLE TRAVIS AS A SNOW MEM-
BER AS HE SEEMS TO BE DOING A GOOD SNOWJOB AT THE [Grace-
land] GATE.

1958

On December 30, 1957, Bill Bullock brought up the idea of Elvis recording with a symphony orchestra using well-known classical pieces (unnamed) which a broader, more conventional audience might very well appreciate. Colonel's response to the suggestion, which Bullock had made before, was direct and to the point. The other project under discussion, which Colonel had first raised some time ago, was released as *Elvis' Golden Records* in March of 1958 and charted for fifty weeks, becoming one of Elvis' all-time bestsellers and once again bearing out Colonel's inclination for what he liked to call "long-term thinking." ■

"It would seem to me like a sideshow medicine pitch. This would not only be unfair to any Classical music but also to ELVIS"

Mr. Bill Bullock   Jan 3rd 1958
Record Department
RCA Victor Division

Dear Bill;
        . . . Regarding your request on the Classical album idea, we do not feel that this would be sound programming for us, I appreciate your offer of sending us a suggested LP; there is no need for this as this idea we cant buy at all. The reasons are very simple from our point of looking at it, also I see no need other than doing something that could very well flare back at us from an angle of trying to sell something that we are in no way connected with, it would seem to me like a sideshow medicine pitch. This would not only be unfair to any Classical music but also to ELVIS. I appreciate the good deal you could make us, and I know that you will

make us another good deal on something else in the future, knowing that you feel so good towards making a good deal with us.

I do hope you will think very carefully regarding a gimmick tie-in on the golden [*Elvis' Golden Records*] LP, for I am very close to sales and what it takes Today to keep something interesting in sales rolling, I am not thinking of a short deal on this LP as I sincerely believe if it is going to work at all, it will have to last a long time, for any LP of this sort will never make it on a short setup. . . .

I am always glad to sit down and work out something when possible to tie-in with anything RCA Victor comes up with as long as it does not take away from our business setups. . . .

Your Pal
The Colonel

Things had been tense between Elvis and his accompanying trio (Scotty Moore and Bill Black, who had been with him from the beginning, and drummer D. J. Fontana, who had joined in September 1955) ever since Scotty and Bill quit four months before. Colonel and Tom Diskin attempted to serve as impartial go-betweens, while Steve Sholes actively campaigned for Scotty and Bill to be replaced by more sophisticated musicians. Film producer Hal Wallis agreed, at least for soundtrack recording purposes.

Scotty and D.J. came back after a month (Bill did not), but things were not the same. Perhaps the reason that Colonel's typing here is even more agitated than usual is his innate dislike of being placed in the middle, but he does take the situation as an opportunity to remind Elvis of the responsibilities of leadership. It is an unusual letter for its uncharacteristically vexatious tone and its almost hammering repetitiousness (some of which I have spared the reader). With the army looming, it is as if, all of a sudden, everything is for the first time up in the air. ∎

"The responsibility that goes with being a star like you is not easy, but you know that we do everything possible to carry our load as much as any-one"

Dear Elvis;   Jan 2nd 1958

I have just completed talking to Scottie Moore and Hal Wallis.

I advised Mr. Wallis that the boy's would be out there on Tuesday, as this is the way he wanted to do it, Mr. Wallis feels that he is using your boy's as a special favor to you as he knows you like to use your own boy's, this he has no objection in doing. However since they do take a long time learning the tunes as they do not read music he feels it only fair that he must have them in town in plenty of time so it does not delay his starting to record when you arive as it did the last time. Mr. Wallis can get all the good musicians he needs for pictures on the Coast that read and can cut it any way you wish, so he is being fair about it. Regarding the deal I only acted as a go between since you did not call the boys yourself or advised them what to do, Scottie was all ready to go on a tour next Week with Bill as they play Texarkana Saturday Nite, however they promised to come by and pickup the car and be out there Tuesday to start working on the tunes. What you do after you get out there with them does not matter at this time, you can work this out in Hollywood, Wallis said he would pay them $250. a week and scale for recording and rehearsal with a 2 week plan for sure, you are to pay their way out there and back and the hotel bill, so this is the way it stands at present, Mr Diskin did not come in Today so I handled this myself. . . .

When I spoke to your Dad Today he informed me that you was upset with a letter from [Elvis' former manager] Bob Neal regarding Neal writing you that he wanted to have you appear Sunday on his show in Memphis, Bob did call me and I told him that it would not be possible, also the notice was too short even if we could do it, Bob asked me if it was alright with me if he spoke to you himself, I told him that I was not a policeman and I had no business advising any-one when they could talk to you or when they could not, Dad tells me that you felt I dumped Neal in your lap, I do not understand how you can feel that way when in his letter Neal himself states that I turned him down. . . .

There are many things that have come up here that I could have dumped in your lap many times wich should have been handled directly by you but we handled them knowing you did not want to be bothered with them. . . . we have at least 800 request for tapes that we have received from all over the Country, also a good many phone calls they want you to make, not counting the many newspaper interviews Daily's and

Weekly's wich we have buffed away from you thru this office, how you can feel with One letter that I dumped something in your lap is beyond me.

Now lets look at it from a point the way you know I work. First if I had told Bob Neal that I wish he would not talk to you or contact you, I am sure you would have thought what is the matter with the Colonel telling Bob not to talk to me, First of all I would be doing exactly what I never do trying to invade your private life. . . . he wrote it from a personal angle as a Friend wich I have no controll over and never would tell any-one that they could not talk to you. [And he goes on to rehash the Neal situation once again from every conceivable angle.]

You have been around long and are smart enough to know that I dont throw any curves to any-one even at my own expense. And you also know my phone number you could have called me when you received the letter and I would have put you straight on the contents, and if you did not believe it you could call Bob Neal up and tell him so. It did not sit well with me when your Dad told me how you felt and you know me well enough that it is only right for me to explain the entire issue since you must have been in doubt about it or you would not have told Dad the way you felt. I have been working here Day and Night trying to plan every-thing for the best when you go into service so things will run smoothly along. There are some details I am trying to work out to save as much as possible any of the deals I had lined up for 1958 and have a steady income while you are in service coming in to your home from all sources, I expect you to saddle yourself right along with me as always and help me in any way you can to make these deals turn out for the good of all of us. The responsibility that goes with being a star like you is not easy, but you know that we do everything possible to carry our load as much as any-one. Bob also told me Today that it was impossible for him to get in touch with you other than by letter. I hope you have received the photos I mailed or rather send to you by Jimmie Snow wich I had received for you from the photographer as I orderred several copies, these are with my compli-ments. Regards to all of you and call me when you have read this letter so we can get things in order for your departure for the Coast.

My best to Your Mother and Dad. The Colonel.

And then the very next day, he wrote a more succinct letter going over some of the same ground while also focusing on the need to maintain strict control over recording (so as not to allow RCA to saturate the market) and, once again, song publishing as well. Here is a brief excerpt. ∎

"I know that you know all this however it does not hurt to bring these facts again to your attention as it is my job to watch this as much as possible from this end"

DEAR ELVIS: Jan 3rd 1958

Enclosed is a copy of a letter I have just written to Bill Bullock regarding plans for 1958 and some of the request they have asked me on future promotion setups, the details I see no need to go into at present with you as they are handled in line with our understanding and with the keeping of what we can and cant do.

As you know we will have to start thinking of some recording dates while on the Coast so we have at least something suitable in the storage bin while you are in service for the First 6 Months, this is very important at the same time we should not worry about having too much on hand also, so we will not have outdated material in the can at a later date, we will not know for sometime how much of the material we will use in the picture that will be suitable for re-lease on records later to tie-in with the Movie re-lease this Fall.

We also must be very carefull so we do not have some of these songs going out without having at least the protection for your return on royalties at a later date when you are in service, as the music checks can only come in from the music firm if we have royalties coming in at all times, everything we do not get some type of royalty set up on will only bring back returns for some-one else and nothing into the music firm later on when you will need it to keep up the Weekly checks that come in every Month from Elvis Presley Music and Gladys Music. These checks as you well know have nothing to do with record royalties, only if Jean and Julian Aberbach and myself get deals on these tunes can we keep payments coming into the Music Firm while you are in service. They have done a tremendous job in getting you cut in on many tunes all the way around, and if you know what some of the artist receive from songs they record against what you have received you would know how important this is to watch as closely as we can. I know that you know all this however it does not hurt to bring these facts again to your attention as it is my job to watch this as much as possible from this end, as you are not on top of this like we are and it is very easy to get slipped up on this with our type of pressure we receive all the time from all sources. . . .

———————————

This is about as perfect a letter as Colonel ever wrote. As he says, "Every sentence has a meaning intended to be understood." Most of all what is to be understood — and what is clearly stated, for everyone at RCA to understand — is that Colonel is in it for the long haul and (no threat intended) everybody else had better be, too. At the same time there is no shortage of affection, or even sincerity, conveyed here. When he says that "when Elvis has donned his uniform we should all put on a new working jacket to show him we are still in front with him regardless of his being in the service," he clearly means it, and I think (though with Colonel one can never be sure) he has little doubt that RCA Vice President and General Manager George Marek and everyone else cc'd here will pick up on it, too. ■

"Short term plans are for people and companies that plan to go out of business"

Mr. George Marek   January 29, 1958
RCA Victor Record Division
155 East 24th Street
New York 10, N.Y.

Dear George:

It was nice talking to you today and we are looking forward to the basket of fruit that you so kindly said you would have shipped to Elvis and his crew here on the set while he is making his new picture. This gesture was most kind as Elvis does not go to cocktail parties or other formal affairs. The ideas and suggestions to make up something for Elvis from the company [prior to his going into army service] were very timely as he has done a great job for all concerned. As you know, the great pains and consideration I have taken were to preserve the career of this artist.

I and all of us in my office have tried to give the best of service and help that was at our disposal, trying to make this grow into a united front pertaining to our business.

None of us have the perfect answer all the time and I make many mistakes and most likely will continue to do so. But I make these in the interest of trying to do the best for this artist. There is no need for anyone to panic just because he has been called to military service. As far as I am concerned, my services will continue as in the past and I do not plan to change this idea of helping to keep this artist in the front line of the entertainment world, to the best of my ability, while he is in the army. It is better to get a quart of milk a day for a long time than it is to get a gallon for a short time. The long range plans for this artist, who was predicted to last 6 months as far back as 3 years ago, will be my main goal and as time goes by I have all the confidence, that with united support, cooperation and understanding from all parties concerned, this will result in long lasting achievements. We may not want to admit it, but the credit due to each and everyone concerned with him, is impossible to measure in time and words. Most of all, the loyal fans that buy his records without seeing him too often, must not be forgotten.

It is much more important to argue the pros and cons and iron out future plans to prepare for two years hence than it is to think about what we are going to do today. Short term plans are for people and companies that plan to go out of business. We only grow old by staying young.

When Elvis has donned his uniform we should all put on a new working jacket to show him we are still in front with him regardless of his being in the service. If we do this, I feel sure that we can maintain the gold record awards and of course the tin plated ones too.

Although a cocktail party is not in order perhaps a real down to earth, peace pipe smoking event with the proper sandwiches, cokes and buttermilk would be a pleasant antidote within the family.

If for some reason anyone of the recipients of this letter should be befuddled or befogged, I will be happy to explain to them in person. This may read like a camouflaged snow job, but rest assured, every sentence has a meaning intended to be understood by this organization. My main object is to prolong the life span and if we stay on the ball, we can have a ball game every day with a winning team. We cannot be anything but happy that the end of the rainbow is a long way off.

Respectfully yours,
Colonel Tom Parker
Manager of Elvis Presley
"A Dollar A Year Man"
(P.S. Please send the buck.)

[This comes accompanied by many ccs.]

Colonel had certainly had his problems with Steve Sholes. By now, though, those problems had for the most part worked themselves out. (Though Steve, unlike Bullock, may never have been a pal, in Colonel's view — and in Sholes'— he would always remain a friend.) It was clear at this point who had won the battle, and Sholes was no longer attempting to assert a primacy that simply didn't exist. Here Colonel deals collegially with Steve and the company on a number of issues, including Elvis' decision to release the Dixieland-flavored soundtrack of *King Creole* rather than rerecord the songs in a more conventional rock 'n' roll setting. Sholes' preference would clearly have been to rerecord the material. But Colonel made his artist's decision perfectly plain, while underscoring once again both his and Elvis' view that movie music is different from music recorded specifically for commercial release and that it would be foolish to conflate the two. ∎

"Elvis is completely aware of everything that is going on"

Mr. Stephen H. Sholes, Manager   March 12, 1958
Artist & Repertoire, Single Records
RCA Victor Record Division
155 East 24th Street
New York 10. NY

Dear Steve:

After I spoke to you on the phone yesterday giving you a rundown on the proposed plans, I again had a meeting with Elvis last night and he feels that under the circumstances, with the music in the picture and tying in with the story of "King Creole" that the majority of fans would like to hear the songs on record just like they are in the picture. He very well realizes that these recordings in the picture are not his regular style of recording and under any other circumstances we most likely would not release another like this without a special reason. The instruments on the sound track fit in with the story and with the producer's idea.

It is apparent also that the suggestion you made regarding the single is proper as we do not think the song "King Creole" is strong enough for a single release.

I have tried to salvage something that the company could work with and tried to make it advantageous for all concerned. You have a right to your own opinion as we have. It may very well be that you are right — who knows? But we are concerned also with the promotion idea and tying it in with the picture. So until further notice from you, after you have worked out the situation with your departments, let me have your thoughts so we can see what can be done in order that everyone will be happy.

I am not going to make any commitments until I am authorized to do so by wire or letter concerning records or releases for RCA Victor as I do not want to be caught in the middle or to step out of bounds. From time to time it seems that I somehow wind up in the middle of things trying to help everybody achieve an advantageous situation. We have spent many hours trying to bring this to a sensible understanding. Trying to work in RCA Victor's, Elvis', and Mr. Wallis' interest is almost like trying to chase a gopher into a mousetrap — which has never been accomplished.

Elvis is completely aware of everything that is going on and this situation has been brought to his attention and also his comments are merely passed on by me as they occur. I have never interfered with the selection of songs or records, but only handle the business end which keeps me pretty busy.

Since you left California I have channeled everything through you for the best working relationship as you expressed a desire for it to be handled that way on your last trip out here. I would be very happy to step out of the picture completely and let RCA Victor handle their own deals and commitments with Mr. Wallis as long as they fit in with our plan of operation from our side. I assume our relationship is one of friendship and cooperation as I do not make any more money by keeping my nose out of it and am sure that you understand this very thoroughly.

Throwing dice with Red West on location for *King Creole,* March 1958. *Courtesy of the Graceland Archives*

I am well aware that merchandising, sales ability, distribution and dealer problems are all a great part of the overall situation and that my contribution is only a small part of this. I really felt that with this setup at Paramount we would all have a good deal if the selection for record release and EP's is connected with this picture. I do not blame you one bit for going on record with such. I will always keep an open mind concerning the entire matter. But after all there will have to be some commitments made in the future that will involve someone's responsibility and I do not intend to take this without 100% backing of all. I have not committed RCA Victor in connection with this picture or Mr. Wallis so

Steve Sholes. *Courtesy of the Graceland Archives*

there is a free road and they can coordinate with me on this. I feel sure that if problems occur between the studio and Mr. Wallis they can be handled as before. I merely have tried to make some merchandise available in connection with this picture. If this material is not acceptable, now is the time to voice those opinions before I put in a lot more work than I have and I can take it up with Elvis before he goes into service.

I fully realize that from all indications, regardless of business recessions, that my artist has delivered his part in merchandising and artistry to the fullest of his ability. Administration, business understanding, promotion, and other details do not concern him one bit as he leaves that entirely in my hands.

Last night I very strongly brought up the entire conversation between you and me to Elvis and he felt the same as you and I do—that it isn't exactly the same as his usual type. But who knows?—a little switching at this time may be better. No one has a crystal ball that works all the time. . . .

Kindest regards,
The Colonel

What the future held in store must have been bothering Colonel a good deal more than he was willing to (openly) let on. Here he reports to Bill Bullock about his visits with Elvis at Fort Chaffee in Arkansas, where he was briefly processed, and Fort Hood in Texas, where he was currently undergoing basic training, and having boasted at some length about Elvis' continuing popularity and the overwhelming number of fan letters that are coming in, he announces in ALL CAPITAL LETTERS to Bullock, and by extension from his point of view the whole world (or at least RCA, and thence the world), his ongoing and exclusive commitment to HIS ARTIST, while trumpeting the unlimited rewards THAT REMAIN TO BE GAINED for each and every one of them all.

"AS FAR AS I am concerned Elvis is in the service but we are not, so we now must even work harder to keep his name alive till he gets out"

Mr. Bill Bullock   April 2nd 1958
RCA Victor Division
Record Album Department
155 East 24th Street
New York City New York.

Dear Bill;

. . . As of Today we have received more than 5000 letters from Ft Chaffee alone not counting the mail coming in from Fort Hood Texas, I hope the LP is holding its own and do let me know how it is rolling.

You would be amused if you knew the artist that have been calling the last 2 Months and more so this week wanting to know if I would take on some of them now that Elvis is in the service. Also some Managers that wanted to work directly thru us from now on. So there is no misunderstanding and you fellows can help a great deal with this as the fans will appreciate this very much. WE PLAN TO GO RIGHT ON LOOKING AFTER ELVIS PRESLEY PRIVATE ELVIS PRESLEY THAT IS. AND THE ONLY OTHER ARTIST THAT WE WORK WITH AND FOR PERSONAL APPEARANCES ONLY IS EDDY ARNOLD THIS OF COURSE YOU KNEW. AS FAR AS I am concerned Elvis is in the service but we are not, so we now must even work harder to keep his name alive till he gets out this I feel we can do if every-ONE PITCHES IN ALONG THE RIGHT TRACK AND MY MAIN PLAN IS NOT TO OVEREXPOSE ELVIS IN ANY WAY. THE WAY BUSINESS IS TODAY ONE MUST BE VERY CAREFULL AND PLAN EVERYTHING THE BEST WAY POSSIBLE, OLD TIME MEDIUMS ARE NOT GOING TO DO THIS, I am always open for suggestions along the promotion line, BUT WHENEVER I CARRY THE

Induction day, March 24, 1958. *Courtesy of the Graceland Archives*

ENTIRE LOAD ON A PLAN I must be doubly carefull FOR IT IS VERY EASY TO GO EITHER WAY IF ONE IS NOT IN THE MIDDLE. I feel sure that MANY GOOD SALES ARE AHEAD FOR RCA VICTOR ON ELVIS PRESLEY BUT THEY MUST BE HANDLED VERY CAREFULLY. After basic training I will know a little more what the plans will be for the Weekends from time to time, as you know we never did overwork TV, Radio and Personals and we will even more be on the Ball not to overdo this, I am sure you know more than any-one that the way this artist was handled the last 2½ Years had a great deal to do with his record sales, any-one that tries to undersell this is a fool for all you have to do is check the list from the top on down on the new talent that started the same time Elvis did, and if they are no fools they must be in compitition with us. I hope to be able to catch up on most of my work in the next 2 Weeks as I have to take Marie and her Mother back to Tampa, Marie's Mother came during Christmas and was to return in 2 Weeks but I have not been able to take the time out to take her back. I thought for awhile that with Elvis in the Army things would let up a little but I was wrong we will have to watch things even more carefully to keep everything rolling as the details are piling up, we are receiving so many request for special shows, appearances and other gimmicks that it almost looks like we are just starting all over again, so watch things closely it may well be that Elvis could be a very important factor again this Year in keeping the Wolf from some DOORS AND I DO NOT MEAN TEDDY BEARS. LET ME HEAR FROM YOU. MY BEST TO ALL THE SNOWERS.

The Colonel.

Nothing could express Colonel's unabashed love and friendship for Abe Last-fogel better or more succinctly than this telegram from the "Madison Branch" of the William Morris Agency. It is in response to Lastfogel's congratulatory wire to both Elvis and Colonel on first seeing a print of *King Creole*. Both men, so cagey in all their business dealings, were able to freely unburden themselves only with each other. ■

"WE KNOW YOUR TRUST AND BELIEF IN US COULD NOT BE BOUGHT WITH A PRICE AND WE HAVE THE BEST DEAL EVER BY HAVING YOUR FRIENDSHIP FOR FREE"

ABE LASTFOGEL   MAY 27, 1958
EXECUTIVE CHAIRMAN OF THE BOARD
WM. MORRIS AGENCY
1745 BROADWAY
NEW YORK CITY, NEW YORK

DEAR ABE
    THANKS FOR YOUR KIND TELEGRAM. ELVIS AND I DEEPLY APPRECIATE YOUR SINCERE FEELING AND CONSIDERATE OPIN-ION ON KING CREOLE. WE KNOW YOUR TRUST AND BELIEF IN US COULD NOT BE BOUGHT WITH A PRICE AND WE HAVE THE BEST

Colonel's Madison house. *Courtesy of Brenda Williams Cohen*

DEAL EVER BY HAVING YOUR FRIENDSHIP FOR FREE. THIS IS
MUCH MORE BINDING THAN ANY AUTHORIZATION WHICH
CAN ALWAYS BE TORN UP AND OUR FRIENDSHIP CAN'T. SO YOU
ARE ALSO GETTING THE SAME BENEFITS AS WE ARE IN OUR
FRIENDSHIP.

WE APPRECIATE YOUR OFFICE GIVING THIS OFFICE THE COUR-
TESY IN THE FUTURE TO ADDRESS YOUR WIRES AS WM. MORRIS
AGENCY, MADISON, TENN BRANCH. THIS WILL ENABLE US TO
PROVE A MUCH MORE LUCRATIVE EXPENSE ACCOUNT IN THE
FUTURE. AS TRYING TO GET MONEY OUT OF [William Morris con-
troller] LOU GOLDBERG IS JUST AS HARD AS CHASING AN ELE-
PHANT INTO A GOPHER HOLE. THE BEST FROM ALL OF US.

> COLONEL TOM PARKER
> WM. MORRIS AGENCY
> MADISON BRANCH

This was by no means the first announcement of Colonel's always forthcoming (but as it turned out never arriving) autobiography and instructional
book, *How Much Does It Cost If It's Free?* but in its imperturbably kidding tone —
and the manner in which it was embraced in kind by both Bullock and all of Colonel's other pals at RCA — it is among the best. ∎

"Many photos of my dear friends and others will be included in this great book"

Mr. Bill Bullock   July 29, 1958
RCA Victor Division
Record Album Department
155 East 24th Street
New York City New York.

Dear Bill;

Enclosed is a special photo wich I know you will be happy to have on
display in your office, I suggest you buy a suitable frame to go with this
photo, by the way I plan to use this photo on the front cover of my Book

entittled HOW MUCH DOES IT COST IF ITS FREE * I have reserved the back cover on my book for the RCA Victor ad wich I spoke to you about sometime ago at a special rate of $2500 Twenty Five Hundred Dollars. I think it would be a good idea to have a letter on this in my files as we do not know at present when the book will be finished and we would have to be sure that the Company is buying this ad as we have no trouble unloading this important space to some-one else this would be of course the only advertising in this important book regarding Records and other material RCA Victor has for sale. I feel that I am giving the company a very good rate having been with you folks such a long time and the value of the advertising will more than pay for the cost, we will of course let you furnish the plate and the layout for this ad at no cost to us. We will at least give you a Six Months notice in advance before the book will be re-leased so you can order at least enough copies for the Company as I know you will want to present a copy to each Fieldman and Distributor, as much information regarding record sales and promotion gimmicks will be included in this great publication, since we are not letting out any advance information on this book at present other than the tittle and we even may change that at a later date, price of the book will be $10.00 Ten Dollars when finished wich is plenty cheap when you can learn so much from it and also will be able to realize so much information on what went on in the past that many of my friends were in on from the start.

This will be the only book with a good story of showbusiness where at the same time the reader will be able to enjoy some very good advertising copy at no extra cost to the readers. To keep in line with our tittle there will be nothing in this book that is free except the reading of it after it has been bought, many photos of my dear friends and others will be included in this great book including some very interesting stories as far back as my dog catching Day's and Circus and Carnival work.

It will always be a pleasure doing business with you and I know that we can count on you to treat this information with due respect.

Your Pal
The Colonel

The tone of this letter, markedly less jovial than his telegram of two days earlier, could in one sense simply be considered to be whistling in the dark. At the same time, it also represents something more than a pro forma attempt to convince Lastfogel of the seriousness of his commitment to put Elvis back on tour if they are unable to come to a more equitable arrangement with Hal Wallis. (One of the firm tenets of Colonel's rules of doing business was, you always need to have your spokesman believe that you are serious if they are to represent your position forcefully.) Why else declare with such disingenuous bravado to an old and trusted friend, who must surely be aware of just what you are doing, "We will have to create a pretty good income for 1960" if a better understanding is not reached? ■

"I am planning a pretty long setup of personal appearances"

Mr. Abe Lastfogel   July 31, 1958
William Morris Agency
151 El Camino
Beverly Hills California

Dear Abe;

Some of the reports I have from friends of mine in the Theatre business are that King Creole has done very well for them to date, In Fla the picture was up to Loving You and better than Jailhouse Rock in receipts. I see no reason why these Friends should tell me this, if it was not so.

I am planning a pretty long setup of personal appearances when Elvis gets out of the Army in event we do not get together with Wallis and Hazen on some setup where they allow us to make the First picture outside. By that time we will have to create a pretty good income for 1960 and we surely wont get it from the Wallis picture.

As I plan to start lining up some of these dates at least a Year or so in advance to secure proper buildings and promoters I suggest that we get some word from Wallis and Hazen as soon as possible, as I do not plan to make any changes after I have setup dates and taken in deposits on same. As we mostly play about 5 dates per Month and I plan to setup at least 25 or 30 of them, you can well see that we surely would not be available for any picture right after Elvis gets out of the service in March 1960. Anything that I have lined up by that time will come First.

I also know that Elvis will want to be home at least a Month before starting on a personal appearance tour, so with the exception of us being able to line-up a good deal on a picture after Elvis gets out of the service we will do whatever is best for us and work out the Wallis setup whenever we have the time to do so. As you know we only owe Wallis One Picture a Year for 3 Years when Elvis gets out, during what time we can make this One picture will be entirely up to the availability of Elvis in any One Year. We surely are not going to get into a setup like we did last Year after getting out to the Coast and have Wallis postpone the shooting several Months when we could have made another picture before King Creole. I am sure You can understand the meaning of me planning to be ready in 1960.

There is not much news it looks like Elvis will be leaving for Germany about the Second Week in September or before. We plan nothing for overthere on anything, and it will be good to alert your London office and Paris that we do not plan to do anything there on TV radio or other work. I think it best along with Elvis that since he is not in special service for him just to be another soldier.

Marie wishes to be remembered to both of you.

[Signed "Tom"]

Here we have yet another prepublication offer, this time to Frank Folsom, the distinguished president of the label's parent company, the Radio Corporation of America, and permanent representative of the Holy See to the International Atomic Energy Agency. Its tone is just as chipper as Colonel's letter to Bill Bullock, once again offering a unique opportunity to Get In on a Good Deal! This familiar mix of kidding and fellow feeling seems in one way to establish to his satisfaction that everyone is on an equal footing — but it also appears to be the one way Colonel has to express admiration and affection. Only with Abe Lastfogel and, of course, Elvis, can he be more direct — and even with them he has his difficulties. ∎

"I want it to be the most up to date and funniest book ever written about showbusiness"

Mr. Frank M. Folsom   August 6, 1958
Radio Corporation of America
30 Rockefeller Plaza
New York City New York.

Dear Frank;

Enclosed is the photo of myself I know you have been waiting for to frame and put on your desk so here it is with my compliments. As you know I have been planning for many Years to write a book with all my background and information from show business hardships my good fortune and about the many interesting people I met and helped me to get where I am Today — it will take sometime before I will get rolling on this book as I want it to be the most up to date and funniest book ever written about showbusiness with all the little gimmicks and details to the fullest, I plan to use the same photo on the front cover as the One just received by you from me as it will suit the purpose very well, the tittle of the book will be. HOW MUCH DOES IT COST IF ITS FREE.

I also plan to sell some advertising space in this book and I have reserved the backcover for RCA Victor as having been with them now well over 15 Years [Colonel's time computations sometimes failed him] and having brought many artist into the company and working along with them on all the other merchandise I feel that this space should be reserved for them, I am of course handling this direct with Bill Bullock when the time comes but I knew you would get a kick out of my plan, to keep in line with my tittle of the book there will be no free copies of this issue, however we will advise my close friends in plenty of time and with plenty of high class pressure so they wont be sorry that they have missed buying the great book. I do plan to give all advertisers a ten percent discount when they buy a book, and in event of any orders over Fifty copies we will of course pay for the shipping.

Some of my close Friends will be included in this book and I of course plan a special advertising rate for them so they wont be left out, the only advertisers that we will not include in our book will be those that fail to answer our advance advertising letter, the release of this great book is pending on our luck in selling enough advertising space so we will be off the nut before a copy is sold, this will make for a happy medium in all our departments. The only reason I am working on the book and getting it ready for the market is because of the pressure from my competitors who want to learn my gimmicks, since I am willing to share most of the things I learned it wouldn't be good business to give this out for nothing as you would be disappointed in me, and it would seem that I had not learned anything from our association, so I am giving them all the privilege of paying for it.

Marie joins me with our best. Your Pal Tom Parker

Frank Folsom. *Courtesy of the Graceland Archives*

For all that I just said, or perhaps in line with it, the following letter would perhaps serve as the most painful example of Colonel's difficulty in sharing (or simply expressing) emotion. He was clearly overwhelmed by the sudden death of Elvis' mother, Gladys, at the age of forty-six, but he was at a complete loss as to how to comfort her utterly devastated son. (At the cemetery, the *Memphis Commercial Appeal* reported, Elvis cried out inconsolably, "Goodbye, darling, goodbye. I love you so much. You know how much I lived my whole life just for you.")

Colonel took care of all the practical details of the funeral. He supervised the response to the more than one hundred thousand condolence cards and letters from the fans and handled all the reporters who had come from all over with uncharacteristic delicacy and respect. But when it came down to expressing his own condolences, in a letter written a full three weeks after the funeral, he found himself unable to do anything but reaffirm his unequivocal commitment to always defend Elvis' interests. It is only at the end of this letter, almost as if he has been trying to avoid the subject all along (I don't think there's any "almost" about it), that he finally gets around to the matter of Elvis and Vernon's loss — and then it is with the homely offering of two scrapbooks he had put together as a "keepsake in her memory." While Elvis remains frozen in his grief, Colonel is just as clearly frozen in his inability to help the one person in the world he would most like to protect. Even the sorrowful shrug of his sign-off indicates his helplessness. There is no appropriate gag, he seems to be saying, no "phony" title, that can take the edge off of grief. ■

"I will do whatever is fair but it is my duty to protect your interest even if people dont like me for it"

Dear Vernon & Elvis;   Sept 6, 1958

. . . I hope you are feeling alright, we hope to see you before long on our way to the Coast, the motion picture meetings are going on full blast and letters are flying back from the Coast Daily, also many phone calls between the Morris office and myself Daily, we seem to have run into a great many legal details wich I will have to smoke out between now and your discharge from the Army as Fox and Wallis are working all to get the First lick under their contracts without giving us any break so far. You can rest assured that I will hold out for the best possible solution on these problems and I am not going to back up as I feel that we are in the right all the way, I will do whatever is fair but it is my duty to protect your interest even if people dont like me for it. It is very easy to have many more fair-weather friends than I have now by giving in and going along with some of their ideas wich would be only good for them and would mean nothing to you. You also would be a great guy if we went along with some of their suggestions but there would not be the money when its over but a big amount of slapping you on the back and many good wishes to go along with the backslapping at the same time. But the cash would be in their saves and not in your bank. . . .

We have finished the 2 books we made up for you and Dad in memory of Your Mother and I know you will be most happy with this keepsake in her memory although we know it is sad, but it also would be what your Mother would know you would want to have from her. Take care of yourself and be strong and keep your chin up I know you can do it. My thoughts are with you even tho I do not see you all the time. Give Dad my best also Your Friends. Your Pal The Admiral Colonel Sergeant Private.

Elvis arrived in Germany for his army deployment on October 1, 1958, a very unhappy young man. With his mother gone, the future in doubt, and for all his public bravado a desperate sense of abandonment, he openly questioned, and not for the first time, what was the point of it all? Had his success been anything more than a cruel delusion? I would say Vernon's panic-stricken telegram reflects the overall mood in the extended Presley household, which at this point consisted of Elvis' father, his grandmother, and two friends from home, Red West and Lamar Fike. (Elvis would soon receive permission from the army to live off base as the sole support of his two family dependents.) Elvis would never have given himself over to such intemperate expression, but it should be kept in mind that Vernon under normal circumstances possessed the most phlegmatic of temperaments. ∎

"WE DO NOT KNOW WHICH WAY TO TURN"

BADNAUHEIM VIA MACKAY   OCT 14 1958
COL TOM PARKER
MADISON (TENN)

DEAR COL IN REGARDS TO OUR TELEPHONE CONVERSATION LAST NIGHT AS I TOLD YOU IT IS IMPOSSIBLE FOR HIM TO LIVE A NORMAL LIFE AS ANY OTHER SOLDIER HERE STOP DUE TO THE PRESSURE FROM NEWSPAPERS AND MAGAZINES ALL OVER EUROPE HE CANT GET OUT LIKE OTHER SOLDIER AND ENJOY HIIMSELF OR SEE ANY OF THE COUNTRY OR ANY ENTERTAINMENT OR LIVE A NORMAL LIFE AS ANY OTHER SOLDIER. THE PEOPLE IN GERMANY ARE VERY FRIENDLY AND NICE BUT DUE TO THE FACT THAT EVERYBODY WANTS TO SEE HIM AND ALL OF THEM WANT AUTOGRAPHS THEY ARE CONSTANTLY MOBBING HIM. MAIL IS PILING UP SO MUCH FROM ALL OF EUROPE AND WE DO NOT HAVE A STAFF HERE TO HANDLE IT

PROPERLY AS IT SHOULD BE. DUE TO CIRCUMSTANCES IT HAS
CREATED STRANGEST PROBLEM THAT WE CANNOT COPE WITH
AND IT HAS GOTTEN TO THE POINT THAT WE DO NOT KNOW
WHICH WAY TO TURN STOP I TRUST IN THE VERY NEAR FUTURE
THAT SOMETHING CAN BE DONE TO LEAVE THIS SITUATION
I WILL KEEP YOU INFORMED ON ANYTHING THAT MAY ARRIVES.
SINCERELY

VERNON

Colonel got back to Elvis and Vernon on the same day. His letter, which I'm
sure was intended to reassure them, certainly filled them in on all the
details. But one has to wonder why he had to fill them in on so *many* of the details.
And the question naturally arises: is Colonel telling Elvis all this simply as an
expression of his own concern or, understandably (maybe there's no either-or
here), so that Elvis will not miss all the looming obstacles that his manager must,
and *will,* overcome? Or, might it even be possible that Colonel himself is feeling
some of the same sense of doubt that Vernon communicates so graphically in
his cable?

No matter. As you will see from just the brief selection of correspondence
that follows, everything would soon work out, and Colonel would emerge triumphant on all fronts. And over the course of the next fourteen months, he and
Tom Diskin would deluge Elvis with dozens and dozens of letters and telegrams —
some of them quite lengthy — offering guidance, good cheer, and, of course,
sound practical advice, while at the same time deploying thousands of telegrams
to movie stars, longtime colleagues, columnists, reporters, magazine editors,
musicians and entertainers, radio stations, recording executives, and politicians,
on births, birthdays, holidays (Mother's Day, Father's Day), stage and movie
openings, anniversaries, and everything in between, all in the name of "Elvis and
the Colonel." His entire professional purpose, he is determined to make clear to
the world, is to serve the interests of his single client, declaring by both deed
and word that he has nothing on his mind but ELVIS.

At the same time the underlying purpose of every one of his letters to Elvis
was to convince Elvis to continue to believe in himself. The same themes were
repeated again and again: he would safeguard Elvis' talent, he would maintain

Elvis' value, despite all the pressure to exploit it at no cost other than deprecia-
tion of its value. Not only would there be no slippage in Elvis' career, he insisted,
his career prospects were only going to improve. That was a certainty. ■

"I know you would want to know how things are going along"

Dear Vernon & Elvis;   Oct 14, 1958

Your wire received I have made a copy of this and mailed this with a
good deal of other information right on to Mr. Ed Cottrell of the special
Army Information center [in Washington, D.C.] with whom I have been
in contact ever since Elvis left Ft Hood, he also handled the New York
setup with me. . . .

I also wired the Mr. John Wiant at Army Times in Franfurtmain
regarding his request for the Christmas show as per blessings of the Army
there, I informed him that all these request must First come from the
Army direct and at that time I would take it up with you, in the meantime
I advised Mr Cottrell about the wire and he told me that he would follow
up and double check on this, as far as he knew the Army had nothing to
do with it. Having already had several other request from Bob Hope for
a Christmas show and having passed this information also on to the Army
it seems best to leave these matters [to] roll themselves up into something
where they will either contact us direct here from Washington on anything like that for this is the only way we would be able to know if anything is being handled properly or if some promoter is using the Army to
get next to Elvis or the other way around. . . .

A charity show of wich Mr Wiant wired would be very nice if it was
just a matter of putting on show for the Orphans, I feel sure that Mr.
Wiant has the best interest at heart, but I also know Mr. Wiant cant
promise us that many other people will want some sort of show for their
charities at some other time, Many of your regular fans that would come
to see you whenever we some Day should perform over there on our own
setup would of course come to see the show and pay the price. And this
money going for Orphans is a good thing and would be a nice presentation
by the Army if it was done by the Army and under a setup whereby the
people know that you are doing this type of work while in the Army. I
have given all this information to Mr. Cottrell in Washington and we will
just wait to see what his answer will be, There must be some line where

you can either be a regular soldier without having to perform at the same time, or work in special service and do whatever can be worked out to please these people.

I also advised RCA Victor that you would not be available for any dealer promotion overthere while you are in the Army, as this also would take up a great deal of your personal time, since you told me that you did not wish to do anything along those lines when you are off duty, also the securety setup on anything like that would have to [be] some-one else responsibility and I just dont see how this can be handled.

I have been in hot water ever since you left with my motion picture setups. I did get a very nice deal from Fox and they are working out the contracts, but we are having a good deal of trouble from Wallis and Hazen as they do not want you to make the First picture for Fox but for them, if you remember we had two pictures to make after King Creole when you was drafted One for Fox and One for MGM, due to the draft we lost the Fox picture and we lost the MGM deal also — Now I was able to get a new deal with Fox but Wallis and Hazen claim you owe the First picture to them when you come out of the Army. . . .

If I had known the way Wallis and Hazen would act after King Creole [Elvis' final picture before entering the army, and a Wallis-Hazen production] I dont think that we would have asked for a extention of the draft to make King Creole as they surely are not giving us a fair break now, Now that they know we can get a deal with Fox for the First picture they want to give us the same deal on the First picture for them as Fox is giving us, but it would not be fair to kick Fox in the face after they have shown us that they believed enough in you when you came out to give us a good deal for the First picture, dont worry about it I will do the best I can along with Mr. Lastfogel. But I know you would want to know how things are going along. I will most likely have to get back out there several times before we will know how far Wallis and Hazen will move, so far they have already had their Lawyers write us several strong letters regarding their rights, we are doing the same thing, I see no reason why we must give in to them when it is not the right thing to do. . . .

I know that Wallis and Hazen are not going to give up trying, as you know they are tough and do not give up easy. I feel that somehow they think we wont go to court with this, and in this they are wrong for we feel that for the cost of the lawyers involved to handle a case like this, we have too much to gain, and can only wind up on the losing end if we give up too easy. Dont worry about it as you know I will fight as long as I feel that you should get a better deal, I see no reason why any-one should get a better deal out of you having to be in the Army.

I am doing everything I can from this end to come up with something but as you know the gates are tight, and I must keep on trying. . . . Take care and give my best to the boys and Grandma.

[Signed "Col"]
The Colonel.

O n November 1 Colonel was finally able to give Elvis some good news: not only had the deal with Hal Wallis been successfully completed, so had the deal with Fox — with just a few details to be worked out on both. (See wrap-up letter of November 18, below.) "This should give you something to look forward to after you get out," Colonel wrote with an understatement that was swiftly obliterated by the jubilant tone of the rest of the letter.

"You know of course without me telling you," he wrote, taking up once again the mutual sense of purpose and achievement that they had always shared, "that I could never have done this without your complete confidence and your unusual talent."

At Colonel's direction Elvis sent out three cables. Here are two of them. (I believe the third went to Jean and Julian Aberbach for all that they had done to safeguard Elvis' song publishing.) Elvis followed Colonel's guidelines, but clearly with some latitude for improvisation. The telegram to Wallis represents a sincerity of feeling (and I think relief) on both their parts. The telegram to Colonel, though it was intended as a kind of informal acknowledgment of the deal which could also be used for publicity purposes, was all Elvis. ∎

MESSERS HAL WALLIS AND JOSEPH HAZEN   November 5, 1958
HAL WALLIS PRODUCTIONS
PARAMOUNT STUDIOS
5141 MARATHON
LOS ANGELES, CALIFORNIA, U.S.A.

DEAR MR. WALLIS AND MR. HAZEN:

THE COLONEL HAS JUST INFORMED ME OF YOUR CONFIDENCE AND BELIEF IN ME WHEN I GET OUT OF THE ARMY. MY FATHER, MYSELF AND THE COLONEL DO APPRECIATE YOUR KIND CONSIDERATION IN THE GENEROUS IMPROVEMENT YOU HAVE MADE IN MY CONTRACT.

I WILL DO MY BEST NOT TO LET YOU FOLKS DOWN WHEN I COME OUT. I WISH THAT I COULD HAVE BEEN THERE WITH THE COLONEL TO SIGN THE CONTRACTS AND SHAKE HANDS WITH YOU BUT YOU KNOW THAT WHEN THE COLONEL SIGNS IT IS JUST LIKE I WAS THERE MYSELF.

GIVE MY BEST TO ALL THE FOLKS AT THE STUDIO AND THE COLONEL.

RESPECTFULLY YOURS,
ELVIS PRESLEY

"THIS SURE IS A LONG TOUR YOU SENT ME ON"

LT COLONEL TOM PARKER   November 5, 1958
BEVERLY WILSHIRE HOTEL
BEVERLY HILLS, CALIF

DEAR ADMIRAL THANKS FOR YOUR LETTER. I HAVE SENT THE CABLES AS YOU REQUESTED. I SURE APRECIATE ALL YOU ARE DOING AND LOOKING AFTER OUR BUSINESS WHILE I AM BOOKED FOR UNCLE SAM. THIS SURE IS A LONG TOUR YOU SENT ME ON. I AM SORRY THE COMMISSIONS ARE SO SMALL [FOR] THIS ENGAGEMENT. THANKS FOR FIXING UP THE PARAMOUNT AND FOX PICTURES DEALS. DADDY SAYS HELLO, ALSO GRANDMA, LAMAR, AND RED WEST. ELVIS

A nd here, with everything fully and finally worked out, is the grand summation of all the good fortune that is coming their way. ∎

"This...will prove to Elvis that he is not backsliding in any way"

Dear Vernon & Elvis;   Nov 18, 1958

Well here is the other news you have been waiting for Have just received the report that 20th Century Fox also is picking up the new deal I worked on the past 8 Months, so this brings the outlook for Elvis in a pretty solid picture for his future, better than it was before he went into the service, I am sure you both will be pleased with this information, this also will prove to Elvis that he is not backsliding in any way, this now brings our picture setup in line with a very healthy setup for the future. And in such a way that now at least I feel that we have what I always wanted to get on the Wallis contract ever since we first started out with them, Elvis knows how I felt about this setup but there was not much I could do at that time except get a little more each time we made a picture for Wallis and Hazen. The Facts are now we do not have to call on Wallis everytime with our hat in our hands to ask for a little extra each time. The improvements I have been able to make will run into at least a couple of hundred Thousand dollars more for the First Wallis and Fox pictures when Elvis comes out plus a percentage. wich we did not have on either before he went into the service, for a time it even looked pretty bad that we would have to [go to] Court on the entire issue, this has all been cleared up. . . .

Another check came in from MGM on the profits wich we of course mailed on to [Elvis' accountant in Memphis] Bill Fisher, this is the Third check so far from MGM on the profit sharing on Jailhouse Rock wich is holding up pretty good. I know this should make Elvis very happy, with the extra gimmicks on photos and the special RCA Victor gimmicks we were able to include this Year Elvis will do even better this Year than he did last Year even while he is in the service. I did not hear from you regarding the letter I wrote giving you the information what the check was from RCA this Month, I hope you received same okay, also enclosed was a wire to be sent to the WSM [Grand Ole Opry radio station] on the DeeJay convention Nov 19th or 20th. Write a line with all the news so we at least know what is going on there. Give our best to Grandma and the boys also from Mrs Parker.

Take care of yourselfs
[Signed "Col"]   The Colonel

With things finally straightened away with Hal Wallis, Colonel sent his sometime nemesis (not really — it was only business) an idea that he had been thinking about for a long time, and which he had broached at least once before. Why not consider an entirely different kind of movie for Elvis, one that could serve as an introduction to Hawaiian music and culture? In Colonel's scenario the Elvis figure would be the unwitting dupe of nefarious record company types and promoters, but no matter, he will emerge triumphant as a genuine avatar of authentic Hawaiian music. Or — and this seems a project even more dear to Colonel's heart — what if the Elvis character were a foundling raised by a freewheeling band of itinerant "Gypsies"? (Remember the young Andreas' childhood experiences, and his lifelong regard for the Romani way of life.) Colonel seems utterly convinced, if not altogether convincing, when he declares that Elvis fans are not about to go for a sappy story that focuses on nothing but love everlasting, thus making a clear argument for his proposed scenarios versus the conventional ones that Wallis is pushing. There is no evidence that Wallis agrees with him, and some that he may be more realistic about the potential audience for the next Elvis movie, and the ones after that. Nor is there any record that he ever took Colonel up on his offer of a new, three-way writing partnership with Wallis and Wallis' partner Joe Hazen. ∎

"I do know that the kids would not buy a smooth story on him with nothing else involved other than love and understanding"

(Col) Hal Wallis   Dec 18, 1958
Hal Wallis Productions
Hollywood, California.

Dear Col Hal;

Thanks for your letter dated December 16, as you can see you are getting an answer in 2 Days wich is pretty good in these hard times, of getting out all our Christmas promotion.

Be sure and watch the Eddie Fisher show Dec 23rd for with the exception that I have been snowed under by the powers in New York there should be a pretty good Elvis Presley plug on this TV show for us. I at least did try to do One of my Second best snowjob in trying to get another plug before the Year 1958 ends, the other was on the King Creole LP last

Sonny Cordes, Colonel, Gayle Kufferath and her mother, Anna. *Courtesy of Gayle Kufferath Behnke*

Summer. Since a spot like that cost RCA Victor about $21,000 for One minute on this Coast to Coast network show you know of course that I have to use a special brand of Snowoil at all times.

I am glad to know that you are interested in my idea of an Hawaiian story My main reason for this idea comes from the type of music these folks play and the idea is that since you myself and Joe Hazen did hold out on getting the King Creole material released just like it was done in the picture, and it surely has proven that it sold very well and the kids liked the songs. And of course Elvis was of the same belief that we were.

Now my thoughts are that with Rock & Roll type of music, The Dixie Land Music we had in King Creole, why it would not be a good idea to try perhaps the Native Hawaiian beat type songs wich more or less are of the same type (wild) and also in ballads very soft and soothing. This type of music brought out into some sort of native Love story with of course some tough elements included in a story and the fine pictorial display that One can get in the Islands seems to me would lend itself to something to think about, also shooting a trip going on a large steamer either to the Islands or coming back with a Love affair included aboard ship by either a Girl from the States or a native Hawaiian Girl perhaps a stowe-away or something like that, My idea is to work a story out in someway where Elvis could be running away from all the [business?] with the fans going wild not knowing where Elvis went, the Recording

Companies being without record re-leases doing everything possible to find him, and somehow a gang of some sort of promoters Con Artist that is snowing Elvis into singing with the natives [and] while he is doing this they would somehow record all this on tape and sneak this into Honolulu and start promoting this new find selling records like Hotcakes and all the time it would be Elvis but no One would know this untill they had to bring Elvis to the Islands to do a show, Elvis not knowing that he has been exploited by these people under another name with these stolen tapes from his singing on the other Island. Of course, he thinks that when he arives in Honolulu that this big reception at the Docks is for him ELVIS PRESLEY OR WHATEVER NAME HE HAS BEING A STAR, but when he goes on the stage and somehow he gets the idea that he has been promoted into something else. I am this far with the story. The idea of course [for] this part of the story is just to give you some idea the way I am thinking, I dont say that this is the right approach. However I have several others I am working on, perhaps with you, Joe [Hazen], [Wallis' associate producer] Paul Nathan and myself we can come up with a pretty good setup and we could keep the story and complete Idea in the WAL-LIS, HAZEN, PARKER, PRESLEY AND COUSINS FAMILY. Knowing that none of us work cheap we know we will come out with a good deal and if all of us are in on it we surely would all be happy with the price.

I also have been thinking of a story regarding Elvis doing a complete turnabout and being the type he is you could also very well use him in some big story regarding Gypsies as he surely is that rugged type that could be cast in this type of story also as a foundling or stolen baby boy by a bunch of Gypsies traveling in wagons sleeping outdoors and whatever that type of life calls for with shows, as you know very well Elvis is at his best in a rugged type of performance with a good love angle involved, this of course also can apply into the Hawaiian setup, I do know that the kids would not buy a smooth story on him with nothing else involved other than love and understanding. . . .

Hope you have a Merry Christmas and Happy New Year, also my best to MR. Joe. and his Family, if the sausage does not arive on time for Christmas you will have to eat it after Christmas.

Sincerely
The Colonel.

om Diskin chimes in here with a voice that sounds very much like Colonel's and yet remains authentically his own. Sending Elvis a book on the Stanislavski method is clearly his own idea, and his advice to Elvis (which boils down to "Trust your own judgment"), while it certainly echoes Colonel's, makes clear that his own belief in Elvis' talent is just as strong as his employer's — and Elvis' should be, too. ■

"You analyze this business pretty well and if any changins to be done then let it be because you yourself feel that you want to go one way or another"

Dear Elvis: December 31, 1958

Thought I'd get a note off to you before 1958 passes out of existence. I had wanted to write on several occasions but between the fifty thousand Christmas cards we had to get out and my running battle with the flu germs I just couldn't dig into anything.

I hope you received my wire on Christmas day. I do want to tell you a little bit about the Christmas present I sent to you. It is a book written by Stanislavski who taught and believed that truly great acting comes from within — or living the character you play. I'm sure you have heard his name from time to time. Much of the book will not interest you for it is about the writers own life story. However, in the last few chapters he explains the simple fact of good acting — be natural. I know, though I haven't read it, that his ideas will be very similar to your own and for that reason I thought you might enjoy reading about something that is very close to you.

Your record (both sides) are in this week's Billboards top ten. Your King Creole [extended-play] albums are #1 and #2. The Christmas cards got a great many column mentions plus being shown on television on about four network shows. We saturated every phase of the business so that just about everyone you can name in the entertainment field received one. I'm sure the Colonel told you all this as he really hit that project with everything he had. . . .

I was listening to the acetates on the stuff in the can and the most genuine sounding thing is My Wish Came True. The stuff you did in Nashville is good but I think the engineer was working as if he were recording a band instead of your voice, for those instruments give you a lot of competition and from my point of view the kids want to hear your voice and not instruments no matter how well they are played. Also, there is something which you will have to give thought to yourself and not allow anyone to influence your judgement and that is about your musicians you have on sessions. The only example I can give you is that Eddy Arnold at one time was genuine, no fancy arrangements, just right down to earth and he was selling records. Then they began to change his musicians, getting more polished performers, making arrangements, and getting away from the real Eddy Arnold. Fans used to say "ole Eddy is going uptown on us", and his record sales began to slide. You analyze this business pretty well and if any changins to be done then let it be because you yourself feel that you want to go one way or another. But I don't think that the character or personality of your performance should be messed with by anyone else. There are plenty of performers who have been polished until they shine but they don't sell any records. The kids and the people want the genuine article not a remake. While you don't have to be worrying about a session at this time it is good to keep these little things in mind.

The past year has brought you much and has taken away much but I hope that 1959 will bring you continued success but more important happiness. Please give my best to your Dad, your grandmother and to the boys. So many kids have asked me to say hello to you for them I couldn't possibly list them so on behalf of a jillion of them "hello". All the best to you.

[Signed "Tom Diskin"]

1959

On January 5, 1959, Colonel wrote to Bill Bullock about a telephone conversation he had just had with Elvis early that morning. What he says at the end is probably true — Elvis very likely did feel warmly toward Bullock, although it also serves as a handy vehicle for expressing his own affection. And he makes the rare admission, however cloaked, that he is still hoping that Elvis might get an early discharge. This is something that he has always vehemently denied in public while privately working every angle with his many army contacts. Still, it is just a dream. ■

"My dream was lost"

Mr. Bill Bullock   Jan 5th 1959
Vice President Records Album Dept.
151 East 24th Street
New York City New York.

Dear Bill;

. . . Will be on the lookout for my ektochromes from you, I am very gratefull to you for typing the wording ektochromes as I did not know how it was spelled, however I understand from Bevo that yours is wrong also. Not wanting to waste a call to Tampa to check with Bevo I will take yours as being correct, I also know my spelling of gratefull is wrong as it only takes 1 L. however I stand on this with 2 LL's on account of me being so very gratefull wich with 2 L'S should mean more to you. I would of course only worry if you did not know what I meant as I do wish to make my letters easy to read for you.

Spoke to Elvis Yesterday or rather he called me at 5 in the Morning to see what I was doing, I told him I was dreaming of him coming back

445

in another Year and that my dream was lost when he called and I would not be able to tell him if he came back sooner. however he said it was snowing over there and he just wanted to talk, he did just that for about an hour and we got a good many details out of the way. He also said to say hello to you and this is no snowjob, I dont know if you know it or not but Elvis has always felt warm towards you, I of course know the reason why, as you have always been down to earth with all of us at all times. . . .

Snowingly yours
The Colonel

Colonel had always felt that Elvis' talent was unique and did not need to be supplemented by any of the usual "gimmicks"— like studio production, for one, or utilizing the services of a record producer, for another. And despite his own lack of any observable religious feeling, he had always recognized the unique pull that "sacred music" had on Elvis — the way it always brought out the best in his performance. What could be more natural, then, especially given his reluctance to see Elvis record in Germany or give RCA anything like a backlog of conventional recordings with which they might be tempted to flood the commercial market, than to propose an utterly new, utterly unique approach to recording his artist, in effect, solo, and totally under his own control?

You can see his enthusiasm grow as the letter progresses (and believe me, however discursively emphatic it may seem in its present form, no opportunity for emphasis or repetition was lost in the unabridged, single-spaced, two-page letter). One wonders a little if this was more an emotional than a well-thought-out suggestion — but on the other hand, Colonel was a man of strong conviction. And who knows, maybe he was onto something. But one is also led to wonder: what can Elvis have thought? In any case, after buying a German tape recorder, he made a lot of home recordings, but it doesn't appear as if he gave any serious thought to his manager's suggestion. Nor, on the other hand, would he be likely to have been surprised that most of these recordings would be released one day as exemplars of untrammeled self-expression. ∎

"I always felt that you['d] do as good a job on your own now than with a recording director by your side"

Dear Elvis & Vernon;   Jan 9th 1959

. . . I want you to think about . . . where no One but you and Vernon
and your own buddies like West and Lamar [Red West and Lamar Fike,
who had gone over to Germany to keep Elvis company] if you wanted
them to be there, you cutting a tape with some tunes all by yourself like
JUST A CLOSER WALK WITH THEE AND PERHAPS ABOUT THREE
MORE SACRED SONGS THAT YOU LIKE YOURSELF AND COULD DO
IN YOUR OWN STYLE IN ANY WAY YOU THOUGHT BEST, ALSO
SOME SONGS BY YOURSELF THAT YOU LIKE EVEN TUNES LIKE
YOU HAD VERNON GAVE ME OVER THE PHONE AND SOME OTH-
ERS WHERE YOUR VOICE AND YOUR OWN PLAYING ON THE
ORGAN OR PIANO OR EVEN IF YOU HAD SOME-ONE THAT YOU
WANTED TO PLAY FOR YOU TO HELP YOU BUT ONLY THE PIANO
ORGAN AND PERHAPS ONLY A BASS, WHATEVER YOU THINK BEST.
Now if you could do this on your own time without any publicity that
you were doing this to any-one not letting any-one know, than you could
work on this until you thought they were good enough for editing and
mail them on to me here I would check all the tunes, than let Freddie
[Hill and Range song representative Freddy Bienstock] see what sort of
deal we could get on any of them, and I would try to make up a couple of
releases or EP'S on them as a special setup with RCA Victor while you
are away, or if you had some tunes in there that you thought would be
good enough for a Single release we could use 2 of the tunes for a single,
also if you did cut 4 sacred songs we could use them for Easter as a special
Sacred EP.

If you remember, the other sacred EP sold well over Half Million
copies over and above the regular releases. WE could do a very good
promotion on this with the promotion geared to ELVIS ALONE. or something like that or some of them ELVIS WHILE OFF DUTY. I know that
you could do a very good job on this and the kids would love it as they
have always been more interested in hearing you sing than the heavy
part of music on records. As you know One Night and Love Me Tender
sure did prove that they like your singing even without much music,
anyway I dont say that you will agree with this but it is something to
think about, I know that it will help a great deal later to have something
to fall back on in event we need it. . . .

I would only be interested if you think you can do it the way you like it, I dont know if you feel as strongly as I do about cutting some songs on your own with just an organ or piano, but believe me Elvis . . . when it comes to sacred songs they would be much better just that way done by you in your own personal mood. IF you could cut Just A Closer Walk with Thee even half as good as you did Tell Me Why [which was judged to be too close to "Just a Closer Walk with Thee" to be released at the time] . . . you would have a hit sacred release with something on the other side that you like to do. Anyway give it some thought as I know you can do it. If you dont feel like doing this on your own its okay I will work things around with Victor the best way I can to make things run longer [i.e., to fulfill Elvis' contractual obligation]. But believe me it sure would be a tremendous promotion and would be good sellers on top of this. But it would have to be done very quietly with no fanfare without any-one knowing about [it] till everything was tied down properly over here after you had mailed the tapes. . . .

Dont say anything about this recording idea to any-one except to the family Vernon, so it does not get out or they will make a big splash on this even if nothing was being done on it. I always felt that you do as good a job on your own now than with a recording director by your side. Except of course when it involves a picture story recording as that is a lot different.

You could even cut some songs that you like yourself very much but never had a chance to do on any session, we can always try to get something on them even for an Album release with 12 of them as a special Elvis records on his off Time In Germany special for his Fans.

Even if you should not feel that you could do this while in Germany I feel sure you should think about something along these lines when you return as I know it would sell very well. . . .

Regards to all
[Signed "Col"]
The Colonel.

PS. I have already gone on record very strongly at RCA that you do not care to record in Germany.

Jan 9th 1959

Dear Elvis & Vernnn;

Enclosed is a note from Mrs Parker for you both, I also wish
to thank you for the Clock and the knives received in good shape and we do
appreciate them very much.I have advised Freddie to start checking on the tunes
you gave on the phone, just to be sure we had them down correct I will list
them here again. LIKE A BABY. THERE'S NO TOMORROW,WHAT A LOVELY THING,
IT WAS NEVER MEANT TO BE. AND SUCH A NIGHT.Freddie said he will get busy on
them and see what can be done to get some sort of deal on these tunes will
advise you as soon as I hear on this from Freddie.The Dick Clark show came off
very good they promised me a tape on this for our collection as soon as we get
it will mail it on to you so you can hear it there .I want you to think about
something like this.What do you think if you could on your own with a piano
or organ in some studio or at the hotel or some place where no One but you
and Vernon and your own buddies like West and Lamar if you wanted them to be
there,you cutting a tape with some tunes all by yourself like JUST A CLOSER
WALK WITH THEE AND PERHAPS ABOUT THREE MORE SACRED SONGS THAT YOU LIKE YOURSELF
AND COULD DO IN YOUR OWN STYLE IN ANY WAY YOU THOUGHT BEST,ALSO SOME SONGS BY
YOURSELF THAT YOU LIKE EVEN TUNES LIKE YOU HAD VERNON GAVE ME OVER THE PHONE
AND SOME OTHERS WHERE YOUR VOICE AND YOUR OWN PLAYING ON THE ORGAN OR PIANO
OR EVEN IF YOU HAD SOME-ONE THAT YOU WANTED TO PLAY FOR YOU TO HELP YOU BUT
ONLY THE PIANO ORGAN AND PERHAPS ONLY A BASS,WHATEVER YOU THINK BEST,now if
you could do this on your own time without any publicity that you were doing
this to any-one not letting any-one know,than you could work on this until
you thought they were good anough for editing and mail them on to me here I
would check all the tunes than let Freddie see what sort of deal we could get
on any of them,and I would try to make up a couple of releases or EP'S on
them as a special setup with RCA Victor while you are away,or if you had some
tunes in there that you thought would be good anough for a Single release we
could use 2 of the tunes for a single,also if you did cut 4 sacred songs we
could use them for Easter as a special Sacred EP, if you remember the other
sacred EP sold well over Half Million copies over and aboe the regular re-
leases.WE could do a very good promotion on this with the promotion geared to
ELVIS ALONE. or something like that or some of them ELVIS WHILE OFF DUTY .
I know that you aould do a very good job on this and the kids would love it
as they have always been more interested in hearing you sing than the heavy
part of music on records,as you know One Night and Love Me Tender sure did prove
that they like your singing even without much music,anyway I dont say that you
will agree with this but it is something to think about I know that it will
help a great deal later to have something to fall back on in event we need it.
No One at Victor would know about this until you and I would have worked out
exactly wich tunes you like anough to be released,also if we got some sort of
deal with the publishers on the tunes,even if that is not possible and you

still wanted to bring some of them out we could use them on some EP's with

Colonel continued to identify with the record company he had been associated with for almost fifteen years now and even worried about its success in the current competitive market. Here he writes to Frank Folsom, president of the label's parent company, with his ideas for what could lift the company out of its commercial doldrums. Free advice? Well, yes, but not in Colonel's view without an eleemosynary angle. What it all comes down to is a classic Colonel lecture about supply and demand, with considerable concern for RCA's slippage in the marketplace (Elvis was doing just fine, thank you). I have left out some suggestions — they are just too wacky — but the overall thrust was to try to bring RCA, a traditionally top-heavy corporation, into the mid-twentieth century not just with proven ideas but with ones that set aside some of the shopworn shibboleths of the past. Other writers, I know, have spoken of how horrified establishment figures like Folsom were at Colonel's brash vulgarity — but I have found no evidence of this in either commentary or correspondence. Folsom in fact seems as charmed as Bill Bullock and all the others. And, of course, he was inaugurated in the very first wave of Snowmen. ∎

"When I was advance man for the circus and put up a twenty four sheet with a big picture of an elephant I didn't have to print what it was for they surely knew it wasn't a giraffe"

Mr. Frank M. Folsom   April 17, 1959
RADIO CORPORATION OF AMERICA
30 Rockefeller Plaza
New York 20, New York

Dear Frank:

It sure was good talking to you yesterday. Marie also enjoyed this very much. She has been feeling rather low the last four weeks with a bad cold and everything else but now that the weather has improved she seems to be getting along much better.

I have been on the road a good deal promoting the latest single release and the LP Album for "LP FANS ONLY". Of course we sell this to other fans and also to none believers.

Enclosed are a couple of charts from Oklahoma City. We have many more but we thought these would give you some idea of what I was trying to tell you about. My only thinking behind this is only for my interest in RCA Victor and not to complain about anyone. Since I am on top of a good many of these outlets and have been very close with a good many disc-jockeys through my travels and personal attention which I give my artist and my work, I do believe that at times in a big company some rules made in the past do not work too well now or in the future and without knowing at times just which rules to correct one misses certain business without knowing exactly why.

When I see a chart with the top fifty records listed and the biggest and most important recording company having only two artists on this chart, it seems that something should be tried to remedy this. I am well aware that a great deal of this is due to over-exposure on television of the older recording artists. But if you will note this chart also shows that most of these artists are young new artists and not the long established recording artists. It shows that my belief for the past years to put something into building new young talent is just as important as engaging new producers and spending money on promoting established artists. . . .

I have always felt that to create a demand is better than to over load even if it hurts a little while creating this demand. . . . It is much better to set up a budget of a certain amount of money to promote and build new young talent for the future than spend too much promoting something that can only, at best, get back the promotion cost. Fancy promotion with long well written merchandising copy and nice pictures displaying the merchandise sometimes does not get the message across to the teen-agers as sometimes the sales message is buried under an elaborate production. But a good flash of a large photo and title of a good tune by a new recording personality will stick with a fan until the next day when they will ask each other, "Did you see the picture of Joe last night on tv and he has a new record out and it's great." Rather than them saying, "I saw something on TV last night about Joe but I don't remember exactly what it was they had cause they had some albums and some girls dancing and something else." When I was advance man for the circus and put up a twenty four sheet with a big picture of an elephant I didn't have to print what it was for they surely knew it wasn't a giraffe.

Believe me, Frank, the top record sellers today on singles are young new artists and they are to be the album sellers of tomorrow. . . . [One reason] trying to get new artists for RCA Victor has been very hard [is] due to the fact that the company has had a policy for several years of paying one cent and a half to music firms in which the artist has an interest for music royalties instead of the standard two cents per record. [The statutory rate for mechanical, or "manufacturing and distributing," royalties was two cents per side, to be paid by the record company to the song publisher, with the sum split equally between songwriter and publisher.] But if an artist does not have his own music setup he can get two cents. Because an RCA artist has an interest in a publishing firm that firm is given only one and one half cent royalty whereas all other firms get the two cent rate. This works against the artist and I sincerely believe that some good tunes and some top artists, some I know of, have been lost to us at RCA due to this setup. I am sure that whoever started this had some good reasons at that time. But I do not think that it has brought in enough good revenue to offset what may have been lost. [Paying the full rate] will help get better recording stars and enable RCA Victor to compete with other companies that are giving better deals to top recording artists to entice them into their firms.

I went along with Presley on this account as not to upset a company policy but I also know that it can't be workable for all parties. When I made my deal with Howard Letts on Presley this was one of the objections I had but when Howard told me that every artist had this type of deal at one cent and a half I told him I would go along on this but if I ever knew of anyone getting the two cent royalty rate and knowing they also have their own music firms or are associated with any I would expect complete payment in full from the time our contract started. Finding now that a couple of very good friends of mine, artist and managers, advised me several times when I saw them that they would have liked to go with RCA Victor upon my advice that they should be with the top company but due to this unfair royalty setup they went to other companies. Knowing that one of these artists has already sold well over three million records with another company in the past seven months I do think it is time that some one recheck the value of this rule. . . . I have advised [RCA Record Division head] George Marek about this on the phone and George said he would check into it.

Believe me, Frank, I am not writing this letter to impress upon you that someone with the company is not doing a job. This is far from my mind as this is not my problem or my business. I stand on my past record of having at all times tried my best with advice in any way possible in the merchandising of our merchandise and any other way to be of help. At times, some of my ideas did not sit too well with some people but they have always been fair about talking about them and going back and forth with me and trying some of them out and happily so they worked to the advantage of all of us. I know of several gimmicks we worked out which we know brought in well over an extra million gross receipt over the long run. Perhaps, we'll never know if this gimmick did the trick but it is better to be happy over something that made money than trying to prove a loss just to say I was wrong. At least this way the money came in, the other way might have done the same but who knows.

My services have always been available to every one at the company. Bill Bullock and George Marek will tell you that there could not be any closer tie-in of working together with a manager. If there was I would have to run a nipper dog kennel to do more.

Times have changed Frank and we are now back to the days of selling the customer everything they want and need instead of giving them what we want them to have. I'd much rather sell five million records in three years and keep the artist alive than sell two million records in one year and say he was a nice guy, I wonder where he went. Our best to you,

> Your pal.
> Tom

Poor Hal Wallis. The first of the two following letters, written on Colonel's jovially self-mocking fabricated stationery, accompanies Colonel's formal signing of the revised deal for Elvis' first post-army picture for "Wallis-Parker-Hazen Productions." The second — well, I suppose you could say he's just rubbing it in. ∎

"In the meantime, I am very happy that my connection with the Salvation Army in the South is strong"

Hal Wallis Productions
Hal B Wallis   Joseph H Hazen
[and, typed in the middle]
Col. Tom Parker
Snow Cable Address: Snowux Madison, Tn.

Messrs Wallis and Hazen   April 28, 1959
Hollywood Office

Dear Associates

On this date, April 28, Tuesday, I hereby present you with the contracts signed by that great artist, Elvis Presley, and approved by your associate, Colonel Thomas A Parker of the Madison Wallis-Hazen office. Now if you two gentlemen will just sign your names in my presence I can take my copies and Elvis's copies and all copies for my office at the Morris agency and bring a close to these negotiations.

As you well know this has been an expensive project, with going back and forth, eating out, sleeping out, telephoning our foreign division or the US Army to bring this project to a final conclusion.

I am sure that both of you will agree that I have endeavored to stay away from both of you as much as possible in bringing this to its conclusion.

I look forward to a pleasant association in the future, especially knowing that something will be coming in the next year when we put this contract to work. In the meantime, I am very happy that my connection with the Salvation Army in the South is strong. As you know they always have kettles in the street during Christmas. Knowing that you don't have to participate in this type of collection, it is with great anticipation that I am looking forward to not having to share whatever I may get out of these kettles with my associates.

Respectfully yours,
You Know Who

"If I should need you for anything call me"

Colonel Hal Wallis &   May 5, 1959
Brigidier General Joseph Hazen
c/o Hal Wallis Productions
Paramount Pictures Corporation
5451 Marathon Street
Hollywood 38, California

Dear Snowers:

First I wish to thank both of you for your generosity in insisting on paying part of the expenses on my many trips to the coast from Tennessee. Naturally knowing that General Hazen was mostly responsible for increasing the amount which enabled me to give you a refund on this partly generous check. This of course does releive me of any further obligations that may come up in the future as it would be tremendously a disadvantage to know that I could get out to the coast but would have no way of getting back. As you know, round trip tickets today do not have any savings attached to them any more. I know that both of you must be brokenhearted that I have decided against doing a closed circuit TV performance next year. But, if there is anything either of you could do to make me feel better, don't hesitate to go to any lengths to achieve this pleasant goal.

Know you are both busy but you will be happy to know that the snow is flying high while I am in New York. There are several big executives that have thrown your name around in the last few days but rest assured that I am protecting both of your reputations, with vigorous protestashuns. I know this of course should be spelled differently but neither I nor my secretary know how to sepell. This will enable both of you to read it without knowing what it means.

I will be home this weekend. If I should need you for anything call me.

> Sincerely yours,
> The Colonel

ps: You should see my suite at the Morris office since we closed the deal for the picture. I am now eight doors removed from the daniker. If you ever worked on a carnival I am sure you know what that means. It looks like the little house behind the big house. That's all for now.

With the IRS threatening the validity of the recording contracts he had negotiated under the careful supervision of William Morris and Hill and Range's top tax lawyers, and with the explicit approval of their language by RCA, Colonel was for once completely flummoxed. The forced jolliness of his tone is belied by the more than usually erratic spelling and lack of punctuation (some of which I have amended for clarity), and by the bleakness of his almost out-of-character conclusion. And signing his name Tom, while it was not uncommon in his correspondence with Steve Sholes, seems like one more indication of the uncertainty he is feeling. ■

"If the ruling should be against this contract, we will all be back where we started 4 Years ago"

Mr. Stephen H. Sholes   June 17, 1959
Recording Director
RCA Victor Division
155 East 24th Street
New York City New York

Dear Stephen;

Your letters received, also the letter with the enclosure on the Army story wich we had already thru our clipping setup. We also knew this story was coming out in advance, these stories are running in the movie magazines and keeps things running all along.

The way it looks right now I will be at home June 25th and 26th One of the main reasons for this, is that June 26th I will be 50 Years old and Marie said if I stayed home she would bake a cake so if you are here you can come over and eat a piece of the cake, I may have to run off to Texas early Monday or Tuesday but if I do I will be back, in time for your visit.

There is not much news, we can talk about whatever you have on your mind when you get here. Perhaps we can sit in the back Yard and get some sun at the same time as I know my chairs will hold you up after having lost some weight from what I hear.

The kids are with us for the next two Weeks so Bobby and Marian [Marie's son and daughter-in-law] can also relax a little and we are of course happy to have them with us.

Marie and the Swami.
Courtesy of the
Graceland Archives

Between you and I there will be an hearing next week in Washington on the Victor contract with the tax division. My lawyer, also Elvis lawyer and our accountants will be there so we will see what happens. If the ruling should be against this contract, we will all be back where we started 4 Years ago, with some new plans to be made to see how we can work this out so Elvis and myself wont be holding the bag all by ourselves on this setup. After all the company had Lets [Executive Vice President of Finance Howard Letts] fly out to California to work out this new contract and on their advise we of course went along with the deal. I know they cant help it should the ruling be against the contract but we cant either. We wont know for sometime what the outcome will be, but I dont have much hopes that it will be in our favor, as they claim it was done to beat the taxes.

> Take care and hope to see you next Week.
> Tom

After, as always, dispensing with the usual amenities regarding family and mutual friends, and running through the particulars of everyday business, Colonel once again returned to counsel and reassurance. There was a great day coming, and soon all their careful planning would pay off. Even if some of the details had not "come out like we would have liked them," Elvis had kept the faith — and now he just had to keep the faith a little longer. They both did. ■

"To me you are still and will always be tops"

Dear Elvis;   July 29, 1959

... Had a nice visit with Dad last Week, went to Memphis had Frankie Connors with me [to] help me drive, had dinner at the house and we talked about many details, Dad looks good and he seemed much more relaxed than when he First arived back, he is now getting ready to return, I already have everything lined up for Grelun [longtime friend and RCA and Hill and Range employee Grelun Landon] to look after the details when he arives in New York next Week, Dad also plans to stop by here on his way back from Louisville this week as he wanted to try and visit there before leaving [Vernon's father lived in Louisville]. . . . Everything is holding up pretty good we are getting good press and also plenty of pressure to record in Germany wich I am turning a deaf ear on as I know you have no interest in recording till you return, and with the present setup on single sales and special material we have planned in Merchandising the old tunes in special LP'S and golden LP and a new Xmas Cover at the regular rate this Fall there will [be] anough merchandise on hand to keep thing rolling in the merchandising market.

First of all I agree with you to the fullest that you must pick your own tunes for the next single very carefully as it will be the First new recording after you have returned from the Army. . . . I feel there will be a bigger demand and a special interest in buying the First record you would have available with your own picking of the tune and special direction by yourself for your First recording to be released wich we can of course promote to the fullest when we do the ABC guest appearance [on the Frank Sinatra special] this would kick the songs off with a tremendous push to hit the Million sale like we have done in the past. I also know that for other reasons wich I am sure you understand it is best not to flood the market with releases as it seems too much like trying to prove something, they have done this with several artist this past year bringing out releases in a hurry if One did not do so well and now after checking around I have found out that some of the bigest record sellers are selling about 200,000 and very seldom over 500,000 even if they hit number One in the charts. You know that the most unpleasant feeling for any artist is to see record sales going down and down, so far we have been able under tremendous hardship in promotion, and with you being out of the pictures to the extent as personal appearances motion pictures, you have done a tremendous job staying up there,

There was an article in one of the papers the other day where Sholes suposedly had said that with no exposure on TV for Presley wich would have helped him a great deal we have done pretty good, Perhaps he said perhaps he did not, it does not matter, you and I know that if you had the exposure on TV like so many others we know have had, that we too would be right now in the 200,000 sales on records or less. . . . The main reason we have always hit the tremendous interest on you has been that very few get to see you in person, they always are looking for you. We have always built up a tremendous interest in you, if every-one could get to you anytime they wanted to do so, we would have no interest before long, and you would be able to walk the streets without any-one trying to get to you, they would say hello Elvis and thats it, or perhaps they would say I saw Elvis on the street Today but no one was trying to stop him or get his autograph, after all you and I know that this is the price we work for.

I know you would be very unhappy if we had a building with 5000 seats and only 800 kids to see your show or to hollor and give you that extra support an artist so much enjoys hearing when they work, so rather than take a chance on something like this I always try to plan for every-thing to be just the other way around. To me you are always so busy that we will try to do what we can, to me you are still and will always be tops as long as you can see the idea behind the entire builtup to keep it hard to get and special, of course without your personality and your talent and the following you have builtup by doing this I could not do this either, but I see so many artist fall by the wayside by trying to get in on everything in a short time and after they have been heard and seen and exploited to the fullest they cant hardly get their picture in the paper as they are not new any-more to any-one,

Look at some of the biggest names in show business that are doing commercials on TV today. I could be wrong on many things and I know that I make as many mistakes on details as other normal people do from time to time, but I do feel that I have been in show business long enough not to try and push anything too fast and too hard in a short time, You have gone thru a period of time that not many artist could do, by sticking to your guns in doing nothing but being a soldier for wich you were drafted, even with all the other details we did work on but most of them did not come out like we would have liked them to be, you held your own and have built such a tremendous special following in respect to the way you have handled yourself that it can only bring great rewards when you return to regular show business again. I have done all I could from this end by sticking to my plan when you went into the army to do nothing but look after your interest. I have been very nice to people that tried to get me to take on other talent and listen to many special snowjobs all around just like you must have had your share of special snowjobs at your end also, I feel that what we have done while you are in the service has been more important to keep our business rolling along the right track than anything else we could have done. . . .

> Best from all of us
> Your Pal
> [Signed "Col"]
> ADMIRAL ALIAS COLONEL.

PS. . . . TELL LAMAR WHAT HAPPEN TO MY SPECIAL PIPE TOBACCO FOR MY BIRTHDAY HE WAS GOING TO SHIP ME? GIVE HIM MY KINDEST SNOW REGARDS.

In the wake of his August visit to Germany for location shots for their upcoming picture, Hal Wallis gave Colonel a full verbal report and sent pictures of his visit with Elvis in Bad Nauheim. (As he and Colonel had long since decided, Elvis did not participate in any way in the shoot.) In his follow-up letters, Colonel continues to needle Wallis, not as I would once have said mercilessly but more like "mercifully," and there is an affectionate undercurrent on the part of both men in their ongoing exchange. At one point Colonel self-demoted himself to "Private," but Wallis would have none of it. And there is, as always, the self-promoting boast leavened by the self-mocking tone, and the obligatory reference to Wallis' partner, Joe Hazen, who really did not like him. ∎

"All I can say as a personal observer neither One of you look very happy. . . . Perhaps both of you were snowing so hard that you were so cold that it was impossible to smile"

Mr. Hal Wallis   Oct 16, 1959
Paramount Studios
Hollywood California

Dear Colonel Hal;

Thanks for your letter received Today, I have just returned from the hospital bringing Mrs Parker back home she has been there about a week, she will have to be at home on a very strict diet, she picked up a bug of some type in the Islands and never was able to shake it off, she lost about 20 pounds to date, now however the Dr after a complete checkup seems to be able to work a new plan on this, so we will see what happens, at least she is feeling better Today.

The pictures [of Elvis and Wallis in Germany] of course arived in your package with the letter, all I can say as a personal observer neither One of you look very happy, Elvis looks like he is ready to jump ship to come home, and you look like you are sorry you went, when you did not have to go wherever you went and why. But the paper is very good the pictures are printed on, or perhaps both of you were snowing so hard that you were so cold that it was impossible to smile.

I saw Colonel Hazen in New York and he was very happy, First of all I did not ask for anything wich always helps with Colonel Hazen Second he knew I was coming and was all prepared with his answers, they were all funny.

Dont know when I can afford to come out to see you but when I do I will let you know. This is about all the news for this time, take care of yourself and dont get snowed under by any-one including yourself, I am leaving tomorrow for Texas where I will be Sunday at Senator Lyndon Johnson Ranch having a special Lunch when he entertains the President of Mexico, wish you could be there to watch the snow fly.

Your Pal
The Colonel.

The question of Elvis' return to civilian life, and just how it should be handled, had been more and more on Colonel's mind. With the help of assistant chief of information for the Department of the Army, E. J. Cottrell, the full ceremony of Elvis' departure from the Brooklyn Army Terminal a year earlier had been perfectly orchestrated, and the interview-and-sound-effects extended-play record that had resulted from it, *Elvis Sails,* had reached number two on the charts. There was even more excitement about his upcoming discharge — many different organizations were clamoring to host a parade, a performance, a civic celebration, and in particular to proclaim with an alarum of trumpets his return to his hometown — but Colonel had other ideas. And here he proclaims them, starting on page 2 of a four-page letter to Elvis and Vernon, on October 27, 1959. ∎

"I feel that you would be a bigger man if you just came home like any other soldier after doing your duty and will be glad to be home and back to your regular work as an artist again"

... We have had many requests from different setups that would like to plan a Welcome Home Parade and such setups when you return to Memphis. I have thought about these very strongly from all sides and wish to pass this on to you for your thinking. ...

I feel that you coming home from the Army as a regular soldier would be better to just arrive home without all that fanfare for you other than whatever we can start up with the fans and fanclubs — not setup but more or less on whatever the fans want to do for you on their own. After all, it is the fans that would more or less be left out on a special prepared parade and welcoming home committee deal, speeches etc.

Also, there are many other soldiers coming home all the time and they get no parade or big welcome and some of them even came from the war some years ago and got no welcome home parade or what have you.

I feel that you would be a bigger man if you just came home like any other soldier after doing your duty and will be glad to be home and back to your regular work as an artist again.

If we were promoting records, movies or personal appearances for something like that it would make good sense and it would be accepted all the way around as another good promotion for Elvis which they know us for. But for returning home from doing your duty and having a big welcome it may look too much like a setup promotion by us. And it would be like using your two years in the army as a gimmick to do it which I know that you have always been very proud in telling the press that nothing we ever did was planned or setup to get publicity other than the natural things the fans did on their own.

Some people of the press and radio may play this up as follows: Why all the promotion for Elvis coming home? He just did his duty in the army, and he did a good job. But why not do this for all the other soldiers that come home and have also done their duty overseas just like Elvis.

Think about it and I will do whatever you think best. I am enclosing a wire you could wire me which I would try to get in the newspapers in Memphis and which would explain everything—how you feel and how much you appreciate everything they'd like to do. But it would not be fair to all the other boys from Tennessee and Memphis if this was done only for you—you feel that you have done no more than any other boy from Tennessee and although you appreciate their thinking this would be best not to do. We surely don't want to use your coming from the army as a promotion for you—you don't need it and knowing you as I do, it is better to have things run in their own way.

The wire will make a bigger guy out of you believe me, all the way around, and will show them that you have done exactly what no one would have expected from the start except real friends.

You know as well as I do that there will be plenty of regular noise from the fans on your return home which we are working on from here on the QT. This is very important as they are the fans that mean the most in our business.

I am also sure that there would be some request later on to do a special personal appearance or other things for whatever group that would promote the "Welcome Homecoming" which you know as well as I do. This way you would not be obligated later on to anyone party whoever they may be for donations or other gimmicks.

Your donations and whatever you wish to give to these different civic clubs should have no connections whatsoever with your personal business appearances and what have you. As most of them are deductible, it is better sometimes to make a donation to some worthy cause than do a personal appearance and give your talent away also. There are many things one can do in the community other than put on shows to raise money. In your income a donation is much better many times than doing a show. Many top stars in Hollywood never do these shows but give a donation towards whatever they are trying to raise money for which is much better all the way around. However, you read everything carefully and let me have either the wire as soon as possible so I can get this planted or advise me if you want to let some of these clubs to go ahead with the plans of having a big splash on your return home. You know, of course, that if we set this up with them that you will have to make yourself available to whatever demands they have to make this go over such as appearances at the luncheons or dinners or make a short speech or whatever gimmick they tie-into this. But as I said in my letter here it is only fair to bring you up to date on this so you can advise me which way you want me to move. I will do whatever you think best but I wanted you to know my thoughts and that they are sincere and for your own interest. . . .

I know you will let me know whatever you think best.

> Your pal,
> The Colonel

And here's the telegram Elvis sent, as per Colonel's instructions, but with a certain flair of his own. ∎

"I WISH TO RETURN TO MEMPHIS THE SAME WAY THAT ANY OTHER SERVICEMAN RETURNS TO HIS HOMETOWN WITHOUT CEREMONY OR FANFARE"

WUA019 120 PD INTL
CD BADNAUHEIM VIA RCA 5 1925
LT COLONEL TOM PARKER
WUX MADISON TENNESSEE

DEAR COLONEL PLEASE CONVEY MY THANKS TO THE VARIOUS GROUPS IN MEMPHIS WHO HAVE SUGGESTED A SPECIAL HOME-COMING FOR ME WHEN I RETURN TO MEMPHIS HOWEVER I WISH TO RETURN TO MEMPHIS THE SAME WAY THAT ANY OTHER SERVICEMAN RETURNS TO HIS HOMETOWN WITHOUT CEREMONY OR FANFARE I SERVED AS THEY SERVED AND WAS PROUD TO DO IT SEEING THE CITY OF MEMPHIS MY FAMILY FRIENDS AND FANS WILL BE THE MOST WELCOME SIGHT IN THE WORLD TO ME I APPRECIATE THEIR KIND GESTURE AND KNOW THEY WILL UNDERSTAND AND I AM GLAD YOU ARE IN AGREEMENT WITH ME ON THIS BEST WISHES TO YOU AND MRS PARKER
    FROM DAD GRANDMA AND MYSELF

                ELVIS,
                921AMC

Here Colonel is taking on a number of issues at once. First, there is his gentle, but unmistakable, endorsement of Elvis' somewhat tentatively expressed, but again unmistakable, desire to reestablish a close relationship with his original guitarist, Scotty Moore, who, along with original bass player Bill Black, had quit with some ill feeling in September 1957. (Scotty came back — Bill didn't.) This, of course, provided Colonel with yet another opportunity to preach the primacy of publishing. (Elvis ended up recording Scotty's song at his first post-army session, with half the song assigned to Elvis Presley Music.) And, finally, Colonel once again encouraged Elvis to put his foot down about the mastering of his records — Steve Sholes needed to be reminded that they had to meet Elvis' standards, they could not be subject to the vagaries of Sholes' own aesthetic judgment. ■

"I know about as much about explaining music to you as an Elephant knows how to get into a gopher hole. But as you well know I do know how to get money for the Elephant"

Dear Elvis & Vernon;   Oct 31, 1959

Enclosed is a tape received here from Scotty wich he and the boys made in Memphis for you to listen to. [This is a song that Scotty wants Elvis to consider for his upcoming session.] . . . As I told you on my last phone talk with you I would approach the Boys setup in some way that would not look too much that you had asked me about them getting back together, I feel that this has been handled up to the present just like you wanted the approach, it is of a business nature and there seems to be an overall feeling of warmth in this new approach wich is what you wanted — after playing the tape you can advise us what your thought are. I can understand from playing the tape here Today that Scotty has tried to the fullest to give you the message of trying to show you that he has a feeling of the type of music you like and what would be good for your way of presentation, You know as well as you have told me, on so many record-ings . . . Mr. Sholes somehow seems to allow the music to overshadow your voice wich is the only complaints we have ever gotten from the kids. . . . Anyway I thought I pass this on to you, I know very well that you are going to watch this even more so yourself from now on as you know more about that than any-one . . . and you know what the kids like to hear and thats You. . . . I also know that to get too smooth a band is not Elvis Presley. Scotty seems to know that much about your thinking as he surely talks that way on the phone and by making this tape special for you to listen I feel he at least has an interest in trying to do whatever you like and what you would feel is best for you. Scotty is mailing you a tape in his own voice explaining the entire setup wich I ask him to do as you know I know about as much about explaining music to you as an Elephant knows how to get into a gopher hole. But as you well know I do know how to get money for the Elephant. Scotty also knows that, and he is also willing to make a deal for his tune with his firm jointly with your Presley

Music to work it out together wich is more than some guys did without us having to push for this first.

Be sure and get me all the answers on all my other requests in my other letters as the pressure here is worse than a fullsteamed cooker.

[Signed "Col"]
The Colonel.

As always, Colonel sought parity with whoever he was dealing with, whether it was Frank Sinatra or the desk clerk at the hotel where he was staying. (Colonel neither kowtowed nor condescended.) Even with someone like Frank Sinatra, the first avenue of approach was humor — well, kidding — which almost always proved a great leveler. Here, after months of setting up the deal for what would be Elvis' first post-army appearance, on Sinatra's "Welcome Home Party for Elvis Presley" television special, he kids his way through a turndown of a Friars Club benefit that Frank is hosting, while at the same time making sure that Frank knows of his contribution to the cause. Sammy Davis Jr. seems to have been the one other member of the Rat Pack with whom he had an ongoing sociable relationship, but it was Frank, a charter member (like Sammy) of the Snowmen's League, with whom he was most anxious to maintain closeness. In later years, after he had established residence in Palm Springs, Colonel would dress up as Santa Claus every Christmas and pay a visit to Sinatra's mother's home. The contractual fine-tuning for Elvis' appearance on Frank's show would continue for some time, but in the end Elvis got a record-breaking $100,000, plus $25,000 for expenses, for singing just two songs plus a little bit of back-and-forth (singing and repartee) with Frank. ■

"Most likely I will be busy trying to sell my Presley Christmas cards around that time to keep something coming in for Elvis and the Colonel while he is in the Army"

Dear Frank: November 1959

The letter from the Friars Club signed by you received here at my Madison, Tennessee William Morris office. Thanks for same. As I have no tux and have no plans to buy one, I don't think I will be in California on November 8 as most likely I will be busy trying to sell my Presley Christmas cards around that time to keep something coming in for Elvis and the Colonel while he is in the Army. I am sorry I will not be able to be at the dinner. However, knowing the fine work you folks do and the many real friends I have that belong to this fine Friars Club and on account of you signing the letter, I am enclosing five hundred dollars for whatever you think best to use in the work you all are doing at the Friars Club. The reason I am mailing you the check is simple, just as you stated in the letter that you had personally asked Joe Cooper to take good care of me or any reservations I may need, I am asking you to see that this check gets to the right people thru you. If they feel that they should do something for the Colonel for not being able to be at the dinner, just tell Colonel Jessel [comedian George Jessel, a true pal] to make a few announcements that Elvis is coming out of the Army in March and that the Colonel felt badly about not being able to be in the lobby to sell a few photos at the Dean Martin table. Anyway, thanks for asking me and it is a pleasure for Mrs. Parker and myself to be able to help a little with the fine work.

Your pal,
The Colonel

Colonel never changed his views about television. In this he was much like Alfred Hitchcock, who famously said, "It can be compared to the introduction of indoor plumbing. Fundamentally it brought no change in the public's habits. It simply eliminated the necessity of leaving the house." In Elvis' case, after getting everything there was to be gained from a dozen bookings on four different shows over the course of his first thirteen months on RCA, Colonel simply stopped. There would be a total of just four more appearances over the next twenty years, with the last three amounting to one-man shows, and the first, the guest appearance on the Frank Sinatra special, something that could be viewed as a genuine career relauncher.

Here, in a letter to Fox publicity chief Harry Brand, one of his favorite Hollywood pals, he delivers himself once again of all his reasons and cautionary tales for not giving anything away (at least not too often) so long as it could continue to be monetized. This is page 2 of a letter probably written around the same time as the letter to Sinatra, though without the missing page it's hard to know for sure. ■

"SELL SOMETHING FOR MONEY ONLY IF NO ONE ELSE CAN GET IT FOR FREE AND YOU NEVER GET ANY COMPLAINTS"

Page 2. Col Brand

... Mr Hal Wallis and anyone else would not go out in making a contract this far in advance [if] they [didn't] know that as far as Elvis and myself are involved we are not going to go on TV shows on and off like some artist do before and in between pictures just to get exposure. I cant see the sense in charging a studio a good price for any artist and than give it away on Television for a small fee and take away the interest of people buying tickets to see the same artist in a Theatre.

When there was no TV Theatres did a very good business even with some bad pictures as this was the only way they could see the stars they had heard so much about. That is One reason why I believe more and more in radio promotion and newspaper promotion Today, at least One can build up a tremendous following but to see the artist they have to go to the theatre. It worked a long time ago and it is working as good Today. I dont even feel that Television clips to advertise a picture do anough to bring in the extra busines, it works the same way in records, check your charts....

Now when a fan sees an artist in a motion picture playing out a part in a picture and singing the song that fits in with the story they are more interested to buy this record than if they see it on TV as Love Me Tender, Loving You, Jailhouse Rock and now King Creole has proven. So far all the records in all these pictures are running neck to neck, they have not slowed down, some sold a little more but they picked up again when they came out in an album or EP. . . . Some producers go to great lengt to promote a picture even at times before they start shooting and go like hell on getting all the promotion they can while they are making the picture, than when the movie is released they have to do everything possible to get some more press and gimmicks as most of the people have forgotten all the other advance promotion that was done while the picture was being made.

I like the old window cards I used to put up when I was with a small circus, we had nothing on it except wait for the big show even when there was no other show coming in before us, but some of them waited and we did business. We are still promoting Love Me Tender, Loving You, Jailhouse Rock, King Creole records and they are still selling so we know that no One ever reaches all the people all of the time, but some of the late comers can be best served all the time by working at it. People that like pictures and shows are all alike, some like One or the other but none will ever come back if they are snowed into something and find out later they could have waited and seen it for free. So my slogan is, SELL SOMETHING FOR MONEY ONLY IF NO ONE ELSE CAN GET IT FOR FREE AND YOU NEVER GET ANY COMPLAINTS.

Love the Colonel.

M ajor General William W. Quinn was an important, if transitory, figure in Colonel's military operation. He had met the general through his friend Colonel Cottrell, who had not only been his principal point of contact for the last year but had even visited Elvis in Bad Nauheim the previous summer. The trip to Washington, he told Hal Wallis, had been "fun," but it touched on a number of significant points, essentially continuing the strategy of persuading the army that his policy of keeping Elvis under wraps made sense from their point of view as well as his own. He followed up his Washington visit by having Tom Diskin write a letter to Colonel Cottrell on his behalf, requesting an autographed picture of the General "because Colonel [Parker] thought him a very fine gentleman." Also, just coincidentally, perhaps General Quinn could let the Colonel know ahead of time exactly where Elvis would be disembarking in a few months so that he could make plans. Evidently, the General got the picture, and in this letter Colonel includes the press release that he was about to put out, which is, essentially, a variation on Elvis' telegram to him. (See above.) ■

"I am sure that Presley will come out of the Army an even greater artist than when he went in"

Maj-General William W. Quinn   Nov 27, 1959
Department of The Army
CINFRO — CHIEF OF INFORMATION
Department of Information
Washington 25 D.C.

Dear General Quinn;

Received the photo I had asked for for my office — Thanks very much, I do appreciate this, One reason I wanted the photo was, That you so fully seemed to understand my feeling that Elvis Presley was trying to be a good soldier in the Army as a soldier and not as an artist, I have at all times tried to follow thru on this with my promotion publicity and whatever help I have been able to give Mr Ed Cottrell in the past, it was indeed refreshing when meeting you for the first time, to know that you agreed with this.

I am sure that Presley will come out of the Army an even greater artist than when he went in, also The Army has been good for Presley and I am happy to know that all the press has been more for Presley as a good soldier than to promote him as an artist while he has been in the service. I have done the best I could to keep his name before his fans as an artist and it was up to Presley to let them know he was doing his duty in the Army as a soldier and not as an entertainer.

Enclosed are a couple of special Albums wich I hope you will enjoy at home with my compliments.

Also a copy of a special Xmas card wich I am putting out this Year to all the RCA Victor dealers with a message to his Fans why Elvis did not record in Germany while he has been in the service there, also a copy [of] a wire wich I am using to all the papers and people requesting special homecomings when he returns, I hope you agree with our thinking along these lines.

                              Sincerely
                              Col Tom Parker
                              Hon Tenn Colonel that Is)

1960

Things were rapidly heating up. All of the plans that had been so carefully laid for the last twenty-two months were finally about to come to fruition. The recording session which would determine the first single (it turned out to be two lengthy recording sessions, separated by two weeks) was the most immediate concern. By Colonel's decree the first single would be released three days after the initial session; the album would follow four days after the conclusion of the second. But it was the Sinatra special, scheduled between the two sessions and broadcast in mid-May, that represented Colonel's masterstroke of promotion. Sinatra was the man who just three years earlier had called rock 'n' roll "the most brutal, ugly, degenerate, vicious form of expression it has ever been my displeasure to hear," and now with his explicit endorsement, on top of Elvis' carefully managed army service, there was every expectation that a new adult audience might very well manifest itself. Colonel as always made every effort to display confidence, but here I think his nervousness shows through, particularly in the check-off choices he gives Elvis at the conclusion of the letter. These might have been intended to read like a gag — but I kind of doubt Elvis took it that way. ■

"Take care of yourself and do sitdown and let me have your thoughts on this letter as I have to make some very important moves in the next 2 Months"

Dear Elvis & Vernon;   Jan 9, 1960

Enclosed are 3 wires that came here last Night thought you would like to have them there, I am saving some of the Birthday and Xmas cards that came into the office till you return . . . along with some other packages and my Xmas present for you and Vernon. I also have a package for Grandma, LaMar [Lamar Fike] and Cliff [Gleaves] wich we did not ship over there. . . . As for Vernon's Xmas present I just keep it here in the locker as I cant use it being a married man. Anyway wanted to explain I had not forgotten you all Xmas.

As I told you in my cable I spoke to Mr. Cottrell in Washington and he was at that time getting in touch with the proper officer in charge overthere to get all the latest information so he can get with me in a few Weeks and give me the lowdown what they were able to do on the arival and discharge setup. I have done everything possible to work this out so you would not be shifted around for several weeks back to some other post, what will happen on this I will know before long and will advise you of this as soon as I know, I of course know that you will keep this strickly to yourselfs and not talk to any-one about it.

The Frank Sinatra ABC show will have to be taped as early in April as possible due to studio rental and rehearsal time and scheduling the show for the network. I am planning to go ahead in getting a correct date on this sometime next Week, so I can start lining up [Elvis' backup vocal group] the Jordanaires and get together with Scotty & D.J. I am trying to get all of them to hold off till Day after Easter so you at least could be home till Easter Sunday, I dont know if I can work this but believe me I am trying my best all the way on this, So if I can get the Sinatra production company to rehearse and tape their ABC show the Week of April 18th. and start the Wallis pre-recording for the picture about April 25th Monday.

If I cant work this out I will try the following: re-hearse and tape the Sinatra show the Week of April 4th finish this up and try to get you to be back home for the Week before Easter and Easter, and return to Paramount for the Picture the week of April 18th to start work there, that way you would at least get to be home for One Week and a few Days before the taping of the Sinatra show and again about Ten Days including Easter before starting at Paramount, or if you did not feel like going all the way back to Memphis perhaps you could stay a week in Vegas or some other place on a short vacation before reporting to Wallis.

As I have tremendous pressure on this do get back to me and let me know wich You would prefer of the Two schedules as I must do my best to keep every one happy without the least extra expenses involved to all parties. As you know the Sinatra ABC TV show is the biggest Guest shot ever sold on TV I was able to get a One Hundred Thousand Dollar Contract [$125,000, with expenses] for this appearance after a Six Months try, all the way around this is the most ever paid to a single artist for One shot and The Sinatra production company has to pay all the other cost, we only furnish your own supporting cast like the Jordanaires and your 3 piece band and music. Also while I think about it, be sure no one traps you into a snowjob on any TV appearance for any reason whatsoever as the ABC contract calls for an exclusive First TV appearance after you get out of the Army or before. That is One reason I was able to make this deal as you have not been on TV for over 3 Years and Frank Sinatra was the only top star and production company that had enough trust in you last Year to signup this deal wich is a tremendous feather in your Cap.

. . . Freddie [song rep Freddy Bienstock] is to bring some tunes for you to look over to be used for the TV show, also when you select any tunes for this show keep in mind that they may also have to serve for the First single re-lease after you get out so we can get the plug on the TV show out of this to help get the record exploited fast as it will have been well over 9 Months since you will have had a single release. It has worked out pretty good so far with everything else being somewhat slow but the Albums selling pretty good all along. I do not know what my meeting with RCA Victor will do in the next Two weeks but I hope to be able to handle all this in plenty of time before you return so I will have at least a bargaining position with them.

Take care of yourself and do sitdown and let me have your thoughts on this letter as I have to make some very important moves in the next 2 Months to get the best most out of everything for us. The way Scotty spoke the last time there seems to be no problem in Scotty and D.J. working with you on this when you get out, I know the Jordanaires are waiting to hear from me on the dates for the re-hearsal of the Sinatra show so they can clear their work here in Nashville out of the way and get off, so let me know wich idea you prefer of the Two, doing the Sinatra show the week of april 4th Return home for Easter or spent a Week in Vegas or some other place before reporting to Wallis right after Easter, or try to get them to do the Sinatra show right after Easter and report to Wallis right after you have completed taping the Sinatra show while you are already out there. I will do my best to try and work either deal you think best for you, but remember the Sinatra show is under pressure to get out of the way and I must know as they must lease the rehearsal studios and setup the entire show to get ready before you get out there. My best to all of you and advise me right away. The Colonel

[Signed "Colonel"]

....

And here Colonel began a separate page.

....

RETURN RIGHT AWAY TO COLONEL PARKER IMPORTANT (SIGNED)

Dear Elvis;   Jan 9. 1960

To make it possible for you to pick the schedule wich you would prefer best under your setup I am enclosing this list marking the schedule Please mark off wich you prefer best and I will do my outmost to clear it. . . .

....

And then he spelled out the choices once again with the direction "SIGN WICH YOU PREFER."

....

Colonel unburdened himself, or perhaps he simply felt like explaining him- self, to his old pal Sam Weisbord at William Morris. The ostensible purpose of the letter was, once again, to seed the ground for schooling yet another new agent for Elvis (in this case a welcome returnee) and to make sure everyone at William Morris was on their toes. But most of all I think he just enjoyed expound- ing upon his philosophy of doing business. ∎

"My Artist does not ever get involved in the business"

Dear Sammy;   Feb 1, 1960

Your letter received, HONESTLY MEAN IT WHEN I SAY YOU DON'T HAVE TO SEND ME JAM OR ANYTHING LIKE IT BECAUSE I SEND YOU ALBUMS. NOW YOU TAKE IT FROM HERE AND QUIT SNOWING.

There is not much news I have been busy getting some of the important plans out of the way for late March, I guess the Boss must be back in New York again by now. Understand Peter Shaw will be my personal contact [at William Morris] on the pictures to help me whenever there is a need, all the big problems if any I will handle of course with my associate Colonel Lastfogel, I did enjoy working with Peter Shaw in the past and I know it will again be nice to be working with him, under my setup we have to have a special understanding as my Artist does not ever get involved in the business and, somehow Elvis seems to want it this way and so far it has worked out pretty good, he never did want to do business with several people on any project, this way I smoke things out screen out the phoney deals and free setups and only present details to him that are cut and dry as to understanding how much and what do I have to do. Since I dont handle his money investments or his personal expenses these are all handled by his Father Lawyer and Accountant in Memphis, it is much better this way, When he gets his checks he can [do] whatever he feels he wants to do with it on the advise of the people that he has to handle this, and not me.

I handle my own, I pay all my own expenses run my own office handle all our own transportation office expenses out of my earnings and this way we have no transaction as to how much I paid out for advertising and other expenses as my artist is not involved in this and does not share in it in any way. Its the cleanest setup I know of any artist Manager re-lationship

Lots of luck and take care best from Marie also.

> Your Pal
> [Signed "Tom"]

Getting out of the army and back to civilian life (Elvis was discharged on March 5, 1960) posed its own set of challenges and expectations. Elvis had brought home with him a newly configured entourage, with Joe Esposito, whom he had met in the army and who would remain with him till the end of his life, as its de facto foreman.

This is the second letter in which Colonel expresses his concern about the new way of doing things. In the first, following a harsh critique of Joe's book-

On the train to Memphis, after Elvis' army discharge: with Tom Diskin and Colonel to Elvis' left; Lamar Fike and sometime security man Ken Moore to his right; and Colonel's brother-in-law, Bitsy Mott, in front. *Courtesy of the Graceland Archives*

keeping methods, he merely (I'm kidding) offers this advice: "You do whatever you like about it. Just wanted to call to your attention that it is a sloppy operation as far as your money is concerned the way it is being handled presently. If I was to do this with my business I wouldn't last very long."

Here he attacks the problem head-on, as he addresses the entire entourage via Elvis and suggests a serious plan of action (re telephone screening, hotel deportment, and every duty that might be expected of them), which I have largely omitted. Mostly, I think, this is an attempt to impress upon Elvis that since, as Colonel says, "I take great pleasure and pride in being able to say that I try to keep my nose out of your personal life in its entirety," Elvis has to take more responsibility himself and let the people who work for him know exactly what *their* responsibilities are — IF they want to go on working for him. These, Colonel emphasized, were serious issues that needed to be dealt with and yielded no easy answers. But, looked at another way, they represent the first real chinks in the armor he had fashioned to sustain the unbreakable connection between his artist and himself, and he was determined to do everything in his power to repair them. And, of course, as the years went by, the problems never went away, and he found himself compelled to address the same issues again and again. Which certainly offers a window into why so many of Elvis' guys (though not Joe, as it turned out, who came to have real respect for Colonel over the years) were inclined to resent him and see him and Vernon as the cause of all their problems. ∎

"I am not angry at any of your friends. I like them all, but I am too old to start raising another family"

Mr. Elvis Presley   April 29, 1960
Beverly Wilshire Hotel
Hollywood, California

Dear Elvis:

I know you will appreciate the fact that rather than sit down and go over all these details again and again like I have in the past on the train, in the hotel, in the dressing room, explaining to these friends of yours the responsibility that goes with their being associated with you.

As you well know from past experience, I take great pleasure and pride in being able to say that I try to keep my nose out of your personal life in it's entirety when you are not working. It is much easier for me to be able after working hours to do what I want to do, socially and otherwise, without having to worry about what is going to happen to your career, either while I am in a movie, visiting friends, or out of town, or back home running my office promoting you. This also applies to Mr. Diskin and currently to my brother-in-law, Bitsy Mott, who I engaged at certain periods to assist in getting you to the studio, getting you up in the morning, seeing that you get calls properly, and in general making sure that at least you can rely on someone to notify you where to be when traveling and keep up with the working schedule, and keep us informed where you are working and where we can contact you if we need you for anything.

It is amazing that out of the five people that are traveling with you none of them have proposed or offered to take some of this responsibility on himself for you. Perhaps it is because you don't tell them. I am paying Bitsy a good salary and his hotel. I don't mind doing this for you and for our business, but I feel sure that the time has come for your own good and your career that you must consider laying down some strict instructions regarding the behavior and services required of those people that you are paying salary to and also expenses and travel.

I would appreciate it if you would set all of them straight, once-and-for-all, explaining to them that I have never been interested in any of them giving me any information regarding you or them, or what they do on their own time when we are not working. I am in no way concerned with this. But I am concerned when people at the hotel and other places keep bugging me about things going on in general that are not in line with the proper protection and behavior for an artist of your standing. Whether some of this information is true or not is entirely up to them and you. I am not a preacher or a social worker, but I am to some extent responsible as a manager, and have put a great deal of my time and effort into the molding of your career. None of our problems today seem to be of a business nature, most of them seem to be social; our business is in very healthy shape at present.

I have already made up my mind that I am not going to do any more preaching to any of them as it seems to fall mostly on deaf ears. I am not singling out any one personality as those that are respectful and on the ball and realize your responsibility to the entertainment world have nothing to be ashamed of or to be called down on. They themselves well know whether they are detrimental to your career, and if they don't have sense enough to think about this then in all fairness to you as a friend they should tell you so and go home.

Whether they do or not is no concern of mine. I like all of them as persons, but I can't sit by any longer and become involved with a daily routine of preaching and advising and looking out for a lot of people that I have nothing to do with as far as my business with you is concerned. If all of them will read this letter the way I mean it to be you will still have all of them with you and perhaps they will understand much better the tremendous responsibility and danger of any simple mistake which can only reflect on your career, even perhaps at no fault of yours. They have nothing to lose but a free berth and whatever you pay them. Your entire career and future is always in jeopardy as you are of tremendous news value and publicity interest and this carries much more responsibility to maintain your standing. They are like me or anyone else living; no one is interested in their doings except in connection with you.

So rather than have to go through the lobby or walk in the room and have any of them give me a dirty look, or the expression of, "I wonder what the Colonel wants now?" or "I wonder what the Colonel has to gripe about this time?", this will be the last time that I will call to the attention of any of them the responsibility they have toward you and your career.

I have always felt reluctant to stick my nose in what they do, where they were going, and how they did it. But the pressure has been too great even for me to all this bugging pro and con, and then trying to straighten these fellows out—at the same time creating some sort of animosity behind my back which I am certainly not entitled to.

I have not been interested in pumping any of the fellows at any time for any information, and this includes Bitsy Mott, as when the time comes that I have to start spying on you to get information from any of the people that travel with you I will be long gone and back in Madison, Tennessee trying to sell snowballs. You know this.

It is up to you to strongly advise these fellows again and again as I have no alternative, Elvis, other than handling my business and doing the best I can as far as you are concerned, to advise you and help you when possible with your social affairs, but only then if you ask me. . . .

So this letter should at least clear up the point that none of them have to ever worry again or be concerned about my coming up stairs or in the dressing room advising them what they should do and should not do. They are all over 21 years old. But at least they now know the problems and I am sure that if their intentions are to be a real friend and appreciative of the fact that they are with you, it was well worth my time and effort to write this letter.

If they were working for me I would know what course to take, and take immediate action one way or another. I must respect and you must appreciate the fact that I realize they are your responsibility, not mine, and I would never over-step my authority as a manager to inject your personal friends into my directing their every day lives other than where it involves your reputation.

I am not angry at any of your friends. I like them all, but I am too old to start raising another family.

Sincerely,
The Colonel

P.S. May I suggest that each one who receives a copy of the letter put it in his suitcase where he can read it from time to time and not let it lay around where someone could pick it up and become suspicious that everything is not kosher, which you well know is debatable.

cc: Lamar Fike, Gene Smith, Joe Esposito, Charlie Hodge, Sonny West, Tom Diskin, Bitsy Mott

---

In the course of going over in considerable detail (and with unimpeachable memory) an MGM deal that the studio had long ago unilaterally abandoned, as well as excoriating Abe Lastfogel's agency for wasting his time by bringing it up again, Colonel proceeds to the unexpected crux of the matter: what is to be the course of Elvis' career over the next few years? His plans will surprise anyone familiar with what that career turned out to be — which was definitely not the world tour that Colonel suggests here or, in fact, any touring at all for the next decade. ∎

"I am still operating under the same banner to pick up some of our neglected personal appearances throughout the world"

Mr. Abe Lastfogel   July 1, 1960
William Morris Agency
151 El Camino
Beverly Hills, Calif.

Dear Abe:

So we will not have to go through the same conversation again on the MGM situation, I would like to clarify in writing the entire situation as I remember it very clearly.

You came to me last year with the same problem, that Mr. Thau [MGM's then studio head Benny Thau] didn't remember having had a deal with us on another MGM picture and the terms discussed. May I recall that you asked me sometime in 1958 to go to Mr. Thau's office to discuss the motion picture problem since Elvis was drafted. If you recall we offered MGM the same deal that we did Twentieth Century Fox, to leave the picture agreement as is and pick up on this when Elvis returned from the Army.

At that time Mr. Thau mentioned that if we could give his company a little better deal he thought he could perhaps go along with this sugges-tion. As we advised him that we could not do so they relinquished this agreement or understanding, whichever term is usually used in a matter like this. . . . I cannot to the best of my ability understand why there is any discussion on it as we gave that picture to Twentieth Century Fox when MGM turned the deal down when they didn't wish to wait for Elvis' return from the Army.

My present plans are in the event we contemplate negotiating another outside picture for 1961 the terms would be $450,000.00 plus $50,000.00 expenses and 50% of the profits, with of course full right of refusal of this offer in the event we got one, as I may contemplate in the event I am still operating under the same banner to pick up some of our neglected personal appearances throughout the world, which are definitely much more lucrative within the same time period as it takes to make a picture, if we were to utilize that many play dates. . . .

I have no desire to push this artist on the open market for another picture so it must only be done from an approach by the interested movie maker who would have a desire to utilize this artist in another motion picture play. In the event there is an interest by a major studio to utilize the services of Elvis Presley in a big production embracing several other movie personalities of importance, I will of course always be happy to sit down and arbitrate a different financial understanding as to the percent-age of the profits. In the event some other personalities are involved in the profits I can very well understand that it would be impossible to take 50% of the profits, but at the same time you must also understand that the guarantee will be substantially raised for the services of this artist. Perhaps it will balance itself out one way or the other.

Hope this will . . . eliminate a great deal of going back and forth on deals that we would not be interested in. We are not interested in any scripts, stories, production deals, or joint participations except under the terms set forth herein.

Respectfully, Your Pal
The Colonel

Despite Colonel's vehement disclaimer here, he did in fact have opinions, often very strong ones, about the suitability, even more to the point the artistic element, of many of Elvis' movie productions and scripts. You have only to look at some of his other correspondence, offering input and suggestions, whether rightly or wrongly, with respect not only to the promotion of the films but to their potential to challenge Elvis' dramatic ambitions and capabilities.

Colonel knew David Weisbart, producer of James Dean's breakthrough *Rebel Without a Cause,* for his championing of Elvis for his initial film role in *Love Me Tender,* and it seems as if he must have been worried that Weisbart would find it natural to put that film's director, Robert Webb (husband of the Mrs. Webb referred to in the letter), in charge once again. Weisbart didn't. Instead he placed the highly regarded Don Siegel at the helm of the new picture, which would eventually be called *Flaming Star* and would present Elvis with the kind of role that called upon his dramatic talents. (Elvis played a half-Kiowan outcast, and the title song was the only musical number in the picture.) The next picture, *Wild in the Country,* made for another producer at Fox with yet another prestigious name attached (award-winning playwright Clifford Odets), was unquestionably one of Elvis' most explicitly James Dean–derived "sensitive-adolescent" roles, also with a minimum of music. Unfortunately, neither film was particularly successful at the box office, or even as an effective dramatic vehicle. And that set the stage for *Blue Hawaii* and all the other frequently vilified Elvis pictures to come, which for the most part (especially *Blue Hawaii*) were big box-office successes.

It's hard to say just why Colonel was so insistent on removing himself from the creative fray here, unless it was the often inscrutable ways of studio politics — or perhaps he simply did not have a very high opinion of Robert Webb as a director and didn't want to go on the record and let Mrs. Webb know. ■

"If someone is using me as a scapegoat I would like to know the reason"

Mr. David Weisbart   July 12, 1960
Twentieth Century Fox Film Corp.
Box 900
Beverly Hills, California

Dear Mr. Weisbart:

As I told you on the telephone today while Mrs. Webb was in my office checking on some information that she had received regarding my being responsible for the selection of a director for the upcoming Elvis Presley picture, supposedly there was a list of directors submitted to me, and as per Mrs. Webb I had checked Mr. Webb's name off of this list. I know of no list ever submitted to me of any directors pertaining to the upcoming picture inasmuch as I did not look for a list or expect one as I have nothing to do with the selection of a director for the picture.

As for me to make the statement that we would need a sensitive director for this picture, it is rather ridiculous to me as I have never seen a script and not knowing anything about production of pictures, I would not know whether you need a sensitive director or some other director even if I had read the script as this is not one of my qualifications.

If someone is using me as a scapegoat I would like to know the reason. My discussions with the studio have never involved the selection of a director, producer or talent pertaining to the picture. I have just completed the promotion of and assistance in a picture for Mr. Hal Wallis at Paramount, and I was never present on the shooting stages at any time until the last day of the production. [I think from pictorial and all other evidence that this was far from the case.]

Even if I voiced any suggestion as to the directors it was only done merely as a suggestion and it surely does not involve me in the selection of same or his engagement for the picture. This to me was a very unpleasant situation and I sincerely hope if this is a political practice within this type of business to use someone as a scapegoat that whoever is doing it will pick somebody else. I am merely here to assist to the best of my ability in the selling and advertising of the picture, which I am doing on my own time without any compensation whatsoever. My responsibilities as a Manager for business is only to deliver the artist to the studio and nothing else. My requirements as such are fulfilled under my contract. Any additional services that I may choose to render are purely voluntary, and I do not choose to work under any unpleasant conditions over which I have no control.

I do not know as of today if you have a director for the picture. I surely have not helped you to select one as of today. The responsibility rests entirely with the studio and it is no concern of mine. Only yesterday I directed a young actor to the Casting Department when he tried to use my influence to get a part in the picture with Presley.

I sincerely hope this will clarify the matter because I do not wish people to feel that I have an axe to grind.

Sincerely,

The Colonel

More from Colonel Parker's Emily Post–like Rules for Doing Business, which focuses here on the importance of always following guidelines of courteousness and consideration. Elvis had at this point established an exemplary reputation in Hollywood for both, and Colonel was determined that he maintain it. Perhaps drawing on past traumatic experiences of his own (and in keeping, for example, with always maintaining the most meticulous records and always paying your bills and taxes in full and on time), he once again underscores one of his first principles of doing business: never give the person in power any additional advantage over you. And, if only to drive this lesson home, Colonel always loved to tell the story of Elvis arriving at the studio one day to find him washing windows with a sponge and a bucket of water. What in the world was he doing? Elvis asked. "Well, if you keep on showing up late," Colonel replied, "we're both going to be back doing the same jobs we were doing before we met. So I figured I might as well get in some practice now." ∎

"It is better for you to wait on them than they wait on us as they are paying the bill"

Dear Elvis,   September 14, 1960

As you know, the first place they call in the morning when you are late is this office. We can only go by the schedule they give us and you know that one of the greatest advantages we have had in the past is the fine compliments we received at every studio that Elvis Presley is always on time. We surely don't want to upset this for any reason, as this is the backbone for making good deals. It is better for you to wait on them than they wait on us as they are paying the bill.

The Colonel

Here once again we find Colonel standing up for Elvis' artistic integrity and once again stressing that the sound of the acetates (similar to test pressings, just a different technology) that were sent to him for approval had to be matched — *exactly* — by the finished vinyl product. The company sometimes suggested that the discrepancy might arise from the audio equipment he was listening on — but Elvis insisted that it was his *ears*. And Colonel insisted that his artist's preferences had to be satisfied. ■

"[Elvis] was very disappointed in the acetates"

Mr. W.W. Bullock   September 19, 1960
RCA Victor Records Division
155 East 24th Street
New York, N.Y.

Dear Bill:

Enclosed are the dubs of "I GOTTA KNOW" and "ARE YOU LONE-SOME TONIGHT" [scheduled to be Elvis' third post-army single] which Elvis likes best and which are much more superior to the one's that we received from your office last week. The breathing in the acetate which you shipped is very dominant. Also, Elvis says that the song has been slowed down. He was very disappointed in the acetates.

Elvis also told me that rather than take a chance in trying to correct it and bring up the quartet a little more he thinks it best just to make an acetate exactly like the one's I am sending you now. Return the new acetates along with the one's I am sending you so we can compare for correctness and similarity as Elvis feels that unless he can be sure they are exactly alike, he had best record these over some time in October.

I regret that we seem to have bogged down on these numbers, but after all Elvis feels that he must be sure before he can OK these two numbers.

Kindest regards,
The Colonel

D espite his seemingly dyspeptic tone, here we find Colonel once again just trying to teach a lesson. He is also, of course, doing his best to underscore just who matters most in this mutual enterprise, while making the point that a movie soundtrack does not necessarily translate into a successful commercial release. There's lots more. He is not telling anyone how to produce motion pictures, but neither should anyone tell him how to promote them — or most of all imagine that they can overlook his artist's musical determinations. ("Only Presley picks and okays [the] recordings.") There is no personal animus (as must be clear by now, he was crazy about Harry Brand), but he reiterates what anyone who knows Colonel has undoubtedly heard many times: there is no cookie-cutter road to success. It all comes down to careful planning, scheduling, and organization — and (something he scarcely needed to repeat, but never failed to) that he has but one allegiance, and one allegiance only: to his artist. ∎

"Whenever you try to fit a song for a picture into a story it is very hard to come up with a commercial recording that has much sales value"

Mr. Harry Brand   OCTOBER 28, 1960
CHIEF OF PUBLICITY
20TH CENTURY-FOX STUDIOS
Box 900
Beverly Hills, California

Dear Harry:

Your two letters received. The reason I have not been able to write sooner is because I have been snowed under with many details here at home [in Madison, Tennessee] having been away for more than five months. I don't know if I will even catch up before having to return to Fox Studios which I may not do for several weeks if I can see where Diskin can handle the details for awhile before returning myself. I have so much to do here that should be done and have devoted so much of my own time at the studios that I neglected many important details here in my own office.

The delay on getting a single record out is mostly due to the waiting in re-recording the tune at the tail-end of the picture just for the title change. [The movie, for months called *Dark Star,* was now to be called

Flaming Star, a determination made only after Elvis had already recorded a title version for the first.] We are not sure if this song is strong enough to bring out on a commercial recording for Elvis. I am trying to work out something to the best of my ability without missing the splendid setup we have had in the past by avoiding bringing out something that is not exactly a Presley tune. As I have told you many times and also all the other folks at Fox, whenever you try to fit a song for a picture into a story it is very hard to come up with a commercial recording that has much sales value. Some of the songs we did in pictures that were just picked because they felt right for the singer did much better. Love Me Tender had no connection whatsoever with the story of the picture but it sold records. . . .

I can never be sure that any songs will be released on records that are in any picture except when it has been cleared and selected in plenty of time to prepare the proper release dates and advance promotion tie-in with RCA Victor. We don't bring out any record on a few weeks notice. I told Mr. Weisbart early at the start of the picture that unless we had the soundtracks soon we would blow the next single release regardless if the song was strong enough. We only release four single records a year and surely won't waste one of these on something we don't think will be ready in time for promotion and at least four weeks before the release of the picture to get the most out of it. We have not had the trouble and delay at the other studios nor did we have any of these problems when we made Love Me Tender. I had an understanding with Buddy Adler and he left the entire music setup up to us. . . .

We are very much thinking of doing away with getting involved with any songs from any pictures in regards to our commercial recording releases as the pressure and the many people that get involved trying to tell us how to run our record business and when to release our records gets to be too much. And we have too much trouble to get a clean cut path from the studio to expedite and assist us to the fullest to get this in the works. I am not a movie producer and have not tried to tell anyone how to make a picture but I do feel that we know our record business pretty well. This is also a very important fact in Presley's career which we can't just pass off by releasing a record at anytime it is convenient to do so to fit in some promotion idea. We have a good promotion outlet and the fact that I did not release a single to date out of "G.I. Blues" goes to prove that

I kept my promise that I made early at the start of the picture. I was trying to save this [next single release] for the Fox picture but [then] we could not get anyone to give us a complete okay on the "Black Star" title and everyone was saying we are waiting to hear from New York before we could go ahead with any plans. . . .

We have never refused to do the songs the producer or director told Presley to sing in a picture but we do reserve the right to determine if they will be suitable for release in our recording setup. This all the studios know. . . . If songs have to be written to fit a story that is okay but most of the times these songs do not fit-in with the current demand by customers in the record trade. They are pretty and they fit a story and most likely must be done that way to make a song fit a picture but they do not always make it possible for record releases that will sell or even get into the record charts on plays or sales.

Our current album "G.I. Blues" you will find is in the best selling charts in less than two weeks and up in the top ten in sales. This is not due to the picture as no one has seen the picture to date as it has not been released. So you know as well as I do that this tremendous advance promotion is only important if the song or songs are strong enough for one of our record releases. I am going to do my best to see if anything at all can be done some other way to assist you and your promotion department in coming up with something after my meeting with Mr. Bullock of RCA Victor. . . . I don't know if anything can be worked out. But whatever can be done we will do our best. However, there is nothing I or anyone else can do about jumping the gun with a release against our regular setup. It would only kickback at all of us with the results being bad business to come out with a release of any song not timely or proper under our regular setup. . . .

It is high time that some of the bottlenecks are unclogged if there is to be a smooth setup pertaining to having the right time to do the right thing if possible in regards to trying to get the most out of all the promotion advantages possible with the release of any picture. I for one have always been for this but I am too old to go back and forth to try out an outdated way of doing this. Times have changed and I try to go along with the current demand of giving the fans what they want and buy when it comes to Presley recordings which only Presley picks and okays. I only handle the promotion and sales gimmicks to get the most for all of us.

The record release and proper tunes and releases is as important to us as it is to you folks. But we can't release any records just for the sake of a radio plug or some other type of tie-in promotion which would be very slim if the record is not commercial. Will take all of this up again should I return to the studio for the next picture. In the meantime, take care of yourself and our best to you and Sybil.

The Colonel

———————————

J ust for fun. But remember: every joke . . .
"Zeke Parkenstein" (or "Rosenberg," or even "Parkowitz") was a name Colonel would occasionally use with his William Morris colleagues, almost every one of whom was Jewish, and at the all-Jewish Hillcrest Country Club, where he and Abe Lastfogel were accustomed to dine several times a week. I would say this is clearly a gesture of fellow feeling from someone who knows himself to be as much of a social outcast as his "fellow" William Morris agents, a number of whom are copied here. But on the other hand, feel perfectly free to take it as no more than a joke playing upon the expectations that derive from every business's moment of truth, the annual Christmas (holiday?) bonus. (Will the lonely Madison, Tennessee, outpost be left out?) And it should be noted that William Morris controller Nat Lefkowitz was not known for his sense of humor and has been described to me by two longtime former William Morris employees as a "crusty, cranky personality who only knew and cared about money down to the cent." (Okay, on the other hand it should be further noted, they were young at the time. I wonder if they knew he was a Snowman in good standing.) ∎

"This is not an emergency letter, but we do request an emergency answer"

[Stamped "CONFIDENTIAL"]
Mr. Nat Lefkowitz   December 7, 1960
William Morris Agency
151 El Camino
Beverly Hills, Cal.

Dear Mr. Lefkowitz:

Welcome to California. Colonel Parker just called to my attention today that you are visiting the main office on your annual deliberation to work out the tremendous problems with your associates of planning your annual profit bonus. Colonel Parker respectfully has requested me to call to your attention the tremendous services that have emanated from the Madison, Tennessee William Morris office. Many projects have been prepared, coordinated and eliminated from this lonely office, as this is by all means an outpost compared with the luxurious surroundings that all of you are benefiting by in New York, Hollywood, London, Paris, Chicago, and other points.

Knowing your tremendous warm feeling toward the infant office in the Smoky Mountains of Tennessee the Colonel has asked me to refresh your memory at this time so you will not feel badly about it at a later date when some of our associates approach you with a remark "What happened?"

You will always be grateful to the Colonel for allowing me to call attention to this matter while you are in a generous mood. We could name so many projects far beyond the call of duty, not even speaking of contractual agreements, that would overwhelm you so much that with your generosity there would not be anything left for anyone else. We of course have no desire to cut anybody out that much, just a little.

In the Madison office with the plaster coming down from the walls and the water pipes leaking and a dilapidated heater which has been in service ever since the Tom Mix days, I know you will appreciate the Colonel allowing me to call attention to these problems.

The Highest of All Potentates is well aware of the situation, his initials are A.L. Some of his associates, S.W. and M.S., will be in a generous mood to go along with this but so far they have gracefully passed the buck, which of course deserves a vote of confidence as they are running true to form.

You, being a member of the Snowmens League of America, will be able to understand that this is not an emergency letter, but we do request an emergency answer. We are not primarily interested in correspondence as much as we are in a certificate, which you will be most likely able to figure out better than we are.

If I am able in this way to help lighten your burden it is just one of the extra services which we render gladly. Do not be burdened with worrying about an answer other than results as we know you are very busy. For any further information you need as to the whereabouts, location or recipients, Colonel Lou Goldberg in the Accounting Department has his finger on all this as he manages to locate us very promptly when the commissions are due.

Your devoted servant,
Zeke Parkenstein

Ccs: Mr. Abe Lastfogel, Mr. Morris Stoller, Mr. Sam Weisbord, Mr. Norman Brokaw, Mr. Joe Schoenfeld

P.S. To protect the favorable results on this letter I deemed it advisable not to discuss this with Mr. Schoenfeld or any other associates that may feel that a favorable answer to me may result in a cut down to them. As a Master Snowman you can understand that I will be unable to advise my associates of your generosity at this time as I don't wish to disappoint them. So a speedy answer will eliminate their worrying as they all have anticipating looks on their faces in the last few days.

1961

Much to his distress, Colonel had begun to hear from relatives in Holland, with whom he had not been in touch since leaving the army in 1933. Evidently one of his sisters had seen his picture in the Dutch weekly magazine *Rosita* (the famous picture of him standing behind Elvis in the doorway of a railroad car as they arrive in Memphis following Elvis' army discharge) and recognized him, she said, because he looked so much like their youngest brother, Jan, now a policeman in Amsterdam. Not long after that, the letters started coming, and Colonel posted this notice in his offices in both Madison and Hollywood. ■

FROM THE DESK OF
Col. Tom Parker
DO NOT OPEN ANY MAIL FROM HOLLAND ADDRESSED TO
COLONEL OR TOM AS PER INSTRUCTIONS 12/7/60
[Each line is double-underlined.]

And then it happened. Colonel's younger brother Adam ("Ad") got his son, Ad Jr., an eighteen-year-old Utrecht University language major, to write a letter in English to his uncle. That letter is lost to history, but Colonel's reply is not, and if ever there was an expression of conflicted . . . what? Feelings? Intentions? Identity?— well, this is it. ■

"You know as well as we do that at times it is better to let the past be as it is and not re-open old wounds"

Dear Ad Van Kuyk; Jr.   Jan 31–1961

Your letter received please do not write again till we have been able to contact Mr. Parker regarding this seemingly personal matter, also advise the others of this request that have been writing as these letters are getting into the fanclub and other hands and perhaps do not understand this. They are opened up by mistake and again mailed on from town to town as Mr. Parker travels most of the time all over the Country. I am sure you will agree that this matter if it involves Mr. Parker must be handled very carefully and privately.

I will take all the letters some of wich we of course are unable to read with me and take this up in person sometime in April or May when I will see Mr. Parker in California or Hawaii, at that time we will try to get back somehow with a contact either by mail or some-one in person to take this matter up so it can be closed out. You know as well as we do that at times it is better to let the past be as it is and not re-open old wounds, if this should be the case I am sure Mr. Parker has felt the same longing and hopes as all of you but must have had a very good reason and many problems so not to bring them to any of his people at any-time, I know he is not that sort of person if he could help it.

This is all we can do at present but we will try to work out some plan to see what can be done in event this is possible you will hear from us later this Year but please dont press or contact us any-more till you hear from Mr. Parker as we do not know what to do at present on anything. There are several Friends that we can depend upon who may help us at a later date in trying to help you. So I suggest that you treat this entire matter till further notice as a Friendship letter and answer.

Believe me if there is anything we can do regarding this matter we will have to handle this from here on a personal private bases in event Mr. Parker feels that this matter is his personal problem.

I suggest you do not show this letter to any-one as there may be some misunderstanding and it would undo so many things that must be worked out if possible, it is hard to explain so many details without knowing the true story of everything, and even harder to understand and be excused if One does not know the entire setup.

Believe me Mr. Parker feels for you and all the other members of your Family the same as you must feel, so bear with us and we will try to help

Jan 31-1961

Dear Ad Van Kuyk,Jr.

          Your letter received please do not write again till we have
been able to contact Mr. Parker regarding this seemingly personal matter,also
advise the others of this request that have been writing as these letters are
getting into the fanclub and other hands and perhaps do not understand this.
They are opened up by mistake and again mailed on from town to town as Mr. Parker
travels most of the time all over the Country.I am sure you will agree that this
matter if it involves Mr. Parker must be handled very carefully and privately.

I will take all the letters some of wich we of course are unable to read with me
and take this up in person sometime in April or May when I will see Mr. Parker
in California or Hawaii,at that time we will try to get back somehow with a
contact either by mail or some-one in person to take this matter up so it can
be closed out.You know as well as we do that at times it is better to let the
past be as it is and not re-open old wounds,if this should be the case I am
sure Mr. Parker has felt the same longing and hopes as all of you but must have
had a very good reason and many problems so not to bring them to any of his
people at any-time,I know he is not that sort of person if he could help it.

This is all we can do at present but we will try to work out some plan to see
what can be done in event this is possible you will hear from us later this
Year but please dont press or contact us any-more till you hear from Mr. Parker
as we do not know what to do at present on anything.There are several Friends
that we can depend upon who may help us at a later date in trying to help you.
So I suggest that you treat this entire matter till further notice as a Friendship letter and answer.

Believe me if there is anything we can do regarding this matter we will have
to handle this from here on a personal private bases in event Mr. Parker feels
that this matter is his personal problem.

I suggest you do not show this letter to any-one as there may be some misunderstanding and it would undo so many things that must be worked out if
possible,it is hard to explain so many details without knowing the true
story of everything,and even harder to understand and be excused if One does
not know the entire setup.

Believe me Mr. Parker feels for you and all the other members of your Family
the same as you must feel,so bear with us and we will try to help in some way
to at least make-up for any mistakes some-one may have made without meaning to
do so.

Remember me to all of them and if you can understand the meaning in this
letter completely you will know and the others will also know this is the only
way we can try to solve this for you.

                    Sincerely and with Thanks.

Colonel replies to his nephew, Ad van Kuijk Jr., January 31, 1961. *Courtesy of Ad van Kuijk Jr.*

in some way to at least make-up for any mistakes some-one may have made without meaning to do so.

Remember me to all of them and if you can understand the meaning in this letter completely you will know and the others will also know this is the only way we can try to solve this for you.

Sincerely and with Thanks,
[Signed "Andre"]

You might think that Colonel had something personal against Steve Sholes — but, in fact, he did not. They had worked together closely with Eddy Arnold for nearly ten years — and they had worked companionably for a year or two with respect to Hank Snow. They had fallen out over Sholes' ideas for Elvis Presley, it's true — but Colonel would have been the first to say that it wasn't anything personal. Sholes hadn't known what to do with Elvis in the studio, Elvis felt that Sholes was patronizing him, and it was clear from the start that the two were not going to be able to work effectively together.

But here, in this letter to RCA General Manager George Marek, the focus was not so much on music as on history, and while it might be thought that Colonel was not particularly dedicated to the study of history in the abstract, his voluminous files and documentation of every aspect of his career (including "dogcatching") would argue otherwise. And it bothered him, for whatever reason, to see everyone either claiming, or assigning, credit for something with which they had little or nothing to do. Colonel himself always pointed to Sam Phillips and, if only out of an old-fashioned sense of courtesy, to Vernon and Gladys Presley, too, as Elvis' "discoverers"— but at the same time he was not above seeking credit for himself. And so he does here, in an account that, while not exactly inaccurate, does not hesitate to applaud his own actions or point out to everyone he was dealing with at RCA at the time — with the sole exception of head of Legal Affairs Coleman Tily and by extension Bill Bullock and Howard Letts — the many errors of their ways. ■

"I have no objections to anyone riding on a broomstick to glory"

Mr. George Marek   April 10, 1961
RCA Victor Records Division
155 East 24th Street
New York, N.Y.

Dear George:

I have just returned from Honolulu and will be working for the next few days in my office at Paramount.

I don't know if Bill Bullock called your attention to the request we had last week to verify a press release that was in the Billboard dated March 20th regarding Mr. Steve Sholes, the discoverer of Elvis Presley, however, as you know, I have never questioned many of the press releases put out by RCA Victor, but I would like to go on record in writing that some of the snow that has been flying out of the Publicity Department at RCA has not always been, as we say in show business language, completely authentic and correct.

I am not concerned too much about some of the stories personally, however, there may be a time in the future where, when we are pinned down for an accurate analysis that the information from RCA Victor will not jibe with the information that we will have to give and which we of course can back up with documentary proof which is in our files, especially pertaining to how Elvis Presley came with RCA Victor and who handled and closed the deal.

I have no objections to anyone riding on a broomstick to glory since we don't handle any broomsticks, but when it comes to an artist that has been milked dry, even in dry seasons, by so many people taking credit for who discovered him, secured him, and brought him into the RCA Victor family that if we had to split royalties with all of them there would be nothing left for us. Fortunately this is not so. However, when a press release released by RCA Victor goes as strong as stating that "A young singer named Elvis Presley was brought to RCA Victor by Mr. Sholes", it is not fair to Mr. Sholes to be put on the spot like that.

First of all, it is hard for anyone to keep going back and forth trying to deny certain things that never happened. But the true story, strictly sticking to the facts is that when Elvis Presley was first offered to RCA Victor by me we received a complete turndown because the price of

$5,000.00 which I thought we could get his contract for was prohibitive from the point of RCA Victor at that time.

Regarding the tapes that were held by Sun Records, which can be verified by Coleman Tiley, 3rd, who was the attorney representing RCA Victor in Memphis when I handled all the transactions and switch-over from one company to the other, and I would like to call your attention to the fact that RCA Victor paid my transportation and expenses and also Mr. Diskin's six months previously to New York to negotiate the possibility of obtaining this artist from Sun Records, at which time we reached a complete stalemate.

Also, it was my money that was put up for deposit with Sun Records 24 hours before the option expiration time because at that time I had been requested by Bill Bullock that RCA would appreciate it if I would put up the money as they could not get it down there fast enough to handle the deal.

I am not going out of my way to correct news stories, but I merely wish to go on record that when we are pinned down we will have to give them the facts as they are and not distorted. I am doing this out of fairness to Mr. Sholes as I know how he must feel to read these items in papers and magazines and it doesn't seem there is anything he can do about it himself. . . .

I am not going into all the facts, but I am keeping a complete file so that there will be no misunderstanding if anyone wishes to challenge this information as not being correct. This includes copies of the Sun Record contract, my correspondence with Sam Phillips, my correspondence with Mr. Bullock. The only representative from RCA Victor working with me at that time in Memphis was the attorney, and Mr. Bill Bullock and Howard Letts, neither of these gentlemen were in Memphis to close the deal. Everything was handled by telephone and I was representing RCA Victor to negotiate the deal as requested and authorized by RCA Victor at that time.

There is no reason for this publicity to be re-hashed every six months just to wave a flag. Everyone connected has benefitted including the artist and the company and all of us, but the pressure that I received last week from different sources to authenticate the story that was in the Billboard left me somewhat puzzled. I managed to dodge the issue fairly well but felt it proper to call this to your attention for the future to keep the record straight. . . .

I'm not pushing the panic button but you and I know when you operate an oil well you don't expect gas.

My best to the Mrs.

Sincerely,

The Colonel

P.S. Would like to pass on my thanks to all the representatives of RCA for the great job in Memphis and Honolulu. Without their help these two benefits could not have been the successes that they were. Elvis and I appreciate everything very much.

———————————

Elvis' benefit concert in Hawaii to raise money for the USS *Arizona* was Colonel's idea, prompted by a story in the *Los Angeles Herald Examiner* that underscored the pressing need to raise money for a monument commemorating the bombing of Pearl Harbor in time for the twentieth anniversary of the attack the following year. That was what Colonel set out to do, and the event was a triumph beyond all expectations. It raised more than $62,000, well over the goal set, and enabled the completion of the monument for its official dedication on Memorial Day, 1962.

Prior to the benefit, Colonel contacted his old friend and Apprentice Snowman Lyndon Johnson, whom he had met with Eddy Arnold at the LBJ Ranch in 1959, and in the immediate aftermath of the show, to which Vice President Johnson had the Secretary of the Navy send a congratulatory telegram, Colonel sent this follow-up message, volunteering his and Elvis' future support.

It's hard to imagine two more widely separated historical figures who could have been better matched, and they remained in touch for many years and seemed to get an equal kick out of each other. (I no longer have the letter in its original format, so I have set it up as best I can.) ■

"We are willing, able and available to serve in any way we can"

Dear Mr. Johnson,   April 22, 1961

We have just completed raising more than $62,000 for the USS Arizona Memorial Fund at Pearl Harbor. Now more than ever we feel it proper to let you know that we are willing, able and available to serve in any way we can, our country and our president in any capacity, whether it is to use our talents or help load the trucks.

> Sincerely, your Friends
> Elvis and the Colonel

Friendship be damned, when it came to his artist, Colonel was not going to let anything get by him. ■

"The wording retroactive is only important to me if we get it"

Mr. W.W. Bullock   October 20, 1961
RCA Victor Records Division
155 East 24th Street
New York, N.Y.

Dear Bill:

Your letter of October 19th received. I would like to be very honest with you. Even with my ability to smoke out circular letters I am unable to come to a stop and analyze this one, and this is no snow job. . . .

I hope your meeting with your associates turned out good for you. I am making up a complete folio and the only thing I need to fill it now is to get the exact interpretation of the artists contracts with RCA Victor that have been so generously favored by RCA Victor with a better remuneration which I was told was not possible when I asked for it. I am always happy for other managers and artists to get a better deal for themselves but it always hurts me a little when we should have been favored with the same proposition when requested in the past, and I accepted the fact that no better deal could be given. For what we have contributed in the past towards the company, not losing sight of the fact that the relationship has been pleasant and lucrative for all concerned and RCA Victor surely have done their part, it doesn't take away the fact that better deals were made with other artists that had not contributed any source of revenue into the RCA Victor coffers. If the company feels that this is not a fair analysis I would agree to the extent that no one else got any different than we did. Surely there can be no objections from anyone when I point out that our track record is such in the past and for the future is at least as promising as anyone else you have signed up so far. So no one can say that the reason they gave someone else a better deal is that they will make more money for the company. I hope they do and I sincerely feel that there should be some overtures to straighten this matter out. If we are wrong I am not too smart to listen to further explanations.

Our present contract was satisfactory to us up until the time that we learned that the company was giving better deals than ours and regardless of the lapse of memory of anyone my memory has not deteriorated so far that I can't recall several instances where I was told that if anyone ever got a better deal we would get the same. The wording retroactive is only important to me if we get it.

If, according to some of the information gathered by us, the more lucrative deal with the other artist is due to a tax advantage they have we feel that we wish to pursue this along these lines and at least get a ruling from the Internal Revenue Department if this is more advantageous to the tax payer, as we know very well as proven in the past RCA Victor does not carry any of the responsibility regarding any tax advantage pertaining to a recording contract for the artist. We surely don't want any unless it is bonified, legitimate and an approved tax ruled situation by the Internal Revenue Department. I feel sure that all our good friends at RCA will want us to have the best advantage for our services and benefits possible as long as they are legitimately so. If the new deals they seem to be coming up with are better for us tax-wise and are so proved by the Internal Revenue Department as being permissible we surely want to take advantage of this, and I know, with your blessing.

Kindest regards,
The Colonel

Though he may not have written this personally revealing account of his life and methods — or even affixed his signature to it — Colonel's fingerprints are all over this 20th Century Fox publicity release concocted sometime prior to the opening of *Wild in the Country* in June of 1961. After a flurry of stories the previous year which focused on his carefully constructed personal mythology (*Time* magazine's May 16 feature being the most prominent), this close-third-person telling of his story appears to have been the final attempt on Colonel's part to put himself front and center. One can only wonder if this relative shrinking from the spotlight (I mean, he never really withdrew from the public eye; he simply became a character actor) might not have had something to do with his brother's visit just prior to the release of the film. ■

"The suspicion has grown in theatrical and journalistic circles that the Colonel is some sort of Svengali who has hypnotized a country boy into becoming one of the great entertainers of our time"

One of the most interesting relationships in show business is that between Elvis Presley and his manager, Col. Thomas A. Parker.

Since Elvis is one of the more withdrawn theatrical personalities and Col. Parker is a breezy extrovert who will talk to anyone at any time, the suspicion has grown in theatrical and journalistic circles that the Colonel is some sort of Svengali who has hypnotized a country boy into becoming one of the great entertainers of our time.

That this happens not to be true has not prevented it from appearing in print along with the rest of the Presley appocrypha [*sic*], which in volume may well exceed the truth written about Elvis.

Col. Parker is Elvis' theatrical manager. He negotiates all the Presley contracts for films, records and personal appearances, although he does not execute them without Elvis' at least perfunctory approval. He is also responsible for all promotional efforts in Elvis' behalf, which is a small industry in itself, and he sees to it that the singing star's living requirements, which because of his sometimes hysterical following are fairly complicated. He oversees the enforcement of contracts for Elvis and sees to it that Elvis lives up to his obligations to the letter.

But the Colonel does not intrude, at least in an authoritative way, on the more private areas of Elvis' life. During the making of "Wild In The

Country", Jerry Wald Production for 20th Century-Fox release, Elvis was asked if the Colonel would object if he married.

"The Colonel would have nothing to say about it," Elvis replied with more than usual emphasis. "I probably would talk it over with him as a friend and a man I respect, but never in the sense of asking his permission."

And Col. Parker has corroborated this attitude.

"When the boy wants to marry, I hope he'll ask me to help him do it," he said.

Like a wise father, Col. Parker takes an interest in the girls Elvis escorts, but doesn't interfere. He probably would step in if he thought Elvis were making some dreadful mistake, but it would be as a counselor not as a commanding officer.

"After all," the Colonel says, "this boy is 25 years old; has served two years in the Army. He's a full grown man and a good man, too. He knows what he wants and how to behave."

In the area of finance, which might be a means of control, Elvis is completely independent of Col. Parker. Elvis' money is handled by his father, Vernon Presley, and has been since the beginning of his career. When asked if Col. Parker objected to his spending $22,000 for a Rolls Royce, Elvis gave an answer almost identical to his reply about the matter of marriage.

Both Elvis and the Colonel assert that Elvis picks his own songs for all occasions, including motion pictures. The Colonel's control in this area consists only of suggestion and through screening the vast amount of material that pours into the Presley organization, eliminating patently unsuitable songs. Even the swivel-hipped style is Elvis' own.

"I had it before I met Col. Parker," Elvis says.

"It's natural to the boy," agrees the Colonel. "It wouldn't have had the appeal otherwise." . . .

Because Col. Parker is not in absolute control in the situations discussed does not mean that he is unimportant as an adviser. It is unlikely that Elvis would take any major step or make any serious decision without consulting him. But there seems [no] reason to believe that Elvis would find himself bound by the Colonel's advice.

Undoubtedly one of the best contract men in the entertainment industry, Col. Parker writes a brutal agreement, not only in terms of money but in all kinds of restrictive clauses. "I'd rather try and close a deal with the devil," is the remark reputed to Producer Hal Wallis, who, nonetheless, has made four of Elvis' pictures and is to produce five more. And—quite possibly with an eye to what he considers the best interests of his young artist—he binds Elvis to the producer's judgement in all matters save only the choice of songs. Elvis, by contract, has no say on script, director or fellow players in his pictures. "We don't know anything about making films," the Colonel says, "and leave all that to the people who do."

This works out to the benefit of the producer and, in some respects, to the Colonel's ideas on showmanship. For example, Elvis hates to pose for still pictures. Left on his own, he probably never could be trapped for the still gallery. But, on the producer's demand, Elvis always appears on time and ready to work. "I know you hate it," the Colonel says blandly, "but, Elvis, it's in the contract."

During the shooting of "Wild In The Country", Elvis, who has become deeply interested in straight dramatic acting, objected to singing a song in a particular part of the picture because he thought it inappropriate to the action. "But," he added, "I know it's in my contract that I have to do it if you say so." He did it.

It is probably in the area of exploitation that Col. Parker's influence is most powerful and decisive. The Colonel, with a carnival and circus background, is flamboyant: Elvis, in the overall picture, is surely conservative. Regardless of what the public image of Elvis may be, his deep attachment for his family; his preference for old friends, his home and his hometown, Memphis, are surely indicative of a reserved nature.

The golden suit was Col. Parker's idea and was a straight publicity stunt, complete with a $10,000 insurance policy against damage to the garment. When Elvis put it on he found the cloth was so heavy that he could hardly breathe, let alone sing and move around in it. But the Colonel persuaded him to wear it for half the performance, anyway, which was enough to send Elvis' picture around the world as fast as wires and radio waves could carry it. . . .

Keeping the Presley name and image before his public, a small industry in itself, is a passion with Col. Parker. For example, he and Elvis send out over a million Christmas cards, mostly distributed through Presley fan clubs. And this is only a detail in the year's operation.

During Elvis' two years in the Army, Col. Parker oversaw the promotion of seven records, previously recorded, each one of which sold over a million pressings. An accomplishment without parallel when it is considered he had to operate without any assistance from his artist whatsoever.

But in interviews with the press, Elvis is on his own. When only a single correspondent is involved, the Colonel is never present. In mass interviews, normally conducted when Elvis first hits town, the Colonel is very much around but only in the capacity of major domo. He sees to the seating, the refreshments if any (never liquor) and any detail outside the interview, itself. But Elvis answers the questions without coaching. Probably because there is no subject on which he has any need to be sensitive, Elvis handles himself magnificently on these occasions. His replies are simple, direct and thoughtful and he never pretends to be anything he isn't. Printed criticisms of Elvis have been confined almost entirely to those writers who have never met him.

Col. Parker likes to see his artist [as] a figure of controversy. "If you and I agree that a certain man is a nice guy, what else can we say about him?" the Colonel inquires. Elvis confesses that criticism has sometimes been painful, but philosophizes: "You can't please all the people all the time."

Although their relationship is an affectionate one, Elvis and the Colonel don't see a great deal of each other. The Colonel is almost never a part of Elvis' social life, rarely appears on his movie sets. As Elvis grows older, he is becoming more restrained in his dress, activities and even his performances. This may be a trifle painful to the Colonel's ideas of showmanship, but he adjusts to it. Elvis has never been "hotter" as a theatrical personality than he is today, and the Colonel probably sees no reason to try to persuade Elvis to a more spectacular operation.

1962

When RCA Operations Manager Norman Racusin took over the Elvis account from Bill Bullock in 1962, clearly he didn't know who he was dealing with. It must have been like walking into a buzz saw, as he sought to impose "normal" business practices on an artist, and a manager, who did not conform to normal paradigms, business or otherwise.

Colonel wasted no time taking umbrage. Their rapid-fire exchange began with Racusin's objection to the form, or perhaps the dating, of Colonel's invoice for his annual production of Elvis calendars, one of the many ongoing staples of his never-ending promotion campaign. Racusin enumerated all the "embarrass-ment," the unintended "vicious and unfavorable" consequences that could ensue if proper procedures were not followed.

Colonel, an implacable foe of bureaucratic stuffed-shirtedness, and a dedi-cated proponent of putting the new fellow in his place, did not hesitate to con-front the problem head-on. As always, he was determined to set the terms for this new relationship, and as always Colonel made sure that Racusin's peers and superiors (including RCA General Manager George Marek) knew of his trans-gression. ■

"You may wish to take another look at your letter . . . perhaps you were writing this to someone else but misplaced his name and used mine instead"

Mr. Norman Racusin   June 20, 1962
RCA Victor Records Division
155 East 24th Street
New York, N.Y.

Dear Norman:

Just as you were quite surprised when you heard from Bill Bullock how my reaction was, I in turn was surprised when I got your letter.

Without going into a lengthy letter, which I am able to do and it would be so long that even I wouldn't know what I am talking about, let me say for the record that I for one at all times am well aware of the procedures of such a large company as RCA having been a stock holder myself and I am still on the Board of Regents for the church that handles our RCA stock. I am well aware when you mention stock holders, management and the people who receive such payments. The only thing that is very confusing in your letter is your mentioning of prescribed procedures, telling me how they sometimes result in embarrassment to all parties concerned. The only way I could embarrass anyone would be if the check didn't come in.

Knowing that I would never get the check unless I signed for it properly, eloquently, and in line with the understanding with the company procedures, I don't understand how we could expose ourselves or Elvis to vicious and unfavorable publicity. This has completely fogged up the situation and if this was your purpose you have achieved it perfectly. Mr. Bullock, as long as I have known him would never turn over one penny to me without my properly signing for it. I had this understanding before he left and I assume he passed this on to the proper parties since he could never have brought the check without it. So you may wish to take another look at your letter and perhaps you were writing this to someone else but misplaced his name and used mine instead.

First of all, I would never become involved in anything vicious and unfavorable for such a small amount; it has to be well up in the millions. The only reason that I am upset is that it is a small amount. You will never hear from me if you increase it. But all in all I was upset because the letter does not make sense with the understanding that I had with Mr. Bullock. If I am digging into the barrell that deep it goes without saying that I have been known to dig down deepest, stay down longest and come up with the least.

If you can top this you will have no problems; just write another check and I will sign again.

Best wishes to all, and am looking forward to seeing you on the Coast, as you say some time this fall, but please come sooner if you have something.

Your Potentate Snowman,
The Colonel

PS: After speaking to Mr. Marek on the phone last night he, himself, was quite upset when he heard that such a small amount was involved, but for this time and like always you guys will always come out on top. Don't worry about the stock holders at present because they have plenty to do checking the daily returns in the stock market, and RCA is still a good buy at any price.

Cc: Mr. George Marek, Mr. W.W. Bullock

———————————

History should record that Racusin sat on his reply for over three weeks, but even then he still could not find the right tone, as he seems to recognize himself. Never bullshit a bullshitter, as the saying goes, never kid a kidder.

Not surprisingly, Racusin was only setting himself up for the comeback that followed, in which Colonel makes a point of the fact that he is typing this letter himself, and while he does not repeat his (deliberate?) misspelling of Racusin's first name as "Noman" (I'm not sure where this occurred in their previous correspondence, but Racusin seizes upon its felicitous omission of the "r"), he seems to be doing everything he can to misspell, misplace, and mispunctuate as many words as possible. One can look at this as a masterpiece of indirection — or perhaps it simply expresses a mild-mannered contempt for those who, on the basis of an Ivy League education or its equivalent (Racusin was a basketball star at Penn State), give themselves airs. But once he got that out of his system, there do not appear to have been any subsequent problems. ■

"You will also know for sure by this that I am not as smart as people think I am"

"Let it snow, let it snow!" The High Potentate of the Snowmen's League of America, with (left to right) Joe Esposito, Gene Smith, Charlie Hodge, Cliff Gleaves, Red West, Elvis, Richard Davis, and unidentified Snowmen, on the set of *Blue Hawaii,* spring 1961. *Courtesy of the Graceland Archives*

Norman Racusin   July 23-d 1962
Vice President & Operation Manager
RCA Victor Record Division
155 East 24th Street
New York City 10, New York

Dear Norman;

Your most welcome and understanding letter arived here from our Paramount office in Hollywood, I had just returned from a promotion trip thru Florida, Alabama and Miss on into Memphis Tennessee and now in Madison Tenn. I will be leaving here in a few Day's to return to the Coast to start the works going on the new MGM picture wich is slated to roll about the First Week in September — with of course good many details to be worked out before that time in getting location housing and other details in order before Elvis arives at the studio, we plan to shoot about One Week at the Worlds Fair.

Now that the decks have been cleared with me waiting for an answer from you on my letter, I can sleep better, as it is always good to know where we stand.

I am well aware of the responsibilities that you have and respect them more than perhaps you think I do. But I do believe me.

I am amtyping this letter myself on a free typewriter so excuse any mistakes as it will make it much more personal when I do it myself and you will also know for sure by this that I am not as smart as people think I am. I was glad to read in your letter that you are a Mole Hill Man [this was comedian Fred Allen's self-characterization as a man who could always make the proverbial mountain out of a molehill], this makes for good stock as it does mean your a man from the Farm also, and perhaps you know how to milk a cow or perhaps even a few goats. Brother Bullock has been snowing me for some time that you are from the Country Money Country that is. I am glad to hear that the Meeting last Week came off with a great Snowjob and a good many of the talks will bring good results I am sure.

Enclosed is a new snowcard wich must be signed by either Bullock, Mareck [*sic*] or Colonel Howard Letts, if neither of these snowers will sign the Card it will be okay to have Sagebrush [Bob] Yorke [RCA's current a&r head] sign it as he is One of the old line POTENTETE* Snowers in Good standing.

This is about all the news and I say it again it was good of you to write.

Take care and my best to all the SNOWERS

Once again Colonel feels let down not so much by the content of Elvis' new movie, *Follow That Dream* (which in fact was dear to Colonel's heart with its disingenuous country-boy humor and a broad comic performance by Elvis that might very well have suggested new possibilities), but by the manner of its promotion, or lack thereof. Once again, just as with *Flaming Star,* the studio's inability to settle on a title for Colonel to promote and the public to grow familiar with nettled him — well, let Colonel Parker speak for himself in a straight-ahead letter to Abe Lastfogel. This is business — but it also touches on something along the lines of professional pride. ∎

"There always seems to be the attitude in some quarters that it is a Presley picture — just advertise it and they will all come flying in. This is not true"

Mr. Abe Lastfogel   August 9, 1962
William Morris Agency, Inc.
151 El Camino
Beverly Hills, Calif.

Dear Abe:

I am sure you recall several months ago and also last year that I called your attention to my feelings when The Mirisch Co. and United Artists decided to change the picture "PIONEER GO HOME" to "FOLLOW THAT DREAM". I objected to this to the fullest as far as my personal feelings and thoughts were concerned. I know they had no official standing as we do not have any rights to advise the studio what they should or should not do with a title, but having been in show business for a few years myself it seemed like a decision made somehow by people without checking into the damage a decision like this could do. Having promoted for more than a year the title "PIONEER GO HOME" with all our promotion outlets, fan clubs, trade papers, etc., also during location, and the book which was entitled "PIONEER GO HOME", it never has and never will make sense to me. I cannot use the wording, "I could be wrong", because I made these statements a long time before the picture was released.

Second, after giving as much as possible of my experience in the past in booking the Elvis Presley type of picture, the tie-in promotion, etc., this also was to my thinking handled entirely away from the best setup to promote and exploit a Presley picture. I am sure that United Artists and The Mirisch Co. are intelligent and know what they are doing and have done in the past with their pictures, but this is a different production and a different type of audience and must be exploited as such. Also, there always seems to be the attitude in some quarters that it is a Presley picture — just advertise it and they will all come flying in. This is not true. A picture must be sold first to fill the house and second for the customers to go out and talk about it. If this is not done even a good picture sometimes falls by the wayside.

"FOLLOW THAT DREAM" is a fine family picture. The comments we have received from the fans have been very favorable, but there are many complaints that the bookings were handled in such a way that in many locations the picture was gone before anyone realized it had been there. Also, the spot booking created the feeling that the picture was in it's second or third run when actually it is the first. Maybe I am wrong about this but the box office receipts surely do not back up this type of thinking. I feel that the picture could have done from half a million to a million dollars more domestic gross already if there had been saturation booking with the full impact in it's entirety exploited at the same time. I understand that 400 or 500 small communities make an impressive booking sheet but if the picture does big in Boaz, Alabama it has no effect on what it will do at the Astor in New York unless advertised and exploited to the fullest at the same time.

As we share in the proceeds of the picture this of course deprives us also of a fair chance to make some extra money if the proper presentation and selling job is not coordinated into the product. I feel sure that [Elvis' immediate Mirisch Company follow-up] "KID GALAHAD" will make a better showing as it does appear that they have taken a new approach in the selling and booking of this picture according to early reports.

I am not complaining but when Mr. Presley is on time, doing his job to the best of his ability, does not have any personal delays in making the picture, and does not contribute to any delays in making the picture, we feel that we are entitled to the best job in selling the product although we have no control over how this is done. I have always been willing to help with advice and information from past experiences. The track record is there. You have a file as thick as a bees nest to prove I am not trying to change horses in the middle of the stream. I advised all parties concerned way in advance on "FOLLOW THAT DREAM" or "PIONEER GO HOME" or whichever it may have been called, how to the best of our knowledge to sell this picture. I sincerely hope that the booking arrangement percentages, etc. with "KID GALAHAD" will be of a nature profiting the box office value of Elvis Presley so we can all benefit properly and not have big grosses but no returns.

Sincerely,
The Colonel

1963

C olonel could not have been more pleased. Hal Wallis had at last come around to the idea Colonel had been pitching to him for the past two years: to place Elvis in the rough-and-ready world of the carnival, the perfect setting for him to deliver the kind of freewheeling, action-packed performance they all knew he was capable of. The film would be called *Roustabout,* it would shine a bright light on the romance of carnival life, and Hal Wallis described the character Elvis would be playing as a "rough, tough, hard-hitting guy."

Colonel threw himself into the project from the moment that Wallis first committed himself to it in mid-1963. As Technical Adviser, which brought him an additional $25,000, on top of $45,000 in bonus payments to be split equally between Elvis and himself, he bombarded Wallis with ideas, though I must admit I'm puzzled by the way in which he suggests to Wallis in this letter that he just might think about peddling those ideas elsewhere — well, maybe we should just read this as one more example of his penchant for teasing Wallis, and Wallis' willingness to take it.

Subsequent correspondence reveals two things: first, his unquestionable enthusiasm for the project, but his equally unquestionable limitations as a scenarist. At times he seems to be unable to stop himself in his pitch — was he selling Tampa, his adoptive hometown? Or was it the romance of the "Gasparillan pirates"? Or was he simply selling himself? But he never wavered in his belief that situating the story within the world of Royal American Shows, the biggest of all the traveling carnivals and the birthplace of his own start in show business, was the key to the movie's authenticity — and, not coincidentally, that he was the only one who could provide the necessary link to his former bosses, the Sedlmayr family.

He carefully scrutinized the script as it developed, coming up with one suggestion after another, from toning down some of the more highfalutin language to injecting notes of actual "business" derived from his own observations and experience. In his communications with Wallis, he was always careful to stress that he would never be party to a picture that in any way denigrated the carnival world; it was a way of life in which all of its participants, including himself, took real, and justifiable, pride.

As it turned out, the finished product, which failed to utilize any of the suggested Tampa locations or take advantage of Colonel's Royal American connections, was something of a disappointment to everyone, but most of all to Colonel, as it almost inevitably would have to have been. Many years later I sent Colonel a copy of *Rain or Shine*, a 1930 film in which a young woman inherits her father's struggling traveling circus, which I thought Colonel might enjoy — but he would have none of it. "The circus presentation is presented as a movie," he wrote to me, "but not as a real tent circus really is or was. But when it is entertainment on film, that's what it is all about anyway." And the star, Louise Fazenda, he reminded me (well, I hadn't actually known), "was married to Mr. Wallis." ■

"There are many aspects that could be worked out to tie in a sensible and authentic story…rather than something with a phoney presentation"

Mr. Hal Wallis   February 27, 1963
515 S. Mapleton Drive
Beverly Hills, Calif.

Dear Colonel:

While you are resting at home I thought you might be interested in looking over the Tampa Tribune with the special spread of the annual Gasparilla invasion of the pirates in Tampa [which came complete with "a pirate ship sailing up into the Bay, pirates in regular pirate costumes, shooting and firing, and beautiful girls"] during the Florida State Fair which is held annually around the first week in February. I attended this Gasparilla celebration for ten to twelve years when I was working on the Royal American Shows which winter quarters at Tampa and is also the largest outdoor carnival in the country today, traveling to the big fairs and the Canadian fair circuit, returning in the fall to Florida to prepare for the Florida State Fair and the Gasparilla carnival.

You may wish to think along the lines of tieing this in as a climax in the event you desire to work out something in connection with The Roustabout, starting off with the gilly show, which is of course a reproduction of a big carnival but actually a carnival of a smaller nature and poor and struggling to exist, before leading into the mammoth carnival. There are many aspects that could be worked out to tie in a sensible and authentic story, which I discussed with you several times, rather than something with a phoney presentation and glamorous to the extend where it looks only ridiculous. . . .

I of course will be glad to sit down with Joe [Wallis' business partner, Joe Hazen] and you if you are interested in discussing the possibility of coordinating this to good advantage for all of us financially and otherwise. I do feel that the Paramount Company should contribute something towards making a more lucrative deal as I am to be involved in helping with whatever little I know trying to make this most commercially successful. I have the idea and I know I could sell it somewhere to good advantage but as I told you, you have the first lick if you desire to go into it. I also have the other idea regarding the personal appearance type picture, so should you have something you think is more advantageous in mind and feel more confidence in I would of course appreciate your advising me to peddly [*sic*] my wares regarding these ideas elsewhere. This I wouldn't do until you say the word.

I don't think we should wait too long as it takes a tremendous amount of preparation and advance work such as scouting the proper locations and making the appropriate tie in's with the carnival and the fair people and city officials, etc., to get the most cooperation. I feel that if properly handled and approached with an open mind this carnival picture could very well be shot completely on location in Tampa and surrounding areas involving and incorporating the entire Gasparilla situation if available . . . and thinking in terms of shooting black and white at the start with a poor aspect of the carnival leading into perhaps a couple of reels of colorful ending bringing the story to a successful conclusion with the finale at the Gasparilla Carnival, which is beyond words.

I feel sure that the Chamber of Commerce in Tampa or the Gasparilla Association would have some colorful film that was taken in the past to look at. So take this for whatever you think it is worth. Having two more motion pictures to do I am sure you will want them to be top notch.

Hope you are feeling better.

Sincerely,
The Colonel

t's the same old problem. It is no wonder that there should have been so much resentment of Colonel among Elvis' crew. From Colonel's point of view it was almost inconceivable that boys from such "good homes" (and here he must have been thinking particularly of Alan Fortas, a special favorite, whose uncle Abe was a confidant of LBJ's and in just two years would be elevated to the Supreme Court), would be so heedless not just of their responsibilities but of basic rules of cleanliness. This was something that couldn't help but offend Colonel, who from early childhood was fastidious to the point of obsession about matters of personal hygiene. It should be noted, though, that Fortas remained close to Colonel until his early death, and Joe Esposito, too, would become an admirer as time went by — at least up to a point. ∎

"There seems to be some reluctance on someone's part to take a stand and stand up for what is right or wrong"

To: Joe Esposito & Alan Fortas   March 7, 1963
From: The Colonel

Dear Joe & Alan:

I am sure that you both will take this letter with the honest acceptance that it is for the interest of Elvis Presley and all concerned.

On several occasions in the past I had made slight remarks off the cuff why someone didn't take enough interest in at least keeping the small kitchen and refrigerator in a healthy and clean condition. This, it seems to me, is a small task for anyone to do who at the same time is getting paid to do these things.

Today, as much as I hate to bring this up, was most disgusting when the refrigerator was opened by the Chief [Ray Sitton] and I saw the conglomeration and collection of good food going to waste, carelessly purchased with no thought in mind of cleaning up food still on hand before purchasing a new supply, such as ham, cheese, baloney, sausage, hot dogs, etc., collected in such fashion that can only lead somehow to spoiled food and perhaps ptomaine poison for someone if not careful.

I am not sure who is responsible for supervising such unnecessary and disgusting neglect of Mr. Presley's money and welfare. I know that if anyone working for me in my situation felt that way by being so neglectful and careless they most likely would have quit on their own rather than have it on their conscience that perhaps they are just along for the ride and what they can get out of it without doing anything for it.

I am well aware that this is none of my business, but I am also aware that it is my business if I make it mine that I cannot sit by and see Elvis Presley's interests and considerations in trying to be a good Joe for all you guys taken advantage of in such a manner. I am also well acquainted with the fact that this is very annoying to Elvis but there isn't much he can do about it except one of these days blow his top and clean out the whole works, for which I wouldn't blame him as I would have done it a long time ago if anyone was so neglectful with my earnings and money when there is no need for it. With so many people starving and looking for work in these times it is a disgrace beyond words to have to see something like this happening.

There seems to be some reluctance on someone's part to take a stand and stand up for what is right or wrong. I don't think that Elvis Presley will ever protect anyone that he knows is not doing the right thing for him, especially when he is paying the bill.

If this letter is somehow annoying to both of you it is meant to be as perhaps knowing that both of you are capable of doing a good job it may very well give a new light on the responsibilities that you have towards looking after Elvis Presley's interests, for which you are being well compensated. Knowing both of you I feel sure that you will take immediate steps to remedy this disgusting situation. . . .

I don't think there is anyone connected with Elvis that if they make up their mind to do a good job they can't do it, but somehow without the proper direction they don't do it. I don't mean to be obnoxious and a sore head but all those responsible for this situation are more or less very fortunate that my organization is not in charge of this or they would be looking somewhere else or at least improve the situation immediately.

It is unfortunate that I have to bring this to your attention. Tax matters, deductions, what you can and cannot deduct, are no excuse for sloppiness and irresponsibility. Both of you know much better than that as you came from good homes and I am sure it would not be allowed to happen if you were at your own house, even without being paid to keep it from happening.

No hard feelings. Yours for better responsibility towards the man who pays the bills.

The Colonel

'm not sure when exactly this letter from Vernon Presley to Joe Esposito was written — perhaps as early as November 1960 when Alan Fortas formally rejoined the group to drive out to California because he wanted to meet Tuesday Weld, Elvis' costar in *Wild in the Country*. Or it may have been written around the same time as Colonel's letter above. In any case I'm sure both subject and tone sound familiar by now and give a pretty good indication of why Vernon and Colonel were so often linked in the "Memphis Mafia's" minds. ■

"So far, we don't seem to be getting through to you"

Dear Joe,

I checked with [Elvis' accountant] Mr. Fisher on the records that you supposedly have been keeping and I find that you are not doing your job as you are suppose to do, which was surprising to me since we have gone over this thing so many times with you trying to explain exactly how the records must be kept. So far, we don't seem to be getting through to you. Of course, I am not your boss, I am only acting in interest of my son, Elvis, who you are working for. According to the rules and regulations of the Internal Revenue Dept. we must have complete records of all expenses for traveling and otherwise, and to do this every penny which is spent by check or cash we must have receipts showing exactly what the money was spent for.

The cash that Elvis spends for his own self is his own business, which I am not talking about. I am speaking of the expenses that you, Alan, or any of the boys who work for Elvis handle. As far as writing a check to cash for expenses it is perfectly alright if you want to handle it that way, but we must have receipts marked, paid in cash for every dime of expense money that goes through your hands or any of the boys hands. Also all of these receipts must be kept daily and mailed to me or Mr. Fisher once a week.

As far as any bills personally made by any of the boys, they are to be paid directly out of their pockets and not charged to Elvis' bill whatsoever. Such as cleaning or anything personal of their own. It is to much of a problem to have to take it out of their checks.

I think if you will try to handle this thing this way that you will find it much easier to keep up with. If this seems to be to much for you to do, Joe, I think it would be the right thing for you to go to Elvis and tell him that you are unable to handle the job. If this is not kept exactly as I have asked you to do I know that Elvis is going to take the matter into his own hands and probably replace some of you guys. After all you are getting paid to do a job, so far your work has not been satisfactory.

I think you should keep your records up to date, daily, Sunday through Saturday night. Start a new week with Sunday and mail each week to me on Sunday and I will receive them Monday.

Joe, I hope you don't think that I am just trying to be hard. I am only trying to point out the things that <u>must</u> be done. I am quite certain that Elvis will go along with me on this.

Now, lets try and see how this works out. If this can't be done, Joe I will do everything in my power to work through Elvis to try to replace you with someone who can do this job. As I said before, this is a <u>must</u>.

That's about all I have to say, except that I hope to get a report from you real soon and every week thereafter.

Sincerely,
Vernon

Colonel kept a whole "binder" of letters like the one that follows, his widow, Loanne, told me, beginning early on and continuing with increasing desperation to the very end. There's no point in going into detail — this one pretty much says it all. And it explains in the most succinct terms the entire basis for Colonel and Vernon's alliance. By the early 1970s they were at their wits' end as to how to control Elvis' spending and — hard as it may be to believe, given the astronomical amounts of money that Elvis made every year — simply how to be sure Elvis could pay his everyday bills. Vernon wrote a self-typed rough draft of this letter, which much like Colonel's far more voluminous self-typed correspondence betrays some of the limitations of each man's formal education. (It doesn't really matter, but I'm not sure that Vernon's figures are correct. According to Elvis' accountants, he made $902,000 from movies in 1962, $775,000 from music and recording. He paid more than $800,000 in taxes.) ■

"I started buying $5,000.00 a month in tax free bonds"

COL. THOMAS A. PARKER   July 7, 1963
PARAMOUNT STUDIOS
HOLLYWOOD 38, CALIFORNIA

Dear Col:

Just a line to let you know how things are. I know it is not your problem. I just wanted you know now since our talk we had in Hawaii about buying tax free bonds for Elvis. When I returned home in May 1962 I started buying $5,000.00 a month in tax free bonds through the Trust Department of the National Bank of Commerce. By the first of 1963 I had $50,000.00 in bonds, also $28,000.00 in a Savings account. Also Elvis had five $10,000.00 E Bonds plus the savings account in Nashville.

Now because the cost of his whole operation is more greater than his income after Taxes I had to borrow $50,000.00 from the Trust Department. Also borrowed $28,000.00 from the savings account, Also $16,000.00 from the E Bonds making a total of $94,000.00 borrowed in June and July of 1963

Also, we are still overdrawn $47,000.00 from the Checking account. Now I am going to borrow from the Savings account in Nashville. Now this is bad. For instance, Elvis' net income for 1962 was $900,000.00. Now after taxes he had around $120,000.00. His payroll alone runs $93,000.00 a year and not more than half of that can be deducted from taxes. By the 15th of July we will need around $150,000.00.

Colonel when I see you I can explain details.

Sincerely,
Vernon Presley

1964–1965

About as succinct an expression of Colonel's feelings of genuine affection for Hal Wallis as you could get. Many have portrayed his contentious contractual battles with Wallis over the years as evidence of personal hostility (I plead guilty), but in fact the two seem to have established a long-term relationship based, I think, on more than just mutual respect. Colonel did not hand out expressions of love very easily, and I have no doubt that he meant it here, nor do I doubt that it was reciprocated, if in a somewhat bemused way — though the same cannot be said in any sense of Wallis' business partner, Joe Hazen. ■

"THE ONLY GIFT I CAN GIVE YOU . . . IS MY SINCERE FRIENDSHIP"

DAY LETTER PAID

MR. HAL WALLIS   Sept. 14, 1964
PARAMOUNT STUDIOS
5451 MARATHON ST.
HOLLYWOOD, CAL.

DEAR COLONEL HAL:
    HAPPY BIRTHDAY. IF I WAS A COOK I WOULD BAKE YOU A CAKE. THE ONLY GIFT I CAN GIVE YOU FOR YOUR BIRTHDAY IS MY SINCERE FRIENDSHIP AND AS YOU KNOW THERE IS NO MONEY INVOLVED IN FRIENDSHIP. I HOPE YOU ENJOY THE GIFT.
    LOVE FROM BOTH OF US.

                    MARIE & THE COLONEL

By 1965 Elvis and Colonel were stuck, if for somewhat different reasons. This is not the time or place to go into all the whys and wherefores, but suffice it to say that Elvis no longer had any real interest in making movies ("It was work. It was a job. I had to be there at a certain time in the morning and work a certain amount of hours, and that's exactly how I treated it"), nor, for that matter, in making music. His entire focus at this point was on pursuing the spiritual studies that he had initiated with the arrival of Larry Geller, a hairdresser with a passion for New Age religion, in the spring of 1964. To that end his primary motivation seems to have become to make as much money as possible in the shortest period of time in order to be free to pursue his studies. (For a fuller account, read "The Magician" in the biographical account at the front.)

Whether for that reason, or for reasons of his own (Was he simply exhausted? This was the time, remember, that Colonel essentially moved to Palm Springs, where he enjoyed what anyone else would have called semiretirement), Colonel appears for the moment to have switched gears and devoted himself not to seeking a creative challenge for his artist but to further perfecting the art of the deal. By the end of 1964 he had completed negotiations for eight pictures scheduled over the next three years at guaranteed salaries adding up to $5,350,000, with in most cases 50 percent participation in the profits.

One result of the exorbitant sums that Colonel extracted from the studios was that there was little left over for production costs, or even other actors' salaries. (The one exception, at least in terms of production, was *Viva Las Vegas*.) The entirely predictable outcome? Well, that is the reason for this letter. Despite an intellect that could easily have figured out a solution to the problem, Colonel simply could not resign himself to the idea that a movie studio, however strapped it might find itself after his salary negotiations, would lack the wherewithal to construct at least a reasonable simulacrum of the kind of Elvis movie that Colonel had taken to labeling "a happy, funny comedy, family picture." Which makes it all the more ironic that he should be complaining here of a shooting schedule that had been dictated by his own demands for his client.

And just as a postscript: talking camel or no talking camel, *Harum Scarum*, for which Elvis received a salary of $1 million plus profit sharing, was the fortieth-highest-grossing film of the year and quickly earned back its investment. ∎

"It would take a 55th cousin to P.T. Barnum to do a good job"

Mr. Robert M. Weitman   June 18, 1965
[Head of Film Production]
Metro-Goldwyn-Mayer Studios
Culver City, California

Dear Mr. Weitman:

After seeing the current Elvis Presley HARUM SCARUM picture and in line with the regular planning to get the most out of our efforts to help promote pictures from our department, I would like to make the following suggestions if at all possible, and I feel sure that the Producer will be at least interested in my suggestions as they are meant to be helpful and nothing else for all concerned:

1. If at all possible I would appreciate if all parties concerned would take a close look at the finale of the picture as it seems rather hard to me to figure out how Elvis got to Las Vegas immediately following the last production shot before the performance in the Las Vegas night club. If somehow a process shot could be used where at least he would be departing by jet where a voice contact could be made at the airport indicating when Elvis gets back to Las Vegas with all the dancing girls that it sure will be some show.

2. In regard to the selling and advertising of this picture it would be very wise to think in terms of selling it as a happy, funny comedy, family picture with tremendous stress that it is not to be confused with a dramatic story of any sort but is strictly good, slapstick, family fun. This may very well help to establish the fact that everyone in the picture is not trying to make an artistic presentation knowingly, but we may receive some credit along the line that they all did a tremendous job of underplaying. This could establish it as being a good comedy that everybody worked hard to leave everybody laughing and happy.

I can very well see that the picture could be tightened up some and I am sure the Producer has plans along that line. I am merely stating the facts so as to help sell it and what we can do to the best of our ability, and this is the only way I can see where I can be of any help in selling it. Even then it would take a 55th cousin to P.T. Barnum to do a good job, but I feel that we must do everything possible to get the most out of the promotion and advertising since this is one of our prime releases during one of our best times, Thanksgiving, to get the money. I would not advise experimenting with this picture by trying to stretch it over a period for a long run. In short, book it fast, get the money, and try again.

It may very well do just as well as [Elvis' 1964 MGM release] KISSIN' COUSINS or a little better if everyone would just take a happy medium approach and sell it along those lines. If any advertising pertaining to this picture is geared along artistic lines dramatizing the story I feel it would bog down financially at the box office; it has a great deal of possibility selling it as a fun picture for the children.

The music is great if it is played up along the lines I have explained. I again must say these are my personal opinions to help sell the picture to the best advantage. If I am wrong perhaps you can try both mediums. I am sure everyone tried their best but it is very important that we do not experiment with Mr. Presley's track record. His current Allied Artists release, TICKLE ME, may be very well worth-while for some of the Sales Department to take a good look at how to sell this type of fun picture as these folks are doing a good job and we are pitching in as usual and so far the box office has been very healthy.

As an afterthought, I feel that on any Presley picture a little more time should be allowed to do a better job. To cram this type of picture into a 15 or 18 day schedule with the principal being in practically every scene does not lend itself to good presentation. There are some pictures such as KISSIN' COUSINS that are of a flavor that one can cover up many shortcomings in acting and presentation, but it is very hard to do in the type of picture like HARUM SCARUM no matter how hard everyone tries. The studio has two more Elvis Presley commitments and I am sure the company will want to get the most out of them, just as much as we do, just as much as any producer or director would want. Enough said.

Respectfully,
The Colonel

[Ccs to many MGM executives]

....

On further thought, just one month later, Colonel came up with a "gimmick" that he suggested (Was he serious? I'll let you be the judge) might help save an otherwise hopeless picture.

....

"Put . . . in a talking camel all through the picture as a narrator in the desert"

Mr. Robert H. O'Brien   July 16, 1965
[MGM President]
Metro-Goldwyn-Mayer Inc.
1540 Broadway
New York, N.Y.

Dear Mr. O'Brien:

Enclosed is a clipping from today's Los Angeles Times on TICKLE ME for Elvis. I thought you would want to show this around to your boys and perhaps they can get some idea on the treatment that is so important when making a Presley picture for the fans, to keep it light and happy and not in an unsaleable serious vein, but making a good musical or light comedy.

It is very important, as I have said until I am blue in the face, to get a good director that understands this type of artist and get the most out of a story with little incidents that are so easily passed over if one does not understand this type of product. I am personally very much upset commercialwise, that unless something is done to take away the flavor of trying to make people think HARUM SCARUM is a serious picture that the investment and all the work involved could be wasted.

The picture could very well be put over best by treating it completely as a farce and comedy. There are some anecdotes that could be injected to make it worth-while to promote but they must be done with intent and interest by all concerned to improve the situation. For instance, it wouldn't cost a great deal of money to research the idea of putting in a talking camel all through the picture as a narrator in the desert, or two camels talking to each other where they converse in camel language or on title strips, that it is unbelievable what has happened to our desert in the modern age; it isn't like the good old days.

That may sound farfetched to you but the picture is also farfetched and it needs something farfetched to make it at least possible as a good family comedy picture. I can't believe that this problem will be shoved under the rug as the results would not be very complimentary and definitely very unprofitable for the company. If I am wrong there is room for improvement. I have tried, talked, and persuaded in my last letter to explain my thoughts.

It is very important that you and your associates take a very good look towards the responsibility of coming up with something worthwhile for the next two pictures to at least protect your investment. There is no room for panic. There is no reason to be despondent except if you do not adhere to your slogan which has been so well publicized in the last year, "M.G.M. is on the move."

Respectfully, faithfully, and for the good of the company,

The Colonel

P.S: I feel sure that the producer and anyone concerned with this picture has the same interest at heart. I cannot believe that anyone connected with this picture for any reason would not want to explore the best opportunity to save all these turkeys for Thanksgiving from being eaten by that tiger we have been advertising.

I know you will be happy to know that Allied Artists [the studio that produced *Tickle Me*] is happy and they can only be happy because they must be getting money.

cc: [This time the many ccs include Abe Lastfogel and Vernon Presley]

Despite not having been able to get his artist into the recording studio for nearly a year and a half now, and despite an alarming dip in record sales (40 percent fewer sales since 1960), and his artist's apparent indifference to his contractual obligations, Colonel was determined to keep up a good front, and toward that end had already begun talks with RCA about a new, improved contract for his artist. Bravado is as bravado does, but Colonel must have given some thought to just how to respond to RCA General Manager George Marek's generous offer of anything that he would like from the RCA warehouse as a birthday gift. It is impossible to miss the delight he still takes in messing with the bureaucrats. (Do I need to point out, there was no such thing as a personal computer at this time? Mainframes were *expensive*.) ∎

"This is better than my million feather deal for TICKLE ME"

Mr. George R. Marek   June 30, 1965
RCA Victor Record Division
155 East 24th Street
New York, N. Y.

Dear George:

What a delightful surprise to find your birthday telegram under my door in Palm Springs. Correction please, Marie found it as I didn't get to go to Palm Springs due to the fact that I had to stay at the studio to help expedite more sales on CRYING IN THE CHAPEL, SUCH AN EASY QUESTION, and the TICKLE ME EP to help the Company make a larger profit this year in our Department than it did last year. I am of course speaking of the Presley Division of RCA Victor. Through the great efforts of the entire staff this of course is always possible.

After carefully studying your kind telegram and checking over everything that you would want us to have that would do us the most good, I would like to have your advice. I am somewhat in a quandary whether I should take your telegram to [RCA West Coast executive] Uncle John West in this territory and order a Spectra 70 computer or one of the outdated Model 501's, which are so ably illustrated in the Electronic Age. I assume that you want me to have the best, since you didn't specify in your telegram that there was any restriction on what I selected. I can only assume that you want me to go first class.

I have never been so fortunate to receive on my birthday a telegram where I could go out and select as a present a computer. I am so overwhelmed that I have already made up my mind that I will pay out of my own pocket for any demonstrations necessary for me to learn to operate it. I am only sorry that you beat John West out with this offer as he has been constantly asking me if there is something the Company could do for me, but you are the first one to come up with this kind of offer.

If you have any other suggestions for other models more advanced please let me know as I don't want to make this selection hastily. Your suggestion to wait until September has completely befuddled, befogged, and bewildered me as I do not know whether you mean this to be in addition to the selection of a computer.

Please feel free to call me collect with the name and address and phone number of the right person to contact for the wonderful gift. I am deeply grateful. This is better than color television.

Respectfully,
Your Obedient Receiver,
The Colonel

PS: This is better than my million feather deal for TICKLE ME now in release throughout the country helping to sell a lot of records. I am ever so grateful for your generosity.

When I went to the Open House at the distributor last week where I received a delightful free dinner, I found a beautiful color television set so much better than anything I have seen. When I asked for delivery they said it would be several months. I surely hope it won't take more than 10 days for me to get my computer.

Cc [to RCA executives]: Mr. Frank M. Folsom, Mr. Charles M. Odorizzi, Mr. John K. West, Mr. Harry E. Jenkins

Elvis in costume for *Frankie and Johnny* with his cousin Billy Smith on Colonel's knee, spring 1965. *Courtesy of the Graceland Archives*

The long-delayed (and even longer-anticipated) meeting between Elvis and the Beatles has taken on an outsize role in Elvis and Beatles mythology. The meeting itself, on August 27, 1965, was pretty perfunctory (maybe awkward would be the better word), but the negotiations could fill a book, and once again, if Colonel's aim was to bring Beatles manager Brian Epstein into the Snowman fold, it should be clear from this that he succeeded. ■

"I figured this assignment would throw anyone but you"

Mr. Brian Epstein   September 10, 1965
Hills House
9 Stafford Street
London W1, England

Dear Colonel Epstein:

Thank you for your nice letter. It was good of you to write. You owe me no thanks for friends don't have to thank each other.

Chris Hutchins [*New Musical Express* reporter, and friend to both the Beatles and Colonel] will relay to you the following. He said you have asked what we would like to have from the boys and yourself. Not being selfish and to make it easy I suggest a couple of midget ponies, but they must be real small. I figured this assignment would throw anyone but you. I wish I could have given Chris a tougher assignment relay. We mean live ponies of course, about 26 inches high, but not over 30, so we can carry them in our trunk and perhaps to Las Vegas to play roulette to keep the dealer looking at the ponies while we pick up the chips.

Regards from all of us.

                      Sincerely,
                      The Colonel

1966–1967

You may have noticed a drop-off in quantity, and I would say quality, too, in Colonel's correspondence over the last couple of years. I have no grand theories. Was his heart no longer in it? I don't think that was it. Maybe the business had just become more defined — at least his business had — and he was carrying out his negotiations at this point almost by rote. Certainly he missed some of his old buddies and fellow kidders like Buddy Adler and Bill Bullock, many of whom had retired or been retired; maybe he just missed the grand battles of the past. In any case his epistolary exchanges were met as often as not with marshmallow bureaucratic replies, and it seems sometimes like he is rehashing old arguments just for the sake of keeping his hand in the game.

Colonel completed negotiations for a new contract with RCA in the fall of 1965 and joined the company in making an announcement early the next year. It seems doubtful that any other manager, faced with such a marked decline in his artist's sales, could have sought, let alone achieved, such a dramatic improvement in his artist's financial fortunes, but RCA put their full faith in Elvis and the Colonel, as they extended the present contract through 1972, with an additional two-year option, while at the same time raising Elvis' guaranteed annual payments from $200,000 a year to $300,000. (There was currently about $1 million owed in back royalties, so the total would come to $2.1 million in guaranteed payments over the next seven years, with only $1.1 million left to be recouped.) In addition, there were various bonus arrangements adding up to something like $400,000, along with further benefits for both Elvis and Colonel.

But if the financial benefits were obvious, there was, from Colonel's point of view, even greater reason for optimism — and a potentially greater payoff to come. By drawing Elvis into a shared mood of celebration (just as in the old days with lots of veiled references and inside jokes) and then, against all precedent, going so far as to share this sense of jubilation with Elvis' guys, Colonel seemed to be doing everything he could to ensure Elvis' implicit agreement to the *terms* of the new contract. Which included, as RCA's Harry Jenkins wrote, recording "two good new singles, possibly more impoi tant one new Christmas single, [and] a complete brand-new religious album." (Remember, Elvis had not at this point entered the recording studio to make a commercial record since January 1964.) And so, without anyone even knowing it, least of all the Colonel (though his belief in his artist never dimmed), the stage was set for Elvis' second artistic renaissance. ∎

"As soon as we are protected contract-wise I will give you the rest of the cake on the new deal. You already have the icing"

Dear Elvis: January 18, 1966

It was nice talking to you last night. . . .

As soon as we are protected contract-wise I will give you the rest of the cake on the new deal. You already have the icing.

Tell your Dad that if anyone contacts him again regarding me selling my contract to refer them to me at the office as I would like to know who is behind the scenes. [There was much talk at this time, not all of it unsubstantiated, about Colonel's openness to the possibility of selling Elvis' contract.] I don't even know how much I should charge as there must be enough for both of us so we both can retire, and what good would it be to buy a deal like that if you and I were not in it?

I called Freddy Bienstock today and told him to get you a good title song on JIM DANDY [Colonel's proposed title for Elvis' next film, which ended up being called *Spinout*] and some fast numbers. He said he was a better Jim Dandy than anybody and I said he'd better come up with a hit tune then.

I will be in Palm Springs over the weekend taking my steam baths and reminiscing of days gone by when we recorded BRITCHES [an embarrassingly bad song that was dropped from *Flaming Star*]. I know this sounds exciting to you.

Best to all of you.

Sincerely,
The Colonel

And when Colonel renegotiated the deal yet again, this time with a new definition of much of his and Elvis' business arrangement as a "joint venture," in which all payments beyond the contractual guarantee would be split 50-50 (see biographical text for elaboration), Elvis sent him a telegram of unfeigned, if deflectional, congratulations, as grateful in its own way (but in a very different way) as the telegram he sent to Colonel in November 1955 after the original RCA deal had gone through. ■

"The Greatest Snowman on Earth"

MEMPHIS TENN   JAN 23, 1967
COLONEL THOMAS A PARKER
MGM STUDIOS CULVER CITY CALIF

DEAR COLONEL. THE GREATEST SNOWMAN ON EARTH HAS CAUSED ANOTHER STORM. LOOKING FORWARD TO ANOTHER GREAT FORECAST FROM YOU RESPECTFULLY

                         ELVIS

1968-1969

Even long after it had to have become clear that there wasn't any point, Colonel couldn't stop trying. Here, once again, he expresses his frustration with the quality, and repetitiveness, of both the movies and the movie roles. Once again he suggests "gimmicks" to make the picture better, including the use of "a great many of the old time talents who carry their wardrobe in hat boxes or duffel bags." But once again his tone seems off, almost wistful, from a man who always prided himself on looking ahead and telling the truth (as in realpolitik), wherever that truth might lead.

The movie, incidentally, was released later in the year as *The Trouble with Girls* and told the story of a traveling Chautauqua company's arrival in a small Iowa town in 1927, with Elvis playing the company's manager. Like *Roustabout,* this was a subject dear to Colonel's heart. A Chautauqua show, a more elevated take on the carnival experience, combined elements of entertainment, education, and lectures on self-improvement, and it has sometimes been suggested that during his first visit to America in 1926–27 a seventeen- or eighteen-year-old Dries van Kuijk traveled briefly with a Chautauqua company. Whether or not he did, it was certainly a way of life with which he was familiar and to which he had always been drawn. The producers don't appear to have paid any attention to Colonel's suggestions — one just wishes, as with *Roustabout,* that he could have found a way to fashion his own lyrical dreamscape of the experience. But, of course, that would have required the services of a screenwriter of sufficient empathy and political sophistication to tailor a screenplay to Colonel's unarticulated dreams and expectations. ∎

"A new image much more acceptable than the regular run of the mill bikini, bathing suit, night club and other current fads which have been in so many Presley pictures"

533

Mr. Clark Ramsay   March 26, 1968
Metro-Goldwyn-Mayer
Culver City, Calif.

Dear Clark:

After our meeting last week I have given some thought to trying to figure out how best to help in the situation of the upcoming production tentatively titled CHATAQUA.

As a suggested title instead of CHATAQUA perhaps the officers will like ONE NIGHT STAND. BONNIE & CLYDE has had tremendous success and world-wide acceptance not only as a profitable picture but in reaction to the period type of clothing worn and the settings of that era. The Chataqua era is even further back than that so it would be negligent on my part not to point out that it would be much more valuable for the picture to go back into the clothing and situations then than to try to up-date it to today's clothing fads.

I sincerely believe commercially the value of the period clothing and sets would be a tremendous asset and would be a new image in presenting this type of picture. It may very well hit a new image much more acceptable than the regular run of the mill bikini, bathing suit, night club and other current fads which have been in so many Presley pictures.

Instead of race cars have an old Model T or similar vehicle of that era. Instead of elaborate stage settings and fancy costumes research into the background of the type of clothing worn in those days.

It will also lend itself to using a great many of the old time talents who carry their wardrobe in hat boxes or duffel bags.

Just wanted to let you know that I have given it some thought trying to help. It would be simplifying the entire story and make for a much better production.

> Kindest regards,
> [Signed "Colonel"]
> The Colonel

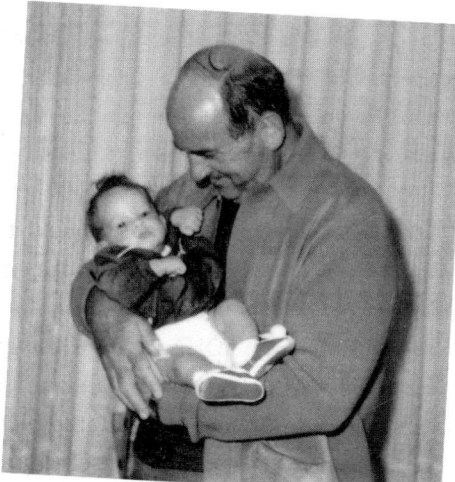

With Lisa Marie
Presley, June 4, 1968.
Courtesy of the
Graceland Archives

The 1968 NBC television special, Elvis' first appearance on television since
1960, was part of an NBC deal for both the show and a movie yet to be
named (it would turn out to be *Change of Habit*, costarring Mary Tyler Moore,
made on a loan-out to Universal Pictures) which between them would bring in
well over $1 million. In addition, the show could only be broadcast three times
after its initial airing (at a cost of $125,000 per broadcast) before ownership
reverted to Elvis and All Star Shows.

It started out, as nearly everyone knows, as a Christmas special, with Elvis
the sole featured performer and the music confined to Christmas themes. This
was Colonel's idea and fit in perfectly with his long-held belief in seasonal entertainment that could be recycled with great success year after year. By the beginning of May, though, Colonel had embraced a very different approach. Alfred di
Scipio, creative director for the show's sponsor, the Singer Company, and NBC
producer Bob Finkel had persuaded him that the show should celebrate Elvis'
entire career, recognizing him "as the initiator of a style of music which has
become an integral part of our contemporary musical culture." Colonel approved
the new format, as per a May 8 memorandum, before the creative team of Steve
Binder and Bones Howe (director and music director) had been hired.

I know, I know, everyone believes that Colonel was the villain in this piece,
that he continued to fight tooth and nail for his original concept of the show right
up to the start of filming — and in some versions of the story, beyond. But that
was not the case. In fact, the only remnant of the original concept that remained

was a commitment on NBC's part to air one Christmas song in the final show. In other words, contrary to popular legend, and even more popular movies, Colonel was not dragged kicking and screaming into the new approach (in fact, he was quite happy with it), and there was never any showdown of any sort with director Steve Binder — at least not until, for whatever reason, Binder left out the one Christmas song that had been filmed for the special, a bluesy version of "Blue Christmas" ("My favorite Christmas song," Elvis announced), in the cut he had put together for all the principals in the Singer, NBC, and Elvis camps. This was when Colonel, as you can see, took extreme umbrage, writing to NBC vice president Tom Sarnoff that he had always taken him to be a man of his word, which Sarnoff proved himself to be.

I don't know about Colonel's description of the gradual chipping away at his thinking. I think he is just playing Sarnoff (though he liked him very much) because there is not a hint of this in any of the extensive documentation of the show's development. Once the new format was decided upon, Colonel encouraged Bob Finkel to get together with Elvis, and Finkel reported back to his various NBC and Singer colleagues that Elvis made the "rather revealing statement . . . that he wants this show to depart completely from the pattern of his motion pictures and from everything else he has done." Several days later it was announced that "Binder-Howe Productions has been confirmed as the production entity," and Steve Binder began the remarkable collaboration with Elvis that resulted in the vibrant, and vibrantly filmed, performances that were the centerpiece of the show.

Two days after the special aired on December 8, Colonel was negotiating a deal for an extended booking at the still-under-construction International Hotel, which would become Las Vegas' largest showroom when it opened in July. ∎

"If the inclusion of one Christmas song poses such a problem as was explained to me last night, for reasons that are hard to understand . . . I suggest we put this show on ice until next summer and do a complete Christmas show for this fall as per our contract"

Mr. Tom Sarnoff   August 21, 1968
National Broadcasting Company
3000 W. Alameda
Burbank, California

Dear Tom:

Last night in the executive screening room at NBC we saw the Elvis Presley Special. With me were Mr. Abe Lastfogel of the William Morris Agency, Mr. Harry Jenkins, Mr. George Parkhill, Mr. Bob Jones and Mr. Grelun Landon of RCA Records and Mr. Tom Diskin. Also present were Mr. Bob Finkel, Mr. Steve Binder, and some other people.

After the screening I had the following discussion with Mr. Finkel and Mr. Binder. I strongly voiced my concern that the Christmas song, BLUE CHRISTMAS, was left out of the show and I strongly insisted that it be put back, on my behalf and also Elvis Presley's. Knowing you were on vacation this is the best I could do at the present.

If you remember, the last time I visited your office I explained to you that the Christmas song, I'LL BE HOME FOR CHRISTMAS, had been deleted from the program. You promised that a Christmas song would be included in the program. I of course took your word for it. I will appreciate your correcting this first of all.

When the deal was consummated it was to be for a Christmas show, 12 to 14 Christmas songs, some old and some new. Then when I was approached about going half-and-half due to the tremendous value of some of Elvis' other material I agreed. Later when it was pared down to just one Christmas song I went along with you, but this was the limit. We have done too much tidying up of promotion gimmicks, radio and otherwise, to have our faces seem red by not having at least one Christmas song in a Christmas special.

After you see the show I suggest that you take a close look at the gospel section, as it seems rather lengthly. There also are some tapes from the informal section that, as I recall, were better tapes of Elvis' voice and action than some I saw on the show last night. I could be wrong but I doubt it. At least it is worth checking.

There are also several good songs on tape that are not being used in this show which also could help tighten the program better than such lengthly production numbers.

I would be negligent in my duties as a manager not to bring up these points. The one that I am strongly opposed to and must be corrected, as you are a man of integrity and always keep your word, is the omission of the Christmas song, which must be put back in the show or we all will lose

Colonel and Elvis on the set of the '68 Special, with producer Bob Finkel's birthday gift to Colonel, a portrait of Finkel costumed as Admiral Nelson. *Courtesy of the Graceland Archives*

a tremendous amount of promotion, not only from my company, All Star Shows, but through many other mediums and the following of Presley fans.

If the inclusion of one Christmas song poses such a problem as was explained to me last night, for reasons that are hard to understand when Little Egypt the fan dancer is included in the program, I suggest we put this show on ice until next summer and do a complete Christmas show for this fall as per our contract, for it does call for a Christmas show.

I have discussed this letter at length with Mr. Presley and he is well aware of all its contents and agrees with me fully. Mr. Finkel knows about the Christmas song. I have spoken to him at length about it.

Hope you had a nice vacation and let me know when we can see the show in its complete form with the Christmas song included.

Kindest regards,
The Colonel

P.S. It is very important that Mr. Harry Jenkins receives as soon as possible all the tapes on all the material whether it is in the show or not, as per our agreement, so we can start planning our fall production to help promote this great TV show for all concerned. We can't wait until the last minute as there is a lot of work to be done.

Copies: Mr. Steve Binder, Mr. Bob Finkel, Mr. Abe Lastfogel, Mr. Harry Jenkins [RCA], Mr. Elvis Presley, Mr. Herb Schlosser [NBC]

E lvis' Las Vegas debut was if anything an even greater triumph than the television special and was promoted with unparalleled aplomb, and in an unparalleled manner. It also brought Elvis and Colonel together with a mutual sense of purpose and commitment that they had not shared in a long time. When Colonel came backstage after the first night's performance, they hugged wordlessly but with a degree of emotion that no one in Elvis' entourage had ever seen before. But then it was back to business, as Colonel jauntily presided over a hastily convened press conference, which Elvis took charge of with all of his easygoing charm and charisma on full display. And while he continued to promote the rest of Elvis' booking (and every future booking as well) in the most extravagant fashion imaginable, taking over the International Hotel as if it were an Elvis Outlet, Colonel did not lose sight of his managerial duties either, suggesting to Elvis in the same way, if in a more muted tone than he had in Batesville, Arkansas, many years ago, that he must never lose sight of the fact that it was his audience that should always be his first consideration. ■

"The pressure is getting a little heavy regarding the off-color material"

Elvis:

Before I left I talked to Joe [Esposito], as the pressure is getting a little heavy regarding the off-color material. I am of course speaking mostly in regard to the dinner show when there are a great many children. I can only relate this to you. You are the only one who can change it. But we are getting pressure even from one newspaper and we surely don't want to undo all the good that we have created during the first part of our engagement. . . .

Colonel

1970–1972

H arry Jenkins had been the intermediary between RCA and the Elvis camp (i.e., Colonel) ever since Bill Bullock's formal retirement in 1963. When things started out badly, Bullock had smoothed the way for him, and Colonel had come to have a good deal of affection for his new point of contact, incorporating him into his very small inner circle for as long as Jenkins remained at RCA. But that didn't stop Colonel from having high expectations of Jenkins — or from expressing them. Nor did it inhibit him in the least from objecting — in this case very loudly — to Jenkins modifying, or altering in any way, Colonel's strong ideas when it came to how an album cover should be designed and presented. Album cover design? Was he kidding? Evidently not. Colonel was very certain of his approach, which went back to the direct pitch favored by the carnivals and traveling shows, but more than that, he knew how much could be lost if you ever ceded ground to an individual or entity with whom you were vying for control. The letter, of course, came with the usual quota of ccs to other RCA higher-ups and lower-downs. ∎

"I am almost sure that the advertising agency was working on a margarine ad instead of ours"

Mr. Harry E. Jenkins   June 2, 1970
RCA Record Division
1133 Avenue of the Americas
New York, N.Y.

Dear Harry:

I know you are a busy man. For the past 28 years [far be it from me to quarrel with Colonel, but it's hard to say where this number comes from] we have had a very pleasant relationship with the Art Department

Designing the cover for the soundtrack album of *It Happened at the World's Fair. Courtesy of the Graceland Archives*

on layouts, covers, and single sleeves, and what have you. There never has been a delay.

I will appreciate if you will double check and make sure that we keep operating the same way we have been doing in the past, unless the superior forces decide that we should change and if they wish to change the policy let me know about it so I can start my retirement plan. I am sick and tired going back and forth with layouts on ad's for approval with a deadline and short notices.

I take a great deal of time to prepare album covers for the company with ideas and know what my artist likes and dislikes. We have an agreement that we have final say so on these and I feel as long as we have sales and merchandise on time this policy should not be changed. Unless somebody comes up with a better gimmick I am not interested in experimenting at your expense.

I am not mad but almost disgusted. I am willing to cooperate but it must be mutual. I am almost sure that the advertising agency was working on a margarine ad instead of ours. Since we are doing all the work out here there is no excuse to get confused from up there.

Regards,
[Signed "Colonel"]
The Colonel

Here we see Colonel once again functioning as movie critic, but this time of the performance documentary, *Elvis: That's the Way It Is,* that had been instigated largely by Kirk Kerkorian, who owned the International Hotel and had recently taken over MGM. As I'm sure will not be lost on any reader, this was Colonel's dream, the ultimate synergistic experience. With a $500,000 fee for the film (plus 60 percent of the net profits, and ultimate ownership of the print), Elvis would now be taking home $1 million for his four-week stint at the International in August 1970. Plus, there would be an RCA soundtrack album to come. But pay attention to Colonel's (almost certainly unsolicited) critique for MGM president Jim Aubrey, which once again shows both Colonel's strengths and weaknesses as a critic, his diplomatic skills, and his inability to let go. Most of all, though, I think it shows his and Elvis' unconditional (and uncondescending) commitment to the fans, a commitment that never wavered in principle (if in Elvis' case it sometimes had to be propped up at certain moments of indecision and self-doubt) over the next seven years, which were taken up for the most part with live performance. ∎

"There is no reason to show an abundance of steaks on a truck . . . when perhaps in Dalton, Georgia where the picture may be showing a family saved up money to see the picture and relinquished their hamburger for that night so they could see Elvis"

Mr. James T. Aubrey   September 24, 1970
Metro-Goldwyn-Mayer Studios
Culver City, California

Dear Jim:

It was nice talking to you this morning. As you know, we are endeavoring to do whatever possible to help assist with the promotion, advertising, exploitation, and in general do a top notch cooperative job with all concerned. I am of course also speaking for Mr. Parkhill of RCA Records who has been tremendously responsible for the top cooperation we received in Las Vegas and Phoenix, plus Mr. Harry Jenkins and the President of RCA Records, Mr. Rocco Laginestra, without whose sanction and permission none of this would be possible as far as coordination is concerned with RCA Records.

It is very important, after seeing the rough cut with my staff the other day, that very close scrutiny be given to double checking, and double checking, the preparation and editing of this ELVIS, THAT'S THE WAY IT IS personal appearance film, notwithstanding the extra footage which will be available at a later date for the subject that we discussed previously.

One of the great climaxes we had on our personal appearances was when Elvis sang the last song, CAN'T HELP FALLING IN LOVE WITH YOU, and the curtain came down and he showed himself briefly underneath the curtain, which is the end of a great performance. I believe that anything after that would take away from the climax of the closing of the picture. Although there is some good footage with Elvis at the piano after that this should be injected into the rehearsal portion and some of the repetitious rehearsal portions that are in the picture cut down.

There are definitely too many cut-in's on the songs on stage, which tend to distort the real life performance with a great disadvantage to getting across seeing Elvis as he really is performing on stage.

The part where the gentleman from the International Hotel very emphatically mentions Frank Sinatra and Dean Martin should be completely eliminated as it is not good or fair to compare other top attractions in an unfavorable expression. Every artist has a right to be big in his own way and there should be no comparison by voice or writing to help sell a picture. We must all stand on our own feet. If we can't do that we have no business being in it.

The complete footage with interviews of the fans should be thoroughly checked where it doesn't become monotonous and take away from the performance, without reflecting upon the value of the artistic viewpoint that may be involved.

I do believe, and my staff concurs with me, that there is no reason to show an abundance of steaks on a truck in this picture when perhaps in Dalton, Georgia where the picture may be showing a family saved up money to see the picture and relinquished their hamburger for that night so they could see Elvis. It has no meaning to the value of the promotion of the picture and it is much better to keep the picture down to earth as much as possible. I think the Maitre d' portion should be only once, not twice.

I believe that with the person being interviewed regarding Elvis' motion pictures the slurs on BLUE HAWAII and G.I. BLUES should be completely removed as these were two of the most successful films ever made by Elvis, box office wise and record sales wise, and they do not deserve to be mentioned as just trash in such a way. If so, we had better eliminate the closing song of ELVIS, THAT'S THE WAY IT IS, which was the hit song out of BLUE HAWAII. It is rather hard to believe that we would allow derogatory remarks about BLUE HAWAII but then stick one of the hit songs in our own picture.

Mr. Diskin has already made up a list of some of the suggestions that should be eliminated, such as son of a bitch, which can only antagonize many of our audience. No profanity is needed or necessary in this picture to sell it. I would hate to think that through an oversight this would be left in when it is so obvious that it should come out. I have a reputation of being a pretty good salesman and I agree fully with that, but I can't sell something that I don't believe is right and vulgarity has no place in this picture. The great MGM lion doesn't need it and we surely don't, at least not in a movie. In a night club there are some reasons for it, I guess, but I don't even approve of those.

On the selling of this picture, it should be borne in mind that it should be sold as a personal appearance film with Elvis doing exactly what his fans would like to see him doing. I can see a tremendous value box office wise if this film is not allowed to escape just as another Presley movie. This is a one time opportunity to get the most value by presenting it properly at the right time and in the right place.

May I suggest multiple bookings on a premiere basis in Las Vegas, Phoenix, St. Louis, Detroit, Miami, Tampa, and Mobile, due to the tremendous sellouts we had a week ago in these markets with Elvis being there in person and us plugging it on stage, "Watch for Elvis' full length personal appearance film, coming soon to your local theatres where you again can see Elvis like you saw him tonight."

I have a lot more that I could put down but this should satisfy your curiosity for several weeks and I will get some more information if you need it.

Mr. Denis Sanders [the critically acclaimed director, who had won one Academy Award already and would soon win another] did a tremendous job with great enthusiasm and dedication. We are endeavoring to help put it together on a professional commercial basis, eliminating some of the features that will not contribute to the box office. After the customer has seen the picture the first impression must be that the first full house and from there on there will be word of mouth advertising. If it is good it will do great. If it is not we will all be able to kick ourselves for not doing the most with everything possible before it is too late.

It is to the interest of the studio and all concerned that we see all of the footage shot as there may very well be some interesting stuff that has been overlooked. We do have a definite promise from you and Mr. Solow [MGM producer Herb Solow] that no footage be destroyed before we see everything.

Jim, as you know — Elvis, you and I believed in this idea from the start. I tried to sell the idea for the past ten years but no one would or could see it. We are all grateful for your belief in it.

Sincerely,
[Signed "Col"]
The Colonel

With the success of the initial Las Vegas bookings, Elvis and Colonel were working more closely than they had in years. In the fall of 1970 Colonel initiated two trial tours in preparation for going out on the road full-time in 1971 and 1972. Their close working relationship was not without its problems, though. One can imagine Elvis at thirty-five might have felt crowded by Colonel's overly fussy need to spell everything out, and then spell it out again. Here we see the old problem of "communication" (literally) rearing its head once again, as it will more and more over the next seven years. "TCB," as every Elvis fan surely knows, means "Take Care of Business" or, with a lightning bolt added, "Takin' Care of Business — In a Flash." Not only had Elvis adopted this as his slogan, he had recently started giving out specially designed jewelry conveying the message to the guys — and Colonel is doing his best here, in a loosely self-typed and somewhat transparently lighthearted vein, to hold him to that standard. ∎

"Remember your slogan TCB but it only works if you use it"

Dear Elvis   December 9, 1970

I happened to pass today thru my affiliates. Tried to make contact with you on several occasions. We have messages which invariably wind up with Charlie [Hodge, Elvis' army buddy] calling Palm Springs for me when everyone knew I was calling from the office. I am somehow getting the feeling that you may wind up in the Bahamas [Elvis had gone there the previous year on what turned out to be a disastrous vacation trip] in a few days, if you do tell Howard hello for me. [The elusive Howard Hughes had recently been reported in the newspapers to be visiting the Bahamas himself.] Our field manager Mr. Tom Diskin who communicates to me thru Charlie has also drawn several blanks. I am sure that this can all be cleared up immediately by your advising one of your lieutenants to communicate immediately, however if I see you before you get this letter you can put it in your scrapbook. First so there will be no misunderstanding I have put my promotion ability to work in the past two weeks for the following. I was advised by Lt Esposito [Elvis' foreman, Joe Esposito] that you needed a 16 mm projector machine for your new home. With a little prodding the RCA family folks were interested in giving you a nice gift for Xmas and your birthday and have generously consented to ship you one of the new ones. . . . We are now currently in the preparation of securing as a Xmas gift and birthday gift for your pleasure for your new home a deluxe model pool table. We do not have exactly the name of the person who will be honored with the courtesy of presenting it to you but we are working on it. In the meantime if you will set up an executive meeting sometime Friday or Sunday evening in Palm Springs before you depart for Memphis it would be very helpful to make sure that nothing has been left undone to keep your organization running first class. My best to the family including the two Brutuses. [Brutus was one of Elvis' three Great Danes.]

Sincerely,
The Colonel

PS Remember your slogan TCB but it only works if you use it.

Poor Harry Jenkins. Here we find Colonel once again taking up the cudgels for his artist's interests (is that what this is?), once again over a matter of promotion — or irresponsible overpromotion, as Colonel portrays it here — in the face of falling sales. I think the only way to look at it is that, whatever the situation, good, bad, or indifferent, nothing was too small to engage Colonel's interest when it came to protecting the Elvis brand. And woe betide anyone at RCA who thought they could ignore any of those intricately carved-out, if unwritten, "verbal agreements," which were to be considered as binding as anything recorded in history's solemn books. ■

"We cannot, and will not stand by and see this great endeavor destroyed by disinterested or greedy personalities"

Mr. Harry E. Jenkins   Spring 1972 [written while on tour]
RCA Record Division
1133 Avenue of the Americas
New York, N.Y.

Dear Harry:

It has come to my attention lately, after speaking with [RCA executive] George Grau Wednesday, pertaining to our royalty statements, when George mentioned to me that he would like to discuss later the heavy returns of Presley material. Before moving into an area of deeper research on this matter, I am sure that you have made some of the new people with RCA Records aware that we have a complete understanding that no Presley product can be shipped on a guaranteed basis, with the exception of a special product, under special circumstances, by letter of agreement.

As you know, many years ago we ran into a similar situation where some eager beaver wanted to make a tremendous sales month by shipping right and left anything the dealers wanted, and stocked the shelves full of products, which made this particular party look like a million dollar award winner in sales. Unfortunately, this sales representative already knew that he would not be with the company to take the responsibility when the products started coming back. We know about a certain percentage for returns, but you also know that this product must be swapped only for Presley products. It cannot be exchanged for other artists.

Until we clarify this matter to the complete satisfaction of all the parties concerned (Elvis and I and his supervisor, Mr. Vernon Presley) we do not wish to release any other product.

We are quite concerned that perhaps all the factors are not known to some of the new people that may have joined the RCA Record family, especially now, when we are on the threshold of a very lucrative new adventure in connection with the record division and this great artist, to utilize all our facilities for all of us to mutually benefit from all our endeavors. [This is in reference to the formation of RCA Record Tours to finance and help promote Elvis' new touring schedule.] We cannot, and will not stand by and see this great endeavor destroyed by disinterested or greedy personalities, if there are any. We don't mind at all being greedy ourselves, but you also know that we don't mind sharing — except we have no intentions of sharing in returned products, as it is not necessary. If a buyer feels he can sell 1,000 albums, don't try to shove 5,000 at him and say, "We'll take 4,000 back at our expense."

I feel sure that whoever is in command of this type of operation in sales can only seriously research this complaint from us to the fullest, for we are positive that this could be the same situation that almost separated this great artist from your company several years ago, when in one instance, after selling more than 1,000 of a particular album which was very good for one city, one of the Company's own representatives wrote a letter that Elvis was slipping and he should be on television, for he had to take back thousands of albums from this particular dealer. But, he failed to say that he had loaded this store to overcapacity on a guaranteed basis, without the proper authorization.

These are cold facts, and they cannot be camouflaged or shoved under the rug. I may wind up not being the most popular manager after you read this letter, but you must admit that I did give you the information.

Sincerely,

The Colonel

P.S. I feel that the RCA Record Division will continue to honor the many verbal agreements that you know exist, but could not be put in the contract due to the complications with other artists.

1973

For everything else that was going on (and there was a lot), read the biographical account. Because 1973 marked a turning point, a sad denouement in Elvis and Colonel's relationship. But it began with a challenge.

Colonel had gotten the idea for a worldwide satellite broadcast performance from watching the live broadcasts of President Nixon's historic trip to China in February. He had had to overcome Elvis' initial opposition, sell the idea to RCA, and get Tom Sarnoff at NBC to go along with it. The fact that it had never been done by an entertainer before was the thing that most intrigued him.

On September 4, 1972, the final day of Elvis' current Las Vegas engagement, Colonel hosted a press conference to announce the date and place of the event. It was to be called *Aloha from Hawaii,* and Elvis and RCA president Rocco Laginestra took questions from reporters, who had already been briefed on all the historic landmarks that this broadcast would achieve by the press kit that Colonel had handed out. It would reach the largest audience ever to see a television show at one time, Colonel's information handout trumpeted with an alacrity not always confined to the facts, "in excess of one billion people" (in fact, after premiering live in the Far East, the show would not be broadcast until later in the day in Europe, and not till April in America) and would also represent "the first time in the history of the record industry" that an album (the follow-up soundtrack) would be released simultaneously on a global basis.

With all those historic firsts, how could Elvis not be just as sold on it, too? It was, Elvis said at the press conference, very hard to comprehend that he had come so far from the place he had started out. And when he met with costume designer Bill Belew in November, he told him that he wanted to present something different with this show, something that would say "America" to the world. "He came up with the American eagle [as a motif for the jumpsuit he would wear]," Belew said, "one of only three times in all the times that we [worked] together that he ever made any requests." In addition, he lost twenty-five pounds in a very short period of time, following a specially prescribed "Las Vegas diet," consisting, among other things, of a daily injection of urine from a pregnant woman.

The show itself met all of Colonel's, Elvis', and the world's highest expectations, achieving, for example, as Colonel announced jubilantly to Elvis at its conclusion, the highest rating ever registered in Japan. And then he wrote Elvis a letter, which expressed in writing a greater degree of shared intimacy than either had declared to the other in some time. And yet one wonders why this intimate, desperately emotional letter needed to be copied to so many other interested parties. It is as if Colonel is telling not just RCA president Rocco Laginestra and three of his own close associates but himself as well that the connection between him and his artist remains undiminished. ■

"I always know that when I do my part you always do yours in your own way and in your own feeling in how to do it best"

Sunday Morning
Three A.M.
January 14, 1973

Elvis:

Enclosed is the copy [of the proclamation] from the Mayor's office I promised to get to you after the show. Also you and I always tell each other by seeing each other on the stage and from the floor by the stage how we feel, so there is no need for hugging each other.

I always know that when I do my part you always do yours in your own way and in your own feeling in how to do it best. That is why you and I are never at each other when we are doing our work in our own best way possible at all times.

Here are a few facts which I know you already know but for you to remember if you hear some of the snowjobs that came to our ears already now that the work has been completed by most everyone but us. I will now have to follow up to get the most mileage out of everything in the future pertaining to this entire production, such as sales for the Satellite album promotion and everything that is tied into this idea. First of all one of the snowjobs that is going full force is the idea for this entire brainchild is completely ignored, except by the RCA people, is that it came from you and me. The title "Aloha From Hawaii" was also ours. Mr.

George Parkhill, myself and all the people from RCA Record Tours were one hundred percent behind us from the start.

Several of our friends that you and I know also told us it was a great idea but did not voice this when they were not with us. Many other people believed in us completely on this but some only came out of the woodwork to take bows after they now have found out that it worked. I know you know all this and just wanted to keep you up to date. There will be some disagreements as to how this will be worked out but that is my job. Just remember you did it all and all of us did our part to help you. Mr. Diskin played a big part. Mr. Diskin and his troupe and all your own selected talent were with you all the way. Without all their help and all your boys' help I would have been stuck to make our ideas work.

You above all make all of it work by being the leader and the talent. Without your dedication to your following it couldn't have been done.

[Signed "Colonel"]

Cc: Rocco Laginestra, George Parkhill, Tom Diskin, Grelun Landon

---

I t wasn't long before everything went back to the way it had been. In fact, it was only weeks.

Elvis quickly regained the weight he had lost, and he had to cancel five shows in his February booking in Las Vegas as well as eight in his Lake Tahoe booking.

By the following summer Colonel was as worried as he had ever been, and Elvis was as out of sorts. Little as he wanted to, Colonel wrote Elvis a letter about the predictability of his show, its lack of energy and innovation, but the effect of his letter can be gauged by the fact that he felt obligated to write the same letter on the same subject exactly one year later. ■

"Without a doubt you are by far the greatest artist I have ever known, and can be even greater if you just believe in yourself half as much as I believe in you"

Dear Elvis: July 12, 1973

Now that the Tour is over and all of us are getting ready to come up with some new ideas for presenting you on your up-coming Las Vegas Hilton engagement, I am sure you will want to think of something new on your stage presentation there. You will be going into your eighth performance there.

There was a good deal of talk during your last engagement whether you would be doing some new songs and perhaps a bit different show format for the opening of your show. I am sure that you just feel the same — that it is time for something different for the opening. Perhaps going back to your first opening with just your boys coming on from behind the curtain.

I would be amiss as a manager if I did not bring up these points. But I'm not telling you how and what to do, as I have always left this up to you — as only you know best how to work it out. Somehow I have to be the one to explain this to you. Everyone involved feels the same way, but no one will come out and tell you about it. Why, I don't know, because I am sure you are too great an artist to be upset with sound suggestions from anyone who has only your best interests at heart.

You are on the threshold of the word being out before long that you are not interested in doing something with songs in Vegas — and will become just another who doesn't change his format. When on concert tour it doesn't matter, as those appearances are always the first time, and we do not stay more than a few days at each location.

During your last appearances in Vegas and Tahoe, you know we had many problems which we managed to overcome. However, I don't feel that we can do this again. We owe the Las Vegas Hilton five performances we missed, for which they paid you, with your promise and mine that they would be made up at some future date. Additionally, we missed eight performances at Tahoe which we must make up at some future date. Everyone involved knows you were sick, and everyone did their part to work things out. We, of course, will do the same in the future.

I will leave it up to your good judgment to prepare yourself to surprise all of those that seem to be under the impression that you're stuck with the same show for Vegas and don't know how to do something new. You have so many of your own block busting songs that will amaze even the biggest unbeliever, and I know you can do it—as soon as you make up your mind to do so. You know I am with you all the way, but I could not say this if I did not honestly express my feelings to you.

Without a doubt you are by far the greatest artist I have ever known, and can be even greater if you just believe in yourself half as much as I believe in you.

Sincerely,
The Colonel

Four days later he attempted once more to inculcate in Elvis one of the fundamental lessons of enlightened self-interest. He was always going to be there for Elvis—that much was understood—but at the same time Elvis must at all times, first and foremost, look out for himself. Earlier in the year, Hill and Range, his publisher from the start, had to all intents and purposes ceased to exist, and Colonel set out to establish an even more lucrative arrangement for Elvis with Freddy Bienstock, Hill and Range's longtime song representative, setting up two new publishers under the exclusive 100 percent ownership of Elvis Presley. Sadly, the new publishing firms never really worked out, most of all because Elvis' records were no longer selling in sufficient numbers (and he was not sufficiently committed to recording) to induce topflight writers to sign up.

But that was not known at the time, and Colonel felt it necessary to remind Elvis once again that friendship was all very well (and true friends in any case could not be bought), but that song publishing would be his one continuing source of income long after his performing days were over. ■

"You have been more than fair and generous with everyone connected with your organization — in some ways even too much so"

Dear Elvis: July 16, 1973

I wish to point out to you again the important decisions that you will have to make, now that you and your father are the principal stockholders in these two new firms. All decisions in regard to securing song copyrights and protecting and signing them legally and properly, should be made without taking into consideration personal friendships and obligations that you may feel toward people in the music business, friends, associates and others. I can see no reason why any of your friends or close associates, especially those that are always heralding their loyalty and devotion to you, should bring any songs for your consideration if they cannot be put into your firms, either Elvis Music, Inc. or White Haven Music, Inc., especially if they are not the writers of the songs and only the promoters. You have been more than fair and generous with everyone connected with your organization — in some ways even too much so. This can, of course, be adjusted by the recipients by being more interested in proving their loyalty by supplying musical compositions that they secure into your firms. As you well know, in many instances some people are only interested in placing one of their songs on the back of one of the good songs so they get a free ride, whether the song is worth it or not, and the same royalties.

As you know, yourself, Lisa Marie and Vernon, your father, are the most important factors in the idea of setting up these two new firms. I personally will not be interested in any way, if we become involved in a free-for-all. Anyone wanting to do business with you can do so, but let them do it in the right and proper way.

Enough said.

                                        Sincerely,
                                        Colonel

Things finally came to a boiling point a little more than a month later. Early Monday morning, on September 3, 1973, at a special 3:00 A.M. show that had been added on to close out his latest four-week engagement at the Las Vegas Hilton (the Hilton hotel chain had taken over the International in 1971), Elvis delivered himself of a rambling onstage diatribe against both the Hilton and Hilton director and CEO Barron Hilton, a longtime supporter of both Elvis and Colonel. The subject was the Hilton's intention to fire his favorite waiter, and Elvis started off with a series of angry references that became more and more disjointed, and occasionally obscene. ("Adios, you motherfucker, bye bye, Papa, too / To hell with the whole Hilton Hotel, and screw the showroom, too," he interpolated in an "X-rated" version of "Love Me Tender.")

Colonel, sitting in his usual front booth with Loanne Miller, who would eventually become his second wife, was absolutely mortified. "He turned to me," Loanne recalled, "and said, 'I've never been so embarrassed in my life. I wish I could just crawl under this table right now.'" And then, without pausing, he added, "Who does he think he is? How am I ever going to face the Hilton people? He can't get away with this."

After the show Colonel stormed into Elvis' dressing room, and the two of them raged at each other behind closed doors in a manner that no one could miss hearing (and no one had ever heard before). Then Elvis went up to the wrap party in his suite, and Colonel sat down and dictated this letter to Loanne. ∎

"We are not judge and jury, but performers, and have a job to do"

Dear Elvis: September 3, 1973

This letter is only intended in the event you aren't up when I come up to see you this evening. After you read it, you can discuss this with me tomorrow afternoon if you wish as I won't leave until early Thursday morning.

I do not want to go into a lengthy discussion in writing regarding the current problem which was created last night during your last performance, when you took it on yourself, on the stage, in front of 2,000 people, to embarrass the executives of the Hilton Corporation with your remarks. Your outburst was a shocking revelation to some of the people — especially after just announcing that they had given you the gold chain.

Your speech regarding the hotel firing this fellow as he was a good man, etc. was completely out of your class — as the hotel does not ask us to hire or fire someone. One of your remarks where you stated you "thought Hilton people were bigger than that" does not fit the consideration they have given you in the past, having knocked thousands of dollars off your bills for the food, beverages and suite over the years, and as much as $20,000 extra on this trip. I can't find anything small-time about them.

I sincerely wish you had taken this up with me before, and perhaps you could have talked to Mr. Lewin [Hilton vice president Henri Lewin, who ran the hotel] regarding your interest in the matter and not taken it up in front of 2,000 customers who had nothing to do with the entire affair and were left somewhat confused by the incident. Mr. Lewin was quite upset when he called me, and I told him I would take it up with you. He felt sure that you had not been informed of the correct details regarding this matter.

But, regardless of that, it should never have been brought up during your performance in front of the public. We are not judge and jury, but performers, and have a job to do on that stage without getting involved with hotel employees during the performance.

I am not aware of the reason for your outburst in this matter, but I am sure you know why you did it, and it has not made things easy to patch up.

If this letter in some way should annoy you, or you perhaps feel I am sticking my nose in something that is not my business, you should know I am only being honest with you, and fulfilling my responsibility as a friend and manager, to keep you informed of the reaction, which is well known — but most of the friends around you are reluctant to pass it on, as they are employees and I am not.

It has nothing to do with us personally, as I am in no way aware of what it is all about. You will have to judge for yourself the responsibility, but I have a feeling that this person [the waiter, Mario] must have given you a pretty good snow job to get you to do this on stage, or if he did not ask you to do it, at least he created a protective feeling from you that he was not able to get somewhere else. It is unfair of this man to take his personal troubles to you, and to take advantage of your prestige as a star and make you a message carrier during your performance. I am sure you will have the feeling that you have been used in this matter.

Sincerely,
The Colonel

Elvis did not find the time to see him that day or the next, and Colonel had gone to bed at midnight, when Elvis called Colonel's aide-de-camp George Parkhill to let him know that if Colonel didn't come up right away, Elvis was coming down to Colonel's room to confront him. Colonel left the room in a cold rage, Loanne recalled. When he returned he announced that he needed to dictate his letter of resignation right away. They worked on it until seven thirty that morning, when Loanne told him she simply couldn't keep her eyes open anymore. But she was back in the office at ten thirty, when Colonel completed the following letter to Vernon. To which a short time later he appended this sorrowful letter to Elvis. ■

"I have tendered my resignation effective immediately"

Dear Vernon: September 5, 1973

As per the understanding between Elvis Presley and yourself, at our meeting at 1 a.m. Wednesday, September 5, 1973, in the Imperial Suite of the Las Vegas Hilton Hotel. It is understood by you and myself that I have tendered my resignation effective immediately, with the understanding for a complete flat settlement on the balance of all contracts in existence, with no exceptions, as per contracts signed by Elvis Presley, on dates thereof listed in each contract to be effective on all his extensions and renewals. [After this, all the contract commitments were listed, including two that were under negotiation at the time.] All services pertaining to the execution of the contracts by Colonel Parker and All Star Shows will be continued on the basis of servicing those contracts only — not as a personal manager. No advertising promotion or outside services, other than as per contract, will be furnished. As listed, there are two proposals: (1) For a complete flat financial settlement within 30 days of receipt of this memorandum with no participation of any percentages or payments due on all existing contracts in the future . . . $5,000,000.

(2) One-half of financial settlement within 30 days from receipt of this memorandum, plus 25% on all overages, personal appearances, television, RCA Record Tours commitments, for the duration of all existing contracts, with no exceptions, in lieu of the flat $5,000,000 settlement as stated above. It is understood that at no time will Colonel Parker, or his staff, be required to be in attendance on any tours or hotel engagements unless mutually agreed.

If settlement #1 is concluded, this will dissolve any and all personal management relationships of any nature for the future. If Elvis Presley so desires, Colonel Parker/All Star Shows, will extend their advice and information, whatever needed, for one week in the event whoever takes over the new management wishes to take advantage of this offer, at no charge, to make this turnover of management as convenient as possible to the artist. The separation of this association, as far as Colonel Parker/ All Star Shows is concerned, pertaining to management, is on a friendly basis, as accepted by Elvis Presley with his statement that he wishes to make a fair settlement, made on these premises on the date listed above at the hour of 1 a.m., Wednesday, September 5, and attended by Mr. Joe Esposito, employee of Elvis Presley; Mr. George L. Parkhill, vice president, RCA Records, RCA Record Tours; Mr. Vernon Presley, father of Elvis Presley; Elvis Presley and Colonel Parker. Colonel Parker/All Star Shows, and his staff, will no longer be an exclusive service to Elvis Presley.

> Sincerely,
> The Colonel

"I have no ill feelings — but I am also not a puppet on a string"

Dear Elvis: September 5, 1973

When I prepared the papers last night I failed to enclose this note I had planned to put in. Also enclosed is a copy of the papers signed by me, to be retained by you.

Please return to me one signed copy of the papers, and indicate which proposal you want to accept — Settlement #1 or Settlement #2. I am sorry you failed to understand that the letter had nothing to do with my response to your questioning this morning. You have always respected my privacy and rest, the same as I have yours. Last night I told Joe Esposito that I would be going to bed. I had waited up until about 9:30 for word whether you were up. This, of course, is okay with me as it is your privilege to sleep as long as you wish. I told Joe I would put in a letter what I was going to talk to you about, so that you could take it up with me this evening, as I would be here until Thursday morning.

I can readily understand you advising me that you would like to see me at a respectful hour, but I could see no reason for a pressure meeting at 1 a.m., as there was nothing that would change the situation. But the main reason was that, after calling my room and I failed to see the light on the telephone, I received the following message from Mr. Parkhill: 'If I did not come up, you were coming down!' This I could not possibly accept as a sensible solution. You knew I was in bed. You were already dressed, and at least you could have told the boys: 'Call the Colonel. I would like to come down to see him.' You have always been able to communicate with me whenever you desired under normal circumstances.

With all the other incidents involved, this is the best solution for all concerned. I have no ill feelings—but I am also not a puppet on a string.

I wish you lots of luck, and I surely will respect the privacy of the confidential nature regarding which of the two settlements is made.

Sincerely,
The Colonel

Without hearing anything further from Elvis or Vernon, Colonel left Las Vegas for Palm Springs on September 6 and wrote yet another sorrowful, businesslike letter to Elvis, either hoping to wrap everything up or—I really don't know. ∎

"I have to move on with my plans"

Elvis: September 6, 1973
    Joe Esposito told me by telephone this morning that you told him you wished to take up the matter of the resignation papers with your father.

Vernon was to call me but he did not. So the record is straight, I did call twice yesterday, but got no action. Since you did not communicate with me before I left, regarding any plans, I take for granted that I must handle this conclusion in my own way. Going back and forth with Joe is a pain in the neck. There is no reason why this could not have been done by sitting down and ironing out all of the problems as to the separation, in a sensible way. In the meantime, regardless of which decision that you make, I have to move on with my plans.

My plans are such that they must be done now, not tomorrow. If no conclusion is reached on the separation agreement, I will have to take immediate steps to cancel whatever is conciliable under the current agreements, and a proper settlement must be made for those canceled, if I am not going to handle them with the people concerned.

The firm contracts you will have to take care of yourself. The signing of the separation papers has nothing to do with this, because you can answer one way or another — which way is immaterial to me — but they stand as they are. If neither is answered, then we must come to an immediate conclusion of a complete separation once and for all, and settlement made as such. You, yourself, stated you wanted to make a fair settlement.

I plan to fulfill any commitments that I made in your name and finish up all the obligations with the people we have done business with, but you must work this out satisfactorily with me before I can do so. The income due for the future can only be achieved if the work is done. We are currently already behind on product for RCA on the new contract, for which you have already been paid. Mr. Parkhill and I have stretched this, so currently we have the single out, but we are definitely behind on the contractual agreement to deliver an album after the last session, which was not completed. It is of the utmost importance that someone advise my office when someone with a truck will pick up at MGM your arrangements and stage equipment which we have been looking after, and other miscellaneous items which will no longer be our responsibility. I am sure you can let Joe Esposito look after this matter of getting the items picked up in Los Angeles. Also we need an address where to have all the mail transferred, as we will not be handling this any longer — whether it should be Memphis or Los Angeles — but we must know. This is not a matter of small-time decisions. They are important and they must be made.

If I am no longer associated with you, I cannot make them for you as I have been doing in the past. I request an immediate solution to the settlement one way or another.

Regards,
The Colonel

———————————

Just to put a finishing touch on this one-way exchange: nothing was ever formally resolved.

Gradually, without anything further being said (or at least without the subject itself being directly addressed), things went back to more or less the way they had been. Colonel continued to harass RCA about all manner of issues; he made sure that Elvis fulfilled his contractual recording obligations to the company; and when he informed his artist that he had worked out a new deal with the Sahara Tahoe (where he had been forced to cancel his engagement the previous year four days short of its conclusion), Elvis sent back a telegram offering congratulations and authorizing Colonel to sign the contract on his behalf.

It was a very rough fall for Elvis. On October 9, 1973, his divorce from Priscilla was finalized. Six days later he was admitted to Memphis' Baptist Memorial Hospital for two weeks for what turned out to be Demerol addiction. Everything seemed quiet in November but then, in mid-December, he had a productive six-day recording session at the Stax recording studio, and sometime during that period he called Colonel and said he wanted to go back to work. "I asked him if he was in shape to do this," Colonel wrote in a recollection some twenty years later, "and he said, 'Right now I am ready.' So I started to put him back to work." And, Colonel concluded, "It was great for a while." But it need hardly be said, it was never the same. And one cannot help but wonder, what if at this point they had simply called it a day?

1975–1976

Not surprisingly, the problems between Elvis and Colonel continued. Many of them can be traced to Elvis' increasing disinclination to communicate with his manager directly, if at all. In place of that, Colonel was forced to go through Elvis' guys, but that left him susceptible to whatever rumors were circulating, whatever roadblocks were set up by a group of men who did not take well to his direction and, while knowing little about his and Elvis' business, often ascribed to him the darkest and most sinister motives.

Elvis himself was more and more prey to dark imaginings of his own, exhibiting increasingly erratic behavior both in his private and professional life. His fall 1974 tour had drawn sharp criticism from reviewers and fans alike. (According to reviewers, he was "bored to death" in St. Paul, hostile and "disappointing" in Indianapolis, sick with the flu in Dayton, and "ill" enough in Wichita that many fans expressed regret that he hadn't canceled.) Then on December 30, when he finally got Elvis on the phone and determined that the rumors which had been filtering back to him were true, Colonel was forced to postpone Elvis' scheduled January 26 opening at the Hilton by nearly two months, after first getting Elvis to send him a telegram authorizing Colonel to "sign any papers necessary for me while I am recuperating." A week later he sent this letter, which attempted to address some of the ongoing issues directly while at the same time reiterating his belief in his artist, if his artist would just make up his mind to turn things around, in language that he hoped could not be misunderstood. ■

"There is no person in this business that I know of that could have shielded everything involved as we have done, or would have taken the abuse from so many sources"

Dear Elvis: January 6, 1975

I am enclosing the press release that we made up for the March 18 opening at the Las Vegas Hilton, instead of the January 26 opening, as per our understanding on the 'phone last week.

I also have advised RCA of the new album dates for recording during this engagement. I, of course, was able to fit the press release in with the opening of the new annex, which I thought would be better than giving the real reason, which I knew you felt bad about if this was to be given for the delay in opening at the Hilton. We, of course, worked very closely with the Hilton people and it was fortunate for us that Bill Cosby could change his dates due to a motion picture commitment. I am still trying to help the hotel secure another attraction in place of our January 26 opening and they are trying very hard themselves to move one of their attractions.

Now that you have the time you feel you need to get ready, I know it will all work out for the best. As soon as you know what you want to do following the March 18 in Vegas, I will try to get some of the concerts I had planned for March back on track. We also should re-open the possibility of the special we planned last year and never were able to close out.

Here it is Monday, January 6. I do not hear much from your staff, so let me know how you are. I just spoke to your dad a few minutes ago and he tells me that some of the boys, or one of them, told you that I said you had money problems. Was the party who told you so concerned that he or they asked you to cut their salaries in half? Whatever I tell these fellows — I have no reservations that they can tell you anything I talk about. My concern has always been to advise them to cut expenses as much as possible when you are not working. If this is wrong the way you look at it, let's get it out in the open. My interest is, and always has been, for what I felt was best for you. I never stuck my nose into your personal affairs. If, after 18 years, you are easily led by phony information it is time for us to settle up and go our separate ways.

I am telling you this just like I told your dad. I have never told these fellows anything that I was ashamed for you to know. How you, or they, interpret this I can't help. However, there is no person in this business that I know of that could have shielded everything involved as we have done, or would have taken the abuse from so many sources. I feel your dad is much closer to understanding how I feel than anyone else at the present.

Sincerely,
The Colonel

I think Colonel's Rules of the Road speaks for itself. ∎

"Graduation in our school of showmanship can never be achieved, not even by us, as there is always something new to learn every day, every month, every year until there are no more concerts"

[ca. February 1975 (written in advance of the spring tour)]

MANUAL FOR TOUR PERSONNEL

The information contained herewith has been compiled for your personal convenience, as it is impossible to run a training school over the telephone.

We also understand that there are not many concert tours that are so particular in handling everything first class. Although we are still a long way from achieving this goal, we are at least trying to do everything right.

For your information, pertaining to buses and trucks, Mr. Pat Kelleher, director RCA Record Tours Transportation and Hotel Reservations Department, is your contact for anything pertaining to these services. Do not contact our Concession Department, but contact Mr. Kelleher.

You have our permission to do all the buck-passing you desire, but do not when you're on the same tour, so it won't interfere with business. We know that all of you involved must have some untapped ability to achieve all of these requirements or Mr. Hulett [Tom Hulett, tour director and Jerry Weintraub's partner in Management III] would not have assigned you to the project.

Graduation in our school of showmanship can never be achieved, not even by us, as there is always something new to learn every day, every month, every year until there are no more concerts.

Should you require extra information in regard to your work, check with our undergraduate, Mr. Charles Stone [another Management III associate], who can tell you all about how it happened to him, and he knows as he has traveled your road before, and is still limping.

Our best wishes to all of you involved.

The Colonel, Mr. Jerry Weintraub, Mr. Tom Hulett

GUIDELINES FOR ADVANCE MEN DOING
PRE-TOUR PREPARATION

In Each Market to Which you are Assigned—

1. Make contact with the individual who is in complete charge of the ticket sales and get the correct telephone numbers of (a) the building where the concert is to be held and its address (b) the name of the building manager, his private telephone number at the building (if any) and his home telephone number in the event Colonel Parker, Mr. Weintraub, or Mr. Hulett wish to call them direct. This information must be telephoned to Colonel Parker and Management Three offices at once.

2. Obtain name of box office contact who can give reports on ticket sales. If tickets are on sale outside of the building box offices, obtain the address and private telephone number, if possible.

3. Get name of the person in complete charge of building concessions, and a telephone number where that person can be contacted.

4. Advise ticket personnel that, when tickets go on sale, the first 14 to 25 rows MUST be sold to fans standing in line. No tickets can be pulled for any favorite customers, etc. THE FANS COME FIRST AT ALL TIMES. Proper security must be secured to line up customers in single file in front of each window and to keep order. Handicapped persons are to be assisted with their purchase of tickets. THERE ARE NO PASSES. EVERYONE MUST HAVE A TICKET TO ENTER THE SHOW.

5. When advance ticket sale is planned, you must furnish Colonel Parker and Management Three the following information immediately— location of ticket sales and address with zip code.

6. Advise name and telephone number of person in charge of stage preparation—backstage manager, operations manager, etc.

7. Secure name of officer as well as work and home telephone numbers, who will be in charge of any hotel detail we may need. Also the

hourly rate of security men as well as the charge for their supervisor. This information must be sent to Management Three by the security officer from his office.

8. Check out the most suitable hotel quarters in the area and advise the hotel manager's name, as well as the address and telephone number of the hotel. (You may be advised to make reservations for the time of the show.)

9. Contact nearest airport and inquire relative to landing facilities and to the largest type of plane they can accommodate, whether they have "starter" facilities, etc.

10. Inform all concerned parties that all advertising for any concert is handled solely through Colonel Parker and Mr. Hulett — WITHOUT EXCEPTION!

11. Acquire the requested information as soon as possible.

12. When you are given a specific time to report to Colonel Parker, Mr. Hulett or Mr. Stone, be on time. Delays can be costly.

13. Do not make promises that you cannot personally fulfill.

14. At any time if you have a problem which you cannot solve after careful consideration, contact your own people and you will be given every assistance in solving the problem. Unless you bring the problem out in the open, there is no way they can help you.

15. Be sensible in the area of expenses — first-class service is often a matter of intelligent approach, rather than lavish expense.

16. Colonel Parker, Mr. Hulett, Mr. Weintraub, or Mr. Stone and the person connected with Management Three handling the advance date, are the only authorized persons to receive ticket sale grosses. Advise each ticket manager not to give out this information to anyone pretending to be calling for the show.

Mr. Hulett and myself hope this information will be of some help to all of you responsible, and will enable you to avoid making unnecessary calls and unnecessary travel back and forth.

Sincerely,
The Colonel

O ne of the most persistent, and pernicious, elements of the Elvis-Colonel mythology is that Colonel, for whatever reason (and the reason cited usually has to do with control, whether financial, psychological, or artistic), was intent on preventing Elvis from exercising his own freedom of creative expression. I think the attentive reader may have gathered that this was not the case — at least not in terms of what was going on behind the scenes. But what about *A Star Is Born*, which many in the Elvis world on just about every level sincerely believe to have been Elvis' last best chance for artistic self-expression?

While this may not be the final word on the subject (it couldn't be), here's the story in brief. Barbra Streisand came to Elvis' show at the Hilton on the evening of March 28, 1975, and met with him in his dressing room afterward. She was accompanied by her boyfriend, Jon Peters, who she said was going to produce and direct her next film, a contemporary adaptation of the classic Hollywood fable of success (this would be its second remake; a third, with Lady Gaga, would be released in 2018), with Streisand in the much-revered Judy Garland role. They wanted Elvis for the male lead (called "Norman Maine" in the two earlier film versions), who drowns his sorrows in drink as he watches his wife's stardom eclipse his own. In this version, rock stardom would replace movie stardom, language would be updated to reflect changes in both era and milieu, and the dramatic climax would come at the Grammys rather than at the Oscar ceremonies.

Elvis could not have been more excited about the project initially (he knew and very much admired the highly emotional 1954 picture), but for whatever reason he didn't tell Colonel about it at first. And when he did, he got the reaction that he may have feared: Colonel was furious that Streisand should have approached his artist so casually, without any regard for the proper channels. And he pointed out that Peters, up till then known primarily as a fashionable hairdresser, was totally inexperienced in filmmaking and that Streisand and Peters as a team would have one interest in mind, and it would not be Elvis'.

The following week Streisand's production company made an offer of $500,000 plus 10 percent of the gross receipts after breakeven, with the movie producers retaining all music and record rights but Elvis and the Colonel free to produce, and profit from, the two live concerts at the heart of the picture. Ten days later Colonel outlined his terms to Roger Davis at William Morris.

Now, two things to keep in mind: For all of his brave talk around the guys, did Elvis really want to make the movie? (His enthusiasm appears to have swiftly

waned, as it did for so many recent plans and projects that required an unequivocal commitment that he no longer seemed prepared to give.) But more to the
point, *could* Elvis have done it? And would it have been to his advantage? Many
in the Elvis camp doubted his ability at this stage to memorize long stretches of
dialogue. And (this is kind of a Hydra-headed two points), most of them probably
agreed with Colonel's underlying, and undoubtedly unspoken, reservation that a
broken-down alcoholic might not be the right role for Elvis to signal his return to
motion pictures. In any case, as everyone knows, the deal was never made (Kris
Kristofferson took the part), but still the final question remains: Was Colonel trying to sabotage any *possibility* of a deal with his demands? Or, if you were in Elvis'
shoes, would you have wanted him to represent you in these negotiations? ■

"I feel very strongly that in this case he should be very much kept up-to-date by us on any negotiations"

MEMORANDUM   April 14, 1975
To: Roger Davis
Re: Elvis movie — Barbra Streisand Contract — A STAR IS BORN

Mr. Presley has indicated he would like to make this movie. I was not
aware until a few days ago that Miss Streisand has been talking this project over with Presley. I have explained to Presley that we would submit
our proposition to them, and that we should hold out for our regular
terms as we have in the past, including some new terms which we have
become aware of in the past years, to protect ourselves when it involves
television sales of a movie.

I am hereby setting forth the basic terms under which Presley will
move forward with this. I know you will have some problems, however,
I advised Presley that we feel he should have the best deal possible for
this project. Since he told me how strongly he feels about doing it I
advised him not to allow this to become a part of making a cheap deal as
they will try to use this as part of the negotiations.

I am also advising you that someone has already started to use this
combination on the news to promote the picture. So far there is no deal,
and I have advised Presley to be handy in case we need him as I feel very
strongly that in this case he should be very much kept up-to-date by us
on any negotiations.

As far as negotiations, I told Mr. Feldman, I believe his name is, we would give him some word on Monday, at least an answer on Presley's feeling. Roger, you can put this in a more readable form from here on. This letter to you is for your information to guide yourself by, and is not to be part of the file on this project for anyone but ourselves. This project should be of the strictest confidence and is not to be a subject of any inter-office memos except our top people.

TERMS:

One Million Dollars ($1,000,000.00) salary for twelve (12) weeks. They told me about three months. We have always had ten weeks, so we make it 12 weeks. No free weeks.

Fifty Percent (50%) of the profit of the picture from the first dollar. One Hundred Thousand Dollars ($100,000.00) Expenses.

All payable from starting date till closing date.

Salary payable as follows: 10 weeks at $75,000.00 per week. First and last week at $125,000.00 per week. Salary to be paid in full on any balance due as picture is completed as far as Presley's service is concerned before the 12 week period. . . .

Regarding movie sound track, this will have to be negotiated separately after we know how many songs, etc. Presley will have to do. Presley reserves the right to reject any song that he feels is not suitable for him.

On duets, if any — any release of these songs on record would have to be worked out in advance of the recording between all parties. No press releases involving Presley can be released unless approved in advance by the Presley office.

Television sale of the movie must be a separate agreement from contract, and Presley is to be paid a fee on the first and second run against his profit participation of not less than $375,000.00 for first run and $250,000.00 for second run if picture is sold for up to One Million Dollars. Over One Million Dollars Presley is to receive $500,000.00 first run and $300,000.00 second run. Film not to be sold in a package deal, but on its own. . . .

Roger, write this up in rough and advise them of our terms first so they will know our thoughts.

The Colonel

....

There is much more, but I think this gives a pretty good picture.

....

L ittle changed. There were still contractual commitments to be met. Elvis was
  desperate to remain on the road to keep up with his ever-ballooning expenses.
It is almost heartbreaking to see how out of control at this point both parties
were, how little was left of a relationship that had once meant so much to
them both.

The organ referred to was an expensive electronic Lowrey organ that Colonel had given Elvis for Christmas, perhaps hoping that it would serve as inspiration if not for the solo recordings he had first suggested when Elvis was in
Germany, at least for the upcoming home recording sessions at Graceland. ∎

**"As you know, we have postponed four times in the past three months
any recording sessions and you have not recorded due to illness, etc.
since last April"**

Dear Elvis: January 6, 1976
As you know, you decided in Las Vegas that you would rather do the
recording the third week in January, after you felt that you could not get
ready in time for your show and also learn the new songs. As you know,
we have postponed four times in the past three months any recording
sessions and you have not recorded due to illness, etc. since last April.
We have somehow managed to scrape enough material from albums to
keep half of your single commitments up-to-date.

As of now, before the end of your RCA Contract Year for 1975, we owe
RCA two albums and four singles on the 1975 contract. I can get by for
the next six months if we can deliver an album and two singles by the
end of January 1976. This we will have to deliver to enable me to bill them
for the 1976 contract payment due early March, which is your large check
for the current contract. So, in order to fulfill this minimum commitment
of one album and two singles, we are setting it up with RCA so that you
can record the first week in February at Graceland in Memphis, live, to

be available for release in late February and complete our commitments for 1975.

We have advised [Elvis' producer, and employee] Felton Jarvis to get everything ready, as per our understanding on the phone last night. We are also advising RCA Records of the new recording dates. If you do not make any tracks it would be best to keep these at a minimum and they would have to be overdubbed at least the next day or the same night, as the album and singles must be made ready for release in late February.

I am sure you want me to keep you informed on this. We can still recoup the commitments but there is nothing we can do at present until we get the recording commitment out of the way for 1975.

Again, Happy Birthday, Happy New Year, and keep playing the organ.

Sincerely,
The Colonel

This is an old story, but an increasingly frustrating one. Vernon once again passes along his son's complaint that his manager has been bad-mouthing him to the guys, undoubtedly knowing that it isn't true, and Colonel immediately replies, undoubtedly knowing that it won't do any good. ■

"To talk about our business to any outsider is absolutely unnecessary. There is no way they can help or do anything about it"

Dear Colonel,   January 16, 1976

Elvis called last night and was very upset about some of the things that you had been saying to Joe, Lamar and some of the group about his financial situation. I don't know what was said, but evidently something upset Joe or Lamar very seriously, in turn they go to Elvis and get him upset about all these things. I think it would be best that Joe, Lamar or any of the other people that work for Elvis do not know anything about our situation. There is nothing they can do about anything, anyway.

I am sure whatever you may have said to them was in good faith, but they evidently did not take it that way. So, I would appreciate very much if you just don't talk to Joe or Lamar or any of the guys about our situation no matter how it is. As I said, there is nothing they can do about it anyway.

So you see, to talk about our business to any outsider is absolutely unnecessary. There is no way they can help or do anything about it.

With all respect to you,

Sincerely,
Vernon Presley

"I do believe we will never be able to eliminate their talking, as there are so many of them"

Dear Vernon:

Your letter of January 16 received, read and carefully noted.

To the best of my ability, I can't figure out what I could have said in any way to Lamar or Joe about Elvis' financial situation, as I don't recall anything that they should be upset about — except if they are upset about something they think themselves, and just perhaps used my name to get their idea across somehow. As far as any of the fellows communicating with me, I hardly ever see them or even talk to them, and never about our personal business, although in some instances I am pumped for information by some . . . which I completely ignore or give a pointless answer. I have told them several times that Elvis does what he wants with his money, as I do not handle his finances and I do the same in my own setup.

I do believe we will never be able to eliminate their talking, as there are so many of them. I like to feel they mean no harm, however you can take it from me there will be no information coming from us. If they say so, bring them around and I will tell them to their faces.

Elvis called me about this, and I told him to put the party on the line, then he said it was a rumor. Well, believe me, a rumor it is, and nothing else. If I had to contact you or Elvis when I heard a rumor, I would be on the 'phone every day.

Regards,
Colonel

W hat is there to say? Colonel writes to Vernon with a helplessness that we have never seen before. Once again, the issue of what Colonel has said (or not said) to the guys rears its head, but it is almost entirely beside the point. The racquetball courts were yet another ill-fated business venture that Elvis had entered into and that Colonel was doing his best to get him out of. Colonel follows up the next day with a letter to Elvis that is equally bleak. ∎

"Perhaps the time has come where Elvis will want to get someone else to handle his career more to his personal liking"

Vernon—   August 19, 1976

So there will be no misunderstanding at a later date, I will bring you up to date as per your request not to communicate with any of the boys in the event there was anything I wished to talk about.

Now I finally pinned down two of the fellows to check if Elvis was getting my calls and my notes, that I had to talk to him, and they told me Elvis had gotten the messages, but they indicated Elvis did not want to see me.

I have no knowledge what Elvis' reason might be. The last time I met with Elvis was in Fayetteville [between August 3 and August 5] and he was very pleased and thanked me for helping him with some of the other problems (as to Joe and advice on the racquetball court that is, how best to pursue this problem). I can readily understand that he wants to be left alone; however there are some contractual business details that I had to bring him up-to-date on.

He has told me many times in the past, when I told him I had called, that he never got the messages. But I also had never been told before by any of his people: "Elvis does not want to see you." Now, if this is the case, I feel I am at least entitled to know why, and whatever the reason, he should face me with it.

If we have come to this, I feel that the time has come that we should work out a settlement on our contract and buy me out . . . or I will try, if he wishes me to do so, to find someone to buy me out and take over, as I am not going to carry on this responsibility without being able to communicate with him—with no response or the reason why.

Regardless what he feels, there is nothing to which I can point as a reason for this unreasonable reaction . . . unless someone has pumped him with wrong details. I really don't know—but he must have some reason of which I am not aware.

At present I am not planning on tour #7 until this matter is cleared up, as I am unable to take this responsibility without communicating with Elvis. Tour #6 is sold out, and we have done our part to the fullest.

As you well know, you have always told me to tell it like it is—and when you asked me last week to tell you how the tour went, I told you what I knew, and what I was told. If the time has now arrived where we must cover up details that can be corrected, I am not the one that can do so, without being able to communicate with the most important party involved. I have covered as much as possible, in a safe legitimate way, some of the firm commitments Elvis has and has been paid for, but we are much too far behind on fulfilling his contracts.

We had a close shave on his RCA contract this year where he at least got paid, but I do not think we can get by with this again, as he is getting too far behind on his recording commitments and these people must have the merchandise. Even if the sales are not as good as they expect, at least they have to pay him if we have the merchandise delivered, as per the contract. If we don't deliver the merchandise, then they will most likely go into the clause that says they pay Elvis when he delivers his albums and records as per contract. We are currently behind three albums and six singles as per contract through 1976. I am only pointing out that none of this pressure has been on Elvis, but on me, and I do not mind but when I can't communicate with him there is not much I can do, except wait until this is at least sensibly straightened out.

Perhaps the time has come where Elvis will want to get someone else to handle his career more to his personal liking. If so, let's do it like grown-up, intelligent people, and settle this on a sensible basis.

In the past, because at various times I have been unable to communicate with him, there have been many decisions that I had to make, which perhaps he might have wanted handled in a different way, but agreements must be handled, and I have done so in the best way I could.

The last time we talked was when Elvis called me in Fayetteville to have a talk, and everything seemed okay at that time.

When I talked to you on the telephone, I was gratified to know that you were in the dark regarding what the problem might be, as much as I am.

As I told you on the telephone, I have eliminated as much as possible any business communications with Elvis' boys and only ask them to relay to him the message to call me, or that I would like to have him stop by to see me (and the reason I ask him to come by, is because of the information I always get from his staff that Elvis would rather stop by to see me than have me coming over to his place, which I do not mind doing any time . . . but the times when I wanted to do this, I was told he would come to my place).

Sincerely,
Colonel

Cc: Elvis Presley

"I will do the best I can under these circumstances"

Elvis —   August 20, 1976

As you know, your special concert engagement [at the Hilton] starting December 2–13 is not too far off. I was able to secure this engagement doing one concert Sunday through Thursday with two concerts on Friday and Saturday with no food service, as per your request in Johnson City, Tennessee.

When you told me you wanted to do more concerts each month, I did schedule six tours, one at the end of each month through the beginning of the next month, to allow you to be off a few weeks and to give me time to set everything up (which gave me no time off except to keep getting tours set up).

Now I feel I must take stock.

First, after we finish tour number six, I will go slow in planning anything further until you advise me that this is what you want to do, as you will have to do some recording before Vegas, as I have delayed this for some time. You owe RCA under your contract, six singles and three albums to complete the 1976/April 1977 contract. As you know, we got in right under the wire with the last album.

You can decide if you wish to do some recording a few weeks after the next tour and do a 10-day tour after that before opening in Vegas. We close September 8 in Pine Bluff. I could try to work out the schedule with Felton [Jarvis] to record the last week in September, and I could try to set up a tour sometime in the middle of October or the last week of October/first week of November, and off until the Vegas concerts.

I had planned to do the seventh and eighth tours before Vegas, but I don't feel things are going as safe as when we did the earlier tours, and get the recording done on time.

Right after the [1975 New Year's Eve] Pontiac concert you said you had to make some money, and I went out and set everything up so you would be able to get out from under your pressure. I will do what I can to keep you going, but as you well know, it has been more than 10 days since I have tried to reach you for a meeting, or to talk to you by telephone, but with no luck. I have left many messages for you to call me (and I trust that you are given these messages, but, of course, I can't be positive that you are receiving them)— with no luck, so I gave up trying.

I will do the best I can under these circumstances.

Sincerely,
Colonel

At the same time that he wrote to Vernon and Elvis about the future, he wrote soberly to tour director Tom Hulett. Hulett had for some time been the person he was closest to on the tour, and he had even talked to Hulett, who had extensive experience setting up international tours, about taking Elvis to Japan or Europe. In the end they had both concluded that it was an impossible situation ("security" was the code word employed — meaning, primarily, Elvis' need to have all his pharmaceutical aids on hand, and the strong probability of his getting busted by overzealous customs officials or local police), and the idea was soon abandoned. ■

"We can no longer take the responsibility of signing contracts and building commitments"

Tom —   August 20, 1976

Due to the uncertain availability of Elvis from time to time . . . and on the advice of the doctor who has been looking after Elvis, who says that unless Elvis adheres to the proper medication and treatment he could not tell us whether Elvis could hold up very long on any concert tour . . . we feel we can no longer take the responsibility of signing contracts and building commitments, except for one tour at a time, and only as long as there are enough finances on deposit to pay off any losses in case of a cancellation during a concert tour.

We had some close calls on the last tour, and we cannot take those chances again. I will go over this with you in person next week.

Sincerely,
Colonel

On the same day he wrote to longtime confidant and first lieutenant Tom Diskin in the same anguished vein. ∎

"It will be a miracle from the way things are at present if we will complete or even start this tour"

August 20, 1976

Tom: It will be a miracle from the way things are at present if we will complete or even start this tour. However, we can't cancel on our own because he will still be ready to go and say, "I did not cancel, you fellows did so I am not responsible." If something should happen, he will have to face the press and tell them himself but he won't take that responsibility. I am only going by what I hear from the boys and also that for 10 days he has not returned any calls or given some indication of his preparedness. . . .

The Colonel

As it turned out, the tour was completed without any cancellations or major incidents, but rock critic and longtime fan Bob Claypool wrote of the August 28 Houston show (this was just one of the clippings that Colonel sent to Vernon) that it was a "heartbreaking [performance], a depressingly incoherent, amateurish mess served up by a bloated, stumbling and mumbling figure who didn't act like 'The King' of anything, least of all rock 'n' roll." Subsequent tours were even more difficult, with each eliciting sharp questions from Colonel as to the state of Elvis' health and readiness, along with reassurances from Elvis that everything was fine — that he wanted to go out again as soon as possible. ■

"We only have about one more chance to stay in there to get back in the groove"

Vernon: September 14, 1976

Here are some reprints of letters and articles that you should see that Elvis gets to read. These are not the worst but a few of the many that are coming in. . . .

We all have the best interests at stake but we now must face a very touchy setup as the word is spreading about the bad performances. Also it would be best for Elvis to show everyone that the rumors that are supposedly going around about his drug and sleeping pill habits are all wrong, and getting on the ball he can disprove all this and show to the fans that these stories don't fit the performances he is doing.

Since we only have about one more chance to stay in there to get back in the groove Elvis must be aware of this. I tried to talk to him on the last tour but it was not possible. He was asleep at times when I had to leave for the next town.

The reason for this letter is very simple. It is meant for Elvis to read but I am sending it to you to make sure he received it. I have written several letters in the past and received no response. Also, Elvis tells me he does not get my calls, however, the boys tell me they give him my messages. So as you can see, something has to be worked out so there will be at least a sensible communication, either through yourself or Elvis direct.

We are having a great deal of trouble booking buildings due to the press reports being released from some disastrous concerts and the many complaints. More than 4,000 people walked out in Houston alone. I am sorry I cannot cover this up any longer as I have tried to do in the past. I know we can climb back in there but Elvis has to do his part so we can again have people believe us when we tell them Elvis will do a great concert as before. We did improve a good deal after Tuscaloosa, but we must be sure that what happened in Houston won't happen again or we will be out of business for sure, as we are now being watched very strongly since there seems to be a feeling that all the stories being circulated about Elvis being unable to perform may be true. He can prove they are wrong.

Sincerely,
[Signed "Colonel"]
The Colonel

1977

The sign-off says it all. The game has nearly played itself out. Mel Ilberman was RCA's fifty-year-old chief financial officer, onetime head of RCA Record Tours, and a great admirer of Colonel's business acumen and hardheaded honesty. Colonel does his best here to deliver the bad news with bravado, but in the end he undercuts the attempt with his signature humor. (Read that any way you like.) ■

"I am glad this was the first time it has ever happened on a concert tour"

Mr. Mel Ilberman   April 4, 1977
RCA Records
1133 Avenue of The Americas
New York, New York 10036

Friend Mel—

As you most likely have heard or read, we had to postpone Baton Rouge, Mobile, Macon and Jacksonville. As these cities were all sold out, we, of course, had to offer refunds in every case . . . so far we are lucky that I was able to reschedule these concerts on the closing of Tour #4, which we just completed setting up. I am enclosing the new schedule of these dates which was some job . . . but that's the concert business.

I am glad this was the first time it has ever happened on a concert tour. We had a great deal of extra expenses, but I was able to bring the tour in with some profit, and there will be a credit to the deposit from Tour #2 to Tour #4 when we mail the contract for Tour #4. We hope to be able to get by without too many refunds, which will only be from people unable to come on these other dates, and whatever comes back, I feel that we can sell these refund tickets.

We are also enclosing the Tour #3 list for your information, together with the reports from Tour #2.

> Sincerely,
> [Signed "The Poor Magician"]
> THE MAGICIAN

P.S. When will we get our storeroom in Hollywood?

I s this all just empty bravado? A laying down of markers and HOW MUCH DOES IT COST IF IT'S FREE? edicts? Wisecracks and jokes? Strict prohibitions? Well, maybe so, but Colonel is clearly determined to stick to his guns to the end.

The occasion was the on-tour, in-performance CBS special, to be filmed in about a month during what would turn out to be Elvis' last tour. In addition to the $1 million–plus guaranteed proceeds from the tour, Colonel and Elvis would divide the $750,000 fee for the special 50-50, the first, and as it turned out only, time Colonel actually applied the full-partnership agreement they had signed more than a year before, with ownership of the special to be shared by the two principals after a single repeat showing. (Despite the agreement, the tour money was divided two-thirds–one-third.)

Money aside, what was the rationale for the special? Well, considered in its best light, it might be seen as a last, desperate attempt to provide Elvis with the kind of challenge that he had always risen to in the past. I think that was what Colonel truly believed. And it may even have been what Elvis believed—or at least what both of them wanted to believe.

But that's not the way it worked out. The show, broadcast a month and a half after Elvis' death, was a disaster, with all of the participants shocked by the reality of what they had actually witnessed. Myrna Smith, the de facto leader of Elvis' female backing group, the Sweet Inspirations, said that she was asked right after the filming how it had gone, "and I said, 'It really went great.' But afterwards, when I watched [the broadcast], I just burst out crying. We were all wearing blinders." Colonel's widow, Loanne, said, "We all believed Elvis could recapture his form if he really wanted to. In retrospect it seems [so] strange. . . ."

It's impossible to know what Colonel himself thought, because, while he often spoke of his rationale for booking the show, he never spoke of the result.

To Loanne alone Colonel confessed his vulnerabilities and his fears. "Colonel needed to be in control," Loanne said, "and there was no way he could control what was happening at this point. He began having nightmares."

But to the world at large, to CBS vice president John Cowden and the producers of the special, he simply carried on as usual, seemingly with nothing else to rely on but the well-worn adage which had guided him all his life: The show must go on. ∎

"Our slogan has always been 'HOW MUCH DOES IT COST IF ITS FREE?'— and this can be quite expensive"

Mr. John P. Cowden, Vice President   May 16, 1977
& Assistant to the President
CBS Television
51 West 52 Street
New York, New York 10019

Good Day, Mr. Cowden:

Regarding your letter pertaining to your information that General Manager Fred Osler of the CBS affiliate in Louisville having terrific footage on the long lines waiting to buy tickets for the Elvis concert at Freedom Hall . . . I, of course, am very happy that you took my advice to get this footage as it is hard to recapture something like that realistically.

I am working in between my regular schedule as much as possible to assist the people on the Coast that are planning to film the concerts in two markets. . . . as Mr. Smith, the Director [Gary Smith, also coproducer of the show], felt that this would be sufficient in addition to all the little extras that I will try to work out with him behind the scenes. . . .

In your letter you state in closing that Mr. Osler plans to write me direct — so far his letter has not caught up with me. However, so we can keep everything in good working condition . . . we do not solicit any special publicity or public relation efforts and Mr. Presley does not do any interviews at any time while he is on a concert tour, and never when he is not working. This has been our policy for twenty-two years and it has worked very well for all concerned, as everything we ever do always seems to be a surprise . . . even to us.

You can rest assured that we will use everything at our disposal to exploit the TV Concert to the fullest in every way possible without calling on anyone connected with the project to involve their personal time and freedom. This is one reason why we hold the longest record of any artist never having been available for panel shows, walk-on shows, and other scale pay projects. The closest we ever came to going on a show just to walk on was the "Laugh In" where my friends at NBC asked me if we would do it for them since they only payed $1,000 to walk on, to which I agreed with the exception that we wanted $49,000 to walk off, making it a special price of $50,000 — which they foolishly turned down. Our slogan has always been "HOW MUCH DOES IT COST IF ITS FREE?"— and this can be quite expensive.

After we start Tour #4 in Knoxville this week, I will give you a call from time to time to coordinate the proper press release with your Barrie Richardson. My thinking is very strongly not to call this project a "special", as this year it seems that "specials" are a dime a dozen. Our title: "Elvis in Concert For You" seems to be more appropriate and if you want something to go with that in place of "special", I will come up with something but it won't be "special". "Elvis in Concert For You" will be very outstanding on the night of the broadcast when other networks will possible be running some of their left-over "specials" and CBS will have "Elvis in Concert For You".

To my thinking the press release should come on your opening day during your Affiliates Conference May 24. If you like, I will be delighted to have Elvis send you a telegram at the opening of your conference which you can read. This would be entirely up to you. Let me know where to send it so you will have it in plenty of time to read at the conference. It is things like this token of direct interest that do the most good. . . .

Sincerely,
[Signed "Colonel"]
THE COLONEL

POSTSCRIPT

Colonel Parker to the Author expressing his pique at authorial temerity, both specifically and in general, from correspondence dating off and on from January 1988 to 1996.

I think I'll omit the tagline here. It's too obvious! But it came in response to an early attempt on my part to establish an accurate rendering of how exactly Colonel came into the Elvis picture.

In any case, the correspondence continued with great goodwill, if somewhat diminished gusto on Colonel's part, and I will always be grateful to him for all the attention and verbal parrying he sent in my direction. One time I wrote to him, "You may think I'm crazy." "Your suggestion is a little late," he cheerfully replied.

Friend Peter: July 10, 1990

Your letter dated July 4 received and carefully read.

I do not wish to waste my time to make corrections regarding the most misinformed information I have ever read in all my career in show business. [He then proceeded to waste some of his time feeding me information that might be useful to me.]

If this helps you any fine — if not, this is all I can do. The TRUE STORY of my entire career has been documented for me and at some future date will be included in my memoirs, which will either be handled by me or my estate, as there is lots to still be added, as I expect to be around for some time. . . .

> Good luck from your friend,
> [Signed "Colonel"]
> THE COLONEL

Peter and Alexandra at Colonel's eighty-fifth. *Courtesy of the author*

Acknowledgments

In writing a book over so long a period (in this case, it goes back to 1995, when I first encountered Colonel's letters en masse), one incurs debts that one can never repay. Literally hundreds of people have helped me with my research and my interviews, and I thank them all. The following are just some of the people and institutions who gave me a hand over the weeks, months, and years.

Julian Aberbach, Academy of Motion Picture Arts and Sciences Library, Mae Axton, Gayle Kufferath Behnke, Freddy Bienstock, Steve Binder, Bar Biszick-Lockwood, Ron Bonja, Bowling Green Music Library and Bill Schurk Sound Archives, Bill Bradley, Bill Bram, David Brokaw, Sandy Brokaw, Lammert de Bruin, Bettie Bonja Byer, Trevor Cajiao, Kathleen Campbell, Dr. Charles L. Clarke, Brenda Cohen, Brenda Colladay, X Cossé, Country Music Hall of Fame and Museum, Mike Crowley, Chick Crumpacker, John Cuthbert, Roger Davis, Jan Donkers, Sander Donkers, Al Dvorin, Ken Emerson, Colin Escott, Joe Esposito, Lamar Fike, Bob Finkel, Trude Forsher, Alan Fortas, Will Friedwald, Anne Fulchino, Joan and Paul Gansky, Gordon Gee, Gregg Geller, Larry Geller, Mychael Gerstenberger, Gary Giddins, Sam Gill, Billy Goldenberg, Stuart Goldman, Paul Gongaware, Michael Gray, Julia Gunn, George Hamilton, Joe Hazen, Lance Hidy, Bob Hilburn, Lenny Hirshan, Ed Hookstratten, Jerry Hopkins, Bones Howe, Suzette Howse, Tom Hulett, Humane Society of Tampa Bay, Adam Iddings, Mel Ilberman, Jim Jaworowicz, Peter Jones, Ernst Jorgensen, June Juanico, Sid Kalcheim, Hal Kanter, James Kaplan, George Klein, Grelun Landon, Shaw Lentz, David R. Lewis, Brian Linn, Hans Luijten, Sanders Marble, Barry Mazor, Liz McCoy, Brad McCuen, Greg McDonald, Bob Merlis, Scotty Moore, John Morthland, Avinandan Mukherjee, David Naylor, Godfried Nevels, Geert Nijland, Loanne Miller Parker, Sam Phillips, Shannon Pollard, Bill Porter, Angela Pratesi, Tom Ricks, Steve Rinaldi Jr., James Roy, Tommy Sands, Joe Sasfy, Jerry Schilling, Flip Scipio, Myrna Smith, Hank Snow, Reverend Jimmy Snow, Jack Soden, Andrew Solt, Stephen Stathis, Gordon Stoker, Michael Streissguth, Pat Sullivan, Ethan Tackett, Adam Taylor, Jordan Taylor, Justin Tubb, Gabe Tucker, Johnny Vallis, Jorrit Van Der Kooi, Jan van Gestel, Ad van Kuijk Jr., Dirk

Vellenga, Monte Warden, Jerry Weintraub, Beth Weiss, Steve Weiss, Richard Weize, Al Wertheimer, Red West, Jonah Wilson, Peter Wolf, Richard Zoglin.

I should also acknowledge the above-and-beyond-the-call-of-duty help I have gotten over the years from Colin Escott, who read the book more than once in manuscript, as did Susan Marsh (several times), whose primacy as a designer is firmly founded on text. Researchers and historians who contributed immeasurably include Brenda Colladay, Ernst Jorgensen, Trevor Cajiao (editor of *Elvis: The Man and His Music* and *Now Dig This*), Stephen Stathis, and Jim Roy, whose Scotty Moore website everyone should check out.

Also, I owe an inestimable debt to Elvis' first biographer, Jerry Hopkins, for providing me with unfettered access to the full range of his interviews and writings; also to Bar Biszick-Lockwood for the interviews she did for her biography of Hill and Range cofounder Jean Aberbach. Thanks to Stuart Goldman and Adam Taylor as well for sharing the information and interview material that they assembled for their 1993 film, *Elvis in Hollywood*.

The Country Music Hall of Fame and Museum should be a destination point for researchers and fans alike. Michael Gray, Adam Iddings, and Kathleen Campbell were among those at the Hall of Fame who offered their help and expertise. I should call special attention to the archival interviews of Eddy Arnold and Steve Sholes, which they provided from the Frist Library and Archive of the Country Music Hall of Fame and Museum. Hal Wallis' correspondence with Colonel is available in the Elvis Presley General Correspondence Files, Hal Wallis Papers, Margaret Herrick Library, Academy of Motion Picture Arts and Sciences, in Beverly Hills.

Michael Streissguth, author of *Eddy Arnold: Pioneer of the Nashville Sound*, could not have been more helpful, or patient, in responding to all of my annoyingly minutiae-centered questions. (Brenda Colladay was a very big help here, too — and equally patient.) And Eddy's grandson, Shannon Pollard, was just as generous in digging up photographs, documents, and information. Barry Mazor fulfilled much the same role as Michael with respect to Gene Austin, and everyone should read his wonderful portrait of Gene, "Gene Austin: The Father of Southern Pop," originally published in *No Depression*, December 2004. And for his insight into the early days at William Morris, and his kind permission to quote from the letters of his father, Harry Kalcheim, I thank Sid Kalcheim, too.

In the Netherlands, Colonel's nephew, Ad van Kuijk Jr., was, of course, the most direct, and generous, primary source with respect not only to his memories but his insights into van Kuijk family dynamics. It was especially kind of him to permit me to publish his uncle's reply to his original 1961 letter on behalf of his father, Colonel's brother Ad Sr., to which he retains all rights. Documentarian Jorrit Van Der Kooi, who filmed Colonel briefly in 1993 and provided me with my original introduction to Ad Jr., offered help in any number of ways, including access to his interviews and articles. Dirk Vellenga, whom I interviewed and corresponded with in the mid-1990s, provided me with the benefit of twenty years of research into Colonel and his family, in some cases offering insights and information that did not find their way into his landmark book, *Elvis and the Colonel*. Geert Nijland, who is currently occupying something like Dirk's old post at *De Stem* in Breda (now renamed *BN DeStem*), helped immeasurably with his unique perspective on Breda and its history. My old friend and doppelganger, Jan Donkers, whose son, Sander, long ago translated the *Rosita* articles for me, has continued to offer advice and support, as has a new friend, Hans Luijten, biographer of Jo van Gogh-Bonger. I've known Jan van Gestel for years (I'm not sure if he introduced me to photographic archivist Ger Rijff or the other way around); he translated a number of pieces for me, as did some of the others. And Lammert de Bruin's podcast series on Colonel Parker for the Dutch public broadcasting system, *Het Geheim van Colonel Parker* (Colonel Parker's Secret), uncovered the documents that revealed Dries van Kuijk's previously unknown (and unsuccessful) voyage to America at the age of sixteen.

Gayle Kufferath Behnke, Brenda Williams Cohen, Ron Bonja, and George Hamilton each provided an entirely unexpected glimpse of a side of Colonel I had never imagined — his lifelong penchant for creating new families everywhere he went. And Greg McDonald, too, who was virtually adopted by Colonel and his wife, Marie, in his early teens, painted a picture of Colonel in Palm Springs that no one else could have.

Jerry Schilling has continued to offer thoughtful and deeply affectionate recollections and insights (I don't think Colonel trusted anyone more in the last years of his life), and Joe Esposito, too, provided me with appreciative reminiscences in our many interviews in the '90s.

I don't think anyone except Loanne could have been a more forceful advocate for Colonel's book, or Colonel's place in history, than Paul Gongaware, who started out with Colonel at Concerts West in the '70s.

At Graceland, Jack Soden as always led the way. And Angie Marchese and her indefatigable Graceland Archives team (including Danielle Forbes, Sarah Bitler, Allison Sights, Dee Dee Antie, and Michelle Wallace) could not have been more helpful or enthusiastic.

Alexandra Guralnick once again patiently read, transcribed, debated, and imagined the details of the story every step of the way. As always, thanks to Jake and Nina for their manifold contributions. And it was a joy to work once again with Barbara Clark not just for her cheerfully stringent approach to copyediting and unmatched work ethic but for her overall positivity and unhesitant readiness to tackle any problem that might arise.

Working with Susan Marsh, whose passionate commitment to elegance of form and unswerving dedication to the text have guided the design of nearly every book I have written since 1979, was, as always, an unalloyed pleasure. After all these years, it was more than a little bit of a shock not to be working with Michael Pietsch, whose honesty, loyalty, editorial insight, and friendship have guided my books for more than thirty years. But he was an early advocate for the Colonel, and now Alex Littlefield has taken his place with much the same spirit of grace, determination, forthrightness, and editorial fidelity that Michael has always embodied.

Obviously, I owe an incalculable debt to Loanne Miller Parker. She provided a depth of knowledge, empathy, and perspective that would have been impossible to find anywhere else. But most of all, of course, I thank the Colonel — for *putting me on the list.*

Bibliography

Arnold, Eddy. *It's a Long Way from Chester County*. Old Tappan, NJ: Hewitt House, 1969.

Austin, Gene, with an uncredited collaborator and a foreword by Gene Autry. *Gene Austin's Ol' Buddy*. Phoenix, AZ: Augury Press, 1984.

Bélard, Paul. *Elvis in Hawaii November 1957*. Greenlawn, NY: Linden Press, 2017.

Biszick-Lockwood, Bar. *Restless Giant: The Life and Times of Jean Aberbach & Hill and Range Songs*. Urbana and Chicago: University of Illinois Press, 2010.

Crumbaker, Marge, with Gabe Tucker. *Up and Down with Elvis Presley: The Inside Story*. New York: G. P. Putnam's Sons, 1981.

Cusic, Don. *Eddy Arnold: I'll Hold You in My Heart*. Nashville: Rutledge Hill Press, 1997.

ElvisMatters: The Travelog-Op zoek naar Colonel Parker. The Netherlands: ElvisMatters, 2010. Travelogue of Ad van Kuijk's 1961 visit published in Dutch by the official Elvis Presley Fan Club in the Netherlands.

Esposito, Joe, with Elena Oumano. *Good Rockin' Tonight: Twenty Years on the Road and on the Town with Elvis*. New York: Simon and Schuster, 1994.

Geller, Larry, and Joel Spector, with Patricia Romanowski. *"If I Can Dream": Elvis' Own Story*. New York: Simon and Schuster, 1989.

George-Warren, Holly. *Public Cowboy No. 1: The Life and Times of Gene Autry*. Oxford and New York: Oxford University Press, 2007.

Goldman, Albert. *Elvis*. New York: McGraw-Hill, 1981.

Guralnick, Peter. *Last Train to Memphis: The Rise of Elvis Presley*. New York: Little, Brown, 1994.

———. *Careless Love: The Unmaking of Elvis Presley*. New York: Little, Brown, 1999.

Guralnick, Peter, and Ernst Jorgensen. *Elvis Day by Day: The Definitive Record of His Life and Music*. New York: Ballantine Books, 1999.

Hoffman, Frank, with Robert Birkline: "Gene Austin." In *Survey of American Popular Music* (online). Huntsville, TX: Sam Houston State University, 2003.

Hopkins, Jerry. *Elvis: A Biography*. New York: Simon and Schuster, 1971.

———. *Elvis: The Final Years*. New York: St. Martin's Press, 1980.

Hurst, Jack. *Nashville's Grand Ole Opry*. New York: Harry N. Abrams, 1975.

Jorgensen, Ernst. *Elvis Presley: A Life in Music—The Complete Recording Sessions.* New York: St. Martin's Press, 1998.

Jorgensen, Ernst Mikael. *Elvis Presley: A Boy from Tupelo.* Copenhagen: Follow That Dream Books, 2012. This is the 527-page book accompanying the boxed set entitled *The Complete 1953-1955 Recordings.*

Kahn, E. J. "The Quiet Guy in Lindy's." *The New Yorker,* April 20, 1946. Profile of Abe Lastfogel.

———. "The Quiet Guy in Lindy's—II." *The New Yorker,* April 27, 1946.

Levy, Alan. *Operation Elvis.* New York: Henry Holt, 1960.

Loper, Karen. *The Elvis Clippings.* Houston, TX: n.d.

McDonald, Greg, and Marshall Terrill. *Elvis and the Colonel: An Insider's Look at the Most Legendary Partnership in Show Business.* New York: St. Martin's Press, 2023.

Nash, Alanna. *The Colonel: The Extraordinary Story of Colonel Tom Parker and Elvis Presley.* New York: Simon and Schuster, 2003.

Pearl, Minnie, with Joan Dew. *Minnie Pearl: An Autobiography.* New York: Simon and Schuster, 1980.

Pugh, Ronnie. *Ernest Tubb: The Texas Troubadour.* Durham, NC: Duke University Press, 1996.

Rose, Frank. *The Agency: William Morris and the Hidden History of Show Business.* New York: HarperBusiness, 1995.

Schilling, Jerry, with Chuck Crisafulli. *Me and a Guy Named Elvis: My Lifelong Friendship with Elvis Presley.* New York: Gotham Books, 2006.

Snow, Hank, with Jack Ownbey and Bob Burris. *The Hank Snow Story.* Urbana and Chicago: University of Illinois Press, 1994.

Streissguth, Michael. *Eddy Arnold: Pioneer of the Nashville Sound.* New York: Schirmer, 1997.

Vellenga, Dirk, with Mick Farren. *Elvis and the Colonel.* New York: Delacorte Press, 1988.

Wallis, Hal, and Charles Higham. *Starmaker: The Autobiography of Hal Wallis.* New York: Macmillan, 1980.

Wertheimer, Alfred, with Gregory Martinelli. *Elvis '56: In the Beginning—An Intimate, Eyewitness Photo-journal.* New York: Collier Books, 1979.

Wertheimer, Alfred. *Elvis at 21: New York to Memphis.* San Rafael, CA: Insight Editions, 2006.

Notes

The endnotes for this book can be found at

Index

Note: Italic page numbers refer to illustrations.

About the Author

Peter Guralnick has been called "a national resource" by critic Nat Hentoff for work that has argued passionately and persuasively for the vitality of this country's intertwined Black and White musical traditions. His books include the prizewinning two-volume biography of Elvis Presley, *Last Train to Memphis* and *Careless Love; Sweet Soul Music; Dream Boogie: The Triumph of Sam Cooke;* and *Sam Phillips: The Man Who Invented Rock 'n' Roll*. His most recent book is *Looking to Get Lost: Adventures in Music and Writing*. He wrote the scripts for the Grammy-winning documentary *Sam Cooke: Legend* and Martin Scorsese's blues documentary, *Feel Like Going Home*.